The Word Became Flesh

The Word Became Flesh

Millard J. Erickson

BAKER BOOK HOUSE
Grand Rapids, Michigan 49516

Copyright 1991 by
Baker Book House Company

Printed in the United States of America

Library of Congress Cataloging-in-Publication Data

Erickson, Millard J.
    The word became flesh / Millard J. Erickson.
       p.   cm.
    Includes bibliographical references and index.
    ISBN 0-8010-3208-3
    1. Jesus Christ—Person and offices. 2. Incarnation. I. Title.
BT202.E75   1991
232' . 1—dc20   91-24728
                                                                   CIP

To the Japan Baptist Church Association
and its leader,

Akira Izuta,

in recognition of faithful service to Jesus Christ

Contents

5

Preface

Several years ago, while writing *Christian Theology,* I found I had to resist the temptation to write a book on the topic of each of the chapters. I concluded that I had the agenda for my next sixty books, and resolved that I would someday attempt to write some of them. The present volume is the first of such efforts.

I have chosen to write on the doctrine of the person of Christ because it is crucial in our day. It has, of course, always been at the very center of Christian faith, but is especially problematic in our time because of several developments in the intellectual world. I am firmly committed to the doctrine of the unique incarnation of God in the person of Jesus Christ, but am convinced that it must be stated in a contemporary fashion, with full awareness of the intellectual climate of our time. It is for this reason that the present volume devotes a considerable amount of attention to recent christological constructions which pose problems for an incarnational Christology. The concluding portion of the book does not claim to provide definitive solutions to those problems, but only to point out directions from which a responsible contemporary incarnational Christology can be expected to come.

Portions of this book are based upon materials utilized elsewhere: chapter 24 is an adaptation of my presidential address to the American Theological Society meeting at Chicago on April 28, 1989; chapter 9 was a paper presented at the annual meeting of the Evangelical Theological Society on November 21, 1985, at La Mirada, California; chapter 14 contains some material from a chapter which I contributed to a festschrift for William Hordern. In each case, there has been a considerable reworking.

I wish to thank those who provided assistance in special ways. Pat Krohn typed portions of the document, especially those mentioned above. Brian D. Anderson of Computer Aid, Inc., provided technical assistance in converting several files from an earlier format. My daughter Sharon Erickson, formerly of Church and Peace, Wetzlar, Germany, and now a Ph.D. student at the University of Colorado, checked my translations from German and helped compile the indexes. Allan Fisher and Ray Wiersma of Baker Book House have again been of great assistance in getting the manuscript into final form. I, of course, assume all responsibility for imperfections of the book.

In his *Little Exercise for Young Theologians,* Helmut Thielicke points out that theology cannot be simply an intellectual activity. It must also involve the person of the student of theology. This is nowhere more true than in the study of Christology. May all who read *The Word Became Flesh* come to understand more fully and love more intensely the Lord whose act of infinite love constituted the incarnation.

Introduction

Throughout its history the church has realized that Christology, or the study of what is to be believed about the person of Jesus Christ, is of the greatest importance. Since Jesus is at the very center of our faith, and since what is believed about him is the very touchstone of our Christianity, this doctrinal endeavor is of paramount importance. In fact, the first real doctrinal controversy and debate occurred in the areas of Christology and the doctrine of the Trinity, namely, the relationship of Christ to God the Father.

While Christology has always been recognized as important, it has never been found to be easy. A whole complex of issues is involved, biblical, philosophical, and historical. Almost endless variations of the teaching seem possible. The formulation of christological doctrine has never been more difficult than at the present, however.

In the past decade and a half, we have seen indications that in Christology and the fields impinging upon it there are, if not a crisis, problematic developments sufficient to warrant a whole rethinking of the orthodox approach to the incarnation. The titles of three books published in this period are sample manifestations of these developments. In a dramatic and rather shocking fashion, *The Myth of God Incarnate*, a symposium by a group of British theologians, called into question some of the most basic elements of Christology. It aroused widespread and in some cases rather angry reaction, not simply on the level of professional theologians, but among parish clergy and even laypersons as well. Its effect was similar to that of John A. T. Robinson's *Honest to God*, Joseph Fletcher's *Situation Ethics*, and the work of the Death of God theologians a decade earlier. A second title, significant especially for its wording, is Jon Sobrino's *Christology at the Crossroads*. Writing from the standpoint of Latin American liberation theology, but well-informed regarding the christological tradition, Sobrino argues that a new approach is needed. Finally, Paul Knitter's *No Other Name?* has stirred considerable controversy with its questioning of Jesus' universal and exclusive status as Savior of all humanity.

These three works indicate that not all of the issues of Christology have been satisfactorily dealt with, and that new issues are arising. It is almost as if a theological tug of war is going on within Christianity, and the person of Christ is the rope being pulled. Each theological group seems to be attempting to pull Jesus into its camp by interpreting him in light of its presuppositions. The response of conservative Christianity to the various christological problems has been fragmentary, yet its very existence depends upon a satisfactory treatment of them.

This book is written with a very definite purpose. It seeks to give an affirmative answer to the question, "Is an orthodox incarnational Christology possible in our time?" In other words, can the doctrine that Jesus was fully God and fully man be so defined that it is intellectually justifiable in light of the current problems of Christology? In a sense, this volume is an attempt to do for our time what the Chalcedonian statement did for its time.

The Council of Chalcedon, in formulating and promulgating its creed, was seeking to draw out the full implications of the biblical testimony regarding Christ. In so doing, it gathered up the results of much discussion that had gone on in the previous 125 years, and also addressed new issues which had just come to the attention of the church. It stated in the categories of its time positive conceptions about Christ and then indicated what was excluded from belief. Because the Chalcedonian Creed does not elaborate on its positive statements, it gives more guidance as to what not to believe than as to what to believe. Although it does prescribe doctrines, it does not really specify the meaning of those doctrines. For example, it gives the formula "two natures, one person" without telling us what that formula means, but only what it does not mean. One of my students several years ago, when called upon to answer the essay question, "What is the orthodox doctrine of the two natures and one person of Christ?" responded, "There is no orthodox doctrine. Every attempt to give some content to the statement was declared heretical by the church." To some extent, that student was right. The Chalcedonian formula may have been all right for its time, as far as it went, but it did not go far enough.

If Chalcedon was not fully adequate even for its era, the problem has been aggravated with the passing of time. For in the more than fifteen hundred years since the council adjourned, many developments have taken place which were not and could not have been addressed by that group of theologians. Surveying the modern situation, Gerald O'Collins indicates six major reasons why classical Christology is under fire: "It is (1) a Christology 'from above,' which (2) remains incarnation-centered, (3) runs into philosophical problems, (4) mixes together historical, theological and mythical language, (5) bypasses the ministry of Jesus, and (6) separates the person of Jesus Christ from his work, that is to say, separates Christology from soteriology or the doctrine of salvation."[1] Much of this challenge to orthodox Christology stems from the Enlightenment and ensuing developments. It may not be an exaggeration to say that there have been more of these epochal developments in the past one hundred years than in all the preceding centuries since Chalcedon.

The extent of the current difficulty is evident in three areas, the first of which is the rising historical consciousness and the formulation of critical methodology for study of the Bible. The use of historical criticism in the study of the Bible is less than two hundred years old. With the application of its methods to Scripture, however, some radical implications for Christology have emerged. The words which once were believed to be direct quotations of Jesus' statements, or accurate reports of his actions, have now come to be viewed with suspicion, as possibly reflective more of the early church's situation and theologizing than of the actual words and deeds of Jesus. An extremely radical form of historical criticism holds that it is virtually impossible to know anything about Jesus. In many cases, the teachings about Jesus that once were so tenaciously held are

---

1. Gerald O'Collins, *What Are They Saying About Jesus?* rev. ed. (New York: Paulist, 1983), p. 5.

coming to be viewed as mythical ideas borrowed from the cultural milieu of New Testament times.

There have also been widespread social and political changes in our world which affect the doing of Christology. For the most part, theology has been done by Westerners, and white middle-class male Westerners at that. The churches which have sent out missionaries have also been the ones to define theology for the church worldwide. Theology has been done largely by northern Europeans and North Americans. In more recent years, however, other groups have begun to promulgate their own understanding of theology: women, American blacks, and Third World persons. Their perception of theological issues has not been quite the same as that which the conventional theologians have disseminated. Now, instead of being viewed as absolute, the majority position is seen as just one more culturally and historically conditioned perspective. In addition, the growth of transportation and communication has given us contact with religions other than Christianity. This global awareness has called into question the universality and normativeness of Jesus.

Finally, there are increasing suggestions that we are in the midst of a cultural paradigm shift. We have for some time been in the so-called modern period. Just as there were certain consensuses which characterized the premodern period, so there also are some general points of agreement in the modern period. They are beginning to break down, however. Increasing numbers of people are suggesting that the modern period, at least as it has been understood, is passing away, and that we are now in what should be referred to as the postmodern period. This means that the whole approach to intellectual problems must be seriously revised or even replaced. As surely as Einsteinian physics replaced the long-held Newtonian model, so must the whole conceptual structure of thought be replaced.

In response to the new situation in these three areas, numerous Christologies have arisen. So O'Collins writes of "new Christological themes"[2] and expounds three Christologies which embody them—the Christologies of James Mackey, Jon Sobrino, and Edward Schillebeeckx.[3] Similarly, John O'Grady refers to

2. Ibid., ch. 2.
3. Ibid., ch. 4.

various "models of Jesus," including Jesus as the incarnation of the Second Person of the Trinity, the mythological Christ, the ethical liberator, the human face of God, the man for others, and personal savior.[4] The plethora of problems has led to a plurality of positions.

In this book we will seek to do three specific things as we pursue the goal of developing an orthodox incarnational Christology for our time:

1. We will seek to understand the basic orthodox interpretation of the person of Christ as it was developed from the biblical materials, synthesized by the ecumenical councils, fulfilled in the Chalcedonian Creed, and refined thereafter.
2. We will examine and evaluate several contemporary christological views, noting the particular problem for orthodox Christology which each presents.
3. We will seek to develop a Christology for today which maintains the orthodox understanding of Jesus as both fully human and fully the Son of God, and yet takes into account and responds to the problems posed by contemporary views.

Such an endeavor may be thought by some to be mere obscurantism, attempting to rationalize a long-held view which is no longer defensible. The author readily acknowledges that he is a conservative, that is, he is convinced that certain basic beliefs must be maintained if Christianity itself is to be retained. He is also, however, what William Hordern has termed a "translator": one who strives to express that unchanging and indispensable essence of the Christian faith in currently meaningful and defensible form.[5]

The reader will note that there are certain limitations inherent in this presentation:

1. Certain customary topics of Christology are not treated specifically, such as the humanity of Jesus and the virgin

4. John F. O'Grady, *Models of Jesus* (Garden City, N.Y.: Doubleday, 1981).
5. William E. Hordern, *New Directions in Theology Today*, vol. 1, *Introduction* (Philadelphia: Westminster, 1966), pp. 146–47.

birth. In that sense, this is not a fully articulated
Christology. The reason the humanity of Jesus, for
example, does not receive separate treatment is that it is
not an issue severely contested in contemporary
Christology; for that matter, it is not contested at all. This
is not to say that it is unimportant. The significance of
Jesus' full humanity will, in fact, be seen in the place
given to it in chapters 21 and 22, which attempt to state a
logically satisfactory understanding of the incarnation.[6]

2. Not every aspect of each view, nor every variety and rep-
    resentative of it, will be treated. This is not a book on lib-
    eration Christology or narrative Christology, for example.
    The chapters devoted to these contemporary Chris-
    tologies are of necessity selective and generalized in
    nature.

3. Not every Scripture passage bearing upon the particular
    issues of Christology that are discussed will be examined,
    nor will there be exhaustive exegesis of any of these pas-
    sages. Relatively little is done, for example, with some of
    the major christological passages in John's Gospel, the
    letters of Paul, and the Book of Hebrews.

Having taken note of our goal, the general method to be pursued, and its inherent limitations, let us proceed to explore the
possibility of developing an orthodox Christology that is relevant
for today. Let us see precisely what is meant when Scripture proclaims, "The Word became flesh."

---

6. Some readers may find in the table of contents indications of an incipient
Docetism; they are urged to read the book in its entirety before adopting such an interpretation.

Part 1

The Formulation of Incarnational Christology

The Biblical Source

We begin our study of Christology where the church began its study of that subject from virtually the earliest times: with the Scriptures, and particularly with the documents which form the

New Testament. In so doing, we are conscious that there has been over the years a great deal of difference of opinion and even controversy regarding the way in which the biblical materials are to be interpreted. Yet since our initial concern is to observe how the developing understanding of the Scriptures contributed to the orthodox prescriptions, we will be assuming the approach which was virtually universal prior to the Enlightenment, namely, that these documents preserve for us a revelation which God has given of himself, his actions, and his purposes for the human race. We will, in other words, assume the orthodox or conservative view of the Bible. That this view is in dispute we do not question. In Part 2 of this treatise we will note various movements which have given rise to doubts about whether the Bible can be so used today as to support the traditional Christology, and then consider whether these objections are valid. But we will not anticipate either of those further sets of considerations in this chapter. Rather, we will look at the Bible as did those who lived in its time and in the first centuries following its writing and canonization. We begin by examining the chief evidences which the various parts of the New Testament present concerning Jesus Christ.

The Synoptic Gospels

Jesus' Self-Designation as the Son of Man

Without question, the title *Son of man* was Jesus' favorite self-designation. The expression occurs over eighty times in the Synoptic Gospels and the Gospel of John, and in nearly every case it is used by Jesus of himself. The only exception is in John 12:34, where the crowd, after Jesus has used the expression, echoes it in the question, "Who is this Son of man?" In the Synoptics, the usage of the term is invariably by Jesus himself. (Later on, Luke does report in Acts 7:56 Stephen's testimony, "I see . . . the Son of man standing at the right hand of God.")

It is, however, no easy matter to determine just what "Son of man" means. It is not a natural expression in Greek, but a literal rendering of the Aramaic *bar nāšā'*, which would ordinarily be understood simply as "man." A great deal has been written on the subject, but it seems likely that Jesus borrowed the term from Daniel 7:13—one "like a son of man," who came with the clouds of heaven. Jesus took this expression and gave his own meaning to it. Hugh Ross Mackintosh suggests that Jesus had some educative purpose in mind. The use of the term *Son of man* prompted reflection and enabled Jesus then to stamp his own impress upon it.[1] Certainly it was a more neutral term than "Son of David," which had politically provocative overtones.

There is fairly general agreement that the Synoptic occurrences of the term *Son of man* can be classified into three groups:

1. The Son of man is at work on earth in a serving role (e.g., Matt. 9:6, Mark 2:10, Luke 5:24; Matt. 12:8, Mark 2:28, Luke 6:5).
2. The Son of man must suffer, die, and rise from the dead (e.g., Mark 8:31, Luke 9:22; Matt. 17:9, Mark 9:9; Matt. 17:22–23, Mark 9:31, Luke 9:44; Matt. 20:18–19, Mark 10:33–34, Luke 18:31–33).
3. The Son of man will return in eschatological glory (e.g., Matt. 16:27, Mark 8:38, Luke 9:26).[2]

The concept of the Son of man was, then, a complex one, involving both humiliation and exaltation. From the Synoptic uses of the term it appears that Jesus thought of himself as a heavenly Messiah fulfilling a ministry on earth for the sake of humans and then culminating in ultimate glorification.[3] The title implies more than just earthly status—it connotes supernatural origin and status as well.[4] Accordingly, it amounts to an implicit claim to deity.[5]

Jesus' Designation as the Son of God

Jesus is also referred to frequently as the Son of God. Although in the Synoptics Jesus never uses this title to refer to himself, he

1. Hugh Ross Mackintosh, *The Doctrine of the Person of Jesus Christ* (New York: Scribner, 1912), p. 23.
2. C. K. Barrett, *Jesus and the Gospel Tradition* (Philadelphia: Fortress, 1968), pp. 32, 79ff.
3. Donald Guthrie, *New Testament Theology* (Downers Grove, Ill.: Inter-Varsity, 1981), p. 281.
4. Robert G. Hamerton-Kelly, *Pre-existence, Wisdom, and the Son of Man* (Cambridge: Cambridge University Press, 1973), p. 100.
5. A. W. Argyle, "The Evidence for the Belief That Our Lord Himself Claimed to Be Divine," *Expository Times* 61.8 (May 1950): 231.

does use the simple term *the Son* in contexts which strongly suggest that it is God the Father to whom he is the Son. "Son of God" is particularly notable in Mark's Gospel, where it is the first title applied to Jesus (1:1) as well as the last (15:39). (Since Mark 16:9–20 does not appear in some of the most ancient manuscripts, we are excluding from our consideration here the references to "the Lord Jesus" in 16:19–20.) The disciples do not use the title *Son of God* in Mark or in Luke, but do so occasionally in Matthew (14:33; 16:16). Even evil spirits refer to Jesus as the Son of God. Especially noteworthy is Mark 3:11, which says, literally, that evil spirits "kept falling down before him and crying out, saying, 'You are the Son of God.'" The verb tenses here point to continuing or repeated action. Satan prefaces his temptations with the words, "If you are the Son of God . . ." (Matt. 4:3, 6; Luke 4:3, 9). At Jesus' trial the high priest poses the question, "Are you the Christ, the Son of the Blessed?" and Jesus replies, "I am" (Mark 14:61–62). Confirmation had come earlier, when the heavenly voice at Jesus' baptism (Mark 1:11) and at the transfiguration (Mark 9:7) identified him as "my beloved Son."

Although in the Synoptics Jesus does not use the full title *Son of God* with respect to himself, he does speak of God as "the Father," "my Father," "my heavenly Father," "your Father," and "your heavenly Father" more than fifty times, with Matthew recording these references most frequently. Jesus' use of "Abba, Father" (Mark 14:36) when addressing God is especially remarkable in view of the Jewish conception of God as very transcendent. This particular expression even carried over into Greek-speaking circles (Rom. 8:15; Gal. 4:6).[6]

A basic question needs to be addressed at this point. Did Jesus consider God to be his Father in precisely the same sense that God is the Father of all, or did he think of his relationship to the Father as being unique? While this question has generated considerable controversy, it appears that Jesus was conscious of having a unique relationship to the Father. For one thing, while Jesus spoke of "my Father" and "your Father," he did not speak of "our Father" except in the Lord's Prayer, which served as his model of how we are to pray; significantly, there is no evidence that he ever prayed it himself. A further consideration is that

6. Joachim Jeremias, *The Central Message of the New Testament* (New York: Scribner, 1965), p. 30.

Jesus taught that we may *become* (Greek, γίνομαι) sons of God (Matt. 5:45), a concept which is never applied to Jesus himself. Donald Guthrie says, "Our approach to the synoptic evidence must, therefore, recognize at the outset a distinction between God as Father of Jesus, and God as Father of the disciples."[7]

Jesus' Humanity

It may seem almost superfluous to examine the teaching of the Synoptics regarding the humanity of Jesus, since that element of Christology has not been seriously questioned in recent years. Yet, as we shall see in the next chapter, the reality and then the completeness of Jesus' humanity came into dispute within the earliest centuries of the Christian era. Although only Mark begins his Gospel with an indication that Jesus is something more than a man, he, more than the other Synoptic authors, concentrates heavily upon the human Jesus. Matthew and Luke, by their inclusion of the birth narratives, focus upon the fact that Jesus' birth (although not his conception) was of the same nature as that of other human beings. He grew as do other children, and he developed in knowledge and social skills (Luke 2:40, 52). He apparently hungered, grew fatigued, and experienced emotions such as do other humans, including sorrow and despair (Mark 14:33–34). He ate, paid taxes, perspired, and did all the normal day-to-day activities that humans do. He underwent real moral testing and temptation. He struggled with the decision between doing what he wanted to do and the Father's will. Yet with all of this, there were indications that he was more than simply another human being. He challenged the forces of nature, forgave sins, and cast out demons. None of the Evangelists, however, calls attention to the apparent incongruity of this fact, or tries to resolve it. It is as if they are unaware of any tension between Jesus' being human and more than human.

Jesus' Sinlessness

Nowhere in the Synoptic Gospels are there specific statements in which Jesus explicitly claims sinlessness for himself. There are, however, corroborating circumstantial evidences that Jesus was sinless and conscious of that fact. Certainly nothing in the

7. Guthrie, *New Testament Theology*, p. 304.

Synopics is incongruous with the later apostolic witness regarding his sinlessness.

One evidence regarding Jesus' own self-understanding with respect to sin is the absence of any confession of sin on his part. Although his ministry began with a call to repentance (Matt. 4:17; Mark 1:14–15), he himself never gave any indication that he needed to repent. Although the baptism of John was a baptism of repentance, Jesus did not give any indication of repentance when he was baptized by John, but instead identified the event with the need to fulfil all righteousness (Matt. 3:13–17). Although the prayer which he gave his disciples as a model for them to pray included a request to the Father for forgiveness of sins, none of his recorded prayers include any such request in his own behalf.

Jesus was subjected to various temptations, a number of which are recorded for us in the Gospels, yet at no point do we find him succumbing. The high standard which he set for his hearers ("Be perfect, as your heavenly Father is perfect," Matt. 5:48), the condemnation which he uttered against the sins of the Pharisees, and the lack of any countercharges of hypocrisy against him are testimonies in their own way to the absence of sin from Jesus' life. In addition, the lack of response to his challenge, "Which of you convicts me of sin?" (John 8:46), and the speciousness of the charges brought against him at his trial offer further confirmation.

One objection raised at times against this claim of sinlessness relates to some instances of Jesus' behavior in the Synoptic Gospels. Should we consider certain of his actions to have been sinful in nature? Was he too severe with the Pharisees, for example, in failing to credit them with any virtue?[8] A close examination of the practice of the scribes and Pharisees, however, indicates that their religion was diametrically opposed to his proclamation. Whereas his teaching stressed personal relationship to God, theirs emphasized the observance of ritual. Apparently, then, he was not excessive in his denunciation of them. Other claimed improper behavior, such as the overturning of the tables of the moneychangers in the temple, when examined in context, proves not to have been excessive.

8. Claude Montefiore, *Rabbinic Literature and Gospel Teachings* (New York: Ktav, 1930), pp. 322–23.

The Virgin Birth

The virgin birth of Jesus is one of the more disputed areas in both Gospel studies and Christian theology. But because our purpose at this point is merely to examine the material with which the church of the first centuries was dealing when constructing its views, we need not and cannot become deeply involved here in questions of Gospel criticism or the possibility of miracles. What we do need to do is to look closely at the Gospels and their witness regarding Jesus' birth. As Guthrie puts it, "Since there is no denying that both gospel writers [Matthew and Luke] describe a birth of a totally unusual kind, and since Luke especially devotes so much space in his book to the nativity stories, the virgin birth of Jesus must form an integral part in any account of early Christian theology, whatever modern interpretations of the evidence are advocated."[9]

In Luke's account, the mode of conception is not initially made an important part of the announcement of the coming birth of Jesus. The fact that the conception will come to pass through the direct intervention of the Holy Spirit is mentioned by the angel only in response to Mary's bewildered inquiry (Luke 1:34–35). No details are given regarding the exact means by which this is to come to pass, but it is clear that a totally unique and unparalleled action of the Holy Spirit will be involved. It is significant that the angel's announcement closely follows Luke's prologue, where the author has pointed out that what he is writing he has carefully investigated. Obviously Luke regards the statement about the conception through the Holy Spirit as authentic, based upon apostolic testimony. He even gives considerable details that support this position, although he does not speculate about how conception apart from a human father could have taken place. That the birth narrative concludes with statements about the human growth of Jesus (2:40), his obedience to his earthly parents (v. 51), and his increase in wisdom (v. 52) indicates that the virgin birth in no way contradicts his true humanity.

Matthew's account is independent of that of Luke, but is wholly consistent with and corroborative of it. The genealogy speaks of Joseph as "the husband of Mary, of whom Jesus was

9. Guthrie, *New Testament Theology*, p. 366.

born" (Matt. 1:16). Mary is said to be with child of the Holy Spirit (1:18). Joseph is told that the child conceived in Mary is of the Holy Spirit (1:20). Matthew states that Joseph did not "know" his wife until she had borne a son (1:25); thus the writer has taken pains to emphasize that there was no human causation involved in the fathering of Jesus. He also quotes from Isaiah 7:14, using the Septuagint text, which translates the Hebrew *almâ* with the Greek παρθένος ("virgin").

Matthew and Luke are the only two authors who refer to the virgin birth. While some have objected to this doctrine because of the silence of other New Testament authors on the subject, this silence did not seem to present any significant problem to the church in the early centuries. It was understood that not every author in the New Testament mentions every aspect of every doctrine.

The Resurrection

The resurrection is another topic which has been under considerable debate over the years, and especially in the nineteenth and twentieth centuries. As with the virgin birth we will here also be concerned simply to note the biblical testimony rather than to debate the nature of the resurrection or its historicity.

In the Synoptic Gospels we find both predictions and reports of the resurrection. Each of Jesus' predictions of his death is linked with assurance of his resurrection which was to follow (Matt. 16:21, Mark 8:31, Luke 9:22; Matt. 17:22–23, Mark 9:31; Matt. 20:18–19, Mark 10:33–34, Luke 18:32–33). Mark has in all of these cases "after three days," whereas Matthew and Luke have "on the third day," but either expression makes clear that the interval will be a short one. That Jesus made the prediction three times may well indicate that he thought his disciples would not understand and believe. Subsequent experience proved that this assumption was correct.

The reason the disciples were unable to grasp and believe the predictions of the resurrection is found in their misconception regarding Jesus' mission. They had expected a materialistic kingdom (Luke 24:21) in which Jesus would be the victorious king. The crucifixion dashed their hopes. Even though Jesus had predicted his death, their faith was so staggered by the event that they did not expect the resurrection.

The biblical testimonies to the resurrection are of several kinds. The first is the empty tomb as found by the women on Sunday morning (Matt. 28:1–8; Mark 16:1–8; Luke 24:1–12). This was followed by a series of appearances of the risen Lord: to the women as they went to tell the disciples what the angel had said (Matt. 28:9–10); to the two on the road to Emmaus (Luke 24:13–35); to all his disciples but Thomas (Luke 24:36–43); to the Eleven on a mountain in Galilee (Matt. 28:16–20). John also reports an appearance amid a gathering of the disciples that included Thomas (John 20:24–29). There also is in Matthew the guards' report to the chief priests of what had happened (Matt. 28:11–15). Thus the Gospel writers duly recorded the evidences of the resurrection; they did not, however, interpret it nor attempt to draw conclusions regarding the nature and status of Jesus.

The Fourth Gospel

When we come to the fourth Gospel, we find ourselves in a very different world from that of the Synoptics. The Johannine terminology and chronology, the concentration on Jesus' ministry in Judea and Jerusalem (rather than Galilee), on elaborate discourses (rather than parables), and on the last days of Jesus' life—these and various other unique features of the book have made many scholars question whether, in the words of George Ladd, "Christian faith has so modified the tradition that history is swallowed up in theological interpretation."[10] Important as are the critical problems today, however, the church in the first few centuries was unconscious of such issues and built much of its Christology upon the Gospel attributed to the apostle John.

One reason for the early church's dependence on the Gospel of John is the strong christological emphasis of the writer. Indeed, he gives as his reason for writing "that you may believe that Jesus is the Christ, the Son of God, and that believing you may have life in his name" (John 20:31). Eternal life is dependent upon a correct relationship to Christ, and that in turn requires a correct understanding of who and what he is. Consequently, Christology is at the very heart of John's Gospel.

10. George E. Ladd, *A Theology of the New Testament* (Grand Rapids: Eerdmans, 1974), p. 215.

One rather obvious indication is the frequency of John's use of the name *Jesus*, some 254 times, more than any other New Testament writer. By comparison, Matthew uses the name 172 times, Mark 93, and Luke 165 (98 times in his Gospel and 67 in Acts). Paul (we are here assuming the traditional attribution of books to him) uses the name a total of 220 times, with the largest number in any single book being 38 in Romans.

Jesus as the Logos

A unique feature of John's testimony is his use of the Greek word λόγος ("Word") in relationship to Jesus. Much debate has centered upon the background of this term, whether it was Hellenistic philosophy, the Old Testament, or something else. There does seem to be a common thread of meaning attached to the term by both Jew and Greek. William Temple has said that the Logos "alike for Jew and Gentile represents the ruling fact of the universe, and represents that fact as the self-expression of God. The Jew will remember that 'by the Word of the Lord were the heavens made'; the Greek will think of the rational principle of which all natural laws are particular expressions. Both will agree that this Logos is the starting point of all things."[11]

In his prologue, John ascribes several amazing attributes and activities to the Word:

1. *Preexistence.* "In the beginning was the Word" seems to be a conscious reference by John to Genesis 1:1. This takes matters back before creation. It also fits with John's report of Jesus' words, "Before Abraham was, I am" (8:58), an allusion to the "I am" self-designation of God in Exodus 3:14.
2. *Deity.* The Logos was with (πρὸς) God and was God (John 1:1). Here we have the teaching that the Word was God and yet not fully identical with him.
3. *Creative work.* All things have come into being through the Logos. Without him nothing that has been made came into existence (1:3).
4. *Incarnation.* The most amazing assertion is that "the Word became flesh" (1:14). The reference is not to some timeless occurrence, but to a specific event at a definite

---

11. William Temple, *Readings in St. John's Gospel* (London: Macmillan, 1939), p. 4.

point in history. Note that John does not say that the Word "appeared as" or "showed himself in" flesh, but that he actually "became" flesh. That this was not only a definite historical occurrence but a continuing fact is seen in the phrase "and dwelt among us" (v. 14). The term is a strong one, which literally means "tabernacled among us" or "pitched his tent among us." It conveys the idea of a lengthy period of residence rather than a temporary visit. The term *flesh* is also a strong one. John did not say, "The Word became man" or "the Word took a body." It is significant that he has just used the term *flesh* to refer to that which is human (v. 13) as opposed to that which is divine (cf. 3:6; 6:63; 8:15). This is a powerful expression of the incarnation. James Dunn, in fact, speaks of "the shocking nature of [John's] assertion" and goes on to refer to it as "otherwise needlessly offensive language [which] can only be understood as deliberately and provocatively directed against any docetic spiritualization of Jesus' humanity, an attempt to exclude docetism by emphasizing the reality of the incarnation in all its offensiveness."[12]

5. *Revelatory work.* The Word has come to reveal life (1:4), light (1:4–5), grace (1:14), truth (1:14), even God himself—"No one has ever seen God; the only Son, who is in the bosom of the Father, he has made him known" (1:18).

John does not make any further explicit use of the Logos concept beyond the prologue. It is clear, however, that the Logos theology "pervades the entire Gospel."[13]

The "I Am" Sayings

The Gospel of John is also distinctive for its use of "I am" (ἐγώ εἰμι) statements. Many of them are predicative or attributive:

1. "I am the bread of life" (John 6:35, 48). Jesus does not simply give bread; he is bread. This was said in a first-century setting in which bread was considered the basic

---

12. James D. G. Dunn, *Unity and Diversity in the New Testament* (Philadelphia: Westminster, 1977), pp. 300–01.
13. Ladd, *Theology of the New Testament*, p. 242.

necessity of life. In a similar vein Jesus said that he had come to give life and to give it abundantly (John 10:10).

2. "I am the light of the world" (8:12; 9:5—in the latter case the emphatic pronoun ἐγώ is not used). Jesus is the source of the world's illumination. This statement confirms what was said of him in the prologue (1:4–9).

3. "I am the door of the sheep" (10:7). Jesus is speaking of the entrance to a sheepfold, but evidently has in mind more than that. He is claiming to be the means by which sheep (his followers) have access into the presence of God and thus receive salvation.

4. "I am the good shepherd" (10:14–18). The imagery here is of care and provision for the sheep. It extends even to the shepherd's laying down his life for them. There is intimate knowledge of the sheep, of each one, and they know their shepherd as well.

5. "I am the resurrection and the life" (11:25). Spoken in response to Martha after the death of her brother, this statement is significant for asserting not merely that Jesus gives or brings resurrection and life, but that he is resurrection and life. In him, the life eternal, are put into proper perspective our life in this world and the death which brings it to an end.

6. "I am the way, and the truth, and the life" (14:6). Here again eternal life is in view: Jesus is the means to and the embodiment of eternal life. The exclusiveness of Jesus as the way to eternal life is underscored in the following statement, "No one comes to the Father, but by me."

7. "I am the true vine" (15:1, 5). Jesus again emphasizes himself as the source of life and underscores the importance of abiding in him.

In addition to these predicative or attributive "I am" sayings, there are passages where John uses the verb *to be* (εἰμί) to express Jesus' absolute existence. While some see allusions to Exodus 3:14 in the various attributive statements we have listed, that is debatable. Where John uses the verb *to be* to express absolute existence, however, we have direct references or parallels to that Old Testament passage. In John 8:24 Jesus calls on his hearers to believe that "I am," and in verse 28 he predicts that when they have lifted up the Son of man, they will know that "I am." The most impressive statement, however, is found in 8:58, "Truly, truly, I say to you, before Abraham was, I am." The Greek here is much stronger than the English translation. What Jesus actually said was, "Before Abraham was born (γενέσθαι), I am (ἐγὼ εἰμί)." Friedrich Büchsel comments, "This is the only passage in the NT where we have the contrast between εἶναι and γενέσθαι."[14] Whatever significance we may attach to Jesus' words, it is instructive to observe the reaction of the Jews: "So they took up stones to throw at him" (v. 59), evidently regarding his statement as a blasphemous claim to equality with God or, in other words, a claim to deity. Guthrie says, "There seems little doubt, therefore, that the statement of 8:58 is intended to convey in an extraordinary way such exclusively divine qualities as changelessness and pre-existence. The divine implication of the words would alone account for the extraordinary anger and opposition which the claim immediately aroused."[15]

Jesus' Self-Designation as the Son of Man

The references in John's Gospel to the Son of man, which are fewer (12) than those in the Synoptics, are significant for two reasons. They show considerable agreement with the Synoptics. They also elaborate some features of the overall picture more explicitly. Always linked in some way either to the salvation Christ brought or to his descent from and glorification in heaven, the references in John's Gospel fall into three basic groupings:

1. *Statements about the origin and destiny of the Son of man.* The theme of the descent of the Son of man from heaven does not occur in most of the pre-Christian Jewish references to the Son of man. By stressing this theme Jesus reveals his preexistence and his having been sent by and from God (John 1:51; 3:13; 6:62). Supporting evidence is found in John 1:1–14 and 17:5. Closely related is the glo-

---

14. Friedrich Büchsel, εἰμί, ὁ ὤν, in *Theological Dictionary of the New Testament*, ed. Gerhard Kittel and Gerhard Friedrich, trans. Geoffrey W. Bromiley, 10 vols. (Grand Rapids: Eerdmans, 1964–1976), vol. 2, p. 399.
15. Guthrie, *New Testament Theology*, p. 332.

rification of the Son of man, mentioned in 12:23 and
13:31. Glory plays an important part in John's Gospel,
not only in connection with a future glorification of the
Son, but also in connection with Jesus' work while on
earth, for John asserts, "We have beheld his glory, glory
as of the only Son from the Father" (1:14), a motif
repeated elsewhere as well (2:11; 5:41–44; 7:18; 8:50–51;
11:4; 12:41; 17:1–2, 22, 24).

2. *Statements showing the authority of the Son of man.* The
Son of man works in conjunction with the Father (6:27;
8:28). He bestows eternal life on believers (3:14–15; 6:27).
His authority is especially linked with the execution of
final judgment (5:26–27).

3. *Predictions of a lifting up of the Son of man.* These passages (3:14; 8:28; 12:33–34) have a dual reference. While
the primary reference is to Jesus' coming suffering and
death, there is also an allusion to his glorification.

Jesus' Humanity

Some have concluded from John's references to the heavenly
origin of Jesus that he could not really be fully human.[16] Yet an
examination of the book indicates that this is not the case at all.
Other people, including Jesus' opponents, frequently speak of
him as a man (e.g., 4:29; 5:12; 7:46; 9:16; 10:33; 11:47). Even
Jesus characterized himself as a man (8:40).

Not only is Jesus referred to as a man, he is also described in
such a fashion as to make clear his fully human nature. Thus he
experiences fatigue (4:6) and thirst (4:7; 19:28). He eats
(4:31–34). He shows concern for his mother (19:26–27). He
experiences human emotions, such as love (11:5), grief (11:35),
anxiety (12:27), and distress (11:33; 13:21).

Jesus' gradual acquisition of knowledge is also an indication
of his humanity. He certainly had some remarkable knowledge,
exceeding that usually found in humans (2:24–25; 5:42; 6:61;
7:29; 10:15). He did, however, have to learn and discover things.
He looked for and "found" the blind man (9:35) and the lame
man (5:14) whom he had healed. He had earlier come to know
that the latter had been afflicted for a long time (5:6). Moreover,

16. Leon Morris, *New Testament Theology* (Grand Rapids: Zondervan, 1986), pp.
244–45.

Jesus withdrew to a mountain when he learned that some people wanted to make him king (6:15). He also asked questions; although some of these were the type of questions that a teacher asks (e.g., 8:43), others were cases of his obviously needing to find out the answer to a question. Examples include his inquiring about the location of Lazarus's tomb (11:34) and the source of Pilate's information (18:34).

A closer examination of Jesus' ministry reveals the extent to which he was dependent upon the Father. Among other things, Jesus depended on the Father for his being, nature, and destiny (5:26; 6:57; 18:11), his authority and office (5:22, 27, 30; 10:18), power (17:2), knowledge (8:16), his mission and message (4:34), his testimony (5:32, 37), his disciples (6:37), the Spirit (1:33), love (17:24–26), and glory (13:32; 17:24). J. Ernest Davey sees dependence in Jesus' obeying the Father (4:34) and in such passages as 8:29, "He who sent me is with me; he has not left me alone." Davey lists twenty-two titles of Jesus found in the fourth Gospel and 1 John, and notes that most of them imply dependence ("Son," for example, implies dependence upon the Father).[17]

Acts

In the Book of Acts is recorded the kerygma, the message of the Christian community immediately following the ministry of Jesus. The speeches of the apostles are especially instructive for us.

Jesus' Humanity

The way in which Jesus is introduced in the apostles' speeches is significant. Frequent reference is made to "Jesus of Nazareth" (2:22; 3:6; 4:10; 10:38; 26:9). In telling the mob at Jerusalem about his conversion, Paul recalls that the risen Lord introduced himself as Jesus of Nazareth (22:8). Jesus is also specifically identified as "a man" in Acts 2:22. The apostles were obviously concerned to make clear to their hearers, as was Luke to make clear to his readers, that they were referring to a specific individual in history.

17. J. Ernest Davey, *The Jesus of St. John: Historical and Christological Studies in the Fourth Gospel* (London: Lutterworth, 1958), pp. 90–157.

The Resurrection

The resurrection of Jesus is prominent in the early church's belief and preaching. It was the major point of Peter's Pentecost sermon. In that message Peter said almost nothing about the life and earthly career of Jesus (2:22). He did not talk about Jesus' character and ethical actions. He said virtually nothing about Jesus' teachings. He made very little of Jesus' deeds, including the miraculous ones. What he really emphasized was that this Jesus, who had been tried, condemned, and executed as a criminal, had been raised from the dead (2:24–33).

The importance of the resurrection is also seen in the fact that the major role of the apostles was to bear witness to it. The one nonnegotiable qualification for an apostle was to have been a witness to Jesus' resurrection (Acts 1:22). Accordingly, Paul takes great pains to emphasize that the risen Lord had appeared to him, a fact mentioned in all three accounts of his conversion (chs. 9, 22, and 26). The resurrection is the central theme of the apostles throughout Acts (3:15, 26; 4:2, 10, 33; 5:30; 10:40; 13:37; 17:31; 25:19). The mighty works done by the apostles are attributed to God's having raised up Jesus (4:10), and salvation can be offered to Israel because of this great miracle (4:12). It is precisely their witness to the resurrection that prompts the first official opposition to the apostles. Ladd neatly summarizes this primacy of the resurrection in the early church's message: "In short, the earliest Christianity did not consist of a new doctrine about God nor of a new hope of immortality nor even of new theological insights about the nature of salvation. It consisted of the recital of a great event, of a mighty act of God: the raising of Christ from the dead. Any new theological emphases are the inevitable meanings of this redemptive act of God in raising the crucified Jesus from the dead."[18]

Pauline Writings

In Paul's writings we have a later stage of the movement of belief in Christ. Paul was not one of the circle of disciples, and was not an eyewitness to the events of Jesus' life. His commission to minister to the Gentiles meant that he had to find ways

---

18. Ladd, *Theology of the New Testament*, p. 317.

of expressing the message to persons who did not have the background in spiritual matters which the Jews had.

The Pauline Understanding of "Christ"

A major terminological change which we immediately notice in Paul's writing is the shift from the use of "Christ" as a title to a proper name. In the Gospels it is almost always used as a title, that is, Jesus the Christ (Messiah). In Paul's writings, however, the usage is almost invariably as a proper name. Among the few instances sometimes cited as possible exceptions are Romans 9:5; 10:6; 1 Corinthians 10:4, 16; and 2 Corinthians 4:4; 5:10. Such a shift of usage probably took place in the Hellenistic churches, where the concept of the Messiah would not have carried any meaning.[19]

Despite this terminological shift, Paul does not minimize the doctrine. Although his recognition of Jesus as the Messiah was of the glorified Lord and led to a radical reinterpretation of the person and function of the Messiah, Jesus still retained in Paul's thinking the functions that traditionally belonged to the Messiah. His coming stands in the stream of redemptive history and fulfils the prophetic promises (Rom. 1:2). His mission is "in accordance with the scriptures" (1 Cor. 15:3). The functions that Paul ascribes to the eschatological Redeemer include appearing in glory to establish his kingdom (2 Tim. 4:1), judging all humans (2 Cor. 5:10), and destroying the wicked with the breath of his mouth (2 Thess. 2:8).

Like the concept of the Messiah, so also the kingdom of God is not much mentioned but has a greater prominence than the limited usage would seem to indicate. Not only would the use of the term *king* have been subject to possible misunderstanding, the proclamation of any king other than Caesar would have rendered one liable to the charge of sedition (Acts 17:7).[20]

Jesus' Humanity

Some have assumed that Paul had little interest in the earthly life of Jesus of Nazareth. It is true that he cites only a few facts about the earthly life of Jesus, yet there are more such references than is generally recognized. Paul tells us that Jesus was born of

---

19. Vincent Taylor, *The Names of Jesus* (New York: St. Martin's, 1953), pp. 18–23.
20. Ladd, *Theology of the New Testament*, p. 410.

a woman (Gal. 4:4), descended from David (Rom. 1:3), had brothers (1 Cor. 9:5), and lived in poverty (2 Cor. 8:9). He underwent death at the hands of the Jews (1 Thess. 2:14–15) by the awful method of crucifixion (Gal. 6:14), was buried, and was raised on the third day (1 Cor. 15:4). Nor was Paul totally devoid of knowledge of Jesus' teachings. He was, as a matter of fact, able to quote some of Jesus' sayings (1 Cor. 7:10; 9:14); on the other hand, he also admitted that there were some topics on which he did not have any of the actual sayings of Jesus (1 Cor. 7:12).

There are significant passages in which Paul either asserts the humanity of Jesus or else alludes to it. He speaks of some of the basic qualities of Jesus' personality, such as his meekness and gentleness (2 Cor. 10:1), his grace, and his willingness to live in poverty (2 Cor. 8:9). At times Paul explicitly refers to Jesus as a man. The argument in Romans 5:12–21 depends upon Jesus' being a man, just as Adam was. This is made especially clear in verse 15, "that one man Jesus Christ." In a similar passage, 1 Corinthians 15:21–22, the same emphasis is found: "by a man has come also the resurrection of the dead." In the pastoral Epistles, Paul speaks of "the man Christ Jesus" (1 Tim. 2:5). Jesus is capable of being a mediator between God and humans because he himself was a man and gave himself as a ransom for all (v. 6), a reference to Mark 10:45.

These references to the humanity of Jesus are basically incidental. One might therefore draw the conclusion that Paul was not much interested in the humanity of Jesus, or even that he did not believe in it. It seems likelier, however, that Paul simply assumed the humanity of Jesus, without which neither the work of Christ on the cross nor the exaltation which was to follow would make sense.[21]

Another relevant passage is Philippians 2:5–11. Here Paul says that Christ Jesus "emptied himself, taking the form of a servant, being born in the likeness of men. And being found in human form he humbled himself and became obedient unto death, even death on a cross" (vv. 7–8). This does not assert humanity in quite so unequivocal a fashion as we might wish, but surely the thrust of the passage is that Christ Jesus took on humanity. His being subject to death presupposes humanity; furthermore, his taking the form of a servant suggests human servanthood to God.

21. Guthrie, *New Testament Theology*, p. 226.

Jesus' Deity

There are a number of passages in which Paul links Christ closely with God without explicitly saying that he is God. For example, the apostle begins many of his letters with the greeting, "Grace to you and peace from God our Father and the Lord Jesus Christ" (Rom. 1:7; 1 Cor. 1:3; 2 Cor. 1:2; Gal. 1:3; Eph. 1:2; Phil. 1:2; 2 Thess. 1:2; Philem. 3; see also 1 Tim. 1:2; Titus 1:4). Sometimes Father and Son are linked in a prayer, "May our God and Father himself, and our Lord Jesus, direct our way to you" (1 Thess. 3:11; see also 2 Thess. 2:16–17).

Paul uses the term *Son of God* quite infrequently in referring to Jesus Christ. An important instance is Romans 1:3–4, "the gospel concerning his Son, who was descended from David according to the flesh and designated Son of God in power according to the Spirit of holiness by his resurrection from the dead, Jesus Christ our Lord." There is widespread opinion that these words did not originate with Paul, but he certainly would not have included them if he did not agree with their thrust.[22] As God's Son, Jesus' mission involved bringing others into the status of sons of God. He was sent as God's Son in order that we might receive adoption as sons (Gal. 4:4–5). This is not to say, however, that Jesus' sonship is simply the same as that of us believers. He is uniquely God's Son. He is God's own Son (Rom. 8:3, 32), and the Son of his love (Col. 1:13). He was not merely a man in history, but a divine person. He preexisted and was active with the Father in creation (1 Cor. 8:6).

We must also give attention to two great christological "hymns," Philippians 2:5–11 once again and Colossians 1:15–20. There has been considerable dispute over whether these were hymns already in use in the church, which Paul then adopted for his own purposes. If they are hymns which Paul utilized, they are indications of the church's belief at a very early stage in its development.[23]

Philippians 2 served as a potent force in the church's christological construction. Its most significant assertion is that Christ "was in the form (μορφή) of God" (v. 6). While the signification

---

22. I. Howard Marshall, "The Divine Sonship of Jesus," *Interpretation* 21.1 (Jan. 1967): 102.

23. Morris, *New Testament Theology*, p. 43.

of this term has been debated at considerable length in recent years, it was interpreted in the early centuries of the church as equivalent to οὐσία. On this basis, Paul was understood as declaring that Christ was of the very same "being" or "essence" as God. In other words, we have here an assertion of the deity of Jesus Christ.

The other major hymnic passage, Colossians 1:15–20, makes several remarkable statements. Christ is spoken of as the first-born of all creation and identified as the one through whom all things have been created and in whom all things hold together. He is the head of the body, the church; he is the beginning, the firstborn from the dead.

Two additional statements served as an especially powerful influence. One is the declaration in verse 15 that Jesus is the image of the invisible God. "Image" was interpreted as being not merely a copy, or a representation, but actual similarity of essence as a son is the image of his father; in other words, Jesus is God as is the Father.[24] The other statement occurs near the end of the hymn: "For in him all the fulness (πλήρωμα) of God was pleased to dwell" (v. 19). What could it mean for all the fulness of God to dwell in someone other than that the person in question must indeed be fully and genuinely God himself? Guthrie cogently summarizes the impact of these terms: "Such concepts as . . . the 'image' and the 'fulness' of Colossians 1 . . . make it impossible to view Jesus as no more than man."[25]

The Resurrection

The resurrection of Christ played an especially significant role in Paul's theology. The best-known passage is 1 Corinthians 15, where Paul discusses the fact and nature of the future resurrection of believers. He ties this inseparably to Christ's resurrection (vv. 3–28). It is his resurrection which constitutes the proof and grounds the hope of the believer's resurrection. Paul takes great pains to establish the reality of Christ's resurrection by reciting his postresurrection appearances and the witnesses to them.

Paul also makes much of the resurrection in Romans. Christ

24. Hermann Kleinknecht, εἰκών, in *Theological Dictionary of the New Testament*, ed. Kittel and Friedrich, vol. 2, p. 389.
25. Guthrie, *New Testament Theology*, p. 365.

has been designated Son of God through his resurrection from
the dead (1:4). He was raised for our justification (4:24–25). The
believer's death and new life are closely tied to Christ's death and
resurrection (6:1–11), a theme repeated in 8:11 with different
imagery. The Christ who died, was raised from the dead, and is
now at the right hand of God is constantly interceding for his
church (8:34).

The resurrection appears elsewhere in Paul's letters as well.
He mentions it in the very opening verse of Galatians. He frequently stresses the idea that not only the future resurrection, but also the present life of the Christian, is a result of
Christ's resurrection (Eph. 1:16–20; 2:5–6; Phil. 3:10; Col. 2:12; 3:1;
1 Thess. 1:10). There can be little doubt that, for Paul, the resurrection is a real event that took place in history and plays an
important part in the justification, present life, resurrection, and
glorification of the believer.

Hebrews

The Letter to the Hebrews emphasizes strongly the greatness
of Christ. Indeed, the entire opening passage is a lauding of
Jesus the Son of God. He is the heir of all things, the one
through whom God made all that is. He is the radiance or reflection of God's glory, and "the exact representation of his being"
(1:3 NIV). He not only was active in creation, but continues to
sustain it. His excellency is demonstrated by a series of favorable comparisons with the prophets (1:1–3), angels (1:4–2:18),
and Moses (3:1–6).

In contrast to this emphasis on Christ's greatness, there is also
a strong emphasis in Hebrews on the humanity of Jesus. This is
conveyed especially through a depiction of the weakness of
human flesh. "In the days of his flesh, Jesus offered up prayers
and supplications, with loud cries and tears. Although he was a
Son, he learned obedience through what he suffered" (5:7–8). He
was made "perfect through suffering" (2:10). "He had to be
made like his brethren in every respect, so that he might become
a merciful and faithful high priest" (2:17). He "has suffered and
been tempted" (2:18); he was "in every respect . . . tempted as
we are, yet without sin" (4:15).

John's Epistles

John's Epistles emphasize Christ's supremacy. John was encountering severe opposition. Some troublemakers had already left the fellowship (1 John 2:18–19); others remained (3 John 9). Many of his opponents claimed to be inspired (1 John 4:1). How was one then to choose between the teaching of John and that of his opponents? The answer was simple—examine their attitude toward Christ.[26] The antichrist, by denying that Jesus is the Christ, is not denying him alone, but also the Father (1 John 2:22). Conversely, whoever confesses the Son has the Father as well (1 John 2:23). Those who have the Spirit of God confess that Jesus has come in the flesh (1 John 4:2). Those who do not confess that Jesus has come in the flesh are not of God, but of the spirit of antichrist. It is imperative to accept that Jesus is the Christ (1 John 5:1), the Son of God (1 John 5:5), to confess him as Son of God (1 John 4:15), and to believe in his name (1 John 3:23; 5:13).

Revelation

The Book of Revelation puts a strong emphasis upon Jesus Christ as the glorious Lord. The author greets his readers with grace and peace "from Jesus Christ the faithful witness, the first-born of the dead, and the ruler of kings on earth" (Rev. 1:5). His first vision is of the Lord in all his glory (1:12–20). He uses a series of titles to convey the greatness of the Lord: "the first and the last, and the living one" (1:17–18); the holder of the keys of Death and Hades (1:18); "the Son of God" (2:18); "the holy one, the true one, who has the key of David, who opens and no one shall shut, who shuts and no one opens" (3:7); "the Amen, the faithful and true witness, the beginning of God's creation" (3:14); "the Lion of the tribe of Judah, the Root of David" (5:5); "a Lamb standing, as though it had been slain" (5:6). The Lamb is extolled in a great song of praise from the four living creatures, the twenty-four elders, and myriads of angels (5:6–14), because he is worthy to take the scroll and open its seven seals. He then in fact proceeds to open those seals. The strong note of victory which pervades the book is inextricably linked with such triumphant actions of the Lord.

26. Morris, *New Testament Theology*, p. 288.

What then was the picture which emerged from the biblical witness regarding Jesus? We have omitted or treated with great brevity many of the considerations which should properly be given greater attention in a full-scale synthesis of the biblical teaching regarding the person of Christ. We have done virtually nothing, for example, with the Old Testament prophetic witness regarding the Christ. We also have not interacted with the critical issues involved in the interpretation of much of the material. Our aim has been simply to draw together the picture of Jesus which is found in the Scriptures, since this is what the church of the first few centuries had to work with in forming its view of Christ. We can now summarize in several brief statements the basic picture which the early church sought to analyze and refine:

1. Jesus was fully human. He possessed both a complete physical body and a complete human psyche (all the personality factors belonging to perfect humanity). He therefore grew and developed, learned, became hungry and thirsty, and could suffer and die.

2. Jesus was also fully divine. He was God in the same sense and to the same extent as the Father. Although he took a temporary role subordinate to and dependent upon the Father, this does not imply any inferiority of essence.

3. Jesus was conceived by a virgin. There was no male human parent; rather, his mother Mary became pregnant through a miraculous work of the Holy Spirit.

4. Jesus was completely sinless. Unlike us he was born without a sinful nature and committed no sin of his own, whether of word, deed, or thought. Although he was genuinely tempted, in all the ways and to the same extent we are, he never sinned.

5. Being fully human, Jesus died a physical death, but he was raised from the dead by the power of the Father. This victory over sin and death was the culmination of his redemptive work.

2

The Development
of Incarnational Christology.
(1) To the Council of Chalcedon

There is no doubt that Jesus made a profound impact upon those who believed in him and considered him their Lord. As they sought to understand more fully who and what he was, they endeavored to integrate their new insights with what they already knew and believed. Not surprisingly, people from different backgrounds held different views regarding the nature of Jesus. Quite early on, some groups denied that Jesus was genuinely divine; others maintained that he was not truly human. Then developed some more sophisticated ideas: he was less than

41

fully divine or less than fully human. Controversy also arose regarding his person: some saw in the biblical Jesus two persons and two natures; others saw one person and one nature. It was not until the Council of Chalcedon in 451 that the standard orthodox definition was formulated: fully divine and fully human, Jesus was one person with two natures. In this chapter we will look at the basic misconceptions that emerged before and led to Chalcedon.

Historical Denials of the Reality of the Two Natures

Ebionism: Denial of the Divinity of Jesus

One of the earliest and in some ways simplest of the misconceptions about Jesus was the movement known as Ebionism. While some have speculated that the name is taken from a founder named Ebion, it seems likelier that it is derived from the Hebrew word for "poor."[1] There were significant numbers of Jews among the believers in the early days of the church. Some of them sought to understand Jesus in light of the basic elements of Jewish thought. Two of these ideas were a strong monotheism and the eternal validity of the Mosaic law. The teachings of this new Christianity appeared to undermine these ideas in significant ways. To a strong monotheist, the deity of Jesus seemed polytheistic. Further, if the law was given by God, it must be final, absolute, and unchanging. The teaching that Jesus was a new and final revelation seemed to conflict with this idea as well. It is notable that primitive Christianity gave some support to the Jewish perspective, particularly the idea of the absoluteness and finality of the law. In Jesus' teaching, for example, there is no criticism of or opposition to the law. He said, in fact, "Think not that I have come to abolish the law and the prophets; I have come not to abolish them but to fulfil them" (Matt. 5:17). While he insisted that the human traditions which had grown upon the law were to be rejected, he treated the law itself with great respect and with recognition of its authority.

The evidence regarding the Ebionites is fragmentary and

1. J. F. Bethune-Baker, *An Introduction to the Early History of Christian Doctrine to the Time of the Council of Chalcedon* (London: Methuen, 1903), p. 63.

somewhat difficult to interpret from the early Christian writings. Justin Martyr (ca. 100–165) spoke of two classes of Ebionites: those who, viewing the law as essential to salvation, required all believers to observe it; and those who attempted to impose its ordinances upon others as well.[2] Justin also spoke of some who regarded Jesus as Christ the Messiah, but considered him simply a man, born in the ordinary way, not of a virgin.[3] Irenaeus (ca. 130–200) emphasized the Ebionites' teaching regarding the person of Christ, observing that their view was similar to that of Cerinthus and Carpocrates,[4] who, while denying the virgin birth and holding that Jesus was an ordinary man, looked on him as surpassing others in righteousness and knowledge.

Eusebius (ca. 260–340) gives the most complete exposition of the Ebionites' Christology. He speaks of two classes, based upon lower and higher conceptions of the person of Christ. Both groups insisted upon observance of the law. The first group held to a natural birth of Jesus, who, although an ordinary human, was characterized by an unusual moral character. The second group, on the other hand, accepted a supernatural birth, but rejected the idea of Jesus' preexistence as the Son and the Logos.[5] Epiphanius (ca. 315–403) distinguished between two sects, the Nazaraeans and the Ebionaeans, but probably drew this distinction inaccurately.[6] These labels persisted as late as Jerome (ca. 340–420), who referred to Ebionites who "pretend to be Christians" and were commonly known as Nazaraeans. While they held to an orthodox belief in Christ, they also insisted upon adherence to the law.[7]

One individual who is generally regarded as an Ebionite is Cerinthus (fl. 100). Because he held to some elements of Gnostic thought, his followers have sometimes been referred to as "Cerinthian Gnostics," as contrasted with "Docetic Gnostics." Most of his doctrines, however, in no way resembled Gnosticism. The similarity to Gnosticism was in terms of the view of the relationship between God and the world. Cerinthus held that God had not created directly, but through angels who served as

---

2. Justin Martyr *Dialogue with Trypho* 47.
3. Ibid., 48.
4. Irenaeus *Against Heresies* 1.26.
5. Eusebius *Ecclesiastical History* 3.27.
6. Epiphanius *Panarion* ("Against Eighty Heresies") 29–30.
7. Jerome *Letters* 112.13.

intermediaries. One of these was the God of the Jews, who gave the law.

Cerinthus's Christology was a form of Adoptionism. According to this view, Jesus was an ordinary human being whom God "adopted" as his Son. Because of Jesus' ethical qualities God gave him a special gift of spirituality. Now God cannot arbitrarily make a person holy. He first had to test Jesus throughout his early life. At the baptism the Spirit of God, the Christ, descended upon Jesus, revealing the Father to him and enabling him to do miracles. Before Jesus' death the Christ withdrew from him. There was no real union between the Christ and Jesus, only a sort of conjunction. The mission of the Messiah was educational rather than redemptive, relating especially to the prophetic office. As the experience of a mere human, his sufferings and death have no special value for us.[8]

A final expression of Ebionism was the Clementines. They were probably Essenes from eastern Palestine who, like Cerinthus, drew a definite distinction between Jesus and the Christ. The Christ, the Son of God, has appeared in a series of incarnations in perfect men. The reason for these appearances is that humans have two orientations. Because they have an inward spirit which is directed toward God, they have an affinity for him; they are the highest of the creatures. They also, however, have a base desire which tends to lower them to earth, and thus they are alienated from God. To save humans from this lower tendency, the Christ has appeared in successive incarnations in the persons of Adam, Enoch, Noah, Abraham, Isaac, Jacob, and finally Jesus. He is the last, and there apparently will be no others. The Clementines attached no special significance to his death and resurrection, however. In their view, his mission was only educational, not redemptive.[9]

Docetism: Denial of the Humanity of Jesus

It was the opposite tendency that proved to be the more formidable threat to orthodox Christology. Docetism (from the Greek verb δοκεῖν, "to seem") was the belief that Jesus was not genuinely human, that he merely "seemed" or "appeared" to possess human nature. This teaching arose very early and was prob-

8. Irenaeus *Against Heresies* 1.26.
9. Hippolytus *Against All Heresies* 9.13.

ably the object of the apostle's rebuttal in 1 John. It may, in other words, have been the original heresy, with the possible exception of the legalism which Paul dealt with in Galatians.

Docetism was not a specific school of thought as such. Rather, it was a characteristic of a number of different theologies. It was especially evident in the theologies which were under the influence of Gnosticism. Gnosticism was a broad cultural trend found not only in Christian forms, but also in Syrian, Persian, and Jewish manifestations. In the words of Gilles Quispel, "Gnosticism minus Christianity is still Gnosticism."[10]

As the name suggests, Gnosticism (from the Greek γνῶσις, "knowledge") placed a great emphasis upon knowledge. It was, in fact, a system of thought which held that the entire cosmos is to be redeemed through knowledge. As might be suspected, any system which places such a strong emphasis upon knowledge naturally accents the spiritual or immaterial as contrasted with the material realm. This is, as a matter of fact, the most fundamental of the major tenets found in the various forms of Gnosticism:

1. *A thoroughgoing metaphysical dualism.* A great chasm separates the spiritual realm and the world of matter. The latter is inherently evil, whereas the supreme God is completely good.[11]
2. *The attribution of creation to the demiurge.* The absolute antithesis between the nature of the supreme God and the world inevitably introduced the question of how the latter could have come into being. To account for creation, Gnosticism posited an intermediate being, the demiurge.[12] Students of philosophy will recognize here the influence of or at least a parallel to a concept found in Plato's *Timaeus.* While some Christian theologians who attempted to integrate Platonic philosophy with Christian theology found difficulty in reconciling the Platonic demiurge with the Christian God, Gnosticism solved the problem by including both in its system. Some Gnostics held that the divine demiurge acted in ignorance when creating the world and especially humankind. Thus the

10. Gilles Quispel, *Gnosis als Weltreligion* (Zurich: Origo, 1951), p. 28.
11. Irenaeus *Against Heresies* 1.4.
12. Ibid., 1.5.

human race did not fall after having been created perfect, but was, instead, created imperfect.

3. *A depreciation of the process of human generation and birth.*[13] Since creation was regarded as inherently evil, anything that came into being through the reproductive process was also viewed as corrupted, as was the process itself, because it involved the material aspect of the human.

From the tenets of Gnosticism it followed that the humanity of Jesus must have been merely apparent. It could not have involved a uniting of the perfect God with real human flesh, since that, as material, must be evil. The docetic thinkers had no difficulty accepting the full deity of Jesus. It was the humanity which constituted the difficulty. Here, as in so many areas, we do not have any direct statements from the proponents of the view themselves. Rather, we have a statement by Justin, "And there are some who maintain that even Jesus himself appeared only as spiritual, and not in flesh, but presented merely the appearance of flesh."[14] Very early in the second century Ignatius similarly protested against "unbelieving" people who claimed that Christ had suffered only in appearance.[15] This could be construed as a reference to the fairly common assertion of that time that someone else had died in Jesus' place. Elsewhere, however, Ignatius vigorously defends the actuality of all of Christ's human experiences, and hints that his opponents did not admit that Christ was genuinely "flesh-bearing."[16]

Just as the Docetic Gnostics had no difficulty accepting the deity of Jesus but only the humanity, so they had no difficulty accepting the idea that Mary was a virgin, but only that Jesus was genuinely born. Mary did not contribute anything to Jesus. The Docetists carefully stipulated that Jesus was transmitted "through" or "by means of" Mary, but was not born "from" or "of" her. That is to say, he derived no part of his being from her. He merely passed through her, as water passes through a tube.[17]

13. Ibid., 1.28.
14. Justin Martyr *On the Resurrection* 5.
15. Ignatius *Epistle to the Trallians* 10; *Epistle to the Smyrnaeans* 2.
16. Ignatius *Epistle to the Ephesians* 7, 18–20; *Epistle to the Trallians* 9; *Epistle to the Magnesians* 11; *Epistle to the Smyrnaeans* 1–3, 7.
17. Irenaeus *Against Heresies* 1.7.

According to one group of Docetists, the Valentinians, Jesus had a spiritual flesh.[18] His humanity, then, was only a vehicle of revelation, utilized briefly for the introduction of the eternal into the world.

The Docetists' conception of the work of Christ follows from their conception of his nature and of human nature. Humans are made up of an earthly part and a spiritual part. Salvation, if it can be called that, is intellectual in character. It is a matter of coming to know the gnosis, the higher truth. The work of Christ was primarily revelatory, appealing to those who are of a higher or spiritual orientation, and made clear by the special truth possessed by the enlightened (the Gnostics).

We noted earlier that Docetism was more a broad cultural trend than a specific movement. Although it may have been more fully and clearly set forth in Gnosticism than elsewhere, it was relatively widespread. Celsus, a virulently anti-Christian Platonist, for example, attacked the notion that a deity could assume a genuine human body: "The body of a god would not have been so generated as you, O Jesus, were. . . . The body of a god is not nourished with such food [as was Jesus]."[19] Marcion, a second-century heretic, while admitting that Jesus had a body capable of suffering in some sense, rejected the idea that it was a material body.[20] Although the distinguished church father Clement of Alexandria was not a Docetist, his division of human nature into body and soul and his depreciation of the former led him to make statements which at times sounded somewhat docetic in their tendency. He made the divine Logos, rather than the historical Jesus, the central motif of his Christology.[21]

Historical Denials of the Integrity of the Two Natures

Arianism: Denial of the Full Divinity of Jesus

Docetism was a heresy against which theologians like Ignatius spoke out emphatically, insisting that Christ "was really born, and ate and drank, was really persecuted by Pontius Pilate, was

18. Tertullian *On the Flesh of Christ* 15.
19. Origen *Against Celsus* 1.69–70.
20. Tertullian *On the Flesh of Christ* 1–5.
21. Jaroslav Pelikan, *The Christian Tradition: A History of the Development of Doctrine*, 4 vols. (Chicago: University of Chicago Press, 1971–1985), vol. 1, p. 47.

really crucified and died. . . [and] really rose from the dead."[22]
Yet the issues did not immediately get worked out. Jaroslav
Pelikan has suggested that the problems raised by Docetism
were somewhat premature, and that its subtle and profound
implications could not be fully dealt with until an equally subtle christological terminology had been created.[23] Furthermore,
before the problem of the relation between the divine in Christ
and his earthly life could be adequately considered, it was necessary for the more fundamental problem of the relation
between the divine in Christ and the divine in the Father to be
treated. Athanasius put it thus, "And how shall he not err in
respect to His incarnate presence, who is simply ignorant of the
Son's genuine and true generation from the Father?"[24] Once the
doctrine of the Trinity had been clarified, the church could
return to deal more adequately with the doctrine of the person
and nature of Christ.

The Background:
Dynamic and Modalistic Monarchianism

Before we move to consideration of Arianism, the heresy that
forced the church to settle the issue of the relation between the
Father and the Son, it is important that we note an intermediate stage which led or at least contributed to the rise of that
movement. This intermediate stage was part of the effort to deal
with the problem of the Trinity. As Christian theologians argued
with increasing effect that the New Testament witnesses to the
deity of Jesus, repeated efforts were made to reconcile this belief
with the strong monotheism of the Old Testament. Two theologies which sought to preserve the emphasis upon the primacy
and singularity of the Father were known as Monarchianism, a
label apparently created by Tertullian.[25] Both Dynamic and
Modalistic Monarchianism aimed to preserve the uniqueness
and greatness of God the Father. Although some scholars have
supposed that the two theologies had a common origin, that
appears unlikely.

Dynamic Monarchianism was a form of Adoptionism. Some
have claimed that the Shepherd of Hermas (a noncanonical

22. Ignatius *Epistle to the Trallians* 9.
23. Pelikan, *Christian Tradition*, vol. 1, p. 174.
24. Athanasius *Four Discourses Against the Arians* 1.8.
25. Tertullian *Against Praxeas* 10.

apocalypse from the second century) is adoptionist in its Christology, but that claim is difficult either to prove or to disprove.[26] The words of Peter in Acts 2:32–36 could be read as adoptionist. The leading proponents of Dynamic Monarchianism, Theodotus the leather merchant (fl. 190) and Paul of Samosata (fl. 260), thought that God came upon Jesus at some point in his life, usually identified as the baptism. Theodotus held that at the baptism the Spirit, or Christ, descended upon Jesus, a supremely virtuous man. As a result, Jesus was able to perform miracles, though he did not become divine. Theodotus and his followers gave a great deal of attention to biblical exegesis, some of it of a rather creative type, appealing especially to texts such as Luke 1:35 (where they read, "The Spirit of the Lord [instead of 'The Holy Spirit'] will come upon you") and Deuteronomy 18:15. They held that the Spirit inspired, rather than indwelt, Jesus.[27] Paul's thought is difficult to reconstruct, but it seems fair to regard his view as similar to that of Theodotus. The chief difference is that Paul incorporated the idea of the Logos into his teaching.

Modalistic Monarchianism was given the same generic name but employed a very different method to achieve the goal of preserving the primacy of the Father. This movement received much greater popular acceptance than did Dynamic Monarchianism. It insisted equally upon two factors, the unity of God and the deity of Jesus. To the modalists, the new concentration on the Logos seemed to endanger the former of these two factors by arguing, as did Justin, that the Logos is somehow numerically other than the Father. In the thinking of modalism, the distinction is only verbal or nominal. Noetus (fl. 200) held that there is only one God, the Father, and that the Father suffered in Christ (Patripassianism).[28] Although Noetus was condemned by the church, his disciple Epigonus found some followers in Rome, notably Cleomenes; even Zephyrinus, the bishop of Rome from 198 to 217, seemed to be somewhat open to this view.[29] Hippolytus summarized modalism as the belief that there is one Godhead to which either the term *Father* or *Son* can be applied.

26. Pelikan, *Christian Tradition*, vol. 1, p. 175.
27. Epiphanius *Panarion* 54.4.1–6.
28. Hippolytus *Against Noetus* 2.
29. Pelikan, *Christian Tradition*, vol. 1, p. 181.

These terms are merely names that are applicable at different times; they do not signify real distinctions.[30]

The person who gave modalism a systematic, philosophical form was Sabellius. He regarded the Godhead as a monad (which he labeled *Huiopatōr*, "Son-Father") expressing itself in three operations. He used the analogy of the sun, a single object (cf. the Father) which radiates both light (cf. the Son) and warmth (cf. the Spirit). Thus the Father is the form or essence of the Godhead, and the Son and the Spirit are modes of his self-expression.[31] So popular did this view become that it appears that Zephyrinus and his successor Callistus (217–222) at least sympathized with it against the beliefs of Hippolytus and Tertullian, which were thought to lead to ditheism.[32]

Modalistic Monarchianism endeavored to solve the problem of the Trinity by in effect removing the distinction between Father and Son. The orthodox response sought to emphasize the distinction, maintaining that the Father and Son, as well as the Spirit, are not the same person viewed in different roles or at different times, but rather are distinct persons. In the process, however, more was demonstrated than had originally been intended.[33]

The Arian Heresy

One passage appealed to by orthodox defenders of the faith over against the Monarchians was Proverbs 8:22–31. These verses clearly indicate the distinction of the Logos (which had come to be used as a term identifying the divine element in Christ). Controversy broke out when Bishop Alexander of Alexandria called upon several presbyters, and especially Arius (ca. 250–336), presbyter of the church district of Baucalis in Alexandria, to give an interpretation of this passage. Arius's interpretation was rendered in light of certain theological a prioris which he brought to the task.

The first of Arius's assumptions was the absoluteness of God. By this is meant in part the singularity of God. He is the one and only, single and incomparable. "One and only" was not suffi-

30. Hippolytus *Against Noetus* 1.
31. Epiphanius *Panarion* 62.1.4–5.
32. J. N. D. Kelly, *Early Christian Doctrines* (New York: Harper and Row, 1960), p. 123.
33. See Arius *Epistle to Alexander* 2, 4.

cient, however. Arius raised this expression to the superlative by affirming that God is "without beginning and utterly one."

Beyond absoluteness there was Arius's conception of the extreme transcendence of God. He is separate and different from everything else. This transcendence meant to Arius that God could not have created by direct contact with the world. There could not have been any involvement with the creation which might conceivably have effected changes in him of the type that would be experienced by a body. This interpretation of transcendence was required not only by the utter oneness of God, but also by the fragility of all creatures, which "could not endure to be wrought by the Absolute and of the Unoriginate."[34]

Arius also relied upon analogical argumentation. He maintained that what is true of a human father-son relationship must also be true of the relationship between God the Father and the Son. Since a human father is prior to his son, and the son cannot have been in existence as early in time as was the father, God the Father, reasoned Arius, must also antedate God the Son.[35]

From these general principles Arius and his followers sought to interpret the relevant passages of Scripture. Several conclusions followed as to the nature of Christ. One was that he is not of the same nature as the Father. Any such continuity between the two would violate the transcendence of the Father. Arius rejected the metaphor comparing the Son's derivation from the Father to a flame's being passed from one torch to another. Whereas the anti-Arians rejected the metaphor as suggesting that the divine essence is something separate from the Father and the Son, the Arians rejected it because it seemed to imply a continuity between the two persons.[36] They regarded the Son as a creature whom the Father made out of nothing. He was, to be sure, the first of the creatures to be made, having been brought into existence before the beginning of time, but he was a creature nonetheless. Unlike the Father, the Son had a beginning.

There is another difference between Jesus and the rest of the creatures. He was made directly by the Father, whereas they were made indirectly, having been brought into being by the action of the Son. He was, thus, less than the Father, but more

34. Athanasius *Defense of the Nicene Definition* 3.8.
35. Athanasius *Four Discourses* 1.15.
36. Arius *Epistle to Alexander* 3.

than other humans. He can be thought of as an intermediary, both cosmologically and soteriologically.[37]

What made it difficult for the opponents of Arianism, both in terms of identifying and of refuting the view, was the fact that the Arians continued to use many of the terms traditionally applied to the Son, while meaning something different from what had usually been meant. For example, they continued to refer to Jesus as the Son of God. In addition, they continued to worship him, to address prayers to him, and to baptize in his name, as well as in the name of the Father and of the Holy Spirit.[38] But when the Arians referred to Jesus as God or the Son of God, they were using these terms merely as courtesy titles. Arius himself said, "Even if he is called God, he is not God truly, but by participation in grace. . . . [He] is called God in name only."[39]

The Arians by no means lacked scriptural documentation for their views. Indeed, they spent much time in exegesis of a number of texts:[40]

1. *Texts which suggest that the Son is a creature.* Proverbs 8:22, especially as rendered by the Septuagint, "The LORD created me," is the specific text that provoked Arius's controversial thinking. Other texts of this type include Acts 2:36, "God has made him both Lord and Christ"; Colossians 1:15, "He is . . . the first-born of all creation"; and Hebrews 3:2, which the Arians rendered, "He was faithful to Him who made him."
2. *Texts which represent the Father as the only true God.* An outstanding example is found in Christ's prayer in John 17:3, in which he said, "And this is eternal life, that they know thee the only true God, and Jesus Christ whom thou hast sent."
3. *Texts which seem to imply that the Son is inferior to the Father.* Jesus himself said, "The Father is greater than I" (John 14:28).
4. *Texts which give evidence of the humanity of Christ.* Here are in view the whole host of passages which attribute

37. Pelikan, *Christian Tradition*, vol. 1, p. 198.
38. Gregory of Nazianzus *Orations* 40.42.
39. Quoted in Athanasius *Four Discourses* 1.2.
40. Athanasius *Four Discourses*, passim; Epiphanius *Panarion* 69.12–79.

weakness, ignorance, suffering, and development to Jesus. Obviously the Arians had a great deal of biblical ammunition with which to support their position.

The Orthodox Response: The Council of Nicea

The Arian view was not acceptable to Alexander, the bishop of Alexandria, so he called a council to meet early in 325 at Antioch. This was a regional council chaired by Ossius, the emperor's theological confidant. It set forth a rather lengthy statement of the divinity of Christ. It described Christ as "not made but properly an offspring, but begotten in an ineffable, indescribable manner," one who "exists everlastingly and did not at one time not exist." It condemned "those who say or think or preach that the Son of God is a creature or has come into being or has been made and is not truly begotten, or that there was a then when he did not exist." Although not mentioning Arius by name, the document contained many verbatim quotations from Arian theologians. Three bishops who refused to subscribe to the statement were excommunicated.[41]

This local council did not really settle matters for the entire church, however. The emperor Constantine, who had established Christianity as the official religion of the state, now convened an ecumenical council to meet at Nicea in Bithynia. It was his desire that agreement be reached in the church, so that there would be ecclesiastical peace within his empire.

It appears that in effect there were not two but three groups at Nicea, although there were really only two camps theologically. On the one hand there were the Arians, who denied the eternality and the full deity of the Son, that is, they held that in these respects the Son is less than the Father. On the other extreme was the group headed by Alexander of Alexandria, whose most articulate spokesperson was Athanasius (293–373). They were determined to maintain the full deity of the Son, his oneness of essence with the Father, and his eternality. But there also was another large group, perhaps the largest of the three. These were bishops who wanted to maintain the status quo. They were not experts in the technical issues of theology. It was their view that if the Arians called Christ God and Son of God, worshiped him and baptized in his name, and professed com-

41. Pelikan, *Christian Tradition*, vol. 1, pp. 200–01.

plete allegiance to Scripture, they were probably sound at heart, and these technical details should not be pressed against them.

These bishops, from Syria and Asia Minor, were considerably influenced by Origen's thought as they understood it. They were fearful of Monarchianism and especially Sabellianism, and thought they saw some semblance of it in the thought and terminology of the opponents of the Arians. They were, moreover, reluctant to use terminology which was new, which, in other words, did not have the sanction of church tradition. They preferred to use simply the terminology of Scripture, and, at least initially, this was their hope. So a whole series of scriptural terms was successively suggested, all of which the Arians were able to accept. Many in the council felt uneasy, however, suspecting that the Arians assigned to these terms a meaning very different from what they themselves had in mind. Real progress began when the friends of Arius produced a creed for the council to endorse. The creed was actually Arian in its content and aroused the anger of most of the bishops. Now that the Arians had revealed what their true views were, it was apparent that the majority of the bishops were not Arian.[42]

At this point Eusebius, bishop of Caesarea, introduced a creed. A significant church historian, he is generally considered to have been the most learned churchman of the time. His own Christology, however, was not carefully worked out. Indeed, J. A. Dorner speaks of Eusebius's doctrine of Christ as chameleon-hued, reflecting all of the unsolved problems of the church of that age.[43] Further, he had shown some real sympathy for Arius, although this was probably due to personal friendship and an aversion to the Sabellian approach. Scholars have long considered the creed which Eusebius introduced to have been the baptismal formula utilized in his own church, but that now appears uncertain.[44] In any event, the statement met with a generally favorable response, but it was not explicit enough to exclude Arianism, so the emperor suggested the insertion of the now famous term *homoousios* (Jesus was "of the same essence" as the Father). A few other small alterations were made, and at the

42. Bethune-Baker, *Early History*, pp. 165–67.
43. J. A. Dorner, *History of the Development of the Doctrine of the Person of Christ* (Edinburgh: T. & T. Clark, 1889), division first, vol. 2, p. 218.
44. Pelikan, *Christian Tradition*, vol. 1, p. 201.

end was appended a list of Arian tenets for anathematization. The creed which was adopted reads as follows:

> We believe in one God, the FATHER Almighty, Maker of all things visible and invisible.
>
> And in one Lord JESUS CHRIST, the Son of God, begotten of the Father [the only-begotten; that is, of the essence of the Father, God of God], Light of Light, very God of very God, begotten, not made, being of one substance (*homoousios*) with the Father; by whom all things were made [both in heaven and on earth]; who for us men, and for our salvation, came down and was incarnate and was made man; he suffered, and the third day he rose again, ascended into heaven; from thence he shall come to judge the quick and the dead.
>
> And in the HOLY GHOST.
>
> [But for those who say: "There was a time when he was not;" and "He was not before he was made;" and "He was made out of nothing," or "He is of another substance" or "essence," or "The Son of God is created," or "changeable," or "alterable"—they are condemned by the holy catholic and apostolic Church.][45]

It is easier to identify from this statement what is being denied than what is being affirmed. Yet, as in so many statements of this type, the list of denials or anathemas is extremely helpful in determining exactly what is being affirmed. We can summarize the Arian tenets that are explicitly denied in the Nicene Creed:

1. There was a time when the Son did not exist.
2. The Father preexisted the Son.
3. The hypostasis or substance of the Son differs from that of the Father.
4. The Son is a creature similar in every way to the other creatures. (Rather, he has been begotten; he has not been made, as they have, either out of nothingness or out of some other material.)
5. The Son is subject to alteration and moral change.

These denials are in turn denials of two underlying assumptions of the Arians:

45. Philip Schaff, ed., *The Creeds of Christendom*, 6th ed., 3 vols. (New York: Harper, 1931; Grand Rapids: Baker, 1990 reprint), vol. 1, pp. 28–29.

1. The Father-Son relationship is literally the same as that between earthly fathers and sons.
2. The birth of Jesus should be equated with his origin or the beginning of his existence.

The positive affirmations are, as we indicated, somewhat less easily identified. Their real core is the term *homoousios*: the essence or substance of the Son is the same as that of the Father. His very nature, that set of factors which makes something to be what it is, is to be identified with the nature of the Father, not with the nature of any of the creatures. He is of the same genus as the Father, not the creatures. He bears no resemblance to the creatures, but is in every respect like the Father.

There is a certain ambiguity in the term οὐσία, on which *homoousios* is built. It can, on the one hand, refer to the substance or stuff common to all the individuals in a class. It can also, however, refer to an individual being or thing as such. Now if the divine nature is understood in the latter sense, the persons of the Godhead who share it must be numerically one. Many scholars have assumed that this numerical oneness of substance is indeed what the council was affirming. Such a concept, however, would be the Monarchian heresy so feared and despised by the majority of the bishops at the council. Another crucial consideration is that in both secular and theological usage prior to Nicea the term *homoousios* was employed primarily in the generic sense. Indeed, Arius himself uses the term in this way in passages denying that the Son is "of the same nature" as the Father; it is Jesus' divinity, not numerical oneness with the Father, that Arius is here denying.[46]

The framers of the confession were also concerned to maintain the soteriological significance of Jesus, and were convinced that this required a certain understanding of his nature. To be delivered from their lost condition, the human race was in need of redemption from without, which could be provided only by the Being who had created the universe and humans with it. Both of these actions—creation and redemption—could be accomplished only by one who was himself uncreated and divine in the same sense and to the same degree as the Father.[47]

46. Kelly, *Early Christian Doctrines*, pp. 234–36.
47. Pelikan, *Christian Tradition*, vol. 1, p. 203.

It might seem to us that the council's action of adopting an anti-Arian statement and banishing Arius and all others who did not accept the verdict would have settled the matter. Arianism should have faded away, never to be heard of again. While the church might have to face new threats to its orthodox Christology, Arianism should no longer have constituted a challenge. In reality, however, this was not the case.

The history of christological discussion and formulation between 325 and 381 is complex, although perhaps no more so than the political vagaries of those years with which it was so closely involved. One of the significant developments was the formation of a party that advocated the term *homoiousios* (Jesus and the Father are "of similar essence"). These were persons, largely Origenistic in their outlook, to whom the major leaders of the Nicene majority, and especially Marcellus of Ancyra, appeared to be leaning toward Sabellianism. In part this misconception was due to the fact that *hypostasis* and *ousia* are equated in the anathemas—those "who assert that the Son of God is from a different hypostasis or substance" are condemned. The underlying problem here is that while the Greek term *hypostasis* is identical in construction to the Latin *substantia* (both are compounds of a preposition meaning "under" and a verb meaning "to stand"), to Greek speakers *hypostasis* signified "individual personality" as well as "essential nature." Western theologians, then, in speaking of one hypostasis in the Godhead, seemed to be obliterating the threeness of God. The situation was further aggravated by the fact that Arius had spoken of three hypostases, and had therefore colored the terminology with the suspicion of heresy. Amid such confusion *homoiousios* was commended as a way of stressing that Jesus is of the same essence as the Father and yet distinct from him. Unfortunately, the term represented different things to different groups. To some it meant virtually what *homoousios* was originally intended to mean in the Nicene Creed. Thus it did not signify any lesser deity for the Son than for the Father, but merely guarded against viewing them as nothing more than different manifestations of a one-person Godhead. Others, however, interpreted *homoiousios* as denoting merely a moral resemblance between Father and Son. A series of councils met over the next fifty years, some proposing improved expressions of the

Nicene Creed, some trying to avoid the use of any terms not found explicitly in the Bible, some actually seeming to favor Arian principles. Marcellus was condemned, and on at least two occasions Athanasius was exiled and subsequently restored.[48]

It was in the context of more distinctly trinitarian discussion that the final disposition of the Arian issue took place. Increasing attention was being focused upon the status of the Spirit. What was his relationship to the Father and the Son? Gradually the Athanasian and the anti-Nicene parties had been coming closer together. The culmination of the theological discussion bearing on the nature and status of the Son was reached at the Council of Constantinople in 381. There, in affirming that the Spirit is "of the same essence" (*homoousios*) as the Father and the Son, the church also reaffirmed the Nicene pronouncement regarding the Son, effectively settling the matter for some time.

Apollinarianism: Denial of the Full Humanity of Jesus

It should be apparent that we are now at a more advanced and thus more subtle stage of the discussion than we were when examining Ebionism and Docetism. Those theories must now appear relatively crude by comparison with the more refined issues being examined. They had, respectively, simply denied the reality of the deity and the humanity of Jesus Christ. Arianism, by contrast, made Jesus more than human, but less than fully God, or in other words a demigod. Not surprisingly, the next major challenge to orthodox theological definition dealt with Jesus' humanity, denying not its reality, but its fulness or completeness.

We should note another shift at this stage of our discussion. We have been examining the relationship between the Son and the Father, and, finally, the Spirit as well. Now, however, we return to the relationship between the two natures (human and divine) in the one person Jesus Christ.

In the fourth century two differing emphases emerged within orthodox christological construction. The Alexandrian school held to what came to be called the "Word-flesh" Christology. On the other hand, the Antiochene school maintained the "Word-man" Christology. As might be suspected, since Arius and

48. Kelly, *Early Christian Doctrines*, pp. 248–50; Pelikan, *Christian Tradition*, vol. 1, pp. 208–10.

Athanasius were both from Alexandria, the Arian controversy occurred basically within the Alexandrian school.

The Word-flesh Christology held that what the eternal Word took in becoming incarnate was human flesh or a human body.[49] Indeed, "incarnate" derives from two Latin words meaning "in flesh." Athanasius insisted that in the incarnation Christ did not merely enter into a man, but actually became a man.[50] To say, as did the Antiochene Christology, that the Word took on man rather than flesh seemed to leave open the possibility of a sort of Adoptionism, according to which the Word united with a preexisting individual human being. Athanasius also saw the incarnation as not altering the transcendent status of the Word in any significant way. While encompassed in a human body, he continued to govern the universe.[51]

In describing what happened in the Word's becoming man, Athanasius speaks of his taking flesh or a body, and of his fashioning a body for himself in the virgin's womb.[52] The Christianity of those who hold that Christ, rather than taking his body from Mary, entered into a holy man, just as he entered into the prophets of old, is called into question. Working with a scheme adapted from the Stoics, Athanasius also holds that the Logos is the animating principle of the entire universe, and that the human soul, a close copy of the Logos, serves as the animating principle of the human body.[53] Christ's human body was a part of the cosmos, and the Logos was the animating principle of this body, just as it was of the entire cosmos.

Apollinarius (ca. 310–390), a supporter of Athanasius, took the Alexandrian position to an extreme. He protests against those who believe that Jesus is not God incarnate, but a man conjoined with God. They hold, Apollinarius claims, to two Sons, the Son of God and the son of Mary.[54] To such a dualism, Apollinarius emphatically objects, since he believes that Scripture clearly teaches that Jesus Christ is a unity.[55] Apollinarius was motivated

---

49. Kelly, *Early Christian Doctrines*, p. 281.

50. Athanasius *Four Discourses* 3.26.

51. Athanasius *On the Incarnation of the Word* 17.

52. Ibid., 8, 9, 10, 18.

53. Athanasius *Letters* 59.2 (to Epictetus).

54. Apollinarius frag. 81 Lietzmann (*Apollinaris von Laodicea und seine Schule*, ed. Hans Lietzmann [Tübingen: Mohr (Paul Siebeck), 1964], p. 224).

55. Ibid., 2, 9 Lietzmann (pp. 204, 206–07).

to a large extent by soteriological considerations. If the divine and the human are separated, then our redemption is jeopardized. Considered merely as man, Christ has no saving power.[56]

To counteract such a dualism, Apollinarius developed an extreme variety of the Word-flesh Christology. He was especially fond of terminology such as "God incarnate," "flesh-bearing God," and "God born of a woman" in describing Christ.[57] In using these terms he did not mean, however, simply that the Word clothed or wrapped himself in human flesh as an outward covering, but rather that the human flesh of Christ was, from the moment of conception, joined with the Godhead in an absolute oneness of being.[58]

In Apollinarius's understanding the flesh is not a complete living entity. It depends for its life on some principle of movement and action. In the case of ordinary humans, this principle is the human spirit or soul. In the case of Christ, it is the Word. The divine Word actually substitutes for normal human psychology. "The divine energy fulfils the role of the animating spirit (psyche) and of the human mind (nous)."[59] In the God-man Jesus Christ, the Word is both the principle of intelligence and the source or basis of life. The flesh has no basis of life apart from the Word, which takes the place of the human soul. Thus we have in Jesus a single entity compounded of the Logos and the flesh, not a duality, nor two complete, self-moving principles (i.e., Logos and human soul).[60]

Apollinarius had no objection to the criticism that his view made Christ different from ordinary humans. He cited texts stating, for example, that Jesus was "made in human likeness" and "found in appearance as a man" (Phil. 2:7–8 NIV).[61] Christ is unique because in the virgin birth the divine spirit replaced the sperm which ordinarily gives life to humans.[62]

We should also take careful note of the fact that Apollinarius was what was later to be termed a Monophysite. He held that Christ had just one nature. His body did not constitute a nature

56. Apollinarius *On Faith and the Incarnation* 9 (Lietzmann, p. 202).
57. Apollinarius frags. 108–09, 49, 52 Lietzmann (pp. 232–33, 216).
58. Ibid., 36 Lietzmann (p. 212).
59. Ibid., 2 Lietzmann (p. 204).
60. Ibid., 107 Lietzmann (p. 232).
61. Ibid., 45 Lietzmann (p. 214).
62. Ibid., 142 Lietzmann (p. 241).

by itself, nor did his divinity. Just as humans have but one nature, so also with Christ.[63]

The postulation of a close connection or even fusion of Jesus' human flesh and the divine Word had several implications. First, Apollinarius regarded Christ's flesh as being glorified; it has become "divine flesh" or "the flesh of God." Second, since Christ's flesh cannot be separated from the Word, it is a proper object of worship. Finally, Apollinarius held to the *communicatio idiomatum*: the flesh shares the names and properties of the Word, and vice versa.[64]

Orthodoxy was clear and definite in its rejection of Apollinarius's view. It first condemned his teachings at a council held at Rome in 377. The condemnation was repeated by synods held at Alexandria in 378 and Antioch in 379, and then by the Council of Constantinople in 381. In a series of decrees issued in 383, 384, and 388, Emperor Theodosius I censured and outlawed Apollinarianism.[65]

The objections to Apollinarianism were several. The most obvious was its docetic perspective: Jesus was not really a man but only appeared to be such.[66] Further, since the most distinctive part of human nature, the psychological, was missing, he was not in the strict sense human, but some strange monstrosity.[67] The depiction of Jesus as lacking human psychology seemed to conflict with the Gospel descriptions of him, according to which he developed, showed signs of ignorance, and experienced human emotions.[68] Most significant, however, was that if Christ did not assume the whole of human nature, the effectiveness of his redemptive work was undermined. Indeed, since the rational human soul, including the will, is presumably the major locus of sin, it is questionable whether he could have achieved our salvation from sin. The most famous phrase in the refutation of Apollinarianism was that of Gregory of Nazianzus, "What has not been assumed cannot be restored; it is what is united with God that is saved."[69] What Christ assumed was the

63. Apollinarius *Epistle to Dionysius* 1.2 (Lietzmann, p. 257).
64. Apollinarius frag. 155 Lietzmann (p. 249).
65. Kelly, *Early Christian Doctrines*, pp. 295–96.
66. Athanasius *Against Apollinarius* 2.4.
67. Gregory of Nyssa *Against Apollinarius* 23, 29, 33, 45.
68. Ibid., 24, 26, 34; Athanasius *Against Apollinarius* 1.4–5.
69. Gregory of Nazianzus *Epistles* 101.

whole of human nature, psychological as well as physical, and thus he saved human nature in its entirety.

Controversy Regarding the Relationship Between the Two Natures

Nestorianism

The next controversy concerned the set of ideas which has come to be known as Nestorianism. In a sense, that label is unfair, for there is real doubt whether Nestorius held the views that have come to be associated with his name. That there were persons who subscribed to such beliefs, however, and that the church in rejecting such ideas more clearly defined its own views, is certain. Also certain is that political considerations had great influence in all of the ecclesiastical decisions that were made.

The controversy arose over the propriety of the term *theotokos* ("God-bearing") as a description of Mary. Nestorius, the newly installed patriarch of Constantinople (428), was asked for his opinion. He was a representative of the Antiochene approach to Christology, which stressed the duality of the two natures of Christ, as contrasted with the Alexandrian school, which emphasized the unity of his person. Nestorius had been taught by Theodore of Mopsuestia, who had taken great pains to emphasize the completeness of Jesus' humanity, as over against any Apollinarian tendency to view his humanity as given life and direction only by the Word.

When Nestorius rendered his judgment regarding the term *theotokos*, his background naturally came into play. He felt that the term was of doubtful propriety unless the term *anthrōpotokos* ("human-bearing") was also used.[70] His own preference was for *Christotokos*. The term *theotokos* was widely used in the Alexandrian school and actually followed from the concept of the *communicatio idiomatum*. While other Antiochenes such as Theodore accepted it with the same qualifications that Nestorius insisted upon, Nestorius used intemperate and provocative language in his pronouncement. God cannot have a mother; no woman can give birth to God.[71] What Mary bore was not God but humanity, the vehicle or instrument of divinity. God cannot

---

70. Nestorius *Epistle to Celestine* 1, 3.
71. Nestorius *Sermons Against* Theotokos ("the Mother of God") 1.

be carried for nine months in a mother's womb, be wrapped in baby clothes, or suffer, die, and be buried.[72] Nestorius felt that such statements were necessary in order to guard against Arianism or at least Apollinarianism.

The form of Nestorius's statements gave his bitter rival, Cyril of Alexandria, grounds for suggesting that Nestorius was proposing that Jesus had two natures joined in a purely moral union.[73] Out of this grew the conception of Nestorianism as the teaching that Christ was actually two distinct persons, one divine and the other human. Nestorius definitely repudiated this teaching, but the conception has persisted nonetheless.[74] Since our study is not of the politics of conciliar theologizing nor of the history of heresies per se, this need not be a major concern for us. What is important is what definition was finally adopted as orthodox. A council was called to meet in Ephesus on June 7, 431. The Antiochene bishops were late in arriving, so on June 22 Cyril was able to persuade the council to endorse his view and condemn Nestorius. When the Eastern bishops arrived, on June 26, they held their own council, deposing Cyril and the local bishop, Memnon, and rejecting Cyril's twelve anathemas which the former assembly had endorsed. When the papal delegation arrived on July 10, they supported Cyril. It is this meeting that has gone down in history as the Third Ecumenical Council.[75]

All was not yet settled, however. There were continual efforts to secure agreement and peace within the church. Major obstacles were Cyril's twelve anathemas and the condemnation of Nestorius. Cyril had spoken of one nature in Christ, and to the Antiochenes this smacked of Apollinarianism. Eventually, in 433, a statement was drafted to which virtually all of the parties could agree, the Antiochenes abandoning Nestorius. This compromise, which uses the term *theotokos*, specifies that Christ has two natures that are united without confusion.[76]

Eutychianism

The settlement reached in 433 proved satisfactory to no one. An extreme group among the Antiochenes persisted in consider-

---

72. Cyril of Alexandria *Letters* 3, 10.
73. Ibid., 10.
74. Nestorius *Sermons Against* Theotokos 1, 2, 4.
75. Kelly, *Early Christian Doctrines*, pp. 326–27.
76. Ibid., pp. 328–30.

ing Cyril a heretic and rankled at the condemnation of Nestorius. The right-wing followers of Cyril felt that he had too easily given up the position that Christ had but one nature. Cyril himself practiced moderation and restrained his more extreme followers. With his death in 444, his successor, Dioscorus, began to reassert the one-nature doctrine, believing that the Fathers supported this position, and that it had been compromised by Cyril only in a moment of weakness.[77]

It was around Eutyches (ca. 375–454), an aged and apparently not too clear-minded archimandrite, that the controversy broke. Because of his favor and influence at the court of Theodosius II, he became the rallying point of all the Alexandrians who disliked the accord of 433. The standing Synod of Constantinople, led by Flavian the local patriarch, met in November 448. Eutyches was repeatedly summoned; after numerous evasions he finally appeared and stated his position that whereas Christ had two natures before the incarnation, there was but one afterward.[78] It is difficult to reconstruct Eutyches' exact views, since the traditional picture of his teaching has been formed by picking out certain of his statements and pressing them to their logical extremes. Some have inferred that he was a Docetist, denying the reality of Jesus' human nature. On the other hand, his belief that the two natures which Jesus had before the incarnation became one after the union may have led Eutyches to conclude that the resulting nature was some type of hybrid, neither divine nor human, or that the humanity was swallowed up by the divinity. Actually, he was a confused thinker who had not come to grips with the issues.

The result of the synod was that Eutyches was deposed and excommunicated, and the one-nature doctrine rejected.[79] Through the use of political influence with the emperor, Eutyches and his followers succeeded in having a council convened in Ephesus in August 449. This assembly restored Eutyches and vindicated his orthodoxy, while condemning and deposing Flavian and the other supporters of the two-natures view. This council, at which threats of physical force were used to coerce the signatures of bishops, has come to be known in history as the "Robber Synod."[80]

77. Ibid., pp. 330–31.
78. Ibid., p. 332.
79. Ibid., p. 333.
80. Ibid., p. 334.

The Orthodox Response: The Council of Chalcedon

It remained for a council convened at Chalcedon in 451 to bring the controversy to a conclusion. This came about when the emperor died after falling from a horse. The new emperor, a professional soldier named Marcian, married the former emperor's sister Pulcheria. Both of them were sympathetic to the two-natures doctrine; with a desire to secure peace in the empire, they were responsive to calls for a general council.[81]

The council took three basic actions. It reaffirmed the Nicene Creed as expressive of orthodoxy. It rejected both Nestorianism and Eutychianism. Finally, it adopted a statement of its own, which was to be the standard of christological orthodoxy for many years to come. Thus it not only settled the immediate issues under contention, but also summed up the earlier decisions in one comprehensive statement:

> We, then, following the holy Fathers, all with one consent, teach men to confess one and the same Son, our Lord Jesus Christ, the same perfect in Godhood and also perfect in manhood; truly God and truly man, of a reasonable [rational] soul and body; consubstantial [coessential] with the Father according to the Godhood, and consubstantial with us according to the Manhood; in all things like unto us, without sin; begotten before all ages of the Father according to the Godhood, and in these latter days, for us and for our salvation, born of the Virgin Mary, the Mother of God, according to the Manhood; one and the same Christ, Son, Lord, Only-begotten, to be acknowledged in two natures, *inconfusedly, unchangeably, indivisibly, inseparably;* the distinction of natures being by no means taken away by the union, but rather the property of each nature being preserved, and concurring in one Person (*prosōpon*) and one Subsistence (*hypostasis*), not parted or divided into two persons, but one and the same Son, and only begotten, God the Word, the Lord Jesus Christ, as the prophets from the beginning [have declared] concerning him, and the Lord Jesus Christ himself has taught us, and the Creed of the holy Fathers has handed down to us.[82]

81. Ibid., p. 338.
82. Schaff, *Creeds of Christendom*, vol. 2, pp. 62–63.

The Development
of Incarnational Christology.
(2) After the Council of Chalcedon

Further Denials of the Two Natures

Monophysitism

One might have thought that the settlement achieved at the Council of Chalcedon would have rendered further debate unnecessary and unlikely. In reality, however, the controversy continued, with only some small shift of ground. The followers of Cyril felt that the formula had been propounded by a council with no more legitimacy than the Chalcedonian fathers had attributed to the Robber Synod. They continued to develop their thought in what has come to be known as Monophysitism. There came to be two major forms of Monophysitism, the Julian and the Severian, named respectively for Julian, bishop of Halicarnassus, and Severus of Pisidia, patriarch of Antioch.

The Julianists were most concerned to preserve the concept

of the unity of Christ. To them, the two-natures doctrine of Chalcedon seemed little different from Nestorianism. They did not believe that the human nature of Jesus was extinguished by the divine at the incarnation; rather, they conceived of it as being quite different from our human nature. As a result of the union of Jesus' divine and human natures, each transmitted qualities to the other. This meant that the substance of his human nature came to be quite different from ours.[1] Dioscorus declared that it would be profane to consider the blood of Christ to be natural. Dioscorus may well have held that from the moment of the incarnation Jesus had the same sort of humanity that he is generally believed to have had after his resurrection.[2] Obviously, part of the difficulty came from a lack of precise delineation of the meaning of "nature" and "person" and of the relationship between the two. As long as this ambiguity persisted, there would be confusion and conflict.

The interplay between the political concerns of the empire and the goals of the church was notable in this period. The emperor naturally wanted to preserve unity. This meant that the Monophysites had to feel themselves in some sense accepted. Accordingly, in 476 Basiliscus the Usurper issued an encyclical condemning the Chalcedonian Creed. More influential was the *Henoticon,* issued by the emperor Zeno in 482. This document did not leave the question of one or two natures an open issue, but came down on the side of the Monophysites. The *Henoticon* declared that the Son of God, while coessential in his deity with the Father and with us in his humanity, is not two but one, and that the miracles and sufferings are to be predicated of the same subject. The Council of Chalcedon was treated as if it had never occurred, the Council of Ephesus was explicitly recognized as authoritative, and even Cyril's anathemas were supported.[3]

The Dyophysites were of course not dissuaded from their position by this action, but found themselves in an awkward situation. Monophysitism could not be vanquished without a definite repudiation of the Council of Ephesus. Yet both Ephesus and Chalcedon were recognized as fully authoritative councils

1. Pseudo–Leontius of Byzantium *On the Sects* 10.1.
2. J. A. Dorner, *History of the Development of the Doctrine of the Person of Christ* (Edinburgh: T. & T. Clark, n.d.), division second, vol. 1, p. 123.
3. Evagrius *Ecclesiastical History* 3.14.

of the church. The rejection of one or both would have serious consequences for the doctrine of church authority. Consequently, the Dyophysites decided not to repudiate the Council of Ephesus, but to reject the *Henoticon*, the major purpose of which had been to affirm the views of Cyril as endorsed by the Council of Ephesus. Thus the church, both Monophysite and Dyophysite wings, found itself retaining both councils, even though their pronouncements were mutually contradictory.[4]

The position of Severus was considerably more moderate than that of Julian and his party. In fact, Severus's conciliatory approach to the problem has made it difficult to determine exactly what his views were. He sought to follow the traditional formulas of the church as closely as possible. Yet he also added qualifications, indicating the sense in which he was accepting those formulas. It is therefore necessary to give careful attention to what he stated.

Severus maintained that while Cyril, who advocated the one-nature position, was nevertheless correct in saying that Christ was "of two natures," Chalcedon wrongly made this to be "in two natures."[5] Pope Leo I, in fact, went as far as to speak of Christ's performing human acts in his human nature and divine acts in his divine nature. Such human activity must have derived from a purely human substratum. Consequently, Chalcedon was viewed as affirming a disunity in Jesus' life. Rather, says Severus, what we find in the life of Jesus after the union of the two natures is unified activity of the God-man. It is not possible to identify separate divine and human activity. In particular, that Christ's redemptive activity was simultaneously divine and human argues for a single, rather than a dual, nature.[6]

On the other hand, however, Severus speaks of ousiai and phy-ses within the person of Christ. He repudiates the teachings of both Eutyches and Nestorius. In criticizing the view of a Julianistic Monophysite named Sergius, he condemns the idea that one nature was annihilated by the other as well as the theory that the two were mixed or blended into some third nature.[7]

How are we to account for these apparently contradictory

4. Dorner, *Development*, pp. 123–24.
5. Severus *Letters to Sergius* 3.
6. Severus *Epistles* 6.5.6.
7. Severus *Letters to Sergius* 1.

statements? J. A. Dorner suggests that Severus is not being duplicitous, but is using the term *nature* in two different ways. On one hand, "nature" may refer to the essence of some quality such as righteousness. In this sense, since Christ has many moral attributes or qualities, it is appropriate to speak of a plurality or multiplicity of physes. Yet these attributes or qualities all unite in one focus, and thus all constitute, in the higher sense of the term *nature*, one physis or hypostasis.[8]

We may, then, summarize Severus's view as follows: In the incarnation, all the divine and human qualities remained unchanged in their nature or essence. However, they were now attached to the one hypostasis, no longer having any center or focus of their own. The substratum or substance was a synthesis of the separate monads, all of the attributes of both the human and the divine subsisting in the one hypostasis or person. Consequently, all of Jesus' activity was a divine-human composite.

One of Severus's favorite arguments utilizes the episode of Christ's walking on the sea. Here is an action which, in the strictest sense, cannot be called human, for humans are not capable of miracles. On the other hand, it cannot be called a purely divine activity, since a divine being, having no physical nature, cannot walk on anything. So Christ's walking on water must have been a divine-human activity. (Severus did not go on to ask what type of act it was that Peter performed when he also walked on the water, or in what sense his act was similar to or different from that of Christ.)[9]

Severus and his followers also argued for their view by using an analogy based on the makeup of human beings. We do not find any difficulty in speaking of individual humans as having one nature, even though they consist of soul and body, which are different substances. Similarly, we should be able to speak of Jesus as of one nature, even though human and divine elements are united in him without alteration. And if we speak of two natures in a state of union, why not also speak of one composite nature?[10]

It can be seen that the orthodox and the Monophysite parties were by this time coming closer and closer together. Indeed,

8. Dorner, *Development*, pp. 137–38. See also Harry A. Wolfson, *The Philosophy of the Church Fathers* (Cambridge, Mass.: Harvard University Press, 1956), vol. 1, p. 451.

9. Dorner, *Development*, p. 138.

10. Ibid., p. 140.

Dorner contends, "We thus see clearly that the two parties were not in reality so far removed from each other as they themselves supposed."[11] It was more a matter of different starting points and emphases than of essential disagreement. Dorner continues:

> The Monophysites, on the one hand, represent the *Nisus* to attain a more intimate union of the natures than was attained by the Chalcedonians; but did no more than the latter to exhibit the inner connection between the divine and human. The Chalcedonians, on the other hand, represent the *Nisus* to preserve to the human element a relative independence without mixture or conversion; but they did not, in reality and logically, get beyond the Monophysite notion of the insubstantiation of the humanity in the deity, although they confessed it not to themselves.[12]

Monophysitism did not die out. Indeed, by this time it had become a separate group outside the Catholic church and even continued to have a life within it. At the Fifth Ecumenical Council, which was held in Constantinople in 553, Justinian tried to satisfy the Monophysites by endorsing the idea that one of the Holy Trinity was crucified for us. There was a growing conviction, however, that Monophysitism would lead to denying the reality of the incarnation. Estrangement from the orthodox church intensified, but the existence of the movement as a separate sect guaranteed that it would long persist.

Monothelitism

One additional sign of the continuing influence of monophysitic tendencies is the Monothelite controversy, which was an internal dispute within the church, which had now officially endorsed the two-natures view. Nothing had been said specifically about Christ's volition, and the Creed of Chalcedon could be read in such a way as to support either the theory that Christ had one will or the theory that he had two wills. Adolf von Harnack asserts that prior to the sixth century no one, not even the Antiochenes, had spoken of two wills within Christ.[13] In the period from 623 to 680, however, this became a heated issue.

11. Ibid., p. 154.
12. Ibid.
13. Adolf von Harnack, *Outlines of the History of Dogma* (Boston: Beacon, 1957), p. 300.

The trouble began when the orthodox party attempted to work out exactly what was implied by the statement adopted at Chalcedon and in the subsequent clarifications. They were motivated by soteriological considerations. In particular, there was a desire to preserve the idea that the redemptive activity of the Savior was the work of the God-man, so that both its infinite value and its applicability to the human race could continue to be maintained.

Whether regarded as the first stage of the Monothelite controversy[14] or a prelude to the actual controversy itself,[15] the initial discussion related not to Jesus' will(s), but to his action(s). The term involved was *energeia*, which Aristotle used technically to refer to "work," "activity," or "operation" (as it came to be translated into Latin), as well as to actuality as contrasted with potentiality. The issue was whether what Christ did should be viewed as the unitary action of a divine-human person, or broken down into human actions and divine actions.

One might assume that the Apollinarians, Eutychians, and Monophysites preferred the monergistic view (i.e., that Christ's action was divine-human), and that those whose sympathies lay closer to Nestorianism thought in terms of divine and human actions. In actuality, both the Monophysites and the Nestorians supported the idea of unitary action. The Nestorians, wishing to keep the two natures distinct and yet wanting to bring them together in some way, found in Christ's action the unity they were seeking.[16]

In the nature of argumentation as it took place in those days, a search was made through the writings of the Fathers to see which position could be better supported. Actually such a search promised little real return, for there was practically no reference in the writings of the Fathers to the action(s) of Christ. The two passages which came in for the greatest amount of consideration were one in Pope Leo's *Tome* (a letter he had sent to Flavian before the Robber Synod) and one in Pseudo-Dionysius. With no variation in the Latin and only a very slight change in the Greek, the grammatical construction of the former could be interpreted

---

14. Dorner, *Development*, pp. 165–66.
15. Jaroslav Pelikan, *The Christian Tradition: A History of the Development of Doctrine*, 4 vols. (Chicago: University of Chicago Press, 1971–1985), vol. 2, pp. 63–64.
16. Ibid., p. 64.

to mean either that each nature does its own actions or that the one incarnate Logos does by means of each nature the acts that are appropriate to it. In the case of Pseudo-Dionysius, there was a question as to whether it was legitimate to emend the phrase "a certain new divine-human action of God made man" to read "a single divine-human action."[17]

The issue, however, as Jaroslav Pelikan has pointed out, was not a matter of grammar or of textual criticism relating to the writings of the Fathers. Rather, the issue was the locus of action in the incarnate Logos.[18] Was the action to be regarded as "hypostatic," that is, belonging to the one hypostasis, or "natural," belonging to the two natures? The confusion was compounded by ambiguity as to what was meant by "energy" or "action." If it was taken as meaning the actual volition or the mode of action, there was a tendency to favor the idea of duality as a safeguard against any sort of Monophysitism, which had been rejected by the church. On the other hand, if "action" was taken as referring to the deed itself or the effect of the volition, there was a tendency to think in terms of unitary, divine-human action, since it was apparent that the person Jesus acted in a unitary fashion.

The debate did not prove profitable. Not only was there a scarcity of both biblical and patristic texts, but each side could levy arguments ad absurdum against the other. The solution to the controversy was to rule the whole question out of court. A compromise solution was the *Ecthesis* written by Patriarch Sergius of Constantinople, promulgated by the emperor Heraclius in 638, and endorsed by the pope, Honorius I. This edict outlawed the use of either formula. The pope commented, "Avoiding . . . the offense of recent innovations, we must not speak either of one or of two actions in our definitions; but instead of the 'one action' of which some speak, we must confess one agent, Christ the Lord, in both natures."[19] This was but an explication of what the *Ecthesis* said: "We, following the holy fathers in all things and also in this, confess one will of our Lord Jesus Christ, true God."[20] Honorius, by his endorsement of the *Ecthesis,* had actually opted for a Monothelite position.

17. Ibid., pp. 65–66.
18. Ibid., p. 66.
19. Honorius I *Epistles* 4.
20. Heraclius *Ecthesis*.

So the issue of Christ's action(s) had been laid to rest. In the process, however, a larger issue had been opened, the issue of one or two wills. Now, instead of a rather obscure issue on which there was relatively little biblical and patristic evidence, a question had been raised with which Scripture seemed to deal directly, especially Luke 22:42, where Jesus prays to the Father, "Not my will, but thine, be done," and John 6:38, "For I have come down from heaven, not to do my own will, but the will of him who sent me." Both sides felt obliged to deal with these passages. The prominence of these and similar passages in the Gospels gave cause to believe that there must be considerable discussion of the issue in the writings of the Fathers.

Neither party in the dispute wanted to fall into the error of Monophysitism or of Nestorianism. Each wanted to be identified with the traditional position of the church. But what was that tradition? Or, perhaps more correctly, what position or positions did that tradition imply, since it had not declared itself specifically and self-consciously on many of these matters?

The dispute between Pyrrhus, the patriarch of Constantinople, and Maximus the Confessor will help us to focus on the positions taken. To Pyrrhus, to admit two wills would lead to a division of the person of Christ, since a will presupposes a person who wills. Maximus, on the other hand, feared that if there were only one will, it must be the divine will; the human will would be subjugated to or eliminated by the divine will, and the humanity of Jesus would thus be compromised. Maximus introduced the Trinity into the discussion. In the Trinity there are three persons and one nature. Further, there are not three wills within the Trinity, but three persons who have one will. Consequently, the will must pertain to nature, not to person.[21]

Controversy on this matter became quite heated, to the point where the emperor, Constans II, fearing a revolution, issued in 648 an edict forbidding all discussion of the subject. This proved to have relatively little effect, however, and the next three decades constituted one of the more grisly periods in the history of the church. Pope Martin I and the Lateran Council of 649 taught that there really and truly were two natures in Christ, and that this required two wills. To deny the two wills was, in their

21. Dorner, *Development*, pp. 179–82.

judgment, to deny the reality of the incarnation. The edict issued by the emperor had to be condemned, because it had the effect of suppressing the truth. In the period from 649 to 680, the emperors regarded such opposition to the edict as political insubordination and attempted to break it by use of violence. The advocates of the Dyothelite position were either martyred or exiled, including Martin and Maximus. The following popes, Eugenius I and Vitalianus, conformed to the imperial decree out of fear. The emperor was murdered in 668; his successor, Constantinus Pogonatus, in time felt the need to work with the pope to reach a settlement. Consequently, the Sixth Ecumenical Council convened in Constantinople in 680–681.[22]

The Sixth Ecumenical Council ruled clearly in favor of the Dyothelite position. The bishops were concerned to preserve the full humanity of Jesus. As a complete human being, he could not have lacked anything that pertains to a human being, including human actions and a human will. If he did, he would in that respect be less than the rest of us and thus not as fully human. But since the difference between Christ's humanity and ours lay solely in "the novel mode of his genesis," that is, the virgin conception, and since in every other way his human nature was like ours, he must have had a human will.[23] Confirmation is found in his desire for food and drink, which had to be an expression of his human will, since his divine nature surely did not need physical nourishment.[24]

Christ's full humanity, then, required two natural wills, but not two natural wills contrary to each other. The human will was completely subject to the will of his divine nature.[25] To preclude the thought of any possible conflict between the two wills, theologians drew careful distinctions. Maximus the Confessor, for instance, spoke of the "natural will," which was ontologically distinct from the divine will, and the "deliberative will," which was functionally identical with the divine will.[26] Since it was the deliberative will that was responsible for decision making, there was no possibility of conflict. In addition, a distinction was

22. Ibid., pp. 184–85.
23. Maximus the Confessor *Theological and Polemical Opuscula* 4.
24. John of Damascus *On the Two Wills in Christ* 26.
25. Pelikan, *Christian Tradition*, vol. 2, p. 74.
26. Maximus the Confessor *Theological and Polemical Opuscula* 16.

drawn between the will as a natural psychological faculty and as "that which is willed, that which is subject to the will."[27]

In the final analysis, the conclusion that Jesus had two wills was a consequence of soteriological concerns. We saw earlier that Gregory of Nazianzus had propounded the axiom, "What has not been assumed cannot be restored."[28] In similar manner, John of Damascus stated, "If [Christ] did not assume a human will, that in us which suffered first has not been healed," since from the fall to the present day it is the human will which has been guilty of sin.[29]

Further Attempts to Understand the Incarnate State

Adoptionism

To complete our investigation of the development of the doctrine of incarnational Christology, it remains for us to examine two attempts to understand and explain the nature of the incarnation. The first was the movement known as Adoptionism, which flourished for a brief time in Spain in the eighth century. It must be seen as coming after the triumph of Dyophysitism and Dyothelitism, and assuming the conclusions of the church on both of those issues. The Adoptionists were disturbed by any approach maintaining that Christ's humanity was in some sense absorbed into his deity, or that the humanity had personality only by virtue of its union with the divine. It was to preserve the genuineness and fulness of the humanity that Adoptionism formed its tenets.

In a sense, the issue can be reduced to the question of whether in the incarnation God took on human nature in general or the human nature of an individual man. There was much in the tradition of Western theology that supported the latter position. According to that tradition, God had selected a specific man as a matter of eternal election.[30] Indeed, this was considered the supreme example and illustration of grace. It was not the case,

27. Ibid.; see also John of Damascus *On the Two Wills in Christ* 21.
28. Gregory of Nazianzus *Epistles* 101.
29. John of Damascus *On the Two Wills in Christ* 28.
30. Augustine *Enchiridion* 36.

then, that Jesus qualified for the incarnation by some merit of his own (a position popularly attributed to Adoptionism).

In the early seventh century Isidore of Seville had asserted that Christ possessed both a name that was his by nature and that which he had acquired by adoption of a man.[31] It was Elipandus, metropolitan of Toledo, who first advocated this idea in an extended fashion. He was concerned to establish that the human nature of Jesus was assumed from his mother, the Virgin Mary. Unlike his deity, it was not directly derived from the Father. The humanity, obtained from Mary, was thus adopted by God. If this was not the case, then the humanity of Jesus would be different from our humanity. Accordingly, Elipandus accused his opponents of being Docetists or Eutychians.[32]

Felix of Urgel developed Adoptionism further. He spoke of two births of Jesus, a fleshly and a spiritual. The first took place when he was born of the Virgin Mary. The second was at the point of his adoption. Although Felix did not say so explicitly, the implication was that the human nature which Jesus took was that of Adam after, not before, the fall. It was necessary that Jesus undergo a second birth, in order that his humanity might become the Son of God. This took place over a period of time, becoming complete only with his resurrection and glorification. To tie the humanity of Jesus to ours, the Adoptionists pointed out that in addition to being "only-begotten by nature" as Son of God, he was also, as Son of man, "first-born among many brethren," not by nature, but by adoption and grace.[33]

The chief opponents and critics of Adoptionism were Beatus of Liebana and Alcuin. One of the major criticisms which they leveled against the thought of Elipandus and Felix was that in the process of trying to make the humanity of Jesus the same as ours, they had removed any real difference between us. Jesus is unique, however, in that even those who are adopted as sons of God do not thereby "begin to be God by nature."[34] It also appeared to the critics that the Adoptionists were in danger of slipping into the same error as had the Nestorians, of dividing the natures so sharply as to virtually sever the person. Viewing

31. Isidore of Seville *Origins* 9.5.20.
32. Elipandus *Epistle to Charlemagne.*
33. Elipandus *Epistle to the Bishops of Francia* 9.
34. Beatus of Liebana *Commentary on the Apocalypse* 1.2.42.

Jesus' sonship as an attribute of his nature(s) rather than his person seemed to lead the Adoptionists to two Sons, a duality, a divided Christ.

Felix was summoned to appear before the Synod of Regensburg (792), and defended himself before Charlemagne. He is reported to have ultimately recanted (the transactions of the synod have unfortunately been lost). Subsequently, however, upon returning to Spain, he renounced his recantation. In 794 the Synod of Frankfurt rejected Adoptionism. Hincmar of Reims summarizes the decision: "There are not two Christs, nor two Sons, but one Christ, one Son, both God and man, because God, the Son of God, assumed a human nature, not a [human] person."[35] Both Dorner and Harnack see here a parallel to the doctrine of transubstantiation. The replacement of the substance of bread and wine by the substance of Christ's flesh and blood is reminiscent of the obliteration of his human ego by the divine, leaving here, also, only the accidents.[36]

Kenotic Christology

Finally, we turn to the kenotic school of Christology, a large and complex movement. In a sense, kenoticism can be found in Christologies dating from virtually the earliest days of theological construction.[37] It was not until the nineteenth century, however, that theologians used this theme as the key to understanding the whole problem of the incarnation.

It should be observed that those who developed the kenosis Christology took the idea of incarnation seriously. They were convinced that the preexistent Word in some sense became related to a human life in the person of Jesus of Nazareth. Had they believed that he was merely a human, or had they adopted a docetic view of his person, there would have been no need for kenotic Christology.

---

35. Hincmar of Reims *On the Deity as One and Not Three* 9.

36. Dorner, *Development*, p. 266; Adolf von Harnack, *History of Dogma*, 7 vols. (Boston: Little, Brown, 1899–1903), vol. 5, p. 291.

37. Donald G. Dawe distinguishes between the kenosis motif, which is found in such New Testament passages as Phil. 2:5–11 and 2 Cor. 8:9, and the kenosis doctrine, specific forms of expression given to this theme in varying theologies. He says of the former, "Kenosis is a theme expressed through Christian literature in every age" (*The Form of a Servant: A Historical Analysis of the Kenotic Motif* [Philadelphia: Westminster, 1963], p. 18).

Concerned theologians took three factors into account in formulating kenotic Christology, the first of which may be termed the biblical factor. Here we have in view the fact that the Bible indicates that in coming to earth the eternal Logos somehow limited or emptied himself. The classic text is, of course, Philippians 2:7—Christ Jesus "emptied himself." Indeed, the key word here, ἐκένωσεν (from *kenoō*), is evident in the very name of the theory—kenoticism. There were other considerations as well, such as Jesus' profession of ignorance of the time of his second coming (Matt. 24:36), and his requesting information which he apparently did not possess (e.g., Mark 9:21). There also were the passages which indicate growth, development, and learning on the part of Christ (e.g., Luke 2:52). Indeed, in one way or another, virtually all of the passages which had led the Arians to their conclusions also contributed to kenotic Christology.

The second factor was the logical problem: How can the finite and the infinite coexist in one person? This question was the stimulus behind many of the developments we have examined in this and the preceding chapter. How can a person be omnipresent, as God is, and yet be restricted in location by a physical body, as each human being is? How can a person be omnipotent, as God is, and yet be limited in power, as every human is? And, of especially great significance for purposes of the current discussion, how can one be omniscient, as is God (who not only knows all truth, but is the source of all truth), and yet have the limitations of a finite human psyche?[38]

The third factor or problem was especially prominent in the nineteenth century and thus explains why kenotic Christology gained the popularity that it did at this particular juncture in the history of the church and of Christian thought. We may term this factor the critical problem, for it stemmed from the newly developing science of biblical criticism. Jesus, pointed out the critics, rather freely quoted from Old Testament books and alluded to Old Testament events. In so doing, he attributed the quotations to the authors to whom they were traditionally credited, and he seemed to assume the historicity of the events to which he referred. Yet historical or higher criticism was in many cases calling into question both the traditional attributions of

38. Ibid., p. 90.

authorship and the historicity of the events. Thus there was a conflict between the conclusions of biblical scholars and the dogma of the infinity, absoluteness, and omniscience of Jesus' divine nature.[39]

We have observed that the motif of kenosis is found throughout the history of Christianity. It was in the nineteenth century, however, that the doctrine was most fully developed, both on the Continent and in Britain. We will examine the thought of the German theologian Gottfried Thomasius and the British theologian P. T. Forsyth as examples of mature kenoticism.

Thomasius was in a sense the first of the modern kenotic theologians. He strongly desired to be perceived as within historic or traditional Lutheranism. At the same time, he did not wish simply to repeat uncritically the formulations propounded in past generations. He took seriously (though he did not accept the final conclusions of) the historical research which was having such profound impact upon the Christologies of his day.

In particular, Thomasius thought that Lutheranism had made an important contribution by its full development of the doctrine of *communicatio idiomatum,* according to which the attributes of each of Christ's natures were communicated to the other nature.[40] He felt, however, that Lutheranism had made a mistake in its one-sided emphasis upon the communication of the divine attributes to the human nature; as a result, the human nature seemed to be virtually obliterated. Thomasius saw two alternatives. One was to give up the idea of *communicatio idiomatum* entirely and to think in terms of a mere togetherness of the divine and human in Christ. The other was to carry through the concept more consistently to a definite self-limitation of the divine in Christ. It was this alternative Thomasius adopted.[41]

In developing his understanding of the incarnation, Thomasius found it necessary to begin by trying to define the nature of God. Here he found himself modifying the conclusions which

39. See, e.g., Alfred E. Garvie, *Studies in the Inner Life of Jesus* (New York: George H. Doran, 1907), pp. 282–83.

40. Gottfried Thomasius, "Christ's Person and Work," in *God and Incarnation in Mid–Nineteenth Century German Theology*, ed. Claude Welch (New York: Oxford University Press, 1965), p. 46.

41. Ibid.

had been reached under the influence of Aristotelian philosophy. The concept of divine absoluteness had been expounded in such a way as to exclude any change and especially any limitation in God. Unchangeable and unmoved by everything within the world, God certainly could not take on himself the limitations of ordinary humans. Thomasius contended, however, that the real meaning of absoluteness is self-determination, not being influenced by anything outside oneself. The ultimate instance of self-determination is self-limitation, the ability to restrict oneself voluntarily. This God has done in the incarnation. To suggest that God cannot so limit himself is to set a limit upon his power of self-determination, and to deny the omnipotence that one professes to be defending.[42]

It will be seen that in many ways this was a real revolution in the understanding of the nature of God. Instead of an unchanging being, Thomasius suggested a God for whom change is the supreme evidence of power. Criticism was quick and sharp. One of the most emphatic critics was Dorner, who had initially been inclined toward the kenotic approach to Christology. He contended that this theory disregarded the real nature of the Trinity. The three members of the Trinity are so closely related to one another that a limitation of one is actually a limitation of all. Thus the limitation of the Son must also be seen as a limitation of the whole divine being, and God would actually cease to be fully God.[43]

Another criticism leveled at Thomasius's theory also had to do with the Trinity. If Jesus really limited himself to a fully human life, then what happened to his earth-ruling function during that time? He certainly could not have divided his mind into human and divine components, so that with one part of his mind he prayed to the Father to calm the storm which he himself was producing with another part of his mind. If he really limited himself to a human consciousness, as Thomasius defined it, then Jesus could have had no part in governing the universe, and the universe would presumably have collapsed.[44] It was in response to such criticisms that Thomasius developed his mature doctrine.

42. Ibid., pp. 46–48.
43. Dorner, *Development*, division second, vol. 3, pp. 252, 258–59.
44. Ibid., pp. 252–53.

The second major proposal made by Thomasius involved an analysis of the divine attributes. In so doing, he followed the lead of the Lutheran orthodox theologian Martin Chemnitz, whose scheme has been extensively used in subsequent theology. Each of the divine attributes can be classified as either immanent or relational. The immanent attributes of God are those which he has in and of himself, independent of the creation. These qualities within the nature of God spring from his inner relatedness as the Trinity. They include power, truth, holiness, and love. They are the basic or essential attributes, those which make God what he is. The relational attributes, on the other hand, have to do with God's relationship to the creation. They are not essential to God in himself. He would be what he is even if he had never created. It is here that we find the attributes of omnipotence, omniscience, and omnipresence. What the Logos did in becoming incarnate was to give up the relational attributes, while retaining the immanent attributes. Thus he continued to be powerful, truthful, holy, and loving, while ceasing to be omnipotent, omniscient, and omnipresent.[45]

From Thomasius's perspective the advantage of this approach was twofold. On the one hand, the relational attributes are precisely those attributes which would conflict with a genuine humanity. By saying that Jesus gave them up, Docetism is avoided. On the other hand, they are not essential to divinity, so there is no loss of the divine nature.[46] This solution provoked a considerable amount of debate, but that goes beyond our immediate concern.

It is in some senses ironic that even as kenotic Christology began to fade in influence on the European continent, it was growing in importance in Great Britain. As in so many areas of theological thought, ideas migrated from the German-speaking to the English-speaking countries, with the English form representing a moderation of the more extreme tenets of German thought. Donald Dawe maintains that there were two tendencies within British theology which produced this effect. The first was hesitancy about the use of speculative reason in theological matters. The second was a greater attention to the biblical witness. The Continental version of kenotic Christology had not been

45. Thomasius, "Christ's Person and Work," pp. 67–72.
46. Ibid., p. 93.

indifferent to the Scripture. Indeed, it had begun its work with attention to the biblical material. It tended, however, to move rather quickly to abstract this material and interpret it in primarily philosophical and psychological ways. To the British, however, the major reason for pursuing kenotic Christology was its grounding in Scripture rather than its usefulness in solving abstract theological problems.[47]

The first introduction to kenotic Christology in the English-speaking world was A. B. Bruce's *Humiliation of Christ*. While the presentation was basically an exposition, it was quite sympathetic to, though not unqualifiedly supportive of, the movement.[48] The first popular espousal of the kenosis doctrine appeared in an essay by Bishop Charles Gore in his book *Lux Mundi*. In discussing the inspiration of Scripture he pointed out that Jesus had at several points in his life been unaware of historical inaccuracies in the Old Testament. Obviously, Jesus' views of the Old Testament were those of any ordinary first-century Jew. Gore concluded that during his earthly ministry Jesus had placed upon his divine omniscience the limitations which are common to all humanity.[49]

In constructing his view, Gore followed Hans Martensen, a Danish bishop, rather than Thomasius. The self-emptying at the incarnation was partial: the Logos retained his divine nature, but surrendered his divine glory and the full functioning of his divine attributes so that Jesus could be fully human. He did not cease to rule the world. The Logos lived a dual life, as unlimited Ruler of the world and as a limited human personality. It should not come as any surprise that critics characterized Gore's position as Nestorianism.[50]

The kenosis theme became quite popular among British theologians, including A. M. Fairbairn, Hugh Ross Mackintosh, Frank Weston, and E. H. Gifford. Earlier, such noted biblical scholars as J. B. Lightfoot and T. K. Cheyne had also dealt with the theme. Their expositions followed the conservative elements within German theology. They were strongly desirous of pre-

47. Dawe, *Form*, pp. 127–28.
48. A. B. Bruce, *The Humiliation of Christ in Its Physical, Ethical, and Official Aspects* (New York: Hodder and Stoughton, n.d.), pp. 134–92, esp. pp. 164–92.
49. Charles Gore, "The Holy Spirit and Inspiration," in *Lux Mundi*, ed. Charles Gore, 5th ed. (New York: John W. Lovell, n.d.), pp. 299–302.
50. Dawe, *Form*, p. 129.

serving the deity of Christ, but they also wanted to give full place to the new critical insights regarding the human consciousness of Jesus.

In some ways, Peter Taylor Forsyth gave the fullest expression to the kenosis doctrine, although his theology is sometimes difficult to discern because of his homiletical style and use of the method which he termed "moralizing dogma." He believed that excessive use of abstract ontological terms often obscures the meaning of the faith and impedes the attempt to expound and declare it. His aim was to restate Christian doctrine in moral and personal terms, which would be more in keeping with its basic nature. The fundamental Christian experience is the experience of forgiveness through Jesus Christ; consequently, Christian faith must be presented as a personal moral experience based upon Jesus Christ. Forsyth's concern was both apologetic and kerygmatic. Because the generation which he was addressing had been profoundly affected by personalism in philosophy and a concern for ethics in religion, a personal moral approach would make the message more intelligible and relevant to them than would one which utilized speculative dogma. It would also bring the doctrines into closer relationship with their biblical sources, which are not primarily speculative but experiential and practical in their orientation. Accordingly, Forsyth's christological affirmations are not so much dogmatic propositions as they are explications of the Christian's experience of forgiveness.[51]

Forsyth begins with the preexistence of Christ. The scope of the Christian experience of salvation is cosmic; it is, in fact, an experience of new creation. It can be such, however, only if there is a unity between the Creator and the Savior. This unity is asserted in the doctrine of Christ's preexistence. Preexistence alone is insufficient, however, for to save us Christ must also be fully human. This requires the doctrine of divine kenosis.[52]

Forsyth gives primary attention to the problem of the divine and human consciousness of Christ. How could the divine consciousness limit itself to a finite form and still retain continuity with its preincarnate form? Forsyth avoids the orthodox view,

51. P. T. Forsyth, *The Person and Place of Jesus Christ* (Boston: Pilgrim, 1909), pp. 1–31, 183–224.
52. Ibid., pp. 282–83.

according to which kenosis involves a mere veiling of the divine consciousness and activity. He also avoids the extreme of modernism, according to which kenosis is the obliteration of the divine consciousness. Rather, he insists that there are both a limitation of and a continuity with the divine consciousness. There is a voluntary contraction of consciousness in response to a higher moral call. The preexistent Christ deliberately limited his divine consciousness to bring forgiveness to humans, but he could do this only by becoming human himself. At the same time, we must bear in mind that there was a continuity between the preincarnate and the incarnate Christ.[53] Forsyth uses an illustration of a young university student who shows great genius for the study of philosophy. In the midst of his studies, however, and at a crucial stage in the family business, his father dies. As the only son, the student must relinquish his pursuit of philosophy to take over the family business. In the course of time he loses his skills in philosophy, yet he retains some recollection both of the content of philosophy and of the joy he once found in it. He has voluntarily accepted a contraction of his consciousness in order to respond to a higher moral call.[54]

Forsyth recognizes a major problem for his view: How can the incarnate Christ be thought of as fully divine? Here he accepts and utilizes one of Thomasius's two major proposals, while rejecting the other. He does not believe that the kenosis involved the renunciation of certain attributes, such as omnipotence and omniscience, and the retention of others. It simply is not possible to split the unitary divine life and action into groups of attributes. The term *self-emptying* is misleading and should be replaced by a term like "self-reduction" or "self-retraction." The divine attributes did not cease to exist. Rather, they entered a new mode of being in which they were concentrated and came to expression in different form.[55]

Forsyth does, however, utilize Thomasius's conception that Jesus' self-limitation is not a diminution of divinity. The acceptance of limitation is not a defect. It is, indeed, the highest expression of self-determination, which in turn is virtually the epitome of divine power. Forsyth observes, "If He could not

53. Ibid., pp. 292–96.
54. Ibid., pp. 297–98.
55. Ibid., pp. 306–07.

become incarnate His infinitude would be partial and limited . . . . It would be limited by human nature in the sense of not being able to enter it."[56]

Does this limitation, however, involve Jesus in sin? Did the restriction of the divine consciousness to human dimensions make him as susceptible to sin as we are? Here Forsyth is emphatic. There was a limit to the divine self-limitation: Christ was unable to sin. The divine self-consciousness was not so retracted or contracted as to allow Jesus to become a sinner. But does this not minimize the humanity of Jesus? Forsyth thinks not. To be a human need not involve the ability to sin. Sin is not a part of true humanity, but merely of empirical humanity, humans as we find them in our experience. What is necessary to genuine humanity is simply the ability to be tempted by sin.[57]

Kenosis is not the whole story. There is also the dimension of plerosis—the exaltation of the resurrection-ascension at the end of Jesus' earthly ministry. The incarnation involves not only the condescending movement of God to man, or kenosis, but also the ascending movement of man to God, or plerosis.[58]

We have reached the end of our review of the development of orthodox incarnational Christology. After several centuries of dispute as to how to interpret the biblical evidence, the Council of Chalcedon had set forth the standard definition. Refinements continued to be made, however. The last of the major refinements was the kenoticism of the nineteenth century. We step now into the twentieth century, which has been noteworthy for its challenges to orthodox Christology.

56. P. T. Forsyth, "The Divine Self-Emptying," in *God the Holy Father* (London: Independent, 1957), p. 33.
57. Forsyth, *Person and Place*, pp. 301–05.
58. Ibid., pp. 323–57.

Part 2

Problems of Incarnational Christology

The Historical Problem.
(1) Critical Christology:
The Possibility of Historical
Knowledge of Jesus

The most conspicuous feature of contemporary Christology is the challenges that have been issued to the traditional formulation. The problems that present themselves can be broadly classified as historical, sociological, metaphysical, anthropological, and logical. We turn first to the historical problem. Our concern in this chapter will be with the critical skepticism as to whether historical knowledge of Jesus is really possible. In chapter 5 we will consider the uncertainty as to whether such knowledge, if indeed attainable, is relevant.

Because the church has long sought to build its understanding of Jesus Christ upon the Bible, biblical studies have always been crucial for Christology; this is truer today than ever. We noted in chapter 1 some of the biblical considerations which led the church to its classical understanding of the person of Christ: he is fully divine but also fully human, one person with two distinct natures that are neither mingled nor confused. Much of this formulation rested upon the assumption that in the Gospels we have a record of Jesus' actual sayings, and thus a report of his self-consciousness.

With the arising and flowering of the science of biblical criticism, especially of the Gospels, this assumption has been called into question. Skepticism about the possibility of recovering the Jesus of history, that is, uncertainty as to whether he was the sort of person that the Gospels portray, has rendered the traditional Christology rather suspect. One who was for some time in the forefront of critical Gospel studies and thus of New Testament Christology was Norman Perrin, who at the time of his death on Thanksgiving Day, 1976, was professor of New Testament at the University of Chicago Divinity School. Coming from a rather conservative background, he had studied with T. W. Manson and then with Joachim Jeremias. Perrin's views evolved considerably over the years.[1] Both in his critical methodology and in the presuppositions of his Christology, he shows considerable affinity for and indebtedness to the approach of Rudolf Bultmann.[2] Although his last contribution to the subject of New Testament Christology was made more than a decade ago, Perrin's outline of the method and the issues still proves especially instructive.

Perrin felt that, just as in his own views, something of a Copernican revolution had occurred in New Testament Christology. In his doctoral dissertation he had basically accepted and defended Manson's relatively conservative position. Then, in the process of doing research for a book on the Son of man, he found himself studying intensively the work of H. E. Tödt, Barnabas Lindars, and others. As a result, Perrin gradually became skeptical about attributing to Jesus any use of the term *Son of man* and, for that matter, of any title such as Son of David or Son of God. He discovered that his own changed convictions

---

1. Norman Perrin, *A Modern Pilgrimage in New Testament Christology* (Philadelphia: Fortress, 1974), pp. 1–9.
2. Perrin contributed *The Promise of Bultmann* (Philadelphia: Lippincott, 1969) to the series *The Promise of Theology*, ed. Martin E. Marty.

were only a microcosm of what was transpiring in New Testament studies: "Although I had reached such a position on the basis of my own work I was conscious of the fact that the change in my own thinking reflected a general change in scholarly thinking about the Christology of the New Testament."[3]

On the occasion of the centennial of the Divinity School of the University of Chicago in 1967,[4] Perrin gave a lecture on "Recent Trends in Research in the Christology of the New Testament." He pointed out that developments in New Testament Christology not only roughly parallel the changes in his own views, but also reflect changes in the way in which New Testament studies in general are being done. He began by tracing general developments in New Testament studies and showing their particular application to Christology.[5] And so, before examining his Christology, we first need to look at his general comments on the critical method of studying the Gospels.

The Methodology of Form Criticism of the Gospels

The Case for Form Criticism of Jesus' Teachings

A suitable place to begin is with Perrin's *Rediscovering the Teaching of Jesus*. In the preface he makes reference to the great impact that has been made upon research into the life of Jesus through the adoption and application of form criticism. As a result, positions as widely differing as those of Rudolf Bultmann and Joachim Jeremias must take a basic set of factors into account. Perrin's stated purpose is "to address particularly the problem of method in life of Jesus research in light of the impact of form criticism and then of the work of, on the one hand, the Bultmann 'school' and of, on the other, Joachim Jeremias."[6]

Perrin observes that a primary task of research into the life of

3. Perrin, *Pilgrimage*, p. 6.
4. Although the present University of Chicago was founded in 1892, its divinity school had been established already in 1867 as the Baptist Union Theological Seminary. As one of the conditions of endowing the new university, John D. Rockefeller insisted that the seminary move from suburban Morgan Park to the Midway and become the divinity school of the university.
5. Perrin, *Pilgrimage*, pp. 41–48.
6. Perrin, *Rediscovering the Teaching of Jesus* (New York: Harper and Row, 1976), pp. 11–12.

Jesus is to reconstruct his teaching from the available sources; and yet the more this research proceeds, the more difficult the task becomes. The Synoptic Gospels are the major source of Jesus' teachings. Close study shows, however, that while this material is ascribed to Jesus, most of it in fact stems from the early church.[7]

How could such a confusing of Jesus' own teaching and the church's conceptions have taken place? There seem to be two major reasons for this, according to Perrin. The first is that the early church did not distinguish between, on the one hand, the earthly Jesus and the words which he spoke during his human existence here, and, on the other, the risen Lord and the words he spoke through his prophets in the church. Similarly, it did not distinguish between the words originally spoken by Jesus and the church's new understanding of those words, a reformulation which it was believed had occurred under the guidance and inspiration of the Lord of the church.[8]

The second reason is the early church's lack of any real concern for historical reminiscence. The pericopes attributed to the Lord were included in the Gospels in order to serve the purpose of the church. What is presented as the teaching of the earthly Jesus is actually what the church understood to be the risen Lord's command to its own current situation. What the pericope conveys is not what Jesus said when he walked this earth (although there may be a "faint echo of the voice of the earthly Jesus"), but, rather, insights into the situation of the early church.[9]

But what of the objection that this is an arbitrary assumption? Could not the church have had historical reminiscence as its purpose in ascribing the teaching to Jesus? While acknowledging that such could have been the case, Perrin still questions whether it actually was the case. His reply is that contemporary scholarship "has been completely successful in explaining pericope after pericope on the basis of the needs and concerns of the early Church, and that over and over again pericopes which have been hitherto accepted as historical reminiscence have been shown to be something quite different."[10]

7. Ibid., p. 15.
8. Ibid.
9. Ibid., p. 6.
10. Ibid.

To substantiate this conclusion, Perrin adduces four arguments. He first examines Mark 9:1 and its parallels, Matthew 16:28 and Luke 9:27. He shows how they differ from each other and seeks to demonstrate that these variations reflect the special concerns of the three Evangelists. What we have here are not the words of the earthly Jesus, but "products of the evangelists, each creating the particular saying." Mark produced a new saying from Mark 13:30 and 8:38, and Matthew and Luke later transformed Mark 9:1 for their own purposes.[11]

The second argument which Perrin employs here is the work of Jeremias on the parables. Perrin contends that Jeremias has successfully shown which elements in the parabolic teaching go back to Jesus and which are simply the product of the church's creative activity.[12]

A third argument is the similarity which critics have detected between the church's handling of the Old Testament tradition and the commentaries (*pesharim*) produced by the Qumran community. Just like the Qumran community, the early church read Old Testament passages strictly in light of their own situation and experiences, and exercised a great deal of freedom with respect to the wording of the texts. For example, Perrin, following Lindars, claims that the pericope of Mark 12:35–37 is clearly the product of early Christian exegesis, not a reminiscence of Jesus' ministry.[13]

A fourth argument is the order of the contents of Mark's Gospel, which reflects the theologically motivated order of the early Christian messages. This Gospel, in other words, gives evidence of being constructed more as a sermon than as a scientific chronicling of Jesus' life and sayings.[14]

Rebuttal of the Opposition to Form Criticism

It is not surprising, of course, that a theory as radical as form criticism has encountered opposition. Perrin is aware of this, and offers rebuttal. Before he does so, however, he makes two general observations. The first is that we must resist the assumption that the ancient world thought as we think. He

11. Ibid., p. 20. While Perrin includes this argument within what he broadly terms "form criticism" (p. 25), it is technically an instance of *Redaktionsgeschichte* ("redaction criticism").

12. Ibid., pp. 20–23.

13. Ibid., pp. 23–24.

14. Ibid., pp. 24–25.

points to some conservative scholars who have treated the New
Testament concept of eyewitnesses as evidence that factual
accuracy was as important an element in ancient Near Eastern
religious texts as it is in a modern Western court of law or a
somewhat literal-minded Western congregation. His reply is
that "this is simply not the case. No ancient texts reflect the attitudes characteristic of the modern western world."[15] Thus any
approach which does not observe this difference is guilty of a
rather large-scale eisegesis of modern culture into ancient texts.
Unless we begin with a sensitivity to this cultural distance, we
will go astray immediately.

The second general observation which Perrin feels we must
keep in mind is the tendency of the early church to identify the
risen Lord of its experience with the earthly Jesus of history.
Whereas we draw a distinction between the two, the ancients
did not. Perrin points to Paul's claim to apostleship upon having
seen the Lord. He is obviously referring to the risen Lord of his
experience on the Damascus road. And when Paul says, "I
received from the Lord" the tradition of the Lord's Supper (1 Cor.
11:23), he is also undoubtedly referring to the risen Christ. It is
possible that this account of the Lord's Supper reflects some
incident that occurred in the life of Jesus, but even if this were
the case, there must certainly have been considerable modification of the original tradition. That would have made no difference to Paul, however, for he made no distinction between the
historical Jesus and the risen Lord. It does not matter at all
whether any of the words ascribed to Jesus in verses 24–25 were
actually spoken at the Last Supper. For the risen Lord's having
spoken them to the church in the Eucharist was no different
from the earthly Jesus' having spoken them to his disciples.[16]

What now of the objections to or attempted rebuttals of form
criticism? The first is that form criticism, in attributing to the
church much (or at least the final form) of the material supposedly spoken by Jesus, is giving the community too much credit
for creativity. That objection, however, overlooks the fact that
form criticism does not deal with some nebulous, generalized
entity termed "the community." Rather, its work has been done
with specific groups, individuals, and traditions. Lindars, for

---

15. Ibid., p. 26.
16. Ibid., pp. 26–27.

example, has dealt with particular Christian exegetical traditions where the creative tendency can be observed. It is not necessary for the entire group, that is, all individuals within it, to be creative, and in every possible way. Only certain individuals or subgroups need show this creativity, and only in limited areas. After concluding that form criticism cannot be refuted by generalizations about the community's lack of creative power, Perrin declares that form criticism can "only be denied by offering an alternative and more convincing explanation of the actual phenomena in the New Testament texts."[17]

A second objection is that form criticism is wrong in thinking that the early church was unconcerned about the historical ministry of Jesus, for such concern can be seen in its appeal to eyewitnesses. Perrin's response is the general point made earlier, that "eyewitness" did not mean then what it does now. Much has often been made of Luke's strong concern for historical accuracy, reflected, for example, in careful investigation involving eyewitnesses (Luke 1:2). We should note, however, that Luke considered Paul an eyewitness. While the exact word used in Luke 1:2 does not appear again in Luke and Acts, a parallel meaning is found in Acts 22:14–15, where Paul is credited with being an eyewitness by Ananias, and in 26:16, where he is so credited by the Lord himself.[18] Obviously the significance of "eyewitness" has changed.

Third, the objection is raised that during the period of the formation of the tradition about Jesus, the first few decades of the life and history of the church, there were persons present in the community, and in vital contact with what was going on, who had been eyewitnesses to the events of Jesus' life. They were a guarantee of the accuracy of the tradition regarding his words and deeds. This argument would be effective, says Perrin, if we could show that these people really were concerned to maintain the separate identity of the historical Jesus, and to preserve this tradition from any change. As we have seen, however, neither they nor anyone else in the early church saw the changes that were made as anything other than the work of the risen Lord, who was, after all, one and the same with the Jesus of history.[19]

17. Ibid., p. 27.
18. Ibid., pp. 27–28.
19. Ibid., p. 28.

These eyewitnesses, Perrin presumes, could have been expected to have greater influence with respect to the narratives than with the sayings. Here we note, however, that there also have been free creation, modification, and interpretation of narratives on the basis of details taken from the Old Testament and elsewhere to serve the apologetic purposes of the church. This is evident from a close study of such events as Peter's confession at Caesarea Philippi and the transfiguration, where eyewitnesses were involved. Perrin is as skeptical of recovering unadorned narratives as he is of identifying the *ipsissima verba*. His judgment seems to be quite similar to that of Bultmann. Perrin says, "The most that the present writer believes can ever be claimed for a gospel narrative is that it may represent a typical scene from the ministry of Jesus, for example the narrative of the Paralytic at Capernaum, Mark 2:1–12 par."[20]

Surveying what he has written about reconstructing the actual sayings of Jesus, Perrin is aware that some might be inclined to despair. He acknowledges that the task of getting back to the original tradition is more difficult than had formerly been thought, and that at points it may not be possible to find our way back to the historical Jesus. Rather than being a deterrent, this should serve as a spur to further activity.[21]

Testing the Authenticity of the Sayings Attributed to Jesus

How, then, shall we go about testing the authenticity of any of the sayings attributed to Jesus? Or, for that matter, how shall we determine, if possible, the correct version of the narrative accounts? Perrin says that we must first establish the history of the tradition. Only the earliest strata can have any claim to authenticity (in the case of the sayings) or to historicity (in the case of the narratives). The work done by Jeremias on the parables is an excellent example of successfully tracing the history of the tradition.[22]

One of Perrin's principles or assumptions is mentioned almost in passing, as if it either were obvious or were virtually inconsequential, yet it is a key factor in what he is doing: *"The nature of*

20. Ibid., p. 29.
21. Ibid., p. 32.
22. Ibid., pp. 32–39.

the synoptic tradition is such that the burden of proof will be upon the claim to authenticity."[23] In other words, a given saying should be attributed to the early church unless it can be clearly linked to the historical Jesus. Beyond this principle Perrin proposes three criteria which can be used to test the authenticity of the sayings attributed to Jesus by the Gospel writers.

The first and most significant of Perrin's criteria is dissimilarity. By this he means that once we have succeeded in isolating the earliest strata of the tradition, we can regard a saying as authentic if it can be shown to be "dissimilar to characteristic emphases both of ancient Judaism and of the early Church, and this will particularly be the case where Christian tradition oriented towards Judaism can be shown to have modified the saying away from its original emphasis."[24] He grants that much in Jesus' teaching, set as it was in the context of Judaism, must have been variations on themes common in Judaism. Yet the most characteristic features of Jesus' teaching are found not in what he shared with his contemporaries, but in those areas where he differed most from them. We should note that those circles of early Christians who were most concerned with the Jews, represented especially by the traditions found in Matthew, had a tendency to tone down those elements in Jesus' teaching which were new and startling.[25]

A second criterion is coherence. This is clearly a secondary criterion, but an important one. Once we have determined the earliest strata of the tradition, we may accept as authentic those elements which can be shown to be coherent with elements already established as authentic by the criterion of dissimilarity.[26] This principle is similar to, but a bit more strongly put than, a criterion used by Jeremias in evaluating even extrabiblical writings: authentic materials are "perfectly compatible with the genuine sayings of our Lord."[27] Jeremias's criterion is somewhat negative, involving the absence of contradiction, which might mean nothing more than that the subject matter is dissimilar, whereas coherence entails specific commonality. The criterion of coherence enables one to move beyond the criterion

23. Ibid., p. 39.
24. Ibid.
25. Ibid., pp. 39–40.
26. Ibid., p. 44.
27. Joachim Jeremias, *Unknown Sayings of Jesus* (New York: Macmillan, 1957), p. 30.

of dissimilarity to those sayings that are not unique or distinctive. It is an indirect use of that criterion, however, because it involves using "material established as authentic by the one sure criterion as a touchstone by means of which to judge material which itself would resist the application of that criterion, material which could not be established as dissimilar to emphases of Judaism or the early Church."[28]

The final criterion which Perrin cites is multiple attestation. By this he means that those sayings which are attested to in all (or most) of the sources which can be discerned behind the Synoptic Gospels are to be regarded as authentic. The usefulness of this criterion is somewhat limited. It is of most help with respect to general themes or motifs of the ministry of Jesus rather than specific sayings, but it should nonetheless not be abandoned. Perrin's preference, however, is clearly for basing decisions regarding authenticity upon the history of the tradition and the criteria of dissimilarity and coherence.[29]

Perrin notes that when the history of the tradition has been established and the criteria are applied, there emerge three areas where it is possible to "reconstruct major aspects of the teaching of Jesus beyond reasonable doubt." These three areas are the parables, the teaching about the kingdom of God, and the Lord's Prayer.[30] In addition, the application of the criteria gives us some degree of confidence about some isolated segments of material whose history does not lend itself to investigation. In such cases the criteria must of course be applied extremely carefully.[31]

One remaining question which Perrin faces is, What about the Gospel of John, the fourth Gospel? For the usual reasons advanced by critics, he is skeptical of its utility and indeed says, "As far as our present knowledge and methodological resources go, the gospel of John is not a source of knowledge of the teaching of Jesus."[32] Perhaps some day a surer command of the Synoptic tradition and more work on John's Gospel will make it possible to use that Gospel, but that time is not yet.[33]

28. Perrin, *Rediscovering*, p. 45.
29. Ibid., pp. 45–47.
30. Ibid., pp. 47–48.
31. Ibid., p. 48.
32. Ibid.
33. Ibid., p. 49.

The Methodology of Critical Christology

Factors Contributing to a New Situation for Christology

Thus far we have examined Perrin's understanding of the method of Gospel research in general. He applies this method specifically to New Testament Christology in his essay "Recent Trends in Research in the Christology of the New Testament." He begins by calling attention to four considerations which have served to create a new situation in New Testament Christology. One of these is the growing acceptance of the thesis that many of the sayings found in the Synoptic Gospels have a history (i.e., have taken various forms) in the tradition of the church. The form in which a saying appears reflects one (or more) of three possible *Sitze im Leben*. There is the setting in the life and ministry of Jesus, the setting in the life and work of the church, and the setting of the writer of the Gospel.[34] Any one or more of these may be reflected in the final form which is recorded in the written Gospel. The major implication of this first consideration is that it casts doubt upon the extent to which the passages formerly believed to give us insight into the self-consciousness of Jesus really do so. Only the earliest form of the saying can tell us anything about Jesus' understanding of himself, and then only after we have determined that it comes from him and not from the church.[35]

A second consideration follows from the first: "If a saying has a history in the tradition then its various forms are evidence for the theological emphases at work in the tradition and its final form in a gospel is evidence for the theology of the evangelist concerned."[36] This is currently considered a commonplace among New Testament scholars, but it is applied in varying degrees. Perrin perhaps takes it as far as any: "for I am of the considered opinion that every single Son of Man saying is a product of the theologizing of the early church."[37] He asserts that the critical evidence is so strong that "today the burden of proof must be held to lie very heavily upon anyone who wants to claim

---

34. Perrin, *Pilgrimage*, p. 41.
35. Ibid., p. 2.
36. Ibid., p. 43.
37. Ibid., p. 45.

that a saying expressing a definite Christology, or using an explicit christological designation, goes back to Jesus himself."[38]

A third consideration is the increased interest in factors in the life of the early church to which developments in Christology may be related. If we wonder why certain modifications in the tradition occurred, we will find the answer in the particular situations facing the church (the second *Sitz im Leben*). For example, Perrin notes the shift in emphasis between Acts 3:20–21, which puts into the future the full realization of God's appointment of Christ to glorification, and Acts 2:36, which puts God's appointment of Jesus as both Lord and Christ in the past. Why did such a shift take place, Perrin asks; he accepts Reginald Fuller's answer, which, despite the fact that the second text appears earlier in the Book of Acts, sees it as evidence of an increasing experience of the Spirit's working in the church.[39]

The fourth consideration is the impact of recent discoveries of extrabiblical materials, especially the Qumran and Nag Hammadi texts. The Old Testament commentaries from the Qumran community lead us to ask if the early Christians may have made similar use of Old Testament texts as the basis for forming their Christology, which emphasized that Jesus is the Son of God.[40]

Trends in New Testament Christology

Having noted these considerations, which constituted the general environment for the doing of New Testament Christology, Perrin goes on to identify specific trends and factors coming to the fore. These trends are in a sense the results of the general considerations we have just discussed. Two of them come in for special attention.

The first is the shift from focusing on the messianic consciousness of Jesus to drawing out the Christology which is implicit in his message. Perrin notes, for instance, the difference between the stance of A. S. Peake in 1924 and that of Fuller forty years later. The primary difference is that the former focuses on Christ's disclosing himself to his disciples, and the latter on the implicit Christology underlying his actions and teachings.[41]

---

38. Ibid.
39. Ibid., p. 46; Reginald H. Fuller, *The Foundations of New Testament Christology* (New York: Scribner, 1965), p. 184.
40. Perrin, *Pilgrimage*, p. 48.
41. Ibid., p. 49.

There are two major reasons for this change. The first is that
the earlier approach, concentrating on the self-consciousness of
Jesus, required a great deal of psychologizing about him. This,
however, involved filling in the gaps by analogy with other persons and resulted in the picture of a person who is either very
much like us or suffering from delusions of grandeur. A glance
at the nineteenth-century searches for the historical Jesus proves
that such a picture is the usual result of psychologizing about
him. The other reason is that critical scholarship now almost
uniformly holds that the more explicitly christological sayings
come from the early church rather than from Jesus himself. This
is not an unsubstantiated theory, but a conclusion stemming
from numerous studies showing that these sayings reflect the
characteristic concerns and theology of the early church and are
expressed in terms reminiscent of its liturgical and confessional
formulas.[42]

Perrin agrees with Fuller that the actions and words of Jesus
imply a tremendous claim for himself and his ministry. There is
a further element, however, to which Fuller does not call attention, but which needs to be observed: while Jesus' words and
deeds imply much about his person, their actual authority
derived from the kingdom of God. In other words, the authority
was not that of Jesus in and of himself, but that of the kingdom.
To view the person of Jesus as the ultimate authority for his
words and deeds is to do violence to his message. "However true
it may be to say that the person cannot be separated from his
words, it is also true that the authority of the historical Jesus was
the authority of the proclamation, not the proclaimer."[43] Perrin
agrees with Bultmann that the proclaimer became the proclaimed in the early church, and as a result the authority of the
proclamation of the kingdom also attached to the proclaimer.[44]

The second trend follows from the first: "a tendency to locate
the beginnings of Christology in the early church, not in the
ministry of Jesus."[45] The message of Jesus is not the starting
point of Christology, nor is even the implicit Christology of that
message. Rather, the theologizing of the early church forms the

42. Ibid., pp. 49–50.
43. Ibid., pp. 52–53.
44. Ibid.
45. Ibid., p. 54.

starting point. This theologizing should not be thought of as a direct response to the message and ministry of the historical Jesus. For the message and ministry "only took on christological significance when they were interpreted in light of the resurrection and when christological emphasis which had developed in early Christianity were [sic] read back into them."[46]

These are the two trends that Perrin sees at work in Christology as it is being done today. They will surely mean that Christology will have a rather different appearance in the future than it has had in the immediate past. And that is as it should be, given the considerations which Perrin has pointed out.[47]

The Content of Critical Christology
The Nature of Biblical Theology

It is important, in seeking to deal with the question of the content of the Christology of form criticism, and particularly that of Perrin, to bear in mind that he is a biblical theologian, and to note in what sense that designation applies to him. Perrin's conception of biblical theology is not far from the definition given by Krister Stendahl in a classic essay.[48] In Perrin's view, biblical theology is descriptive in nature rather than prescriptive. New Testament theology concerns itself with defining and presenting the theology of the New Testament authors or of the early church. The proper locus of biblical Christology is the study of what was held or written about Jesus. The question of what is the true understanding of Jesus Christ, or of what we are to believe about him, belongs to an entirely different discipline.

What, however, does the biblical theologian answer to the person who says, "So this is what Luke, Mark, and Paul believed about Jesus. What ought I to believe about Jesus?" Note that there are two possible dimensions to this problem. One is the fact that we are nearly two thousand years removed in time from the New Testament situation. That is not what we are facing here. The question is, "If I were a first-century individual living in the years immediately following the life of Christ, what,

46. Ibid., p. 55.
47. Ibid., p. 56.
48. Krister Stendahl, "Biblical Theology, Contemporary," in *The Interpreter's Dictionary of the Bible*, ed. George A. Buttrick, 4 vols. (New York: Abingdon, 1962), vol. 1, pp. 418–32.

according to Perrin, ought I to believe about Jesus?" Does New Testament theology give any prescriptive answers or only descriptive answers to this question?

Three Types of Knowledge About Jesus

One place where Perrin deals with this question is in an essay entitled "The Significance of Knowledge of the Historical Jesus and His Teaching."[49] In this essay, he takes us through a survey of the search for the historical Jesus, concluding with Bultmann and then the new quest. In presenting his own view, he differentiates three types of knowledge about Jesus:

1. *Historical knowledge.* Basic to Christology are straightforward, descriptive facts about Jesus of Nazareth. We know, for example, that Jesus ate with tax collectors and sinners, that he accepted his death as a necessary consequence of his proclamation of the kingdom, and that he went to the cross with the confidence that it would serve, not hinder, God's purpose. In a parallel example, Socrates accepted his death as the consequence of spreading his convictions and drank the hemlock with serenity. A more recent example is the fact that in March 1912 Captain Lawrence Oates, who was too ill to travel farther, walked out into a blizzard to save his companions in the Scott expedition to Antarctica.[50] These are matters of mere "happenedness" or *Historie*, in the language of Martin Kähler and Rudolf Bultmann.

2. *Historic knowledge.* Historical knowledge can, under certain circumstances, come to have a direct significance for the present. Jesus' acceptance of the cross or, for that matter, the actions of Socrates and Captain Oates can influence a future time. This is a direct or existential influence. This historic significance is, of course, directly related to historical knowledge. If Jesus had railed against God, Socrates had to be forced to drink the hemlock, or Captain Oates had to be driven out into the blizzard, the historic significance would be quite different.

49. Perrin, *Rediscovering*, pp. 207–48.
50. Ibid., p. 236.

3. *Faith knowledge.* Some knowledge has significance only within the context of a particular faith, belief, or commitment; for instance, in a context where Jesus is acknowledged as Lord and Christ. Here we are in the realm of a transhistorical and then nonhistorical reality, the realm of God and his activity. Whereas to say, "Jesus died," is a matter of historical knowledge, to say, "Christ died for my sins in accordance with the Scriptures," is a matter of faith knowledge. It introduces the idea that Christ's death fulfilled God's purposes and was accepted by him.[51] Perrin says, "That Jesus died nobly or showed confidence in God are historical statements, subject to the vicissitudes of historical research, but that his death fulfilled the purpose of God in regard to 'my sins' is certainly not such a statement, and it lies beyond the power of the historian even to consider it, even though, as a Christian, he might believe it."[52] Here it should be borne in mind that while "historical knowledge can come to have this significance . . . so can myth, legend, saga—and any combination of these!"[53]

What, we must ask, is the relationship between these types of knowledge? This, Perrin holds, is the proper form of the "question of the historical Jesus." He notes that faith knowledge of Jesus arises in response to the church's proclamation. He has been convinced of this from two sources: the recent discussion and his own experience. There are many forms of proclamation, including historical narrative and legend, but they all have one distinguishing characteristic: "the ability to mediate the encounter of faith with the Christ present to faith in them."[54] This experiential and pragmatic validation of faith knowledge (the faith image) is further expounded by Perrin: "What gives this faith-image validity is the fact that it grows out of religious experience and is capable of mediating religious experience; that it develops in the context of the complex mixture of needs, etc., which originally created,

51. Ibid., p. 237.
52. Ibid., pp. 237–38.
53. Ibid., p. 236.
54. Ibid., p. 243.

and continues to create, an openness towards the kerygma; and that it can continue to develop to meet those needs."[55]

What is the role of historical knowledge? First, it contributes to the formation of the faith image. While the content of that image comes from many sources, among them the church's proclamation and one's own personal religious experience, it may also include historical knowledge.[56] After all, Christian faith is faith in something, and historical knowledge can help to provide the content.

There is a second role which historical knowledge serves with respect to faith knowledge. While the first of these roles is positive, the second is primarily negative. There are many faith images extant, many conflicting and competing kerygmata, many different Christs. How is one to choose among them? Here there is something of a dilemma for Perrin, because, as he says, "we must fully admit the highly individualistic character of a believer's faith-image, and yet, at the same time, face the question of which, if any, are to called 'Christian,' and so face the necessity of distinguishing true from false."[57] He believes he has the right to appeal to "our limited, but real, historical knowledge of Jesus."[58] While thus recognizing that the potential contribution of historical knowledge is limited, he nonetheless identifies it as real. Recognition of the limitation is apparent in his speaking of "consistency" with historical knowledge rather than "coherence": "The true kerygmatic Christ, the justifiable faith-image, is that consistent with the historical Jesus."[59] In this sense, and to this limited extent, historical knowledge validates the Christian kerygma, but as Christian rather than as kerygma.[60] That is to say, it can tell us which beliefs Christianity proclaims must be accepted to receive salvation, but it cannot prove those beliefs.

A basic point of Perrin's which we observed earlier is now introduced, namely, that the early church identified the earthly Jesus of Nazareth with the risen Lord of Christian experience. Indeed, the Epistles include sayings of both the earthly Jesus

55. Ibid., p. 244.
56. Ibid.
57. Ibid.
58. Ibid.
59. Ibid.
60. Ibid.

and the risen Lord without distinguishing them. This identification Perrin believes to be a justification for saying that we must use historical knowledge to test the kerygmata about Christ.[61]

There is a third role of historical knowledge. Perrin asserts that "historical knowledge of Jesus can be directly relevant to faith, apart from aiding in the formation of the faith-image."[62] He arrives at this conclusion through an examination of the Synoptic Gospels. In particular the equation of the earthly Jesus with the risen Lord means that the ministry of the historical Jesus has applicability to the life of the church and the Christian today. Using Mark 8:27–9:1, Perrin draws a number of parallels:

Earthly Jesus	Risen Lord
Peter	Typical Christian disciple
Situation in Jesus' earthly ministry	Situation faced by the early church
Instruction to the disciples	The risen Lord's instruction to the early church

If, then, a believer in response to the kerygma stands in a relationship to God parallel to the relationship in which a Galilean disciple stood in response to Jesus' proclamation, Jesus' instruction to the latter is directly applicable to the former; indeed, it is applicable to believers in any age. It was for this reason that some of the earthly Jesus' teaching was incorporated into the Synoptic tradition.[63]

While thus maintaining that knowledge of the historical Jesus can be relevant to faith in any age, Perrin does acknowledge one major difficulty: "the practical problems involved in crossing the barrier of two millennia and radically different *Weltanschauungen*."[64] Nowhere is this more apparent than in the treatment of the resurrection of Jesus, a topic with which Perrin deals in his little book *The Resurrection According to Matthew, Mark, and Luke.* After carefully surveying and examining the evidence for the resurrection as found in the three Synoptic Gospels, he faces the question of what actually happened that

61. Ibid., p. 245.
62. Ibid., p. 246.
63. Ibid., p. 247.
64. Ibid., p. 248.

first Easter morning. He maintains that this is "essentially a modern question, alien to these ancient religious texts."[65] None of them is concerned about giving us what we would call historical information. Nonetheless, a modern writer must face that question's challenge.

To answer the question of what really happened on Easter, Perrin notes the several passages in Paul's writings bearing witness to the resurrection: 1 Corinthians 9:1–2; 15:3–8; Galatians 1:15–16; and Philippians 3:7–11. The stories of Jesus' post-Easter appearances are the main consideration, the account of the empty tomb being relatively late.[66] Paul is the only claimed witness whom we may interrogate, but he presumes that the other witnesses would give a similar response, could we also interrogate them. What can we then say?

> In some way they were granted a vision of Jesus which convinced them that God had vindicated Jesus out of his death, and that therefore the death of Jesus was by no means the end of the impact of Jesus upon their lives and upon the world in which they lived. Very much to the contrary, since Jesus as risen commissioned them to new tasks and to new responsibilities, they found confidence in themselves and in the future of the world in which they lived precisely because they were now living in a world in which Jesus was risen.[67]

This is as far as Perrin feels he can go, and he again reminds us that "Did Jesus really rise?" is a twentieth-century, not a first-century, question.

Evaluation

How shall we assess Perrin's Christology? We must note first several commendable aspects of his thought:

1. Perrin is to be commended for having carefully thought out his view of biblical theology and adhering to it. While he does not always make his view explicit, and does not spell out the

---

65. Norman Perrin, *The Resurrection According to Matthew, Mark, and Luke* (Philadelphia: Fortress, 1977), p. 78.
66. Ibid., p. 80.
67. Ibid., p. 83.

relationship between biblical theology and systematic theology, he is careful to stay within the bounds of his definition.

2. He has strenuously endeavored to determine the teaching of the biblical authors. He has gone to great lengths to discover the cultural and linguistic backgrounds of the concepts they employed.

3. He has carefully spelled out his methodology. One does not have to wonder where he stands with respect to the approach of Kähler, Bultmann, or the new quest.

On the other hand, there are a number of shortcomings in Perrin's Christology which give us real reservations:

1. Perrin at times is quite selective in his use of Scripture. Of course, he is not a systematic theologian and so is not required to make inductions from all portions of Scripture, but we are referring here to writings by the same author, Paul, and even within the same book and chapter, as when Perrin draws upon certain portions of 1 Corinthians 15, but not other portions. And while there may be certain texts that he does not consider authentic or regards as suspect on critical grounds, we are refer-ring to his neglect of crucial texts regarding which he does not introduce such considerations.

2. An inadequate understanding of the nature of inductive proof leads Perrin to frequent overstatements of the degree of certainty of his conclusions. It is not uncommon for him to refer to conclusive demonstration, as if deductive proof had been given. What one would expect instead is some indication of the degree of probability.

3. Closely allied to this is a tendency to stipulate the terms of the debate. In particular, Perrin insists that the burden of proof rests upon any claim that a specific word of Jesus as found in Scripture is authentic. Perrin thus gives himself a great advan-tage in the debate. Is this a fair stipulation, however? In courts of law, witnesses are deemed reliable unless their credibility can be impugned.

4. Hidden assumptions are at work in Perrin's treatment of the resurrection. He resolutely refuses to state that the early Christians really believed that Jesus was bodily risen. He care-fully restricts the resurrection to "a vision of Jesus which con-vinced them that God had vindicated Jesus out of his death," whereas the witnesses claimed that Jesus had been raised, and

in a fashion which strongly suggested bodily resurrection. Although Perrin speaks of "Jesus as risen," he hesitates to use stronger language. Could it be that there are assumptions at work similar to Bultmann's conception of the closed continuum, according to which everything that occurs in the universe abides by the laws of nature? Something seems to preclude a supernatural interpretation of what happened on Easter.

5. In his treatment of the resurrection, Perrin also maintains that the witnesses and the Scripture writers did not ask questions such as, "Did it really happen?" Such considerations were not part of their way of thinking. But what about Paul's statement in 1 Corinthians 15:12–19? Here he seems very concerned about whether the resurrection really happened and expostulates on its significance. Yet while citing verses 3 to 8 of this chapter, Perrin without any justification stops short of verses 12–19.

6. Perrin's effort to spell out the relationship of historical knowledge to faith knowledge is deficient. Historical knowledge contributes to the formation of faith knowledge, but the real value seems to be in the negative role. Any variety of faith knowledge that is not consistent with historical knowledge is thereby shown not to be true. The problem is that there may be two or more types of faith knowledge that are consistent with historical knowledge, but not with one another. What does one do then? It hardly seems sufficient to refer, as Perrin does, to the "highly individualistic character of a believer's faith-image," which tends to fall into subjectivism.

7. On the basis of the parallelism between the earthly Jesus and the risen Lord, and between situations in the ministry of Jesus and in the early church, Perrin contends that knowledge of the historical Jesus is relevant not only to the early church, but to believers in all ages. He is aware of the practical problem of moving from the early church to the present-day church, with the barrier of two thousand years and different *Weltanschauungen*, but apparently feels that this problem can be easily solved, for he simply slides over it. Yet this problem, from the standpoint of the systematic theologian, is extremely large, at least as large as the problem of moving between the historical Jesus and the early church.

8. Perrin repeatedly refers to the early church's identification of the words of the risen Lord with those of the earthly Jesus,

but he does not grapple with the underlying reason for this identification. He also makes reference to the belief of the early
church that the risen Lord spoke to them through prophets, but
he never considers the possibility that such inspiration and revelation really did occur in the early church. This is another indication of his antisupernaturalistic assumptions.

Perrin insists that his Christology is based solely on the conclusions of historical research. Such a flat statement grows out
of a naturalistic or positivistic conception of history, such as that
espoused by Bultmann. But this view is very strongly disputed
today by Wolfhart Pannenberg and others who argue that one
must proceed upon the assumption of an open universe. Since
Perrin's Christology rests upon the results of his historical investigation, which in turn is based upon an arbitrary assumption
about the nature of reality, it is Perrin upon whom the burden
of proof must rest.

5

The Historical Problem. (2) Existential Christology: The Relevance of Historical Knowledge of Jesus

GOTTHOLD LESSING
SØREN KIERKEGAARD
RUDOLF BULTMANN
EVALUATION

One of the questions with which Christology must deal is the relationship between history and faith. Specifically, what is the relationship between one's reasoning about the historical Jesus and the internal commitment of faith which the believer makes to him? We have already considered the problem of whether historical knowledge of the man Jesus of Nazareth is possible; now we must consider whether it is relevant and necessary.

We shall examine this question in several steps. We will first consider the famous "ugly ditch" proposed by Gotthold Lessing. Then we will investigate Søren Kierkegaard's adaptation and modification of this concept. Finally, we will note some twentieth-century developments in the thought of Rudolf Bultmann. The nuances introduced at these several stages of the discussion should help us to understand the issue more fully.

111

Gotthold Lessing

Gotthold Ephraim Lessing was born in 1729, the son of an orthodox Lutheran pastor who in 1746 sent him to Leipzig to study theology. His real interest at this point in his life, however, was the stage, so upon receiving permission from his father he gave up the study of theology. A combination of factors, however, led to his return to theology: the failure of a theater in which he was employed in Hamburg, a growing interest in theology, and the offer of a post as librarian at the Duke of Brunswick's library in Wolfenbüttel. There he found Hermann Samuel Reimarus's four-thousand-page manuscript defending deism, portions of which he published as *Wolfenbüttel Fragments by an Unnamed Author*. As a result, Lessing found himself under attack by a number of defenders of orthodoxy, most notably Johann Melchior Goeze, chief pastor of the Lutheran Church of Saint Catherine in Hamburg. In the process of responding to Goeze, Lessing's own views, rather than those of Reimarus, came increasingly under contention. Finally, when the exchange became too heated, the duke decreed that Lessing's writings would have to be censored. He then resorted to his earlier love, casting his ideas into dramatic form rather than first-person expression.[1]

It was in the exchange with Goeze that Lessing declared, "The accidental truths of history can never become the proof of necessary truths of reason."[2] This dictum, through its many interpretations, has been very influential upon Christology, theology in general, and even philosophy. It is, in fact, the topic of this chapter.

The idea that historical truth can never prove necessary truth was not original with Lessing. He especially appreciated the position of Gottfried von Leibniz, who had written, "The original proof of necessary truths comes from the understanding alone, and all other truths come from experiences or from observations of the senses."[3] He also wrote, "Truths of reason are necessary and their opposite is impossible; those of fact are contingent and their opposite is possible."[4] Thus truths of fact, scientific and his-

---

1. The biographical details in this paragraph are taken from the introductory essay in *Lessing's Theological Writings*, trans. Henry Chadwick (Stanford, Calif.: Stanford University Press, 1957), pp. 9–29.
2. Ibid., p. 53.
3. Gottfried W. von Leibniz *New Essays on the Human Understanding* 1.1.5.
4. Gottfried W. von Leibniz *Monadology* 33.

torical, are less certain and more untidy than are truths of reason, such as mathematics. Lessing also gave much attention to another rationalist, Benedict de Spinoza, who maintained that natural divine law does not depend on the truth of any historical narrative: "The truth of a historical narrative, however assured, cannot give us the knowledge nor consequently the love of God, for love of God springs from knowledge of him, and knowledge of him should be derived from general ideas, in themselves certain and known, so that the truth of a historical narrative is far from being a necessary requisite for our attaining our highest good."[5] As a representative of empiricism, a school whose epistemology was directly opposed to that of rationalism, John Locke had put it thus: "If the evidence of [a divine revelation's] being a revelation, or that this is its true sense, be only on probable proofs, our assent can reach no higher than an assurance or diffidence, arising from the more or less apparent probability of the proofs."[6]

Lessing's major contribution regarding historical truth was made in his essay "On the Proof of the Spirit and of Power." The real issue underlying this discussion is not the rationality or verifiability of the biblical revelation, but the relationship of faith to past historical events. He distinguishes between miracles and fulfilled prophecies which he himself experiences firsthand and those of which he merely hears through the testimony of others. They are quite different from one another. He comments, "If I had lived at the time of Christ, then of course the prophecies fulfilled in his person would have made me pay great attention to him. If I had actually seen him do miracles . . . I would have gained so much confidence that I would willingly have submitted my intellect to his, and I would have believed him in all things in which equally indisputable experiences would not tell against him."[7] Lessing evidently is in this respect a confident empiricist, having no doubts about the reliability of his sense experiences, even if they include phenomena which seem to be supernatural in nature.

5. Benedict de Spinoza *Tractatus Theologico-Politicus* 4 (*The Chief Works of Benedict de Spinoza*, trans. R. H. M. Elwes, 2 vols. [New York: Dover, 1951], vol. 1, p. 61).

6. John Locke *Essay Concerning Human Understanding* 4.16.14.

7. Gotthold Ephraim Lessing, "On the Proof of the Spirit and of Power," in *Lessing's Theological Writings*, pp. 51–52.

The effect which removal from firsthand experience has is made clear by Lessing. If miracles and fulfilments of prophecy were occurring in his time, he would have no difficulty believing. The problem is that he lives in the eighteenth century, "in which miracles no longer happen."[8] He adds, "These, the prophecies fulfilled before my eyes, the miracles that occur before my eyes, are immediate in their effect. But those—the reports of fulfilled prophecies and miracles—have to work through a medium which takes away all their force."[9]

One of the confusing aspects of Lessing's thought is that he tends to intertwine several different considerations without explicitly distinguishing them. Here we encounter one of those situations. For when the issue is historical knowledge of miracles and prophecy fulfilled in the past, we face not merely the difficulty of removal in time and the lack of immediate experience, but also the problem of the miraculous. When he says that miracles no longer happen in the eighteenth century, he is implicitly invoking the principle of analogy: our ability to understand and to believe an event which allegedly occurred in the past is dependent upon our experiencing something similar in the present.

Lessing now introduces the dictum we looked at earlier with its crucial distinction between accidental and necessary truths: "Accidental truths of history can never become the proof of necessary truths of reason."[10] He is here working with the familiar rationalist distinction between necessary truths, which can be demonstrated deductively, and contingent truths. Necessary truths are those whose negation is self-contradictory. They cannot be false; they cannot not be true. Since it is impossible for them to be false, they are necessarily true. Contingent truths, on the other hand, do not have to be true. Their negation is not self-contradictory. They simply happen to be true, but it could be otherwise.

We should note that the nature of the issue here is quite different from what it has been. The issue is not temporal distance. It is now the distinction between the apodictic certainty of logical or mathematical truths and statements involving mere prob-

8. Ibid., p. 52.
9. Ibid.
10. Ibid., p. 53.

ability. This is different from the distinction between knowledge gained by personal experience and knowledge gained from historical reports.

We must also note that there is ambiguity when Lessing says that no historical truth can be demonstrated. Is he denying that people in all times and places can know for certain that a given event occurred at one time and place in history? If so, he is referring to the epistemological problem, the question of the possibility of gaining knowledge of the past. Or does he mean that it is not possible to know past historical occurrences well enough to be able to draw conclusive meaning from them, as he seems to be saying when he asserts that his not having witnessed Jesus' miracles makes it impossible to draw any personal significance from them? If so, he is referring to the metaphysical problem, the question of the significance that a historical event can have for dogmatic belief.

Suppose, Lessing argues, that on historical grounds we had to allow that Christ both raised persons from the dead and himself rose from the dead; would we not also have to grant the truth of his statement that God had a Son of the same essence as himself, and that he, Jesus, was that Son? "This would be quite excellent!" Lessing laments, "if only it were not the case that it is not more than historically certain that Christ said this."[11] The problem here, then, is epistemological; there is insufficient information to be able to determine with requisite certainty that Christ made such a claim for himself. It is in this context, uncertainty as to what Jesus actually said and did, that Lessing makes his famous "ditch" statement: "That, then, is the ugly, broad ditch which I cannot get across, however often and however earnestly I have tried to make the leap. If anyone can help me over it, let him do it, I beg him, I adjure him. He will deserve a divine reward from me."[12]

What did Lessing do to negotiate this ugly ditch? In the treatise which we have been examining, he basically leaves the problem unresolved. Elsewhere, however, he continues to deal with it in different form and to share with us something of the solution at which he arrived. In the process he moves the issue from the epistemological toward the metaphysical realm. The ques-

11. Ibid., p. 55.
12. Ibid.

tion then becomes, How can necessary truths, among which he reckons religious truths, be related to contingent historical events? Basically what Lessing appears to do is to affirm that the truths of religion are true irrespective of any particular historical events. Since what we require are necessary, not contingent truths, secondhand testimony and even direct experience become irrelevant. It is not insignificant that Lessing concludes his treatise "On the Proof of the Spirit and of Power" with a mathematical reference.[13]

In the rationalistic and deistic framework in which Lessing was working, the true is not true because it derives from certain historical occurrences which can be demonstrated in some conclusive fashion. Rather, the true is the set of universal truths. In his treatise "On the Origin of Revealed Religion," he says we are all bound and committed to natural religion according to the capacity of our powers. Since this capacity varies from person to person, everyone's natural religion will be somewhat different. Out of the religion of nature it is necessary to construct a positive religion, just as a positive law is constructed out of the law of nature. All positive religions are equally true and equally false.[14]

Lessing makes this very point in a different literary form. In his drama *Nathan the Wise* a man has a valuable ring which is desired by each of his three sons. In order not to disappoint any of them, he has two duplicates made. He gives the genuine ring to one son and the duplicates to the others. When the three rings are inspected, no one can tell the difference. It is therefore concluded that the original has been lost, and that all three are copies. This, it should be noted, is Nathan's answer when he is questioned as to which of the three religions, Christianity, Judaism, or Islam, is true.[15]

Together with the shift in the understanding of the nature of religion is a shift in the understanding of the universality or normativeness of Christianity. One area in which the historical issue usually has special pertinence is Christology. For Lessing, however, Christology is not a matter of predications, metaphysical or otherwise, about the nature of Jesus. Rather, the concern is

13. Ibid., pp. 55–56.
14. Gotthold Ephraim Lessing, "On the Origin of Revealed Religion," in *Lessing's Theological Writings*, pp. 104–05.
15. Gotthold Ephraim Lessing, *Nathan the Wise*, quoted in *Lessing's Theological Writings*, p. 27.

with Jesus as a teacher of universal moral truths. Consequently, the effort to bridge the gap between the historical account of the life of Jesus and traditional christological assertions does not have to be made.[16]

Finally, there is a shift in Lessing's thought from emphasis upon the external, the publicly observable events of Jesus' life, potentially accessible to and verifiable by all persons, to the internal state of the religious person. This is, for example, one of the points of *Nathan the Wise:* what is important is not the external differences in the doctrines and ritual of the three religions, but what is within each of the worshipers, namely, sincerity. It is also implied in the reference to mathematics at the end of "On the Proof of the Spirit and of Power." Earlier in this essay Lessing, in regard to an old pious legend that conveys a religious truth, remarks, "What does it matter to me whether the legend is false or true? The fruits are excellent."[17] Gordon Michalson, Jr., comments regarding Lessing's solution: "We settle the question of religious truth by looking within ourselves, not by appealing to matters of historical fact or adjudicating competing doctrinal formulations."[18] Emphasis on the internal state also seems to be implied by Lessing's statement comparing the possession and the pursuit of truth: "If God held all truth in his right hand and in his left the everlasting striving after truth, so that I should always and everlastingly be mistaken, and said to me, 'Choose,' with humility I would pick on the left hand and say, 'Father, grant me that. Absolute truth is for thee alone."[19] The subjective activity of searching for the truth is more desirable than the possession of objective truth.

Søren Kierkegaard

It is in the thought of Søren Kierkegaard, the melancholy Dane, that we find the most complete discussion of the issues which Lessing had introduced with his concept of the ugly ditch.

16. Karl Barth, *Protestant Thought: From Rousseau to Ritschl* (New York: Simon and Schuster, 1969), p. 125.

17. Lessing, "Proof," p. 55.

18. Gordon E. Michalson, Jr., *Lessing's "Ugly Ditch": A Study of Theology and History* (University Park, Pa.: Pennsylvania State University Press, 1985), p. x.

19. Gotthold Ephraim Lessing, *Eine Duplik* (Lachmann-Muncker, 13. 23–24), quoted in *Lessing's Theological Writings*, p. 43.

Kierkegaard brought his own concerns to the discussion and thus gave the entire subject a new turn. Indeed, much of the popular conception of what Lessing says is actually Kierkegaard's interpretation and adaptation of Lessing.

Kierkegaard discussed the problems in two major works. His *Philosophical Fragments* is a brief, terse "thought experiment" posed in terms of a dialogue between the pseudonymous Johannes Climacus and an imaginary reader. It is an abstract and formal treatment, whereas the *Concluding Unscientific Postscript* is a more extended discussion, in which the framework is easily identifiable as the Christian religion.

Michalson has offered a helpful and perceptive analysis of the issues. He suggests that two questions are intertwined in Kierkegaard's handling of the ugly-ditch issue. The first is the historical, namely, whether we can obtain sufficient historical information about the person of Jesus to have him as an object of faith. The second is the philosophical problem, namely, the relationship between historical revelation and philosophical reason. Here the question is how the historical references of Christianity to specific occurrences at particular times and places shall be related to philosophy's endeavor to speak of universal, temporally independent truths.[20] For Christology the issue is how the specific events of Jesus' life, the actions which he performed, are to be related to matters such as his humanity and deity. How does one get, for example, from a statement about Jesus' hungering and thirsting to the doctrine of his humanity? How does one get from accounts of his performing miracles to the doctrine of his deity?

What we have mentioned so far are objective issues regarding the question of the truth of Christianity in general. There is another issue which concerns Kierkegaard greatly and occupies much of his thinking and discussion. That is the subjective problem, the truth of Christianity for the individual. In some ways Kierkegaard's extended discussion of subjective truth is his answer to the objective issues posed above.

At the very opening of the *Philosophical Fragments* Kierkegaard asks, "How far does the Truth admit of being learned?"[21]

---

20. Michalson, *Lessing's "Ugly Ditch,"* p. 64.
21. Søren Kierkegaard, *Philosophical Fragments*, trans. David F. Swenson (Princeton, N.J.: Princeton University Press, 1936), p. 5.

This way of putting the question moves it from the purely historical into the philosophical realm. Here the context must be understood. Kierkegaard is reacting to Georg Hegel's organic idealism, which holds that all particulars are related to a whole (the Absolute), and all questions about reality can be answered rationally. He is also responding in a sense to the whole idealistic tradition, which, in one way or another, poses an ontological connection between ourselves as knowers, the world, and God. This means that we have epistemological access to the world.

The epistemology of idealism is in some cases quite simple. Because both we and our world have been created by God, common patterns of structure and rationality are present in all three. With this commensurability of subject and object, knowledge is possible. Socrates believed that all humans actually possess knowledge within themselves antecedently. This is usually interpreted to mean that in an earlier existence we had contact with the pure essences. In the Socratic process of learning, truth is not so much discovery as recovery. The truth lies unrecognized within the person, and error consists in failure to recognize this truth. Thus the role of the teacher is not to impart truth, but to help the person recognize the truth which is within. The teacher does not give birth to any truths, but is like a midwife, helping others to give birth to their own ideas. This, indeed, is Socrates' favorite designation of himself. The teacher is not essential to the learning process, as one who must impart some truth not possessed by the learner. Rather, the relationship is an accidental one. What the teacher helps learners discover is something which they could conceivably discover without the teacher, since they already possess the truth. Ignorance is not absence of the truth, but failure to recognize that one possesses the truth.

Kierkegaard gives the virtual opposite of this Socratic epistemology. Suppose, he says, that we are not really in possession of the truth at all. What if our ignorance is a matter of our state of being rather than our state of knowing and learning?[22] What if the truth is not within us but outside, so that learning is not a matter of recollection but of true discovery? Then the problem is not epistemological but metaphysical. It is not the case that we possess a hidden truth which we are unable to identify, but that we are completely cut off from the truth!

22. Ibid., p. 9.

Cut off as we are, we must not only come into contact with the truth, which is external to us, but must place ourselves in a condition receptive to that truth. Kierkegaard describes what we as learners need under such circumstances:

> One who gives the learner not only the Truth, but also the condition for understanding it, is more than teacher. All instruction depends upon the presence, in the last analysis, of the requisite condition; if this is lacking, no teacher can do anything. For otherwise he would find it necessary not only to transform the learner, but to re-create him before beginning to teach him. But this is something that no human being can do; if it is to be done, it must be done by God himself.[23]

In Kierkegaard's depiction of the process of coming to truth, he observes not only that we are devoid of the condition for obtaining the truth, but also that this is a condition which we once had and of which we must therefore have been deprived. This deprivation could not have been by the action of the God who created us, thus giving us the requisite condition in the first place. That would be a contradiction. Rather, the deprivation must have been a willful act on our part, a theme that recurs in Kierkegaard's view of faith, which, as we will see, he defines as a willful act opening ourselves to what seems to be paradoxical.[24]

We need to recognize, moreover, that it is not simply the inadequacy of historical reasoning that obstructs faith. If this were the case, total access to the data that would resolve the historical questions conclusively (e.g., did Jesus really rise from the dead?) would constitute the basis for belief. And the eyewitnesses to the events would have an advantage over those of us who, coming at a later time, must rely upon their testimony. This notion is effectively laid to rest by Kierkegaard in the *Fragments*, however.

The problem is the contingency of history. Necessity pertains only to matters of logic, which could not be otherwise; historical events, by contrast, could have been otherwise. Logic deals with that which is. History, however, deals with that which comes to be.[25] And it is this coming to be which makes historical knowledge contingent, both for the person who is years removed from the event and for the firsthand observer, the eyewitness. In a long

---

23. Ibid., p. 10.
24. Ibid.
25. Ibid., pp. 60–63.

and rather turgid "interlude" Kierkegaard makes the point that although the observer can witness that which has come into being, it is not possible to witness the actual coming into being. All knowledge of coming into being is inferential. While second-hand knowledge may appear more inferential because it is somewhat farther removed and involves more steps, it is of the same genus as the firsthand knowledge possessed by the contemporary disciple.[26]

Kierkegaard goes on to affirm that historical knowledge is not only inadequate to produce faith, as if the problem were merely a lack of sufficient information, but irrelevant to faith. On one hand, an unbeliever may have more historical information than does a believer, and on the other, an eyewitness may be a believer, but not by virtue of being an eyewitness. For Kierkegaard, "the historical in the more concrete sense is a matter of indifference,"[27] and faith "cannot be distilled from the nicest accuracy of detail."[28]

Part of the difficulty in basing faith upon history is the unique nature of the type of faith Kierkegaard is discussing. For the object of this faith is the paradoxical, and indeed, the supreme paradox, the idea that the eternal God has entered time. This is the thought which reason cannot conceive. Here again Kierkegaard's opposition to all idealism and rationalism becomes evident. The aim of idealism is to render everything intelligible, and it is confident that such can be done because of its underlying belief in the essential connectedness of the human with the Creator and with all created truth. Here, however, we have the collision between time and eternity, underscoring the essentially transcendent nature of God. Any human attempt to think of the eternal and transcendent must inevitably fail.

To a large extent, the *Concluding Unscientific Postscript* is an effort to develop on a broader scale the underlying principles of the *Fragments*. We have said that history can never be a basis for faith because historical research gives us insufficient knowledge and the wrong kind of knowledge. There is a fundamental antithesis between historical reasoning and faith; they deal with quite different objects. We noted earlier that for Lessing the solution to the problem of the ugly ditch was found in a turn inward to the

26. Ibid., pp. 66–71.
27. Ibid., p. 48.
28. Ibid., p. 87.

subjective dimension of life. We find in Kierkegaard a parallel or, rather, a stronger form of the solution.

The difference between objective and subjective thinking is fundamental. Objective thinking is the type of thinking which goes into all research where the goal is to understand some object as completely and accurately as possible. Thus, inquiry is made with greater and greater refinement into the nature of that object. The supreme paradigm of such endeavor is, of course, the natural sciences. Here the exact chemical makeup of the substance is investigated, or the precise weight, length, color, or pressure. The social sciences have in recent years endeavored to fulfil this ideal as well. History also seeks to identify as accurately as possible what has occurred and why.[29]

In objective thinking the emphasis is upon the object. The subject, or the person making the inquiry, is not to intrude into the consideration. The attitude of the subject should not be a factor, for that could skew the results. Ideally, the exact nature of the outcome ought to be a matter of total indifference to the investigator. Objectivity is strongly desired, since that helps guarantee accuracy.[30]

What goes on in objective thinking is an ever-increasing approximation to the truth. As more and more experiments are developed, as the means of controlling the variables improve, as instruments for measuring results become more refined, as the techniques of investigation become ever more sophisticated, knowledge comes closer and closer to the object as it actually is. While absolute knowledge is not possible, since humans are not omniscient, knowledge can come closer and closer to that ideal.[31]

Subjective thinking is the opposite. Here the emphasis is not upon the object, but upon the subject, or upon how the object of knowledge affects the knower. Our concern is not turned outward, but inward.[32] The focus is upon our relationship to the object rather than the object itself. How something is said is considered far more important than what is said.[33]

29. Søren Kierkegaard, *Concluding Unscientific Postscript* (Princeton, N.J.: Princeton University Press, 1941), p. 173.
30. Ibid.
31. Ibid.
32. Ibid., pp. 175, 178.
33. Ibid., p. 181.

Subjective thinking is especially appropriate with respect to God. Some people attempt to approach God by an objective approximation process, seeking to gain ever more information about him until there is certainty. That must inevitably fail, however, because God is not an object; he is a subject. Thus the way to truth about him is the antithesis of the objective approximation process.[34] There comes a point where the objective swings off, as Kierkegaard puts it, where objective knowledge is placed in abeyance. There, amid and precisely because of objective uncertainty, the inwardness of passion which constitutes subjective truth is increased. This subjective truth is of inestimable value: *"An objective uncertainty held fast in an appropriation-process of the most passionate inwardness is the truth,* the highest truth attainable for an existing individual."[35] The truth is precisely that venture which chooses the objectively uncertain with the passion of the infinite. While one might attempt to find God by contemplating the order of nature and discover there his omnipotence and wisdom, "I also see much else that disturbs my mind and excites anxiety."[36] This definition of truth as inward passion for the objectively uncertain is also a definition of faith, according to Kierkegaard:

> Without risk there is no faith. Faith is precisely the contradiction between the infinite passion of the individual's inwardness and the objective uncertainty. If I am capable of grasping God objectively, I do not believe, but precisely because I cannot do this I must believe. If I wish to preserve myself in faith I must constantly be intent upon holding fast the objective uncertainty, so as to remain out upon the deep, over seventy thousand fathoms of water, still preserving my faith.[37]

Again we see not only the insufficiency of objective knowledge, whether historical or philosophical, for faith, but the actual antithesis between historical knowledge and faith. The less the objective certainty, the greater the inward passion that inspires and even constitutes faith. Objective certainty is inversely proportional to faith. In fact, Kierkegaard poses the question of whether

34. Ibid., p. 182.
35. Ibid.
36. Ibid.
37. Ibid.

the objective conception is at all necessary. In a famous passage
seeking to discover the basic nature of religious truth, he contrasts
two worshipers and then asks which one has the greater truth:

> If one who lives in the midst of Christendom goes up to the house
> of God, the house of the true God, with the true conception of
> God in his knowledge, and prays, but prays in a false spirit; and
> one who lives in an idolatrous community prays with the entire
> passion of the infinite, although his eyes rest upon the image of
> an idol; where is there most truth? The one prays in truth to God
> though he worships an idol; the other prays falsely to the true
> God, and hence worships in fact an idol.[38]

Here truth and the nature of one's relationship to God are not
determined by the correctness of one's conception of God, but by
the passion with which one prays. While many defenders of
Kierkegaard have sought to modify or blunt the full impact of this
passage, its literal meaning must not too quickly be dismissed.

The view which we have developed of the relationship of truth
to historical and other objective data is supported by Kierkegaard's concept of the stages on life's way or, perhaps more accurately, the spheres of existence. Although they may be steps
through which one moves sequentially, they should be thought of
primarily as orientations to life, sets of values, or ways of living.

The first stage is the aesthetic stage. This is the approach to
life that lives for the enjoyment of the moment. The epitome of
this stage is a Don Juan whose pleasure is found in the pursuit
and conquest of members of the opposite sex.[39] Another example
is the pursuit of health, or of riches, honor, and position, or the
development of a talent.[40] In all of these cases the enjoyment is
immediate.[41] Unfortunately, however, in a sense the aesthete has
no self.[42] The experiences do not mold a permanent character;
rather, the aesthete simply continues to savor the enjoyment of
the moment.[43] There is an absence of any commitment, except to
the pursuit of pleasure. Variety is the key to this pleasure, requir-

38. Ibid., pp. 179–80.
39. Søren Kierkegaard, *Either/Or*, 2 vols. (Princeton, N.J.: Princeton University Press,
1944), vol. 1, p. 105.
40. Ibid., vol. 2, pp. 153–65.
41. Ibid., p. 150.
42. Ibid., p. 152; *Postscript*, p. 478.
43. Kierkegaard, *Postscript*, p. 265.

ing abandonment of the pursuit just when its object is about to be possessed.[44]

The second stage is the ethical stage. Utterly unlike the aesthete, individuals at this stage have committed themselves to something; they have accepted responsibility. Here the model is marriage, in which one pledges oneself to another and to certain ways of living.[45] If the key word characterizing the first stage is "enjoyment," the key word for the second stage is "struggle." Here the object is not so much some finite external value as it is the development of a character, a moral fiber within the person. Choice—in particular the choice of a self and determination to become that self—is a fundamental component of the ethical sphere of existence.[46]

The third stage is the religious. Here the key word is "suffering." There must be a double movement—infinite resignation and faith. One gives up everything and then, against all rational expectation, possesses it again in faith. An example of this is Abraham, who is the central character of Kierkegaard's *Fear and Trembling*. Abraham was willing to sacrifice his son Isaac to God.[47] And then, in the face of all rational expectation, Isaac was restored to his father.[48]

There is also in Kierkegaard's thought a distinction between two types of religion, which can be simply termed religion A and religion B. Religion A believes the self to be in continuity with God. We submit ourselves to the divine, who is immanent within us. Any imperfection, which manifests itself as guilt rather than sin, can be changed through a process of self-transformation.[49] Religion B, which is more distinctly Christian, sees the human personality as devoid of truth. Inward effort results only in a consciousness of distance from God, of an absolute difference between God and us.[50] We can come to know truth only through a revelation of God in history. That revelation, however, by its very nature is paradoxical and offensive to reason.[51] To be com-

44. Kierkegaard, *Either/Or*, vol. 1, pp. 234–35.
45. Ibid., vol. 2, pp. 252, 255.
46. Ibid., p. 141.
47. Søren Kierkegaard, *Fear and Trembling* (Garden City, N.Y.: Doubleday, 1954), pp. 65–66.
48. Ibid., p. 67.
49. Kierkegaard, *Postscript*, pp. 494, 498, 516.
50. Ibid., p. 439.
51. Ibid., pp. 187–88.

prehended, it requires more than simply a bit of assistance from a God who is immanent within us. It requires a transformation of our person by a transcendent God.[52]

What is especially significant for our purposes here is the way in which one moves from one of these stages to another. This does not take place in response to a carefully reasoned judgment. One does not, for example, conclude that there are ten good reasons for adopting the ethical orientation in preference to the aesthetic orientation. Rather, the transition is an existential decision in which one moves from one to the other by a leap, which may be without rational basis and even in the face of logical considerations. Aesthetes move to the ethical way of life because of boredom, the inability of their activities to produce the enjoyment previously prized. We move from the ethical to the religious stage because of despair or frustration with our inability to meet the standards which we have set for ourselves.[53]

In these converging motifs Kierkegaard, like Lessing, has demonstrated that for him religion has taken a "subjective turn." Religion is not a matter of doctrines, objective descriptions of the nature of God and reality, or rational proofs of the object of our faith, but a matter of inward subjectivity stemming from the offense occasioned by the encounter of the intellect with the paradoxical, and leading to a decision to adopt a particular mode of life. The ugly ditch has been crossed, not by building a bridge across it, or by fording it, but by making a leap which is beyond the comprehension of reason. By transforming the ugly ditch from a rational to an existential matter, the problem has been set aside.

Rudolf Bultmann

Rudolf Bultmann's program of demythologization sets out from a different starting point and yet reaches a conclusion rather similar to that of Lessing and Kierkegaard. Bultmann concerned himself with critical study of the Gospels. Skeptical regarding the possibility of reconstructing with any finality the life and teachings of Jesus,[54] he concluded that much of what is

52. Ibid., p. 517.
53. Kierkegaard, *Fear and Trembling*, p. 59; *Postscript*, p. 306.
54. Rudolf Bultmann, "The Study of the Synoptic Gospels," in Rudolf Bultmann and Karl Kundsin, *Form Criticism* (New York: Harper, 1962), pp. 71–74.

attributed to Jesus in the Gospels cannot be taken as a literal report of what he said and did. There are two reasons for Bultmann's arriving at this conclusion. One is that his form-critical approach led him to the idea that the Gospels were written by persons of faith, not by impartial reporters. They had a significant stake in the life of Jesus. They wrote to persuade others of their point of view. Their purposes were so different from those of modern historians that it is not possible to construct a history from their writings.[55] Further, the Gospel materials incorporate the oral traditions passed down by the church, and reflect the experiences of the church and the influences upon it. To a large extent, what we find in the Gospels are the *Sitze im Leben* of the church and the Gospel writers rather than the ministry of Jesus. Both the church's tradition and the authors selected, modified, rearranged, and even created the words attributed to Jesus. Bultmann said in 1934, "For no single word of Jesus is it possible to produce positive evidence of its authenticity,"[56] although he did feel that we can identify the earliest strata and from them come up with at least a consistent representation of the message of Jesus.

If this suggests a somewhat agnostic view of the possibility of reconstructing Jesus' life and teachings, Bultmann in some cases expresses conviction that what is reported could not have happened. His thinking reflects a historical positivism which rules out much of the miraculous element in the Gospels. Many of the events reported did not happen, simply because such things cannot happen, being contrary to the laws of nature.[57] Thus on two grounds, the inadequacy of the testimony and the impossibility of the events reported, Bultmann asserts that faith cannot be based upon historical reconstruction of what happened in Jesus' life.

Bultmann solves the problem with a twofold classification of history, following the lead of Martin Kähler of the late nineteenth century.[58] There is *Historie*, which is factual history or

55. Ibid., p. 70.
56. Ibid., p. 54.
57. Rudolf Bultmann, "The New Testament and Mythology," in Rudolf Bultmann et al., *Kerygma and Myth: A Theological Debate*, ed. Hans Werner Bartsch (New York: Harper and Row, 1961), pp. 4–8.
58. For excellent discussions of Bultmann's view, especially in relationship to Kähler, see Norman Perrin, *The Promise of Bultmann* (Philadelphia: Lippincott, 1969), pp.

what actually occurred. This is subject to the usual type of research and proof with which historiography concerns itself.
Historie is the historical, or history external to the person.
There is also *Geschichte*, which is the impact made upon the
person by these historical events, whatever they were. This is
significant or internal history. *Geschichte* is the historic, often
expressed through the literary form of myth.[59] What seem to be
literal reports of events that took place in objective history are
in many cases merely myths giving expression to human self-
understanding.[60] We are not to interpret them literally, as do the
fundamentalists, or discard them, as do the liberals, but retain
them, take them seriously, and demythologize them; that is, we
are to discover and appropriate their existential meaning. We
must ask what the disciples were trying to do in their messages
and writings. They were people who had been profoundly influenced by Jesus, and who were attempting to give expression to
this influence in a way which would lead their hearers and
readers to belief in him.[61] Thus we should not take, for
example, their accounts of the resurrection of Jesus as reports
of something which actually occurred in his life, but as expressions, in mythological form, of the fact that they had been resurrected from defeat and pessimism to faith and hope.[62]

Here the solution to the problem of the ditch is to concede its
reality but deny its importance. In a very real sense, we cannot
get across the ditch. But it is equally true, according to Bultmann, that this difficulty does not matter. Truth is on our side
of the ditch. The message is not fundamentally about something
external which happened some nineteen centuries ago. It is
about each of us, our own experience of existence. Bultmann
has shifted the locus of the message from external history in

---

37–46; and *Rediscovering the Teaching of Jesus* (New York: Harper and Row, 1967), pp.
219–23.

59. Bultmann develops his view in numerous places, especially "The Primitive
Christian Kerygma and the Historical Jesus," in *The Historical Jesus and the Kerygmatic
Christ*, ed. Carl E. Braaten and Roy A. Harrisville (New York: Abingdon, 1964), pp.
15–42. See also *Jesus and the Word* (New York: Scribner, 1958); *Theology of the New
Testament*, 2 vols. (New York: Scribner, 1951, 1955); and "New Testament and
Mythology" and "Reply to the Theses of J. Schniewind," both in *Kerygma and Myth*, pp.
1–44, 102–23.

60. Bultmann, *Kerygma and Myth*, p. 10.

61. Ibid., pp. 22–24, 34–43.

62. Ibid., pp. 40–41.

Palestine so long ago to the internal history of each person in every moment of existence. Though their solutions are radically different, Bultmann is just as emphatic as Kierkegaard in asserting that subjective truth (*Geschichte*) is the truth.

Evaluation

We have looked at Lessing's ugly ditch between the particularities of history and faith, and have examined three attempts to deal with the problem. While it is to some extent, especially in the work of Bultmann, stated in terms of the insufficiency of historical material to establish faith, the problem for the most part is not quantitative but qualitative. Historical research and faith are of such different nature that no amount of the former, even if exhaustive of all of the data, can produce faith. The gap formed by the ditch is not quantitative, either in terms of the years that have elapsed since the biblical events or the degree of probability attainable in determining the past, but qualitative— the difference between objective assessment and subjective commitment.

We must now inquire into the adequacy of this analysis by noting both its strengths and its weaknesses. We begin with the positive aspects:

1. The views of Lessing, Kierkegaard, and Bultmann show congruence with the biblical text in their insistence that it is possible to know and accept certain historical facts without thereby developing faith. One excellent example is the scribes and Pharisees in Jesus' day, who, seeing his miracles, fully believed that they had happened and even that Jesus had performed them. They did not thereby come to believe, however, that Jesus was divine, nor even that the miracles were divinely accomplished. Their explanation, to the contrary, was that it was by Beelzebub, the power of the demons, that Jesus performed miracles. Historical assent does not equal biblical faith.

2. To go a step beyond: even acceptance of correct doctrine, or the orthodox interpretation of the events, does not equal biblical faith. Kierkegaard criticized the doctrinally orthodox but spiritually dead State Church of Denmark. This theme that mental assent is insufficient echoes through the New Testament from Jesus' "Why do you call me 'Lord, Lord,' and not do what I tell you?" (Luke 6:46), and "He who has my commandments and

keeps them, he it is who loves me" (John 14:21), to James's statement that faith without works is dead (James 2:17, 26). Faith is more than orthodox belief.

3. Lessing, Kierkegaard, and Bultmann have correctly observed and reminded us that the persons upon whose recollection and reporting we are dependent for historical knowledge of Jesus were not unconcerned, uninvolved spectators. They were fervently committed to the person, message, and cause of him whom they preached.

4. The theologians we have been discussing have also reminded us that history is not a perfect science. Even when done expertly, history suffers from the fact that its events are not susceptible to scientific controls. Nor are the events which it studies repeatable—they cannot be confirmed by being duplicated in a laboratory. Further, it is never possible to observe and record every factor in every situation. Value judgments have to be made regarding which items to include and which to omit, and these value judgments can be assessed only in retrospect, when it is too late to correct mistakes.

5. The theologians being considered have taken into account the Kantian dichotomy of noumena and phenomena, although these categories are anachronistic in reference to Lessing, who wrote before Kant's major works were published. It is apparent, however, that he was reacting to the same issues Kant expounded later. Kierkegaard, in particular, saw that the problem of history is only a special form of the larger problem posed by Kant, so that the eyewitness or the disciple with firsthand experience is not spared the difficulty faced by later generations. Kant gathered together several streams into one statement of the problem (or set of problems) which made nineteenth- and twentieth-century theology significantly different from all that had preceded. Any theology that hopes to exercise influence in the present time must come to grips in some way with the Kantian critique. This Lessing, Kierkegaard, and Bultmann attempted to do.

Several significant negative observations must also be made:

1. The theories we are considering do not fit the biblical picture of the relationship between faith and reason, including historical considerations. We could offer several examples. One is the response when the disciples of John the Baptist asked Jesus whether he was the one they had been looking for, or whether

they should be looking for someone else (Luke 7:18–23). Jesus called attention to what he was doing: healing the blind, the lame, lepers, and the deaf; raising the dead; and preaching the good news to the poor (v. 22). There certainly was no separation here of the facts of history from faith. A second example is Paul's emphasis on the reality of Jesus' resurrection (1 Cor. 15). The validity of the Christian experience and message rests upon the genuineness of Christ's resurrection (vv. 12–19). A third consideration is Luke's obvious concern to attain correct information for his writing (Luke 1:1–4; Acts 1:1–5). While our first example might be affected by critical study of the passage, the second and especially the third confirm that the split between faith and historical reason is not part of the biblical picture.

2. A more general objection relates to whether the views at issue are psychologically sound, that is, whether they correctly represent the way we function in life. Is it really the case that our commitment to a person and fervency for a cause are independent of, or even contrary to, the objective evidences? Not at all. Most persons tend to make their commitments on the basis of the most compelling considerations (although these may be pragmatic); even in desperate straits they choose the alternative that has the most evidence supporting it, even if that evidence is relatively small. Objective certainty has been shown to be a major factor behind success in virtually every human activity, largely because it produces greater effort and application. Uncertainty generally results in tentativeness and, consequently, ineffectiveness.

3. A related consideration is the possibility that our theologians, and especially Kierkegaard, may well have confused one type of passion or emotion, namely, insecurity and anxiety, with passion in general, or even with another specific passion, namely, fervor and commitment. But this is an illicit transition, for the differences are not inconsequential.

4. Bultmann in particular has correctly observed that the New Testament believers were committed followers of Jesus, but has then drawn the conclusion that this made them less accurate observers and reporters of what happened. The assumption is that their positive bias toward Jesus and his cause made them less careful in reporting what they observed and in preserving it; they even exaggerated somewhat in the interest of promoting

belief in him. Such arguments are usually made with the assistance of an analogy involving courtroom testimonies. But a different analogy, drawn from a classroom setting, may be closer to the situation of the Gospel writers, who were, after all, disciples of the Teacher. In a classroom, who is likelier to catch every word the teacher says and to record correct and complete notes, the casual listener or the student strongly committed to the teacher's view? We would prefer the notes of the latter in virtually every case. They most carefully retain the wisdom of the teacher, because the person writing them down believes they will have value beyond the final examination. As believers in the special value of all that Jesus said, the disciples surely made extra efforts to preserve his teachings accurately.

5. The view of historiography we have been examining is rather nineteenth-century in assuming that the universe is a closed continuum in which all that happens is under the control of laws of nature, and is to be understood as analogous to our present experience. This, however, has been challenged in recent times by a number of historians, biblical scholars, and theologians, perhaps the most significant for our purposes being Wolfhart Pannenberg.[63] Basic questions about metaphysics deserve to be asked.

6. A perennial problem plagues every view which emphasizes the subjective dimension of Christian experience: How is this subjectivity to be prevented from slipping into subjectivism? Does there need to be an object to which one relates? If so, why, and does it matter what that object is? Does it matter whether one is a Buddhist or a Christian? Kierkegaard's story of the two worshipers, if taken seriously, seems to say that it does not matter; and yet he places much emphasis upon the incarnation, the supreme paradox. And Bultmann has been criticized, both from the right and from the left, for retaining some mythological elements, an indication that he does not follow his emphasis on the subjective dimension to its natural conclusion.[64]

---

63. Wolfhart Pannenberg, "Response to the Discussion," in *New Frontiers in Theology: Discussions Among Continental and American Theologians*, vol. 3, *Theology as History*, ed. James M. Robinson and John B. Cobb, Jr. (New York: Harper and Row, 1967), pp. 264–66.

64. See, e.g., John Macquarrie, *The Scope of Demythologizing* (New York: Harper, 1960).

7. What is the measure of subjective truth? Lessing's criterion is fruitfulness, but how is that to be measured? For Kierkegaard, it seems that the ideal subjective state is that evoked by the supreme paradox, the absurdity that God should become a man. But is that really the supreme paradox? Would it not be more paradoxical and absurd for God to have become a worm?[65] And whose subjective truth is the greatest? Is there any way to communicate subjective truth (i.e., give it intersubjectivity), or would it then lose its subjective nature? Kierkegaard suggested using indirect discourse or the Socratic method. But if there is no objectivity, can there be any real dialogue regarding religion? Can such efforts ever be anything more than a shouting match of testimonials?

65. Edward J. Carnell, *A Philosophy of the Christian Religion* (Grand Rapids: Eerdmans, 1952), pp. 485–86.

The Sociological Problem.
(1) Liberation Christology

Having examined the historical challenge to traditional Christology (Is knowledge of Jesus possible and relevant?), we turn to the sociological problem posed by three contemporary theologies: liberation (ch. 6), black (ch. 7), and feminist (ch. 8). Certain segments of society object to Christology as usually done. Noting that discussions of Christology are dominated by white Western males who picture Jesus as being like themselves, various members of other classes object that this traditional Christ is not relevant to them. They cannot relate to him. Their objection may range from relatively mild to violent. In the former case, the contention is usually that certain aspects of the person or doctrine of Christ have been overlooked; in the latter case, the very idea of God incarnated in an individual who was a member of specific social classes is believed to result in the oppression of those people who happen to fall into other social classes.

Perhaps no school has generated more discussion and writing in the 1980s than has liberation theology. The number of books by liberation theologians and about liberation theology is growing at a rate which virtually precludes one's keeping pace. Beginning as a Latin American endeavor, it has generated worldwide interest.

As we commence our examination of liberation theology, a caveat offered by Roger Haight is well worth observing. In the phrase *liberation theology* the word *theology* has a connotation somewhat different from what it has in "scholastic theology," for example. Scholastic theology (and, to some extent, systematic theology in general) "points to a finished theological system in which the language is more or less stable and in which all of the major doctrines have been examined." Liberation theology, however, is more a movement than it is a theology. It is not yet a systematic theology. Being still an emergent movement, it has not attained the level of refinement and sophistication usually sought by theology.[1]

There is an additional problem, according to Haight. Liberation theology is not really a unified whole, a school of thought. There are many liberation theologies and liberation theologians, not all saying the same thing. While the most common variety is Latin American, liberation theology is also to be found in Africa, Asia (India and the Philippines), and the United States; indeed, European political theology is a not too distant cousin.[2] As we have observed elsewhere, diversity is a characteristic not only of liberation theology, but of theology in general in this latter part of the twentieth century.[3] It should serve to remind us to exercise a certain amount of restraint when we speak of the position of liberation theology on a particular subject.

1. Roger S. Haight, *An Alternative Vision: An Interpretation of Liberation Theology* (Mahwah, N.J.: Paulist, 1985), p. 15.
2. Ibid.
3. Millard J. Erickson, *Christian Theology* (Grand Rapids: Baker, 1986), pp. 61–62.

The Nature and Methodology
of Liberation Theology

A New Definition of Theology:
Critical Reflection on Praxis

As with any theology, we must begin with an examination of its basic nature and method. Yet to do that, it is first necessary to observe the context within which it arose. The theology of liberation has arisen out of an awareness of the poor and their predicament, and a desire to do something to alleviate their situation. Some liberation theologians see an antecedent in Bartolemé de Las Casas, a sixteenth-century priest who cast his sympathy with the Indians who were oppressed and exploited by the Spanish colonizers of the New World. It was not until the 1960s, however, that awareness of the predicament of the poor in Latin America led to a definite school of thought reflecting upon their situation. Deane Ferm sums up South American liberation theology: "Basically it is the effort to relate the teachings of the Christian faith to the lives of the poor and oppressed. Theology begins and ends with the downtrodden and their vision of life."[4] It is not to be thought of in the traditional sense of correct thinking about the nature of God, with the goal of convincing the unbeliever of God's reality. Rather, theology is reflection upon the condition of the oppressed poor, with the aim of understanding and explaining that condition. Explication is not the final step, however. Rather, the explication is for the ultimate purpose of alleviating the condition of the poor.

This conception of theology is fundamentally different from the traditional definition. Liberation theology is not so much concerned with correct thinking as it is with correct action. Not orthodoxy so much as orthopraxis must be pursued. Indeed, Gustavo Gutierrez sees praxis as the very matrix of theology.

Basically, theology is critical reflection. The nature of that reflection has taken several different forms throughout history. At times it was wisdom. This was the case, for example, in the early years of the church, when meditation was closely allied with the attainment of spiritual growth. In about the eleventh

---

4. Deane William Ferm, *Contemporary American Theologies* (New York: Seabury, 1981), p. 62.

century, theology became more clearly identified as a science or rational knowledge of the content or objects of the Christian faith. Gradually, however, especially after the thirteenth century, it was reduced to systematization and clear exposition. At least initially, this role of theology was linked with the goal of spiritual growth. From about the fourteenth century on, however, spirituality and knowledge came to be separated.[5]

Gutierrez considers both of these functions of theology legitimate in our time as well as in the past. He proposes to retain the reflective outlook and style, but not the specific end products it has brought forth in historical contexts different from one's own. The two functions must be salvaged from the division which has taken place. The resulting definition of theology has by now become classic in liberation-theology circles: critical reflection upon praxis.[6] Gutierrez contends that this is not as novel and revolutionary as some might think it to be. Its roots are to be found in the early centuries of the church's life, one excellent example being Augustine's *City of God*, which "is based on a true analysis of the signs of the times and the demands with which they challenge the Christian community."[7]

It was not easy to arrive at this conception of theology as concerned with praxis, or as Gutierrez puts it, to view praxis as the very matrix of theology. For many Latin Americans were indifferent to their predicament of poverty, because they had been exposed to the theological tenet that the hereafter is of primary importance. The present life is only a preliminary stage where one's eternal destiny is determined; the heavenly realm alone is real. This lower, profane world, including politics, is fleeting and transitory. It is unreal. Although all of this was professed, Gutierrez observes that the preoccupation with the spiritual realm did not prevent the upper classes from making sure that they had sufficient material security within this earthly realm. Any claimed goodwill of these people had little beneficial impact upon the conditions of the poor. Further, they reinterpreted Christian values in such a way as to reinforce the existing order and the domination of one social class by another.[8]

5. Gustavo Gutierrez, *A Theology of Liberation* (Maryknoll, N.Y.: Orbis, 1973), pp. 3–6.
6. Ibid., p. 6.
7. Ibid.
8. Gustavo Gutierrez, "Liberation Praxis and Christian Faith," in *Frontiers of Theology in Latin America*, ed. Rosino Gibellini (Maryknoll, N.Y.: Orbis, 1979), p. 3.

The Hermeneutical Circle

The most thorough treatment of the methodology of libera-tion theology by a member of the school is Juan Luis Segundo's *Liberation of Theology*. This book, which is based on a course Segundo taught as a visiting professor at Harvard Divinity School, analyzes the methodology of liberation theology as a radical and consistent application of the hermeneutical circle, "hermeneutical circle" being a term he uses to designate a bipolar hermeneutic as contrasted with a monopolar hermeneutic.

The aim of a monopolar hermeneutic is to get back into the setting in which a biblical passage was originally written and thus ascertain the author's intended meaning. This meaning is then applied to the contemporary situation. The assumption here is that the meaning was fixed in the past by the process of divine inspiration, which conferred a unique authority upon the original text. In a very real sense, the present situation is pas-sive. It merely supplies a receptacle, as it were, into which the original meaning is poured.

Bipolar hermeneutics, on the other hand, emphasizes the interpretive role of the present time and situation. In varying forms and to different degrees, the setting of the interpreter con-tributes to the understanding of the message and, occasionally, even to the message itself. Bipolar hermeneutics is inclined to say that the meaning which a passage had when first written was its meaning for that time and those people, but is not nec-essarily its meaning for today.

Segundo observes that in the monopolar approach, theology is attached to a particular book in the past and does not in any sense see itself as independent of that book and that past. It is bound to them. Furthermore, says Segundo, theology does not declare its independence from the sciences that help us to under-stand the past, including general history, the study of biblical lan-guages and ancient cultures, and form and redaction criticism. And yet he speaks of the autonomy of theology under a mono-polar hermeneutic, for it either implicitly or explicitly asserts its independence from the sciences which deal with the present. This is the result of the conviction that the past is the exclusive or at least primary key to the meaning of the text and thus to truth, and that the present has little if anything to contribute.[9]

---

9. Juan Luis Segundo, *The Liberation of Theology* (Maryknoll, N.Y.: Orbis, 1975), p. 7.

Segundo clearly opposes the monopolar approach: "Now a liberation theologian is one who starts from the opposite end. His suspicion is that anything and everything involving ideas, including theology, is intimately bound up with the existing social situation in at least an unconscious way."[10] While the traditional academic theologian gives virtually exclusive attention to the past, the liberation theologian "feels compelled at every step to combine the disciplines that open up the past with the disciplines that help to explain the present."[11] Accordingly, liberation theology has a greater interest in sociology than in history.

Segundo states that there are two preconditions for a hermeneutical circle in theology. There must first be questions arising out of our present situation which cause us to change our most basic conceptions, what German theologians (and those who follow them) would call our *Weltanschauung*, although he and other liberation theologians would not use a term so characteristic of traditional academic theology. He has in mind the "customary conceptions of life, death, knowledge, society, politics, and the world in general."[12] There must be such a change in, or at least a pervasive suspicion about, our ideas and judgments regarding these matters if we are to reach the truly theological level and theology is "to come back down to reality and ask itself new and decisive questions."[13]

The second precondition relates to what is done once our basic conceptions have changed. There must be a willingness to change our interpretation of Scripture as well. If this is not done, if we try to answer our new questions on the basis of the old understandings of Scripture, the hermeneutical circle is immediately terminated. Unless our interpretation of Scripture changes, the questions will go unanswered, or worse yet from Segundo's perspective, they will receive "old, conservative, unserviceable answers."[14] The assumption here is that the world has changed so significantly that the answers of the past cannot merely be adapted or reapplied to the new situation. In this regard, liberation theologians must be classified as transformers rather than translators of the Christian message; that is to

10. Ibid., pp. 7–8.
11. Ibid., p. 8.
12. Ibid.
13. Ibid., p. 9.
14. Ibid.

say, they are willing to alter, rather than merely restate or re-apply, the basic message from the past in order to make it deal directly with the present state of affairs.

Segundo says that unless these two preconditions are present, theology will always be a conservative way of thinking. This, to him and to the other liberation theologians, is unacceptable, for theology will then serve to justify perpetuation of the status quo, as it has so often in the past. And that status quo, regarding which the liberation theologians are so concerned, is the condition of poverty which afflicts so many people, together with the oppression and injustice accompanying it. His objection to conservative theology is not so much its content as its lack of *here-and-now* criteria for judging the present situation. It judges the present situation in terms of how well it accords with "guidelines and canons that are . . . ancient and outdated."[15]

Once the two preconditions have been met, a hermeneutical circle can be formed. In summing up, Segundo notes that there are actually four factors involved in the process:

1. A new way of experiencing reality, leading to "ideological suspicion."
2. The application of this suspicion to the whole ideological superstructure, and particularly to theology.
3. A new way of experiencing theological reality, leading to exegetical suspicion that the prevalent interpretation of the Bible does not take important pieces of data into account.
4. A new hermeneutic, a new way of interpreting the Bible that utilizes our new experiences.[16]

The Pragmatic Nature of Theology

Theology as understood by the liberation theologians is pragmatic. This means not merely that theology is concerned with, but that it actually is the practice of the Christian life, or praxis as they are fond of saying. Of course, if taken in isolation, Gutierrez's definition of theology as critical reflection upon praxis could be understood as categorizing theology as merely a

15. Ibid.
16. Ibid.

reflective matter. Segundo might also be understood as viewing theology as concerned merely with defining correct practice when he says, "The most progressive theology in Latin America is more interested in *being liberative* than in *talking about liberation*. In other words, liberation deals not so much with content as with the method used to theologize in the face of our real-life situation."[17] Gutierrez's emphasis upon the eschatological character of theology corrects this misconception, however. Theology does not merely begin with praxis and reflect upon the action of the Christian; it must also lead to praxis. It leads to the building up of the world. In this vein the encounter of theology with Marxism leads the church to ask "what its own reflection might mean for the transformation of the world."[18]

We might borrow here an analogy from ethical theory. In Bernard Mayo's "three-tier model," the ethical agents, those actually engaged in moral (as contrasted with amoral) behavior, are on the first level or ground floor. On the second floor are the moral critics or ethicists, who discuss the actions of the persons on the first tier. These critics are concerned with determining good and bad, right and wrong. On the third tier are the metaethicists, who discuss the language and the categories being employed by the ethical critics on the second tier, those who are making the judgments about what is right and what is wrong.[19] For a number of years, the dominant approach in Great Britain and English-speaking North America was metaethical. Gradually there has been a shift toward a more normative ethics. Some students have demanded that ethics professors practice their trade, that they be activists for causes considered morally significant. The analogy can be applied to other subjects as well, for example, aesthetics. Performing and creative artists would be on the first level. The critics would be on the second tier, making judgments as to what is good and what is bad art or literature, though they themselves may be incapable of artistic creativity. On the third level would be the aesthetician, discussing the meaning of concepts such as beauty.

Now by way of application of this analogy to the issue at hand, liberation theology most assuredly does not consider theol-

17. Ibid.
18. Gutierrez, *Theology of Liberation*, pp. 9–10.
19. Bernard Mayo, *Ethics and the Moral Life* (London: Macmillan, 1958), pp. 9–14.

ogy to be merely a third-tier activity. It is concerned with reflection upon correct praxis as well, which would be a second-level activity. But it also insists that theology does not simply define correct belief and activity, but actually engages in praxis. It is not merely correct thinking about reflection on praxis (the third level) and thinking about correct praxis (the second level). It is praxis. Theology is not only cognitive, it is functional as well.

The Epistemic Nature of Praxis

What we have just said about theology can, with a slight twist, also be said about praxis: praxis is not only functional, it is cognitive and epistemic as well. In fact, one cannot have knowledge of the reality upon which theology seeks to reflect (i.e., praxis) without engaging in praxis. This is most clearly spelled out by Leonardo and Clodovis Boff in their book *Introducing Liberation Theology*. Their chapter on "How Liberation Theology Is Done" spells out the methodology as clearly as does any writing on the subject. Because the Portuguese edition was published in 1986 and the English translation in 1987, we have here a fairly recent statement.

According to the Boffs, we must begin with a living commitment to the poor. Before one can do theology one must do liberation. One must participate in some way in the activity of liberation. "The essential point is this: links with specific practice are at the root of liberation theology."[20] To be a theologian involves more than using methods skillfully. It means being imbued with the theological spirit. This is what liberation theology is, not a new theological method, but a new spirit. This spirit can be acquired only through an "effective connection with liberating practice."[21]

This commitment to the poor will take place on one of three levels. The first is more or less restricted. It might entail sporadic visits to poor communities, occasional meetings, or somewhat more regular endeavors such as pastoral work on weekends. The second level alternates periods of scholarly work with periods of practical ministry, such as pastoral work in a local church. The third level is to live and work permanently among

20. Leonardo Boff and Clodovis Boff, *Introducing Liberation Theology* (Maryknoll, N.Y.: Orbis, 1987), p. 22.
21. Ibid., pp. 22–23.

the people. "Whichever level is chosen, one point is paramount: anyone who wants to elaborate relevant liberation theology must be prepared to go into the 'examination hall' of the poor. Only after sitting on the benches of the humble will he or she be entitled to enter a school of 'higher learning.'"[22]

After the initial commitment to the poor come three stages or mediations of theology, which correspond to the three traditional stages of pastoral work: seeing, judging, and acting. The first stage, socioanalytical mediation, asks why there is poverty. There are three ready-made explanations. The empirical explanation is that poverty is vice, resulting from individual laziness, ignorance, or wickedness. Here the solution is aid in any of several forms, all of which treat the poor as objects of pity. The second explanation is that poverty is economic or social backwardness. The solution is to reform the situation through economic or social development. The final explanation is the dialectical or historicostructural explanation: poverty as oppression. It shares with the second explanation the idea that poverty is a collective phenomenon, but adds the idea that the problem can be overcome only by replacing the present system with an alternative. The means of effecting this transformation is revolution.[23]

The second stage, hermeneutical mediation, attempts to find out what the Scriptures have to say about poverty. This is the stage in which *formal* theology occurs.[24] Bearing the whole weight of the problems, sorrows, and hopes of the poor, the liberation theologian seeks light and inspiration from the divine Word. This is a new way of reading the Bible: the hermeneutics of liberation.[25] The liberation theologian does not anticipate the response of the Scripture to the problem of poverty and oppression, but approaches the task with an openness to God's Word. "This means that the response of the word can always call the question itself into question. . . . There is no denying that the lead in this dialectic belongs to the sovereign word of God, which must retain primacy of value, though not necessarily of methodology."[26]

It would appear that, in one sense at least, liberation theolo-

22. Ibid., p. 24.
23. Ibid., pp. 24–27.
24. Ibid., p. 33.
25. Ibid.
26. Ibid.

gians cannot be accused of eisegesis. They are willing to let any given text speak for itself, correcting the reader if need be. There is, however, a deliberate departure from traditional hermeneutics in terms of selectivity. While traditional hermeneutics looks at the message of the Bible as a whole, liberation theologians look for those dimensions of Scripture which especially speak to the questions being brought. They readily acknowledge that their hermeneutic is not the only legitimate one. For the Third World, however, it is the obvious one, since it is vital to seek out those texts that speak to the situation of the poor.[27] The Boffs even give a list of "biblical books favored by liberation theology." They mention especially Exodus, the Prophets, the Gospels, the Acts of the Apostles, and Revelation, pointing out that certain passages of other books are also favored.[28]

The final stage in doing liberation theology is the practical mediation. Liberation theology begins with action, and it leads to action.[29] While the kind will depend upon the theological level of the individual, whether professional, pastoral, or lay, some practical action must be present if theology is to be complete.[30] Note that this stage is itself theology, not the application of theology, and that the action is heuristic or epistemic. More knowledge is gained from praxis than from theory, from experience than from thought. Therefore, wisdom and prudence are more useful at this stage than is analytical reasoning. And in this, ordinary persons are often way ahead of the learned.[31] It is clear that what we have here is an instrumentalist or pragmatist theory of learning. Actually engaging in a situation of need and working to change it are the means to discovery of truth.

The Secular Nature of Theology

We need to observe that liberation theology is in many ways a thoroughly secular theology. By this is meant that it takes very seriously the world in which the Christian and the church live. In a sense, all theologies except those which are thoroughly ascetic take the world seriously. Many of them, however, see the

27. Ibid., p. 32.
28. Ibid., pp. 34–35.
29. Ibid., p. 39.
30. Ibid., pp. 39–40.
31. Ibid., p. 41.

world simply as a fallen and sinful place, a place in need of redemption or salvation. It is not a source of truth. The truth or the defining authority is located in a sacral realm, whether transcendently in heaven with God or in some events and documents from the past. The present world is taken seriously, but not determinatively, in terms of the method and content of theology. In liberation theology, however, we have a reversal. Instead of being interpreted and judged by the Scriptures and the church, the here-and-now world gives us the perspective from which to interpret and judge the Scripture and the church. In a very real sense, the present world, or at least our experience of it, is normative for theology. Another way of putting this would be to say that present experience has priority over past authority.

This is an oversimplification, however. It would be more accurate to say that liberation theology, while conscious of history, does not absolutize past documents and events. There is an awareness that all events in history are influenced by the circumstances in which they occur, be they scientific, political, economic, philosophical, or whatever. Even our own situation, including what we believe and how we understand the past, is profoundly conditioned by these factors. This has two effects upon the hermeneutical process. The first is that it is not possible to take certain events or writings of the past and lift them out of this relativizing process, thus absolutizing them. The second is that the way we understand or interpret the past is not a purely objective matter. It is relativized by our being part of the process of history.

This brings us to the observation that liberation theologians have doubts about the possibility of objectivity. Not that they doubt that there is anything objective for us to know, but that they question our objectivity in knowing it. In other words, it is relativism, not subjectivism, that they are espousing. Haight sees this as a product of Vatican II, since most liberation theologians are Roman Catholic. Vatican II released Roman Catholic theology from "an authoritarian point of departure and from a kind of theologizing that consists in an objective analysis of purely objective data and meanings based on authority."[32]

32. Haight, *Alternative Vision*, p. 18.

The de-emphasis of past authority means that sociology plays a large part in the method of liberation theology. Since the first step in the hermeneutical process is exegesis of the present historical situation, appropriate tools must be used to interpret it. It is not sufficient simply to perceive or to feel the predicament of poverty. There must be an analysis, an understanding of the structures behind this condition.[33] The role once played by the original languages in determining the meaning of the biblical texts is now played by sociology to give us an understanding of the contemporary social situation. It supplies the categories and the methods appropriate to the object with which we are concerned.[34]

The Methodology of Liberation Christology: The Jesus of History as the Starting Point

Having surveyed the general background of liberation theology, we must now turn to its specific treatment of the person of Christ. A number of books written by liberation theologians have developed a Christology as such. One of the first was Leonardo Boff's *Jesus Christ Liberator*.[35] The main virtue of the book is its clear delineation of methodological issues. One of its drawbacks is that it does not have any distinctively Latin American character. A number of reviewers have suggested that it could just as well have been written by someone from any continent, perhaps even Europe, who happens to hold the same general principles.[36] José Miranda's *Being and the Messiah: The Message of St. John* is, as its subtitle suggests, a study in the Gospel of John more than a systematic treatise in Christology.[37] The single most thorough and systematic book-length treatise to date has been Jon

33. Leonardo Boff, "Salvation in Liberation: The Theological Meaning of Socio-historical Liberation," in Leonardo and Clodovis Boff, *Salvation and Liberation* (Maryknoll, N.Y.: Orbis, 1984), pp. 4–5.

34. Segundo, *Liberation of Theology*, ch. 2.

35. Leonardo Boff, *Jesus Christ Liberator: A Critical Christology for Our Time* (Maryknoll, N.Y.: Orbis, 1978).

36. Emilio A. Nunez, *Liberation Theology* (Chicago: Moody, 1985), p. 207. For a comment on such criticisms see Hugo Assmann, "The Power of Christ in History: Conflicting Christologies and Discernment," in *Frontiers of Theology in Latin America*, ed. Gibellini, p. 137.

37. José P. Miranda, *Being and the Messiah: The Message of St. John* (Maryknoll, N.Y.: Orbis, 1977).

Sobrino's *Christology at the Crossroads.*[38] The discussion in the next few pages will rely primarily upon Sobrino and Boff.

One immediately evident characteristic of liberation Christology is its strong emphasis upon the Jesus of history. Boff notes that the answer of imperturbable faith to the question of who Jesus is had traditionally been that he is "the Christ, the only begotten and eternal Son of God, sent as man to liberate us from our sins."[39] The eighteenth century, however, with the breakthrough of critical reason, raised questions about the teaching of the Scriptures. Various critical methodologies jeopardized the status of the Gospels as objective historical sources from which biographies could be constructed. The Gospels were now seen to be the witness of faith, a theological interpretation rather than a disinterested account of the events in the life of Jesus.[40] Accordingly, some abandoned the search for the historical Jesus and instead placed their trust in the Christ of faith, the figure found in the preaching of the early church. Rejecting such an alternative, Boff returns to the hermeneutic attempt to get at the historical Jesus found in the Gospels, but notes that this is a very difficult and complex problem.[41] He then proceeds to apply the best in critical methodology to the Gospels, including a particular hermeneutic that he developed elsewhere. He attempts to determine what type of person Jesus was, what he did, and what he taught.

Even more clearly spelled out is Sobrino's starting point. He states almost at the very outset, "My starting point is the historical Jesus. It is the person, teaching, attitudes, and deeds of Jesus of Nazareth insofar as they are accessible, in a more or less general way, to historical and exegetical investigation."[42] Before expanding on that theme, however, he surveys briefly various other possible starting points which he has rejected. He mentions them for two reasons: (1) they influence us unconsciously, and (2) by contrasting his viewpoint with others he will be able to make clear just what he means by the historical Jesus.

Sobrino is emphatic in rejecting the traditional Catholic

---

38. Jon Sobrino, *Christology at the Crossroads* (Maryknoll, N.Y.: Orbis, 1978).
39. Boff, *Jesus Christ Liberator*, p. 2.
40. Ibid., pp. 2–3.
41. Ibid., pp. 32–33.
42. Sobrino, *Christology*, p. 3.

approach of "Christology from above," which starts with the dogmatic formulation of the Council of Chalcedon that Christ has two natures, human and divine, in one person. Sobrino has some difficulties with terms such as "nature" and "person," but his real objection is on a more fundamental theological basis: "The Chalcedonian formula presupposes a Christology of 'descent.' It starts off with God and then goes on to affirm how the eternal Son became man. But Scripture tells us that the proper approach should be exactly the opposite. It starts off from the man Jesus and then goes on to reflect upon his divinity."[43]

Sobrino also objects to Chalcedonian Christology because it is heavily influenced by Greek philosophy. It presupposes what he terms an epiphanic conception of God, according to which the realm of the divine and eternal bursts into the here-and-now world. What he is protesting is Chalcedon's transcendent view of God as over against an immanent view of his working. "Thus God is presented in terms of epiphany rather than in the biblical terms of *being at work* in the world. The Chalcedonian formula does not make it clear that God is at work, through his own free choice, in the struggle for justice and the expectations of hope."[44] While it is valuable for its indication of the limits of any Christian understanding of Christ, the Chalcedonian formula is too abstract to be the starting point of Christology.[45] With this judgment Sobrino has already revealed one of the operative presuppositions underlying his Christology: the immanence of God, his working in the world for the cause of justice.

We may summarize briefly the other proposed starting points for Christology which Sobrino rejects as inadequate:

1. *A biblical focus on Christ.* This approach, which is not necessarily historical, investigates the various titles for Jesus or the major events of his life. Here, as with the Chalcedonian dogmatic approach, both the titles and the events reflect a later stage of theologizing about Jesus. Further, there are a variety of Christologies to be discovered, not just one. The problem is to find a means of unifying these several conceptions. Since it is the concrete

43. Ibid., p. 4.
44. Ibid., pp. 4–5.
45. Ibid., p. 5.

figure of Jesus, rather than some later theologizing, that unifies the several Christologies found in the New Testament, the Jesus of history, argues Sobrino, is the logical starting point.

2. *The experience of Christ as present in cultic worship.* There are problems with using Christ's presence in liturgy and sacrament as the starting point of Christology. How can we distinguish his genuine presence there from illusion? After all, he was taken away in the ascension, and cultic contact cannot replace acquaintance with the concrete Jesus. Further, such cultic contact can be and has been subject to various interpretations, some of which are directly contrary to the reality of Christ.

3. *The resurrection of Jesus.* Sobrino points out that adopting the resurrection as the starting point entails special hermeneutical problems which can be resolved only from the standpoint of the historical Jesus.

4. *The Christ of the kerygma.* Rudolf Bultmann has pointed out that beginning a Christology with the Christ of the kerygma does not give us sufficient concreteness regarding the nature of "authentic existence." It also rests upon an existential philosophy which is excessively individualistic.

5. *The teaching of Jesus.* Viewing Jesus as a model of bourgeois morality, nineteenth-century liberals made his teaching the starting point of Christology. This approach overlooked certain central features of his person, however, particularly his eschatological character, which cannot be made to support a bourgeois set of beliefs and practices.

6. *Soteriology.* Finally, Sobrino rejects the rather common approach of getting at Jesus' person through his works. While there is much about soteriology that is important for Christology, it cannot be made the primary basis for the latter. If our interest in salvation were the starting point, Christology would be just another variable in anthropology, promoting our own self-concerns. The fact is, however, that the cross of Jesus breaks quite sharply with the interests which have brought people to him.[46]

46. Ibid., pp. 5–8.

Upon completing this survey Sobrino clearly declares his approach and his reasons for adopting it:

> We choose to adopt the historical Jesus as our starting point here for several reasons. Our Christology will thereby avoid abstractionism, and the attendant danger of manipulating the Christ event. The history of the church shows, from its very beginning as we shall see, that any focusing on the Christ of faith will jeopardize the very essence of the Christian faith if it neglects the historical Jesus. Finally, we feel that the historical Jesus is the hermeneutic principle that enables us to draw closer to the totality of Christ both in terms of knowledge and in terms of real-life praxis. It is there that we will find the unity of Christology and soteriology.[47]

Sobrino advances two reasons why the historical Jesus is a particularly appropriate starting point for liberation Christology. The first is that there is a clear resemblance between the Latin American situation and that in which Jesus lived. While it is important to recognize that the passage of time has brought about extensive changes, and not to see parallels where none exist, the resemblance is nonetheless genuine.[48] The second is that the first Christian communities did not have any fabricated Christology. They had only the testimonies of those who had seen Jesus. From this they constructed their own Christologies, utilizing two poles: Jesus of Nazareth and their own concrete situation. What they did is what theologians today must do as well.[49] Sobrino therefore proposes to investigate the historical Jesus, looking for those traits of his which can be most definitely established. Sobrino wants to make sure that, rather than viewing Jesus directly from his own twentieth-century situation, he sees what really happened two thousand years ago. At the same time, he acknowledges that he will be looking at Jesus from a definite standpoint: "Certain traits of his will take on importance precisely because we will be viewing them from the concrete situation of Latin America."[50]

47. Ibid., p. 9.
48. Ibid., p. 12.
49. Ibid., p. 13.
50. Ibid., p. 14.

Substantive Christology

The Kingdom of God

When we look at this Jesus of history, we find that his teachings were strongly centered upon the theme of the kingdom of God. This echoes the familiar thesis of Adolf von Harnack that Jesus' message did not refer primarily to himself but to the kingdom. Sobrino says: "This is our first basic thesis about Jesus: He did not preach about himself or even simply about God, but rather about the kingdom of God. This thesis enables us to properly appreciate the activity of Jesus as liberation."[51] Similarly, Leonardo Boff says, "The theme of Christ's preaching was neither himself nor the church but the kingdom of God."[52]

As Sobrino expounds the kingdom of which Jesus spoke, it becomes apparent that it is not merely a cognitive concept, but pertains especially to praxis. For the kingdom is not and cannot be limited to verbal proclamation. The proclamation must be accompanied by action to bring about that reign; orthopraxis must take priority over orthodoxy.[53] Boff emphasizes that there are two dimensions to the kingdom: there must be personal conversion, and there must also be a structuring of the human world. "The kingdom of God means a total, global, structural revolution of the old order, brought about by God and only by God."[54]

It is important to note also that there is a definite connection or correlation between this concept of the kingdom of God and liberation. Jesus dealt primarily with people who had no real hope. Most of his acts of forgiveness of sin were extended to individuals who were not only alienated from God but also socially ostracized. So we find him addressing his message to prostitutes, drunkards, and tax collectors. Sobrino says, "The type of sinner pardoned by Jesus is the person who is living under oppression, the person who is despised by those who are just in society according to the law and who is condemned to a life with no future by the law itself."[55] This theme of liberation of the oppressed is the key to understanding the whole of Jesus'

51. Ibid., p. 60.
52. Boff, *Jesus Christ Liberator*, p. 63.
53. Sobrino, *Christology*, p. 45.
54. Boff, *Jesus Christ Liberator*, pp. 63–64.
55. Sobrino, *Christology*, p. 50.

activity. Boff expresses the same idea when he says that Jesus "breaks the social conventions of the period."[56]

The kingdom of God is not thought of as merely a liberation in the past, however. There is a definite eschatological character to it. And this eschatological character is not purely future, but has a distinct application to the present as well. Sobrino speaks of the historicotemporal character of the kingdom. There is a negative aspect in that no present reality exactly corresponds to the kingdom, but also a positive aspect in that a kind of existence that does correspond to the kingdom is presently being revealed. We are both to wait for the coming of the kingdom as something which must be divinely introduced, and to seek, as did Jesus, to live a personal and social life in accord with the kingdom.[57]

Following Jesus

Let us note further the nature of the relationship which liberation theology postulates between the Christian believer and Christ. This is seen in the concept of following Jesus, which Sobrino argues plays a heuristic or epistemic role: "The following of Jesus, understood as a praxis rather than as a theory, [is] the basic hermeneutic principle for comprehending who God is, and . . . who the Christ of faith is."[58] Boff's explication of the concept is even stronger: "This following of Christ must not be reduced to a moral category. It attaches us profoundly to the resurrected Christ and allows him to act in us. It inserts us into his new reality . . . . The resurrected Jesus is present in all sincere Christians, even those who are not in full communion with the Catholic church."[59] This personal internalization of Christ is what the expression *following Jesus* came to mean after his resurrection and ascension.

One issue that frequently is raised when the soteriological role of Christ is discussed is the question of whether salvation is primarily of individuals or society. This was a major topic of disagreement in the modernist-fundamentalist controversy of the early twentieth century. To put it into the categories being employed here, how is the kingdom of God to be realized? Is it

---

56. Boff, *Jesus Christ Liberator*, p. 73.
57. Sobrino, *Christology*, pp. 65–66.
58. Ibid., p. 60.
59. Boff, *Jesus Christ Liberator*, p. 221.

to be through individual conversions, or through structural changes within society? Sobrino's initial response is to say that it is both. He is not about to adopt the social-gospel approach that structural change can solve the problem of the need for personal change of the individual.[60] Conversely, the view that the conversion of individuals is the solution to the structural problems of society is oversimplified. Sobrino sees individual conversion and structural justice as inextricably bound together:

> If we take due note of Jesus' demand to bring about the kingdom, and even more of his own personal example, then we are forced to conclude that personal conversion must always be associated with social praxis. Speaking in terms of justice, we are forced to conclude that Jesus sees people becoming just only insofar as they do the work of justice. In systematic terms people become "children"of God by doing the work of "brotherhood." So even the aspect of personal justice is inseparably bound up with some form of social justice.[61]

Gutierrez describes the relationship between individual and social considerations in a somewhat less dialectical fashion:

> But in the liberation approach sin is not considered as an individual, private, or merely interior reality—asserted just enough to necessitate a "spiritual" redemption which does not challenge the order in which we live. Sin is regarded as a social, historical fact, the absence of brotherhood and love in relationships among men, the breach of friendship with God and with other men, and, therefore, an interior, personal fracture. When it is considered in this way, the collective dimensions of sin are rediscovered.[62]

Thus, when fully stated, the initial expression of the understanding of sin as collective is broadened and modified to include a personal dimension. Similarly, in discussing Paul's statement in Galatians 5:1 about Christ's setting us free for freedom, Gutierrez characterizes sin as a selfish turning in upon oneself, a breach of one's relationships with God and with one's neighbor. Behind unjust structures, then, there is a personal as well as collective will responsible. Thus, "a social transformation, no mat-

60. Sobrino, *Christology*, p. 121.
61. Ibid.
62. Gutierrez, *Theology of Liberation*, p. 175.

ter how radical it may be, does not automatically achieve the suppression of all evils."[63]

Traditional Issues of Christology

For the outsider looking at liberation theology from a more traditional perspective, there will always be a natural tendency to ask how this view relates to the usual questions of Christology. Especially prominent are the Chalcedonian issues of the deity, humanity, and incarnation of Jesus. Can such questions actually be put to a liberation Christology?

Leonardo Boff takes a rather conservative approach to such questions. He does have some reservations about the particular way in which Chalcedon dealt with some issues and failed to deal with others.[64] At no point, however, does he call into question the reality of the deity or the humanity of Christ, or of the union between the two, but he endeavors to clarify these issues. He notes that most studies of the incarnation begin with an abstract analysis of divinity and of humanity, and then attempt to explain how they could be united in one person. Boff makes an approach quite similar to that of Karl Barth, in effect saying that we know what true divinity is and even what true humanity is only by studying them in Jesus.

Boff states his commitment to the deity and humanity of Jesus in quite direct fashion:

> If we accept in faith that Jesus was a human being who could relate to God and be in God to the point of being his Son (i.e., the personal identity of Jesus with the eternal Son), and if we accept in faith that God can empty himself of his own self (cf. Phil. 2:7) in such a way that he fills the complete openness of Jesus to the point of becoming himself human, then we accept and profess what Christians profess and accept as the Incarnation; the unconfounded, immutable, indivisible, and inseparable unity of God and humanity in one and the same Jesus Christ; God remains God and the human being radically human. Jesus was the creature that God wanted and so created that he could exist totally in God, so created that the more he became united to God, the more he became himself, that is, human.[65]

63. Ibid., p. 35.
64. Boff, *Jesus Christ Liberator*, pp. 189–94.
65. Ibid., pp. 197–98.

While this might be construed as Adoptionism, that does not seem to be what Boff has in mind. It is deity and humanity in the full orthodox sense that he is advocating here, although, to be sure, he sees certain limitations of the Chalcedonian formula:

1. It does not take into account the evolution in Christ seen in the Gospels.
2. It does not perceive the transformation that occurred in the resurrection, from Logos-flesh to Logos-spirit.
3. It makes the kenosis difficult to understand.
4. It lacks a universal, cosmic perspective.
5. It runs the danger of placing God and humanity on the same level.[66]

Sobrino prefaces his discussion of christological dogma with an explanation of the nature of dogma. Its function is not to provide us with *additional* knowledge beyond what is already known. Its function is, rather, to give a better understanding, a logical explanation of what is in Scripture.[67] It attempts, for instance, to clear up the element of mystery in certain historical statements in Scripture which speak of God in his essence. Dogmatic statements express in theological language what is also expressed in the liturgical hymns of praise and thanksgiving as well as in the language of praxis in real life.[68]

When Sobrino applies his understanding of dogma to the subject of Christology, he deals first with the Chalcedonian formulation. And like Boff, he follows Barth's suggestion that we are not able to begin with some antecedent knowledge of the meaning of divine and human. We do not know what God is like, or what human nature is, apart from knowledge of divinity and humanity in Jesus Christ.[69]

Sobrino makes a strong distinction between what he calls Christologies of descent, which emphasize the concept of God's becoming man, and Christologies of ascent, which emphasize the idea of the man Jesus' becoming God. Sobrino's preference is clearly for the latter. While this may seem to argue for some

66. Ibid., p. xx.
67. Sobrino, *Christology*, p. 318.
68. Ibid., p. 325.
69. Ibid., pp. 329–30.

form of Adoptionism, he counters that both models necessarily involve some element of mystery. The difference between the two, and the advantage of the Christology of ascent, is that it enables one to maintain an emphasis upon the historical Jesus. While both approaches are dogmatic in nature, Sobrino notes that the Christology of descent really cannot stand without the Christology of ascent. Thus, he evidently regards the latter as logically prior.[70]

Sobrino is conscious of his vulnerability to the charge that he is less than fully orthodox on this point. He tries very hard to avoid such vulnerability. The issue, he says, is not one of ontology, but of epistemology:

> The believer who has gone through the whole process of reflection as just described can and should end up with the doxological statement that the Son became man. But one must have first observed how Jesus went through the process of becoming the Son for the process of reflection to be possible at all. An authentically orthodox Christology must end up with the ontological affirmation of the Incarnation. Epistemologically, however, it must work in the opposite direction. It must examine the divinization of Jesus.[71]

Yet having said this, Sobrino goes on to make statements which call into question the qualitative uniqueness (and hence the divinity) of Jesus:

> The Son does not simply reveal the potential filiation of all human beings with God. He also reveals the very process of filiation, the concrete way in which human beings can and do become children of God. If Jesus is the Son, then human beings can be children of God. But Jesus went on to reveal a very concrete sort of filiation, with a concrete path all its own; hence human beings have been shown the path to filiation.[72]

A Transforming Praxis

When all has been said and done, however, Sobrino is quite clear that these questions are not his primary emphasis. Of

---

70. Ibid., pp. 338–39.
71. Ibid., p. 339.
72. Ibid., p. 340.

greater moment is the fact that every Christology must respond to the challenge posed by the Enlightenment. That is a twofold challenge, to credibility and to relevance. Each Christology must determine whether it is chiefly concerned with justifying the truth of Christ before the bar of reason or before "the demands and yearnings for a transforming praxis."[73] In Sobrino's judgment, history indicates that European Christology has concerned itself primarily with the former. By contrast, Latin American Christology has been more concerned with the latter: "It seeks to show how the truth of Christ is capable of transforming a sinful world into the kingdom of God."[74]

Analytical Summary

We now need to make some general analytical observations about the Christology of Latin American liberation theology, although this will result in some oversimplification.

1. There is a strong emphasis here upon the historical Jesus. Instead of abstract dogmatic reflection an attempt is made to get back to the concrete actions and teachings of Jesus. The emphasis is strongly upon a "Christology from below."

2. This leads to a distinction between the message of Jesus and the message about Jesus, not greatly unlike the distinction made by Harnack. Jesus' message was primarily about the Father and even more so about the kingdom of God, not about himself.

3. Liberation theologians make rather free use of the methodology of form criticism, as evidenced in their distinction between the Jesus of history and the Christ of faith.

4. Liberation Christology has a strong pragmatist basis:

> a. There is a pragmatist or functionalist epistemology. Knowing is a result of doing. Thus, one comes to know Jesus only in the process of doing his will.
>
> b. The person of Christ is approached through the work of Christ. Thus, in a very real sense, Christology is secondary to, or dependent upon, soteriology, although Sobrino formally disavows this.

73. Ibid., p. 348.
74. Ibid., p. 349.

c. Verification is done pragmatically. The Chalcedonian Christology is, at least in part, verified by its results. As Sobrino says, "The Chalcedonian formula continues to be true insofar as there really continue to be followers of Jesus."[75]

d. Orthopraxis is at least as important as orthodoxy. Another way of putting this is that genuine discipleship is measured not by what one thinks about Christ, but by whether one follows and obeys his teaching.

5. There is a strong developmental dimension to the understanding of christological dogma. Dogma is not taken as having been given permanent form in the past, but as unfolding historically. There is almost a sense in which Jesus becomes something different with each new period of history.

6. There also is a secular note in liberation Christology. The world, and even the world outside the church, is taken very seriously as a source and norm of truth. The truth is not something introduced from without or from above, which Paul Tillich would have spoken of as a heteronomous use of reason.

7. Finally, we should note that there is a strongly existentialist flavor to liberation Christology. This is seen especially in the focus upon the human predicament. It is also seen in the relative impatience with intellectualism and with the formulation of abstract doctrines. In many ways, will seems to prevail over intellect and rationality, a tendency that carries over even into the formulation of christological beliefs.

Evaluation

It is now necessary for us to attempt some sort of evaluation of the theology which we have just discussed. We begin with the positive considerations:

1. Liberation Christology has emphasized the aspect of Jesus' ministry that related to basic human needs, material and physical. In the eagerness to understand his eschatological message, this dimension of concern with the here and now, which is found both in his teachings and in his actions, has often been muted.

75. Ibid., p. 342.

2. Liberation Christology has also offered an important corrective to overly spiritualized conceptions of faith and of the mission of the church. This follows from our first point. If Jesus was concerned only about the future and about heaven, then that should also be the concentration of the church. If, on the other hand, he taught about the needs of the poor and gave himself to healing the ill, then the church should engage in similar concerns.

3. Liberation Christology has corrected the overly intellectualized conception of Christ. Asking who and what he was, rather than what he did and what he was seeking to do and what he asks of us, tends to make him simply an object of speculative or rational thought. Like any other area of theology, however, Christology is not an end in itself. It is intimately involved with ethics and practical Christian conduct.

4. Liberation Christology has pointed out that conservative and evangelical Christologies have at times been selective in utilizing Scripture to construct their understanding of the person and teachings of Christ. There has been much more emphasis on Jesus' statement to Nicodemus, "You must be born anew," than on his statement to the rich young ruler, "Sell all that you have and distribute to the poor."

5. While there is a tendency to criticize liberation theology for having too closely identified with the values of a particular society or part of the world, its spokespersons have rightly pointed out that more-orthodox Christologies have been guilty of the same offense, having been utilized to justify imperialistic endeavors.

When we look more closely at liberation Christology, however, it becomes clear that there are some definite points of weakness as well:

1. One of the most readily apparent problems is the selective use of Scripture. It is indeed true that the historical Jesus attended to certain basic human needs and showed particular concern for the poor. Yet this was only a part of his message. He had a great deal to say about personal piety, about the spiritual aspect of life. He also spoke at length of heaven and of the life hereafter.

2. While liberation theologians in giving answer to the preceding criticism will respond that the real starting point for

Christology is the existential human predicament in which we find ourselves, and especially the situation of the poor and exploited, the fact is that Jesus did not tailor his message in quite this way to the specific situation of the persons whom he met. To be sure, he was concerned with the unique situation of the man born blind, the rich young ruler, and the Samaritan woman. He did not, however, become involved with the political predicament and problems of the Jews of his day. There was no attempt to address the political domination of the Jews by the Roman Empire. In fact, there was nothing approximating the prophet Amos's denunciation of exploitation of the poor. Rather, Jesus was more concerned with universal problems related to sin and righteousness. Furthermore, his message never took the form of an answer to the people's perception of their situation. Rather, his message first defined what their problem was and only then gave the answer.

3. Liberation theology displays a lack of clarity regarding the normative element or elements within any given formulation of Christian belief. On the one hand, one sometimes gets the impression that the message is to be recontextualized for each generation and situation. On the other hand, a normativeness seems to attach to the original message. A dilemma emerges. Either there must be some timeless criteria by which each contextualized formulation can be evaluated, or all of them are equally legitimate. In the latter case, it is hard to understand how a particular position can be advanced as though other persons were to believe it.

4. Another form of the same criticism is the question of whose experience is to be regarded as authoritative. Suppose that there is a conflict between two persons' experiences. Whose then shall prevail? For example, let us think of the situation in South Africa. It is not difficult to conclude that the Latin American liberationists consider the experience of the blacks to be the authoritative one. But what of the Afrikaners, whose experience is quite contrary? They are just as convinced as the blacks that right is on their side. How does one then mediate between these two? It is not completely clear how one is to arrive at the answer.

5. Liberation Christology is vague when some of the issues under discussion are pressed. For example, in what sense is the

deity or divinity of Jesus Christ qualitatively unique, as orthodox Christianity has always insisted? Or what can the
Christology of ascent respond to the charge of Adoptionism?
Sobrino's answer that there is some element of mystery on both
sides is scarcely an adequate response. Now of course a general
response that can be given to all such questions is that theology
is not exclusively or perhaps even primarily concerned with
issues of orthodoxy. It is focused most of all on orthopraxy. But
liberation theologians will also on occasion argue that one particular view is preferable to another, that the praxis depends to
some extent upon the doctrine. That being the case, it would be
helpful to make the doctrine being advocated fairly specific.

7

The Sociological Problem.
(2) Black Christology

The phenomenon known as black theology has many different facets. It has more varieties and nuances than do most other types of liberation theology. Further complications include the need to distinguish black theology from other movements within black American culture and even to distinguish between the earlier and later thought of some theologians, James Cone being a particular example. A number of considerations do, however, enable us to sort out the several black theologies.

To some extent, black theologies can be classified by the degree to which they have affinity for and are influenced by the black-power movement. A related means of classification is the

163

attitude toward nonblacks. Some black theologians see whites as the enemy and totally reject any possibility of common concern or endeavor. Others have as their goal some sort of reconciliation between blacks and whites. They see the need of love for the white. In a sense, the issue here is whether the model is Martin Luther King, Jr., Stokely Carmichael, or Malcolm X. A further consideration is the degree of concern for other oppressed groups, such as women and Latin Americans. To some extent, this last issue is the question of globalization: Is the concern exclusively for American blacks, or does it extend to blacks outside of North America, such as those in Africa?

The Starting Point of Black Theology: The Black Experience

Each of the black theologies emphasizes the uniqueness of the black experience. There is a sense in which one can understand what it means to be black only if one is black. Together with this go a whole black history and black culture, which must be taken into account.[1] One has no choice about being black in a white racist society. It is a given received with the color of one's skin. When the black moves from color blindness to color consciousness, blackness becomes a resource for developing a self-understanding and a philosophy of life. There is a choice of what sort of philosophy one will develop from the fact of blackness. One can become a thoroughgoing advocate of black power, or one may choose to utilize blackness to help interpret and enrich the Christian faith.[2]

There is a consciousness of a need for developing a uniquely black theology to correspond to and elaborate this black experience, for theology has been done in a fashion just as imperialistic as was the colonializing of an earlier generation. Theology has been done in a Western or Greek framework. All theologians really were cousins, whether English, German, or French. Virtually all of them were white and male, and there was a general presumption of the superiority of Western culture. The philosophical heritage brought to the theological endeavor was Greek,

---

1. Olin P. Moyd, *Redemption in Black Theology* (Valley Forge, Pa.: Judson, 1979), p. 24.
2. J. Deotis Roberts, *Liberation and Reconciliation: A Black Theology* (Philadelphia: Westminster, 1971), p. 14.

either Platonic or Aristotelian. If one was to do theology, it had to be within the ground rules established by this tradition. Although there were sharp disagreements among theologians, these were mainly family disputes. Whoever came to the task of theology from outside this context either had to assimilate the methodological framework and presuppositions of this tradition, and accommodate to it, or face expulsion for being somehow different or heretical.[3] This became another form of oppression or enslavement. The black, the Hispanic, and the woman had to think in white, Western, and male categories. While other forms of subjugation controlled what the oppressed did, how and where they lived, the rigid philosophical structure had the effect of controlling what and how they thought. Being the more subtle, this form of oppression was also in some ways the more dangerous.

White-male theology has been the means of justifying other less subtle forms of oppression. Cone identifies two: (1) regarding the theological task as unrelated to black suffering (the liberal Northern approach) and (2) defining Christianity as compatible with black suffering (the conservative Southern approach). The former is basically what we have just described. Its instruction to be dispassionate in doing theology ruled out the emotional experience of oppression, and was equivalent to urging blacks to be patient with their lot, since there would be deliverance in the heavenly life to come. While the latter more obviously justified the political conditions that created and permitted deprivation to persist, both approaches regarded theology as the servant of the state. This had death-dealing effects upon blacks (sometimes literally so); and as a result, many blacks found it increasingly difficult to remain part of organized Christian religion.[4]

All of this seemed satisfactory as long as the homogeneous situation prevailed. Little theology was being attempted by persons other than Western (and Northern) white males. This was because the Christian churches in other parts of the world had not sufficiently educated their members. In those countries there was little consciousness of the unique nature of Chris-

3. J. Deotis Roberts, *Black Theology in Dialogue* (Philadelphia: Westminster, 1987), pp. 11–12.

4. James H. Cone, *A Black Theology of Liberation*, 2d ed. (Maryknoll, N.Y.: Orbis, 1986), p. 4.

tianity, so only a very few members of those cultures broke into the relatively exclusive guild of theologians. All of this has changed, however, for we are now in a revolutionary situation.

An independence or autonomy not previously found in minority groups has developed. Contextualization plays a significant role here. Instead of being seen as *the* theology, the only way that theology can be done, Western white-male theology is seen as simply the expression of the way in which Western white males think theologically. There are equally valid alternative ways of doing theology, by blacks, for example, seeking to give expression to their unique experience of oppression. The major problem with adopting the theological reasoning of white males is that they have not experienced oppression. They are therefore unable to take into account a portion of the experience of blacks, and a very important portion at that.

Varieties of Black Theology

As we have already noted, there is a considerable spread of positions among black liberation theologians. Some, such as James Cone, are extreme to the point that whites are seen as an absolute enemy. This approach views the white oppressors as wholly in the wrong, and there is no sense of any sin of which the oppressed need to repent. Others, such as J. Deotis Roberts, are more inclined to be self-critical, and to seek some sort of accommodation or reconciliation with whites.

James Fowler has sought to delineate the various stages by which faith develops. In classifying the major black theologies of liberation in terms of these stages, he emphasizes that he is not saying that one group is necessarily more mature or more Christian than the other.[5] Fowler terms the more radical group ideological theologians. Their theology is especially characteristic of his fourth stage, which he terms individuative-reflective faith. At this stage individuals begin to be critically aware of their operative values and attitudes. The major goal here is the maintenance of firm, clear boundaries. Therefore issues are seen in dichotomies with sharp distinctions involving clear either/or

---

5. James W. Fowler, "Black Theologies of Liberation: A Structural-Developmental Analysis," in *The Challenge of Liberation Theology: A First-World Response*, ed. L. Dale Richesin and Brian Mahan (Maryknoll, N.Y.: Orbis, 1981), p. 82.

choices. Theology is frankly regarded as utilitarian. Fowler classifies James Cone, Albert Cleage, and their critic, William R. Jones, as ideological theologians.[6]

The other major group Fowler categorizes as theologians of balance, representing his fifth stage, conjunctive faith. Whereas individuative-reflective faith draws sharp distinctions between opposites, persons with conjunctive faith tend rather to take polar opposites into themselves; either/or has become both/and. Individuals with conjunctive faith affirm both particularity and universality for their theology. They speak from the standpoints of both subjectivity and objectivity. To such theologians, the line between oppressor and oppressed does not pass between but through peoples and groups. Black and white are not mutually exclusive experiences, in which the former possesses all of the truth and the latter none of it; but rather they are complementary experiences, both of which are necessary for the full attainment of truth. Fowler identifies as representatives of this group Joseph Washington (at least as represented in *Politics of God*), J. Deotis Roberts, Major J. Jones, and Warner Traynham.

With this background, we may now look more closely at the differing types of black theology and then their Christologies. Here we face a paradox of sorts. On the one hand, the ideological theologians appear somewhat more liberal, in the sense of restructuring the conventional nature of theology, whereas the more moderate theologians of balance seem relatively conservative or traditional. On the other hand, however, the ideological theologies seem more conservative in taking the Bible in a somewhat more literal fashion and more as a unique and singular source of authority. In the case of James Cone, this seems to reflect the neoorthodox view of biblical authority. Theologians of balance, on the other hand, tend to have a more nuanced view of the Bible, and to draw upon external sources, even including dialogue with representatives of religions other than Christianity.

Liberation from Oppression (James Cone)

James Cone's very definition of theology immediately sets him in the camp of ideological theology: "Christian theology is a theology of liberation. *It is a rational study of the being of God in*

6. Ibid., pp. 82–83.

the world in light of the existential situation of an oppressed com-
munity, relating the forces of liberation to the essence of the gospel,
which is Jesus Christ."[7] Here we have an instance of stipulative
definition. All understandings except Cone's are excluded. There
is just one reason for doing theology: to so explain God's activity
in the world "that the community of the oppressed will recognize that its inner thrust for liberation is not only *consistent with*
the gospel but is the gospel of Jesus Christ."[8] The sine qua non
of theology is identification with the humiliated and abused.
When theology ceases to arise out of the community of the
oppressed, it ceases to be theology.

Cone then demonstrates that his conception of theology arises
chiefly from the biblical tradition itself. While he does not make
the Bible the exclusive source of theology, it is the major source
apart from the experience of oppressed people. For Cone, the
account of the exodus is definitive of God's purpose. Indeed, we
might say that for liberation theologians of all varieties Exodus
1–3, rather than Genesis 1–3, is the most important portion of
the Bible for understanding human nature and the human
predicament. God elects the people of Israel in light of their condition and his purposes to free the oppressed from human
bondage.[9] This is not the only biblical source for the belief that
God's chief purpose is to deliver the oppressed. The prophetical
writings also offer much support for this view. And in the
Gospels Jesus declares that his great purpose is to proclaim
release to the captives (Luke 4:18–19).[10] Black liberation theology is legitimate theology because it arises from an oppressed
community and has as its purpose the inspiring of that community to risk all to obtain freedom. It is also Christian because it
focuses upon Christ. It has Jesus Christ as its point of departure.
Cone says, "Though black theology affirms the black condition
as the primary datum of reality to be reckoned with, this does
not mean that it denies the absolute revelation of God in Jesus
Christ. Rather it affirms it."[11]

To sum up Cone's view: A major dimension (if not the whole)

7. Cone, *Black Theology of Liberation*, p. 1.
8. Ibid.
9. Ibid., p. 2.
10. Ibid., p. 3.
11. Ibid., p. 5.

of God's activity in the world is the liberation of oppressed people. Theology arises out of the experience of such people, in this case, the black community. Theology's purpose is to inform and inspire them to arise and liberate themselves. For Cone, then, theology is strictly utilitarian. It has two sources: the experience of oppressed people and the biblical revelation. The former is primary in that it is the point where the theological quest originates; the latter serves to confirm this approach to theology.

Bridge Building (J. Deotis Roberts)

When we come to the theologians of balance, we find a somewhat more complex conception of the nature of theology and therefore also of its methodology. We take as our primary example J. Deotis Roberts. His most mature and recent statement is found in his book *Black Theology in Dialogue*, the title of which is indicative of its thesis. He maintains that black theology has now come of age. Instead of its more parochial orientation in earlier years, it now has entered into dialogue with theological developments around the world. It is to be seen as a bridge-building enterprise. In particular, he emphasizes that blacks in the United States are Afro-Americans. Though they live in the United States, they must recognize that their heritage is rooted in the Third World.[12]

Roberts believes that the new situation calls for some rather different dimensions to the theological task. He particularly emphasizes that theology must be done in context, and expresses admiration for what Paul Tillich has labeled an answering theology, which moves back and forth between the two poles of the authority of the Bible and the specific situation of a given society. Roberts similarly believes that a dialogical rather than monological approach is needed.

Tillich's position, while very helpful, was not fully adequate as he developed it. This is because no one philosophy can expect to frame satisfactorily all the questions which the present situation poses. For this reason, any single philosophical bias, such as process philosophy or Marxism, will be inadequate. Cognizant of this problem, Roberts makes ten suggestions as to how to carry out theological reflection in context:

12. Roberts, *Dialogue*, p. 7.

1. Theology should be more interdisciplinary. In the past, theology has been interdisciplinary in the internal sense: systematic theology has interacted with disciplines such as biblical study and the history of doctrine. Now, however, it is necessary for it also to be interdisciplinary in the external sense, conversing with disciplines such as the social and natural sciences. It is instructive to note Roberts's own enumeration of the sources of his book: "Various disciplines have been used as a resource for this theological expression. Insights from metaphysics, moral philosophy, the history of religions, the behaviorial sciences, and biblical interpretation have been used in the development of a contextual framework for the doing of theology."[13]
2. Theology needs to be ecumenical. While denominational affiliation will continue to be important, discussion must transcend the boundaries of denomination as well as of sex, race, and culture, for no single category has all of the truth.
3. There needs to be what Raimundo Panikkar has termed *ecumenical ecumenism*. By this is meant discussions not only with other denominations within the Christian religion, but also with other religions. Theologians should enter into conversations not only with biblical specialists, but also with historians of religions and cultural anthropologists.
4. There needs to be a centering upon the Bible in our theological reflection. This means genuine dialogue in which the Bible influences the construction of theology, and in which biblical scholars in turn heed the challenge of theological questions.
5. The historical perspective must be taken seriously. This means historical research into the Christian movement. In face of the pluralism in our world, such research will be a help in determining what is God's will for our own situation.
6. Theological reflection should be rooted in the life and worship of the church. Theology and ministry should influence one another.

13. Ibid.

7. Theology should be political, but not partisan. It should be sensitive to injustices and the violation of human rights. At the same time there needs to be a realization that the oppressed's being chosen by God is not a sign of being better than others, but is instead a call to servanthood. We need to realize that God also has a salvific concern for oppressors, and that the oppressed are sometimes themselves oppressors.

8. Theological reflection in context should be holistic. The whole person—body and soul; cognitive, volitional, and affective aspects—is the proper concern of theology.

9. Theology must be particular but not provincial. There must be concern for the entire human race. This means putting an end to all oppression sponsored in the name of God, to the religious intolerance which is a basic cause of so much suffering today.

10. Theology needs to be passionate without being irrational. There must be a careful thinking through of epistemology. Though we may adopt ways of thinking that are not normative in the West, we must continue to think clearly.[14]

The Sources of Black Theology

Sources and Norm (Cone)

We turn now to an analysis of the basic tools of black theology. Here we begin again with James Cone and the more radical black theologies. Cone distinguishes between the sources and the norm of black theology. The sources provide the relevant data for the theological task, the materials from which theology is to be done. The norm, on the other hand, provides the guide or rule for the use of the sources. It is "the criterion to which the sources must be subjected."[15] It frequently is the case that different theologies share the same sources. What causes them to differ from one another is that they have different norms, which entail different utilizations of the sources and different emphases.[16]

14. Ibid., pp. 15–19.
15. Cone, *Liberation*, p. 21.
16. Ibid.

Cone proposes that there are six different sources for black theology:

1. *Black experience.* It should be apparent from what has already been said that the black experience is a very prominent component in the formulation of the theology. It keeps the gospel from being turned into theological catchphrases. The black experience must be correctly conceived of, however. By "experience" Cone does not mean anything like what Friedrich Schleiermacher had in view when he defined religion as the feeling of absolute dependence. It is not mere introspection. Rather, it is the totality of black existence in a white world of oppression and exploitation; even quality education is defined by college administrators in the light of white values. The black experience means more than existence in a system of white racism, however. It means blacks' making decisions about themselves, affirming the goodness of blackness, accepting responsibility for themselves. This black experience seeks to relate the biblical revelation to the situation of blacks in America. It identifies God's presence with events that serve to liberate the black community.[17]
2. *Black history.* An important source of black theology is general knowledge of the way in which blacks have been treated from the time they were brought to this country as slaves. Black history is not, however, merely what whites did to blacks. It is also black persons saying no to white brutality. For black power is not new. While the task of showing how black history reveals God will not be easy, it is essential![18]
3. *Black culture.* Another source of theology is the self-expression of the black community in music, art, and literature—"the creative forms [that flow] as one reflects on history, endures pain, and experiences joy."[19] Simply defined as the way in which persons live and move in the world, culture is important because it molds thought forms. Cone says that black theology must take seriously the cultural expressions of its community, so that it can

17. Ibid., pp. 23–25.
18. Ibid., pp. 25–27.
19. Ibid., p. 27.

speak relevantly to the black condition. He recognizes here the potential criticism that he is identifying the word of human beings with the Word of God. But while this was a valid warning for Karl Barth to issue, given the situation to which he spoke, it does not apply to blacks in America today. They need a direct correlation between divine salvation and black culture, because Christ has too long been depicted as white.[20]

4. *Revelation.* Cone is aware that some will criticize him for placing revelation fourth rather than first, but says that there is no significance in the numerical order. Revelation, in his judgment, is not comprehensible apart from a prior understanding of its concrete manifestation in the black community. With Barth, he holds that revelation is an event, a happening in human history, God's self-manifestation through occurrences like the exodus. This revelation is not restricted to past events, but incorporates God's present redemptive activity in behalf of blacks. That is why black experience, history, and culture are listed among the sources of theology.[21]

5. *Scripture.* True to his Barthian heritage, Cone insists that the Bible is not revelation; only Jesus is! It is, however, an indispensable witness to God's revelation, so that it is a primary source for Christian thinking about God. It serves as a guide for checking our contemporary interpretation of God's revelation. It is, in fact, the source of our knowledge that God is a God of liberation.[22]

Cone has little time for the idea that the Bible is God's infallible witness. His objection is not primarily ideological but pragmatic, for preoccupation with this doctrine leads to concern about unimportant matters and a concomitant neglect of really significant issues: "It matters little to the oppressed who authored scripture; what is important is whether it can serve as a weapon against oppressors."[23] Cone believes that there is a close correlation between political and religious conservatism, so that

20. Ibid., p. 28.
21. Ibid., pp. 29–30.
22. Ibid., p. 31.
23. Ibid.

those whites who insist upon verbal infallibility often are
the most violent racists. The literalistic view of the Bible
has too frequently been used to instruct slaves to obey
their masters, and the oppressed to turn the other cheek.[24]

Scripture, then, does not give us answers or make
decisions for us. Cone quotes with approval John Macquarrie's statement that the Bible is a theological source
because of its power to "renew for us the disclosure of
the holy which was the content of the primordial revelation." The power of the Bible does not lie in its words per
se, but in its ability to point us beyond itself to the current activity of God in the world.[25]

6. *Tradition.* Cone's last source of theology is the church's
   reflection upon the nature of Christianity from its beginnings to the present. This is an important guide to interpretation of the Bible. Black theology is not uncritical of
   tradition, however, for it has at times been used to justify oppression. In fact, black theology holds that the
   spirit of the authentic gospel has sometimes been better
   expressed by heretics than by the orthodox tradition.[26]

What makes the difference among theologies, according to
Cone, is the norm which is adopted, that is, the hermeneutical
principle which specifies how the various sources are to be used.
It determines their relative importance and distinguishes relevant from irrelevant data. This norm must not be individualistic, but must spring from the black community as community.
With this in view, Cone states his norm:

The norm of black theology must take seriously two realities,
actually two aspects of a single reality: the liberation of blacks
and the revelation of Jesus Christ. With these two realities before
us, what is the norm of black theology? *The norm of all God-talk
which seeks to be black-talk is the manifestation of Jesus as the
black Christ who provides the necessary soul for black liberation.*
This is the hermeneutical principle for black theology which
guides its interpretation of the meaning of contemporary
Christianity.[27]

24. Ibid., p. 32.
25. Ibid.
26. Ibid., pp. 33–34.
27. Ibid., p. 38.

Reading the Bible from Black Religious Experience (Roberts)

Roberts, representing a less militant form of black theology, expounds a view of the Bible which has strong points of agreement with Cone, but also significant differences. Roberts looks to African roots. He notes that when black slaves were introduced to the Bible, they eagerly embraced it. This was because of their understanding of life as sacred, as whole, as community.[28] When they interpreted the Bible, however, they found a message quite different from what their white slavemasters found in it.

Roberts sets for himself the goal of rereading the Bible from the standpoint of black religious experience.[29] He cites with approval the observation of Thomas Hoyt that there is no pre-suppositionless exegesis. Thus, what blacks are doing is relating the Bible to their social context. Indeed, the black slaves were in a situation which rather closely resembled that of the Hebrews in Egypt, and thus, in a sense, were better able to understand the Bible than were whites.[30]

It is important that blacks develop a cadre of biblical scholars. Roberts is not confident about this happening, however. While some black biblical scholars are lured away from the field by more attractive offers, most of the others continue to repeat uncritically their Euro-American sources. It may be necessary for black theologians to do their own exegesis and develop their own hermeneutic. This is precisely what theological pacesetters such as Barth and Tillich had to do, and perhaps for similar reasons.[31]

Substantive Christology

We come now to the examination of the actual Christology resulting from the assumptions and methodology we have described. We shall see that there are basically two different conceptions of the person and work of Christ, just as there are two different views of the Bible and of the nature of theology. We will find, however, that the two views have more in common than they have of difference.

28. Roberts, *Dialogue*, p. 24.
29. Ibid., pp. 24–25.
30. Ibid., pp. 26, 36.
31. Ibid., pp. 36–37.

The Black Christ (Cone)

James Cone reflects his Barthian education with a statement that "Christology begins and ends with Jesus Christ. He is the point of departure for everything to be said about God, humankind, and the world."[32] Cone is definite that Jesus Christ is the essence of Christianity. It would be unthinkable to discuss Christianity without continuous and explicit reference to him.

Having said this, however, Cone cannot permit the discussion to remain on an abstract level. It is fine to speak of Jesus as the essence of the Christian gospel, but we must also ask what this means to oppressed blacks. Determining Christ's significance for blacks is not easy to do in a white society which uses Christianity as an instrument of oppression. The Christ which it presents is a white Christ, tailored to the values of white suburban Christians. Cone is quite clear about the need for a different Christ: "If Jesus Christ is to have any meaning for us, he must leave the security of the suburbs by joining blacks in their condition. What need have we for a white Jesus when we are not white but black? If Jesus Christ is white and not black, he is an oppressor, and we must kill him. The appearance of black theology means that the black community is now ready to do something about the white Jesus, so that he cannot get in the way of our revolution."[33]

Cone, together with other black theologians, places strong emphasis upon the historical Jesus. It is important to know who Jesus was, because otherwise we cannot know who he is. Without continuity between the Jesus of history and the kerygmatic Christ, the gospel becomes merely the subjective reflections of the early Christian community. If that is the case, there is no possibility of excluding whatever subjective interpretations of Jesus might be given. With disjunction between the Jesus of history and the Christ of faith, "we not only separate [Christianity] from history, but we also allow every community the possibility of interpreting the kerygma according to its own existential situation. Although the situation is important, it is not the gospel. The gospel speaks to the situation."[34]

32. Cone, *Liberation*, p. 110.
33. Ibid., p. 111.
34. Ibid., p. 113.

Theology must move back and forth between two poles, as Paul Tillich prescribed, the changeless gospel and the changing situation, and must be careful not to confuse the two. That was the mistake of Rudolf Bultmann, but not only of him. "Black theology also sees this as the chief error of white American religious thought, which allows the white condition to determine the meaning of Jesus. The historical Jesus must be taken seriously if we intend to avoid making Jesus into our own images."[35]

Cone believes that when we turn to the New Testament to find Jesus as he truly was, a clear picture emerges:

> Taking seriously the New Testament Jesus, black theology believes that the historical kernel is the manifestation of Jesus as the Oppressed One whose earthly existence was bound up with the oppressed of the land. This is not to deny that other emphases are present. Rather it is to say that whatever is said . . . must serve to illuminate Jesus' sole reason for existence: to bind the wounds of the afflicted and to liberate those who are in prison. To understand the historical Jesus without seeing his identification with the poor as decisive is to misunderstand him and thus distort his historical person.[36]

Cone recognizes the need of demonstrating this contention. He traces the major events of Jesus' life and finds in them evidences that Jesus' identification with the oppressed is the "distinctive historical kernel in the gospels." The birth of Jesus is one of the most obvious indications. Even though there is question about the historical accuracy of some features of this narrative, such as the stable and manger and Herod's killing of the babies, they possess mythic value, since they reflect the early Christian community's conception of Jesus. This, together with the economic, social, and political status of his family, makes it clear that he was one of the humiliated and the abused, even in his birth.[37]

The baptism and temptation of Jesus also reflect his identification with the poor and oppressed. John's baptism was for repentant sinners; Jesus' willingness to submit to it indicates that he identified with sinners. And Jesus' refusal of the tempter's offers, such as all the kingdoms of the earth, "may be interpreted

---

35. Ibid.
36. Ibid.
37. Ibid., pp. 114–15.

as his refusal to identify himself with any of the available modes of oppressive or self-glorifying power."[38]

Jesus' ministry also focused on the oppressed. His declaration that the kingdom of God was at hand meant that slavery was about to end; the divine reign would displace all human authorities.[39] Cone rejects any interpretation that views certain biblical accounts as justifying wealth, such as the apparent discipleship of Joseph of Arimathea, a rich man; Jesus' association with wealthy persons; and Zacchaeus's offer to give away half, not all, of his wealth. In assessing Jesus' ministry Cone concludes, "It seems clear that the overwhelming weight of biblical teaching, especially the prophetic tradition in which Jesus stood unambiguously, is upon God's unqualified identification with the poor precisely because they are poor. The kingdom of God is for the helpless, because they have no security in the world."[40]

Finally, the death and resurrection of Jesus confirm this contention. Black theology agrees with much contemporary theology in seeing the cross and the resurrection as extremely important for understanding Jesus. By taking upon himself the totality of human oppression and being resurrected, Jesus discloses "that God is not defeated by oppression but transforms it into the possibility of freedom."[41] This means that men and women who live in an oppressive society do not have to look on death as the ultimate. They no longer have to fear dying. They are free to resist an oppressor who threatens them with death.[42]

It is necessary, continues Cone, to take seriously the significance of the historical and resurrected Jesus for our times. Both emphases must be maintained if the gospel message is to be understood. Taking seriously the historical Jesus means that we are not free to make Jesus whatever we wish. He is who he was, which we can determine through historical-critical study of the New Testament accounts of his life. By focusing upon the contemporary significance of the resurrection, Cone, unlike Wolfhart Pannenberg, is saying that "the soteriological value of Jesus' person must finally determine our christology."[43] There is a heuris-

38. Ibid., p. 115.
39. Ibid., p. 116.
40. Ibid., p. 117.
41. Ibid., p. 118.
42. Ibid.
43. Ibid., p. 119.

tic dimension to this work of Christ in that the living reality of his resurrection as present victory over oppression gives us knowledge of him:

> We know who Jesus was and is when we encounter the brutality of oppression in his community as it seeks to be what it is, in accordance with his resurrection.
>
> The christological significance of Jesus is not an abstract question to be solved by intellectual debates among seminary professors. The meaning of Jesus is an existential question. We know who he is when our own lives are placed in a situation of oppression, and we thus have to make a decision for or against our condition. To say no to oppression and yes to liberation is to encounter the existential significance of the Resurrected One. He is the Liberator *par excellence* whose very presence makes persons sell all that they have and follow him.[44]

Cone's Christology is summed up in the idea of the black Christ. As the Oppressed One, Jesus is the black Christ. Because the black community is an oppressed community, he will be relevant to blacks only if he identifies with the oppressed, that is, only if he himself is black. He must be either for the poor or for the rich, for the strong or for the weak. Although some whites will contend that he is for both, this simply cannot be.[45] The meaning of Christ as incarnate is that in him God becomes oppressed (black) humanity and thus demonstrates that the achievement of full humanity is not inconsistent with divine being.[46]

Cone addresses the question of whether Jesus was literally black. That question, he says, is irrelevant. Blacks are not oppressed on the basis of their blackness. If they were, lighter blacks would be less oppressed than darker blacks. This is not the case. Yet it is true that Jesus was black, theologically and literally. He was, as Albert Cleage says, a black Jew. The point is that blackness is a symbol that translates the first-century situation of oppression into relevant concrete meaning for today.[47]

Cone also identifies the black revolution as the kingdom of God becoming real in America. The kingdom does not refer primarily

44. Ibid., pp. 119–20.
45. Ibid., pp. 120, 122.
46. Ibid., pp. 121–23.
47. Ibid., p. 123.

to material security. It has more to do with the quality of life
and the realization that persons are more important than property. Entering the kingdom is entering into the state of salvation,
the condition of blessedness. And this salvation is not merely a
spiritual blessedness. It is deliverance from oppression.[48]

The Black Messiah and Reconciliation (Roberts)

Roberts's most complete discussion of his Christology is found
in his 1971 work, *Liberation and Reconciliation*. He immediately
points out in his chapter on the black Messiah that he is using
the term in a symbolic rather than literal sense. He believes in
an actual historical Jesus, but not that he was literally black:
"My use of *symbol* and *myth* in the understanding of the black
Messiah does not mean that I am prepared to give up a historical-
literal understanding of the incarnate Lord."[49] Roberts holds
that Christology is the fortress of the Christian faith, and that
anyone who makes a radical restatement of the doctrine of the
person and work of Christ must have good reason for doing so.
His concern is "psychocultural." His approach is to restate the
teaching about the universal Christ in such a way as to particu-
larize God's redemptive act for a specific group of people in a
specific situation. Christ is the Redeemer of the entire human
race, but also of each and every specific people. Those people
must be enabled to identify with Christ. It is legitimate for the
Japanese to visualize Christ as Japanese, and also for black
people to conceive of him as black. This is especially important
for American blacks, since in America Christ has been accultur-
ated into the image of a middle-class white.[50]

Roberts draws upon the thought of a number of contemporary or at least modern theologians. Without identifying the
source, he appears to follow Paul Tillich's concept that a symbol
participates in and also points beyond that which it symbolizes:

> The black Christ participates in the black experience. In some
> sense Christ makes contact with what the black Christian is aware
> of in his unique history and personal experience. He *encounters*
> Christ in that experience and is *confronted* by the claims of Christ

48. Ibid., p. 126.
49. Roberts, *Liberation and Reconciliation*, p. 134.
50. Ibid., pp. 134–36.

also in his black experience. But at the same time, the *confrontation* of the black Christian with the black Messiah, who is also the *universal* Christ, points him beyond the mere symbolism that is rooted in his experience.[51]

Roberts also utilizes Søren Kierkegaard's idea of the contemporaneity of Christ. Through faith black Christians experiencing suffering, rejection, and loneliness in a white racist society find Christ to be their contemporary. The black Messiah is right here and now and understands the black persons' needs because he is one of them.[52] Roberts holds that the suffering which black persons experience enables them to understand Christ in his suffering and resurrection more fully than do white persons.[53]

Roberts holds, as does Cone, that Christ's work involves the liberation of blacks from their oppression. There is, however, one especially significant difference between the two Christologies. Roberts includes reconciliation in the work of Christ. This involves what he terms an awesome task for black theology:

> While we speak *externally* to liberation from white oppression, we must speak *internally* to the need for forgiveness from sin and exploitation within our own group life. Black theology must speak of liberation within from black men and liberation from without from white men. But, at the same time, it must speak of reconciliation that brings black men together and of reconciliation that brings black and white men together both in a multiracial fellowship of the body of Christ and within the world where a multiracial society must be built.[54]

Analytical Summary

It is now time to draw together some general characteristics of black theology. This will involve both summarization of what has already been noted and additional observations. There will also be some drawing of distinctions within the general movement of black theology.

1. As in all liberation theologies, there is a strong emphasis upon the situation of oppressed people. This is both a source

51. Ibid., pp. 139–40.
52. Ibid., pp. 140–42.
53. Ibid., pp. 143–49.
54. Ibid., pp. 151–52.

and also a norm for the construction of theology. Existential and pragmatic concerns play a large part in the formation of black theology.

2. There is a strong concern with the historical Jesus. Who Jesus is for oppressed people today is inseparably tied to who he was. Historical criticism, then, has a major role to play.

3. There is a basically orthodox view of the deity of Christ, the incarnation, and the resurrection. While this view is seldom presented in a direct and extensive way, it seems always to be assumed in what is said and done. There seems little reason to take at other than face value the statements black theologians make on these issues.[55]

4. There is a strongly soteriological cast to black Christology. Jesus is approached in terms of what he does or can do for the transformation of black consciousness. This salvation is thought of in primarily this-worldly or secular terms. The idea of salvation as "an objective act of Christ in which God 'washes' away our sins in order to prepare us for a new life in heaven" is rejected by Cone as white salvation, even though some blacks have been deluded into adopting the idea.[56]

5. There is variation in the degree of exclusiveness of black theologies. On the one hand, James Cone rejects any suggestion that blacks might need to repent of their sins, or that there might be validity to whites' conception of Jesus. He gives the impression that there is an inherent antithesis between blacks and whites, who must be regarded as the enemy. Roberts, on the other hand, as a theologian of balance, sees the need for blacks to repent of their sins, and urges that effort be made to bring about reconciliation not only among blacks, but between blacks and whites as well.

Evaluation

Having examined these views, what shall we now say by way of evaluation? We need first to note the strengths or positive values:

1. The black theologians have rightly reminded us of the universality of Christ. Although he had a definite identity as Jesus

55. E.g., Cone, *Liberation*, pp. 118, 121; Roberts, *Liberation and Reconciliation*, pp. 134, 137.
56. Cone, *Liberation*, p. 127.

of Nazareth, in one sense his specific time and place in history are incidental. We can make inferences about his skin, hair, and eye color with some probability, but the Gospel writers never make mention of these matters. They were incidental to faith. But for the necessary connection with the covenant nation of Israel, Jesus could just as well have been Chinese or African. It is appropriate for each national and ethnic group to think of him as one of them.

2. The black theologians have correctly reminded us of the danger of acculturating Jesus to our own group. White Christianity has often accommodated Jesus to its own social values.

3. Attention has been called to the fact that Christianity and even the doctrine of Christ have been used at times to exercise domination over blacks. Submission and nonviolence have been emphasized in such a way as to ignore some of the other values which Jesus taught.

4. Jesus' identification with the poor and deprived, and his abhorrence of the exploitation of others, have been appropriately pointed out.

5. The black theologians have meaningfully joined an emphasis upon the past historicity of Jesus with the existential contemporaneity of Christ. There is a powerful pastoral value in teaching this theme.

There are, however, certain problems as well, some of which apply more to one branch of black theology than to the other:

1. Particularly in the writings of James Cone, there is a tension between the black-power movement and the traditional black religious experience. As his brother Cecil has pointed out, there are contradictions between these two influences, and failure to choose one as paramount produces internal problems: "Because he does not consistently hold to [the traditional black religious] experience in the development of his theological analysis, the theology itself loses its integrity. Cone must make up his mind concerning his confessional commitment: Is it to the black religious experience or to the Black Power motif of liberation with a side-long glance at the black religious experience? As long as it is the latter, so long will he suffer an essential inconsistency."[57]

57. Cecil W. Cone, *The Identity Crisis in Black Theology* (Nashville: AMEC, 1975), p. 122; see also pp. 96–97, 103, 118.

2. There also is an inconsistency in James Cone's appeal to both the historical-critical method and the black religious experience. Cecil Cone points out that historical criticism is alien to black experience and also to black theology:

> It should be obvious to anyone acquainted with black religion that Cone is not dealing with questions his community is able to ask and still be true to itself. . . . The problem of the historical Jesus is not a problem in the black community, and cannot be in the nature of the case. Schweitzer, Bultmann, and their followers are dealing with problems that arose in a culture and from a perspective that is European, and not African or Afro-American. In effect, the quest for the Jesus of history represents an apologetic for Christianity on the part of those western theologians who are culturally committed to the historical critical method. Thus, one wonders why Cone feels the need to spend time on issues alien to his community, since he claims to be writing a Black Theology, a theology of and for black people. But the answer is clear enough when his work is examined. Cone has committed himself to an alien theological methodology, and that is why he asks questions his people are not asking. Even white theologians, the people from whom Cone derived his concern for history, are beginning to recognize the futility and the dangers of the historical method.[58]

3. There is a form of fideism or voluntarism in James Cone's thought that at times approaches anti-intellectualism.[59] Frequently taking a position diametically opposed to that of whites, he does not give any justification for doing so other than the black experience of oppression. His conclusions, he says, are somehow self-evident from the black experience. The problem is that the opposite conclusions may be equally self-evident from the white experience. (And we might note that in the past, when Cone was concerned only about blacks, Latin Americans and women were just as sure about their views.) Such confidence that one's own view is right and that of others wrong is sheer unsubstantiated opinion. In such a situation we will eventually either have to admit that the competing viewpoints may be equally valid, which leads to a type of relativism, or else, if we insist that our truth applies to everyone, find ourselves in a shouting match. But

58. Ibid., pp. 109–10.
59. J. Deotis Roberts, *Black Theology Today* (Lewiston, N.Y.: Edwin Mellen, 1983), p. 42.

then we are not engaged in an argument but in a quarrel; we are engaged not in persuasion so much as in propaganda. In actuality, Cone does not seem to care about persuading whites, only attacking them. If so, white readers may save themselves the time they would spend reading Cone's books.

4. There is a selectivity involved in the use of the Bible. Only those passages which substantiate the position being defended are given attention. This is seen most dramatically in James Cone's ignoring of passages that enjoin us to love our enemy and to turn the other cheek. These are rejected on the grounds that they have been used by whites to oppress blacks. But here we have a norm arrived at arbitrarily: any biblical evidence that would count against Cone's position is rejected, and then the remaining data are used to support the norm. Surely this is circular reasoning, and in a rather tight circle at that.

5. James Cone exhibits the very type of attitude that he criticizes in whites. Are his seeming hatred of and desire to destroy whites any better than the actions of the white oppressor? Roberts is sharply critical of Cone's statement that blacks should resort to any means necessary to win their freedom: "The statement appears to be an ethic of no ethic. This was a reckless and irresponsible statement in the midst of a tense and explosive situation. Young angry black militants were seeking guidance. They asked for bread; he cast them a stone. A moral paralysis remains inherent in Cone's theological method."[60]

6. There is a theodicy problem for black theology, especially as stated by James Cone. William Jones has pointed out that blacks have undergone an inordinate amount of suffering. If God is all-powerful, why has he not done something about it? This is particularly a problem for a theology which identifies blacks as God's specially favored people, as Cone does. The argument is much like Richard Rubenstein's discussion of Auschwitz.[61] The problem of evil is of course a severe problem for all strong theisms, but Cone has stated his view in such a fashion as to make it especially vulnerable.

7. Finally, we need to note one criticism directed especially at Roberts's view. In his most recent writing, he has argued for a

60. Ibid., p. 39.
61. William R. Jones, *Is God a White Racist? A Preamble to Black Theology* (Garden City, N.Y.: Anchor, 1973), pp. 185–202.

dialogical approach to doing theology. He contends that there should even be "ecumenical ecumenism," or dialogue with other religions besides Christianity. It is not completely clear, however, what the purpose of this dialogue is. What are the criteria for determining what the theologian should receive from such interchange? There needs to be clarification to determine just what is normative about the Christian tradition.

There has been, over the years, a softening and modifying of the rather extreme motifs of the earlier strident message, even to some extent by James Cone. There has been a much greater tendency towards self-criticism by those within the movement. What is needed is a fuller development of a black theology along the positive lines suggested by Cecil Cone, which would incorporate the most valid insights of black theology with a better balance of sources. Though he has not achieved this goal in any comprehensive sense, his words give hope for a black theology of the future:

> If Black Theology takes seriously the black religious experience, it will become not so much a theology of and for black people but of and for the glorification of God. . . .
>
> The divine and the divine alone occupies the position of ultimacy in black religion. Indeed, an encounter with the divine is what constitutes the core or essence of that religion. Such an encounter is known as the black religious experience. This experience is continued in black churches today and is to be found wherever two or three are gathered in the name of God for prayer, song, or sermon. Black Theology must come to terms not with black people as such, but with the God of black people, the One who encountered the people in their concrete and peculiar circumstances and gave them "the imagination to think of a good reason to keep on keepin' on," and the power "to make the best of a bad situation."[62]

---

62. Cone, *Identity Crisis*, p. 143.

The Sociological Problem.
(3) Feminist Christology

As a species of liberation theology in the broad sense, feminist theology shares many characteristics of Latin American theology and black theology. It has, however, some unique characteristics as well. In general, feminist theology is constructed upon the premise that male theologians have overlooked certain aspects of theological truth precisely because they are male. This premise may be stated mildly: for example, there are perspectives on the Bible which males fail to see because they have not

187

experienced them and therefore cannot understand them. Or the claim may be that feminine experience itself is the criterion and source of truth; therefore, truth is not available to anyone who is not female. In any event, there is the contention that the female voice has not been heard in the construction of theology, even though women have a unique contribution to make to theology. This contention may take the form of a simple statement that the theology traditionally done by males is one-sided and therefore in need of supplementation, or may go beyond to say that, at least for women, masculine-dominated theology is wrong.

To understand feminist Christology, it will be necessary to see the whole structure of feminist theology in general. For feminist Christology is an application of the general principles of feminist theology to the specific area of the doctrine of Christ. In so doing, we will note that feminist theology is not a monolithic whole. While there was a general consensus in the early stages of the movement, that has been largely displaced by a variety of perspectives. We now speak of radical feminist theology, represented most emphatically by Mary Daly; moderate feminist theology, of which Rosemary Radford Ruether is the most articulate spokesperson; and a number of positions in between.

Methodological Issues

The Starting Point of Theology: Human Experience

For virtually all feminist theologians, the starting point is human experience. The beginning is not with God and the transcendent. That would involve some external principle being applied to the issues of theology. As Pauline Turner and Bernard Cooke put it: "It has become a truism that humans—their being and consciousness and history—are the basic phenomena that must be studied as a springboard for some insight into the transcendent."[1] This is not to be understood as advocating an anthropomorphism in which human characteristics are projected onto a god. Rather, it is an epistemological statement that the only possible starting point for doing theology is "our shared experience of being persons in relation to one another."[2]

---

1. Pauline Turner and Bernard Cooke, "Feminist Thought and Systematic Theology," *Horizons* 11.1 (Spring 1984): 125–26.
2. Ibid., p. 126.

In a relatively conservative approach like that of Ruether, the hermeneutical method is a circle between our own experience and the Scripture. She says, "Clarified hermeneutics lies in being conscious of the questions one brings from one's own situation and the response that one reads from the scripture, either negatively or positively, about these concerns."[3] So theology consists in seeking for biblical truth, or at least a biblical understanding, that relates to the most pressing issues of our times. She is quite clear that the dialogue between Scripture and contemporary concerns must be a two-way relationship. While the Scripture questions us and challenges our values, we must also challenge it at points. And here we sometimes find it wanting. "We cannot abstain from coming, at times, to a provisional judgment that the world of the Hebrew Bible or New Testament falls short of values which we must affirm. There are indeed tribalistic triumphalism, sectarian rancour, justification of slavery and sexism in parts of scripture. The text then becomes a document of human collective moral failure, rather than a prescriptive norm."[4]

A somewhat mediating position is found in the thought and writings of Sheila Collins. She holds that the core of feminist theology, which stems from the experience of oppression, is the shared search for transcendence.[5]

From the left wing of feminist theology, Mary Daly says that her method "obviously is not that of a 'kerygmatic theology,' which supposes some unique and changeless revelation peculiar to Christianity or to any religion."[6] She carries this objection further, denying even the possibility of objective knowledge about reality. Accordingly, she does not attempt to correlate with the immediate experience of feminine consciousness certain "eternal truths," captured and expressed in a fixed and limited set of symbols.[7] Indeed, she is reluctant even to accept the designation of "theology" for her statements, since that would mean applying "doctrine" to women's liberation, which she most emphati-

---

3. Rosemary Radford Ruether, *To Change the World: Christology and Cultural Criticism* (New York: Crossroad, 1981), p. 3.

4. Ibid., pp. 4–5.

5. Sheila D. Collins, *A Different Heaven and Earth* (Valley Forge, Pa.: Judson, 1974), p. 45.

6. Mary Daly, *Beyond God the Father: Toward a Philosophy of Women's Liberation* (Boston: Beacon, 1973), p. 7.

7. Ibid.

cally does not intend to do. Her agenda is quite different: "Rather, my task is to study the potential of the women's revolution to transform human consciousness and its externalizations, that is, to generate human becoming. If one must use traditional labels, my work can at least as accurately be called philosophy."[8]

The Hermeneutical Task

Elisabeth Schüssler Fiorenza has stated that her hermeneutical aim is to give a biblical interpretation which will relate to the feminist position. Beyond that, however, her intention is to develop a feminist hermeneutic. In other words, not only the feminist teachings found in or justified by the Bible, but a feminist methodology of biblical study. Her feminist biblical interpretation incorporates not merely the results of her study of the Bible, but also the basic principles of the discipline:

> I have focused on problems concerned with the Bible and biblical interpretation in church and academy. In this way I seek to develop a feminist biblical hermeneutics, that is, a theory, method, or perspective for understanding and interpretation. In doing so I also seek to contribute to the feminist articulation of a new scholarly paradigm of biblical interpretation and theology. Feminist theology begins with the experiences of women, of women-church.[9]

Her starting point is identified even more clearly a few pages later: "The spiritual authority of women-church rests on the experience of God's sustaining grace and liberating presence in the midst of our struggles for justice, freedom, and wholeness of all. It rests not simply on the 'experience of women' but on the experience of women struggling for liberation from patriarchal oppression."[10]

The Bible has all too often been used to justify oppression of women, claims Fiorenza. This abuse is still found today in numerous pulpits and fundamentalist television programs. While the Bible does contain certain texts which *are* patriarchal in their original function and intent, they have been misapplied to attack

8. Ibid., p. 6.
9. Elisabeth Schüssler Fiorenza, *Bread Not Stone: The Challenge of Feminist Biblical Interpretation* (Boston: Beacon, 1984), p. x.
10. Ibid., p. xvi.

women's rights and freedoms.[11] In light of this situation, Fiorenza develops a hermeneutics that not only correlates the biblical text with the feminist ideal of liberation, but also critically evaluates that text from the perspective of the struggle. The criterion for such evaluation of the Bible is "not a revealed principle or a special canon of texts that can claim divine authority. Rather, it is the experience of women struggling for liberation and wholeness."[12]

It has been customary to identify revelation with the Bible in some sense. What Fiorenza claims instead is that the Bible is not a "normative immutable archetype," but an experiential authority, an enabling resource for the creation of "women-church." It can therefore become Holy Scripture. Revelation is not limited and restricted to certain texts from the past. It is "found among the discipleship community of equals in the present and in the past . . . in the experience of God's grace and presence among women struggling for liberation from patriarchal oppression and dehumanization."[13]

In somewhat more conservative settings where Christianity is considered a "revealed religion," there is the belief that some communication of the divine has been given to humans. Even here, however, it is emphasized that such communication can take place only in people's (i.e., some people's) experience.[14] Thus we are back at the familiar premise that human experience is the source and ground of theology.

Inclusive Experience and New Ground Rules

When we examine further this body of experience as the basis of theology, we note another distinctive of feminist theology. What is in view is not the experience that has usually been drawn upon in doing theology, that is, the experience of white Western males. Because they were limited to their maleness, they sensed only a portion of the reality that there is within human experience. Therefore, only one form of expression was recognized for theology.[15]

Women have indeed been victims of the rules' being set by

11. Ibid., p. xii.
12. Ibid., p. xvi.
13. Ibid., p. xvii.
14. Turner and Cooke, "Feminist Thought," p. 126.
15. Sheila D. Collins, "Feminist Theology at the Crossroads," *Christianity and Crisis* 41.20 (14 Dec. 1981): 344.

men, according to Daly. Theology has been thought of as a rather cerebral activity. But the emerging creativity of women is more than a cerebral process. Consequently, even the term *method* must be reinterpreted. It must be wrenched out of its usual semantic field. The power of defining has been stolen from women. They have not been free to define themselves, the world, or God. In the Genesis story, Adam names the animals independently of Eve. Thus it has been also with the theological activity of the past. Men defined, described, and named on the basis of their experience of the world; and their definitions were false, because their experience was partial.[16]

Theological scholarship up to this time has been almost exclusively androcentric. It has taken *man*, males, as the paradigm of what the human being is. This is part of the very mind-set of our culture, which promotes the idea that women's experiences and cultural contributions are not as valuable as those of men. Against this, feminist theology seeks to include all human experience. It identifies the male experience as *one* particular experience of reality.[17]

Sometimes the limitations of male theologians have been relatively benign. At other times, however, the very way in which men have perceived reality has been not only supportive of men's rights, but downright denigrating of women. Tertullian considered women the devil's gateway. Augustine held that women were not made in the image of God. Thomas Aquinas, following Aristotle, thought that women were misbegotten males. Martin Luther stated that whereas God made Adam the head of the entire creation, Eve spoiled it all. Nor is this bias restricted to the distant past. Karl Barth, perhaps the greatest theologian of the twentieth century, wrote that the woman is ontologically subordinate to the man, who is her head.[18]

What most feminists seek in doing theology is not to construct merely a female version of reality. That would be as partial and thus inadequate as the traditional androcentric theology. Rather, what is sought is a truly inclusive view. To accomplish this goal requires initially a challenging of the male assumptions

16. Daly, *Beyond God the Father*, p. 8.
17. Fiorenza, *Bread Not Stone*, p. 2.
18. Daly, *Beyond God the Father*, p. 3.

and androcentric language.[19] At that point feminists introduce a radical shift in the traditional theology. Their central commitment is not to the church, the tradition, or the Bible as a whole, which are male-dominated and supportive of androcentric language and ideas. Rather, their commitment is to "women in the churches . . . , a feminist transformation of Christian traditions . . . , the liberating Word of God finding expression in the biblical writings."[20]

The Practical Orientation of Theology

It should be apparent from what has been written here that feminist theology does not intend to be an objective description and definition of reality. Rather, it is by its very nature practical in orientation. In the more radical form of feminist theology, Daly disavows any attempt to be a disinterested observer seeking objective knowledge about reality. Male-oriented theology has often sought this goal, but has never achieved it. Male theologians could afford such a luxury, for the position of the male was already secure. Daly resents male authors who fail to see that the new feminist consciousness involves more than objective knowledge; it is an "emotional-intellectual-volitional rebirth."[21] In the more moderate form of feminist theology, Fiorenza sees the Bible as "a structuring prototype of women-church rather than as a timeless archetype, as an open-ended paradigm that sets experience in motion and structures transformations."[22] Like Latin American liberation theology, feminist theology puts a strong emphasis upon praxis. This is not to say, however, that theology consists in putting fixed principles into practice; rather, theology is reflection upon fundamental issues in the light of experience.

The Feminist Doctrine of God

Before moving on to examine the feminist treatment of Christology per se, it is important that we look closely at feminist discussions of God. For as we shall see, the basic ideas or tenets about God go a long way toward setting the framework which

19. Ibid., p. 2.
20. Ibid., p. 3.
21. Ibid., p. 200 n. 9.
22. Fiorenza, *Bread Not Stone*, pp. xvi–xvii.

serves to define the person and work of Christ. We will note the contrasting approaches of Mary Daly and Rosemary Ruether.

God as the Verb of Verbs (Mary Daly)

Mary Daly states in very clear and direct fashion the feminist objection to the traditional Christian conception of God: the Supreme Being is understood as male.

> The biblical and popular image of God as a great patriarch in heaven, rewarding and punishing according to his mysterious and seemingly arbitrary will, has dominated the imagination of millions over thousands of years. The symbol of the Father God, spawned in the human imagination and sustained as plausible by patriarchy, has in turn rendered service to this type of society by making its mechanisms for the oppression of women appear right and fitting. If God in "his" heaven is a father ruling "his" people, then it is in the "nature" of things and according to divine plan and the order of the universe that society be male-dominated.[23]

Daly argues that what must be done is to castrate God.[24] By this she means that there must be a complete transformation of the collective imagination. The idea of a Supreme Being distinct from the world but controlling it according to his plan and keeping human beings in a state of subjection is divine patriarchy. It is a projection of the patriarchal societal structures in place at the time that the Judeo-Christian tradition was being formulated. This view of God has been used oppressively against women in at least three ways: (1) the subordination of women has been proclaimed to be God's will; (2) the human relationship to God has customarily been symbolized in terms of one sex (we are "sons" of God), thus making women feel alienated and outsiders; and (3) detachment from the concrete realities of the human struggle against oppression has been encouraged. Even the theologies of hope, such as those of Jürgen Moltmann, Wolfhart Pannenberg, and Johannes Metz, are guilty of this third fault—their vision of eschatology lacks concrete grounding in the experiences of the oppressed, probably because they have not themselves experienced oppression. One would expect Paul Tillich's view of God as the ground of being to be more helpful

23. Daly, *Beyond God the Father*, p. 13.
24. Ibid., p. 19.

than the patriarchal image, but it does not address the specific fact of sexual oppression.[25]

Daly is quite explicit about her basis for evaluating and even constructing a doctrine of God. The experience of women—oppression and liberation—is the sole consideration:

> It is becoming clear that if God-language is even implicitly compatible with oppressiveness, failing to make clear the relation between intellection and liberation, then it will either have to be developed in such a way that it becomes explicitly relevant to the problem of sexism or else dismissed. In asserting this I am employing a pragmatic yardstick or verification process to God-language in a manner not totally dissimilar to that of William James. In my thinking, the specific criterion which implies a mandate to reject certain forms of God-talk is expressed in the question: Does this language hinder human becoming by reinforcing sex-role socialization? Expressed positively . . . the question is: Does it *encourage* human becoming toward psychological and social fulfillment, toward an androgynous mode of being, toward transcendence?[26]

What Daly proposes in constructing her view of God is something very much like Tillich's ground of being. While some would assume that the women's movement could simply dispense with God and any discussion of him, she points out that the continued effort by women toward self-transcendence requires continued awareness of ultimate transcendence. In what is almost a form of the cosmological argument for the existence of God (while everything in our experience is caused by something else, there must at some point be an uncaused cause or necessary being), she points out that we have no power over the ultimately real and that, on the other hand, such power as we do have derives from participation in ultimate reality.[27]

Reifying God as a definite object has generally been part of patriarchalism. Daly proposes that instead of viewing God as a static noun, we should instead think of God as a verb, which would be infinitely more personal.[28] This would also avoid the

25. Ibid., pp. 20–21.
26. Ibid., p. 21.
27. Ibid., pp. 28–29.
28. Ibid., p. 33.

dichotomization so characteristic of patriarchalism, for this Verb of Verbs is intransitive. There is no object to limit its dynamism. "That which it is over against is nonbeing."[29] This means that as women engage in the struggle of self-affirmation, the struggle against nonbeing, they are participating in the Verb, that is, God. Having experienced the shock of nonbeing and then the surge of self-affirmation, they are inclined to perceive transcendence as the Verb in which they now participate—live, move, and have their being.[30]

As women engage in their revolution, they are involved in the unfolding of God.[31] While not speculating regarding other movements, Daly sees a generalized presence of the Verb within the women's movement: "When women take positive steps to move out of patriarchal space and time, there is a surge of new life. I would analyze this as participation in God the Verb who cannot be broken down simply into past, present, and future time, since God is form-destroying, form-creating, transforming power that makes all things new."[32]

God as Not Exclusively Masculine (Rosemary Ruether)

In this area as in others, Rosemary Ruether takes a more moderating approach than does Daly. She seeks to show that the biblical picture of God does not unequivocally support the patriarchal approach. While acknowledging that there are factors in the Bible that seem to support patriarchy, she calls attention to four countering or balancing factors:

1. *The prophetic God.* The predominantly male images and roles of God would seem to support patriarchalism. By patriarchalism is meant not only the domination of women by men, but all similar domination such as of serfs by aristocrats and slaves by masters. Yahweh, however, has liberated people from bondage. The prophets in the Old Testament protest against ruling-class privilege and deprivation of the poor. While these pronouncements were not directed against gender discrimination, the New

29. Ibid., p. 34.
30. Ibid.
31. Ibid., p. 40.
32. Ibid., p. 43.

Testament extends this prophetic consciousness to all marginalized groups. "Consequently, it is possible to recognize as liberated by God social groups overlooked in Old Testament prophecy. Class, ethnicity, and gender are now specifically singled out as the divisions overcome by redemption in Christ. In the New Testament stories, gender is recognized as an additional oppression within oppressed classes and ethnic groups."[33]

2. *The liberating work of the sovereign God.* Though represented as King and Father, God has through Jesus freed us. Accordingly, Jesus calls his followers "friends" rather than slaves. And the church he establishes does not take the form of a patriarchal family, but of a community of brothers and sisters.[34]

3. *The proscription of idolatry.* Israel was prohibited from making any picture or graven image of God. Ruether argues that this must be extended to verbal images. Taking the word *Father* literally, to mean that God is male and not female, makes it idolatrous.[35]

4. *Equivalent images for God as male and female.* Ruether points out that the Bible contains feminine as well as masculine images for God. For example, God is referred to as "Abba," a loving, trustworthy parent who is maternal and nurturing. Moreover, in the parallel parables in the Synoptic Gospels God is represented by female as well as by male characters—the woman who searched for her lost coin and the shepherd who sought his one lost sheep.[36]

On the basis of such considerations, Ruether asserts that we must not think of God as exclusively masculine. Indeed, although Christianity has in her opinion relied excessively upon the model of God as parent, with its depreciating of autonomy and free will, and its perpetuation of spiritual infantilism, she declares that if this imagery is to be used, it is as appropriate to refer to God as Mother as it is to use the term *Father*.[37]

33. Ruether, *To Change the World*, p. 63.
34. Ibid., pp. 64–65.
35. Ibid., p. 66.
36. Ibid., pp. 67–68.
37. Ibid., p. 69.

Feminist Views of Christ

When we come to the understandings of the person of Christ, we find the same spread of positions that we noted earlier. Perhaps the most conservative position is that which seeks to demonstrate the continuity of Jesus' teachings and praxis with the concerns of women in general and feminists in particular. An example is Leonard Swidler's article entitled "Jesus Was a Feminist."[38] Closely allied is the work of Rosemary Radford Ruether, who examines three images of Jesus; she rejects the first two as destructive to the welfare of women, but draws upon the third, which she feels holds the key to reversing the present order.[39] Carter Heyward argues that the traditional doctrine of the unique and exclusive divinity of Jesus has contributed to the oppression of women, but that there are less exclusive understandings of his divinity which may actually have a positive effect.[40] The most liberal and radical view is again that of Mary Daly, who steadfastly maintains that the traditional understandings of Jesus, which she refers to as "Christolatry," help confirm sexual hierarchy and thus, being incompatible with the liberation of women, must be rejected. We will begin with this last and most liberal view.

The Rejection of "Christolatry" (Daly)

Daly presents three basic reasons for her rejection of the traditional ("mythological") view of Jesus as the unique and exclusive incarnation of God. The first objection stems from the way in which this idea has been used to reinforce male supremacy. Since the incarnation is held to have taken place in a single historical person at one point in time, and that one person was a male, it has frequently been assumed that God could not have become incarnate in the so-called inferior sex.[41] But given the fact that women are no longer consenting to the assumption of male supremacy, the view that God could not become incarnate in females is being undermined. Daly shows some surprise that

---

38. Leonard Swidler, "Jesus Was a Feminist," *Catholic World* 212, no. 1,270 (Jan. 1971): 177–83.

39. Ruether, *To Change the World*, pp. 45–56.

40. Carter Heyward, *Our Passion for Justice: Images of Power, Sexuality, and Liberation* (New York: Pilgrim, 1984).

41. Daly, *Beyond God the Father*, pp. 69–70.

the Death of God phenomenon did not also result in the death of Jesus. Even in a theology as radical as that of Thomas Altizer, there are still a fixation upon and a primacy of Jesus. This Christian idolatry of the person of Jesus is likely to be overcome only through the feminist revolution. Daly comments, "It will, I think, become increasingly evident that exclusively masculine symbols for the ideal of 'incarnation' or for the ideal of the human search for fulfillment will not do. As a uniquely masculine image and language for divinity loses credibility, so also the idea of a single divine incarnation in a human being of the male sex may give way in the religious consciousness to an increased awareness of the power of Being in all persons."[42]

Daly's second objection is to the idea of Jesus as a Savior. This idea of a unique male Savior, she says, is just "one more legitimation of male superiority."[43] The doctrine of original sin is very much tied up with this conception of Jesus as Savior. But the story of the fall of Adam and Eve into sin has been characterized as the hoax of the millennia, a description with which Daly agrees. The related dogma of the hypostatic union of the God-man (God-male) to save us from our sin is also beginning to appear to women to be some sort of cosmic joke. The real original sin is sexism! Liberating the human race from it is a role which no male figure can perform.[44]

Daly's third objection is to the model of Jesus as the supreme scapegoat. This model, projected upon women and others for them to imitate, has contributed to their victimization. Taking on the idealized qualities of a victim, such as sacrificial love, passive acceptance of suffering, humility, and meekness, has reinforced women's subservient role.[45]

Daly also takes issue with Swidler's argument that Jesus was a feminist. In the first place, it is irrelevant or superfluous. Many women will respond, "Fine. Wonderful. But even if Jesus wasn't a feminist, *I am*." The feminist convictions of modern women do not need any support from Jesus. Daly also finds two inherent difficulties with Swidler's approach. The first is his assumption that it is possible to extract "religious truths" from "time-

42. Ibid., p. 71.
43. Ibid.
44. Ibid., p. 72.
45. Ibid., pp. 75–77.

conditioned categories." The implication is that we can get back to some pristine purity of the original revelation. This backward-looking approach assumes some superiority of past history over present experience, as if the former were necessary to legitimate the latter.[46] The second difficulty is closely related to the first: the belief that adequate models can be found in the past. There are inherent problems in setting up Jesus (or anyone else) as a model to be followed. Slavish imitation of a master or father figure with an almost blind devotion is part of the patriarchal mind-set. The modern feminist consciousness is critical of all ready-made models. While there are strong and free women who have our admiration, their influence on us should not take the form of imitation, but of inspiration and courage to affirm our own unique being.[47]

Theologians have, for the most part, not faced the problem of the conflict between the christological tradition and the growing feminist consciousness. There are several reasons for this: First, the vast majority of theologians are men and consequently are not sensitized to the problem of patriarchal conditioning. Second, any challenge to orthodoxy often carries with it guilt feelings. Third, negative sanctions set up by seminaries and denominations can lead to professional disadvantages for those who do not "think right." Finally, there are positive rewards for those who remain, or at least appear to remain, "orthodox."[48]

Daly points out that certain methods are used to avoid insight into the conflict between feminism and Christianity, and especially those areas which she calls Christolatry:

1. *Universalization of the problem of the oppression of women.* It is argued that Jesus not only was not female, he also was not black or elderly. So, it would seem, women are not the only outsiders. This argument, however, fails to observe that the particularity of Jesus' maleness has had an effect which his Semitic identity and his youth have not. Non-Semites and persons over the age of thirty-three have not been excluded from the priesthood and the Protestant ministry as women have.[49]

46. Ibid., pp. 73–74.
47. Ibid., p. 74.
48. Ibid., p. 78.
49. Ibid., p. 79.

2. *Particularization.* Another argument is that the oppression is limited to particular times and places. Protestants find it in Catholicism; Catholics, in the medieval period. This fails, however, to recognize the universal presence of patriarchy.[50]

3. *Spiritualization.* Some theologians quote Galatians 3:28 or say that when women attain equality, it will not matter that God came as a man. But such approaches distract from the present oppression and the obligation to do something about it. They insist upon clinging to a myth which perpetuates the oppression.[51]

4. *Trivialization.* It is argued that women's rights and equality are not so important. Women should instead turn their minds to more serious questions.[52]

All of these evasions, when seen for what they are, lead us to one basic conclusion. The doctrine of the deity of Jesus Christ—that God became uniquely incarnate in one particular male human being—contributes to and has supported patriarchalism, which is diametrically opposed to the feminist consciousness. And since that consciousness is the unquestioned starting point, the a priori of persons like Daly, Christolatry, the myth of the unique deity of Jesus, the God-man, must be rejected. In practice, then, any value of Jesus' actions and teachings is disregarded.

Jesus as Valuable Though Not Uniquely Divine (Carter Heyward and Rita Brock)

A second type of feminist Christology also denies the idea of a qualitatively unique incarnation of the Divinity in Jesus, but does emphasize his value to us, including women. One who has especially represented this position is Carter Heyward, who has characterized herself as a white lesbian feminist. She questions the necessity of holding to the divinity of Jesus, who himself pointed us elsewhere: "We ask why the divinity of Jesus, when as it appears to some of us, Jesus himself tried his best to shift focus from himself to God and to get his friends

50. Ibid., pp. 79–80.
51. Ibid., p. 80.
52. Ibid., pp. 80–81.

to take themselves—their power—as seriously as he took his, by the grace of God."[53]

Heyward holds that the feminist theological agenda "pushes us into *discontinuity* with orthodox Christology, beyond even the most adventuresome theological spokespersons of the past and present Christian male collegium."[54] She raises two questions: Are belief in and commitment to Jesus Christ as God the Son, the only Lord and Savior, inherently damaging to most of humankind? If so, what constructive relation might Christians have to Jesus? In common with Daly, Heyward replies yes to the first question. In contrast to Daly, however, she seeks to articulate the value of Jesus for us.

Like Daly, Heyward considers belief in Jesus Christ as Lord and Savior of all a stumbling block for women, who are thereby required to look up constantly to a man for inspiration, leadership, role modeling, and redemption.[55] She broadens her perspective to include Jews and various other groups that have been victims of social injustice which has been supported and perpetuated by this Christolatry. This doctrine is not merely obsolete. It is inherently improper:

> I believe with increased faith that the doctrine of Jesus' divinity is false, as is any theological teaching that grows out of and feeds into unjust social relations. It is not that Jesus' "fully divine" nature was, once upon a time, an appropriate, truth-bearing doctrine that has simply passed its time, nor simply that we have moved beyond Greek metaphysics in our theoretical constructions of reality. It is rather that neither then nor now has this teaching represented justly the true and dynamic relation between God and *all* people, who may be Jews or Christians, Muslims or Hindus, Quakers or Unitarians, practitioners of Wicca or nonpractitioners of any religion.[56]

Rita Brock takes a rather similar stance in relation to traditional Christology. There is an inherent contradiction between traditional Christology and feminism. Feminism values images of wholeness in a pluralistic world. The traditional Christ, how-

---

53. Heyward, *Our Passion for Justice*, p. 13.
54. Ibid., p. 212.
55. Ibid., p. 214.
56. Ibid., p. 217.

ever, promotes dualism and hierarchy.[57] He divides the world into true believers and heretics. Claims about the exclusive divinity of one male, Jesus of Nazareth, have damaging effects upon women. A change will be necessary, if feminism is to be Christian. "If Christology is to be reclaimed in feminist visions, the image of an exclusive divine presence in a 'perfect' man called Jesus who came to be called the Christ is disallowed. The doctrine that only a perfect male form can incarnate God fully and be salvific makes our individual lives in female bodies a prison against God and denies our actual, sensual, changing selves as the locus of divine activity."[58]

It may seem to some that the nullifying of the unique, authoritative status of Jesus costs Christianity its objective and absolute basis. Brock counters that the demand for allegiance to one paradigmatic and central symbol does not fit the complexity of the pluralistic universe in which we live.

Where Heyward and Brock part company with Daly is in emphasizing the value which Jesus, properly understood, can have for the human race and particularly for feminists. Heyward does so by broadening and potentially universalizing the meaning of the term *Christ*. This suggests that Jesus' role was not a unique and exclusive one. He serves to reveal to us what "Christ" is, and to make it possible for us to experience the reality of Christ in our lives at the present time:

> This being so, might it be that Jesus, by his manner of life in relationship to God, redefined that hypothetical one [the Messiah or Christ] for whom Israel had been waiting? Might it be that, by his life with God, Jesus showed us that "Christ" is the love relation between the human and the divine, manifest in human life that is lived in right-relationship to God? Just as Jesus himself lived as this "Christ," and in so being, becomes our Christ, we ourselves can discern in him who we are at our best, in right-relation to God. Or, as we affirm at the end of the Eucharistic Prayer, "by Christ, in Christ, with Christ," we come to know ourselves as we are meant to be.[59]

57. Rita Nakashima Brock, "The Feminist Redemption of Christ," in *Christian Feminism: Visions of a New Humanity*, ed. Judith L. Weidman (San Francisco: Harper and Row, 1984), p. 57.

58. Ibid., p. 68.

59. Heyward, *Our Passion for Justice*, pp. 17–18.

Heyward thus moves the incarnation from a purely past event
to the present and even to the future. "Rather than proclaim the
mystery of our faith as we Episcopalians do in our new liturgy
by focusing our attention on a singular and unique Christ-
being—Jesus of Nazareth—when we say, 'Christ has died. Christ
is risen. Christ will come again,' we might well sing out in cele-
bration that 'Christ is dying. Christ is rising. Christ is here
again,' manifest in and through our own lives, in our own times,
revealing God's being to us, and us to ourselves."[60]

Brock also gives a special place to Jesus. Her aim is to
"redeem" Christ; she hopes to reclaim him. Dedivinizing Jesus,
however, is necessary in order to reclaim him as a remarkable
man for his time. There must be a separating of Jesus from the
patriarchal Christ that has been created by theologians, for that
Christ does not contribute to the feminist quest for wholeness.[61]
While patriarchal cultures are preoccupied with death and
destruction, the life-giving image of Jesus as a healer is more
helpful for today.[62] It is important to note, however, that the
emphasis in the biblical accounts is not always upon Jesus as
the source of healing. In some stories, the faith and vulnerability
of the sufferer usher in the miracle. Further, healing does not
belong exclusively to Jesus. There are others who heal (Mark
9:38–41; Luke 9:1–6; Acts 3:1–10).[63] The impact which the
theme of healing has on the cause of feminism is defined by
Brock in one particularly clear paragraph:

> The healing Christological images are not the center of our faith,
> but they can nourish faith when they feed our power, an erotic
> power that helps us save the images that restore us and lead us
> back to each other. We redeem Christ when we recognize the
> images of Jesus Christ that reflect our hunger for healing whole-
> ness and claim those images as resources for hope because we
> belong to a community of transformation and empowerment.
> Christ as healer need not be an image of exclusive power and
> authority. Christ is an image of shared power that works and is
> increased only in the sharing.[64]

60. Ibid., p. 18.
61. Brock, "The Feminist Redemption of Christ," p. 69.
62. Ibid., pp. 70–71.
63. Ibid., p. 73.
64. Ibid., p. 74.

Jesus as a Champion of Women (Ruether)

A third feminist approach to Christology is proposed by Rosemary Ruether. While recognizing the problems between traditional Christology and feminism, she is ready neither to abandon Jesus, as is Daly, nor to generalize the meaning of incarnation to include all persons, as do Heyward and Brock. Rather, she examines several interpretations of Jesus and then selects one which sees him as a champion of the cause of women.

Ruether is clear in her assessment of the danger in orthodox Christology: "Christology has been the doctrine of the Christian tradition that has been most frequently used against women."[65] In addition to the historical statements of Thomas Aquinas that the woman is a misbegotten male and therefore the incarnation had to take place in a male, and of Augustine that woman by herself does not represent the image of God, there are more recent problems. The ordination of women has been opposed in the Roman Catholic and Anglican churches on the grounds that Jesus chose only male disciples. Further, as the head and bridegroom of the church, Christ must necessarily be male. Therefore, those who represent him (priests and ministers) must also be male. Behind these arguments of the necessary maleness of Christ and his representatives lies the assumption of the maleness of God.[66]

Ruether notes that Mary Daly and other radical thinkers have concluded that the maleness of Christ is so fundamental to Christianity that women cannot see him as their Redeemer. Instead, they must seek a female Divinity and Savior. The question of whether a male Savior can save women is not merely a theoretical or speculative issue. It is a very practical issue, for many women have already left the church for alternative feminist communities.[67]

Ruether explores three alternative models of Christology to see whether they might prove more compatible with feminism. The first of these she terms the imperial Christ. This represents a fusion of two basic symbols from Hebrew messianism and Greek philosophy. The Messiah not only is the warrior-king overthrowing empires for the benefit of the oppressed nation Israel, but

65. Ruether, *To Change the World*, p. 45.
66. Ibid., p. 46.
67. Ibid., p. 47.

also governs the whole universe. While this model might have been used to level hierarchy, it came instead to justify hierarchy, patriarchy, slavery, and Greco-Roman imperialism. Just as the nous of God governs nature, so must Greeks, masters, and men govern barbarians, slaves, and women respectively.[68]

The second alternative model is the androgynous Christologies which have represented Christ as unifying male and female. This model has usually been found in groups regarded as marginal or heretical, with the exception of Protestant Pietism. It has led to a dilemma within the women's movement today, as to whether to get into the "man's world," which is evil but real, or to hold out for a better, utopian (i.e., nonexistent) world incorporating "feminine" principles that are still unempowered.[69]

The third alternative holds more promise. It is the prophetic iconoclastic Christ, a Christology being elaborated by liberation theologies. This Christology is based upon the Jesus of the Synoptic Gospels. The iconoclastic Jesus exposed the leaders of the religious establishment as hypocrites and blind leaders of the blind. The outcasts of society, the poor, publicans, prostitutes, and Samaritans, were given opportunity to hear the gospel. This was not merely an overturning of the hierarchy of that time, but the introduction of a new order where any type of hierarchy was out of place.[70]

The prophetic iconoclastic Christ went particularly to the downcast, the oppressed. They in turn had a special affinity for the gospel. Though women were the very bottom of the hierarchy, Christ dealt directly with the Samaritan woman and the Syrophoenician woman. Unlike the models of Christology which have been used to justify patriarchalism and oppression, the iconoclastic Christ is well able to be a Savior of women, because he is opposed to the system of domination and embodies the new humanity of service and mutual empowerment.[71]

Jesus as a Feminist (Leonard Swidler)

A final position argues that it is not necessary to reject the picture of Jesus in the Gospels. For they portray him as a friend,

68. Ibid., p. 48.
69. Ibid., p. 53.
70. Ibid.
71. Ibid.

not a foe, of women's efforts to obtain equal status and access to the opportunities within society. While a number of persons have developed this view, one of the more forceful presentations is that of Leonard Swidler.

Swidler's basic thesis is simply that Jesus was a feminist. By "Jesus" he means "the historical person who lived in Palestine two thousand years ago, whom Christians traditionally acknowledge as Lord and Savior, and whom they should 'imitate' as much as possible." By "feminist" he means a person who "is in favor of, and who promotes, the equality of women with men, a person who advocates and practices treating women primarily as human persons (as men are so treated) and willingly contravenes social customs in so acting."[72] Swidler corroborates his thesis with both negative and positive proofs. The negative proof consists in simply reading through the four Gospels and noting that nowhere did Jesus treat women as inferior beings. In fact, he took pains to make it clear that they were one of the classes to whom he had been particularly sent—the poor, the lame, sinners, and women.[73]

There are two special factors which, taken together, serve to highlight the negative proof that Jesus was a feminist: the status of women at the time and the nature of the Gospels. In first-century Palestine, women were clearly regarded as inferior. They were not allowed to study the Torah, they were not subject to the obligations regarding prayer that were incumbent on men, they could not speak in the synagogue, and even had to sit in a separate place. Within marriage they did not have the rights which men had. Their primary function was to bear and rear children. They were almost always under the tutelage of a man. The rabbinic writings characterized them as evil, undesirable, and unworthy.[74]

Swidler also points out that the Gospels are not like the straightforward factual accounts that we find in modern newspapers. Rather, they are in part reflections of the assumptions and attitudes of the four different communities of faith from which they come. Consequently, these accounts of the life of

72. Swidler, "Jesus Was a Feminist," p. 177.
73. Ibid.
74. Ibid., p. 178.

Jesus could be expected to detail certain concepts and customs which had no special religious significance. "The fact that the overwhelmingly negative attitude toward women in Palestine did not come through the primitive Christian communal lens by itself underscores the clearly great religious importance Jesus attached to his positive attitude—his feminist attitude—toward women: feminism, that is, personalism extended to women, is a constitutive part of the Gospel, the Good News, of Jesus."[75]

Proof of Jesus' affirmative attitude toward and treatment of women is abundant and various. His first appearance after his resurrection was to women, whom he then commissioned to bear witness to the Eleven. He did this despite his knowledge that the law disqualified women from bearing witness. The only time he violated the ceremonial laws about touching the dead was in the case of a woman, Jairus's daughter. He rejected the taboo against contact with women experiencing a blood disorder. He had women disciples who learned from him, followed him on his travels, and ministered to him. He spoke to the Samaritan woman, deliberately violating the common code regarding men's relationship to women. He rejected the stereotype of women as sex objects. (We might note here that although Swidler utilizes critical methodology, he cites the story of the woman taken in adultery [John 8:1–11] as if there were no textual problem involved.) Jesus also rejected the stereotype of women as being only housekeepers, encouraging them to study and discuss his teachings. His teaching on marriage and divorce presupposed that women had the same rights as men. He even used feminine imagery when referring to God, especially in the parable of the woman who found her lost coin (Luke 15:8–10). It was as if Jesus was deliberately pointing out to the scribes and Pharisees, who held a low view of women, that women no less than men reflect the image of God.[76]

From these types of considerations, both negative and positive, Swidler draws what he feels is a clear conclusion: "Jesus vigorously promoted the dignity and equality of women in the midst of a very male-dominated society: Jesus was a feminist,

75. Ibid., p. 179.
76. Ibid., pp. 179–83.

and a very radical one." He poses the question: "Can his followers attempt to be anything less—*De Imitatione Christi?*"[77]

General Doctrinal Characteristics of Feminist Christology

Having surveyed the stances of several feminist theologians on the person of Christ and related aspects of Christian doctrine, we need to draw our observations together.

1. We note first that feminist theology is anthropocentric and experience-based. It does not begin by applying some external authority, such as the Bible, to the issues of life. This is because feminist theology is not primarily concerned about a God who is superior and transcendent to humans. That is the approach of patriarchy, which begins with a God who rules the world as an omnipotent and sovereign Father. It is his will, then, that is important; it is he who must be satisfied. Like other liberation theologies, feminist theology begins instead with human experience, human concern, human need. By human experience we do not mean empirical data or sense perceptions, but rather an awareness of modern life in general, including the problems and needs which must be met. Collins observes:

> Feminist theology shares with all other forms of liberation theology a rootage in the historical experience of oppressed and obscured subcultures that have existed within and over against dominant white Western male culture. For this reason these theologies are critical theologies, beginning with a hermeneutics of suspicion. . . . The starting point for feminist theology, as for black theology and Chicano theology, is experience, as against a priori propositions or tradition.[78]

Dorothee Soelle says much the same thing in different language when she makes faith rather than theology one of the components in the process of liberation, because theology is "only the late-coming reflection upon what happens to people in the concrete praxis of their living."[79] Daly and Ruether similarly

---

77. Ibid., p. 183.
78. Collins, "Feminist Theology at the Crossroads," p. 343.
79. Dorothee Soelle, "Remembering Christ: Faith, Theology and Liberation," *Radical Religion* 3.2 (1977): 18.

begin with actual human experience. The one exception is
Swidler, who utilizes the Bible to establish that Jesus was a feminist. Two observations qualify even this exception, however. The
first is that Swidler is not necessarily a true feminist, and in the
judgment of many within the movement could not possibly be,
since he is male. The second observation is that his exposition
of Jesus' feminism was undoubtedly motivated by present-day
human concerns, a desire to show that the real Jesus did not, by
his words or actions, contradict the feminist consciousness.

2. A second significant generalization is that feminist theology
views the traditional or received understanding of God as contradictory to and destructive of the values of women, oppressed
women. The idea that God is male has led to the inference that
he does not identify with women, but somehow disapproves of
and discriminates against them. Accordingly, the feminist theologians are unanimous in insisting that God is not male, or at
least no more male than female. Many of them, to avoid the word
Father and the masculine pronoun in referring to God, use inclusive language (e.g., either "Divine Parent" or "Father-Mother God").

Beyond the masculinity connoted by "Father," there is also an
aversion to the concept of the lordship and domination of God.
This is seen as implying gradations of being within the creation
and within society. Given such gradations, it is natural to
exclude certain persons, such as women, from full participation
in the church and access to its privileges and responsibilities.[80]

3. Since the traditional doctrine of the person of Christ is
closely tied to this patriarchal view of God, feminist theologians
aver that it contributes to the oppression of women in a similar
fashion and to a similar degree. That he is the Second Person of
the Trinity means that all humans must submit themselves to
him. Women are particularly degraded by subjugation to this
divine representative of the male gender. The idea of incarnation
in one particular person is sexist as well, for it has led to the
view that God could not have become incarnate in a woman.
What emerges in feminist Christology is that Jesus is not
uniquely divine. It may well be that God was in some sense
incarnate within him, but not in a way qualitatively different

80. Geoffrey R. Lilburne, "Christology: In Dialogue with Feminism," *Horizons* 11.1
(Spring 1984): 11.

from his presence (at least potentially) within each of us. Even Swidler's argument does not require a unique divinity for Jesus.

4. Jesus' person is approached through his work. There is a strong soteriological orientation to feminist theology. Salvation liberates us from an existential condition of oppression. Whatever Jesus was and is must be understood in the light of the role he plays in the liberation of women. Just as the Bible is in a sense secondary to the experience of oppression, so the nature of Christ is understood in the light of the human predicament from which deliverance is needed. Here feminist Christology is following a tradition which reaches back in some respects to Philipp Melanchthon. It should of course be noted that traditional and feminist Christology conceive the condition that requires salvation quite differently. Consequently, the nature of salvation and the nature of the liberator are also quite different. Whereas traditional theologians argued that the human predicament required the Christ to be divine, the opposite conclusion is drawn by the feminists. Heyward says that any attempt to give Jesus a unique status above other humans must be resisted.[81]

5. There is a marked tendency in feminist Christology to concentrate upon the historical Jesus and, even more narrowly, upon what some have termed the Synoptic Jesus as contrasted with the doctrinal construction of the Christ. This is somewhat paradoxical in a sense, since the historical Jesus was clearly and unequivocally male, whereas the doctrinal Christ, as elaborated by theologians, can perhaps be thought of more androgynously. The problem is that the doctrinal Christ reflects patriarchalism, which is so destructive of feminine welfare. The historical Jesus is seen as a feminist, or at least one whose views are harmonious with the concerns of feminism. It remains to be seen whether the picture of the historical Jesus drawn by the feminists is selective or fully rounded.

6. While on the surface the feminist theologians appear to approach Christology from below, that analysis must be carefully weighed. There is, of course, a strong emphasis upon the human person of Jesus of Nazareth. Actually, however, the feminists come to the human Jesus with a presupposition regard-

81. Isabel Carter Heyward, *The Redemption of God: A Theology of Mutual Relation* (Ann Arbor, Mich.: University Microfilms, 1981), pp. 33–34.

ing the doctrinal or (perhaps a more accurate term) ideological Christ. He cannot be divine in such a way as would support patriarchy and hierarchy. Thus, on the ideological level there has been a decision about the type of person this historical figure must be. There is, then, a movement downward, so to speak, although the expression *Christology from above* seems somewhat inappropriate in the case of those theologians who regard Jesus as only human.

Evaluation

Having examined several varieties of feminist Christology, we need to offer some evaluation. We will first note the positive contributions:

1. Feminists have shown the conflict between the biblical understanding of God and various popular views. The conception that God favors males—that he created women inferior, and therefore they are to be subjugated to men—has gained considerable favor in some circles. One argument used by feminists to demonstrate that God is not a sexist is his treatment of women. His utilization of women to work in his kingdom and the praise of virtuous women in the Bible indicate that those who consider women to be incomplete males have drawn their ideas from sources other than the divine revelation.

2. The feminist theologians have clarified the gender issue with respect to God. It can be shown from Scripture that God is not merely male or female; nor is he both male and female; he is in a sense neither, for he transcends such distinctions. He can, however, appropriately be called Father, for he has revealed himself especially under that imagery. Such imagery does not preclude his possessing the qualities more commonly associated with mothers.

3. The feminist theologians have, further, clarified Jesus' attitudes toward women. Swidler and others have documented well, especially against the background of the culture of that day, that Jesus was rather radical in his teachings about and treatment of women. While Jesus did not face many of the issues of our time, it is significant that he went out of his way to show special attention to women.

4. The feminists have helped to clarify the biblical doctrines of humanity and of salvation. While they have neglected some

aspects of these doctrines, they have called our attention to other features that have been overlooked. Since both male and female are made in the image of God (Gen. 1:27), men's treatment of women as somehow less than fully human is a violation of the doctrine of humanity. And the inhumanity of men to women is certainly one manifestation of the fallenness of the world in which we live. Salvation, to be complete, must therefore include the elimination of sex discrimination, just as it precludes race discrimination.

5. The feminists have pointed out that an exclusively masculine doing of theology is insufficient. There are certain aspects of biblical truth to which men tend to be blind, simply because they have not experienced them. The vigorous statements that we have examined have served to call these neglected truths to the attention of men.

Having observed these points of strength in feminist Christology, we must, however, point out several areas in which there is considerable inadequacy:

1. The feminist Christologies may have purchased cogency at the expense of objectivity. To the extent that feminist theologians emphasize that men cannot understand because they cannot experience what oppressed women experience, they have argued against the intersubjectivity of their ideas. Daly in particular speaks of a virtually nonrational immediate experience somewhat reminiscent of the wild imagery and intuitive vision of Thomas Altizer. If this is presented as something that all, including men, should believe and act on, there must be some evidence that men can pick up for themselves. It must be possible to experience vicariously what these women are talking about. Their ideas need to be accessible to all.

2. Daly claims that any language that even implicitly can be made compatible with oppression must be rejected. This is a most unusual statement. It is not enough that our language not support oppression; it must be incompatible with it! It must be made "explicitly relevant" to the problem of sexism. That, however, is to make oppression (or, more correctly, liberation) the one issue that must be addressed in all theological discourse. All statements that fail to address that issue must be rejected. This is stipulative determination of the proper topics of theological discourse. Daly's thought, then, is a new type of authoritarianism

very similar in some ways to the authoritarianism that she believes has been at the core of oppressive patriarchalism.

3. In many forms of feminist Christology, there seems to be an excessive response. If a patient has a gangrenous toe, amputating at the hip will doubtless solve the problem. It is also possible to solve it, however, by amputating at the knee, the ankle, or preferably at the toe joint. Similarly, rejecting the deity of Christ will refute anyone who attempts to demonstrate the essential inferiority of women on the basis that Jesus was male. Argumentation like Swidler's, however, shows that it is possible to refute sexist views without going to this extreme.

4. There appears to be a narrow understanding and application of the doctrine of sin. It is true that men have sinned by acting selfishly. Are women, however, exempt from such behavior? In this regard the self-criticism of the movement by Collins and others is more realistic than is the highly ideological thinking of Daly, but even the more moderate feminists tend to overlook the possibility that women may have their own shortcomings.

5. As a result of the narrow understanding of sin, there is also an inadequate understanding of salvation. Is it as simple as the liberation of women and other oppressed groups? What of the oppressors? Does salvation for them consist in the release of their victims from oppression? And what of the character of the oppressed? If, as some feminists contend, the oppressed are not guilty of sin, does the concept of salvation have no further meaning for them once liberation from social, political, and economic oppression is achieved? And what, then, are we to make of Jesus' words about loving one's enemy? Do they not argue that the oppressed should show some concern for the oppressor? The feminist use of Jesus' actions and teachings about sin and salvation appears to be somewhat limited.

We must take seriously the types of considerations to which the feminist theologians have pointed us. But we must also realize that these considerations in no way require us to give up such basic conceptions as the qualitatively unique deity of Jesus Christ.

The Metaphysical Problem.
(1) Functional Christology

Incarnational Christology has a very large stake in metaphysics. For to speak of someone's being both God and a human being is to speak in terms which require some understanding about the ultimate nature of things. The Chalcedonian formulation expressed the doctrine of incarnation in Greek metaphysical categories, "person" and "nature." Is it possible to express this doctrine in ways more suited to today? In the next two chapters we will examine two objections to the Chalcedonian formula, and implicitly to any traditional understanding of metaphysics. Functional Christology objects that such an approach is inconsistent with the biblical revelation. Process Christology argues that the usual conception of incarnation is incompatible with contemporary ways of understanding reality.

It may seem to some that to examine again the nature and value of functional Christology is unnecessary, this view having been sufficiently scrutinized and disposed of. One who has underscored the general consensus that a pure functionalism is untenable is Gerald O'Collins: "There can be no satisfactory account of what Jesus does if we dismiss as unimportant the question who he is. Every soteriological statement has its Christological implications. This point has won wide acceptance and in any case seems obvious enough. To go on insisting that one cannot pursue a functional approach without somehow taking an ontological stand looks like exhuming and beating a thoroughly dead horse."[1]

So then, we will not engage in a thoroughgoing equine thanatology at this point. Nevertheless, we must note that although the more extreme forms of functional Christology are less common today than they were in the 1950s and 1960s, numerous varieties of functionalism are still alive. Many of the contributors to *The Myth of God Incarnate* appear to espouse basically a functional Christology.[2] And the issues involved are still very much with us. Klaas Runia even suggests that "nearly all alternative [i.e., nonorthodox] Christologies opt for a functional Christology over against an ontological Christology."[3]

We may define functional Christology as an approach to the person of Christ which emphasizes what he did rather than what he is. Based upon a belief that this was the biblical writers' concern, functional Christology often includes the idea that it is either unnecessary or improper to go beyond them. William Schutter observes that there is a nearly limitless variety of functional Christologies. One common belief is found in all of them, however: "Jesus is not God; he is God's tool. Jesus is God's agent and representative. The more traditionally oriented the functional Christology happens to be the more stress there is upon Jesus' uniqueness as agent."[4]

There have been precursors of this twentieth-century view.

1. Gerald O'Collins, *What Are They Saying About Jesus?* (New York: Paulist, 1977), pp. 27–28.

2. E.g., Frances Young, "A Cloud of Witnesses," in *The Myth of God Incarnate*, ed. John Hick (Philadelphia: Westminster, 1977), pp. 18–21.

3. Klaas Runia, *The Present-Day Christological Debate* (Downers Grove, Ill.: InterVarsity, 1984), p. 95.

4. William L. Schutter, "A Continuing Crisis for Incarnational Doctrine," *Reformed Review* 32.2 (Winter 1979): 84.

Dynamic Monarchianism understood Jesus not as God, but as a person who did the miraculous works of God through the power of the Spirit.[5] Philipp Melanchthon penned the famous statement that "to know Christ is to know his benefits."[6] In the nineteenth century Albrecht Ritschl approached doctrine in terms of value judgments; accordingly, he stressed what Christ does for us instead of what he is.[7] In the twentieth century Emil Brunner declared that the work of Christ is the route of access to the person of Christ,[8] and a full-fledged functional Christology made its appearance in the work of Oscar Cullmann, Hans Küng, and John A. T. Robinson.

The Basic Tenets

The Biblical Approach to Christ: Functional, Not Ontological

Our major task in this chapter will be to expound and then evaluate functional Christology, which can best be presented in a series of propositions. The first of these tenets is that the biblical writers did not discuss the nature(s) of Jesus in any metaphysical sense. They did not ask who Jesus was or what he was like. Rather, their discussions of Jesus stressed what he did.

The starting point is Jesus' own testimony regarding himself. The functional Christologists, like many other New Testament scholars, employ the techniques of form criticism and redaction criticism to try to isolate Jesus' words from the interpretations introduced by the early church community and by the Gospel writers. Only the Synoptic Gospels are used in the endeavor to get at Jesus' sayings and self-understanding; the fourth Gospel is deemed unreliable for this purpose.[9] Ob-

5. This is particularly true of the views of Theodotus. See J. N. D. Kelly, *Early Christian Doctrines* (New York: Harper and Row, 1960), p. 116.

6. *Melanchthon and Bucer*, comp. Wilhelm Pauck, *Library of Christian Classics* 19 (Philadelphia: Westminster, 1969), pp. 21–22.

7. Albrecht Ritschl, *The Christian Doctrine of Justification and Reconciliation* (Edinburgh: T. & T. Clark, 1900), pp. 385–484.

8. H. Emil Brunner, *The Christian Doctrine of Creation and Redemption* (Philadelphia: Westminster, 1952), pp. 271–74.

9. Hugh Williams Montefiore, "Towards a Christology for Today," in *Soundings: Essays Concerning Christian Understanding*, ed. A. R. Vidler (Cambridge: Cambridge University Press, 1962), p. 158.

serving this limitation the functional Christologists turn to examine the data.

The most striking feature in Jesus' self-testimony is that he made no claims to being of the nature of God. Hugh Montefiore says, "Negatively, he did not describe himself as God: indeed, he even seems implicitly to have denied this ('Why do you call me good?')."[10] Montefiore sees this text, Mark 10:18, as a *crux interpretationis*. Jesus is at least implying a contrast between himself and God, a contrast reinforced by the Gospel references to Jesus' prayers to his Father.

What did Jesus mean, then, in referring to himself as "Lord" and "Son of man"? Montefiore insists that Jesus' self-concept was in functional terms rather than ontological:

> In using these titles of himself, Jesus did not make ontological statements about himself: he was using biblical *imagery* to describe his messianic functions and his relations to God and to his fellow men. When he spoke of himself as Son and of God as "My Father," he did not mean that he was "of one substance with the Father." He was using the language of relationship. The use of Father for God by the Jews did not imply an idea of God but a characteristic attitude of piety.[11]

What is true of Jesus' self-understanding and self-testimony is also the witness of the rest of Scripture, according to the functional Christologists. The Scripture writers were not interested in who Jesus was, but in what he did. "The New Testament hardly ever speaks of the person of Christ without at the same time speaking of his work. . . . When it is asked in the New Testament 'Who is Christ?' the question never means exclusively, or even primarily, 'What is his nature?' but first of all, 'What is his function?'"[12] In presenting Christ's person in this way, the biblical writers were reflecting the Jewish understanding of messiahship:

> Jewish Messiahship does not yield a Christology of *status* in metaphysical terms of "human" or "divine" *origin* at all. That

10. Ibid.
11. Ibid.
12. Oscar Cullmann, *The Christology of the New Testament* (Philadelphia: Westminster, 1959), pp. 3–4.

question is quite irrelevant to the Jewish conception. It yields instead a Christology of *function* in terms of history. And in those terms the Jewish evidence about "Messiahship" is decisive. The *function* of the Messiah is a Divine function; His bringing in the "Kingdom of the Heavens" is God's own bringing in of His own Kingdom; the Messiah's action in history is starkly identified again and again with God's own action in history, even when (*e.g.* in the *Psalms of Solomon*) the Messiah is described as a human Davidic King.[13]

Hans Küng is one of the theologians who emphasize the functional role of Jesus. While making much of the titles Jesus bore—Son of man, Messiah-Christ, Lord, Son of God, Logos— Küng does not interpret them as expressions denoting Jesus' nature(s). Küng says, for example, that the title *Son of God* initially *"had nothing to do with Jesus' origin but with his legal and authoritative status.* It is a question of function, not of nature."[14] This is not to say that Jesus should be thought of merely as a representative of God. More than a representative, he should be thought of as "personal messenger, trustee, indeed as confidant and friend of God."[15] Küng, it should be observed, does not opt for a functional Christology completely devoid of ontological dimensions.[16] It is significant, however, that he apparently does not see ontological elements within the biblical testimony.

The Dichotomy Between the Hebrew and Greek Mentalities

The avoidance of ontological matters is traced to the very nature of the biblical material and the mentality of the Hebrews. Not only are there no metaphysical or ontological references to the nature(s) of Christ, there are no ontological references of any kind in the Bible. Not only did the biblical authors not think metaphysically about Jesus, they *could not*, for they simply were not of a metaphysical frame of mind. They did not ask such questions. Montefiore puts it most clearly: "The biblical revela-

13. Gregory Dix, *Jew and Greek: A Study in the Primitive Church* (Westminster: Dacre, 1953), pp. 79–80.
14. Hans Küng, *On Being a Christian* (Garden City, N.Y.: Doubleday, 1976), p. 390.
15. Ibid.
16. Ibid., p. 448.

tion is not expressed in philosophical terms, because the Jews did not think philosophically. They were concerned not with ontological definition but with dynamic function and with personal relationship."[17]

Robinson describes the Hebrew mentality somewhat differently, but the net result is much the same. He speaks of the Jewish categories as representing a mythological way of thinking that centered on God's act of sending his Messiah as Savior and Judge.[18] The person of Jesus could not be thought of in terms of two natures until a fundamental shift in the way of viewing reality took place, that is, until Christology replaced the Jewish mythological categories with Greek ontological categories. Here the functional Christologists are adopting the commonly held tenet of the biblical-theology movement that the Hebrew mentality is eminently distinguishable from the Greek mind-set.[19] The work of Johannes Pedersen, although not basically theological in nature, laid the foundation for this theory.[20] In Thorleif Boman's *Hebrew Thought Compared with Greek*, the implications for biblical studies were spelled out.

The Hebrew mentality, as Boman described it, understood reality to be dynamic rather than static. He states his conclusion in categorical fashion:

Our analysis of the Hebrew verbs that express standing, sitting, lying, etc. teaches us that motionless and fixed being is for the Hebrews a nonentity; it does not exist for them. Only "being" which stands in inner relation with something active and moving is a reality to them. This could also be expressed: only movement (motion) has reality. To the extent that it concerned Hebrew think-

17. Montefiore, "Towards a Christology," p. 157.
18. John A. T. Robinson, *The Human Face of God* (Philadelphia: Westminster, 1973), p. 33.
19. Brevard S. Childs, *Biblical Theology in Crisis* (Philadelphia: Westminster, 1970), pp. 44–47. The expression *biblical theology* as used in this context refers to a definite movement which arose in the 1940s, flourished in the 1950s, and declined in the 1960s (see James D. Smart, *The Past, Present, and Future of Biblical Theology* [Philadelphia: Westminster, 1979], p. 10). This movement should not be confused with the discipline of biblical theology, which is the study of the doctrinal content of the Old and New Testaments (for further explanation, see Millard J. Erickson, *Christian Theology* [Grand Rapids: Baker, 1986], pp. 23–25).
20. Johannes Pedersen, *Israel: Its Life and Culture*, 2 vols. (London: Oxford University Press, 1926, 1940).

ing at all, static being as a predicate is a motion that has passed over into repose.[21]

When Boman discusses verbs that indicate condition or quality, he draws a further distinction: "It is really more correct to say that we are dealing here with neither a 'being' nor a 'becoming' but with a dynamic third possibility, more an 'effecting' as in the case of the verb 'lighten' which means not only to be bright or become bright but also to make light effective, i.e. illuminate."[22] Boman also maintains that the Hebrews understood personal being in terms of an individual's movement and activity: "an inner, outgoing, objectively demonstrable activity of the organs and of consciousness is characteristic of the person."[23] This is a reference to what the person *does*.

The strong alignment of functional Christology with the biblical-theology movement appears quite clearly at this point. Both Cullmann and Robinson, of the persons we are considering here, were identified with the movement virtually from its beginning. Consequently, their interpretation of the biblical witness to Christ is colored by that movement's understanding of the nature of biblical thought.

It should be borne in mind that, in the view of the biblical theologians, Hebraic thought was not restricted to the Old Testament, nor was there a contrast between the Old and New Testaments. The Hebrew mentality actually underlay both Testaments, even though the New Testament was written in Greek. While some scholars such as F. C. Baur had in an earlier period argued that Paul was the chief culprit in Hellenizing the original Hebraic mode of thought,[24] most of the biblical theologians felt the transformation occurred much later.[25] Gregory Dix represents well the usual conclusion of the biblical-theology movement: "S. Paul has by now stood his trial on the charge of 'Hellenising' Christianity to make it acceptable to the Greeks— and the verdict is decisively 'Not Guilty.'"[26]

21. Thorleif Boman, *Hebrew Thought Compared with Greek* (Philadelphia: Westminster, 1960), p. 31.

22. Ibid.

23. Ibid., p. 46.

24. F. C. Baur, *The Church History of the First Three Centuries*, 2 vols. (London: Williams and Norgate, 1878–1879).

25. Adolf von Harnack, *History of Dogma*, 7 vols. in 4 (New York: Dover, 1961), vol. 2, p. 275.

26. Dix, *Jew and Greek*, p. 3.

The Postbiblical Shift
Toward Ontological Christology

The third tenet of functional Christology relates to the construction of an ontological Christology. This, according to the functional Christologists, did not occur within the biblical period; indeed, it could not. Rather, this type of theological construction came into play at a later point, when Greek categories became dominant and could be employed even by Christian theologians.

Greek thought is characterized by terms like "substance," "nature," *prosōpon*, and *hypostasis*. The Greeks, despite variations among them, had in common a concern to examine the nature of being, that which *is*, and to determine what *truly is*.[27] With the exception of Heraclitus, with his uncharacteristic emphasis upon change, the Greek philosophers thought of reality as static, unchanging. Indeed, the basic contrast between Greek and Hebrew thought is to be found in their respective interests in bodies at rest and bodies in movement.[28]

Greek thought was also abstract, rationalistic, and theoretical. It was more concerned with determining what something is than what it does. It was logical thinking rather than psychological understanding.[29] It had as its focus "that which is," the objective and unchanging. Its aim was to attain correct information about the object under investigation. There were even basic physical differences between the Greek and Hebrew approach. Hebrew thought centered on time, Greek thought on space. For the Hebrew the decisive reality of the world of experience was the *word;* for the Greek it was the *thing.* Thus, to experience truth the Hebrew depended on hearing, whereas sight was the predominant sense for the Greek.[30]

In the first four or five centuries following the New Testament period, Christian theologians began to use Greek philosophical categories as they reflected upon and attempted to interpret the biblical evidence regarding Jesus Christ. This was part of a general shift in the way in which reality was viewed. According to Robinson, the transition from a mythological to an ontological way of thinking "is reflected in Christology in the shift from

27. Boman, *Hebrew Thought*, p. 53.
28. Ibid., p. 55.
29. Ibid., pp. 194–95.
30. Ibid., p. 206.

Jewish categories to Greek. The former viewed finality in terms of the eschatological act of God in history, embodied in the sending of his Messiah as saviour and judge of everything in heaven and earth and under the earth. The latter saw ultimate reality not in terms of final act but of timeless being, in the categories of substance rather than will."[31]

It was natural for the Chalcedonian Christologists to think of Jesus in terms of what he was. It also was necessary, for they were combating heresies regarding the person of Christ which were being formulated in fundamentally ontological categories. This resulted in an alteration of the picture of Christ. According to Cullmann, there was a greater emphasis upon the nature of Christ than upon his work. This represented an orientation and set of conclusions different from the Hebraic or biblical view.

> As a result of the necessity of combating the heretics, then, the Church fathers subordinated the interpretation of the person and work of Christ to the question of the "natures." In any case, their emphases, compared with those of the New Testament, were misplaced. Even when they did speak of the work of Christ, they did so only in connection with discussion about his nature. Even if this shifting of emphasis was necessary against certain heretical views, the discussion of "natures" is none the less ultimately a Greek, not a Jewish or biblical problem.[32]

There is consensus among the functional Christologists that the Chalcedonian formulation was different from the biblical witness regarding Christ. There is disagreement, however, as to whether this divergence was appropriate. Some hold that the Chalcedonian formulation legitimately extends the biblical view. Others see it as a distortion: what is stated there does not make explicit what is implicit within the Scriptures, but introduces something foreign.

One who sees the Chalcedonian construction as a distortion of the biblical testimony is Montefiore. He quotes with favor the words of G. L. Prestige: "Jesus Christ disappears in the smokescreen of the two-nature philosophy. Formalism triumphs, and the living figure of the evangelical Redeemer is desiccated to a

31. Robinson, *Human Face*, p. 33.
32. Cullmann, *Christology*, p. 4.

logical mummy."[33] Similarly, Montefiore approves of William
Temple's statements that the Chalcedonian definition represents
"the bankruptcy of Greek patristic theology," and that as a solution to christological problems it "marks the definite failure of
all attempts to explain the Incarnation in terms of Essence,
Substance, Nature and the like."[34] While conceding that some
critics have not done justice to the Nicene fathers because of
failure to recognize that they were using a Platonist metaphysic,
he at the same time asserts that "the early Fathers were compelled by their tradition of thought to formulate the Incarnation
in terms that were sub-personal."[35] Similarly, Robinson speaks
of the ontological approach as employing rather "bloodless" categories.[36] Along with Dix he observes that we who are trained in
Western culture, with its ontological ways of thinking, tend naturally to see the development of an ontological Christology as a
heightening of Christology.[37] In Jewish terms, however, it is not
possible to say anything higher about the Messiah than that his
action in history is to be identified with God's action in history.
It is therefore no improvement or advance upon the Jewish conception to construct an ontological Christ with two natures.[38]

Others, however, see the Chalcedonian Christology (or at least
some Greek or ontological Christologies) as legitimate exten-
sions or inferences from the biblical testimony. One is Cullmann.
In *Christology of the New Testament* he made certain statements
which some have interpreted as unqualified criticisms of ontological Christology and as affirmations that functional Christology cannot be improved upon. For example, "In the light of
the New Testament witness, all mere speculation about his
natures is an absurdity. Functional Christology is the only kind
which exists."[39] It is not clear how this statement is to be interpreted. Cullmann might be asserting simply that there is no
ontological Christology in the New Testament. Or he might be
asserting the fundamental untenability of any endeavor to go

33. Montefiore, "Towards a Christology," p. 156.
34. Ibid.
35. Ibid.
36. Robinson, *Human Face*, p. 34.
37. Ibid., p. 33; Dix, *Jew and Greek*, p. 79.
38. Dix, *Jew and Greek*, p. 80.
39. Cullmann, *Christology*, p. 326.

beyond the New Testament to discuss the natures of Christ. Later, however, in an article written in response to his critics, Cullmann affirmed that his insistence upon the "acting" of God did not exclude "being." The fact is that while presupposing the divine being and person of Christ, the New Testament "regards these not from the perspective of their origin or their nature, but of their *manifestation* in the history of salvation."[40]

Cullmann mentions two biblical passages which explicitly refer to the being of Christ: John 1:1 and 1 Corinthians 15:28. These two passages, which mark the extreme limits of the history of divine action (before creation and after the culmination of the history of salvation), "rest content with the substance without really venturing affirmations relative to the nature."[41] They stop at the threshold without crossing it. Cullmann also mentions Philippians 2:6 and the birth narratives, which presuppose the divine nature of Christ, but do not view it independently of his function.[42]

Cullmann still must face the issue of whether posing the question of the natures and using categories not found in the New Testament constituted a deviation. He has said that it was necessary for the church to do so. Beyond that, he states that the church did not let itself be led away upon a dogmatic enterprise contrary to the New Testament. He believes the final formulae of the great early councils remained in contact with the Christology of the New Testament—which is what is crucial. Although he does consider some later Catholic dogmatic developments to have been spurious, his final statement on Chalcedon is that "the dogma formulated by this Council [on the question of the natures] corresponds to what the Christology of the New Testament presupposes."[43]

The Contemporary Mood: Functional, Not Ontological

The final tenet in the argument is that the mood of today is functional, not ontological; consequently, Christology for today

---

40. Oscar Cullmann, "The Reply of Professor Cullmann to Roman Catholic Critics," *Scottish Journal of Theology* 15 (1962): 40.
41. Ibid.
42. Ibid., p. 41.
43. Ibid., p. 43.

should be constructed in a functional mode. The first step is to assert that the Greek ontological thinking that underlay the Chalcedonian ("two natures") formulation is obsolete and untenable for us today. This may be expressed in a relatively mild statement, as that the particular form of metaphysics which the Greeks employed is now outmoded. This is Montefiore's position: "It is inevitable that a developed Christology should use language that is philosophical, but the particular philosophical tradition which underlies the Chalcedonian Definition is outmoded today."[44] The tendency of modern thought is to evolve dynamic concepts, in large part because of the influence of science and the new interest in the meaning of history. As a result, the concept of "substance" has faded.[45] While some might think this to be a real and serious problem, Montefiore does not:

> There is nothing sacrosanct about the philosophical categories of the patristic period. God did not reveal to us a particular philosophy: he revealed himself to us in Jesus Christ. Unless we believe that the Chalcedonian Definition is binding upon Christians for all time—and the Anglican concept of authority does not encourage such a view—then we need not feel ourselves bound by the terms in which Christology is defined in the formula, although we shall be very chary of rejecting what underlies these forms of expression.[46]

Robinson states the issue somewhat more strongly. He maintains not only that the ontological approach is passé, but that this is necessarily so, for there has been a change in the very way in which reality is represented. Just as the mythological way of thinking about reality gave way to the ontological, so we are now moving from the ontological to a functional way of thinking.[47] We think about reality in terms of what happens rather than what is, of verbs rather than substantives or substances.[48] This way of viewing reality "comes naturally to an empirical, scientifically trained generation."[49] But if such a way of thinking is modern, it is also primitive. Robinson says, "It is

44. Montefiore, "Towards a Christology," p. 156.
45. Ibid., p. 157.
46. Ibid.
47. Robinson, *Human Face*, p. 38.
48. Ibid., p. 183.
49. Ibid., p. 184.

much nearer the Hebrew prophetic tradition before it was influenced by the streams of thought that entered Judaism in the centuries immediately before and after the Christian era."[50] While he has distinguished the mythological from the functional ways of thinking, it now appears that the two have more in common with each other than either has with ontological thinking. Similarly, Montefiore has described both the biblical and the modern mentality as concerned with dynamic concepts.[51] Thus, modern functional Christology is actually closer to the biblical Christology than are the Chalcedonian and other ontological Christologies.

What does such a Christology entail? Robinson has very clearly summarized the view:

> The Christ is the one who does what God does, who represents him. He stands in the place of God, speaking and acting for him. The issue is not where he comes from or what he is made of. He is not a divine or semi-divine being who comes from the other side. He is a human figure raised up from among his brothers to be the instrument of God's decisive work and to stand in a relationship to him to which no other man is called. The issue is whether in seeing him men see the Father, whether, in mercy and judgment, he *functions* as God, whether he *is* God to and for them.[52]

This, then, is the modern functional Christ: one who acts on behalf of God. That is what constitutes his deity, not some metaphysical nature. And in adopting this perspective, according to the functional Christologists, modernity has managed to return to the biblical view.

The Philosophical Background of Functional Christology

We have seen that those who advocate a functional Christology do so because they believe that the current environment is open to a functional approach to truth, but not to a more speculative or intellectualist view. They also maintain that

50. Ibid.
51. Montefiore, "Towards a Christology," p. 157.
52. Robinson, *Human Face*, pp. 183–84.

functionalism and the biblical view are closer to one another than they are to the metaphysics of the Chalcedonian construction. While many varied streams of contemporary thought relate to functionalism, it is most fully embodied in the philosophy known as pragmatism.

Pragmatism is in many ways a distinctly American philosophy, although its influence has been much more widespread than that. It was in many ways the dominant philosophy in the United States during the first quarter of the twentieth century. While it has ceased to be a dominant, clearly organized school of thought, it has lingered on in diffused form in many areas of culture. H. S. Thayer says, for example: "And in this alteration of the philosophical scene, some of the positive suggestions of pragmatism have been disseminated into current intellectual life as practices freely adopted and taken for granted to an extent that no longer calls for special notice."[53] It is in these general influences that pragmatism has had an impact upon the framing of functional Christology.

The first major exponent of pragmatism was Charles S. Peirce. He considered ontological metaphysics to be absurd. Rather, he was especially concerned with the practical meaning of ideas: "Consider what effects that might conceivably have practical bearing you conceive the object of your conception to have. Then your conception of those effects is the WHOLE of your conception of the object."[54]

Pragmatists are not concerned about absolute truth. Nor are they interested in questions of ultimate reality. "The pragmatist is not even interested in the question as to what the world 'really' is."[55] Such questions are unanswerable; even if answers could be found, they would be unintelligible.

William James took Peirce's scientific conception and generalized it to other areas of human culture and inquiry.[56] Donald Mackay maintains that the pragmatic movement should be

53. H. S. Thayer, "Pragmatism," in *Encyclopedia of Philosophy*, ed. Paul Edwards, 8 vols. (New York: Macmillan, 1967), vol. 6, p. 435.

54. Charles S. Peirce, "The Essentials of Pragmatism," in *Philosophical Writings of Peirce*, ed. Justus Buchler (New York: Dover, 1955), p. 259.

55. Walter G. Muelder and Laurence Sears, eds., *The Development of American Philosophy* (Boston: Houghton Mifflin, 1940), p. 312.

56. Gertrude Ezorsky, "Pragmatic Theory of Truth," in *Encyclopedia of Philosophy*, vol. 6, p. 427.

thought of as merely an attempt to extend the experimental attitudes and procedures of science into other fields such as philosophy.[57] Instead of seeking to get at the real essence of things, the aim is simply to examine what they do or how they affect human behavior. John Dewey applied the pragmatist approach to educational theory and practice; among the later pragmatists of note are C. I. Lewis, English philosopher Ferdinand C. S. Schiller, and even a few other Europeans.[58]

To see how the pragmatic method bears upon a field like Christology, let us look for a moment at Peirce's discussion of the concept of hardness. Instead of attempting to get at the "real" meaning of hardness, Peirce looks at the concept functionally: "If in certain situations the operation of scratch-testing is performed on O, [and] the general result is: O will not be scratched by most substances," that is the meaning of "O is hard."[59] Similarly, pragmatists approach the person of Christ not in terms of his ultimate nature, but in terms of his effect both on his contemporaries and on individuals today.

Critical Scrutiny of the Four Major Tenets

The Biblical Approach to Christ: Functional and Ontological

Having noted both the fundamental tenets of functional Christology and the philosophical conception which underlies it, we now need to scrutinize each of the claims in turn. The first, the reader will recall, is the contention that the references to Christ in the New Testament are primarily functional in nature. Cullmann claimed that the relatively few biblical treatments of Jesus' nature(s) are always found in connection with, and subjugated to, statements about his function. But is this really so?

One who dissents is Reginald Fuller. He agrees that much of the New Testament Christology is purely functional, especially in its Jewish phases. Though it has been pointed out that even this Palestinian kerygma does not restrict itself to what God has done, but uses christological titles such as "Son of God" and

57. Donald S. Mackay, "Pragmatism," in *A History of Philosophical Systems*, ed. Vergilius Ferm (New York: Philosophical Library, 1950), p. 397.

58. Ibid., pp. 388–89; Thayer, "Pragmatism," p. 431.

59. Thayer, "Pragmatism," p. 432.

"Son of man," they are found almost without exception in sentences which speak of Jesus' action. Fuller says, "They assert what the Christ has done, is doing, or will do; not what he is, ontically."[60] In the mission to the Gentiles, however, the church advanced beyond its purely functional statements to make what Fuller terms "ontic" statements.[61] It is not proper to refer to them as "ontological," for we do not find here a thoroughly developed ontology. There is no systematic treatment of the being or nature(s) or metaphysical makeup of Jesus. There are, however, statements about who Jesus was and is, not merely what he did or what was done through him.

A passage of particular note is Philippians 2:6–11. It had been common, following Ernst Lohmeyer's interpretation, to regard this passage as an Aramaic hymn, and to view it in an Aramaic framework. "The form of God" (v. 6) was understood as a parallel to the image or the likeness of God in Genesis 1:26, and "emptied himself" (v. 7) was equated with "poured out his soul" in Isaiah 53:12.[62] There is now stronger evidence, however, that what we find in Philippians 2 is Hellenistic in nature rather than Semitic. F. W. Beare writes: "The terminology is best interpreted within the framework of Hellenistic (syncretistic) religious thought. . . . The 'form of God' and the thought of 'equality with God' are hardly compatible with any late form of Judaism. The whole tone is peculiarly and distinctively Christian, and Christian against a Hellenistic, non-Jewish background."[63] Fuller rejects Beare's assumption that the terms and tone of Philippians 2 can be traced to the Gnostic myth of a redeemer. He insists, however, that the passage cannot be reduced to a functional Semitic conception. While he admits that the term μορφή ("form") had lost the classical meaning of "underlying reality" and in verse 6

60. Reginald H. Fuller, *The Foundations of New Testament Christology* (New York: Scribner, 1965), p. 248.

61. Ibid.

62. Ernst Lohmeyer, *Kyrios Jesus: Eine Untersuchung zu Phil. 2, 5–11*, 2d ed. (Heidelberg: Carl Winter, 1961); Lionel S. Thornton, *The Dominion of Christ* (London: Dacre, 1952), pp. 91, 95n; H. Wheeler Robinson, *The Cross in the Old Testament* (Philadelphia: Westminster, 1955), pp. 57, 104–05; Joachim Jeremias, "The Servant of God in the New Testament," in Walther Zimmerli and Joachim Jeremias, *The Servant of God*, rev. ed. (Naperville, Ill.: Allenson, 1965), pp. 97–98. For a contrary view see Ernst Käsemann, "Kritische Analyse von Phil. 2, 5–11," *Zeitschrift für Theologie und Kirche* 47 (1950): 313–60.

63. F. W. Beare, *A Commentary on the Epistle to the Philippians* (New York: Harper, 1959), p. 77.

means "mode of existence," the point is that "the pre-existent One dwelt in an existence which was equal to that of God."[64] If this is not a theoretical reference to the metaphysical deity of Christ, it certainly is at least an implicit statement of his divine nature.

There are other considerations as well. Passages like Colossians 1:18 and 2:9 and Hebrews 1:3 are difficult to interpret on any basis other than a genuine incarnation. While they do not fully develop the doctrine of two natures, they certainly have more than a merely functional deity in view.

Jesus' self-designations and terms which others used of him have also been cited as references to ontological deity. The functional Christologists have offered an alternative explanation of most of these terms. When we look at how they are actually employed in the New Testament, however, we find that the explanation on functional grounds usually does not work.

One of the titles cited as a reference to ontological deity is "Son of God." Some theologians, however, looking at the Old Testament background, maintain that this title refers merely to a faithful covenant partner. Hendrikus Berkhof, for example, points out that in the Old Testament it is used of Israel as a whole and of the king, and that the New Testament refers to believers as children and sons of God.[65] When we look at the Gospels, however, we find that the scribes and Pharisees apparently did not understand Jesus to be claiming a merely functional deity for himself. Because of his use of the term *Son of God* and his claim to be able to forgive sins, they accused him of blasphemy. The Jews sought to kill him "because he not only broke the Sabbath but also called God his own Father, making himself equal with God" (John 5:18). Somewhat later we read that they said to Pilate, "We have a law, and by that law he ought to die, because he has made himself the Son of God" (John 19:7). (We recognize, of course, that the functional Christologists do not admit the Gospel of John as evidence of Jesus' deity. We cannot help wondering, however, whether the high Christology of the Gospel of John may not be a factor in its exclusion from their considerations.)

Jesus' preexistence is also rejected by the functional Christologists. The passages that are cited as evidence of preexistence

64. Fuller, *Foundations*, p. 208.
65. Hendrikus Berkhof, *The Christian Faith* (Grand Rapids: Eerdmans, 1979), p. 282.

they reinterpret as Jewish or Hellenistic descriptions of God's initiative in Jesus' life.[66] The term *Son of God* and the references to preexistence cannot so easily be taken in a general way, however. Runia says, "They are so deeply embedded in the New Testament and stated in such an unequivocal manner that we have to take them seriously. Indeed, they can be explained only in terms of 'incarnational' theology. It is really not enough when Frances Young speaks of 'incarnational elements' in the New Testament. The New Testament Christology can be understood properly only in terms of a real incarnation."[67]

The passages which speak of a real incarnation—of God's actually coming in the person of Jesus—are not incidental or obscure or rare. As I. Howard Marshall points out, that doctrine is not found on the fringe of the New Testament.[68] Rather, it is found everywhere, in all parts of the New Testament. As Runia says, "For all these writers [John, Paul, Peter, and the author of Hebrews] it is the 'organizing principle of their Christology.' And it is not a matter of functionality only, but it has its ontological basis in Jesus' unique, pre-existent Sonship."[69]

James Barr's Disproof of a Hebrew-Greek Dichotomy

The second point to be considered is the alleged dichotomy between the Hebrew and Greek mentalities. There had been all along some rather isolated objections to this concept. And then in 1961 James Barr's *Semantics of Biblical Language* presented a thoroughly devastating criticism. Ironically, it was not Barr's express purpose to criticize the notion of an ideological contrast between Hebrews and Greeks. He says early on in the book: "The validity of the thought contrast is no part of our subject; our subject is (a) the way in which the thought contrast has affected the examination of linguistic evidence, and (b) the way in which linguistic evidence has been used to support or illustrate the thought contrast."[70]

---

66. Ibid., p. 289.

67. Runia, *Present-Day Christological Debate*, p. 94.

68. I. Howard Marshall, "Incarnational Christology in the New Testament," in *Christ the Lord: Studies in Christology Presented to Donald Guthrie*, ed. Harold H. Rowdon (Downers Grove, Ill.: Inter-Varsity, 1982), p. 13.

69. Runia, *Present-Day Christological Debate*, p. 95.

70. James Barr, *The Semantics of Biblical Language* (New York: Oxford University Press, 1961), p. 14.

Barr has two major objections to the argument usually presented. One is the failure to examine the relevant languages closely, Greek and Hebrew. The other is the failure to relate what is said about them to general linguistic theory. Indeed, Boman took to task such linguists as Carl Brockelmann, Hans Bauer and Pontus Leander, and Gotthelf Bergsträsser for failure to give adequate attention in their treatments of the verb system to the unique Hebrew understanding of time and the dynamic nature of reality.[71]

When Barr proceeds to examine the actual nature of the Hebrew language, he finds several problems with the evidence and the reasoning offered for distinguishing between the Hebrew and Greek mentalities. For example, one of Boman's proofs for saying that Hebrew thought was dynamic rather than static (or, as Boman preferred to say, "harmonic") was that Hebrew has only one verb to express the two meanings of "to lie": "to be lying" (a static condition) and "to lie down" (motion).[72] In this, however, Barr points out, Hebrew is no different from a number of other languages, including English, Greek, and Egyptian.[73]

The same type of deficiency is found in the contention of Boman and the biblical-theology movement generally that the Israelites were not interested in "existence," and that consequently and correspondingly the Hebrew language has no means of expressing existence.[74] Barr points out that the word yēš, "there is," is used to express the idea of existence. It cannot be rendered "is present," so that, for example, Psalm 14:1 would read, "There is no God present."[75] Barr contends that the emphasis upon the verb as the basis of Hebrew speech is not only dubious, but fails to do justice to important words like yēš and 'ayin, which are distinctly not verbs. Further, in certain contexts they come near the idea of absolute existence and nonexistence.[76]

Part of Barr's criticism of the work of Pedersen and Boman is their failure to apply their principles consistently to other lan-

71. Boman, *Hebrew Thought*, pp. 23–24, 26.
72. Ibid., pp. 27–31.
73. Barr, *Semantics*, pp. 50–54.
74. Ibid., pp. 59–60.
75. Ibid., p. 62.
76. Ibid., p. 63.

guages. For example, on the basis that there are different and unrelated verbs for "go up," "go down," "go in," and "go out," Pedersen argues that the Hebrews did not engage in abstract thinking. In English, by contrast, we have one word which is supplemented by adverbs to indicate the direction of movement. This, he says, is because English has an abstract idea of "going," which Hebrew thought lacks.[77] But, as Barr points out, the same contrast can be drawn between English and French. Are the French therefore possessed of a more concrete thought, and are they less capable than English-speaking peoples of conceptualizing abstractly?[78]

These are only small samples of the type of criticism brought by Barr against the arguments for distinguishing between the Greek and Hebrew mentalities on the basis of the character of the languages themselves. To examine Barr's comments in detail would require a complete book on the subject, and a rather large one at that. His criticism served to accelerate the "cracking of the walls" of the biblical-theology movement.[79] In the three decades since publication there has been no adequate rebuttal or refutation of Barr's book. The verdict of Brevard Childs is worth noting:

> In reflecting on the effect of Barr's book, one cannot help being impressed with the success of his attack. Seldom has one book brought down so much superstructure with such effectiveness. Barr's argument seemed to most English scholars and the majority of Americans to be fully convincing. When reservations did come, it was in terms of an overly negative style of argument, and in regards to the outer limits of his criticism. But even among those Biblical theologians who remained unconvinced, there was agreement that the emphasis of the Biblical Theology Movement on a distinctive mentality could never be carried on without a major revision.[80]

Functional Versus Ontological Christology— A False Dilemma

The third tenet we examined was the postbiblical construction of an ontological Christology. The question arises, Is this

77. Pedersen, *Israel*, vol. 1, p. 111.
78. Barr, *Semantics*, p. 31.
79. Childs, *Biblical Theology*, p. 72.
80. Ibid.

Christology consistent and harmonious with the functional Christology of the Bible? To some extent, this question has already been answered, since we have shown that the biblical witness regarding Christ is not of an exclusively functional character. But even if it were, would that be enough in itself? Can we simply stop at the point of saying that Jesus acted for God, or that he did God's work, or that he is God to us? Is that in itself a sufficient statement of who Jesus was and is?

A growing number of theologians and even New Testament specialists have come to insist that the function of Jesus cannot be separated from his nature. Walter Kasper, for example, dismisses the dilemma of an ontological and a functional Christology as "illusory and a position into which theology should not allow itself to be manoeuvered."[81] Gerald O'Collins says, as we have in part already seen, "Jesus' value and function for us demand that we examine and recognize his status at the level of his being. His saving work indicates both *who* he was and is—both in himself and in his relationship to the Father. There can be no satisfactory account of what Jesus does if we dismiss as unimportant the question who he is. Every soteriological statement has its Christological implications."[82] Edward Schillebeeckx also acknowledges the inseparability of the issues of Jesus' work and his divine nature: "We cannot separate God's nature and his revelation. Therefore in the definition of what he is, the man Jesus is indeed connected with the nature of God."[83] And, as we have seen, although Cullmann contended that "functional Christology is the only kind which exists,"[84] he later explained that he was saying merely that a Chalcedonian type of reflection is not New Testament exegesis. And having made that clarification, he went on to affirm that the dogma formulated by the Council of Chalcedon "corresponds to what the Christology of the New Testament presupposes."[85]

There are even those who would contend not merely that it was necessary for the Greek fathers to formulate an ontological

---

81. Walter Kasper, *Jesus the Christ* (New York: Paulist, 1976), p. 24.

82. O'Collins, *What Are They Saying*, p. 27.

83. Edward Schillebeeckx, *Interim Report on the Books Jesus & Christ* (New York: Crossroad, 1981), p. 142.

84. Cullmann, *Christology*, p. 326.

85. Cullmann, "Reply," p. 43.

Christology, but that this type of thinking is a universal necessity or tendency of the human mind. Fuller, for example, says that "it is not just a quirk of the Greek mind, but a universal human apperception, that action implies prior being—even if, as is also true, being is only apprehended in action."[86] This is not to say that the particular variety of ontological Christology formulated at Chalcedon is an exact representation of the teachings of the New Testament. But it is to say that the endeavor not only was not incompatible with the New Testament, but was a necessary result of it.

The Contemporary Concern with the Nature of Things

We must now examine the fourth tenet as well, namely, that the mood of our time tends toward a functional and empirical approach to reality. People today are interested in what something does or how it functions rather than what it is, particularly in a metaphysical sense. It must be acknowledged immediately that the twentieth century has been characterized by a profound suspicion of, and even hostility toward, any type of metaphysical thinking. Most of the dominant philosophical movements of our time have rejected the metaphysical endeavor as illegitimate. Logical positivism affirmed that a synthetic statement (i.e., a nondefinitional, nonmathematical statement) is meaningful if there is a set of sense data which will verify or falsify it. Existentialism minimized the objective approach, in which the primary concern is to describe an entity correctly, emphasizing instead the subjective approach, which focuses on the effect of the entity upon the individual who perceives it. And pragmatism insisted that the meaning (or even the truth) of a proposition is its practical effects.

But is contemporary thought really that unconcerned with the nature of things, with analysis and explanation? To be sure, there is a strong orientation to observation and the empirical method. And given this orientation, practical implications are more important than speculation about real essences. Yet scientific inquiry is constantly forming constructs to account for the

86. Fuller, *Foundations*, p. 248.

phenomena under investigation. What an electron really is (i.e., is it ultimately matter, an idea, or what?) may not be ascertainable or even important. Indeed, whether there actually are such things as electrons may not be an issue of ultimate importance. But it is of great importance to physics to formulate such concepts to account for the phenomena. To the degree that these concepts can be refined, prediction and control are facilitated.

The same is true in a realm such as psychology. Behaviorism is perhaps in some ways the fullest expression of the twentieth-century outlook. Here there are no probings into theories of personality. Rather, observable behavior is the locus of inquiry. One finds no components of personality such as Freud's id, ego, and superego. And yet there is an emphasis upon conditioned responses, which, though not reified, are nonetheless very real.

It should be noted further that even philosophical functionalism is not so consistently opposed to intellectual theorizing as has been represented. We observed earlier that pragmatism defined meaning (in the case of Peirce) and truth (in the case of James) in terms of the consequences or implications for human conduct. Yet James began with a definition of truth that goes beyond a pure functionalism: "Truth, as any dictionary will tell you, is a property of certain of our ideas. It means their 'agreement,' as falsity means their disagreement, with 'reality.' Pragmatists and intellectualists both accept this definition as a matter of course. They begin to quarrel only after the question is raised as to what may precisely be meant by the term 'agreement,' and what by the term 'reality,' when reality is taken as something for our ideas to agree with."[87] It is evident that James proposed pragmatism less as a theory of the nature of truth than as a test for truth, a test with rather rigorous criteria.

It would appear from the foregoing that the claimed parallel between functional Christology and the modern intellectual milieu will not bear close scrutiny. Contemporary thought in general has a stronger interest in precise definition than is displayed by the functional Christologists. There is a concern to discover the entity (be it electrons, human nature, or truth) behind the function. An equivalent concern on the part of functional Christologists would lead them both to ask what sort of being

87. William James, *Pragmatism* (New York: Meridian, 1955), p. 132.

Jesus must have been in order to have performed the functions which he did, and to specify those functions much more clearly.

Evaluation

We have noted four major tenets of functional Christology and its philosophical framework. We then examined each of these tenets and challenged some of the bases on which they rest. We must now analyze and evaluate a bit more fully, observing first the positive features:

1. A real strength of functional Christology is its emphasis upon the work of Christ. In the final analysis, the biblical treatments of who Jesus is and was are at least implicitly and usually explicitly related to what he did. The Second Person of the Trinity did not become incarnate simply to be the God-man, but to reveal God and redeem the human race. Further, the teaching about who he is was not given merely to supply us with some information, but to bring us into fellowship with the God from whom our sin has separated us.

2. Functional Christology is in effect essentially an evangelistic Christology, calling upon us to respond to the divine invitation.

On the other hand, there are a number of areas in which functional Christology proves deficient:

1. While correctly interpreting many biblical passages which present what Jesus did, functional Christology is not sufficiently comprehensive to account accurately for the full sweep of the biblical data. Cullmann's rather grudging reference to passages that, marking the extreme limits of the history of divine action, allude to the being of Christ, is virtually a tacit admission of that deficiency.

2. A basic cause of the insufficiency of functional Christology is that its exponents have espoused a limited twentieth-century view of meaning and truth. Some, such as Robinson, have done so consciously. Others either are not aware of what they are doing or simply have not acknowledged their presuppositions. Yet presuppositions are part of the framework which the functional Christologists bring to the task of biblical exegesis and biblical theology. And these presuppositions affect their perception of the biblical content.

All exegetes work with presuppositions, which affect what they find in the text and how they regard it. These presuppositions are like tinted glasses. If one is wearing glasses with blue lenses, skies and waters will be deeper in color, grass will be aqua, clouds will be pastel blue, and human complexions will be quite peculiar. And if one's glasses are also of the wraparound style, so that no parts of the visual field are unaffected by the lenses, the whole world will take on a different hue. Now none of us really knows that we are not each individually looking through colored lenses. If we are aware of their presence, we will be able to some extent to compensate for them, telling ourselves, for example, "The sky is not really as blue as it appears." But if we do not realize how our perception is being affected, we will simply continue under the illusion.

Some exegetes quite openly acknowledge their presuppositions. Rudolf Bultmann is an example, with his overt espousal of existentialism. Others, however, proceed in apparent naiveté regarding their methods. For this reason, I always urge my students to inquire critically regarding the presuppositions of writers and speakers, to look for factors which would bias the conclusions. It is wise to inquire about the presuppositions even of those who give us the tools used in exegesis, such as grammars and lexicons, so that we can avoid doing unconscious eisegesis while attempting exegesis.[88]

What is being suggested here is that the functional Christologists to some extent find functionalism in Scripture because they bring it with them. They have seen the effect of Greek metaphysical presuppositions upon the persons who formulated the Chalcedonian Creed, yet have failed to see their own presuppositions, or perhaps even to recognize that they themselves have presuppositions. They are the more likely to be influenced by their presuppositions as a result. This may be a case akin to what Henry Cadbury had in view in his discussion of archaizing. He was referring to neoorthodoxy, but the point is appropriate here as well:

It is not much different from modernization since the current theology often is simply read into the older documents and then

88. Although many exegetes use the term *tools* to refer to techniques or methods of exegesis, such as form criticism and redaction criticism, I reserve the term for the actual devices employed, such as grammars, concordances, and lexicons. Exegetical methods are to these devices what the carpenter's technique of sawing is to the saw.

out again. It is the old sequence of eisegesis and exegesis. I do not
mean merely that modern words are used to describe the teaching of the Bible like demonic or encounter, and the more philosophical vocabulary affected by modern thinkers. Even when the
language is accurately biblical, it does not mean as used today
what it first meant.[89]

But what of the ontological Christologists? Are they not also
biased by their presuppositions? And how, then, does one determine whether ontological or functional Christology is closer to
the correct interpretation of Scripture?

One of the basic principles of textual criticism will be helpful
in sorting out such questions: when we are faced with alternative readings, the one which would have been more difficult for
the copyist is to be preferred. By extension, a conceptual interpretation that is contrary to the contemporary milieu of the
exegete-theologian is preferable to one in accord with it. A
potential problem here lies in defining the contemporary milieu,
for there are many different milieus extant at a given time, and
the particular mind-set or worldview of the exegete may itself be
contradictory to that of the dominant subculture.

3. Another consideration is that we should choose the exegetical method which can deal with more elements of the biblical revelation with less distortion than can the alternatives. Recurrent distortion may well be a sign of conceptual mismatch between the
method and the material being examined. And here functional
Christology frequently runs into difficulty, for it approaches the
biblical text with some fundamentally antisupernatural presuppositions. We might well expect that some of the functional
Christologists will develop a functional doctrine of God the
Father. And some indeed have already done so. We might also
expect that a functional view of Jesus' humanity would emerge as
well; that is, he was not really human, but only acted on behalf of
humanity, or did the work of humanity. Why has this view not
emerged? Perhaps because an antisupernatural bias is operant.

What I am calling for is a willingness to challenge the contemporary mind-set as we engage in the process of exegesis and
theology. It seems to me that Scripture sets forth an explicitly

89. Henry J. Cadbury, "The Peril of Archaizing Ourselves," *Interpretation* 3 (1949):
333.

metaphysical scheme of things. This is admitted even by the opponents of biblical authority, who of course reject those metaphysical elements. Although the particular type of metaphysic employed may vary from one era to another, it is imperative that this distinctive be maintained as an antithesis to any contemporary philosophies which reject an ontological God and an ontological deity of Jesus Christ. For to fail to do so is to lose part of the essence of Christianity.

10

The Metaphysical Problem.
(2) Process Christology

Process Metaphysics

Process Christology must be seen as part of the larger movement of process theology in general, which in turn can be understood only as an application of process philosophy. Accordingly, we will begin with a brief account of the development of process metaphysics.

Ancient Greek philosophy was from virtually the beginning concerned about the relationship between permanence and change, being and becoming, the one and the many. Heraclitus emphasized the change within the universe about us, while others, among them Zeno, argued that such change is only appar-

243

ent, not real. Eventually, something of a compromise was struck: substances are real and permanent, but change can occur in their accidents, or one substance may be substituted for another. "Substance," the underlying set of characteristics or qualities that makes something what it is, is the basic unit of reality. This form of metaphysic was the assumed basis of theology for a long period of time. When Thomas Aquinas adopted Aristotelian philosophy as the basis for his theology, the traditional Greek metaphysic, with some variations, became virtually standardized. Even the Reformers, in rejecting Roman Catholic theology, did not abandon, but merely modified the view that substances are the fundamental building blocks of reality.

It remained for the twentieth century to produce an alternative conception. Alfred North Whitehead, a mathematician, began reflecting and writing upon issues of philosophy and particularly of metaphysics. He proposed that the most basic units of reality are not fixed substances, but processes and events. Instead of emphasizing the permanence of reality, he emphasized the change. Thus, reality was thought of not so much as static but as dynamic. This fit well with developments in physics. The traditional focus on substance had fit well the Newtonian understanding of the universe, with its commonsense ideas of time and space as fixed and absolute. In an Einsteinian universe, however, where space and time are relative, a more dynamic or relative conception appears fitting. In Whitehead's understanding, all of reality, which includes God, exhibits the same characteristics, or to put it differently, the same laws govern the entire universe. Thus God, like the rest of the universe, is characterized by change and process rather than fixity and absoluteness.

At the University of Chicago, a theology called "naturalistic theism" developed along the lines of process metaphysics. Probably the leading exponent of this view was Henry Nelson Wieman, although others, such as Bernard Loomer and Bernard Meland, joined in the effort. Yet this theology did not gain widespread acceptance. Parallel movements were occurring elsewhere. In Roman Catholicism, for example, Pierre Teilhard de Chardin's idea of cosmic evolution was indirectly related; but it, too, was not a widely popular view.

Gradually, however, through philosophers such as Charles

Hartshorne, who adopted Whitehead's metaphysic and applied it to the philosophical issues of religion, an increasing number of theologians began to construct a process theology. Among the more prominent have been Norman Pittenger, Daniel Day Williams, Schubert Ogden, John Cobb, and David Griffin. As thoroughly systematic thinkers, they have included Christology among the areas they have reformulated in the light of process categories.

In some ways, process thought can be conceived of as a reaction against a variety of other systems of thought, some of which are contradictory to one another. On the one hand, process thought rejects the analytical and linguistic philosophies that exclude metaphysics. It also rejects Karl Barth's assertion that pure biblical theology must be done without the contaminating effects of any philosophical metaphysic. With a touch of irony Pittenger notes that in rejecting metaphysics both of these competing systems are actually presupposing some sort of metaphysics.[1] Process thought, too, recognizes the weakness of the older metaphysics, which was too grandiose, presumptuous, and inclusive. But instead of rejecting metaphysics out of hand, process theology attempts to construct a much more modest metaphysics, which begins with concrete human experience, then makes generalizations that extend to other areas, and returns again and again to experience for evaluation and validation of these generalizations.[2]

Pittenger has given us a convenient summary of the process understanding of reality.[3] While he is usually identified as one of the leading process theologians of the twentieth century, he does not restrict himself to process thought. He also draws upon the insights of other movements such as emergent evolution, personalism, and existentialism.[4] He notes eight basic tenets of process philosophy:

1. Norman Pittenger, "Process Thought as a Conceptuality for Reinterpreting Christian Faith," *Encounter* 44.2 (Spring 1983): 110.

2. Ibid.

3. Ibid., pp. 111–13; Norman Pittenger, "Christology in Process Theology," *Theology* 80 (1977): 187–88. Other concise summaries of process thought can be found in David R. Griffin, *A Process Christology* (Philadelphia: Westminster, 1973), pp. 167–92; and John B. Cobb, Jr., *God and the World* (Philadelphia: Westminster, 1969), pp. 67–86.

4. Norman Pittenger, *The Word Incarnate: A Study of the Doctrine of the Person of Christ* (New York: Harper, 1959), pp. 146–65.

1. The world is not to be thought of as a collection of things or substances which are essentially static, but of events, occasions, happenings, or occurrences. These events are foci of energy. Reality is, in other words, dynamic.
2. Thus, reality is to be thought of as a process from the past (which is given) through the present (where decisions are made) into the future (which is potential). This process should not necessarily be thought of as progress, however. There is always change, but not invariably for the better.
3. Reality is organic or organismic. It should not be thought of as a collection of disparate events, occurrences, or foci of energy, but as a whole in which everything is related to everything else, and everything influences everything else. Reality is so structured that everything grasps or "prehends" everything else, to use Whitehead's neologism. In a sense broader than the usual meaning of the term, everything "feels" or "grasps" what has gone before, and uses it for its own advance within the process. Whitehead spoke of events in the present prehending those in the past. Pittenger also uses the term to depict the relationship between present events and the future. Decisions made in the present use the content or the influence of the past to actualize the potentialities of the future.
4. There is genuine freedom within this whole system. While the past is utilized within the present, it does not determine the present or the future. This freedom runs throughout the entire universe, but is most fully expressed in human decision. There appears to be a sense in which there is freedom or spontaneity within nonhuman events as well. Given the chance or random factors within the creation, the process of the universe is not completely predetermined and thus not fully predictable.
5. There is a bipolar character to all events. There is, on the one hand, the concrete actualization and, on the other, the abstract possibility. We must think in terms of both what is and what can be. Each event or actual entity has what Whitehead called an "initial aim" or given possibility. Whether that possibility becomes actuality depends

upon whether the entity makes that initial aim its own "subjective aim." If it does, the potentiality is realized. If it does not, the potentiality is not realized.

6. All events are important. Their value varies greatly, however. An event which indicates and contributes to what is going on within the creation is of greater value; an event which merely repeats or reverts to earlier states of affairs is of lesser value.

7. Persuasion, lure, or love is in the long run more effective than coercion or force. The most complete and lasting realizations of the potential which is contained within the cosmos are attained by enticing or eliciting responses of free choice rather than by compelling acquiescence.

8. The fundamental cause of what occurs within the universe is the supreme reality which religion refers to as God. This is by no means the sole cause, for all events have a measure of self-determination. Nor is this God somehow outside of or opposed to that whole of which we are a part. He (or it) is the supreme exemplification of process and of freely chosen actualization of potential. God cannot be surpassed by anything, but is capable of self-surpassing by making use of that which is occurring within the creation.

The Nature of God

We have been looking at broad considerations that form the background against which process theology in general and Christology in particular are constructed. The consideration which bears most heavily upon Christology is the nature of God. The primary attribute of the God of process theology is immanence. We have noted that the process thinkers see all of reality as being of one piece. The characteristics, rules, and processes that pertain to the whole of reality pertain to God as well. Any understanding of God as remote, isolated, and removed from the world is rejected. The idea of a First Cause or a Creator who afterward ceased to be involved in the creation; the idea of God as a lawgiver, moral governor, or justifier of the status quo; the idea of a self-subsistent perfect being—these are all unacceptable to the process theologians. These ideas of God are regarded as either false or inadequate for genuine religion. Instead of beginning with some abstract conception believed to be revealed in some special way, the process theologians hold that the best clue to understanding God's nature will be found by observing human experience and its cosmic setting.

Since God, like everything else in reality, has a bipolar nature, he is not perfect. He is identified with the world, although not identical with it. His participation in the temporal process is different from our limited and defective participation. He has a primordial or abstract pole, which entails his being the source of all creative possibility.[5] He chooses the good for the creatures, and then lures them to accept and thus fulfil this divine intention.[6] God also has a consequent nature: he has goals and possibilities toward which he is moving, or which he is seeking to actualize. He not only affects the world, but is also affected by it. He is moved by what goes on in the creation, being either enriched or saddened by what he encounters. He is not to be thought of as absolute in the sense of being unable to change or grow. He is not omnipotent. There are aspects of the creation which he cannot alter. He works in relationship with it, not by compelling or coercing its members to carry out his desires, but by luring or inducing or persuading them to actualize the goals which he sets for them.[7]

God is not to be thought of as a static possessor of attributes and qualities, but as an active, dynamic, creative being.[8] He is what he does, and what he brings about in others. This means that he is revealed, then, in the whole of the creation. Each event is a revelation of him. Having said this, however, we must observe that there are various degrees of revelation. The degree of revelation is particularly high in those events that adequately disclose what is going on and afford us opportunity to cooperate with God in his ongoing activity.[9]

According to process theologians, the absolute qualities usu-

5. Griffin, *Process Christology*, pp. 181–82.
6. Ibid., p. 175.
7. Ibid., p. 187; Lewis S. Ford, *The Lure of God: A Biblical Background for Process Theism* (Philadelphia: Fortress, 1978), pp. 20–21.
8. Schubert Ogden, "The Reality of God," in *Process Theology: Basic Writings*, ed. Ewert H. Cousins (New York: Newman, 1971), p. 123.
9. Pittenger, "Process Thought as a Conceptuality," p. 114.

ally associated with God are all to be reconceived by analogy with ourselves.[10] Certainly omnipotence cannot be literally true, for God is consequent as well as primordial. Influence is not a one-way street in this scheme. Just as God influences the world, so he is also influenced by it. He must work through events to realize his goals. Nor is he omniscient. While his memory of his past is complete and unfailing, he does not have a similarly exhaustive knowledge of the future. He is dependent upon the occurrence of events to know what they will be.[11] Because there is genuine freedom or spontaneity within the creation, God can only design or intend what is to be, but cannot guarantee or compel the outcomes. In a sense, God can be said to be omnipresent, since he is influentially at work in all parts of the universe, but this is not what has traditionally been meant by that term.

God's primary attribute is love. He is not a divine sovereign who compels by his power. Rather, he respects the freedom of each actual occasion. He works by drawing, luring, enticing, rather than by threatening, forcing, driving. This is the basic attribute of God, Love-in-act, in terms of which all his other attributes must be interpreted. Pittenger says, "Therefore omnipotence can only mean the power of Love, omniscience the wisdom of Love, omnipresence the immediate presence and availability of Love, transcendence the inexhaustibility of Love, immanence the identification of Love with the world in which it is operative."[12]

The Starting Point of Process Christology

Faithfulness to the Doctrinal Aims of the Tradition (Norman Pittenger)

The various methodologies of process Christology can be best understood by noting the respective starting points of each theologian. Norman Pittenger has given more attention to Christology than have the other process thinkers. For him, as an Anglican theologian, the Christian tradition is of more importance than it might be for a Baptist or a Methodist. Thus he points out that he is writing from the perspective of one who is both a "Catholic"

10. Ogden, "The Reality of God," pp. 124–25.
11. Griffin, *Process Christology*, p. 182.
12. Pittenger, "Process Thought as a Conceptuality," p. 115.

and a "modernist." By "Catholic" he means one who stands within the great institutional community of Christianity, and who "values . . . the historical experience of the Christian fellowship conveyed to us all through the sacramental and institutional structures which have come down to us from the past."[13] He also notes early on in what he says will be his final work on Christology that when he speaks of Christ's deity, he is emphasizing the act of God in Christ. This reflects his adoption of the process thinking of Whitehead and Hartshorne.[14] To deal faithfully with the question of Jesus Christ, however, is also to deal faithfully with the Christian tradition, and Pittenger is aware that at this and a number of other points he is in conflict with the tradition.[15]

What does it mean to be faithful to the tradition? To some, faithfulness to the tradition means repeating what has been said. If this is the case, then to remain faithful to the tradition of the patristic age would require Christology to speak of the incarnation in terms of two natures in one person. Others follow the formula of Vincent of Lérins, who held that the task of the theologian is not to speak of new things, but of old things in a new way.[16] Pittenger believes both of these approaches to be mistaken. He cites with approval the statement of Maurice Wiles that true faithfulness to the age of the Fathers goes beyond repeating and building upon their doctrinal conclusions to consciously continuing their doctrinal aims.[17] The essence of the doctrinal task is to do justice to the witness of Scripture, of worship, and of salvation.[18] When we attempt to do this, we inevitably find ourselves not merely saying the old things, even in a new way, but saying new things. But since it is an abiding reality about which we speak, continuity with the aim and objective of traditional theology guarantees that what we say will not be entirely new, though it will be new.[19]

We noted earlier that Pittenger sees himself as not only a Catholic, but also a modernist. By "modernist" he does not mean

---

13. Pittenger, *Word Incarnate*, p. xiv.
14. Norman Pittenger, *Christology Reconsidered* (London: SCM, 1970), p. 2.
15. Ibid., pp. 3–4.
16. Ibid., p. 5.
17. Ibid., p. 4.
18. Ibid., p. 5.
19. Ibid., pp. 5–6.

someone who minimizes the great central affirmations of the Christian faith, but who attempts to penetrate to their essential meaning, and to rethink, reinterpret, and restate that meaning.[20] This sounds as if he is attempting merely to say the old things in a new fashion, and he in fact identifies himself with Thomas Aquinas. His goal is that of George Tyrrell: to reconcile "a perfect loyalty to the fundamentals of the Catholic tradition with an equal loyalty to the claims of scientific truth and moral sincerity."[21]

Already in 1959, however, Pittenger was conscious that he was at points departing from the orthodox christological tradition.[22] By 1970 he was more explicit about the need for actually altering the tradition, and doing so intentionally. There are good reasons why this change is inevitable. All of them are in essence varieties of the truth that much water has gone under the bridge since the creation of the tradition. The world, especially the intellectual world, has changed irreversibly, so that it is not possible to continue to say what the tradition has said.

One of the areas that need rethinking is our understanding of the Bible. The critical study of the Scriptures and especially of the Gospels cannot be undone. We cannot uncritically use the material written about Jesus as if it were straightforward biography. Pittenger accepts the major principle of form criticism that the oral tradition which eventually was put down in writing in the New Testament documents had been modified and shaped by the beliefs and practice of the primitive church community. In writing up the stories of Jesus, the church tended to modify them in the direction of the element of wonder. We should not think of this as deliberate misrepresentation by the early Christians; rather, we should recognize that they were affected by the same influences and laws that governed all such communities in that period of time.[23]

There is another reason why certain elements of the Gospel accounts cannot be accepted and retained. They reflect a first-century worldview which we simply do not and cannot hold today. Pittenger agrees with Rudolf Bultmann that we cannot be

20. Pittenger, *Word Incarnate*, p. xv.
21. Ibid., pp. xv–xvi.
22. Ibid., p. xiv.
23. Pittenger, *Christology Reconsidered*, pp. 14–15.

modern persons and hold the view held and taught by the New Testament writers. The cosmology of the Bible is no longer tenable. Its quasi-scientific, quasi-philosophical orientation became obsolete centuries ago. There is no longer a question of whether we should hold such a view; we cannot.[24]

Pittenger's concern goes even further. It is not merely the particular picture of reality found in the tradition that is unacceptable. We today have a wholly different way of conceiving of the nature of reality. The middle-Platonic and later the neo-Platonic philosophies were dominant in the time of the Fathers. Thus, patristic theology was done within this framework. To do theology today, however, requires a different type of metaphysics. There are two reasons why we can no longer accept traditional metaphysics. First, most of us do not think in static categories. Second, static categories distort the biblical conception of God as living and as vitally related to the world.[25]

Divine Self-Revelation (David Griffin)

More complex is the methodology of David Griffin. In the preface to *A Process Christology* he states that he is attempting to bring together three dimensions of recent theology, all of which have some validity and therefore should be preserved: "(1) the new quest for the historical Jesus, (2) the neo-orthodox emphasis upon God's self-revealing activity in history, and (3) the theology based primarily on the process philosophy of Alfred North Whitehead and Charles Hartshorne."[26] In a sense, it could be argued that Griffin is not a pure process theologian—he is more than a process theologian, for his Christology also incorporates neoorthodoxy and the quest for the historical Jesus.

Griffin recognizes that combining these three dimensions of recent theology will not be easy. In particular, the neoorthodox tended to belittle the quest for the historical Jesus. They also rejected, in the name of divine revelation, any attempt by human rationality to evaluate the Christian faith. Griffin sees process thought as the key to tying together these seemingly competing positions. His thesis is stated in clear and succinct fashion: "I find that the conceptuality provided by process philosophy

---

24. Ibid., pp. 15–16; Pittenger, *Word Incarnate*, p. 18.
25. Pittenger, *Christology Reconsidered*, pp. 16–17.
26. Griffin, *Process Christology*, p. 9.

allows one to maintain both his formal commitment to rationality and his substantive conviction as to the truth of the essentials of Christian faith, at the center of which I place the notion
of the self-revealing activity of a personal God. This can be considered the major thesis of this essay."[27]

Griffin's first step is to show the rationale for using revelation
as the starting point of Christology. He argues that it is through
the cognitive dimension, our outlook on reality, that Jesus first
has saving significance for us. His saving significance for the
affective and volitional dimensions of experience is indirect,
being mediated through the cognitive dimension. Although
Griffin does not want to commit himself to a primarily intellec-
tualistic anthropology and acknowledges Whitehead's emphasis
upon the priority of the affective and the unconscious, he notes
that Whitehead also said that, in the long run, character and
conduct of life depend upon one's ultimate convictions. The
assumption behind Whitehead's statement and Griffin's approach
is that we are in essence religious beings that want to be in harmony with the ultimately real.[28] Appropriate feelings and
actions will follow from a correct understanding of what Jesus
was like.[29]

One objection which has been raised to making the concept of
revelation central to theology is that it is not central in the New
Testament. But there is a good reason why the concept is given
little emphasis in the New Testament, namely, Jesus' view of reality was simply that of the Judaism from which he emerged. In
our day, however, with the variety of ways of viewing reality, and
with the many difficulties attaching to the concept of revelation,
it has become a central component of the Christian faith.[30]

Christ as Transforming Force (John Cobb)

John Cobb develops his Christology against the background
of his earlier work in the field, which included what he calls a
"Jesusology."[31] Seeking to set his Christology in a broader context, he takes note of three characteristics of the present setting:

27. Ibid., p. 10.
28. Ibid., p. 16.
29. Ibid., p. 17.
30. Ibid., pp. 19–20.
31. John B. Cobb, Jr., *Christ in a Pluralistic Age* (Philadelphia: Westminster, 1975), p. 13.

(1) the commitment of the modern mind to the profane and the pluralistic; (2) openness to other religious traditions; and (3) the need to live together on spaceship Earth.[32] His endeavor is frankly apologetic, an attempt to locate Christ in contemporary experience. He has chosen to begin with the present, with our experience, and then to work through the past to the future.[33] He begins by showing how Christ is experienced in the present; he then relates this experience to the Jesus of Scripture and Christian tradition, and afterwards to some images of hope.

Cobb notes that there has been a loss of the sense and the pertinence of Christ. The traditional ways of thinking of Christ are no longer relevant.[34] Attempting to find a new way to experience Christ, Cobb turns to art. He traces the way in which Western art has depicted Christ. It seems on the surface that art has triumphed over Christ, since Christ is in the Christian tradition particularized, while art has tended to generalize. In reality, however, Christ is the force inducing the process of "creative transformation."[35] Cobb takes the biblical concept of the Logos and gives it a Whiteheadian twist. The Logos supplies each event or actual entity with its initial aim, its potentiality, and lures it to do more than simply repeat habitual existence, that is, entices it to realize that potentiality. The enabler of this creative transformation is the "incarnate Logos," the "Christ."[36]

Cobb then shows how the life of Jesus fits into this pattern of creative transformation. Jesus did not simply repeat that which was already present within Judaism, nor did he bring into being something totally new. Instead, he transformed the tradition. In turn, Jesus has had a transforming effect upon the history of our world and in personal encounter with us. This suggests a special relation of the incarnate Logos to Jesus of Nazareth. When the incarnate Logos evokes such a total response of creative novelty, the self involved can be said to be constituted by the Logos. Jesus so realized the potentiality supplied by the incarnate Logos that we can say that Jesus was Christ.[37]

32. Ibid., pp. 18, 22.
33. Ibid., p. 23.
34. Ibid., p. 17.
35. Ibid., pp. 43, 61.
36. Ibid., pp. 76–78.
37. Ibid., p. 142.

Substantive Christology

The Humanity of Jesus

As we turn now to the substantive issues of Christology, we come first to the humanity of Jesus. Here there is a general agreement among the process theologians that Jesus was indeed human. They assert that this is the one common point of agreement among most Christologies today.[38] Yet there are still some significant questions as to what that means.

Pittenger has pointed out that virtually all contemporary theologians have rejected both outright Docetism, according to which Jesus only seemed to assume humanity, but did not really do so, and partial Docetism, the view that Jesus took all of the physical aspects of humanity, but not the human center of personality.[39] Now if Jesus was truly human, Pittenger asks, what can we know about his person and life? This is the question of the historical Jesus of Nazareth. The issue is important, for belief in the full humanity of Jesus makes little real difference if we cannot place him at certain times and locations. If the historical Jesus is for us an unknown quantity, there is little significance in asserting that he lived.

There must therefore be historical research into Jesus' person and the type of man he was. And there must be no short-circuiting of the process. Some attempt to do this in a most peculiar way. They affirm the importance of the historicity of Jesus. Yet at the same time they deny that there are data of such a nature that a secular historian would be compelled to acknowledge them. One might expect that these theologians would therefore give up belief in the historical Jesus. Instead they affirm that the very existence of the Christian faith, with its theological demand that a supposed incarnation must have been historically grounded, establishes the actuality of the historical event. Without identifying the authors, Pittenger rejects such Christologies as both absurd and incredible.[40] He cites a comment by Dean William Inge about the superstructure supporting the foundations.

---

38. See, e.g., Pittenger, *Christology Reconsidered*, p. 22.
39. Ibid.
40. Ibid., pp. 23–24.

Pittenger points out two senses of the term *historical* as applied to Jesus. First, it means that we can affirm, on the basis of reasonable induction from the available evidence, that there was such a person and that he was involved in certain specific events. Second, it means that Jesus and the events of his life have modified attitudes and created new convictions and insights. Pittenger believes that Christian theologians must declare that Jesus of Nazareth was historical in both senses.[41]

Pittenger takes note of how New Testament criticism has changed the issue. It is no longer possible to take the Gospels as firsthand accounts of what certain observers heard Jesus say and saw him do. Form criticism has rendered that impossible. We now know that what we have in the Gospels are the results of the passing on of an oral tradition by the church. We have only the church's interpretation of Jesus. This should not lead us to skepticism, however. We may not be able to be absolutely sure of the details, but we do have, "at the very least, a highly probable portrait of a real man."[42]

To emphasize Jesus' connectedness with us, Pittenger underscores that Jesus was a person of his time. Since no one nowadays questions the genuineness of Jesus' human body,[43] it is with respect to his psychological humanness that this emphasis needs to be made. Psychological humanness

> entails being limited by those processes through which men come to know whatever they know, think whatever they think, and share in those depths of consciousness which, whether inherited from our ancestors or established in us through our social relationships, have so much to do with determining what we shall know and think. . . . [Jesus] thought like a Jew, he understood as a Jew understood. . . . It is not only theologically wrong to see him in any other light; it is also untrue to the evidence which we possess.[44]

He learned by experience, just as we do. An example is to be found in the story of the Syrophoenician woman whose daughter Jesus is said to have healed (Mark 7:24–30). Until he encountered this woman, Jesus held the common Jewish conception

41. Ibid., pp. 24–25.
42. Ibid., p. 30.
43. Ibid., p. 35.
44. Ibid., pp. 35–36.

that salvation was only for the Jews.[45] Moreover, there is no doubt in Pittenger's mind that on some matters Jesus was mistaken. For example, he held, as did the Jews of his time, that certain kinds of illness, especially what we today call emotional illness, were caused by demon possession. He could not have believed otherwise, if his humanity was genuine.[46]

Pittenger is clear that he is talking about Jesus' being a flesh-and-blood man, not some generic humanity. Jesus was a concrete human individual who lived in a definite time and place. Of course, if he had been some abstract form of humanity, we might evade the fact of his limitation. There can be no denying, however, that his was a humanity which went all the way through.[47]

To some extent, the real test of a view of Jesus' humanity is its conception of his status vis-à-vis human sin. Seeing this issue as important, Pittenger starts his discussion further back than do most writers. He begins by considering just what the meaning of sin is, and that involves a thorough consideration of what human nature is. Here his process thought asserts itself quite clearly. As might be expected, Pittenger does not think of humanity in static fashion. Rather, he sees us essentially as "dynamic creatures with a thrust or drive towards the realization of potentiality."[48] Three factors are operant here: the past, which involves the whole of our memory, both conscious and unconscious; present involvement in a whole constellation of relationships; and an aim or general direction we are to pursue.[49] The initial aim which God has provided for each of us is the actualizing of a deep, comprehensive love uniting us with one another and thus with the source of that love, God.[50] When human nature and purpose are understood this way, sin is seen, not as the breaking of commandments, but as the distortion of our aim.[51] Sin is failure to accept and seek to fulfil the initial aim which God has for us, namely, becoming what we are capable of being through love. Sinfulness and sinlessness are, then, more a matter of our direction than of our specific acts.

45. Ibid., p. 37.
46. Ibid., p. 38.
47. Ibid., p. 44.
48. Ibid., p. 47.
49. Ibid., pp. 47–48.
50. Ibid., p. 50.
51. Ibid., p. 51.

Is it possible to demonstrate from the material available to us that Jesus was absolutely sinless? Pittenger answers that question in the negative. He is not bothered primarily by the portions of Scripture that seem to suggest some sort of imperfection in Jesus. For he believes that most of them can be explained away. Rather, the overriding consideration is that there are vast segments of Jesus' life about which we simply have insufficient information. And so Pittenger suggests that we view the issue from a different perspective. The question which must be asked is whether the material in the Gospels is sufficient to assure us of the direction of Jesus' life.[52] Pittenger answers this question in the affirmative. Though Jesus shared in the deficiency of the human situation, and though he had to learn obedience, nonetheless the direction of his life was unswervingly toward fulfilment of the aim given to him initially by God—he made God's aim his own.[53] Whatever be the actual incidents which lie behind the stories of the baptism and the temptation in the Gospels, those stories show a person who, although he struggled to fulfil his mission, remained true to his decision to realize fully the potentiality God intended for him.[54] This view of Jesus' sinlessness does not remove him from humanity, as do some Christologies which proclaim that sin is a universal and essential part of human nature. Jesus was fully human, and yet by perfectly actualizing his aim, he can also be said to have been sinless.[55]

In Griffin's Christology, the humanity of Jesus is presupposed. The crucial question is whether and in what sense the assertion that God was uniquely present in Jesus can be harmonized with the assertion of his full humanity. For if we cannot show that a statement incorporating both of these assertions is not a self-contradiction, this key christological doctrine is merely a meaningless combination of words.[56] Griffin's uncompromising commitment to the complete humanity of Jesus is also seen in his thoroughgoing criticism of Friedrich Schleiermacher's view, which he regards as at least partially docetic.[57]

---

52. Ibid., p. 55.
53. Ibid., p. 57.
54. Ibid., pp. 59–60.
55. Ibid., pp. 63–64.
56. Griffin, *Process Christology*, p. 142.
57. Ibid., pp. 123–34.

Cobb is concerned lest his conception of Jesus as embodying the Logos be misconstrued as precluding his full humanity. One way of avoiding this is to point out that the Christ is present within all human beings, and even within all of reality. Thus, if on this ground Jesus cannot be fully human, neither can we.

There is another aspect of Cobb's explanation. We must re-examine what it means to be human. It is commonly assumed that the word *human* refers to some fixed mode of being.[58] Accordingly, it is not possible for an entity to enter a human being without in some way displacing part of that person. Thus, according to traditional Christology, for God to have been present within Jesus would have required the displacement of some part of his human nature, whether physical, psychological, or both. In process thought, however, this is not so. There is not a fixed quality to the nature of a human being. Rather, a person is a dynamic, changing set of relationships. So entity A can be present within B without displacing any part of B. Rather, B prehends A; that is, A is incorporated into B's existence. "B would not be what it is apart from this presence. B does not first exist and then incorporate A; rather this incorporation is constitutive of B's coming into existence."[59] Thus, for God to be present and active within Jesus in no sense diminishes his genuine humanity.[60] Repeatedly, Cobb emphasizes not only his belief in the humanity of Jesus, but its importance and even indispensability.[61] He summarizes his essential contention: "The one God was thus uniquely present in him. At the same time, Jesus was fully human and no aspect of his humanity was displaced by God. It was a thoroughly human 'I' that was constituted by God's presence in Jesus."[62]

The Divinity of Jesus

We now turn to consider whether and in what sense we may speak of Jesus as divine, or, to shape the question to process

58. John B. Cobb, Jr., "A Whiteheadian Christology," in *Process Philosophy and Christian Thought*, ed. Delwin Brown, Ralph E. James, Jr., and Gene Reeves (Indianapolis: Bobbs-Merrill, 1971), pp. 383–84.
59. Ibid., pp. 384–85.
60. Cobb, *Christ in a Pluralistic Age*, p. 140.
61. Ibid., pp. 170, 184; Cobb, "A Whiteheadian Christology," pp. 383, 390.
62. Ibid., p. 394.

theology, in what sense Jesus is an incarnation of God. Pittenger named his first book on Christology *The Word Incarnate: A Study of the Doctrine of the Person of Christ*, thus indicating how strongly he believed in the incarnation. He argues that we may properly call the divine action and operation in the world, whether in nature or in history, "the Word of God."[63] He emphasizes that the relationship of God and the world is not an occasional or special matter: "God and man are always in relationship—by the fact of man's creation, by the continual grounding of human life in the Divine Logos or Word, by the union however incomplete of the purpose of God and the will of man, and in many other ways."[64] This activity of God in humans is found most fully in Christ. Rejecting concepts like substances and natures, process theologians see this internal working of the Word as the grounds of the divinity of Jesus: "That which the divinity of Christ denotes is the *act* of God the Word in him; and the unity of the divinity and manhood in him is the *coincidence* of the divine and human acts, the act of God and the act of man."[65]

In *Christology Reconsidered*, Pittenger emphasizes the meaning of human personhood. He points out that a person is not some fixed, isolated entity, but rather is the focusing of one's past history, present relationships, and future influence.[66] God's activity in an individual must be understood as occurring in and through this whole constellation. His activity in the event which we call by the name of Jesus must be seen in the entirety of that event, not merely in the discrete individual who was at its center. "It is entirely appropriate that the name of Jesus should be given to the event whose central figure he is, but it would be a false abstraction to isolate the central figure from his context."[67]

Pittenger stresses, as do all of the process theologians, the importance of the response to or acceptance of the divine initiative. God does not coerce or control history. The human response is as essential as the divine initiative. The positive reaction of Mary in Luke 1:38, "Let it be to me according to your

63. Pittenger, *Word Incarnate*, p. 180.
64. Ibid.
65. Ibid., p. 181.
66. Pittenger, *Christology Reconsidered*, p. 78.
67. Ibid., p. 81.

word," is a very significant but frequently overlooked component in the nativity story. The human response was also a vital factor during Jesus' earthly life and in the attitudes taken toward him afterward. God's ability to act is conditional upon the willingness of persons to have him act. Summarizing his understanding of the incarnation, Pittenger says:

> In conclusion, we may suggest that the answer to the question of the location of the Incarnation should be along these lines. The *locus* of that specific activity of God which we designate when we say Jesus Christ is the total complex of event, compounded of long Jewish preparation, the appearance and life of Jesus himself, the response made to him as he was received in the days of Palestine, in the experience of him as risen from among the dead, and in the primitive and continuing Christian community which also responded to him—and, by a legitimate extension, the totality of his impact upon human history down to the present moment. The man of Nazareth is indeed the centre, or as I have phrased it the focus, of that activity of God. Hence the activity is appropriately and even necessarily called by his name, since what he was remembered to have been has qualified the forms in which it has been understood, received, and implemented. . . . In the words of [John] Knox . . . it is Jesus-in-the-midst-of-his-own—past, present, future—who constitutes the proper location of God's activity which Christians have come to denote by the word incarnation.[68]

Griffin, as we have noted earlier, approaches Christology from the perspective of revelation. Significantly, the central chapter of his book *Process Christology* is entitled "God's Supreme Act of Self-Expression."[69] Griffin understands Jesus to be a special act of God, and indeed God's supreme act. Three considerations are stressed here: (1) Jesus' message, both in word and in deed, expresses a particular vision of God's character and purpose; (2) Jesus' active ministry was rooted in God's aim for him; yet (3) it is not to be understood as rooted only in God's aim for him. Griffin sees the message of Jesus as presupposing the vision of reality found in Judaism. What was new about his message, then, was not some innovative element, but the way in which the various constitutive elements were weighted.

68. Ibid., p. 86.
69. Griffin, *Process Christology*, p. 206.

Because of the tradition from which Jesus came, he was particularly well situated to be given by God a special initial aim which directly reflected the divine purpose and character. His acceptance of that aim, however, was not automatic. There had to be, and there was, a free decision by Jesus to accept it.[70] Thereafter, his active ministry was completely rooted in God's aim for him.

Griffin focuses on the fact that there was something special about Jesus' relation to God. If this were not the case, it would be inaccurate to refer to him as God's supreme act. This means that Jesus' life is the supreme example of the way in which God acts in relation to the world.[71] That action of God is not coercion or absolute causation, but sympathy and love—God is affected by and responds to what transpires in the world.[72] There is nothing about Jesus' life to suggest that God completely controls the acts of humankind. The crucifixion is an excellent demonstration of that.[73] To climax the argument on the uniqueness of God's presence in Jesus, Griffin utilizes Schleiermacher's conception of religion as God-consciousness: "In Jesus the consciousness of God was dominant over the other elements. Hence the presence of God in Jesus constituted his selfhood in a way that was not the case in other men."[74]

Cobb, as we pointed out earlier, approaches Christology by tracing the power of creative transformation within culture. This power he terms the Logos or the Christ. He argues that the Logos is incarnate in all things. To say, therefore, that the Logos is incarnate in Jesus is true but insufficient. What Cobb sees in Jesus is the paradigm case of incarnation: "In the fullest incarnation of the Logos, its presence must constitute not only a necessary aspect of existence but the self as such. Embodiment of this structure of existence explains Jesus' certainty and authority."[75]

What would be involved in an embodiment of the Logos? Cobb notes that the "I," the organizing center of human experience, is usually understood as being continuous with the "I" of preceding moments of experience. And the call to the Christian life is

---

70. Ibid., pp. 216–20.
71. Ibid., p. 223.
72. Ibid., p. 224.
73. Ibid., pp. 225–26.
74. Ibid., pp. 227–28.
75. Cobb, *Christ in a Pluralistic Age*, p. 138.

usually understood as coming from without.[76] There is another possibility, however, in which the Logos actually constitutes selfhood, or is "identical with the center or principle in terms of which other elements in experience are ordered."[77] In such a case the "I" is in each moment constituted as much by the "subjective reception of the lure to self-actualization that is the call and presence of the Logos" as by continuity with the personal past.[78] This picture of a human person fits with what we know of Jesus. Because of his unity with God's present purposes for him, he could even set aside the rules which embodied God's past purposes. He presented his teachings without citing textual or empirical support. This he could do because his perspective on things was coconstituted by the Logos within him.[79] The Gospels give indication, however, that Jesus was not totally free from the struggle between the "I" and the Logos. That was part of his being fully human. What was new about him was the full incarnation of the Logos in him. We do not know whether this may have been true of any others. That is an open question, since we do not have exhaustive knowledge of all persons within history; but so far as we know, Jesus was unique.[80]

The Uniqueness of Jesus

We must now deal with the crucial question of the uniqueness of Jesus. The argument of all of our process theologians has been that God was at work in Jesus. In view of this divine activity, it is appropriate to speak of Jesus as divine. Throughout, however, the process theologians are also careful to point out that God is at work everywhere in his world, and especially with humans. We must ask whether there is any sense in which God was at work in Jesus but not in other humans. Here we may note the classification of process Christologies by Thomas Idinopulos. Cobb and Griffin maintain that Jesus is very special and therefore can be appropriately referred to as unique. Pittenger, Schubert Ogden, and Peter Hamilton, on the other hand, hold that Jesus Christ is just a special, not a very special

76. Ibid., pp. 138–39.
77. Ibid., p. 139.
78. Ibid., p. 140.
79. Ibid., p. 141.
80. Ibid., p. 142; Cobb, "A Whiteheadian Christology," p. 394.

revelation, and therefore is different only in degree, not in kind, from God's other revelations.[81]

Let us look first at Pittenger's thought. He faces the issue very directly, even entitling a chapter of *Christology Reconsidered* "Different in Degree or in Kind?" He there states, "In *The Word Incarnate* I argued that the difference could be much more satisfactorily stated in terms of degrees than in terms of kind. I should still maintain this position, although with certain qualifications which will appear as we proceed."[82] It thus appears that Idinopulos has been fair in his categorization. Pittenger would object, however, to any inference that a difference in degree is inherently slight. There may be the greatest possible difference in degree. Although he does not like arithmetical ways of speaking, he would hold that the difference between Jesus Christ and even Francis of Assisi is enormous.[83] On the other hand, the humanity of Jesus was ordinary; it was the same as ours. He did not have some peculiar channel of communication with God or powers not available to others. Jesus was unique in the sense that every human is unique. There is something about each person's humanity that is special. Jesus, however, fulfilled his potentiality, God's original aim for him, to a degree that stood out from others of his time and of other times. Pittenger comments:

> Jesus, in the dynamic existence which was his, fulfilled the potentialities which were also his in a manner that impressed those who companied with him as being extraordinary without being a violation of the ordinary conditions of manhood. . . . His degree of realization was not the same as that of other men whom his companions knew; it was immeasurably different yet not utterly removed from the experience of manhood elsewhere seen.[84]

We may, then, speak of Jesus as qualitatively different from other humans, but only in the sense in which each human is qualitatively different from every other.[85] When Pittenger specifically faces the question of the uniqueness of Jesus, he notes that,

81. Thomas A. Idinopulos, "A Critical Appraisal of Differing Process Christologies," *Encounter* 37.2 (Spring 1976): 212.

82. Pittenger, *Christology Reconsidered*, p. 111.

83. Ibid., p. 112.

84. Ibid., pp. 119–20.

85. Ibid., p. 121.

technically, "uniqueness" means "absolutely and completely different from anything else."[86] If unique in this sense, Jesus would be removed from the realm of the human and historical. Pittenger appeals to C. F. D. Moule's distinction between uniqueness of exclusion and uniqueness of inclusion. The former admits of no parallels or similarities. The latter, which is the sense in which the word *unique* can be applied to Jesus, "is regarded as including within it, but in some eminent manner, values or characteristics or qualities which have been found elsewhere but in a much less adequate fashion."[87] We may speak of a certain uniqueness of Jesus, but it does not take him from his context. Indeed, it emphasizes his context within Judaism. He penetrated to the very heart of the Jewish awareness of God and united with it a fresh understanding of humankind; in so doing he "established a new intensity in the relationship between God and man."[88]

Pittenger denies any conception of Jesus that would exclude from authentic existence or salvation any who do not accept him.[89] This false Christocentrism, which would make Jesus an exclusive revelation of God, he steadfastly rejects. The major problem is that it contradicts the basic Christian insight, namely, that God is love.[90] What makes Jesus "unique" in the inclusive sense is that in the love which he exhibited as a man there is the most intense and most generous revelation of God's love that we find anywhere.[91] This love is not different in kind, but only in degree, from other instances. Indeed, Pittenger takes exception to Anders Nygren's *Agape and Eros*, with its qualitative distinction between the love of God and human love.[92]

Griffin and Cobb emphasize much more than does Pittenger the specialness of Jesus. Cobb sees this specialness particularly in contrast with the prophets. Unlike them, Jesus' "I" was not in contrast with the divine "I." Rather, he saw his authority as that of God.[93] It was not that the Logos was more fully incarnate in

86. Ibid., p. 125.
87. Ibid.
88. Ibid., p. 128.
89. Ibid., pp. 89–93.
90. Ibid., p. 93.
91. Ibid., p. 94.
92. Ibid., p. 130.
93. Cobb, "A Whiteheadian Christology," p. 392; *Christ in a Pluralistic Age*, p. 137.

Jesus than in anyone else, but that the Logos constituted his self-hood. In all respects Jesus *was* Christ.[94]

Griffin takes much the same approach. He insists that "unless there is something about God's action in Jesus that differs from his action elsewhere, it is misleading to speak of Jesus as God's special or decisive act."[95] This requires that there be something special about his relation to God.[96] Griffin cites with approval Schleiermacher's description of Jesus as supremely conscious of God. He then appeals to Cobb's historical argument distinguishing Jesus from the prophets. He differs from Cobb, however, in emphasizing not merely Jesus' sense of authority, but the content of his message:

> In summary, then, the Christian belief that Jesus is God's decisive revelation can be understood to be a real possibility in terms of the following conceptualization. Partly because of the content of the divine aims given to Jesus during his active ministry, and partly because of Jesus' conformance to these aims, the vision of reality expressed through his sayings and actions is the supreme expression of God's character, purpose, and mode of agency, and is therefore appropriately apprehended as the decisive revelation of the same. The finality of this expression is due to the fact that at least at decisive moments Jesus identified himself with the divine aims for him, so that he provided no hindrance to the expression of the divine Logos other than that which is inherent in human nature as such.[97]

Analysis

How shall we appraise the value of process Christology or, to be more accurate, this cluster of Christologies? Because we are dealing here with a genuine Christology which presents a clear alternative to traditional or orthodox Christology, it is important that we evaluate it carefully. Before we do so, however, it would be well to make some general analytical observations.

Process Christology is clearly built upon a self-consciously developed metaphysic. Indeed, it begins with the adoption of a

94. Cobb, *Christ in a Pluralistic Age*, p. 142.
95. Griffin, *Process Christology*, p. 220.
96. Ibid., p. 221.
97. Ibid., pp. 231–32.

particular philosophy deemed to have potential for use in constructing a theology. The basic concepts of process philosophy have been applied to each of the traditional areas of theology, such as human personality, the nature and activity of God, and, most important for our present purposes, the person of Christ. The process theologians come back repeatedly to the elements of this philosophy as they construct their Christology.

We have here a Christology built on the idea of an immanent God. It is true that Pittenger, reserving the term *immanence* for the work of the Holy Spirit, rejects it as a christological designation for the relationship of the Word to the creation.[98] Nonetheless, a God who is involved in every aspect of reality, who shares the characteristics of the rest of reality, and is governed by the same laws must surely be referred to as immanent.

In the process theologians we also have a case of what William Hordern has termed "transformers" as contrasted with "translators."[99] Whereas translators endeavor to maintain the essence or basic meaning of Christianity and express it in forms and terms intelligible to the present time, transformers are willing to make significant alterations or even deletions of major elements of the traditional faith in order to make it acceptable to the modern world. The process theologians are open about their willingness and even eagerness to transform what they see as outmoded ways of thinking.

There is also a thorough commitment to historical-critical study of the Bible. This is perhaps most evident in Pittenger's use of the conclusions of form criticism, but it is also prominent in Cobb's writing. To affirm the historicity of the incarnation, they maintain, requires research into the actual history of the man Jesus. It is notable, however, that they utilize Scripture in a rather broad and general fashion. There are very few citations of specific passages of Scripture.

Finally, there is a strong and unquestioning commitment to the humanity of Jesus. This is scarcely argued, being an underlying assumption. Care is taken, however, to avoid anything resembling Docetism. The strong emphasis upon the oneness of Jesus with the rest of the human race and his participation in a

98. Pittenger, *Christology Reconsidered*, p. 113.
99. William E. Hordern, *New Directions in Theology Today*, vol. 1, *Introduction* (Philadelphia: Westminster, 1966), pp. 141–46.

typical constellation—past history, present relationships, and future influence—where God's activity occurs leads to a diminution of any radical uniqueness of Jesus among humans. While Cobb and Griffin emphasize the very special nature of Jesus, and Pittenger insists that there are extreme differences in degree (though not in kind) between Jesus and others, the question remains, Is there anything about Jesus that could not also, at least theoretically, be true of us as well? It appears that the answer of process Christology is no.

Evaluation

Let us now seek to evaluate process Christology, beginning with the positive features:

1. The process theologians have made a definite and concerted effort to develop a theology by using a well-worked-out metaphysic. We have come through a period in the history of Christian thought when any use of philosophy was eschewed. This was most notably true of the writings of Karl Barth, but also, to lesser extent, of the work of a number of other theologians. Yet when we deal with the doctrine of God or the doctrine of the person of Christ, it is very difficult to ignore the metaphysical issues. The process theologians have seen that questions such as the relationship of God to the world are metaphysical issues. To fail to address them consciously is to answer them unconsciously and thus poorly. Everyone necessarily has a metaphysic, whether implicit or explicit; the process theologians have chosen to make theirs explicit.

2. There also is an attempt to do a genuinely new metaphysic. In a sense, there has been no full-scale treatment of metaphysics since the various forms of nineteenth-century idealism. This is perhaps due in some measure to the aversion to metaphysics on the part of a number of twentieth-century schools—analytical, existentialist, and pragmatic. Philosophy, redefined by those movements, largely abandoned the attempt to give ultimate, synoptic answers. Theology, however, of necessity must make some of those judgments. With full consciousness of the objections raised in the twentieth century, process theology has tried to deal with such issues. It has attempted to construct a metaphysic and thus also a set of theological doctrines based upon some of the

contemporary understandings in fields such as physics. There is a consciousness that to be relevant, or at least to be perceived as relevant, a theology must address the questions currently posed by general learning and even secular culture. Process theology, then, has a genuinely apologetic dimension.

3. There is a rightful objection to the rather static and immobile conceptions sometimes attached to the orthodox view of God and even of Jesus Christ. While this objection more often than not takes the form of a caricature which orthodox theologians have denied, there is a need for dissociating Christian theology from some aspects of Greek thought.

4. Process theologians recognize that the form in which Christology was discussed in the past is not meaningful today. It may well be that terms like "person" and "nature" carried meaning for the fourth and fifth centuries, but they do not convey that same meaning for the twentieth century. Moreover, some of the issues discussed in the past are now recognized to have been pseudoproblems or cases of excessive hairsplitting. Such doctrines as the *communicatio idiomatum* are shown to be meaningless or unintelligible or superfluous.

5. Process Christology has endeavored to preserve the doctrine of the genuine humanity of Jesus. While there has been little real Docetism in the twentieth century, little real denial that Jesus was fully human, there has been a certain amount of practical Docetism. It has been contended, for example, that the historical life of Jesus has no significance for faith, or is inaccessible to us, or that Jesus' humanity was in some sense removed from our humanity. In some cases the implications of his full humanity have not been drawn. By contrast, process Christology has made a genuine effort to take Jesus' humanity and his place within history very seriously.

6. A strong emphasis upon the love of God mirrors correctly the biblical stress upon this aspect of God's nature. At times process theology offers an interpretation or draws an inference that is difficult to reconcile with the biblical view of God's love, but the general emphasis is appropriate. Love, rather than some sort of mechanical force, is declared to be the basis of the relationship between the divine and human in Jesus. In like manner, love, rather than coercion, is declared to be the basis of God's dealing with his human creatures.

7. Process Christology attempts to engage in dialogue with various non-Christian religions, and to recognize the value in them, while still in some way maintaining the uniqueness and special place of Jesus. This endeavor varies with different process theologians, and with different religions, being most prominent in John Cobb's interest in Buddhism.

What, then, are the difficulties and weaknesses in the process Christologies? A large number of problems have been pointed out by various thinkers, including some from within the general school of process thought:

1. We find a lack of clarity regarding the status of Scripture, which is a basic issue for any theology. Presumably, every Christian theology must give some attention to the Bible. In process Christology, however, we find an imprecise, inconsistent, and selective use of Scripture, suggesting a poor assimilation of the doctrine of Scripture into the system. There seems to be a tendency to utilize the general themes of Scripture, but with very little specific citation and very little of what would ordinarily be called exegesis. Beyond that, those general topics that are drawn upon are narrowly selected. There is a lack of treatment of themes such as creation, evil, and eschatology, vital issues for a Christology to address. Gabriel Fackre has pointed out that Cobb pays little attention to the Old Testament, even though he maintains Jesus built upon the Old Testament traditions.[100]

2. More generally, the issue of authority is not adequately addressed. There has been considerable discussion of the general nature of process philosophy and its specific tenets, but the question of authority (as contrasted with the issue of methodology) has been addressed only by Ogden.[101] And his treatments of the subject tend to be generic to liberalism rather than specific to process theology.

3. There is a clear commitment to dialogue with contemporary culture. We must ask, however, whether more has been conceded than need be. If the entire agenda of a theology is allowed to be set by secular culture, is that theology really a message spoken to

100. Gabriel Fackre, "Cobb's *Christ in a Pluralistic Age*: A Review Article," *Andover Newton Quarterly* 17.4 (March 1977): 313–14.

101. Schubert Ogden, "The Authority of Scripture for Theology," *Interpretation* 30 (July 1976): 242–61; idem, "Sources of Authority in Liberal Protestantism," *Journal of the American Academy of Religion* 44 (Sept. 1976): 403–16.

its culture, or is it simply an echo of secularism? And why should one choose that theology as an alternative to secularism? Fackre pointed out already in 1977 that analysts of culture are now making less sweeping assessments of both the extent and the irreversibility of the secularization process.[102] One of the problems which liberalism had was too close a tie to and articulation with the secular culture of its time, so that it was either constantly changing, or else failing to maintain its claim to relevance.

4. Process Christology seems to assume that the new is more valuable than what has preceded it. However, as Mary Rattigan has pointed out, change is not necessarily for the better.[103] What criteria has process theology been utilizing in making such a judgment? Indeed, does it have any real basis for such a judgment, or is this simply an a priori?

5. A number of doctrines which have a vital connection with Christology seem to be omitted or at least inadequately developed; among these are sin, Jesus' preexistence and virgin birth, the crucifixion and resurrection, the apocalyptic expectation of his return, and the question of our personal immortality.[104] Perhaps the most serious omission is the lack of any real emphasis upon creation, which forms the backdrop of so much of biblical discussion. It may, of course, be replied that these doctrines assume a rather literal and authoritative understanding of Scripture, which the process theologians do not hold; but the real difficulty is their lack of a clearly defined view of Scripture, as pointed out earlier. The result is the impression that the ideas they expound are derived from a philosophy rather than the Christian tradition.

6. There is insufficient basis for maintaining the unique status of Jesus as a religious teacher, even within the Judeo-Christian tradition. Cobb and Griffin struggle mightily to demonstrate a specialness, and do so particularly by pointing to Jesus' complete acceptance of God's initial aim for him, and to his God-consciousness and sense of authority, in which he clearly surpassed the prophets. Idinopulos, however, responds to Cobb that

102. Fackre, "Cobb's *Christ*," p. 311.
103. Mary T. Rattigan, "The Christology of John Cobb," *Encounter* 47.3 (Summer 1986): 208.
104. Gilbert Sanders, "Christology and Norman Pittenger," *Encounter* 44.2 (Spring 1983): 121–24; Fackre, "Cobb's *Christ*," pp. 314–15.

"on my reading of the Bible, Jesus' authority and consciousness do not appear to be at all different from the authority and consciousness of the Prophets, and if there were a difference we would have no way of knowing it."[105] The key words here are "on my reading of the Bible," for there does not seem to be a great deal of difference between the way in which Idinopulos and Cobb read the Bible. Given process theology's imprecise use of the Bible, how does one really know what Jesus' God-consciousness and sense of authority were?

7. More broadly, the case for the specialness or uniqueness of Jesus is rather unconvincing in all of the process Christologies. Can the distinctiveness of Jesus really be maintained? There seems to be no reason for saying that what happened in Jesus could not happen in others as well, including us, and perhaps to a greater degree. Cobb states that someone of whom we have no record may have approximated Jesus, but that this is idle speculation.[106] Griffin argues that Jesus was God's supreme act of self-expression, for (1) God's initial aim for him directly reflected, to an unsurpassable degree, his own eternal character and purpose; and (2) Jesus fulfilled that aim, also to an unsurpassable degree.[107] Lewis Ford, however, says, "We could confess that for us God has appeared in Jesus to an *unsurpassed* degree, but have we any warrant for saying that it is impossible in principle for this revelation ever to be surpassed in the future, or by intelligent life elsewhere in the universe?"[108] It seems evident that on the grounds advanced, the answer must be no. Griffin has moved from "unsurpassed" to "unsurpassable," an illicit transition.

8. One of the aims of process theology has been a continued openness to and dialogue with other religions, but it appears that in at least one case there is difficulty. Clark Williamson points out that Cobb calls for an openness toward Judaism, but that the structure of Christian existence transcends prophetic existence and, by implication, Judaism. If Jesus has effected a creative transformation of the tradition in which he was nurtured, how can there be openness to a system which rejects that

105. Idinopulos, "Critical Appraisal," p. 212.

106. Cobb, *Christ in a Pluralistic Age*, p. 142.

107. Griffin, *Process Christology*, p. 216.

108. Lewis S. Ford, "The Possibilities for Process Christology," *Encounter* 35.4 (Autumn 1974): 293.

transformation?[109] Openness to Judaism would create a serious dilemma as to whether the Logos is to be regarded as universal or uniquely embodied in Jesus, a man whose very identity was formed by the Christ.

9. The final criticism has been implicit in many of the preceding comments. At what point do we have to say that we can no longer identify process Christology as Christianity? How many of the distinctive features of what has traditionally been termed Christianity can be safely discarded before we have to say that what is left is a generic religion that is not entitled to the designation *Christian*? Even process philosophers allow for some strand, some abstract essence, to be carried over from each occasion to the next.[110] What, precisely, is that abstract essence of Christianity which distinguishes it from other religions, ways of life, and philosophies? Rattigan puts this criticism neatly:

> In a series of transformations of beliefs, a consequence of not adhering to any specific doctrines about Jesus might well be a view of the person of Jesus having no features in common with previously held Christian understandings. At least there is nothing to prevent this from happening. And so we ask: How elastic can we expect Christology to be? How far can we expand our understanding of Jesus through other insights without being destructive of Christian self-identity?[111]

Perhaps at the very root of the difficulties of process theology is an unresolved dilemma, or even a contradiction. There is a desire to identify Jesus with the rest of humanity, and yet to make him unique and supreme for faith, but without appealing to abstract essences or substances. If this tension is not to have fatal effects for process theology, it will have to be resolved.

109. Clark M. Williamson, "Anti-Judaism in Process Christologies?" *Process Studies* 10.3–4 (1980): 86.

110. Griffin, *Process Christology*, p. 211.

111. Rattigan, "Christology of John Cobb," p. 215.

11

The Anthropological Problem.
(1) Universalist Christology

It is sometimes observed that the doctrine of the incarnation is a statement as much about God as about Christ. In many ways that is true. It is not the entire truth, however, for the doctrine of the incarnation also says a great deal about the human race. It maintains that God entered the human race in incarnational fashion once and only once in all of history. Consequently, this one unique incarnation is the basis of salvation for everyone, at all times and in all places. In this sense, the entire human race is alike. There is just one true religious understanding and way of life, and there is a qualitative difference between biblical Christianity and all other faiths.

Anthropology is a discipline which has expanded greatly in the past century. Contact with persons of other cultures has particularly accelerated in the late twentieth century. One effect of these new relationships has been to call into question the uniqueness of the Christian religion vis-à-vis the beliefs, practices, and leaders of other religions. This in turn challenges the idea that the incarnation as a once-for-all occurrence is normative for all persons at all times. The result has been the growth of a universalist Christology.

There has been another anthropological development as well. Some scholars suggest that a whole cultural paradigm shift has occurred. The way we think about things is changing. This means that the whole underlying system of rationality on which the doctrine of the incarnation is based is no longer tenable for some individuals, and will progressively become so for increasing numbers of people. To help cope with this change, a postmodern Christology has arisen. That will be the subject of chapter 12. First, however, we will take a close look at universalist Christology.

The exclusivism implicit within the orthodox view of Christ as God incarnate presents a problem for a number of twentieth-century theologians. Actually, the issue has been with Christianity virtually from its beginning in the form of universalism, the teaching that everyone, not merely those who believe in Christ, is to be saved. In recent years, however, with the phenomenon of globalization, or the growing contact of Christianity and of Western culture in general with other cultures and other religions, the problem has become more pronounced. The shrinking world has resulted, for some Christians and theologians, in a shrunken Christ.

Among the theologians troubled by the exclusivism of Christianity is John Hick, an Englishman who has taught at a number of institutions both in Great Britain and in the United States, and who currently holds an appointment in the religion department of the Claremont Graduate School. Another is Paul Knitter, a Catholic theologian who has enunciated a pluralist view. A former missionary, he is now professor of theology at Xavier University (Cincinnati). His book *No Other Name?* surveys various views of the uniqueness of Jesus and of Christianity. Raimundo Panikkar, an Indian Catholic priest, and Stanley Samartha, also an Indian and a presbyter of the Church of South India, defend the pluralistic view growing out of interfaith dialogue. Also deserving mention is Eugene Hillman, who served as a Catholic missionary to the Masai people of what is now Tanzania. From this experience and correspondence with the Catholic theologians Karl Rahner and Edward Schillebeeckx, he came to a position which goes well beyond that of Rahner and Schillebeeckx. He has taught at Yale University, Weston School of Theology, the University of San Francisco, and St. John's University.

Because of the extensiveness and clarity of Hick's writings, we will rely most heavily upon them. Hick himself has had an interesting spiritual journey.[1] He was raised in the Church of England, but found the Anglican services infinitely boring. While in college, he was converted to a strongly evangelical and even fundamentalist variety of Christianity. He became very active in the Inter-Varsity Fellowship and the Christian Union at the University of Edinburgh. Gradually, however, his views broadened. He comments that anyone who is either born or "born again" into the conservative-evangelical tradition, and who has a questioning mind, will face challenges to that belief system, and will almost certainly be led by rational or moral considerations to modify or discard certain of its elements.[2]

Factors That Challenge the Exclusivism of Orthodox Christology

Diversity of Religions

A number of factors give Hick cause to doubt the exclusive claims implicit in traditional Christology. One is the simple fact of the variety of religions found in the world; Christians are clearly in the minority. Most people who have been raised in Christianity and have had no real contact with other religions

---

1. John Hick, *God Has Many Names* (Philadelphia: Westminster, 1982), pp. 13–19.
2. Ibid., p. 16.

think of its basic tenets as being fairly obvious. Automatic acceptance is becoming less widespread, however. One reason is the growing contact with other cultures and religions through increased travel, especially by persons at the upper economic and educational levels. In addition, worldwide news on television exposes most of us to views and practices other than our own.[3]

Close examination of the status of the Christian religion raises a disturbing consideration. Christianity has assumed that it is the true religion, and that therefore it is God's will that all persons, including adherents of the other religions, be converted to it. Christians, however, constitute only about one-third of the world's population. And although total membership is growing, that increase is not keeping pace with the world population. Thus, Christians are gradually becoming a smaller proportion. Instead of becoming relatively more Christian, the world is becoming less so.[4] Hick introduces a pragmatic argument here: "This thought casts a massive shadow over any assumption that it is God's will that all mankind shall be converted to Christianity."[5]

The Tie Between Ethnicity and Religion

A related consideration is the correlation between one's place of birth and religion. In the great majority of cases, perhaps 98 or 99 percent, what religion one holds and practices is a consequence of where one was born.[6] This is easily verifiable. It is also a fact which any credible religious faith must take into consideration.[7] Can we, in light of what we now know of the diversity of cultures and religions, hold that being born where and when we were gave us a special access to the truth?[8] Rosemary Radford Ruether speaks of "ecclesial ethnicity," referring to her commitment as a Roman Catholic; and Hick speaks of "religious ethnicity."[9] One is a Christian, Muslim, or Hindu by virtue of having been born an American, an Arab, or an Indian.

Now if we subscribe to the religion we do because of where

3. Ibid., p. 60.
4. Ibid., pp. 60–61.
5. Ibid., p. 61.
6. Ibid.; John Hick, *God and the Universe of Faiths: Essays in the Philosophy of Religion* (New York: St. Martin's, 1973), pp. 100, 132.
7. Hick, *Names*, p. 61.
8. Hick, *Universe*, p. 132.
9. John Hick, *Problems of Religious Pluralism* (New York: St. Martin's, 1985), p. 47.

we were born, and if only those who are believing and practicing Christians are saved, what happens to the Christian doctrine of a loving God who desires all persons to be saved? He has evidently ordained that humankind must be saved in a way that precludes the majority. Hick says, "It is the weight of this moral contradiction that has driven christian thinkers in modern times to explore other ways of understanding the human religious situation."[10] This exploration has made it apparent that the Christian view of other religions has often been a caricature. Today we have objective and accurate studies instead. We no longer see other world religions as crude and inferior, but as parallels and viable competitors to Christianity.[11]

Lack of Missionary Success

The relative lack of missionary success by the Christian religion is another consideration. For it is apparent, as we study the growth of world religions, that the success being experienced by Christian missionaries is generally "downwards," that is, in lands where the relatively primitive religions hold sway, rather than "sideways," in territories dominated by the more sophisticated religions.[12] Most of Christianity's converts are coming from animism and polytheism. Knitter says, "When confronted by living religions, especially if they are undergirded by some kind of intellectual system, Christian missionaries have had practically no success of conversions."[13]

The Quality of Religious Life in Non-Christian Religions

Closely tied to the lack of missionary success is the quality of faith and spiritual life among adherents of religions other than Christianity. It is common for any religion to magnify the instances of outstanding spirituality found among its followers. Thus, Christianity has made much of its saints. The assumption is that they led holy lives because of their commitment to

10. Hick, *Universe*, pp. 122–23.
11. Hick, *Names*, pp. 61–62.
12. Hick, *Universe*, p. 138.
13. Paul F. Knitter, *No Other Name? A Critical Survey of Christian Attitudes Toward the World Religions* (Maryknoll, N.Y.: Orbis, 1985), p. 4.

Christianity, and that such spirituality cannot be found elsewhere. This assumption flies in the face of the facts, however. This "Ptolemaic Christianity," as Hick terms it, "does not easily square with the evidences of salvation within other faiths in this present life—the evidence of saints, prophets, martyrs and mystics who have been intensely aware of the divine presence and whose lives have demonstrated the reality of their devotion."[14] In a similar vein, Hillman expresses gratitude to "the Masai people who taught me the meaning of religious pluralism and demonstrated in their lives that God's grace is not less operative among non-Christians than it is among Christians."[15]

The Phenomenological Similarity of Religions

A broader version of the same argument is found in Hick's observation that visitors to non-Christian places of worship encounter a shocking discovery—"that phenomenologically (or in other words, to human observation) the same kind of thing is taking place in them as in a Christian church."[16] Exclusivists, assuming that only Christianity is authentically in contact with the true God, hold that there must be a considerable difference between Christianity and other religions in their worship and prayer practices. And there are, to be sure, considerable differences. The prescribed attire of the worshipers may be quite different. Some worship involves the use of musical instruments, some does not. These are not crucial differences, however. On the other hand, "there is an important sense in which what is being done in the several forms of worship is essentially the same."[17] Hick quotes from Jewish, Muslim, Sikh, Hindu, and Bhakti hymns and prayers, and shows that they are basically expressing the same type of experience.[18] A viable Christian theology must take these parallels into account.[19]

Knitter's arguments are similar in many ways, although his base is broader. He notes three types of reasons for what he

14. Hick, *Universe*, p. 130.
15. Eugene Hillman, *Many Paths: A Catholic Approach to Religious Pluralism* (Maryknoll, N.Y.: Orbis, 1989), p. x.
16. Hick, *Names*, pp. 62–63.
17. Ibid., p. 63.
18. Ibid., pp. 63–66.
19. Ibid., p. 66.

terms "unitive pluralism."[20] First is the philosophical. The processive-relational view of reality emphasizes change, development, and relationship as the keys to understanding the world.[21] This is closely related but not restricted to process philosophy. Everything, including religion, is in the process of becoming, which takes place through interrelating. This means that in the interfaith dialogue each religion, while retaining its own uniqueness, "will develop and take on new depths by relating to other religions in mutual dependence."[22]

The second type of reason for unitive pluralism is sociological-psychological. If we are to move on to a postconventional understanding of personal identity and social morality, our values will have to take on a universal quality. This means that our identities must be "universalistic," which in turn will require interacting with persons from other cultures. Thus, in order to be good citizens of our own nation, we will have to be *world citizens*.[23]

Knitter's third reason for pluralism is political and economic. No longer can we see the world as composed of economically and politically independent nations. Geopolitics and worldwide economics are realities. Instead of contributing to this unity, however, religions have engaged in aggressive egocentric activity. They must now collaborate in building a common world.[24]

Views of the Relationship of Christianity to Other World Religions

Exclusivism

A number of responses have been given to the question of the relationship of Christianity to other world religions. The most common traditional response is what Hick labels exclusivism. It has been especially embodied in the Roman Catholic dogma of *Extra ecclesiam nulla salus* ("Outside the church, no salvation"). The nineteenth-century Protestant missionary movement held a similar view, which was, in effect, "Outside Christianity, no salvation." More than a mere ignoring of non-Christian humanity,

20. Knitter, *No Other Name?* p. 7.
21. Ibid., pp. 7–9.
22. Ibid., p. 9.
23. Ibid., pp. 9–13.
24. Ibid., p. 31.

this was a positive declaration that a majority of the human race were unsaved.[25]

Hick sees a direct correlation between the juridical conception of salvation and exclusivism. If salvation consists of a change in status from a guilt deriving from Adam's fall to a forgiveness based upon personal acceptance of Christ's sacrificial death, then of course salvation is restricted to the Christian community of faith.[26]

Hick refers to exclusivism as the first phase in the development of the Christian attitude toward other religions; it is based upon ignorance of those religions.[27] In some cases where there is contact (as through missionary endeavor), exclusivism flows rather from being "blinded by dark dogmatic spectacles through which [the Christian] can see no good in religious devotion outside his own group."[28]

The most serious flaw that Hick sees in exclusivism is its understanding of God. As noted earlier, if we are virtually predetermined to our religious commitment by where we are born, and if we can be saved only by being consciously committed to Jesus, then God has apparently consigned the majority of humans to eternal frustration and misery. This is simply not reconcilable with Christian teaching, for "to say that such an appalling situation is divinely ordained is to deny the Christian understanding of God as gracious and holy love, and of Christ as the divine love incarnate. Thus the attitude of total rejection, expressed in the dogma that outside Christianity there is no salvation, implies a conception of God radically questionable from the standpoint of Christian faith."[29]

Inclusivism

The force of the argument against exclusivism has been felt by numerous Christians. Thus there have emerged several qualifications of the traditional position. These qualifications Hick calls inclusivism[30] or the "phase of the early epicycles,"[31] the lat-

---

25. Hick, *Pluralism*, p. 31.
26. Ibid., p. 32.
27. Hick, *Names*, p. 30.
28. Ibid., p. 31.
29. Ibid.
30. Hick, *Pluralism*, p. 32.
31. Hick, *Names*, p. 31; Hick, *Universe*, pp. 124–25.

ter being an analogy recalling a futile attempt to preserve the Ptolemaic view of the universe, according to which the planets and stars, including the sun, move around the Earth. Upon discovering that the movement of the planets did not fit this scheme, certain astronomers introduced the concept of epicycles. In addition to their circular path around the Earth, the planets were thought to revolve in smaller supplementary circles, the centers of which lay on the larger circle. This theory yielded planetary pathways which were considerably more complicated and closer to the actual movements. As more and more complications were added, however, the system eventually collapsed under its own weight. The law of Ockham's razor or, as it is called in science, the law of parsimony prevailed. According to this principle, more factors than necessary should not be introduced to account for any given phenomenon.[32]

Essentially, inclusivism maintains that while Christianity is the true religion, and salvation is through Christ and him alone, all persons are included in the benefits of his work. The idea of human guilt and need for atonement is retained, but Christ's sacrificial death is seen as applying even to those who have not consciously placed their trust in him.[33] In another variety of inclusivism, salvation is seen not as juridical forgiveness of sins, but as a gradual transformation of human life which can take place in various religious contexts in addition to the Christian. In all of these contexts, however, it is still Jesus Christ who is the source of the transformation. Thus it is possible to speak of the "unknown Christ of Hinduism."[34]

Inclusivism has taken many different specific forms; or, as Hick would say, a variety of epicycles have been posited as a means of maintaining the theoretical truth of exclusivism while negating its practical implications:

1. Pope Pius IX's Allocution of 1854 maintained that someone who is invincibly ignorant of the true religion as revealed in the Roman Catholic Church is not guilty in the eyes of the Lord.[35]

32. Hick, *Universe*, pp. 124–25.
33. Hick, *Pluralism*, pp. 32–33.
34. Ibid., p. 33.
35. Hick, *Names*, p. 33; Hick, *Universe*, p. 123.

2. A related theory is the concept of implicit faith or baptism by desire. Some people who are ostensibly outside the church are unconsciously within it because they have an implicit faith, that is, a sincere desire to do God's will. This idea was enunciated in a letter from the Holy Office in Rome to the archbishop of Boston in 1949.[36] It is also found in Karl Rahner's concept of the anonymous Christian, which Hick regards as the best attempt of its kind. According to Rahner, one may be a Christian without knowing it.[37]

3. Hans Küng has proposed perhaps the most radical of the inclusivist views. He argues that there is an ordinary way of salvation within the world religions, and an extraordinary way within the Catholic church. This seems to be a virtual elimination of the exclusivist scheme.[38] Küng, however, maintains that the ordinary way of salvation is only an interim state; it obtains until one comes to explicit Christian faith. It is the duty of non-Christians to seek Christ within their own religion until such time as they are directly confronted with the claims of the Christian religion.[39]

4. A variety of inclusivism found more frequently in liberal Protestantism than in Roman Catholicism is eschatological universalism. According to this teaching, everyone will come to conscious acceptance of Christ as Lord and Savior. Whoever has not done so in this existence will be given an opportunity in the life to come.[40] Even in contemporary evangelicalism one can find representatives of this view, for example, Clark Pinnock. While he does not maintain that we will have a second chance at salvation, he does argue, on the basis of 1 Peter 3:19–20 and 4:6, that everyone will have a first chance. If it does not come during one's lifetime, it will occur at death.[41]

36. Hick, *Names*, p. 33; Hick, *Universe*, pp. 123–24.
37. Hick, *Universe*, p. 127; Hick, *Pluralism*, p. 33.
38. Hick, *Names*, pp. 34–45; Hick, *Universe*, p. 128.
39. Hick, *Names*, p. 35; Hick, *Universe*, pp. 128–29.
40. Hick, *Names*, p. 35.
41. Clark H. Pinnock, "The Finality of Christ in a World of Religions," in *Christian Faith & Practice in the Modern World: Theology from an Evangelical Point of View*, ed. Mark A. Noll and David F. Wells (Grand Rapids: Eerdmans, 1988), pp. 165–66.

Knitter divides Christian inclusivism into two camps. One is the mainline Protestant model, which holds that general revelation has the effect of making persons aware of the existence of God and of their own lack of righteousness. There is, then, a positive value in the world religions, but only as a preparation for the gospel, not an alternative to it.[42] The other camp Knitter terms the Catholic model of "many ways, one norm,"[43] which Hick identifies with Vatican II and subsequent Catholicism. Here the belief is that persons who are not consciously and overtly adherents of Christianity can be saved. That is, the boundaries of Christianity are broadened to include anonymous Christians.

Hick finds all of these attempted qualifications of the traditional exclusivism to be unconvincing. For one thing, any religion could use this tactic. Just as the inhabitants, if there were such, of Mars or Jupiter could develop by the use of epicycles a Ptolemaic theory that their own planet is central in the universe, so could the adherents of religions other than Christianity make their faith central. Thus a Hindu could maintain that Christians and the followers of other religions are "implicit Hindus."[44] Epicycles could be added and sustained indefinitely. The problem here is not logical possibility, but psychological plausibility. At some point human candidness will find it unprofitable and perhaps even undignified to go on defending in this fashion a view that so evidently clashes with the facts.[45] Hick says that a better explanation for the apparent salvation available through other religions must be found.

Pluralism

The alternative which Hick proposes in place of exclusivism and inclusivism is pluralism. Rather than holding that one religion is supreme and that all persons must somehow be participants in this one religion, as does inclusivism, pluralism maintains that there is one reality, and that all religions lay hold upon it. The various doctrines and practices of the world faiths are simply the same truth refracted in different ways.

---

42. Knitter, *No Other Name?* pp. 97–119.
43. Ibid., pp. 120–44.
44. Hick, *Names*, pp. 36–37, 70–71.
45. Hick, *Pluralism*, p. 53.

An initial argument advanced by Hick is the commonality of
the religious experience of persons from differing traditions.
This is substantiated both by personal testimony and by comparative observation. We earlier noted his use of the similarities
in worship as an argument against the exclusivism of any one
religion; now they are an argument for the commonality of the
object of worship in various faiths. The personal testimonies in
song and poetry that Hick cites are instructive.[46] It would be
interesting to abstract them from their non-Christian contexts
and then read them to Christians. It is quite possible, perhaps
even probable, that many devout Christians would think them
to be beautiful expressions of Christian piety and adopt them as
appropriate renditions of their own faith in God. Would not this
be an implicit argument that the various religions are worship-
ing the same God?

It is not just the expressions of worship and prayer, however,
that are similar in different religious traditions. Their conceptions of the higher power often show some significant resemblance. What comes through in all religions is a sense of transcendence, conviction that there is something which goes
beyond one's own experience, and therefore is worthy of a certain kind of commitment or reverence.[47]

Hick also observes that the various religions are engaged in a
similar quest. So he likens them to groups of people marching
in the same direction in different valleys. Unaware of the others
as they march along, each group develops its own songs, ideas,
language, and stories. Then they discover the existence of the
others as they all emerge on the same plain, the plain of modern communications. They wonder what to make of each other.
We might expect that they would greet one another as pilgrims
on a common journey. Instead, the unique traditions that each
group has developed keep them apart. So it is with the several
religious traditions, each traveling the same route, but each
developing songs that affirm that we are the only such travelers,
and our songs are the only true ones. Each tradition virtually
denies the legitimacy of the other groups.[48]

46. Hick, *Names*, pp. 64–66; Hick, *Universe*, pp. 139–43.
47. Hick, *Names*, pp. 90–91.
48. Ibid., pp. 40–41.

Hick makes use of a parable said to have been told by the Buddha. Each of several blind men ran his hands over a different part of an elephant. The man who felt one of the elephant's legs identified it as a tree; the man who felt the elephant's trunk thought it was a snake; the man who felt the tail said it was a rope. Each of them was describing what he perceived.[49] This is a picture of the way in which different religions describe the supreme reality. Two additional observations need to be made. First, the details of the parable should not be pressed too much. Whereas each of the blind men took hold of a different part of the elephant, the different religions are not speaking of different parts of the supreme reality. The variety in the descriptions is not an indication of diversity in God, but of "different human mentalities forming and formed by different intellectual frameworks and devotional techniques."[50] Second, Hick is not suggesting that all conceptions held by the various religions are equally valid. Some are closer to the truth than are others. He proposes, as a criterion, that "every conception of the divine which has come out of a great revelatory religious experience and has been tested through a long tradition of worship, and has sustained human faith over centuries of time and in millions of lives, is likely to represent a genuine encounter with the divine reality."[51]

Hick also anticipates and deals with an objection. What is the vantage point from which the pluralist can make the judgment that all religions are nonabsolute understandings of the supreme reality? How can one know that matters are as Hick has described them? Hick replies that pluralists do not profess to know that their view is correct, if by "know" is meant some sort of infallible knowledge. Pluralism is a hypothesis, just as is true of all other views, whether exclusivist or inclusivist. It is inductively arrived at from the fact that "many human beings experience life in relation to a limitlessly greater transcendent Reality—whether the direction of transcendence be beyond our present existence or within its hidden depths."[52]

Hick develops a historical hypothesis of the rise of the various religions. There has been a universal tendency in human

49. Hick, *Pluralism*, pp. 37, 96; cf. Hick, *Universe*, p. 140.
50. Hick, *Pluralism*, p. 96; Hick, *Universe*, p. 141.
51. Hick, *Universe*, p. 141.
52. Hick, *Pluralism*, p. 37.

life to give a religious interpretation to reality. In its earliest forms, this involved a belief in sacred objects, ancestral spirits, and quasi-animal forces.[53] Our knowledge of these early stages of religious development, derived from archaeology, indicates a tendency to conceive of spiritual forces in our own image, as being humanlike in nature.[54] From about 800 to 200 B.C., which Karl Jaspers has called the axial period, there was a virtual outburst of religious development. Most of the major religions of the world either were founded or definitively developed during this time.

In dealing with the other religions Christian inclusivism is quite satisfactory as long as one works solely from the Christian perspective. Here it serves as an adequate explanation of a fact which is rather embarrassing to exclusivism: that there are persons explicitly outside the Christian fold who seem to display some of the qualities which are highly esteemed as Christian virtues. The difficulty comes when one realizes that these qualities can be explained in a parallel way from other perspectives. That is to say, it would be quite possible to formulate a Hindu, a Buddhist, or a Jewish inclusivism. From such a perspective, Christians would be implicit or anonymous Hindus, Buddhists, or Jews. Thus inclusivism can be as ethnocentric as is exclusivism.

There is in Hick's pluralism a basic epistemological relativism. We have seen that he holds that all religions (or at least the major religions which he has examined) are in contact with and describe the same reality. Thus there is no need for an adherent of one religion to be converted to another. All believers, no matter their specific faith, have experienced ultimate reality at revelatory moments. The problem is, If all of them are basically perceiving the same reality, why are their conceptions and descriptions so different from one another?

Here Hick draws upon certain features of the epistemology of Immanuel Kant, although he does differ from Kant on some important details. The commonsense view of the knowing process is that our environment is simply reflected in our consciousness in a direct and simple way without our understanding it. But this is true only at the most basic physical level, which is lim-

53. Hick, *Universe*, pp. 133–34.
54. Hick, *Names*, p. 44.

ited to what is necessary for our biological survival and flourishing. Kant made a major contribution by pointing out "the creative part that thought, and the range of concepts in terms of which it functions, plays in the formation of conscious experience."[55] For knowledge, both reason and sense impressions are necessary. This is parallel to Kant's distinction between the noumenal and the phenomenal. The noumenal is the real world, the world as it is in and of itself behind the appearances. The phenomenal is the world that appears to our consciousness. Knowledge is possible only by processing sense data through the categories or concepts of the understanding, for example, unity, causation, and negation.

Although Kant himself did not believe that we experience God as we do our sense impressions (for God is noumenal), Hick proposes that God is known in a similar way.[56] Hick contends that while no one experiences God simply as an abstract, undifferentiated concept, such as "the uncreated Creator of the universe," we do experience him schematized or concretized in a range of divine images. And just as our sense impressions are processed by the Kantian categories, so are those divine images processed by "the continuum of historical factors which have produced our different religious cultures."[57]

Hick would also say that two basic concepts dominate religious experience: the concept of Deity or God (the Real as personal), and the concept of the Absolute (the Real as nonpersonal). These concepts are always found in specific forms, never in terms of Deity in general or the Absolute in general. Moreover, these specific forms are found in great variety because they arise in different historical and cultural settings. Hick explains: "There are different concrete ways of being human and of participating in human history, and within these different ways the presence of the divine Reality is experienced in characteristically different ways."[58]

One additional point which arises is whether it is possible to do any evaluation or grading of religions. Is there any way in which greater or lesser religious adequacy can be identified? And

55. Hick, *Pluralism*, p. 40.
56. Hick, *Names*, p. 104.
57. Ibid., p. 105.
58. Hick, *Pluralism*, p. 41.

is it conceivable that we might come to rank one of the great religions ahead of the others? Hick has devoted an entire chapter of his *Problems of Religious Pluralism* to this issue ("On Grading Religions"). He declares that he will derive his criteria from an inductive or empirical study of religions and religious practice. He does not, then, adopt and use the criterion employed by most people, namely, the assumption that their own religion is complete and unmixed truth. Rather, he holds that there are two tools for grading religions: "One is reason applied to their beliefs; and the other is conscience, or moral judgement, applied to the historical out-working of those beliefs."[59]

Hick's first test of a particular faith is actually pragmatic: reason measures whether the complex of religious experience, belief, and behavior is soteriologically effective. That is, does it transform human existence from self-centeredness to Reality-centeredness?[60] The second test scrutinizes the spiritual and moral fruits of this basic religious experience and vision. We have to look both at the ideal, as found in the lives of the saints of a given tradition, and also at the lives of the millions of ordinary believers.[61] Here Hick notes that in their own way all of the great religions lead to the desired goal: "If every Christian and Muslim, every Hindu and Buddhist, fully incarnated their respective ideals, they would live in a basic acceptance and love of all their fellow human beings. For they would have turned away from the self-centeredness which is the source of acquisitiveness, dishonesty, injustice and exploitation."[62]

It is not possible, Hick concludes, to weigh the different religions over against one another. The devotees of each naturally point at the benefits that have issued from their own faith and the drawbacks or dark moments of the history of the others. In actuality, each has its positive and negative points. Even the contention of Christians that their history and tradition gave rise to the modern conception of universal human equality is not a decisive argument. For equality is an idea which has been as much opposed as supported by Christian churches and is also

59. Ibid., p. 79.
60. Ibid., p. 80.
61. Ibid., p. 81.
62. Ibid., p. 83.

found in secular movements such as Marxism and humanism.[63] In the final analysis, then, no one religion has the advantage:

> Whilst we can to some extent assess and grade religious phenomena, we cannot realistically assess and grade the great world religions as totalities. For each of these long traditions is so internally diverse, containing so many different kinds of both good and evil, that it is impossible for human judgement to weigh up and compare their merits as systems of salvation. It may be that one facilitates human liberation/salvation more than the others; but if so this is not evident to human vision. So far as we can tell, they are equally productive of that transition from self to Reality which we see in the saints of all traditions.[64]

Knitter calls pluralism the theocentric model. By contrast, Christian exclusivism and inclusivism consider Christ to be the center of faith. The grounds of any salvation attained within another religion is Christ's presence there, perhaps unknown to the adherents of that faith. Pluralism, however, puts God, not Christ, at the center. There then are many ways to the center. Those who hold this view question the finality and definitive normativeness claimed for Christ and Christianity.[65] Knitter lists Hick, Panikkar, and Samartha among their number, as well as theologians involved in the Jewish-Christian dialogue, such as John Pawlikowski, Rosemary Ruether, and Monika Hellwig, and certain political-liberation theologians, including Dorothee Soelle, Tom Driver, and Ruether.[66] This is the view which Knitter himself espouses and defends in light of the shortcomings of exclusivism and inclusivism.[67]

Pluralism and the Incarnation

Pluralism seems clearly to be threatened, however, by the traditional doctrine of the incarnation. For as usually understood, that doctrine proclaims that God's presence and activity in Jesus were radically different from his presence and activity in other

63. Ibid., p. 85.
64. Ibid., pp. 86–87.
65. Knitter, *No Other Name?* pp. 145–46.
66. Ibid., pp. 146–65.
67. Ibid., pp. 165–67.

human beings. Thus, the way to contact with God must be through faith in Jesus and conversion to Christianity.[68]

Jesus' Belief

A first issue with respect to the threat which the incarnation poses to pluralism is whether Jesus himself believed and taught the traditional view. For a long period of Christian history it was thought that this was indeed the case. But biblical criticism has disputed the grounds which led to such a conclusion. Hick's own position is quite clear: "It is extremely unlikely that Jesus thought of himself, or that his first disciples thought of him, as God incarnate."[69] In particular, the critics claim that sayings like "I and the Father are one" (John 10:30) were never in fact spoken by Jesus of Nazareth. "It seems altogether more probable that they reflect the developing theology of the church toward the end of the first century."[70]

What did Jesus think about himself then? Hick suggests that he was, so to speak, a Buddha. He had attained true knowledge of and direct access to pure reality. He was aware that God was present in his teachings and actions, powerfully encountering men and women to give a positive response.[71]

The Development of the Doctrine of Incarnation

If Jesus and the earliest disciples neither believed nor taught that he was God incarnate, how did that conception come to be part of the tradition? It is important to keep in mind that there had been a great event, which Hick, along with many others, refers to as the Christ event. This event, or complex of events, constitutes the essence, the abiding defining content, of Christianity.[72] The church sought to interpret, or to give itself a fuller understanding of, the Christ event. In the process the church made use of the concepts and language available in that day, including the Old Testament concept of divine sonship. In Psalm 2:7 God had referred to the king of Israel as "my son," and in Isaiah 42:1 to the Suffering Servant as "my chosen" (or "my

---

68. Hick, *Names*, pp. 19, 58.
69. Hick, *Universe*, p. 114.
70. Hick, *Names*, p. 73.
71. Hick, *Universe*, p. 115.
72. Ibid., p. 111.

son"). In these contexts, however, the term *son* has a meaning completely different from what is found in the trinitarian idea of God the Son.[73] That came later, a result of the culture in which the Christian movement was developing. Hick says, "What seems to have happened during the hundred years or so following Jesus' death was that the language of divine sonship floated loose from the original ground of Jewish thought and developed a new meaning as it took root again in Graeco-Roman culture."[74]

It is important to bear in mind that the early Christians had encountered God. This was a matter of absolute importance, and could be expressed only in the language of absolutes. Expanding westward into the Greco-Roman world, to which the message had to be explained, Christianity seized upon the Greek concept of substance. And so the idea of divine sonship, which was utilized to interpret the Christ event, was explained in terms of substance, which entailed a static set of attributes. Thus the early Christians' original idea that in Jesus they had encountered God led eventually to the teaching that Jesus was of the same substance as the Father, and then to the doctrine that Jesus was God incarnate, the Second Person of the Trinity.[75]

In a sense, according to Hick, this doctrinal development was an accident of history. If, instead of expanding primarily westward, Christianity had made its move eastward into Asia, Christology might have evolved quite differently. If, for example, it had early moved into India, where Buddhism was then becoming a powerful influence, "it is likely that instead of Jesus being identified as the divine Logos or the divine Son he would have been identified as a Bodhisattva who, like Gotama some four centuries earlier, had attained to Buddhahood or perfect relationship to reality, but had in compassion for suffering mankind voluntarily lived out his human life in order to show others the way to salvation."[76]

The question arises, If Christianity had spread primarily eastward, would Christology have undergone a wrong development, or simply a different development? Hick says that "once we understand that theology is the human attempt to state the

73. Ibid., pp. 115–16.
74. Ibid., p. 116.
75. Ibid.
76. Ibid., p. 117.

meaning of revelatory events experienced in faith, we realize that many different theologies are possible—like the many different projections by which the three-dimensional earth can be represented on two-dimensional maps."[77] Theology, then, is merely a culturally conditioned response to the Christ event.[78] And so, as Christianity developed westward, the form of theology varied greatly through different periods; there were even radically dissimilar forms in any given period.[79] What these different theologies had in common, enabling all to be referred to as Christian, was not an identity of doctrines, but the same origin—the Christ event.[80]

Seeing these matters in this light has a freeing effect upon us. We are no longer compelled to hold to specific theological doctrines, which we can now see to be culturally conditioned reactions to and interpretations of the Christ event. But what about the Christ event itself? Is it so unique that we must continue to maintain the supremacy of Christianity among the various religious faiths? What we must do instead, says Hick, is to carry the Copernican revolution into theology. By this is meant that we must shift from a Jesus-centered model to a God-centered model of the universe of faiths.[81] Just as the Christology that developed was one way in which Christians sought to give expression to the God they had encountered, so other religions represent the endeavor of their adherents, in most cases from rather different cultures, to give expression to their encounter with the ultimate reality.[82]

Degree Christology

To achieve a God-centered model, we must shift from a Christology that holds that Jesus is unique in kind (and therefore Christianity is supreme among religions) to a Christology that holds that he differs from other humans only in degree. This shift is already taking place, for reasons other than to facilitate pluralism.[83] Hick points out that the substance approach to

77. Ibid.
78. Ibid.
79. Ibid., p. 118.
80. Ibid., p. 119.
81. Hick, *Names*, p. 18.
82. Ibid., pp. 18–19.
83. Hick, *Pluralism*, p. 35.

Christology has had to be rejected because of theology's inability to treat the incarnation factually. It certainly has never been understood to mean that God literally was the father of Jesus in the sense that the Holy Spirit filled the role of the male parent in conception, thus making Jesus a divine-human figure such as is found in Greek mythology, for example, Hercules. While rejecting such an idea, Christian theology has not been able to supply any satisfactory alternative. Hick says, "Whenever in the history of Christian thought theologians have tried to spell out its meaning in literal, factual terms the result has been heretical."[84] Instead, says Hick, the real heresy is treating the incarnation as factual. "The reason why it has never been possible to state a literal meaning for the idea of the incarnation is simply that it has no literal meaning."[85]

Instead of trying to explain the incarnation in some literal fashion, Hick maintains that we should understand it metaphorically. He gives an analogy to illustrate what he means:

> Incarnation, in the sense of the embodiment of ideas, values, insights in human living, is a basic metaphor. One might say, for example, that in 1940 the spirit of defiance of the British people against Nazi Germany was incarnated in Winston Churchill. Now we want to say of Jesus that he was so vividly conscious of God as the loving heavenly Father, and so startlingly open to God and so fully his servant and instrument, that the divine love was expressed, and in that sense incarnated, in his life. This was not a matter (as it is in official Christian doctrine) of Jesus having two complete natures, one human and the other divine. He was wholly human; but whenever self-giving love in response to the love of God is lived out in a human life, to that extent the divine love has become incarnate on earth.[86]

Incarnation, then, is a figure of speech indicating that Jesus is our living contact with the transcendent God.[87]

When incarnation is understood this way, one can see that Jesus was not unique in kind, and that Christianity is not therefore the only way to God. Instead of understanding incarnation in terms of substance and a divine nature in Jesus, Hick defines

84. Hick, *Names*, p. 74.
85. Ibid.
86. Ibid., pp. 58–59.
87. Ibid., p. 74.

it as "the activity of God's Spirit or of God's grace in human lives, so that the divine will is done on earth."[88] He finds particular affinity between this definition and two British Christologies. Donald Baillie uses as a model of incarnation Paul's experience that the good, the positive spirituality, he found in himself was not his doing, but the working of the grace of God within him.[89] And Geoffrey Lampe sees as a clue to understanding incarnation in Christ the activity of the Holy Spirit within human life.[90] In both of these Christologies, God's presence and activity in the life of Jesus are not qualitatively, but only quantitatively different from the way in which he is present and works in other believers. Both systems are therefore what Hick calls "degree Christologies" rather than "substance Christologies." Although the work of theologians who believed in the supremacy of Jesus and of Christianity, they do not necessarily lead to such a conclusion:

> If, with Baillie, we see in the life of Christ a supreme instance of that fusion of divine grace and creaturely freedom that occurs in all authentic human response and obedience to God, then the situation changes. For we are no longer speaking of an intersection of the divine and the human which only occurs in one unique case, but of an intersection which occurs, in many different ways and degrees, in all openness and response to the divine initiative. There is now no difficulty in principle in acknowledging that the paradox of grace was also exemplified in other messengers of God or indeed, more broadly, in other human beings who are markedly Reality-centred rather than self-centred.[91]

Hick recognizes, of course, that some who hold to a degree Christology may still insist upon the supremacy of Christianity over other faiths; they claim that Jesus more fully exemplified authentic response to God than has any other human being. The situation is now greatly changed, however. For the claim that Jesus' response to God was unique and absolute

> is no longer . . . a necessary inference from the nature of God's action in Jesus, but must instead be a judgement based upon his-

88. Hick, *Pluralism*, p. 35.
89. Ibid., pp. 59–61.
90. Ibid., pp. 61–62.
91. Ibid., p. 63.

torical evidence. And the main problematic question that arises, for any Christian who is familiar with the modern scholarly study of the New Testament, is whether we have a sufficiently complete knowledge of the historical Jesus to be able to affirm that his entire life was a perfect exemplification of the paradox of grace or of divine inspiration.[92]

The Relational Uniqueness of Jesus

Knitter states that the underlying question for him, which he calls the "gadfly-question," is the uniqueness of Jesus Christ: "Is Jesus unique among the religious figures of history? If so, how?"[93] He finds all of the varieties of Christology that argue for either an exclusive uniqueness or an inclusive uniqueness to be inadequate on two counts: "All these traditional Christian claims are insufficiently sensitive to the way they contradict contemporary awareness of historical relativity and to the way they impede authentic dialogue with believers of other faiths."[94] The search for a theocentric Christology grows out of these two considerations. What Knitter proposes in the place of exclusive or inclusive uniqueness of Jesus is *relational uniqueness*. This is "a uniqueness defined by its ability to relate to—that is, to include and be included by—other unique religions."[95]

Knitter's first move is to examine the New Testament proclamation of Jesus. At the heart of this endeavor is Knitter's hermeneutic. He follows Hans Georg Gadamer's concept that every text has two horizons—that of the author and that of the reader. In Knitter's adaptation, it is not sufficient to interpret a text within its historical context. Both the text and its context can be understood only "within the 'horizon' of experience and meaning as that horizon expands through history."[96] This is what Panikkar has called the "universal context" or the "texture" of the text, a dimension which is essential to really hearing and being faithful to the true meaning. In contradiction to those who believe that fidelity to the text means simply repeating what it signified in its original setting, Knitter says, "Unless the text and

92. Ibid., pp. 64–65.
93. Knitter, *No Other Name?* p. 171.
94. Ibid.
95. Ibid., pp. 171–72.
96. Ibid., p. 172.

its context are continually being reheard in the ever new texture, one is really not hearing what the text means. And where there are real shifts or changes within the texture, especially when human experience evolves from the tribal to the global, there *must* be new interpretations of the text. Otherwise, we are not being faithful to the New Testament; we are not hearing what it really means."[97]

Knitter shows that there has been an evolution in the texture of human experience, so that it is very different today from what it was at the time of the New Testament and past dogmatic statements. He is what William Hordern termed a "transformer"— one who holds that the world has changed in such significant ways since biblical times that what is needed is an actual modification or restructuring of the content of the message, not merely a restatement or reexpression (translation). The elements which Knitter finds in this new context are by now familiar:

> This texture includes a new "historical consciousness" of the relativity of all cultures and historical achievements, a new awareness of pluralism, and especially a clearer realization of the need to fashion a new form of unity among people. Not to understand Jesus anew in this texture, not to open oneself to the possibility of a new christology, is to run the risk of confining the past in an idolatrous "deposit of faith." Secure in such a deposit, one can comfortably avoid the call of the past to conversion and action in the present.[98]

When Knitter examines what the best in recent New Testament scholarship has to say about Jesus, certain fairly clear conclusions begin to emerge. One is that Jesus himself was theocentric in his message and ministry. Very little can be discerned from the New Testament about how Jesus understood himself. With the possible exception of "Son of man," none of the New Testament titles for Jesus were self-designations. Jesus gave us no Christology, according to Knitter. Probably the most that can be said is that he understood himself to be the eschatological prophet, whose message was about the kingdom of God.[99]

It was the early Christian community or, to be more accurate,

97. Ibid., pp. 172–73.
98. Ibid., p. 173.
99. Ibid., pp. 173–74.

communities that transformed this theocentric message of Jesus into a christocentric message. Most of Jesus' titles and the proclamations about him originated in the early Christians' experience of him, which Knitter calls a "big-bang experience that transformed persons' lives," a saving experience, an experience of revelation.[100] Unlike Hick, he rejects the old approach which saw a unilinear development from Jewish to Greek titles. Instead, New Testament scholars now speak in terms of "trajectories," various credal perspectives which developed simultaneously in different social contexts and intermingled. There were basically four of these trajectories:

1. The *maranatha* ("Come, Lord") or *parousia* Christologies conceived of Jesus as Lord of the future and Judge of the world.
2. The *divine man* (*theios anēr*) Christology depicted Jesus as a divine agent able to perform mighty deeds.
3. The *wisdom* and *logos* Christologies drew upon the Jewish idea of God's creative, revelatory, and redemptive activity in the world.
4. The *paschal* or *Easter* Christology emphasized the crucifixion and resurrection of Jesus, and especially their effects on the community of believers.[101]

Study of the New Testament trajectories has yielded the conclusion that even from the beginning of the church there was diversity in the understanding of Jesus. Beyond that, early christological activity was dialogical, which is to say that Christology was built out of material taken from the cultural heritage of the period. It crystalized elements which were already there, such as the Greek idea of the universal logos and the Jewish conception of wisdom. Finally, the New Testament Christologies must be understood as part of a gradual unfolding, a process to be pictured as following the contours of a spiral rather than a straight line.[102]

From his study Knitter derives certain guidelines which he feels should be utilized in doing christological work:

100. Ibid., p. 175.
101. Ibid., pp. 176–77.
102. Ibid., pp. 177–79.

1. The christological trajectories of the early church are to be viewed as *interpretations* rather than definitions. They are more like impressionistic paintings than photographs.
2. No one of the trajectories should be absolutized or allowed to absorb the others.
3. We must bear in mind that all of these images, taken together, do not exhaust who Jesus was or what he means for Christians and for the world.
4. Just as in New Testament times, the continuing evolution of Christology will require dialogue with other cultures and other religions.
5. What is needed in our doing of Christology is a return to or renewal of the theocentrism which marked Jesus' understanding of his mission and of himself. Such a Christology not only avoids the impediments to genuine dialogue that characterize exclusivism and inclusivism, but also remains faithful to its origins.[103]

What are we to do, however, about the exclusivism which rather obviously characterizes the church's proclamation in texts like John 1:14; 14:6; Acts 4:12; 1 Corinthians 15:21–22; 1 Timothy 2:5; and Hebrews 9:12? Knitter maintains that all of the "one and only" statements that pertain to Jesus and the way of salvation were more a requirement of the medium than they were the core message of the New Testament. Given the historical context, the message of the early church needed to have a universal or absolute quality. For one thing, the Christians were working in a culture which thought of truth as unitary, unchanging, certain, and normative. To have any impact in such a culture, Christians had to express their message in absolutist fashion. Further, the philosophy of history which the first Christians inherited from their Jewish religion led them to expect a new and definitive stage of history; accordingly, they proclaimed with great conviction the beliefs which they had so recently acquired. Finally, we should not overlook the fact that as a minority movement the church had to "arm itself with clear identity and total commitment." If we see the absolute statements as attempts to insure the survival of the community rather than as once-and-for-all definitions, we

103. Ibid., pp. 180–82.

can adhere to the basic worldview of the early Christians without taking an exclusivist position. In fact, given the contemporary milieu, this is what we are called to do.[104]

We must see the absolutist language of the early church as confession and testimony, not as science, philosophy, or dogmatics. It is what Krister Stendahl calls "love language, caressing language." The early believers were not expressing metaphysics, but their personal relationship with and commitment to God. The absolute language is like that which a husband may use in speaking of his wife as "the most beautiful woman in the world, the only woman for me." Such language is not intended to be taken literally or scientifically.

In addition to showing that Scripture does not claim an exclusive or inclusive uniqueness, a normativeness, for Jesus, Knitter examines several types of contemporary Christologies. Among these are Karl Rahner's transcendental Christology, process Christology, and liberation Christology.[105] Each of these in its own way supports his contention that we can construct a Christology which has a unique but not normative Christ. He believes that this further substantiates his own theocentric Christology.

A final problem for Knitter is the resurrection, which seems to set Jesus apart from other religious leaders. Knitter adopts what he terms a "reputable, though controversial, understanding of the resurrection."[106] He follows the approach of Edward Schillebeeckx, Norman Perrin, Reginald Fuller, and Hans Küng, who attempt to steer a course between purely objective and purely subjective interpretations of the resurrection. In a nontraditional sense there was an objective factor, namely, the experience of conversion or forgiveness. The resurrection accounts are to be understood as "attempts to express and give more tangible form to these conversion experiences rather than as photographic statements of what took place."[107] As such, they are not greatly unlike the attempts by adherents of other religions to give expression to their experiences, though other terms may be used. Thus the founders of other religions also live on in a spiritual,

104. Ibid., pp. 182–84.
105. Ibid., pp. 186–97.
106. Ibid., p. 197.
107. Ibid., p. 199.

but *real* way. Knitter concludes in regard to these other religions: "What happened, therefore, to the early Christians and to Jesus after his death might possibly have happened to their believers and their saviors. The resurrection of Jesus, in all its authentic mystery and power, does not necessarily imply 'one and only.'"[108]

Knitter realizes that for some Christian believers the proposal of a theocentric Christology will be profoundly disturbing. They need a Christ without parallels. Knitter points out, however, that a husband's appreciation for his wife is not diminished by recognizing that other women also have admirable qualities. Indeed, a secure marital relationship and a deep commitment will increase one's ability to appreciate the attractive qualities of others. Knitter then suggests that perhaps it is an insecure Christian faith that craves an exclusively unique Jesus.[109]

What Knitter proposes instead is a confessional approach. Here we simply confess what we have experienced in Jesus, rather than taking the apologetic approach of attempting to demonstrate his superiority to other religious leaders. In the long run, not putting the followers of other religions on the defensive will make Christianity more attractive and thus will be more effective.[110]

Evaluation

How shall we evaluate this attempt to maintain both a commitment to Jesus Christ and an equal validity for the other great world religions? There are some strengths to universalist Christology:

1. Universalist Christology respects the sincerity of the adherents of religions other than Christianity. All too often Christians, convinced of the truth of their faith, have failed to realize that Hindus, Buddhists, and Muslims are equally committed to their beliefs and practices. As a result, Christians have sometimes ridiculed those beliefs and practices. In many ways this is no different from ethnocentrism and consequent insensitivity to other cultures and societies. Theologians like Hick and Knitter, on the other hand, have shown greater cultural breadth and sensitivity,

108. Ibid., p. 200.
109. Ibid., pp. 201–02.
110. Ibid., pp. 200–04.

enabling them to relate to persons of quite different religious orientation.

2. The universalist theologians have recognized the psychological principle (which seems to transcend cultures) that a predominantly negative or critical approach does not prove useful in attempting to convince others of the truth of one's own religion. The tendency to speak without being willing to listen, conveying the impression that the other person has nothing to say which is worth hearing, has not advanced the cause of Christianity. The universalists, by contrast, have engaged in genuine dialogue.

3. The pluralists have attempted to deal honestly with the genuinely virtuous and positive lives of non-Christians. Some Christians, theologians and laypersons alike, maintain that it is axiomatic to Christianity that there can be no genuine goodness in anyone who is not a Christian. They have consequently sought to minimize or explain away the good qualities in the adherents of other religions, failing to realize that non-Christians could apply the same techniques to the lives of Christians and even of saints. All of this conveys the impression of a certain lack of intellectual integrity. The theologians we are discussing in this chapter, however, have honestly admitted that Christianity does not have a monopoly on human virtue.

4. The universalist theologians have dared to ask themselves, "What if Christianity is not true, at least in the exclusivist sense in which it has been traditionally interpreted?" Another way of putting this is that they have asked whether the received form of Christianity has rightly dealt with the facts. This ability to be critical of one's own tradition is certainly commendable.

5. Pluralist theology has recognized and declared that religion has social, economic, and political dimensions. It is not simply a spiritual phenomenon, which we can analyze and understand by using only theological categories. Its sources and effects are intricately related to the other dimensions of human reality.

There are, on the other hand, several points of inadequacy in this christological view:

1. There is an inadequately developed epistemology. The universalists contend that experience, and especially the experience of encounter with other religions, is to be the determining force in construction of a theology. But why should this be given pri-

ority over revelation or the other traditional grounds of theology? There is a begging of the question here rather than an argumentation of the point.

2. On a number of other points the pluralists do not offer adequate argumentation. This is especially the case when they postulate the source of certain of Christianity's conceptions. Similarity does not prove that one idea or movement derived from another, or that they had a common origin.

3. The universalists are occasionally guilty of a genetic fallacy; that is, they incorrectly suppose that temporal priority signifies causation. For example, Knitter assumes that the early church's absolutist proclamation regarding Christ was due to the historical context: such a presentation was necessary in the face of societal opposition to minority movements. But although this could have been the case, it has not been established that the exclusivism of early Christianity would not have arisen in any other historical context.

4. Pluralism has overstated the resemblances between the various world religions and oversimplified their differences. While there are some definite points of similarity between Christianity and certain forms of Buddhism, for example, the theologians in question have incorrectly interpreted the similarity as sameness.

5. The pluralist theologians may have accomplished something other than what they intended. Their assumption is that they have established that all religions are true. What they may actually have established is that all religions are equally false, or at least that none of them is true. They do not make an adequate case to establish that there is some objective truth in religion.

12

The Anthropological Problem.
(2) Postmodern Christology

The Definition of Postmodernism

The movement which we are now going to discuss can be called postmodernism, because it challenges many of the beliefs which have come to be associated with modernism, or the spirit of the modern age. Several different streams of thought and several different influences feed into the general worldview which we are about to consider. It can be thought of as a theory of literary criticism, the French philosophical and literary movement known as deconstruction and associated especially with the Heideggerian philosopher Jacques Derrida. Or it can be thought of as a theory of the nature of history, identified in the United States as the new historicism. It also includes the American philosophical movement termed neopragmatism. For the most part, the postmodernists have been working independently of

305

one another in different fields of study, so there has not been much conscious cooperation. Nevertheless, each of the streams of postmodernism—aesthetics, philosophy of history, and epistemology—displays certain family characteristics. There has been a shared mood derived from a .common milieu; it is this shared mood which is referred to as postmodernism. Moreover, the influence of a given area of study occasionally spills over into adjacent fields; Derrida, for instance, is both a philosopher and a literary critic.

Postmodernism is such a diverse collection of concepts and agendas that it is difficult to gather them under one umbrella. What they all have in common is a dissatisfaction with what is broadly referred to as modernism. There is a sense that just as modernism displaced certain other views, it can and should itself be displaced. Far from possessing some absolute truth or final status in itself, it is simply one more way station in the onward march of the human race and its culture.[1]

Theology is one of the fields being affected by postmodernism. David Griffin divides modern theology into an early and a late period. The early period, represented perhaps most clearly by the deism of the eighteenth century, was characterized by an attempt to accommodate theology to the modern worldview by reducing its content. The hope was that this would lead to a universal religion embodying the positive qualities that all religions hold in common. That endeavor proved to be a failure. As a result, late modern theology gave up the goal of universality and accepted pluralism.[2] In so doing, late modern theology made two further adjustments. First, in contrast to the public verifiability that served as the test of truth in science and science-based philosophies, theology increasingly began to rely upon much less objective tests. Subjective truth, as highlighted by Søren Kierkegaard, and revelation to a specific community, which then passed on what it had learned, became the measures. Faith virtually conceded the arena of public discourse to the modern worldview; theology was not subject to public or universal cri-

---

1. David R. Griffin, "Introduction to SUNY Series in Constructive Postmodern Thought," in *Varieties of Postmodern Theology*, ed. David R. Griffin (Albany: State University of New York Press, 1989), p. xi.

2. David R. Griffin, "Introduction: Varieties of Postmodern Theology," in *Varieties of Postmodern Theology*, p. 2.

teria of verification or falsification. Second, late modern theology began to spread the idea that one's personal piety is a private matter without relevance to public policy, as John F. Kennedy strove mightily (and successfully) to establish in the 1960 presidential campaign.[3]

The several theologies termed postmodernism are agreed in their understanding of what modernism is. They also are agreed that the era of modern theology is over. Where they differ from some of the earlier reactions to modernism is that they hold that "the modern world has produced unparalleled advances that must not be lost in a general revulsion against its negative features." These new theologies, then, are truly postmodern, not premodern. They are calling, not for a return to an earlier era and its conceptions, but for progress beyond the modern view.[4]

Four Types of Postmodernism

Except for their agreement upon the nature of modern theology and its inadequacy, the postmodern theologies display great diversity. Griffin gives a helpful summary of four basic types of postmodernism:[5]

1. *Constructive* or *revisionary postmodern theology* sees Western culture as changing rapidly. Part of the reason is that the objective approach to reality, instead of supporting the modern worldview, is pointing to a postmodern worldview. In keeping with this change, theology must now become public in two senses: (a) it must make its case objectively, by appealing to the criteria of self-consistency and ability to explain the generally accepted facts of experience, and (b) it must be relevant to matters of public policy.
2. *Deconstructive* or *eliminative postmodern theology* believes that an objective approach to facts leads to the paradoxical conclusion that an objective approach is not possible. This undermines the modern worldview along with all other worldviews. The result is an increasingly relativistic scheme.

3. Ibid.
4. Griffin, "Introduction to SUNY Series," p. xiii.
5. Griffin, "Introduction: Varieties," pp. 1–7.

3. *Liberationist postmodern theology* emphasizes the need for transforming society. It also emphasizes that theologians should not allow themselves to be shaped by the modern worldview, which, in the judgment of Harvey Cox, is too concerned with objective arguments that meet the standards of self-consistency and ability to explain facts.

4. *Restorationist* or *conservative postmodern theology*, which thus far has appeared only in Roman Catholicism, has much in common with constructive postmodernism. Its best-known representatives, Pope John Paul II and George William Rutler, emphasize going beyond postmodernism, but at the same time holding on to those elements which it has in common with premodernism.

It is worth observing that most postmodernists are not theologians per se. There are, however, theologians who have taken the major thrusts of postmodernist writings in other fields and made theological applications of them. These are the deconstructionist theologians, the most conspicuous of whom is Mark C. Taylor.

Three Aspects of Postmodernism

A number of different streams feed into postmodernism. They have been analyzed and classified in various ways. While certainly oversimplifying, we will examine this movement briefly in terms of three aspects: deconstruction in literary criticism, neopragmatism in philosophy, and the new historicism in history.

Many of the postmodernists see their work as a continuation of the concerns of the nineteenth century. Indeed, there are frequent references to Immanuel Kant, Georg Hegel, Søren Kierkegaard, Friedrich Nietzsche, and others. There is relatively little talk of the philosophical movements of the twentieth century, such as analytical philosophy, other than to speak somewhat derisively of them. It is as if such movements represent false paths taken in the pursuit of the solutions to the problems posed by the nineteenth century, and the various postmodernists and deconstructionists are attempting to go back to the spot where Western culture lost its way.

Perhaps the best introduction to deconstruction in literature is a point Richard Rorty made in discussing epistemology. He tells of a cosmologist who held, as many ancients did, that the world rests upon the back of an elephant. When asked what the elephant stood upon, he replied, "It's elephants all the way down." Reality, says Rorty, should now be understood in a similar fashion—"It's words all the way down."[6] The prevailing view had been that the words of our theories and discussions must ultimately rest upon some reality that is other than verbal. Now the search for that nonverbal reality has been abandoned. For it is declared that what words are referring to are merely other words, which in turn are related to yet other words, and so on ad infinitum.

Derrida has engaged in a deconstruction of what is sometimes called logocentrism, the attempt to locate and describe what is ultimately real or rational. That has been the role of what he calls "speaking," which he defines as the attempt to mirror the logos, the underlying nonverbal reality, an activity sometimes referred to as the ontotheological way of viewing things.[7] "Writing,"on the other hand, which Derrida makes primary, with speaking being derivative, does not try to get back to some basic referent. Rather, it deals with signs, which in turn deal with other signs. Every instance of writing supplements that about which it writes, which in turn supplemented that about which it wrote, and so on.[8]

In part, Derrida's view can be seen as a reaction against structuralism. Structuralism shifted the locus of meaning and literary investigation away from the author's intention to certain universal structures or patterns found within the text. Structuralism, then, is objective in the sense that it holds that there is meaning in the text, though the author did not consciously place it there.[9]

Derrida's emphases were picked up by a group of scholars at Yale, Paul de Man, Geoffrey Hartman, J. Hillis Miller, and Harold Bloom. At times they extended Derrida's criticism to all referents. This means that the literary critic alone, rather than the literary critic in conjunction with the work of literature, determines its meaning.[10]

6. Richard Rorty, *Consequences of Pragmatism: Essays 1972–1980* (Minneapolis: University of Minnesota Press, 1982), p. xxxv.

7. Jacques Derrida, "Structure, Sign, and Play in the Discourse of the Human Sciences," in *Writing and Difference* (Chicago: University of Chicago Press, 1978), p. 291.

8. Jacques Derrida, *Of Grammatology* (Baltimore: Johns Hopkins University Press, 1976), p. 159.

9. Mark C. Taylor, *Erring: A Postmodern A/theology* (Chicago: University of Chicago Press, 1984), pp. 86–87.

10. See, e.g., Harold Bloom et al., *Deconstruction and Criticism* (New York: Seabury, 1979).

This movement away from finding meaning in the object to finding it (at least partly) in the subject is paralleled in philosophy by neopragmatism. Neopragmatism is largely a reaction against the correspondence theory of truth, which holds that truth is a quality of ideas that agree with or accurately reflect that to which they refer. In explaining the new philosophy Rorty distinguishes two principal ways in which we humans place our lives in a larger context in order to give them meaning. One of these is objectivism. The practitioners of this approach seek to relate to an "immediate" nonhuman reality. They are what Rorty calls "Truth-seekers."[11] The other way to give one's life meaning by placing it in a larger context is what he calls solidarity. Those who follow this approach seek to contribute to a community, either the one in which they live or an imaginary one populated by heroes and heroines. This approach, the neopragmatic, views truth as what is good for us to believe. It holds that we do not need an account of the relations between beliefs and objects, nor an explanation of human abilities which establishes that we can indeed come to know reality. Advocating a hermeneutical attitude rather than method, he calls us "to abandon the notion of discourse proceeding within a preexisting set of constraints, and instead open ourselves to the course of conversation." We must reject "the Kantian notion that there is something called 'a structure of rationality' which the philosopher discovers and within which we have a moral duty to remain."[12]

The third area of consideration is history. Here we may see the issues most clearly by contrasting the premodern and modern periods with the postmodern. William Dean has given an especially helpful analysis. In the premodern period, it was common to look for the meaning of history in something transhistorical, which was the source of everything that happened within history and also the explanation of history. Thus, the real meaning of history was to be found in something outside of it. For Christians this was the will and activity of God. In a more secular vein, Plato developed his theory of pure forms as the explanation of what transpired in the visible world, which was only a shadow of the real or ideal world.

11. Richard Rorty, "Solidarity or Objectivity?" in *Post-Analytic Philosophy*, ed. John Rajchman and Cornel West (New York: Columbia University Press, 1985), pp. 3–4.
12. Richard Rorty, "A Reply to Dreyfus and Taylor," *Review of Metaphysics* 34 (1980): 39.

The modern world rejected this type of transcendentalism. Indeed, it rejected all sorts of classical and medieval structures, social, ecclesiastical, and governmental. It did, however, look for some types of universals within history. If premodernism was basically Platonic on the question of universals, then modernism was basically Aristotelian. It looked for the patterns of history or the universal factors not in some transcendent realm, but in the contingencies of history. Modernism was simply carrying into history the approach which had been established in science: external factors were disregarded or even discarded. This new outlook, which we shall call the old historicism, took a number of forms. The first, historically, was the rationalist approach, epitomized by René Descartes. The rationalists found universal or objective factors in the pattern of human reason and thought; the order of the human mind, they said, corresponds to reality. The empiricists, represented by David Hume, found constant patterns in their experience of the world, which they called the laws of nature. The humanists, ranging all the way from Friedrich Schleiermacher to Kierkegaard, fixed the locus of meaning in the individual self.[13]

The modernists certainly did not have a transcendental view of reality. They did not find the meaning of history in some external realm. Nonetheless, their view was still metaphysical in the sense that they held that history has some meaning which is not subject to contingent events and thus is transhistorical. There is some abiding reality which holds history together and gives it meaning. There is something universal to be discovered within space and time. It is something objective, in the sense that its existence does not depend upon someone's knowing it. Historians must take into account this universal factor within the realm of nature.[14]

The role of the modern historian has more in common with the premodern than the postmodern historian. Though modern historians rebelled against the premodern attempt to find meaning in some external realm beyond the events of history, they nonetheless were seeking to discover a universal factor within those events. They engaged in what might be called a mimetic

13. William Dean, *History Making History: The New Historicism in American Religious Thought* (Albany: State University of New York Press, 1988), p. 4.
14. Ibid.

use of their imagination to discover and reproduce in their accounts the meaning of the past.[15]

In postmodern historicism, much has changed. To be sure, here also there is a genuine limitation of inquiry and explanation to the actual experiences of history. The difference is that the role of the imagination is no longer merely mimetic, but integrative or creative. It does not simply discover and reproduce history. The imagination constructs history, "sometimes rather freely and always with the contribution of the interpreter and its community."[16] The communication with past historical particularities is not just to reproduce, but to interact, initiate, and create, just as one does in a conversation.

As one might expect, this creative role of the imagination has earned the new historicists the charge of subjectivism. On the contrary, maintains Dean, they have been quite conservative. With nothing beyond the experiences of history to which to appeal, they have necessarily relied heavily upon its most visible institutions, including the church.[17]

How have the new historicists arrived at their views? Not through the discovery of some transcendent or extrahistorical principles, but through a sort of cultural sensibility which, for want of a better term, we designate postmodernism. Essentially, this includes a radical empiricism which holds that one experiences only what can be experienced within time and space.

Dean summarizes the major tenets of the new historicists, beginning with three negative points:[18]

1. *A rejection of foundationalism.* The new historicists deny the idea that there are some kinds of foundations beyond history. This view they share with the modernists or the old historicists. They see no point in a return to a medieval or premodern understanding of reality and specifically of history.
2. *A rejection of realism.* The new historicists deny the existence of any realities (metaphysical as well as historical) independent of human experience. They do not believe in

15. Ibid., pp. 3–4.
16. Ibid., p. 3.
17. Ibid., p. 5.
18. Ibid., pp. 6–7.

the existence of objective universals which are there to be discovered and understood.

3. *A rejection of the idea of universal subjective characteristics.* The new historicists deny that some sort of transcendental attribute is inherent in all persons. This contradicts the thought of such disparate figures as Immanuel Kant and Sigmund Freud.

From the perspective of the new historicists, the old historicism had the right objectives, but stopped short of complete realization of them. It clung to the concept of extrahistorical entities. By contrast, the new historicists understand themselves to be carrying the objectives of the old historicism through to their natural conclusions. In the process, they espouse three positive tenets:

1. *A radical pluralism.* The new historicists embrace what Dean terms an unlimited pluralism. This is understandable, since they deny the existence of universals beyond the multiple particulars of history. There are, to be sure, generalizations from experience, but they are not to be thought of as anything more than that. They are not real entities, but mere abstractions; they are attempts to describe the particulars of one's world, not actual objects that exist in their own right.

2. *Pragmatism.* Because of their denial of extrahistorical foundations, objective realities independent of human experience, and universal subjective characteristics, the new historicists turn to pragmatism in evaluating any given view. For such judgments they introduce relativistic criteria. In the confusion caused by the absence of absolute criteria, they arbitrate disputes between opposing beliefs, not by appealing to extrahistorical factors, but "by asking which ideas contribute more satisfactory historical consequences."[19] They do admit, however, a primary problem for pragmatism, namely, a pure pragmatism unsupplemented by other perspectives always remains unclear about the meaning of "satisfactory."

3. *The centrality of interpretive imagination.* The new historicists attribute growth in history to the interpreter, the

19. Ibid.

historian. Unlike their predecessors, they see the imagination as creating its ideas rather than receiving them from something abiding within or beyond history. In finding sense in history the individual makes a genuine contribution to that history instead of merely extracting from it some inherent meaning. This is not to be taken as an unrestricted creativity, however. There are checks upon it, both from the past, which limits the signification the present interpreter can supply, and from the future, which will reject those present interpretations that fail to produce satisfactory historical consequences.[20]

To analyze how postmodernism compares with other epistemologies, we turn to an old story which, with some modification, may help us better understand this phenomenon, which is more of a mood than a movement. Three baseball umpires were discussing the calling of balls and strikes. One said firmly, "I call them as they are." That was the rationalist, possessed of such absolute or indubitable certainty as one can have only with clear and distinct ideas. The second said, "I call them as I see them." That was the empiricist, allowing for the possibility of error or of approximation, a disadvantage which is inherent in reliance upon sense experience. The third said, "They ain't neither balls nor strikes until I call them." That man should probably be termed an existentialist, creating reality or calling it into being by his own act of will.

That story is good as far as it goes. But now we must add another umpire, a postmodern person. What would he say? Like the existentialist, he would undoubtedly disavow the existence of any sort of objective criteria for judging pitches to be balls or strikes. He would, however, deny as well that definite classes of pitches are created by his action of calling balls and strikes. He would say something like, "Judgments of balls and strikes do not really describe any specific objects. Our very discussion of the subject is just talk about talk; it helps to create the material with which we deal. We can observe certain clusters of characteristics of what we call balls or strikes; these, however, are not inherent qualities, but just general marks of things. It is helpful

20. Ibid., p. 7.

to have some such sorting, because that works out best for most people most of the time. But such a classification is not a proof of what a particular pitch really was."

The emphasis on creative interpretation is also found in the postmodern approach to understanding the Bible. "Reader-centered criticism" is one label that has been used to describe this approach. It involves the reader in the meaning of the text in ways not ordinarily found in either premodern or modern biblical interpretation. Edgar McKnight describes it as follows: "Radical reader-oriented criticism is postmodern in that it challenges the critical assumption that a disinterested reader can approach a text objectively and obtain verifiable knowledge by applying certain scientific strategies."[21] In postmodernism, by contrast, the reader is directly involved in the meaning of the text. There is, in fact, in this approach an interdependence between the reader and the text. "The text is actualized by the reader in a fashion that the text may be said to actualize the reader."[22]

The Postmodern Theology of Mark C. Taylor

Having examined the background factors which enable us to understand better the general mood or milieu in which postmodern theology is being done, we need to look at a concrete example. Although relatively little has been written thus far by theologians, it is apparent that religion is one of the fields where the implications of postmodernism are the strongest. We shall give primary attention to one person who has clearly identified himself with the deconstructionist movement, and who has attempted to utilize it as a resource in doing theology. Mark C. Taylor, professor of religion at Williams College, issued a major manifesto with his book *Erring*, although its basic ideas had already been anticipated in his *Deconstructing Theology*, as well as in a volume edited by Thomas Altizer, *Deconstruction and Theology*. Taylor has since produced *Altarity*. It is *Erring*, however, which most clearly spells out the principles and procedure of his deconstructionist theology. The book consists of two parts,

21. Edgar V. McKnight, *Postmodern Use of the Bible: The Emergence of Reader-Oriented Criticism* (Nashville: Abingdon, 1988), p. 15.
22. Ibid.

one negative and the other positive. The former he terms "Deconstructing Theology" and the latter, "Deconstructive A/theology."

The Irreversible Change in the World

It is apparent that for Taylor the world has changed decisively and irreversibly. The old ways of doing theology, as well as several other disciplines, simply cannot be pursued. He speaks of postmodernism's opening with a "sense of *irrevocable* loss and *incurable* fault"; we have been wounded by an overwhelming awareness of death, beginning with the death of God and ending with the death of our selves.[23] While the death of God was anticipated in the thought of Hegel, Kierkegaard, and Nietzsche, it was not until the present century that it became fully realized. Unfortunately, many contemporary philosophers of religion and theologians seem unaware of the death of God. Too often they simply try to recapture a past which is decisively gone. Such an attitude and such actions are indefensible.[24]

This sense of the irreversible change in our world admittedly leaves us in a quandary. We must begin where we are, but there is confusion over where that is.[25] People are unsure of where they have come from and where they are going. The old answers no longer seem to mean much; and instead of a unified answer to our questions, we are getting manifold and conflicting answers.[26] We are in what Taylor terms "a time between times and a place which is no place."[27] Thus, if we are to do our work of theology at all, we must do it with a sense of dislocation.

This news of the death of God has brought differing reactions, as we might well expect.[28] First we have those who treat it with indifference. These are relatively unreflective people, who are totally immersed in their everyday activities. A second group is troubled by the implications of postmodernism and even of modernism for traditional religious beliefs. They usually respond with an emphatic rejection of these critiques. The solution gen-

23. Taylor, *Erring*, p. 6.
24. Ibid.
25. Ibid., p. 3.
26. Ibid.
27. Ibid., p. 16.
28. Ibid., pp. 4–5.

erally followed and recommended is a reassertion of traditional orthodoxy. The members of a third group welcome the news of the death of God with great enthusiasm, for they now have a sense of liberation from the constricting authoritarianism which they associate with a transcendent God. There is a fourth group, however, that especially interests Taylor. These are the marginal people, individuals who find themselves in a sort of "no man's land" or, as we would probably term it now, "no person's land." These are persons to whom the question of religious belief is of interest and concern, but who find themselves suspended between the loss of the old certainties and the dearth of new beliefs. They "constantly live on the border that joins and separates belief and unbelief." They are searching but do not find. Taylor's special interest in this group is revealed in his comment: "It is to these marginal people (among whom I count myself) that this study is addressed."[29]

Essentially, then, *Erring* is intended to be a piece of apologetics, and should be viewed that way. It may not be the traditional apologetics with which we are familiar, but insofar as it is an attempt to facilitate belief, or to make it possible for persons to understand and to exercise faith, it is apologetics. Taylor observes that in the twentieth century one of the most effective ways of addressing people who find themselves between belief and unbelief has been to employ insights from contemporary philosophy. The ideas of such widely differing philosophers as Martin Heidegger, Ernst Bloch, Ludwig Wittgenstein, and Alfred North Whitehead have been pressed into service. Some of the innovative developments in theology, such as process theology, liberation theology, the theology of hope, existential theology, and hermeneutical theology might not have been possible without the contributions of contemporary philosophy. Taylor notes that the philosophy known as deconstruction seems especially appropriate for this role, although it has not thus far made much impact upon philosophy of religion and theology. On the surface, of course, deconstruction seems an unlikely and inappropriate potential partner for theology, since it appears to be avowedly atheistic. Derrida himself has said that deconstruction "blocks every relationship to theology." And yet deconstruction

29. Ibid., p. 5.

is of potential use to theology in that it faces squarely the fact of the death of God and draws the implications of that fact for various areas of thought. Indeed, Taylor asserts that it would not be too much to claim that "deconstruction is the hermeneutic of the death of God," a statement that he emphasizes by italicizing it in his book.[30]

The inability or unwillingness to come to grips with the fact of the death of God has made it impossible for most Western theology to embrace postmodernism. This inability or unwillingness is at least in part a result of failure to recognize the effects that the death of God has had in certain closely related areas. In Christian theology God, self, history, and the Book are part of an intricate network, a complex web. The self is made in the image of God and mirrors its Creator. History is the realm where divine guidance and human initiative meet. The Book weaves a unified story of this interaction between God and the self. Being bound in this intricate relationship, these concepts are not isolated from one another. What happens to one inevitably affects what happens to the others as well. Thus, we cannot come to grips with the death of God until we have fully recognized its effects or echoes, as Taylor terms them, in these other areas: the disappearance of the self, the end of history, and the closure of the Book.[31]

Taylor proceeds to observe that Western theological tradition rests upon what he calls a polar or, more precisely, a dyadic foundation. On a full page he lists various opposed concepts, such as God and World, Life and Death, Centered and Excentric, Depth and Surface. Much modern thought struggles to overcome this polarity in which each member of a pair can profit only by diminishing or defeating the other. So some resort to radical revolution. It is not enough, however, to achieve a mere reversal, where the usually subordinate member of a pair is made supreme. What must be achieved instead is an inversion which is simultaneously a subversion of the whole system. Taylor says, "What is needed is a critical lever with which the entire inherited order can be creatively disorganized. It is at this point that deconstruction becomes a potential resource for the a/theologian."[32] Deconstruction unravels the very fabric of

30. Ibid., p. 6.
31. Ibid., p. 7.
32. Ibid., p. 10.

Western theology and philosophy, but it does so from within. As long as theology remains bound to its traditional approach, that is, to dyadic opposition, deconstruction will oppose and exclude theology. But by challenging the pattern of opposition, by "inverting and subverting the poles between which Western theology has been suspended, deconstruction reverses itself and creates a new opening for the religious imagination."[33]

The Procedure of Deconstructing Theology

It is necessary to observe Taylor's procedure as he begins his actual work of detailing the deconstruction of theology. We must recognize that he is not giving us a usual type of theological argument. In the words of Peter Hodgson, "Taylor's argument does not advance conceptually, logically, or indeed argumentatively in any conventional sense."[34] Rather, he establishes connections by engaging in wordplay and word associations. He particularly likes to trace the etymology of a word and to list all of its possible meanings. He plays with words, utilizing puns, hyphens, slashes, and parentheses to draw out possible meanings. It should be noted that such practices are quite in keeping with his understanding of language. Following the lead of his mentor, Derrida, he holds that language does not refer to objects, but to other signs, meanings, and interpretations, and that the use of language is generative of meaning. In a sense, what is said does not matter as much as how it is said. Taylor is to be commended for illustrating this point by the very form of his expression. The reader, however, especially one trained in logic, objectivistic linguistics, or analytical philosophy, will have to labor very hard indeed to enter into what Taylor is doing. Trying to follow his procedure will, at the very least, prove to be what Hodgson has termed "an unusual experience."[35]

Taylor gives us an initial example of his method by explaining the title of his book. He takes the term *err* and "roams through the labyrinth of the word," to gain an understanding of its meaning. He spends almost the equivalent of a page listing its derivations, various meanings, and cognates in other languages, to illustrate

---

33. Ibid., p. 25.
34. Peter C. Hodgson, review of *Erring* by Mark C. Taylor, *Religious Studies Review* 12.3–4 (July–Oct. 1986): 256.
35. Ibid.

how he will wander through the concepts that he intends to examine throughout the book.[36] In so doing, he will deviate (err) from some of the conventional or well-established approaches.

When he comes to discuss the death of God, Taylor initially points out that humanistic atheism is merely a modern form of this belief. The Death of God theology actually received its original impetus from the Reformation, especially from Martin Luther's *pro nobis* (Christ lived and died "for us"), with its emphasis upon the subjective self. An additional step was taken with Descartes's *cogito*, which makes the human self supreme and God merely one more object of the self's thought.[37] Because God has heretofore always been experienced as our master and as that which blocks our struggle for autonomy and deprives us of our own birth, that is to say, as death, the putting of God to death is a positive move. It is both the assertion of the self as its own master and the seizing of life.

Deconstruction takes this process one step further. In mastering an external object (e.g., God), we necessarily also internalize it. And in putting to death and thus "possessing" this object (the other), we in turn become possessed by it. The external object, now inside us, is experienced as both a repressive master from without and a seductive demon within. In Sigmund Freud's terminology, the superego forms and gradually comes to dominate the ego. The aggression that was formerly directed against the other is now internalized. In addition, when we internalize the other, we internalize its unknown aspects and so come face to face with the unknowableness of at least a part of the self. Thus, says Taylor, "the repressive master and the seductive demon join forces to split the subject."[38] The result is that the self is itself destroyed.

The humanist resists the death of the self, failing to see that it is entailed by the death of God. The deconstructionist, on the other hand, sees the inevitable connection, for God and self are parts of the network or web of which we spoke earlier. Nihilism, then, can be a mark either of weakness or of strength. Unable to accept the loss and death of the self, the partial nihilism of the atheistic humanist is a sign of weakness. But the complete nihilism of Taylor and those who like him follow the path of

36. Taylor, *Erring*, pp. 11–12.
37. Ibid., pp. 21–22.
38. Ibid., p. 31.

deconstruction is a sign of strength. "For the writer who suffers the crucifixion of selfhood, nihilism is the mark of the cross. On Golgotha, not only God dies; the self also disappears."[39]

For someone who avowedly adopts the deconstructionist (a)logic, Taylor follows a surprisingly logical pattern in the overall structure of his presentation. Each of the two parts of his book is divided into four chapters, each of which corresponds to a parallel chapter in the other part. And each chapter leads into the next by an overlapping of the argument. The chapter on the death of God is the beginning of the discussion of the disappearance of the self. The chapter on the self adumbrates the discussion of the end of history, which leads in turn to the subject of the closure of the Book. Here we have, of course, what Taylor deems the four basic parts of the network of Christian theology.

In developing his deconstructive a/theology, Taylor picks up Derrida's theme that all writing is rewriting. Thus, Taylor's task in the second part is "not to initiate a new departure but to elaborate the implications of insights that have already begun to emerge."[40] Now he makes another key point: on the subjects of the end of God, of self, history, and the Book, "Hegel has emerged as a pivotal figure. On the basis of insights gathered in the first part of the inquiry, it would not be too much to suggest that Western philosophy and theology reach closure in the Hegelian System."[41] Yet it is Kierkegaard's willful misreading and misinterpretation of Hegel and even the middle ground between those two as provided by Nietzsche's doctrine of the will to power that prepare the way for Derrida's idea of writing.

To set the stage as it were for the whole concept of a/theological tenets, Taylor refers to "a parable of word," the story of Jesus' appearance to the two disciples on the road to Emmaus (Luke 24:13–35). They did not recognize Jesus when he was present with them, but only after he left them. Thus "they recognized presence in absence and absence in presence."[42] (It should be noted that the biblical account does not say quite what Taylor suggests; Jesus was recognized and *then* vanished [v. 31]!)

39. Ibid., p. 33.
40. Ibid., p. 98.
41. Ibid.
42. Ibid., p. 103.

Christology

A very important positive point now emerges, perhaps the most significant statement in the book in terms of clarifying Taylor's theology, and certainly the most significant for our present study of Christology:

> The main contours of deconstructive a/theology begin to emerge with the realization of the necessary interrelation between the death of God and radical christology. Radical christology is *thoroughly* incarnational—the divine *"is"* the incarnate word. Furthermore, this embodiment of the divine is the death of God. With the appearance of the divine that is not only itself but is at the same time other, the God who alone is God disappears. The death of God is the sacrifice of the transcendent Author/Creator/Master who governs from afar. Incarnation *irrevocably* erases the disembodied logos and inscribes a word that becomes the script enacted in the infinite play of interpretation. To understand incarnation as inscription is to discover the word. Embodied word is script(ure), the writing in which we are inscribed and which we inscribe. Like all writing, the carnal word is transgressive. Inscription inverts the traditional understanding of the God-world relationship and subverts all forms of transcendence. A/theology is, in large measure, a critique of the notion of the transcendent God, who is "self-clos'd, all-repelling."[43]

Taylor proceeds to elaborate upon this statement, and gives one of the most undialectical expositions of the entire work. He makes it clear that he is not simply reverting to the orthodox view that at a particular point in space and time God became incarnate in a concrete individual, Jesus of Nazareth:

> In order to avoid unnecessary confusion, it is important to realize that in radical christology the divine is *forever* embodied. The word is *always already* inscribed. Incarnation, therefore, is not a once-and-for-all event, restricted to a specific time and place and limited to a particular individual. Rather, inscription is a continual (though not necessarily a continuous) process. To insist that God *"is"* eternally embodied in *word* or that the divine *"is"* incarnate *word* is to imply that "there is a sense in which the word 'God' refers to the word 'word' and the word 'word' refers to the word

43. Ibid., pp. 103–04.

'God.'" God is what word means, and word is what "God" means. To interpret God as word is to understand the divine as scripture or writing.[44]

This is a rather large chunk of quotation and thought to digest. Comparison with other views will prove helpful before going on. The Hegelian background of Taylor's thought shines through quite distinctly here. In Hegel, the antitheses of the transcendent and the immanent, of God and the world, are synthesized. The absolute is all things, not an external something which is other than all finite things. Further, in Hegel, particular events of history are not significant, except insofar as they illustrate or, more correctly, exemplify the repeated patterns of history and ongoing truths. Thus, Jesus was not a once-for-all incarnation of God, but an example of God's continual relating to the world. Taylor similarly abandons the notion of a transcendent God and teaches that incarnation is an eternal occurrence. Particularity gives way to universality, and transcendence gives way to immanence.

It should also be noted that Taylor's interpretation of the death of God has much in common with the doctrine of the Death of God theologians of the mid-1960s, especially Thomas Altizer. By "the death of God" Altizer meant that the transcendent or, as he termed it, "primordial" God had become completely immanent within the human race. This was not a once-for-all occurrence, but a process completed in Jesus of Nazareth.

Yet Taylor exhibits some significant differences from Altizer's view, at least as expounded in *The Gospel of Christian Atheism*. Altizer maintains that there has been a change in God's status: he metamorphosed from the primordial God into the incarnate God over a period of time.[45] Taylor does not seem to hold that there ever was a time in which God had transcendent status, but only that there was a time when people were able to conceive of him that way and did so. The change, in other words, has been in human understanding, a view which more closely approxi-

---

44. Ibid., p. 104. The quotation "there . . . 'God'" is from Robert Scharlemann, "The Being of God When God Is Not Being God: Deconstructing the History of Theism," in Thomas J. J. Altizer et al., *Deconstruction and Theology* (New York: Crossroad, 1982), p. 101.

45. Thomas J. J. Altizer, *The Gospel of Christian Atheism* (Philadelphia: Westminster, 1966), pp. 102–12.

Problems of Incarnational Christology

mates that of another of the Death of God theologians, William Hamilton.[46] Further, Altizer thinks of the change as progressive, so that it comes ever closer to completion as time passes. Taylor, on the other hand, seems to think of the change as something that happens *in toto* repeatedly, that is to say, continually rather than continuously. Finally, Altizer's view is that God becomes incarnated in individuals, including Jesus, and possibly secondarily in groups or organizations. For Taylor, incarnation seems to be in an activity, namely, writing. He utilizes Derrida's concept of writing as virtually a substitute for the discredited concept of God. In the traditional understanding of language and of writing, a sign (word) is believed to refer to an object. That notion is tied to the ontotheological scheme in which God is the "transcendental signified," functioning as "the purported locus of truth that is supposed to stabilize all meaningful words."[47] Taylor introduces instead the idea of a continuous interplay of signs. Signs refer not to objects but to other signs; all signification takes place within a "complex signifying web." He quotes Derrida as saying that this network of signs is "the functional condition, the condition of possibility, for every sign."[48]

Taylor spends considerable time distancing his view from the traditional dyadic view referred to earlier. In conventional theology the opposing concepts of each dyad endeavor either to absorb or to disperse one another, but in Taylor's system they are held in constant tension with each other.[49] This dynamic interplay of opposing words and concepts is actually the basis of reality: "Writing is the forceful play of differences that forms the nonoriginal origin of everything."[50]

Analysis

Let us pause for a bit of analysis, difficult as that may be in light of the opacity of Taylor's writing. He is obviously dependent on both Hegel and Derrida. Like Hegel he holds that there

46. William Hamilton, "The Death of God Theologies Today," in Thomas J. J. Altizer and William Hamilton, *Radical Theology and the Death of God* (Indianapolis: Bobbs-Merrill, 1966), pp. 38–42.
47. Taylor, *Erring*, p. 105.
48. Ibid., p. 107.
49. Ibid., p. 109.
50. Ibid., p. 113.

is an organic character to reality; each part is what it is only in relationship to the whole. Here, however, the basis or ground of everything is words and their continuous interplay in writing. In Taylor's thought, writing plays the role that mind does in Hegel's, or that the dialectic does in dialectical materialism. It is the moving force, as it were, that causes what happens to happen. And it serves to fill much the same sort of role that God does in classical theism. There is, however, a significant departure from Hegel here. In Hegel, the thesis and the antithesis become synthesized, each being "lifted up" into a new entity. In Taylor, however, the differences do not get lost. They continue to exist in tension with one another, constantly interchanging. This is Kierkegaard's either/or rather than Hegel's both/and.

We have noted the similarities to the Death of God theology of the 1960s. Of the persons who formed the core of that group (Thomas Altizer, William Hamilton, Paul van Buren, and, to a lesser extent, Gabriel Vahanian), Taylor's ideas, style, and method of argumentation most strongly resemble those of Altizer. Here one senses the apocalyptic vision of Altizer rather than the cool, logical analysis of van Buren. Yet with the substantive and stylistic similarities, there are some differences.

For one thing, Taylor does not display the sense of loss or of grief over the death of God that one finds in the earlier theologians. Perhaps it is that Taylor has had more time than did Altizer to contemplate and thus adjust to the conclusion that God has died. There is reference to the irrevocable loss occasioned by the death of God and of one's self,[51] but the angst, the pathos, is missing. Further, Taylor's proposed course of action in view of this loss differs from what one finds in the Death of God theologians. Believing that God is now incarnated in all of our fellow humans, Hamilton advocated practical action (such as involvement in the civil-rights movement) as a means for recapturing the sense of the divine.[52] Taylor proposes instead an intellectual playing with words, perhaps because the locus of incarnation for him is not persons, but words and ideas.

We also need to make some observations regarding the nature of Taylor's Christology. Incarnation, in his view, is a diffused

---

51. Ibid., p. 6.
52. Hamilton, "Death of God Theologies," pp. 46–50.

presence of God rather than a concentrated, once-for-all event.
This dispersion of divinity, one might be inclined to say, is
Taylor's Christ, for he speaks of a "radical christology [that] is
thoroughly incarnational. The carnality embodied in the free
play of carnival and comedy overturns every form of repressive
transcendence."[53] He is reluctant to use the term *Christ*, or
christ, of this process or of that which underlies it. In fact, the
word appears only seven times in the book, and frequently the
context is a reference to the traditional, logocentric approach. It
is even more evident that Jesus is not central or determinative,
the word *Jesus* appearing merely four times and only in passing,
the first three times in reference to the traditional Christian
view, and the fourth as an illustration.[54] All of the traditional
functions of Christ—revealing God, sustaining reality, delivering
humans from their predicament—have been reassigned to the
free play of words and ideas.

There is another point which needs to be made about this
postmodern Christology, a point which Taylor does not make
explicitly, since he says so little about Christology, but which
seems to follow logically from his basic principles. We have seen
that the various manifestations of postmodernism deny that
there is some fixed objective truth which we should strive to
attain. Historians, literary and art critics, and philosophers actually create or contribute to truth by their discussions. History (in
the sense of the writing down of what has occurred) makes history (in the sense of the events which have occurred and are
occurring), as Dean has pointed out in the title of one of his
books (*History Making History*). The study of religion is not of
extrahistorical realities or even of the social context of the Bible
and sacred institutions, but of the spiritual community's interpretation of its God. Thus, "religion's own interpretations of God
could be understood to in part alter the meaning of God, for the
signifier is always capable, to some extent, of altering the meaning of the signified."[55] By our discussion of Christology we are
contributing to the incarnation of God and thus, to the extent
that we use the term, to Christ. Just as history makes history, it

53. Taylor, *Erring*, p. 168.
54. Ibid., pp. 15, 55, 65, 103.
55. William Dean, *American Religious Empiricism* (Albany: State University of New
York Press, 1986), p. 7.

is theology (the discussion of the doctrine) that makes theology (the doctrine believed) and Christology that makes Christology.

Evaluation

We have examined briefly the rather remarkable postmodern philosophy and a/theology. It is apparent that if taken seriously, it constitutes a major challenge to theology and specifically to traditional Christology. We now need to evaluate this scheme of thought, beginning with the positive:

1. We must commend the postmodern theologians for their sensitivity and responsiveness to recent developments in the intellectual world. They have made the effort to work through difficult but important writings coming from outside the field of theology. They thus bid to introduce these influences to theology and to be among the first to interact with them. They have taken cognizance of the fact that a virtual paradigm shift has taken place in the intellectual world, and are seeking to deal with it.

2. The postmodern theologians have made an effort to be genuinely apologetic, in the sense of seeking to make the message of Christianity intelligible and even credible in an age when that seems quite impossible to many persons. They have singled out for their attention a group of disenchanted or indifferent persons for whom no one else is manifesting much concern.

3. The scholars in question have shown genuine honesty and courage. In discussing theology they are willing to look at any and all considerations, and to follow the truth wherever it may lead them. In this sense, they are truly modern or postmodern persons.

These are commendable objectives and accomplishments. There are, however, some significant problems for postmodern theology:

1. There is a problem with both meaning and truth. The question is, How shall we decide whether a view is true, or even whether that matters? Let us assume that what is being presented to us is in some sense a claimant to belief. How shall we evaluate it? Given the type of linguistic play that postmodernism engages in, can we establish whether something is right or wrong? For example, is postmodernism itself a (re)mark(able) tale/or should it be mark(ed down as) tailor(ed) goods? How can comments like this count for or against acceptance of a particu-

lar view? What we have here are the kinds of word games that children and even adults sometimes play—puns, tongue twisters, and the like. But do such activities have any bearing upon the question of truth and falsity?

Now, to be sure, we must recognize that we are not dealing with a rationalist view. Indeed, Taylor has been quite explicit about repudiating the dyadic structure of logocentrism. But at the same time he seems to present a rational type of argument to persuade us to accept the system of belief he is advocating. I submit that what we have here is not a proof, but only the illusion of a proof.

We are all familiar with optical illusions, which appear to the eye to be something that they are not. There are also intellectual illusions, which appear to the mind to be something that they are not. Søren Kierkegaard maintained that accumulating various proofs for the existence of God will ultimately prove futile. No conclusion about an entity's quality can emerge from merely quantitative additions. One instructor illustrated this point by telling his class about "nis balls," which are small, hard, white spherical objects similar to golf balls but without the dimples. If we have one nis ball and add another, we have two nis balls, then three, four, eventually nine nis balls, and then, by simply adding one more, we have tennis balls. Voilà! We have a new kind of ball as the result of adding more of the old kind. A new quality has been quantitatively produced. But that is not really the case. What we have is just one more of the same kind of ball. The apparent qualitative change is an intellectual illusion. The same is true of Taylor's endeavors. Do we prove anything by punning on a name, or by introducing hyphens, brackets, parentheses, or slashes? If we have studied all the etymological possibilities of a word (a dubious lexicographical endeavor at best) and examined all the variant definitions, have we established what the meaning is to be in a particular instance? If we think we have, we are probably victims of an intellectual illusion.

2. If, on the other hand, Taylor is to be interpreted as not arguing that his statements are true, then what is he doing at this point? Do we not have to question whether there can be any real exchange of information? Can what one person perceives as true be properly designated as true by and for another? Must we not simply say, "That is how it is for you, but not for me"?

Deconstructionists have been charged with subjectivism, but is this not a valid criticism in view of the arguments they have raised against the objective logocentric and dyadic approaches? Have they built into their arguments objective criteria that prevent subjectivism?

3. There appears to be inconsistency in Taylor's procedure. He attempts to demolish (or deconstruct) the use of objective arguments to support the traditional approach. Yet that seems to undercut the very possibility of his convincing others of his point. What is the status of an argument that seems to be attempting to prove objectively that objective proofs are impossible? He cannot have it both ways.

One response to this criticism is that Taylor is not trying to offer persuasive logical or rational arguments. He is merely using rhetorical devices to evoke a nonrational or intuitive apprehension. But if so, we ought to have a definite explanation of his procedure. Consider, for comparison, Kierkegaard's use of indirect discourse, the maieutic method, and Socratic midwifery.

In making the same criticism Eric Holzwarth says of a fairly typical passage that it is neither philosophy nor criticism, but a new kind of writing which has partially dissolved the boundary between primary (literary, religious) and secondary (critical, theological) texts. Thus, he says, "we also risk dissolving the boundary between reflection upon religious experience and religious experience itself."[56]

There is another aspect to Taylor's inconsistency. At times his approach seems to contradict his beliefs. For example, there is a rather definite logical organization to his book: each chapter in the first part is paralleled by a corresponding chapter in the second part. And despite his decrying the logic of historical progression, he himself tells us how things have been in the past, are now, and will be.[57]

4. There seems to be no real dimension of ethical concern. By contrast, the Death of God theologians pointed out how their view entails ethical concerns and leads to action. Virtually all Christian theologies at some point draw ethical implications

56. Eric Holzwarth, review of *Erring* by Mark C. Taylor, *Religious Studies Review* 12.3–4 (July–Oct. 1986): 261.

57. Walter Lowe, "A Deconstructionist Manifesto: Mark C. Taylor's *Erring*," *Journal of Religion* 66.3 (July 1986): 324–25.

from their tenets. This kind of sensitivity and seriousness seems lacking in Taylor's writing, as Peter Hodgson has pointed out: "Taylor is very much attuned to the hedonism of the American Derrideans."[58] Taylor calls upon us to engage in endless, aimless wandering. But, says Hodgson, "this acceptance of the given leaves utterly unchallenged the structures of domination and oppression from which the great majority of earth's population suffers."[59]

5. Postmodernism seems to be an elitist view of the world. To be sure, religion is not the same as theology, and one cannot expect that all religious persons will be able to understand and assimilate the theology of the professor, or that pastors will be able to preach it from the pulpit. Responsible theology, however, should be translatable into religion. This is not true of post-modernism, which seems to be an attempt to deal with the intellectual problems of an important but exceedingly small group. It has no message for others. Postmodernism is not a theology for professors in church-related seminaries, for pastors, and certainly not for the lay people in the pews. What does one who holds a deconstructive a/theology have to say, for example, to the parents of a teenager who is addicted to cocaine, or to a wife whose husband has just left her for another woman, or to a man who has just been informed that he has a fast-growing terminal malignancy? Deconstruction is only for university students and for professors in university departments of religion who read papers on the subject at professional societies. We have here a sort of Gnosticism for those initiated into the secrets of the free play of words. Perhaps we also have here a sort of snobbery. Without minimizing Taylor's personal angst, we must recognize that he does not touch the problems of the major segments of society. Hodgson's words may be unduly severe here, bordering on ad hominem, but they do make the point eloquently:

> Taylor's god, it appears to me, is for those who don't need a real God—a God who saves from sin and death and the oppressive powers—because they already have all that life can offer; this is a god for those who have the leisure and economic resources to

58. Hodgson, review of *Erring*, p. 258.
59. Ibid.

engage in an endless play of words, to spend themselves un-
reservedly in the carnival of life, to engage in solipsistic play primarily to avoid boredom and attain a certain aesthetic and erotic
pleasure. Taylor's god is a god for the children of privilege, not
the children of poverty; a god for the oppressors, not the oppressed (although of course he wants to do away with all the
structures of domination); a god for the pleasant lawns of ivied
colleges, not for the weeds and mud of the basic ecclesial communities; a god for the upwardly mobile, not for the underside of
history.[60]

6. It is difficult to assess in what sense deconstructive a/theol-
ogy is to be called Christian. In particular, so little is made of the
historical person of Jesus of Nazareth that one wonders whether
there is any justification for calling the movement Christian.
Perhaps it is not intended to be Christian. At times, in fact, the
movement shows resemblance to Buddhism.

7. When, as William Dean points out, neopragmatists seek to
justify beliefs without a correspondence theory of truth, there is
frequently a lack of agreement about what "works."[61] Do we not
require some understanding of human nature and of history and
its directions (human destiny)? And to determine whether an
idea or action actually results in a desirable outcome, do we not
require something approximating the correspondence theory of
truth? Indeed, William James himself accepted such a theory, at
least in a broad sense.[62]

8. There is an apparently self-destructive facet to postmodernism. If it is true, it, like all philosophies, is false, or
meaningless, or irrelevant. When deconstruction succeeds in
accomplishing its task, has it not done too much, as we implied
above, and deconstructed itself?[63] And since life has practical
dimensions that go far beyond the realm of abstract thought, is
not postmodernism an untenable, or at least unworkable, view?

---

60. Ibid., pp. 257–58.
61. Dean, *History Making History*, pp. 6–7.
62. William James, *Pragmatism* (New York: Meridian, 1955), p. 132.
63. Allan Bloom suggests that deconstruction is "the last, predictable, stage in the
suppression of reason and the denial of the possibility of truth in the name of philosophy" (*The Closing of the American Mind* [New York: Simon and Schuster, 1987], p. 379).

13

The Logical Problem.
(1) Mythological Christology

The doctrine of the incarnation is a logical conception: Jesus was simultaneously fully God and fully human. This idea is subject to some serious potential difficulties, including some which have become particularly problematic in the last part of the twentieth century. An age-old problem is the charge of logical contradiction: deity (infinite) and humanity (finite) simply cannot coexist in one person. This apparent contradiction has led some scholars to conclude that the traditional concept of incarnation is meaningless. Accordingly, mythological Christology contends that the concept should not be taken in a literal fashion; it should instead be understood in a symbolic or poetic fashion. It is also argued that the traditional concept was derived from postbiblical culture rather than from divine revelation.

In chapter 14 we will look at yet another dimension to the logical problem. The idea that the Christian message should be presented and analyzed propositionally is believed to be mistaken. Instead of the discursive approach of traditional systematic theology, the narrative theologians propose concentrating on the stories that carry the key ideas of Christianity. While less explicitly opposed to traditional incarnational theology than is the mythical interpretation, narrative Christology also in effect redefines the doctrine of incarnation.

Rejection of Literal Incarnation

One might have expected that the interpretation of the incarnation as a myth would have died with the decline and fading of the demythologization school of Rudolf Bultmann. Scarcely any clearer evidence of the repeatable nature of theology can be found, however, than the book *The Myth of God Incarnate*, which appeared in 1977. A symposium edited by John Hick, it includes contributions by several scholars, both biblical and theological, arguing for the dispensability of the concept of incarnation.

It is difficult to find any clear thesis for the book. The closest approximation to a thesis comes in the preface, where Hick quotes with approval the words of T. S. Eliot, "Christianity is always adapting itself into something which can be believed."[1] He observes, for example, that in the nineteenth century Christianity made two major adjustments in response to the increase of knowledge. It accepted the doctrine of evolution, with the concomitant idea that the human race is part of nature. It also accepted the idea that the Bible, having been written by a variety of humans in a variety of circumstances, cannot have been verbally inspired.[2] The contributors to the symposium are convinced, says Hick, that a third adjustment is necessary in the last part of the twentieth century. "Growing knowledge of Christian origins [has resulted in the] recognition that Jesus was (as he is presented in Acts 2:22) 'a man approved by God' for a special role within the divine purpose, and that the later conception of him as God incarnate, the Second Person of the Holy Trinity living a human life, is a mythological or poetic way of expressing his significance for us."[3]

The statement here is plain enough: Jesus was not actually the incarnate Son of God. He was a man chosen by God for a spe-

1. *The Myth of God Incarnate*, ed. John Hick (Philadelphia: Westminster, 1977), p. ix.
2. Ibid.
3. Ibid.

cial role. The doctrine of the incarnation did not originate in Jesus' time and is not to be taken literally. Rather, it is a later reflection that seeks to express in poetical or nonliteral form the unique character of his life.

Maurice Wiles in the opening chapter states the issue clearly. Christianity, he says, is often described as an incarnational religion. Now there are both a looser and a stricter sense of the word *incarnational*. In the looser sense, it means simply that Christianity is "a religion in which man's approach to God is through the physical world rather than by escape from it." In the narrower sense, it means that Christianity is "a faith whose central tenet affirms the incarnation of God in the particular individual Jesus of Nazareth." It is this narrower sense that is at stake here. The issue is whether this conception is essential to Christianity.[4]

The argument of *The Myth of God Incarnate* is complex and involved. As a symposium the book is composed of a series of chapters not always clearly related to one another. In general, the first step is to examine the biblical materials relating to the person of Christ and to assess the degree to which the doctrine of incarnation stems from the life and teaching of Jesus himself and from the testimony of those contemporaries who knew him best. The second step is more theological in character—examining the nature of myth and the role which it plays in theological construction.

Literal Incarnation as a Product of Postbiblical Theologizing

It will be helpful to analyze the case presented in the several chapters of the treatise. The first argument against the view that Jesus was the Second Person of the Trinity incarnated in a human is that it is not part of the genuine biblical tradition. It is, rather, a product of theologizing either in the later biblical period or after the completion of the canon. The second argument is that the idea of a literal incarnation is both untenable and undesirable. It is untenable because it is incoherent and internally contradictory; it is undesirable because it has unfortunate consequences for both our belief in and relationship to God.

---

4. Maurice Wiles, "Christianity Without Myth?" in *Myth of God Incarnate*, ed. Hick, p. 1.

The conclusion that literal incarnation is not part of the genuine biblical tradition stems from an investigation of the New Testament with the usual methods of form criticism. In her essay "A Cloud of Witnesses," Frances Young begins by pointing out that statements about the person of Christ are parasitic upon soteriology; the New Testament is itself a great "testimony-meeting," a collection of documents witnessing to the saving effects of the life, death, and resurrection of Jesus.[5] Young readily acknowledges the presuppositions of form criticism and redaction criticism regarding the material that was selected for preservation in the New Testament: "The faith of the church in a given historical setting affected the preservation and handing on of traditions about Jesus; and the faith of the gospel-writers in another given situation affected their selection of material, its arrangement and preservation."[6] That is to say, the New Testament writings reflect "the witness of communities and individuals to the effects of faith in Jesus Christ in their own particular situation." Young's stress, then, is on "the historical particularity of the documents and the cultural particularity of the images and concepts used to express faith in Jesus Christ."[7]

Young notes that recent discussion of New Testament Christology has tended to concentrate upon the christological titles. In existence and use before the time of Christ, these titles were adopted and adapted by the Scripture writers to give expression to their own personal response to Jesus; significantly, he never used these titles in reference to himself.[8] When we look closely at the New Testament, we find that their uses and contexts, the particular Christologies they help to construct, vary greatly, a reflection of the differing difficulties and crises of faith which the church and the biblical authors were facing.

It is Young's contention that in none of the New Testament Christologies do we find a genuine incarnational view. She illustrates this point by examining Paul's writings. Paul taught that Jesus was a person who acted on God's behalf for our salvation. He was exalted by God. In none of the Pauline passages which she examines, however, does Young find any suggestion of an

5. Frances Young, "A Cloud of Witnesses," in *Myth of God Incarnate*, ed. Hick, p. 14.
6. Ibid.
7. Ibid., p. 15.
8. Ibid.

incarnational view. What she finds instead could anachronistically be called Adoptionism.[9] There is a developing conception of a preexistence, of a man from heaven, but not of a divine being. This man alone has always been "the true 'image of God' as man was created to be."[10] Young concludes: "The notion of God being incarnated in the traditionally accepted sense is read into, not out of, the Pauline epistles, and I suggest that, space permitting, the same could be argued for the other New Testament documents."[11] At the same time she concludes that, on the whole, the New Testament is thoroughly christocentric. It presents a being who "'stands for' God, and is the focus through which God is revealed to those who respond." Jesus is "the one intermediary through whom God is revealed and can be approached with confidence."[12]

It was in the patristic period of theologizing that the doctrine of incarnation was developed, a product of both the cultural situation in which Christians found themselves and the political situation within the church. The doctrine is, then, culturally conditioned. Young maintains that the church during this period was seeking to respond to two questions: How is the exalted Jesus, whom we worship as Lord, related to the one and only God? and How is God related to the world?[13] Although there is danger of oversimplification, Young maintains that the dominant philosophy of the period was a type of Neoplatonism. Congenial in many ways to the ethical monotheism of Judaism, Neoplatonism was extensively used in formulating the Christology of the period. In particular, the Greek philosophy had always been puzzled about the relationship between the one and the many. This problem was finally solved by the doctrine of the incarnation, according to which the eternal Logos actually came into the world and assumed its conditions.[14] On the other hand, the variations between the Christologies that arose during the patristic age, such as those of Arius and of Athanasius, were the result of differing conceptions of salvation.[15] Thus, bearing the

9. Ibid., p. 20.
10. Ibid., p. 22.
11. Ibid.
12. Ibid., pp. 22–23.
13. Ibid., p. 23.
14. Ibid., p. 25.
15. Ibid., p. 27.

marks of both the prevailing philosophical presuppositions of
the time and the political wranglings within the church, these
Christologies, like the New Testament expressions, can be said
to have been culturally conditioned.[16]

There are reasons to see this doctrinal development not as a
providential uncovering of truth given implicitly by the Holy
Spirit, but as a historical process which led, according to Young,
to "the blind alleys of paradox, illogicality, and docetism."[17] We
are faced, then, with the question of what we shall do with these
ancient formulations. Some have simply dismissed them as
based upon outdated philosophical categories involving concepts like "substance." This is not the approach which Young
takes, however. She asks what it was that led theologians to
make such formulations, what essential value they were seeking
to preserve. She comments: "It is . . . important to recognize that
the sense of salvation received through [Jesus] was the driving
force of the subsequent philosophical and doctrinal formulations. It was the dynamic reality of their experience which they
sought to preach and articulate for their contemporaries."[18]
Young suggests that we emulate their example. We can become
part of the group of witnesses in the New Testament and the
early church by seeking to do what they did—expressing, in our
own time and in our own thoughts and words, our personal
experience of the redemptive effect of faith in this same Jesus.

At this point Young's position seems remarkably like that of
Rudolf Bultmann.[19] It is even, in some ways, like that of Harry
Emerson Fosdick and other modernizers of the Christian faith.[20]
For she is saying that certain ways of expressing the Christian
experience are outmoded and therefore untenable and indeed
unnecessary to the preservation of the Christian faith. The solution is to preserve the essential experiences of Christianity,
which are, in the broadest sense of the word, soteriological in
nature. While no longer interpreting the biblical and patristic

16. Ibid., p. 28.
17. Ibid., p. 29.
18. Ibid., p. 30.
19. Cf. Rudolf Bultmann, "The New Testament and Mythology," in Rudolf Bultmann
et al., *Kerygma and Myth: A Theological Debate*, ed. Hans Werner Bartsch (New York:
Harper and Row, 1961), pp. 1–44.
20. Cf. Harry Emerson Fosdick, *The Modern Use of the Bible* (New York: Macmillan,
1933), pp. 97–130.

writers literally, we should continue to follow their chief objective: giving expression to the redemptive experience.

Michael Goulder pursues further the quest into the origin of the incarnational myth. He begins autobiographically, as do a number of the contributors to *The Myth of God Incarnate*. He notes that early in his ministry he held to the doctrine of the incarnation, basing his belief largely upon John 1:14, "The Word became flesh and dwelt among us," together with similar statements in Philippians 2 and Colossians 1, and hints in other Pauline letters and Hebrews. He asked himself where John got this incarnational idea, and the usual answer was that he received it as a truth from God by inspiration. Historical study, however, proves to be the enemy of the theory of inspiration, for it removes the mist from such matters, and with it the mystery as well. It is Goulder's hypothesis that the church drew its teaching of incarnation from two sources. One is the Galilean eschatological myth, the other the Samaritan Gnostic myth. He acknowledges that as a reconstruction of history his hypothesis can never be anything more than probable. He recognizes that others may trace the doctrine of incarnation to different historical sources; indeed, some of the other contributors to the volume have done just that. Having admitted the uncertainty of his theory, he turns his attention to the Samaritan myth.[21]

Goulder takes note of the opening chapter of Acts, where Luke describes the expansion of the church as taking place in Jerusalem, in all Judea and Samaria, and to the uttermost parts of the earth. In the rest of the book there is a disproportion in the attention given to these various stages of the church's expansion. While sixteen chapters are given to the mission beyond Palestine (chs. 13–28), only twenty-two verses are devoted to the Samaritan mission (8:4–25).

Goulder summarizes five features of Samaritan theology:

1. Though God cannot be experienced through history, he is experienced through revelation (i.e., Scripture).
2. God's revelation should often be spoken of as mysteries and secrets.

---

21. Michael Goulder, "The Two Roots of the Christian Myth," in *Myth of God Incarnate*, ed. Hick, pp. 64–65.

3. Being remote, God is to be spoken of by abstract names.
4. God is a duality. Simon Magus took himself to be an incarnation of one of the persons of the dual Godhead (see Acts 8:9–13).
5. There is no resurrection of the dead.[22]

Goulder suggests that Paul was flexible and would on occasion adopt the positions and arguments of his opponents, including Samaritan missionaries who were propagating their own brand of theology. His early writing, such as Thessalonians, was done before he had any contact with the Samaritans, and shows no sign of an incarnational Christology. In his later writings we find a distinct change. Goulder explains: "Paul appropriated the idea of Jesus' incarnation in the course of dialectic with the Samaritan missionaries in Corinth and Ephesus between 50 and 55."[23]

Young expands upon this particular line of argumentation in her chapter "Two Roots or a Tangled Mass?" Here she affirms the basic soundness of Goulder's argument, but suggests that there are many additional sources from which the idea of incarnation might have come into Christian theology. For example, she mentions the report that Plato was the son of a human mother and the god Apollo.[24] Alexander the Great, Romulus, and others were also said to have been born miraculously of divine descent.[25] Such reports may well have been the background of the tradition regarding Jesus' incarnation.

Young also points out that the early Christian titles for Jesus closely paralleled the terminology used in the various ruler-cults of antiquity. From the time of Alexander on, it was common to give kings and emperors divine honors. Indeed, the Jews suffered great torture rather than confess Caesar as their master, since God alone was their Lord. It is even possible to see hints or echoes of this situation in passages such as 1 Corinthians 12:3.[26]

Another strong candidate for the source of the doctrine of incarnation is the Hellenistic concept of the *theios anēr* ("divine

22. Ibid., pp. 69–74.
23. Ibid., p. 79.
24. Frances Young, "Two Roots or a Tangled Mass?" in *Myth of God Incarnate*, ed. Hick, p. 89.
25. Ibid., pp. 95–96.
26. Ibid., pp. 98–100.

man"). We find accounts of miraculous births, disappearance after death, and other strange manifestations in connection with various exceptional persons. These motifs were borrowed from ancient Greek mythology. Young says, "One cannot dismiss out of hand the view that something of the same thing happened in the case of Jesus."[27] Although it would be difficult to establish direct influence, "people living at roughly the same time do seem to have produced mythological accounts with parallel motifs."[28]

Young examines a number of other possible parallels and influences. Among these are Philo, Jewish rabbis, and the apocalyptic books of Enoch. She recognizes that none of these theories can be established; indeed, all of them have been criticized, partly because in each case the evidence is sparse or late, and partly because none of them provides an exact parallel to the Christian claims regarding Jesus. Nonetheless, she maintains that what no one theory can do in isolation is accomplished by the cumulative impact of the several theories taken together: "There is at least sufficient evidence to have produced each suggestion as a serious possibility, and the total impact of the evidence has led to widespread acceptance of the view that it was the Greek-speaking Gentile converts who transformed Jesus, the Jewish Messiah of Palestine, into an incarnate divine being."[29]

And so while recognizing that objection could be made to the specifics of Goulder's theory, Young declares that the argument of the book does not rest upon any one construction or explanation of the genesis of the Christian doctrine of incarnation. Any of a number of explanations could be substituted for that of Goulder. It is sufficient for us to observe that the general cultural atmosphere in which Christianity originated and grew was conducive to the rise of an idea like incarnation. Accordingly, we should seek the origin of this doctrine in the general syncretistic religion of the period.[30] Young concludes by saying, "Whether or not we can unearth the precise origins of incarnational belief, it is surely clear that it belongs naturally enough to a world in which supernatural ways of speaking seemed the highest and best expression of the significance and finality of

27. Ibid., p. 101.
28. Ibid., p. 102.
29. Ibid., p. 98.
30. Ibid., p. 117.

the one . . . identified as God's awaited Messiah and envoy."[31] In light of some of the criticisms which have been leveled at the book, it will be important for us to retain the form of its argumentation, and especially to determine exactly the basis of Young's conclusion.

There follow additional explanations of the way in which the doctrine of incarnation may have arisen. Leslie Houlden begins by noting that there is not just one Christology in the New Testament, but many. Not only did each writer have his distinctive view, but one of them, Paul, shifted his view in the course of his career. The customary way of treating their views is through an examination of the different titles they used to refer to Jesus. Houlden, however, proposes to distinguish the views on the basis of "their degree of closeness to renewed personal vision."[32] He notes that there are two basic stages of theological creativity, the experiential and the credal. Especially at the beginning of a new religious movement some persons have a heightened awareness of God's presence and power. They now know God differently from before. The existing formulas are inadequate to express their experience. Consequently, new words are invented, or old words are given new meaning. The vividness of the experience often results in imprecision, incoherence, or even inconsistency.[33]

This experiential stage sooner or later yields to the credal stage. Here the link between experience and expression is weakened, lengthened, and altered. It is weakened because the experience is now often secondhand and imitative. It is lengthened because the surging spring of inspiration has been interrupted by a process of reflection, ordering, and systematization. It is altered because other considerations, such as institutional needs and policy, enter in.[34]

Houlden maintains that we find both stages in the New Testament. At the experiential stage the titles for Jesus were not so much labels attached to his person as they were oblique statements about God. They were formally attached to Jesus because he had been the agent by which the early church had been intro-

31. Ibid., p. 119.
32. Leslie Houlden, "The Creed of Experience," in *Myth of God Incarnate*, ed. Hick, p. 127.
33. Ibid., pp. 127–28.
34. Ibid., p. 128.

duced to a new relationship with God or a new dimension of relationship. At the credal stage these titles came to be thought of as a literal description; the imagery of the experiential stage became doctrine. Now all Christians agree at the experiential level, says Houlden, about "the centrality of Jesus for all that concerns man's relationship with God and understanding of him." They also agree upon God's deep and intimate involvement with the world. But are these two general points of agreement equivalents of the statement that "the Word became flesh" and of the Nicene and Chalcedonian conceptions of Jesus? Houlden indicates that, in the final analysis, the pressure of general truth makes certain credal expressions outmoded and irrelevant. In striving to make the message pertinent, it will be necessary to identify in plain terms the earliest experience of God that the primitive church had and we have through Jesus. This may well inspire others to give expression to this experience in terms which are genuine for today.[35]

Literal Incarnation as Untenable and Undesirable

The contributors to *The Myth of God Incarnate* buttress their case against the idea of a literal incarnation. In addition to being the product of postbiblical theologizing instead of a New Testament teaching, it is untenable. In particular, they contend that the idea of incarnation is incoherent or internally contradictory. In a sense, this is not really argued, but assumed in much of what is said. The most extended discussion of the orthodox doctrine of incarnation comes in Don Cupitt's chapter, "The Christ of Christendom." He notes that not since H. P. Liddon in 1865 has a British writer given a scholarly defense of the full deity of Christ. The theological leader who succeeded him, Charles Gore, could not bring himself to defend the traditional view of the incarnation. Instead, he developed the kenotic view that Christ voluntarily gave up his divine attributes to become human.[36]

Cupitt claims that the idea of literal incarnation distorts or contradicts certain traditional tenets of Christianity. It results in anthropomorphism, pagan notions, and even blasphemy. It is,

---

35. Ibid., pp. 131–32.
36. Don Cupitt, "The Christ of Christendom," in *Myth of God Incarnate*, ed. Hick, p. 134.

then, not merely untenable, but also undesirable and negative in its effect. In the long run, as Cupitt puts it, the dogma of the incarnation had "damaging effects upon belief in God, and upon the way man's relation to God was conceived."[37] Cupitt levels four criticisms against the orthodox view:

1. The idea of God's becoming permanently united with humanity in the incarnation suggests a synthesis between the divine and the things of this world. This, however, is to fail to keep separate what Jesus distinguished. Particularly in his parables, Jesus maintained a disjunction between the things of God and the things of humankind. The divine view is very different from the worldly perspective.

A prime example is the kingship of Jesus, which in the Gospels is contrasted sharply with the Gentile kingships. In Christendom, this contrast came to be lost completely, so that Jesus was eventually depicted as crowning the emperor, a case of his stooping only slightly to someone who was but a single step lower on the scale of being. This blurring of the distinction between temporal lordship and the eschatological lordship of Christ led to the erroneous belief that Christ is the "manifest Absolute of history," the basis of present political and ecclesiastical power. And Bultmann made the mistake of rejecting the Jesus of Jewish history in favor of a Greek ecclesiastical Christ. Just as the fundamentalists' absolutized view of the Bible prevents them from understanding it, so too the absolutized view of Jesus keeps us from seeing the rich and complex ways in which he revealed God.[38]

2. The orthodox doctrine claims that at the moment of conception began an indissoluble union of the divine and the human in Jesus. That this miraculous union took place prior to and thus independently of his earthly life means that the suffering and moral struggles which he underwent for our redemption were peripheral and irrelevant. Orthodoxy has attempted to reply to this objection in two ways, neither of which is satisfactory, according to Cupitt. One is the view known as Dyothelitism, according to which Jesus had both a divine and a human will. The other is the idea that the incarnation was dissolved upon the death of Jesus and restored at the resurrection; thus

37. Ibid., p. 140.
38. Ibid., pp. 140–42.

the passion was real. In either case, Cupitt questions whether the orthodox or Chalcedonian formulation does justice to Jesus' priestly and mediatorial office.[39]

3. If the incarnation is literally true, then it is possible to have direct worship of Jesus. This gives rise to a cult of Christ, as contrasted with a cult of God. Cupitt traces to some of the "orthodox" opponents of Arianism in the fourth century the beginning of the practice of praying directly to Christ, rather than praying to God through Christ. He believes that this process of the paganization of Christianity led to the decision of the World Council of Churches to adopt as their doctrinal basis "acknowledgment of our Lord Jesus Christ as God and Saviour"—and nothing more. It may have led finally to the strange view of "Christian Atheism." Cupitt says, "Chalcedonian christology could be a remote ancestor of modern unbelief, by beginning the process of shifting the focus of devotion from God to man. It could not put up any resistance to the focusing of piety upon the glory of the incarnate Lord rather than the glory of God, and then upon the humanity of Christ, and then upon humanity in general. On the contrary, it appeared to legitimate a cult of humanity."[40]

4. If in the incarnation God has permanently assumed human form, then it is possible to depict God in human form. The result has been anthropomorphism and restoration of the pagan notion that God is a superhuman person with gender. This trend was reinforced by use of the traditional Father-Son imagery.[41]

Cupitt has outlined these specific detrimental effects which the doctrine of the incarnation has for theology. Some more general effects are mentioned in other essays in *The Myth of God Incarnate*. Frances Young speaks of what could be called the practical or perhaps even the political effects of doctrinal formulation in general, and the doctrine of incarnation in particular:

1. Living witness and faith are distorted into a set of definitions and propositions.[42]
2. Arrogant and intolerant attitudes are encouraged among the orthodox believers.[43]

39. Ibid., p. 142.
40. Ibid., p. 143.
41. Ibid., pp. 143–45.
42. Young, "Cloud," p. 38.
43. Ibid., pp. 13, 39.

3. The potential richness and variety of christological insights and images are obscured by subordinating everything to the one model of the incarnation of God in Jesus.[44]

4. Any attempt to produce a creed that captures the truth exclusively is divisive in nature. We should ask not whether a particular statement is true, but whether it is healing and constructive rather than dangerous and harmful.[45]

The Alternative: The Mythological Interpretation of Jesus

We have seen the major arguments against the doctrine of the literal incarnation of God in Jesus Christ. It is not part of the original biblical tradition, but arose through the assimilation of external traditions both during the later New Testament era and during the patristic period of doctrinal formulation. It is also internally incoherent and therefore cannot be believed. Finally, insisting upon literal incarnation has adverse doctrinal and sociopolitical effects. Having reviewed these arguments, we now need to examine the alternative advocated in *The Myth of God Incarnate*.

The Nature of Myth Explained and Illustrated

It is not easy to determine the exact meaning of myth or what the function of myth is believed to be. Hick, as we saw at the beginning of this chapter, says that the conception of Jesus as God incarnate is "a mythological or poetic way of expressing his significance for us." This suggests that myth is a legitimate and desirable nonliteral way of giving expression to an experience, in this case to the significance which Christ has in our lives.

A more extended discussion of myth is given in Maurice Wiles's chapter "Myth in Theology." He begins by discussing the introduction of the term *myth* into theology in the nineteenth century. He then examines usage of the term in more-recent theological writings. Here he merely mentions Rudolf Bultmann's

44. Ibid., pp. 13, 38.
45. Ibid., pp. 38–39.

treatment of the term and then moves on to the definitions given by Norman Pittenger and Wolfhart Pannenberg. The statements of Gordon Kaufman, Emil Brunner, and John Knox are explained in greater detail and compared. Wiles proceeds to consider three basic Christian myths: the creation, the fall, and the resurrection of the dead and final judgment. He notes that sometimes a distinction is drawn between these three myths and the incarnation, for it alone refers to what in the proper sense can be thought of as a historical event—the first two are prehistory, and the final judgment is posthistory. By asking how myth functions in these other instances, he tries to determine the nature of myth, particularly in the case of the incarnation.

Wiles quotes Alasdair MacIntyre to the effect that a myth is living or dead, not true or false. It is not something that can be refuted; regarding it as refutable is to treat it not as myth but as a hypothesis or history.[46] Wiles does not fully agree with MacIntyre, who was writing primarily about Platonic myths. Considering the statement too sweeping, Wiles declares that the truth or falsity of a myth is not as simple and straightforward as the truth or falsity of a statement like "the cat sat on the mat" or a directly testable scientific hypothesis. Like poetry, a myth is capable of being interpreted at different levels, and may have more than one interpretation even at the same level. There are, however, limits to the possible interpretations of a myth; and hence there are not an indefinite number of states of affairs with which a myth may be compatible. Wiles says that "in so far as [myths] express certain fundamental aspects of the human condition, they may do so in a way which (apart from extremely far-fetched and implausible interpretations) turns out to be false. Thus while it is bound to be extremely difficult to apply the categories of truth and falsity with any confidence, I do not think it is a procedure which ought to be ruled out in principle in advance."[47]

Wiles points out that the myth of the creation excludes and is excluded by certain types of statements: "If the universe as we know it is a wholly self-contained and self-evolving system, in no

---

46. Maurice Wiles, "Myth in Theology," in *Myth of God Incarnate*, ed. Hick, p. 158.
47. Ibid., p. 159.

way dependent for its existence on anything other than itself, then the creation myth would seem to me to be religiously inappropriate or false." On the other hand, "if the world is in fact dependent on a transcendent, creative source, as the Christian theist claims, then the myth would be appropriate or true."[48] It is not necessary, then, that all the details sometimes attached to a myth like creation be true. For example, the lack of correlation between the biblical account of the order in which the world was created and the order of its evolution as a matter of historical fact does not falsify the myth.[49]

Similar statements can be made about the myth of the fall. It is sometimes viewed as a theodicy explaining the origin of evil in God's world. Wiles declares that when the myth is understood in this way, that is, as attributing evil wholly to wrong human choices, it is false. Yet, he continues, "I am still prepared to treat it as religiously appropriate or true, because I believe it is true that men fall below the highest that they see and that they could achieve."[50]

Wiles holds that the myth of the resurrection of the dead and the final judgment is even more difficult to interpret. The reason is not simply that we are less able to check up on the truth or falsity of this myth than on the truth or falsity of the others, but also that there is a wider variety of beliefs that are in fact felt to be compatible with it. "In my judgment," says Wiles, "for the myth to be religiously appropriate or true, it would need to be true that in some sense man lives on beyond his physical death."[51] Others would not require this much; some hold that the myth is true because they see it as signifying nothing more than the possession of hope, even if that hope is delusive. While he cannot refute this latter interpretation, Wiles feels that resurrection is a highly inappropriate metaphor for so natural a concept as hope.[52]

The Meaning of the Myth of Incarnation

Wiles summarizes his position before moving on to inquire about the more controversial case, that of the incarnation:

48. Ibid.
49. Ibid.
50. Ibid., p. 160.
51. Ibid.
52. Ibid.

The criterion by which I have been trying to distinguish between true and false interpretations of [myths] might be expressed something like this. There must be some ontological truth corresponding to the central characteristic of the structure of the myth. But such a criterion is not at all easy to apply. For one thing if the ontological truth were one that could be expressed with full clarity and precision there would be less need for the myth. In the case of creation I have spoken of the dependence of the world on a transcendent creative source other than itself. In the case of the fall I have spoken of men's falling below the highest that they see and could achieve. In the third case I have spoken of some kind of survival of human life beyond physical death. Thus while I would wish to allow room within Christianity for a wide range of interpretations of these central myths of the faith, I also want to claim that where interpretation of them abandons any ontological element of the kind I have tried to delineate, then the myths are being interpreted in what seems to me an inappropriate way and it would be better to abandon the use of them.[53]

What, then, is the meaning of the myth of the incarnation? There must be, of course, some ontological reality corresponding to the myth. The traditional interpretations insist upon "an identity between the personhood of Jesus and the Second Person of the Godhead." This direct metaphysical understanding has serious inherent difficulties. Can there be other, less direct interpretations which retain the ontological correlation which Wiles requires?[54]

Wiles notes that the doctrine of the incarnation has never been seen as simply a statement about something in the past. It has also been seen as that "which makes possible a profound inner union of the divine and the human in the experience of grace in the life of the believer now and more broadly in the life of the church as a whole."[55] He points out as well the use of such expressions as "the body of Christ" and even "the extension of the incarnation" to refer to the church. May it not be, then, that the union of divine and human in our persons is the ontological truth involved in the myth of the incarnation?[56]

53. Ibid., p. 161.
54. Ibid.
55. Ibid.
56. Ibid.

Wiles notes, however, that there is something peculiar about this particular myth as compared with the others which he has examined. The myth of the incarnation is especially linked to the historical Jesus. Wiles inquires whether it is reasonable to link the incarnation so specially with the historical figure of Jesus while we interpret it as a mythological depiction of the potential union of God and human in every individual. He points out that in order to answer we must take into account the nature and mission of Jesus together with the relationship between Jesus and the distinctively Christian experience in the later life of the church. While there has been great flexibility in the historical claims made regarding Jesus, two statements in particular need to be affirmed for the incarnation myth to be specially applied to him: "First that his own life in its relation to God embodied that openness to God, that unity of human and divine to which the doctrine points. And secondly that his life depicted not only a profound human response to God, but that in his attitudes towards other men his life was a parable of the loving outreach of God to the world."[57] Wiles believes that this much can be firmly established as part of the historical tradition. Although we cannot be certain of all the other details, it is unlikely that any further discoveries will jeopardize the historical certainty of what has here been affirmed.[58]

As Wiles observes, the appropriateness of linking the myth of incarnation especially to Jesus does not depend merely upon his personal character. It also depends upon the historical relationship between Jesus and the experience of grace in the lives of believers. Affirmation of a special relationship may take either a weaker or a stronger form. The weaker form is a simple statement that the truth about our experience of grace first came alive in our tradition through Jesus. The stronger form insists that his life and all that has stemmed from it are essential to the full union of divine and human in our lives. The sole grounds for making such an assertion are historical and psychological reflection on the formation of our spiritual life. Only the course of future history can validate the claim.[59]

57. Ibid., p. 162.
58. Ibid., pp. 162–63.
59. Ibid., p. 163.

Evaluation

The time has now come to make some evaluation of mythological Christology. There appears here the same difficulty found throughout our exposition, namely, the fact that the several writers and their essays do not exactly agree. What we have to do is to discern some common themes or general agreements, and make our response on that basis. A few positive values are worthy of note:

1. The proponents of mythological Christology have pointed out that the Christian revelation came in a definite cultural context. It took the form that it did, at least in part, because it was contextualized to that situation.

2. By seeking sources and parallels in the general culture of the time, the authors of *The Myth of God Incarnate* have, perhaps unwittingly in some cases, called attention to the characteristics of the biblical revelation and the incarnation.

3. The question of the exact denotation of the biblical doctrine of incarnation (and thus, potentially, of all biblical doctrines) has been grappled with. Is this doctrine really expressing something objective, and if so, what is that content?

4. The conditioned character of several of the doctrinal expressions which we use has been brought to our attention.

5. The advocates of mythological Christology have understood that, regardless of the essence of a doctrine, it must be communicated in such a way that it relates to contemporary ways of conceptualizing.

The weaknesses of mythological Christology far outweigh its strengths, however:

1. Mythological Christology seems to involve, to an unusual degree, the genetic fallacy. It is assumed that explaining how a particular conception like the incarnation came to be held determines the issue of its truth or falsity. This seems to be the assumption in Michael Goulder's and Frances Young's extended treatments of the philosophical and theological backgrounds. They attempt to show parallels between the Christian doctrine of incarnation and certain features in Judaism or in other theological systems of the Greco-Roman world. At times they point to a non-Christian parallel with the post–New Testament construction of Christian doctrine. At other times the parallel is with certain New Testament teachings, especially those of Paul.

By proceeding in this manner they substitute an explanation of how the doctrine of incarnation came to be held for a discussion of whether it is cogent. In other words, they confuse two senses of the word *why*: why the doctrine is held and why it should (or should not) be held.

Maurice Wiles objects quite strenuously to this criticism, which has been raised by a number of reviewers. He acknowledges that if his colleagues were really arguing that historical antecedents and parallels determine the truth or falsity of an idea, the argument would be a very bad one. They were, however, making two quite different points. First, they were responding to the claim that the Christian doctrine of incarnation was so different from other views of the time that it must have been based on something that actually happened. The thrust of their argument was to nullify that contention. Their second point was to show the culture gap between the first century and the twentieth.[60]

We must note, however, that if Goulder and Young were misunderstood, they themselves contributed to the misunderstanding. This is especially noticeable in Goulder's title, "The Two *Roots* of the Christian Myth" (emphasis added). The reader will recall that Goulder introduces his discussion with the doctrine of inspiration: traditional orthodoxy holds that it was through the Holy Spirit's inspiration that John wrote of incarnation ("The Word became flesh and dwelt among us," John 1:14). Goulder counters: "Historical study is the implacable enemy of such a view of inspiration: when we remove the mist, we remove the mystery. It shows, I believe, two roots to the Christian myth, that is, the Christian account of what went on, goes on and will go on behind the scenes of this world. One is the Galilean eschatological myth . . . ; the other is the Samaritan gnostical myth."[61] It appears from this that it is not the doctrine of the incarnation that these scholars are attempting to explain away. Rather, it is the doctrine of inspiration. But if this is the case, they are aiming at least indirectly at the doctrine of incarnation as well. And regardless of the subject addressed, the genetic fallacy remains.

The second aspect of Wiles's reply also deserves attention. He

60. Maurice Wiles, "A Survey of Issues in the Myth Debate," in *Incarnation and Myth: The Debate Continued*, ed. Michael Goulder (Grand Rapids: Eerdmans, 1979), pp. 11–12.
61. Goulder, "Roots," p. 65.

contends that the point of *The Myth of God Incarnate* was to show the great cultural gap between the first century and ours. The implication was that the changes that have occurred have rendered untenable a view which seemed quite acceptable at that earlier time. It is apparent to us that considerable changes have taken place over that span of time. It should be noted that these changes have not all taken place during the last century or two, although there is no question that with the knowledge explosion of recent decades the change has accelerated. In view of the continued change down through the centuries the mythographers (as Basil Mitchell terms them) claim that there is no identity between the doctrine of biblical times and that of the present. Mitchell, however, questions this: "But I have to confess, as a layman, that when I turn from the hymns of Fortunatus to those of Luther, Wesley, and Newman, I do not feel myself confronted by sheer discontinuity. The 'family resemblance' is strong and deep and this becomes even more evident if we compare them with characteristic expressions of Hindu or Buddhist piety."[62] Thus the point the mythographers are making, which is in effect that there is no orthodoxy per se and that what they are doing is not radically different from the activities of the early theologians, is less persuasive than appears to be the case.

2. Mythological Christology exhibits a deficient understanding of the nature of inductive proof. There is, of course, an inherent difficulty in any type of argument involving inductive logic. At best, only a high degree of probability can be established. There can never be total or absolute or final proof. The degrees of certainty of inductive conclusions can be plotted on a continuum: conceivable-plausible-possible-probable-highly probable. Now the ideas of the mythographers are in some cases barely conceivable, or at most plausible. An idea may be true, but evidence must be offered establishing that it is true. The mythographers do not appear to be sufficiently aware of this need.

Of the two mythographers who concentrate most upon reconstructing the origin of the doctrine of incarnation, Young seems considerably more aware of the partial and inconclusive nature of the argument than does Goulder. She says, for instance, that

---

62. Basil Mitchell, "A Summing-Up of the Colloquy: Myth of God Debate," in *Incarnation and Myth*, ed. Goulder, p. 236.

his essay "provides a very good example of the kind of hypothetical reconstruction which is possible."[63] She also says of her own endeavor that she is proposing no specific theory, but simply offering a sample of the type of evidence that could be relevant and outlining some theories which have been suggested.[64] Yet she eventually concludes, "Whether or not we can unearth the precise origins of incarnational belief, it is surely clear that it belongs naturally enough to a world in which supernatural ways of speaking seemed the highest and best expression of the significance and finality of the one . . . identified as God's awaited Messiah and envoy."[65] At some point the argument seems to have taken on greater certainty than the preceding material would seem to allow.

Another example of faulty logic is found in Young's initial chapter. Here she begins by observing, "Exclusive claims that there can be only one way of understanding salvation in Christ have never been 'canonized' in creed or definition, though they have often caused intolerance between Christians."[66] Accordingly, she deplores the exclusive claim that there is only one way to understand the nature of Christ, namely, in terms of a unique divine incarnation. This she regards as having had an impoverishing effect, obscuring the potential richness and variety of christological insights.[67] At the end of the chapter she says, "If we admit the primacy of soteriology, we inevitably open the gates to a multiplicity of christologies, rather than insisting upon one to which all are expected to conform."[68] Note the various assumptions she has made: a multiplicity of soteriologies, the primacy of soteriology, and a consequent multiplicity of Christologies. All of these premises are suspect.

Young's presupposition of a multiplicity of soteriologies rests upon the fact that there has never been an official canonizing of the doctrine of salvation. In making this assumption, she ignores the equally well known fact that the various doctrines of Christian theology did not develop simultaneously. Whereas the doc-

---

63. Young, "Tangled Mass," p. 87.
64. Ibid.
65. Ibid., p. 119.
66. Young, "Cloud," p. 13.
67. Ibid.
68. Ibid., p. 38.

trines of the Trinity and the person of Christ received attention early and were formulated by ecumenical councils, the work of Christ was not fully discussed until the eleventh and twelfth centuries, and the doctrine of salvation not until the sixteenth century. It is highly questionable, moreover, whether any definitive statement about the Trinity or the two natures of Christ could have been made in the later centuries, given the difference in environment. The political oneness of the church which had obtained during the patristic period and the heyday of the Holy Roman Empire had passed from the scene. This may seem to argue Young's point, namely, that there is no single correct position on the person of Christ. In reality, however, what it does is explain the absence of a single official position on soteriology; it does not argue for a variety of views of salvation. To be sure, there are several aspects to the redemptive work of Christ, each of which has become the basis for a different theory of the atonement. These several aspects are not mutually exclusive, however. In fact, I have argued elsewhere that all of them center on the idea of penal substitution and thus require not a variety of understandings of the person of Christ, but rather the incarnational view.[69]

Young also assumes the primacy of soteriology. An old principle going back to Philipp Melanchthon, it does not appear to be established by Young's argument. She says at the beginning, "In the light of this historical study [which will constitute a major part of her essay], the primacy of soteriology becomes plain,"[70] but the subsequent demonstration is far less categorical than this promise leads us to expect.

Finally, Young assumes that the variety of understandings of soteriology requires a variety of understandings of Christology, but this does not follow. It would be true only if there were divergent testimonies within Scripture regarding the work and person of Christ. Perhaps, as we have already suggested, the rich variety of the aspects of Christ's atoning work rests upon there being only one basic position. Indeed, would not our understanding of the Christian life be impoverished rather than enriched by surrendering the exclusivity of the doctrine of incarnation?

69. Millard J. Erickson, *Christian Theology* (Grand Rapids: Baker, 1986), pp. 801–23.
70. Young, "Cloud," p. 14.

One of the problems with the logic of the mythographers is the regular occurrence of the fallacy of an undistributed middle term. This is quite common with any type of inductive logic; indeed, inductive logic may actually rest upon it. The fallacy consists in assuming that because two objects have some characteristic(s) in common, one of the objects must be an instance of the other. A simple example is, "Cows have four legs. That horse has four legs. Therefore, that horse is a cow." All too often the mythographers similarly assume that a superficial resemblance between the doctrine of incarnation and an element of some other theology or philosophy establishes common origin or causality.

3. In some cases, the mythographers' argument is historically wrong. This is particularly the case with respect to their use of Scripture. Space does not at this point permit us to go into detail on this matter, but the problems with their approach will become clear when we turn to Scripture to construct a contemporary incarnational Christology (see, e.g., pp. 461–79). For the moment, however, we might point to C. F. D. Moule's argumentation in *The Origin of Christology*.[71] Although written before the publication of *The Myth of God Incarnate*, it anticipates and deals with many of the considerations raised therein. Indeed, Stephen Neill says of Moule's book, "If it had been available a little earlier, I wonder whether the book under consideration [*The Myth of God Incarnate*] could have been written in anything like its present form."[72]

4. There is within the writings of the mythographers a relativism which at times becomes a virtual subjectivism. Young, for example, says, "There is no suggestion that [my] approach . . . will be meaningful or acceptable to everyone. Genuine faith in Jesus Christ does not take the same form in all believers."[73] This remark admits of several interpretations. On the one hand, she may simply be saying that different people have slightly different ways of expressing the same truth. To some extent, this point will be conceded by anyone other than the most rigid absolutist.

71. C. F. D. Moule, *The Origin of Christology* (Cambridge: Cambridge University Press, 1977).

72. Stephen Neill, "Jesus and Myth," in *The Truth of God Incarnate*, ed. Michael Green (Grand Rapids: Eerdmans, 1977), p. 64.

73. Young, "Cloud," p. 38.

Or she may be saying that all are in contact with the same truth, no matter how conceived and expressed. This is the underlying theme of Hick's essay on comparative religions.[74] Or she may be repeating the Kierkegaardian emphasis that subjectivity is truth. The important thing about a doctrine or idea is the subjective response it evokes, not its objective correspondence to some external reality. At times this seems to be what Young and the other contributors to the symposium are saying. But if this is the case, how can they argue as they do that the traditional view of incarnation is not tenable? Is not this view one of the possible options? One cannot maintain a subjectivist position and at the same time argue against a particular interpretation on seemingly objective grounds, that is, by appealing to evidences which everyone can examine.

5. A remaining issue is whether one can, on the basis of the argument advanced by the mythographers, maintain any form of faith which can appropriately be called Christian. This raises the question of what is the essence of Christianity, a topic pursued in several late-nineteenth-century books. Is the idea that the only true and living God at one point in history entered the human race by becoming metaphysically (not merely influentially) present in one person, Jesus of Nazareth, in a way (and not merely to a degree) that he had not been and will never be present in any other person, indispensable to Christianity? One of the distinguishing marks between the mythographers and their critics is that the former answer this question in the negative, while the latter answer it in the affirmative.

One issue underlying this question is whether the existence of variations affects the essential nature of an idea. It is not possible to resolve that issue within the brief scope of this treatise. It may suffice, however, at this juncture to observe the effects which abandoning the traditional view of the incarnation will have elsewhere within Christian doctrine. We will address this matter positively, asking what it is that the doctrine of the incarnation testifies to.

It has been said that the doctrine of the incarnation is more a statement about God than it is about Jesus. While the prime purpose of this observation may be to emphasize the direction

---

74. John Hick, "Jesus and the World Religions," in *Myth of God Incarnate*, pp. 167–85.

of the initiative (i.e., from God downward rather than from the human upward), it is also a profound indication of how much the incarnation tells us about God. First, it testifies to the *personal* character of God. In Jesus, one individual person, we meet God. We encounter God most directly not in his generalized influence everywhere in the creation, nor in his dealing with all humans, nor even in the life of all Christians, but in Jesus. That God is present, in an unequaled fashion, in the person of Jesus shows that he is not merely the force which creates personality; he is personal! He is not less but more personal than we are. The qualities of divine personality were encountered by those first-century persons who interacted with Jesus. Through their testimonies and our own encounter with Christ, we also come to a knowledge of the divine personality.

Second, the incarnation testifies that God is love. The full extent of God's love is seen not in his announcing his love, nor in his assisting humanity in its predicament, but in his actually coming, in person, to die to save us from our sins.

Finally, the power and dominion of God are seen in the incarnation. That which no human could do—reunite the separated spiritual partners, that is, cross the gulf that separates God and human beings—he has done. What we could not even conceive, he by his coming has proved himself able to do. This is not a human accomplishment. It is a divine gift.

Clearly, the incarnation stands at the very heart of what has always been meant by Christianity. To abandon or redefine it would so alter the meaning of Christianity as to make it scarcely worth calling by that name.

14

The Logical Problem.
(2) Narrative Christology

Narrative Christology represents an attempt to do Christology in a genuinely new and creative way. To understand this Christology, we must first examine narrative theology in general, which in turn rests upon an innovative conception of the status and nature of theology today in light of the present cultural situation.

Narrative Theology
The Contrast Between Narrative and Propositional Theology

We may gain an understanding of what narrative theology is by observing what it is not. A good way to proceed is to contrast

359

narrative theology with the customary type of theological method, namely, propositional theology.

Terrence Tilley begins his analysis of the nature and function of narrative theology with a discussion of metaphor. Metaphors, he says, are "locomotives of meaning," bearing the freight of insight from place to place.[1] Inevitably people want to know the meaning of a metaphor, so that they can decide whether they agree or disagree with it. There are different ways to get at this meaning. One is to translate or parse the metaphor into a set of similes and dissimiles until the content of the metaphor has been exhausted. There is nothing wrong per se with the process of parsing a metaphor. Three problems occasionally attend it, however. It often exhausts the patience of the analysts long before the full depth of the metaphor has been exhausted. Dissection robs metaphor of its power to evoke new insight. Parsing also tends to obscure a key function of religious metaphor: the provision of a "bridge over which faith moves from the tradition of the community into the life of the individual."[2] A better way of elucidating a metaphor's meaning, suggests Tilley, is to place it in a story, to explore it in a definite context.

What has been said about metaphors applies to Christian doctrines as well, for the key Christian ideas are "metaphors which have been conceptualized by inclusion in prototypical narratives"; they are "metaphors at rest."[3] Being metaphors, these ideas can be paraphrased and analyzed. Such a process will result in propositions that express and dogmas that fix their meaning. This is "propositional theology": "the analysis, exploration, transformation, systematization, and proclamation of the canonical metaphors, the concepts of Christianity."[4]

Tilley is quick to say that there is nothing wrong with doing propositional theology. It has several drawbacks, however, reminiscent of the difficulties of parsing metaphors:

1. Propositional theology can lose the oak of metaphor in a forest of paraphrase.
2. It can rob important Christian concepts of their power to evoke new insight.

1. Terrence Tilley, *Story Theology* (Wilmington, Del.: Michael Glazier, 1985), p. 1.
2. Ibid., p. 3.
3. Ibid.
4. Ibid.

3. It has difficulty showing how faith enters into the lives of individual believers.

It is this last difficulty that is most serious. Only after propositional theology has finished its work can pastoral or practical theology begin to show how this "systematized structure of doctrine" enters into the life of the believer.

There are two more-direct ways to carry the meaning of a Christian idea into the lives of believers. One is through their participating in rituals or enacted metaphors. This approach is most suitable for the doctrine of the Eucharist, but is used for other doctrines as well.[5] The second approach is through the stories in which the metaphor is incorporated. The telling and retelling, the adopting and adapting of the stories, especially in the form of autobiography, provide "the bridge for canonical images and metaphors from the community or tradition to the individual."[6] Whereas the primary purpose of propositional theology is to analyze and explore the meaning of metaphors, narrative theology retells and adapts the stories which contextualize key Christian ideas. Tilley says, "That process of discovering, creatively transforming, and proclaiming the stories which carry the key ideas of Christianity is the distinctive work of a Christian narrative theology."[7]

The concerns of the two types of theology are in many respects similar. The ways in which they carry out these concerns are significantly different, however. Both attempt to show Christians the central and distinctive meaning of their faith. Propositional theologians "concentrate on presenting true propositions, defending them, and reminding the faithful of them."[8] They often use stories as illustrations of these profound truths, but the stories are secondary to the doctrinal propositions. Narrative theologians, on the other hand, "tell, evaluate and re-tell the stories." They, of course, use whatever help propositional theology can give.[9]

Tilley lists some of the other significant differences between the two types of theology, including their presuppositions:

5. Ibid., p. 4.
6. Ibid.
7. Ibid., p. 5.
8. Ibid., p. 15.
9. Ibid., pp. 15–16.

1. While both agree that Christian metaphors and ideas must be distinguished from those that are incompatible with the faith, they differ regarding the criteria of incompatibility. For the propositional theologians the doctrines of the tradition are the test; for the narrative theologian, the stories of the tradition.[10]

2. Propositional theology assumes that narratives are dispensable portrayals of Christian faith, whereas narrative theology maintains that one must study the content and structure of the stories to discover the basic elements to be believed.[11]

3. Propositional theology sees its task as formulating and reformulating systems of doctrinal truths. Narrative theology sees its task as making religious tradition vibrant by setting old stories in fresh contexts and telling new stories. Propositional theology views revelation in terms of God's giving to scribes systematic statements to write down. Narrative theology has a more personal view of revelation, which calls for a corresponding change in the task of theology.[12]

4. Propositional theology seeks to give a single, unified, and definitive statement of the correct system of doctrine. Narrative theology, on the other hand, "recognizes the irreducible and provocative multiplicity in Christianity."[13]

The Various Roles of Narrative

Narrative is seen as performing several different roles in the theological task. As a matter of fact, narrative theologies can be classified by the number of these roles which they incorporate and the relative importance assigned to them.[14] In general, narrative has three basic roles:

1. *The communicational role.* Narrative theologians have observed that theology as usually done is quite abstract

---

10. Ibid., pp. 11–12.
11. Ibid., pp. 13–14.
12. Ibid., p. 14.
13. Ibid., p. 16.
14. For a more detailed discussion of the several roles of narrative see Millard J. Erickson, "Narrative Theology: Translation or Transformation?" in *Festschrift: A Tribute to Dr. William Hordern*, ed. Walter Freitag (Saskatoon: University of Saskatchewan Press, 1985), pp. 30–34.

and difficult to communicate. This propositional theology also has difficulty exciting the believer and attracting unbelievers to faith. So there is great admiration for the rabbinic way of answering questions, not with didactic or discursive responses, but with a story. This is the best way to impart relevant truth, a goal which Tilley emphasizes strongly. Creative propositional theologians have a similar goal, but see the core of the message as lying in propositions, which constitute the end to which the stories are mere means. The propositions of a doctrine are the best embodiment and preserver of the Christian tradition. The narrative theologian, on the other hand, sees stories as the best embodiment of the tradition. Pictorial power is ultimately preferable to analytic precision.[15]

2. *The hermeneutical role.* The content of Scripture is usually assumed to be the basic standard of the Christian faith. According to the theologies under discussion, it is specifically the narrative portions of the biblical text that constitute the normative factor. They are, then, the key to interpreting the remainder, and biblical religion is to be understood as essentially narrative in nature. Slightly more complicated is a bipolar or two-horizon view which holds that meaning is an interaction between the biblical narrative and the interpreter, and the interpreter's self-understanding is crucial to true comprehension.[16]

3. *The heuristic or epistemological role.* The content of the Christian faith is not final and fixed, but constantly growing. The stories of saints within the history of the church and, beyond that, our own stories serve to increase our knowledge of reality.[17]

The Reason for the Rise of Narrative Theology

But why has narrative theology arisen? In the judgment of many of the narrative theologians, fundamental shifts in the ideological environment have taken place, requiring correspond-

15. Belden C. Lane, "Rabbinical Stories: A Primer on Theological Method," *Christian Century* 98.41 (16 Dec. 1981): 1307.

16. Darrell Jodock, "Story and Scripture," *Word and World* 1.2 (Spring 1981): 133.

17. George W. Stroup, *The Promise of Narrative Theology: Recovering the Gospel in the Church* (Atlanta: John Knox, 1981), pp. 200–01.

ingly radical changes in the way in which theology is done. To a large extent, these changes are of relatively recent occurrence. Throughout most of church history there had been a basic agreement upon the nature of the theological enterprise. Although the currently popular and prominent forms varied with the passing of time, there was something of a consensus about the general nature of theology. This is changing, however. Thus, James McClendon says, "Where are we now in theology? A shift is in progress. The old landmarks set by Barth and Rahner, by Tillich and Congar, are slipping away, or perhaps the changing countryside makes the old features unrecognizable. What seemed so durable when the present generation was in school may seem quaint or incredible."[18] Note the scope of this shift. Both Protestant and Catholic theology are undergoing major changes. Not only the relatively conservative theology of Karl Barth, but also the progressive or liberal theology of Karl Rahner and Paul Tillich is undergoing metamorphosis. We might say there is a change not merely of theologies, but of the very conception of theology itself. A paradigm shift is taking place.

Similarly, Tilley speaks of the shaking of the foundations of theology during the early 1960s.[19] Once again both Catholic and Protestant theology are in view. The Second Vatican Council offered Catholic theologians a genuinely creative role. The only role allowed them previously had been the writing of footnotes to the theology of Thomas Aquinas. In Protestantism there was the waning of the age of giants—Barth, Tillich, Rudolf Bultmann, and Reinhold Niebuhr. In their place arose the radical theologians, most notably the Death of God theologians. These various reactions were all attempting to provide a new central focus for Christian faith, but none received widespread acceptance.

Both McClendon and Tilley see this upheaval in theology as part of a widespread shift in the entire cultural and intellectual mood of the day. McClendon sees it not simply as religious, political, aesthetic, or moral, but as pervading all of these realms.[20] Tilley sees challenges coming to theology from a variety of areas.[21]

18. James McClendon, *Biography as Theology: How Life Stories Can Remake Today's Theology* (Nashville: Abingdon, 1974), p. 13.
19. Tilley, *Story Theology*, pp. 18–20.
20. McClendon, *Biography*, p. 13.
21. Tilley, *Story Theology*, p. 20.

McClendon believes not only that the shift in mood is not primarily religious, but that it cannot be seen as clearly in the religious realm as in some others. And so he proposes to examine the new mood in ethics instead. Utilitarianism has dominated the secular age which is now dying. There was a sort of calculus of right and wrong, good and bad, which many, especially younger people, now reject. Its aim was to effect the greatest good for the greatest number. Since that involved the loss of liberty and even of life for some, the system was seen as dehumanizing and even brutalizing. It turned persons into things.[22] The alternatives from the religious realm, namely the "decisionism" of Joseph Fletcher and the "realism" of Reinhold Niebuhr, were no better. They did not lead to national morality. Consider, for example, the Watergate scandals and the Vietnam War.[23]

What is needed instead, according to McClendon, is a "character ethics," or what he would prefer to call, were it not such an awkward expression, the ethics of character-in-community.[24] The closest approach to such an ethic is H. Richard Niebuhr's posthumous *Responsible Self* (i.e., as long as the emphasis is placed upon the self rather than upon responsibility).[25] According to Niebuhr, the locus of morality is not our acts, which may be done out of a variety of motives, some good and some bad, but our character. Now character is not a matter merely of traits but of convictions as well. And here we find a great common interest between ethics and theology, for both deal with convictions.

McClendon's understanding of theology is quite different from the traditional definition, just as his view of ethics differs from the traditional utilitarian view. He believes that "the best way to understand theology is to see it, not as the study of God (for there are godless theologies as well as godly ones), but as the investigation of the convictions of a convictional community, discovering its convictions, interpreting them, criticizing them in the light of all that we can know, and creatively transforming them into better ones if possible."[26] Convictions, then, are not considered

22. McClendon, *Biography*, pp. 14–16.

23. Ibid., pp. 16–28.

24. Ibid., p. 29.

25. Ibid.; H. Richard Niebuhr, *The Responsible Self: An Essay in Christian Moral Philosophy* (New York: Harper and Row, 1963).

26. McClendon, *Biography*, p. 35.

merely in themselves, but in relationship to the persons and communities that hold them. The theologian is interested not only in whether the God that is believed in actually exists, but also in the difference which God's existence and the belief in it make to individuals and communities.[27]

What is the role of narrative and of biography in all this? It is important to understand that "Christian beliefs are not so many 'propositions' to be catalogued or juggled like truth-functions in a computer, but are living convictions which give shape to actual lives and actual communities."[28] McClendon notes that from time to time, either within a community or near it, there arise persons who embody and exhibit its convictions in a new, striking, and dramatic fashion. The example of their lives stirs up the community's moral vision as well as what might be properly termed its doctrinal convictions. These, of course, are objects of study not only for Christian biographers and church historians, but also for the theologian. McClendon says: "Such lives, by their very attractiveness or beauty, may serve as data for the Christian thinker, enabling him more truly to reflect upon the tension between what is and what ought to be believed and lived by all. To engage in such reflection, however, is the proper task of Christian theology. That the task can be fulfilled in this way is the theme of the present book."[29]

Tilley deals with the changes in the cultural environment in both broader and more detailed fashion. He finds four factors in the transformation of the intellectual culture, all of which favor viewing theology in terms of narrative (he speaks of "story theology") rather than as a discursive or propositional endeavor.

The first factor is the "empirical-analytical philosophers." The earliest of this group, the logical positivists, had a very rigorous view of what constitutes a meaningful statement. They laid down the dictum (which came to be known as the verifiability principle) that meaningful statements were those which "pictured the way things were in the world and could be verified by a person."[30] The later analytical philosophers, instead of specifying what language must do if it is to be meaningful, tried to

27. Ibid., pp. 35–36.
28. Ibid., p. 37.
29. Ibid.
30. Tilley, *Story Theology*, p. 20.

discover the particular function which various sorts of statements have. While certain statements (namely, scientific statements) do operate according to the specifications of the logical positivists, statements in other realms have different functions. According to R. B. Braithwaite, religious statements express an intention to live in a certain way.[31] Therefore, the stories we associate with such intentions have religious significance. These stories need not be true, nor need we believe that they are literal. We need only entertain them so that they help us carry out our declared intentions.[32] Here the link between literature and religion is reestablished.

The second factor which Tilley cites as contributing to the rise of story theology is "the recovery of the realization that human experience is inherently narrative in form."[33] Here he follows the argument of Stephen Crites.[34] Human experience has conventionally been thought of as a series of events unconnected with one another. Crites, however, claims that we should think of experience as patterned in and through time. This means that experience is an incipient story. He likens experience to music. It is possible to think of music as a group of notes combined into a whole piece. It is better, however, to think of music as a whole piece divisible into individual notes. Similarly, since our experience is basically durational and the present is simply the point of division between the past and the future, we should think of our experience as a whole piece, a narrative or story as it were. Such stories must, of course, be analyzed critically.[35]

The third factor bearing upon the rise of story theology has been the evolution of biblical criticism. It is no longer possible to naively take the Bible as conveying literal accounts of what transpired in the past. Essentially, biblical criticism has given us a fresh understanding of the nature of the Bible. Three major conclusions have emerged: Jesus' teachings are especially recognizable in his parables; the Gospels are not history or biography, but stories about him that express the effect which he had upon

31. Ibid., p. 22.
32. Ibid.
33. Ibid., p. 23.
34. Stephen Crites, "The Narrative Quality of Experience," *Journal of the American Academy of Religion* 39.3 (Sept. 1971): 291–311.
35. Tilley, *Story Theology*, pp. 25–26.

the narrators; the Old Testament is really a set of stories of God and his people rather than nascent science or divine commands illustrated by stories. Whereas previously the Bible had been thought of as containing stories, we know now that it is composed of stories. These stories occur in a great variety of forms, including myths, legends, satires, allegories, histories, apocalyptic, and parable.[36]

The fourth factor in the rise of story theology has been the erosion of the Enlightenment myths, the set of beliefs which together have exalted the rationality of humanity. These beliefs include the autonomy of the individual; the inevitability of evolution and progress; the existence of a world which is independent of our ideas, and to which we must seek to make our ideas agree; and the distinction between science as cognitive and hard, and art as imaginative and soft.[37] Together they constitute the myth of modernity, which tells us we have outgrown stories. Auguste Comte saw humanity as moving from religion (in the form of stories) to philosophy (in the form of metaphysics) to science with its exactness. This, however, is itself a story. And we thus have a contradiction, suggesting that our need for stories has not been outgrown.[38] Indeed, narrative is indispensable to the doing of theology.

The Methodology
Identification of Jesus

Narrative Christology has as its purpose the identification of Jesus. It asks who he is. This goal is not greatly different from our desire to come to know anyone else. We are, however, sometimes distracted by the fact that Jesus is a special case. We therefore are inclined to think that the method involved in determining his identity is and must be different from that followed with other human persons. Robert Krieg contends, however, that this need not be the case: "The language of Christology is similar to our usual attempts to say who someone is."[39] The works of

36. Ibid., pp. 26–30.
37. Ibid., pp. 30–34.
38. Ibid., pp. 35–36.
39. Robert A. Krieg, *Story-shaped Christology: The Role of Narrative in Identifying Jesus Christ* (New York: Paulist, 1988), pp. 5–6.

Walter Kasper, Edward Schillebeeckx, and Franz van Beeck have recognized this, and have followed the familiar way of making a personal identification.

How do we usually go about identifying a person? We generally begin by giving a name and a title. Beyond that, we give a description of the person. This may be a physical description, but that does not go deep enough. More particular is the use of narrative, telling anecdotes and even forming a biography. Finally, one can resort to conceptual discourse, using ideas more than images.[40]

This leads us on to the matter of personal identity, or that which remains the same in an individual throughout life. A person, says Krieg, consists of three dimensions: length, breadth, and depth. Length is one's persistence through time. Breadth is one's relationships with the world, especially with other people. Depth is one's self-consciousness or self-understanding. Biography is especially appropriate for identifying a person, since it "encompasses the unfolding of events, the interaction of agents, the relating of men and women, and their self-reflections."[41] That is to say, biography deals with the person as agent, in relation, and as subject.[42]

When we come to consider who Jesus is, there are some unique dimensions to the endeavor. Jesus Christ is now known in light of his resurrection. Whereas in discussing other persons we eventually shift to the past tense, this is not true in the case of Jesus. He is a living reality, and thus is contemporaneous with every age. In identifying Jesus Christ, then, our language will not be the same as, but analogous to the pattern followed with other persons.[43]

In beginning with Jesus' name and titles, we seem to be doing what we do with others, but his name is unique and his titles apply in a special way. For example, we may speak of someone as a son or daughter of God, but Christians speak of Jesus as the Son of God. To supplement his name and titles, we have no sources giving a physical description of Jesus, and historical materials for constructing a biography are also lacking.[44]

40. Ibid., pp. 6–8.
41. Ibid., pp. 9–11.
42. Ibid., p. 11.
43. Ibid., pp. 14–15.
44. Ibid., p. 16.

How then do we go about establishing the identity of Jesus? Krieg's answer is definitive for a particular type of narrative Christology:

> We can speak about the identity of Jesus Christ, I propose, by relying on three different kinds of narratives. Whereas we can ordinarily grasp who someone is by telling biography, in the case of Jesus Christ we need not only a rough biographical sketch, but also something more. We need narratives that allow us to convey the continuity of this life beyond death. Two such kinds of narratives are the Gospels and biographies of exemplary Christians. Through the use of historical narratives about Jesus, the Gospels as stories, and critical recollections of the saints' lives, we are able to perceive Christ from three perspectives.[45]

To summarize: an analysis of the way in which we usually identify a person and recognition of the uniqueness of the person of Jesus Christ lead to the conclusion that the use of narratives is especially appropriate in doing Christology. These will include historical narratives about his earthly life as well as two additional sources which give us insight into the living, resurrected Jesus: the Gospels viewed as stories, and stories about the saints (later believers).

The Sources

One of the most important methodological issues in any theology concerns the sources from which that theology is drawn. An examination of the sources of narrative Christology will take us far toward understanding its images of Jesus.

We begin with Walter Kasper, who did not explicitly identify himself with narrative theology. This may be due in part to the fact that his *Jesus the Christ* antedated the full development of the movement. Narrative Christology is found only in latent form in his thought, yet he set the agenda for much of what has followed, particularly the contributions of Krieg.

Kasper notes that the issue of the identity of Jesus cannot be restricted to the question of who he was, but must also deal with who he is. Christology must focus upon both considerations. We dare not neglect either the historical Jesus or the present life and faith of the church:

45. Ibid., p. 19.

The church belief . . . has in the earthly Jesus, as he is made accessible to us through historical research, a relatively autonomous criterion, a once-and-for-all yardstick by which it must continually measure itself. Nevertheless it is impossible to make the historical Jesus the entire and only valid content of faith in Christ. For Revelation occurs not only in the earthly Jesus, but just as much, more indeed, in the Resurrection and the imparting of the Spirit. Jesus today is living "in the Spirit." Hence we are granted not only an historically mediated, but a direct mode of access to Jesus Christ "in the Spirit."[46]

Part of this dual concern is the psychological fact that it is within the community of the church that one comes to knowledge of Jesus Christ. That Kasper is a Roman Catholic may be a factor here. He emphasizes that only through the Holy Spirit can one grasp or be convinced of the New Testament witness, and that the locus of the Spirit's present activity is the church: "Only where the message of Jesus Christ is alive and believed, where that same Spirit is alive who enlivens the writings of the New Testament, can the testimony of the New Testament be understood as a living witness. Even today, therefore, the community of the Church is the proper location of the Jesus tradition and encounter with Christ."[47] The pietistic conception of a solitary individual finding a Bible, perhaps a Gideon Bible in a hotel room, reading it, and coming to understanding and faith is foreign to Kasper.

What Kasper appears to be doing at this stage of explaining his method is to distinguish between the psychological and the logical bases of faith in Christ and thus also of Christology:

The starting-point of Christology is the phenomenology of faith in Christ; faith as it is actually believed, lived, proclaimed and practised in the Christian churches. Faith in Jesus Christ can arise only from encounter with believing Christians. The proper content and the ultimate criterion of Christology is, however, Jesus Christ himself: his life, destiny, words and work. In this sense we can say too that Jesus Christ is the primary, and faith of the Church the secondary, criterion of Christology. Neither of the two criteria can be pitted against the other. The question is of course how the two criteria are to be joined together. That is one

46. Walter Kasper, *Jesus the Christ* (New York: Paulist, 1976), p. 35.
47. Ibid., p. 27.

of the fundamental questions of modern theology. It is posed with special emphasis in modern research into the life of Jesus.[48]

This leads Kasper to the concept of a Christology of reciprocity, that is, a Christology which moves back and forth between "the earthly Jesus *and* the risen, exalted Christ."[49]

Drawing the familiar distinction between the Jesus of history and the Christ of faith, Kasper envisions a systematic study of three distinct but complementary sources: historical investigation, the Jewish-Christian Scripture and tradition, and the life and thought of the contemporary church. Theologians must utilize the best of historical methodology to investigate the life and ministry of Jesus, although it will never be possible to develop a full-scale biography of him. In addition, the early church's kerygma, the message which it preached about the Christ in whom it believed, is a vital source.[50] What is of most interest to us, however, is the third element: the contemporary life of the church. For Kasper holds, as we noted earlier, that God's revelation continues into the present time. The modern church is therefore a proper source and subject matter for the construction of a Christology. As Kasper proceeds to construct his own Christology, however, he gives little indication that his view of revelation is not the traditional one.

Krieg's discussion of the sources of Christology follows Kasper, as well as Schillebeeckx and van Beeck. He particularly likes the threefold division which Kasper makes. Accordingly, he makes use of three specific narratives: (1) Mark's Gospel, which represents the revelation preached and tradition handed down by the early church; (2) a historical reconstruction of the ministry of Jesus of Nazareth; and (3) the life story of a modern disciple, Dorothy Day. Though different, each of these focuses upon Jesus in a special way.[51] Krieg then critically reflects on these three narratives.[52] While the narratives show us who Jesus is, Krieg's reflection tells us who he is.

Although using different terminology, Tilley also employs the same three general sources. Focusing on the stories of Jesus,

48. Ibid., p. 28.
49. Ibid., pp. 35–36.
50. Ibid., pp. 15, 35.
51. Krieg, *Story-shaped Christology*, pp. 111–21.
52. Ibid., pp. 121–35.

which include both the stories which Jesus told and the stories told about him, Tilley reminds us of the need for a thorough use of biblical criticism in approaching even such seemingly straightforward sections of the Gospels as the parables.[53] In addition to the narrative and didactic portions of the New Testament, there are the kerygmatic elements, such as Paul's theme of the new Adam, and Peter's applying to Jesus the Suffering Servant motif.[54] Finally, in a chapter entitled "The Body of Christ," a reference to Paul's imagery for the church, Tilley points out that questions which we might apply to ourselves, namely, where would we be without our bodies, and what would we do without our bodies, can be applied to Jesus as well. Tilley reasons: "If the church is the body of Christ, its members continue the work of Christ in the world and continue to make his presence felt in the world. To continue to tell the story of Christ is to tell the stories of the members of his body."[55] He proceeds to make the claim that certain contemporary saints actually reincarnate the atonement.[56]

In his book *Biography as Theology*, McClendon has concentrated on the third of these elements, stories of present-day believers. He treats the lives of Dag Hammarskjöld, Martin Luther King, Jr., Clarence Jordan, and Charles Ives, and suggests that they can tell us a great deal about Christ. A similar position is taken by Johannes Metz, who maintains that knowing Jesus requires following him:

> Every attempt to know him, to understand him, is therefore always a journey, a following. It is only by following and imitating him that we know whom we are dealing with. Following Christ is therefore not just a subsequent application of the Church's christology to our life: the practice of following Christ is itself a central part of christology, if we do not wish to identify the Logos of this christology and of Christianity in general with the purely contemplative Logos of the Greeks, for whom ultimately Christ could only ever be foolishness.[57]

53. Tilley, *Story Theology*, pp. 73–78.
54. Ibid., pp. 128–31.
55. Ibid., p. 147.
56. Ibid., pp. 161–74.
57. Johannes Metz, *Followers of Christ: The Religious Life and the Church* (New York: Paulist, 1978), p. 39.

Metz contends that biographical and autobiographical material about people who follow Christ plays a communicational and heuristic role: "Christological knowledge is formed and handed on not primarily in the form of concepts but in accounts of following Christ."[58] Such accounts are "the genuine material" of Christology.

We have seen, then, that narrative Christology draws upon three sources: historical reconstruction of the life of Jesus from the Gospels; the kerygma of the early church, and in the case of Catholic theologians, the continuing tradition of the church; and the present-day experience of the resurrected Christ in his church. Critical reflection upon these narrative materials is also vital, a point stressed most prominently by Krieg.

Substantive Christology

Jesus as a Figure of Unparalleled Originality

We now need to examine the actual Christologies which emerge from this endeavor. Kasper posits several models or images of Jesus. One of these is that Jesus is to be understood as a figure of unparalleled originality. Kasper's research on Jesus is fueled by the post-Enlightenment search for a new kind of freedom in history, the modern commitment to liberation. He is convinced that we must be aided if we are to ever realize our longing for freedom. Accordingly, his discussion of the historical Jesus incorporates the idea of freedom. And his discussion of the risen Christ combines the modern search for freedom with Scripture and tradition. The result is three representations of Jesus, as Son of God, Son of man, and mediator—a truly unique and original figure! Noting that the writing here is dense and that the use of narratives is only implicit, Krieg supplements Kasper with several explicit narratives, some of them biographical and even fictitious in nature.[59]

Jesus as the Founder of a New People of Compassion

In doing his christological work Krieg, as we have already observed, examines three sources. He first turns to Scripture and

---

58. Ibid., p. 40.
59. Krieg, *Story-shaped Christology*, pp. 39–49.

finds in Mark's portrait of Jesus an inaugurator of the kingdom of God.[60] He then turns to a historical reconstruction. While the material is insufficient to construct a full biography, there is nonetheless a consensus among exegetes and historians about many details of Jesus' life. The question "Who was Jesus of Nazareth?" is answered, "He was a charismatic Jewish teacher who, at approximately age thirty-five, was crucified outside the walls of Jerusalem during the reign of Tiberius Caesar. He died preaching the coming of God's kingdom."[61] The final source, a contemporary Christian experience, is the life of Dorothy Day, who after her conversion in her twenties founded over forty shelters for the urban poor. Here the question "Who is Jesus Christ?" is answered, "He is God's compassionate presence."[62]

Combining all of these elements, Krieg comes up with a view of Jesus as the founder of a new people of compassion.[63] Each of these terms—"founder," "new people," and "compassion"—is carefully examined in the light of the three narratives: the Gospel according to Mark, the historical review of Jesus' ministry, and the life of Dorothy Day. Although dissimilar in nature, these narratives elucidate the three key terms in complementary ways.[64]

Having examined figurative terms like "founder," Krieg takes the reflection one step further, to more conceptual terms. While this has the disadvantage of losing the specificity of figurative speech, it has certain merits, namely, it provides the clarity of thematic discourse, thereby shedding further light on Jesus Christ. The primary concept considered is that of personal agency, first the idea of Jesus as self-agent and then as God's agent.[65]

Reincarnations of the Atonement

Tilley examines the lives of a number of Christians, first of saints in the history of the church, and then of some contemporary saints. He sees these individuals as reincarnating the atonement. Like Jesus, the mediator between God and humans, all of

60. Ibid., pp. 113–16.
61. Ibid., pp. 118–19.
62. Ibid., p. 121.
63. Ibid.
64. Ibid., pp. 121–27.
65. Ibid., pp. 128–34.

them "have given their lives for unity, reconciliation, and some have even died in that quest."[66]

As we examine narrative Christology, no one single version of Jesus emerges. The pictures are rather general in nature, such as "agent of God," "a figure of unparalleled originality," "founder of a new people of compassion," and "mediator between God and humans." It appears, then, that there are several narrative Christologies.

Evaluation

We must now seek to make some evaluation of narrative Christology. Although there is variation among its different forms, some generally applicable comments can be made. We begin with a few positive observations:

1. Narrative theology has recognized the communicational power of narrative. Many abstract treatises in Christology could be made both more interesting and more understandable with the use of clear illustratory narratives. One amateur theologian who utilized this technique effectively was C. S. Lewis. His Narnia chronicles are vivid statements of Christian truth whose appeal is not restricted to children. Theology must not only communicate meaning but grip the heart as well. Narrative is useful here in that it often brings otherwise prosaic truths to life in a dramatic fashion.

2. Narrative theology has reminded us that the work of Christ is in many ways continuing. While it is important to bear in mind that the life of a Christian cannot perfectly express the life of Christ, Christian truths which were initially enacted centuries ago are further elucidated when enfleshed in human experience of today.

3. Narrative Christology has reminded us that understanding is not always best achieved by a disinterested or neutral approach, and certainly not by a negative or hostile orientation. Empathy is helpful in understanding truths of a personal or social nature. Thus the insistence upon following Jesus if we want to know him is very much in order.

66. Tilley, *Story Theology*, p. 174.

4. We have been reminded of the need for spiritual vitality in the life of the theologian, and particularly the specialist in Christology. The end of Christology is not simply to know about Jesus. It is to know him, to love him, to obey him, to pattern oneself after him.

On the other hand, narrative Christology also has several shortcomings:

1. The theologians we have been discussing have shown the problems with the traditional approach to Christology. This is particularly true of the writings of McClendon and Tilley. They have not fully considered the difficulties inherent in their own theologies, however, difficulties which may be more numerous and serious than those of the Christology they are rejecting. Of course, no theory is totally devoid of difficulties or unresolved problems. It is not, therefore, a simple case of one theory's being right and another wrong. It is, rather, a matter of better and worse, more and less satisfactory views. Even if the criticism of propositional theology were conclusive, narrative theology would not be established thereby. Yet the narrative theologians assume that theirs is the only alternative, and that such a choice is a necessary one. May it not be that neither propositional nor narrative theology is correct, but that some other option is to be preferred? Or may it not be the case that no Christology at all is the choice to make? The narrative theologians seem not to have adequately established the necessity of there being a Christology at all.

2. In some instances the narrative theologians have prechosen their conclusions. For example, Tilley seems to have accepted Braithwaite's view of the nature of religious language because it fits his own preexisting theory. Tilley does not bother to establish for himself that this view indeed is true. This being the case, we are here confronted not with reasoning, but with rationalization.

The same phenomenon appears elsewhere as well. Why are particular stories and biographies selected for attention? Some of them seem to have been chosen to fit a particular conception of Christ. For example, Tilley uses stories that lead to understanding Christ and Christian discipleship in terms of social action. Yet Kasper has pointed out that Jesus' behavior in befriending tax collectors had little "to do directly with what is normally thought of today as social concern or revolution," since these tax collectors "were in no sense the exploited but the exploiters, who collaborated with the Roman power."[67]

3. To put this issue somewhat more broadly, narrative theology has difficulty stating the criteria for its selection and interpretation of narratives. This may seem to make it no different from other Christologies, which in limiting themselves to the biblical material may yet have difficulty interpreting narratives and selecting which ones to emphasize. At least, however, for these Christologies the range of possible material is limited. But for narrative Christology, which incorporates contemporary Christian biographies, the range is almost unlimited. One can find examples of almost any conceivable Christian lifestyle. The peril here is that we, like the nineteenth-century liberal Protestant searchers for the historical Jesus,[68] may be accused of looking for our own image in the stories of Christ and later saints.

4. Why should Christ's story be selected? Does it really matter what religious leader we choose to follow? John Hick and Paul Knitter, as we saw in chapter 11, suggest a religious pluralism which would make Buddhist or Hindu narrative theology equally valid. Tilley recognizes the problem and rejects two responses to it—the determinist view that some are foreordained to believe and others are not, and the egalitarian view that it really does not matter whom one accepts as a model for one's life. He dismisses both on the grounds that they are reactions to a world dominated by doctrines and the idea that valid doctrines must be true. What he offers instead are a world of metaphors and the idea that valid metaphors are not true, but good, effective, powerful, and live. An ingenious proposal to be sure, but has he really avoided the problem?

5. It is ironic that little of the actual discussion of narrative theology is done in narrative form. Rather, it is done in discursive or propositional form. This is reminiscent of a debate regarding various teaching methods. Four seminary instructors each made a presentation extolling a particular approach. The professor advocating the lecture method was last. His presentation consisted of just two sentences: "I simply wish to point out

67. Kasper, *Jesus*, pp. 66–67.
68. George Tyrrell, *Christianity at the Cross-Roads* (London: Longmans, Green, 1910), p. 44.

that the case for each of the other methods was made by the use of a minilecture. I rest my case." We may well ask, If narrative is the best way to communicate meaning, why do the narrative theologians take a propositional approach? Now it may be argued that doing theology and analyzing the doing of theology are activities of different levels, and that the use of discursive theology on the second level says nothing regarding the relative utility of narrative and propositional theology on the first level. But while this may be a valid argument, the narrative theologians fail to present it adequately. Krieg's model balancing narrative and critical reflection is not widely followed. Tilley seems to utilize the greatest number of narratives, but in most cases he is merely illustrating or embellishing his propositions.

6. The narrative theologians celebrate the diversity within the Christian tradition and boast that one of the virtues of narrative theology is its ability to accept and accommodate variety. Yet they are not willing to accept endless variety. What, then, are the limits, and what are the criteria by which they judge whether those limits have been exceeded? There is insufficient clarity here.

7. Narrative theology gives considerable evidence of conforming to the pragmatist view of truth. This is especially characteristic of Tilley's presentation. There is, however, the danger of slipping from subjectivity (the testing of reality by standards set by the individual), which the narrative theologians very much desire, into subjectivism (the theory that reality is limited to conscious experience), which they presumably do not. The strong rejection of the concepts of true and false doctrine, and the claim that stories are "true" when they are revealing, coherent, and authentic, tend to contribute to this problem.

Part 3

The Construction of a Contemporary Incarnational Christology

15

The Reliability of the Historical Evidence for Jesus. (1) The Synoptic Gospels

As we come now to the constructive portion of our study, we begin by asking a question which has been asked repeatedly and with great intensity over the past century and a half: Can we know enough about Jesus to be able to place our faith in him?

383

Who was this Jesus of history, and what was he like? Has the modern advance of historical criticism rendered it impossible to say with certainty what sort of person he was?

Definitional Matters

The Meaning of "History"

There are, of course, a number of major senses of the word *history*. The first is the mere fact of occurrence, or what happened. This is the subject matter or the object of consideration of the discipline termed history. The second is this endeavor itself, the study of the events that have transpired, the attempt to chronicle and to interpret them. History, or perhaps a better term would be "historical research" or "historiography," is thus the discipline which studies the objects of history, the events, persons, movements of the past. There is, moreover, a third sense of the word *history*, namely the product of history in the second sense, or that which the historian produces or writes as the record of history in the first sense.

Now surely there was a Jesus of history in the first sense. And there is research into the Jesus of history, some of it quite intense and sophisticated. That is the second sense of the Jesus of history. Using this and the next chapter as a foundation, we will attempt to produce the Jesus of history in the third sense, to utilize the research in such a way that our knowledge of Jesus approximates as closely as possible the actual historical Jesus.

Approaches to Research into the Jesus of History

We need to note initially that the whole question of the Jesus of history can be approached in several different ways. John A. T. Robinson has described four attitudes with regard to the question of the New Testament, its historical reliability, and biblical criticism: the cynicism of the foolish, the fundamentalism of the fearful, the skepticism of the wise, and the conservatism of the committed.[1] Though Robinson himself acknowledges that these are in a sense caricatures, there nonetheless is value in observing the different tendencies in dealing with the issue of

1. John A. T. Robinson, *Can We Trust the New Testament?* (Grand Rapids: Eerdmans, 1977), pp. 13–29.

the reliability of the New Testament. I am firmly committed to orthodox, conservative, or evangelical Christianity and its view that the Bible is the fully inspired and authoritative message of God. Some who hold this view of the Bible believe that it is sufficient simply to rest upon that commitment of faith. Since the Bible, being inspired, must be fully truthful in all that it asserts, we need not deal with critical problems. This is a kind of fideism, for it assumes that no rational support of one's faith is necessary, nor perhaps even possible, and yet that one's belief in the Bible's truth is not at all diminished thereby.

Some Christians, primarily theologians but also some laypersons, have tended to approach the Bible with virtually the opposite attitude. They are prepared to accept only those portions which can be established as genuine by the use of historical criticism. These persons follow an approach in history roughly parallel to the natural theologians' use of philosophical reasoning. Sometimes this has been accompanied by considerable inherent skepticism, and in particular a naturalism or antisupernaturalism regarding the events dealt with in Gospel research. The miracles, it is declared, are unlikely to have occurred. The resurrection presents a particular problem. Thus, a priori considerations have limited the possible conclusions of historical research.

Many evangelicals have also seen value in the various methods of critical study of the Gospels. But they have customarily adopted somewhat different presuppositions with respect to those methods. In particular, they have protested against any notion of a "closed continuum," such as Rudolf Bultmann assumed in his form-critical methodology. Being thoroughgoing supernaturalists, they believe that miracles can occur and that we cannot make an antecedent judgment as to whether a miracle has occurred or not. It is possible to fall victim to a sort of secondary naturalism, however, that is, a naturalism at another level. While holding that at least some of the events can be and should be given supernatural explanations, we may treat the production of the biblical accounts of those events as if a fully natural explanation were the sole type of explanation needed and desired. This secondary naturalism is a somewhat Thomistic approach.

On the other hand, it is possible to steer a middle course somewhere between the fideistic and the naturalistic viewpoints toward history. Augustinianism, for example, has been generally characterized as "faith seeking understanding." It is possible to approach the critical study of the Gospels with the assumption that they are divinely inspired and fully reliable historically, and then seek to test that hypothesis against the relevant data. The contention here is that while the ideal would be a completely objective or uncommitted investigation, what we have in the real world are differing approaches which come with their own set of assumptions, and that we may test the validity of a given set of assumptions by asking whether it can handle a wide sweep of the data more accurately and with less distortion than can competitive approaches and their sets of assumptions. Does the hypothesis that the Gospel authors wrote under the supernatural influence of the Spirit of God which is called inspiration fit the data of the Gospels better and with fewer attendant difficulties than do the other views?

Note that we are not suggesting that we should accept only those portions of the Gospels which we can demonstrate by historical research to be reliable. The affirmations of the Gospel writers are inspired and true, regardless of whether we can demonstrate them to be so. We should not confuse the issue of being with the issue of knowing. The question in dispute is whether we must take the Gospels only by faith. The point of greatest concern is whether the transmission of the Gospel materials from the time of actual occurrence or utterance to the time of their being recorded in writing preserved or distorted the content. To put the matter differently, we are herein contending that it is possible to establish sufficiently the historical reliability of enough of the Gospels to construct a Christology (or at least a partial Christology) upon that material.[2]

The Assumption of Antithesis Between Theology and History

In evaluating the historical reliability of the Gospels it is frequently assumed that the Evangelists were not historians, but theologians. Because they were persons who wrote with a particular purpose, who were seeking to communicate their own

---

2. As Robinson points out, the great English New Testament scholars, J. B. Lightfoot, Brooke Foss Westcott, and F. J. A. Hort, saw that the answer to bad criticism is better criticism, not none (*Can We Trust the New Testament?* p. 16).

convictions about Jesus, they did not possess the necessary objectivity to make them good sources upon which we can base and develop our historical picture of Jesus.

It should be conceded immediately that "Evangelist" is an apt description of the Gospel writers—they sought to persuade others of the understanding of Jesus to which they themselves had come. John puts it most baldly: "These are written that you may believe that Jesus is the Christ, the Son of God" (John 20:31). All of the other Gospel writers had a similar purpose. It is also evident from a careful reading of the four documents that each author tailored his writing to communicate most effectively to his specific audience. And there is no reason to believe that those from whom the Evangelists received their material did not also have such a motivation. Once we have acknowledged the writers' motivation, it is, as R. T. France puts it, a short but an illegitimate step to say that therefore the Gospels are not to be trusted as historical records.[3]

What lies at the heart of the issue is the assumption that the Evangelists' passion to communicate necessarily militates against the possibility of historical accuracy. We noted this presupposition in our examination of Norman Perrin's work (see pp. 92–93). He puts the point quite directly: That "early Christian preaching . . . was interested in historical reminiscence [is an assumption] for which we have absolutely no evidence. The opposite view, that it was theologically motivated, is the one for which we have evidence."[4]

But is the assumption that theological motivation precludes historical accuracy justified? Is there evidence to support such an assumption upon which so much is made to hinge? Is it the case that the only way to get across one's message about a person is to misrepresent the facts, either intentionally or unintentionally? How much biography is written by authors who are indifferent to the person about whom they are writing? One of the reasons why authors write about certain subjects and persons is an interest in the topic. And biographies are usually written because the author believes that others could learn from the life of the person under consideration. Indeed, it may well be that

3. R. T. France, *The Evidence for Jesus* (Downers Grove, Ill.: Inter-Varsity, 1986), p. 102.

4. Norman Perrin, *Rediscovering the Teaching of Jesus* (New York: Harper and Row, 1976), p. 24.

this type of interest in the person being written about guarantees even greater than normal diligence in ascertaining the facts. France asks, "Is a *Christian commitment* and an *evangelistic* aim somehow more destructive of historical concern or integrity than other motives for writing? Many would want to argue the opposite."[5] Furthermore, since the apostles risked their lives to proclaim what they did, there is probably additional basis for believing that they were accurate in ascertaining and reporting what had happened. In light of these considerations, we must maintain that the assumption that theological motivation precludes historical reliability cannot be sustained, and that arguments which rest upon that assumption are to be discarded.

The Dates of Writing

It may seem to some that the time the Gospels were written is a matter of indifference to the question of their reliability. After all, if they are true, they are true regardless of when they were written. Yet we should note that two factors make this question significant. If oral tradition tends to be modified with the passage of time and with the number of retellings, then the greater the length of time that elapses from the event until the account is written, the greater the likelihood of modification or distortion. The second factor is that the later the writing and circulation of the Gospels, the less the likelihood that eyewitnesses to the original events were still alive and able to confirm, contradict, or clarify what was written. The date of writing is therefore an issue of considerable importance.

In actuality, there is a correlation between the dates scholars assign to the Gospels and the degree of historical reliability attributed to them. One of the most radical negative arguments is that of G. A. Wells, who questions whether Jesus actually existed at all. Wells indicates how dependent his argument is upon a late dating of the New Testament documents: "The earliest references to the historical Jesus are so vague that it is not necessary to hold that he ever existed; the rise of Christianity can, from the undoubtedly historical antecedents, be explained quite well without him; and reasons can be given to show why,

5. France, *Evidence*, p. 103.

from about AD *80 or 90,* Christians began to suppose that he had lived in Palestine about fifty years earlier" (emphasis added).[6] Indeed, Wells dates even Mark, which is generally considered the earliest of the Gospels, as late as A.D. 90.

On the other hand, a number of scholars have shifted their dating of the Gospels to significantly earlier dates. Perhaps the most thorough and in some ways the most surprising is the work of John A. T. Robinson, whose *Redating the New Testament* represents quite a change of conviction from his earlier writings, such as *Jesus and His Coming*. He notes that Adolf von Harnack underwent a similar conversion.[7] It should be observed that Robinson is utilizing the same critical methods the form critics employed to require a later dating. He contends that by the criteria the form critics used elsewhere, the Gospel accounts must be quite early.

Robinson points out the way in which the consensus which has prevailed was constructed. Very few absolute dates are available for the New Testament. Consequently, most of the dating has been done on a relative basis. A basic tenet of the critics was that each of the processes they studied required a certain minimum amount of time.[8] Since redaction criticism assumed the results of form criticism, and form criticism assumed the conclusions of source criticism, the datings arrived at early on have not been reexamined or reevaluated in some time. When they are reexamined, "one realizes how thin is the foundation for some of the textbook answers and how circular the arguments for many of the relative datings. Disturb the position of one major piece and the pattern starts disconcertingly to dissolve."[9]

For Robinson, that one piece was the Gospel of John. While some had earlier dated it as late as the end of the second century, most scholars, both conservative and liberal alike, had

---

6. G. A. Wells, *The Historical Evidence for Jesus* (Buffalo, N.Y.: Prometheus, 1982), p. ix.

7. John A. T. Robinson, *Redating the New Testament* (Philadelphia: Westminster, 1976), pp. 90–91. Harnack's change of position is found in his *Date of the Acts and the Synoptic Gospels* (New York: Putnam, 1911), pp. 90–135.

8. For example, if Mark was written earlier, and Matthew utilized Mark in writing his Gospel, a certain amount of time was required for Matthew to do the necessary reworking of Mark. Similarly, form criticism maintained that the development of theological themes in the Christian community during the oral period involved certain minimum amounts of time.

9. Robinson, *Redating the New Testament*, p. 9.

come to agree on a date near the end of the first century. For Robinson, however, the arguments for dating it as late as 90–100 began to lose their force, first because of a growing recognition of John's dependence upon the Synoptics, and then, after 1947, because of the discovery of linguistic parallels in the Dead Sea Scrolls. He began to wonder if the Gospel of John did not belong to the period prior to the Jewish revolt of 66–70. But this then raised questions regarding the Synoptic Gospels. Either they would have to be dated still earlier, or the commonly held view of their priority would have to be abandoned.[10]

The major, but not the only factor influencing Robinson's dating of the Gospels is the fall of Jerusalem in A.D. 70. Here, certainly, is a most significant event which provides a benchmark for chronology, since its date can be definitely established from secular sources. Robinson finds it striking that this event is never once mentioned in the New Testament documents as a past fact.[11] To be sure, there are prophetic references which liberal critics have interpreted as instances of *vaticinium post eventum*. He finds this an artificial and unwarranted assumption, however, as does Bo Reicke: "An amazing example of uncritical dogmatism in New Testament studies is the belief that the Synoptic Gospels should be dated after the Jewish War of A.D. 66–70 because they contain prophecies *ex eventu* of the destruction of Jerusalem by the Romans in the year 70."[12]

In fact, on form criticism's own grounds there are some surprising things to be found. An example is in Mark 13:1–4, where in response to the disciples' exclamation about the temple Jesus comments that its stones will be cast down. Then they ask him what the signs of these things will be, but he does not answer the question. Now if this Gospel had been written after the fall of the city, that event would certainly have been much on the minds of the church community and the people to whom Mark was writing. The lack of detail in the report, and the fact that Mark does not give Jesus' answer, are hard to account for on form-critical grounds if this Gospel were indeed written after

---

10. Ibid., pp. 9–10.
11. Ibid., p. 13.
12. Bo Reicke, "Synoptic Problems on the Destruction of Jerusalem," in *Studies in New Testament and Early Christian Literature: Essays in Honor of Allen P. Wikgren* (supplement to *Novum Testamentum* 33), ed. David E. Aune (Leiden: Brill, 1972), p. 121.

A.D. 70. For the form critics stress that the Gospels clearly reflect the *Sitz im Leben* of the church. Here, certainly, it is difficult to speak of prophecy shaped by prior events.[13]

And what of the other Synoptics? They contain passages which seem to describe events with greater resemblance to the fall of Jerusalem and destruction of the temple. One thinks, for example, of Matthew 22:7 and Luke 21:20–24. K. H. Rengstorf has shown, however, that the vocabulary of the former passage represents a fixed description of ancient expeditions whose purpose was to mete out punishment.[14] And C. H. Dodd argues that the latter is simply a general description of war, and that Josephus's account is much more specific.[15]

When all the passages in the Synoptic Gospels are examined, it seems peculiar indeed that if they were written after the fall of Jerusalem, there are no explicit references to the event. This is strange enough in the case of one writer, but as C. C. Torrey has pointed out, how can it be that three or even four writers all failed to make mention of it?[16] While this argument is from silence, it is extremely cogent in light of form criticism's stress on the *Sitz im Leben*.

Another argument for an early dating of the Gospels is the abrupt conclusion of the Book of Acts. The narrative takes the reader up to the point of the trial of Paul, but then the book comes to an end without informing us as to the outcome of that trial. Harnack goes as far as to liken this to telling the story of Jesus and then ending the account with his delivery to Pilate.[17] Nor for that matter is there any reference to the persecution under Nero, the taking of authority by Ananias the high priest at the death of Festus the Roman governor, the death of James the brother of Jesus at the hands of Ananias and the Sanhedrin

13. Robinson, *Redating*, pp. 15–16, 21.

14. K. H. Rengstorf, "Die Stadt der Mörder (Mt. 22:7)," in *Judentum-Urchristentum-Kirche: Festschrift für Joachim Jeremias* (supplement to *Zeitschrift für die neutestamentliche Wissenschaft* 26), ed. W. Eltester (Berlin: Töpelmann, 1960), pp. 106–29, especially 125–26.

15. C. H. Dodd, "The Fall of Jerusalem and the 'Abomination of Desolation,'" *Journal of Roman Studies* 37 (1947): 47–54; reprinted in Dodd, *More New Testament Studies* (Grand Rapids: Eerdmans, 1968), pp. 69–83.

16. C. C. Torrey, *The Apocalypse of John* (New Haven: Yale University Press, 1958), p. 86, quoting his earlier book, *The Four Gospels* (New York: Harper, 1933).

17. Harnack, *Date of the Acts*, pp. 95–96.

before the new governor arrived, and the deposition of Ananias by Agrippa to put himself and the Jews on the right side of the Romans. The matter of Ananias would have served ideally Luke's apologetic to show that Christianity posed no threat to the Romans—it was the Jews who were the real enemies of the gospel. All of these omissions require some explanation, but none of those which have been offered appear as plausible as that the Book of Acts had been completed before these events took place. But if Acts was finished before A.D. 70, then what shall we do about Luke, which evidently had been composed previously (Acts 1:1)? Must we not date it earlier yet?

An additional consideration relates to the apocalyptic portions in the Synoptic Gospels. Robinson had earlier observed that the closest parallels to these texts, which seem to be the latest materials in the Synoptic tradition, are to be found in the letters to the Thessalonians, probably among the earliest New Testament writings. At that time he was unable to explain the time lag between the similar texts.[18] Now, however, he suggests that the ideas found in Thessalonians were already present in the Matthean community and its version of the gospel by the year 49. The apocalyptic elements in Matthew 24 do not, he contends, require a late date.[19]

One final consideration, at which we have already hinted, is the silence of the Gospels regarding the death of James the brother of Jesus. This omission is in itself of great interest. In addition, there is no mention of James's successor as bishop of Jerusalem (or, as nonepiscopal scholars would prefer to say, as acknowledged leader of the Jerusalem church), who Eusebius tells us was Symeon, the son of Clopas, Joseph's brother. Although the Gospels mention a number of other persons who would be of significance to the later church, including Clopas (John 19:25), Rufus (Mark 15:21), and Salome, the mother of James and John, the sons of Zebedee (Matt. 27:56; Mark 15:40; 16:1), Symeon is nowhere named. Robinson suggests that this is because the death of James (A.D. 62) followed the writing of the Gospels.[20]

These are only samples of the arguments that could be

18. John A. T. Robinson, *Jesus and His Coming* (New York: Abingdon, 1958), pp. 105–11.

19. Robinson, *Redating the New Testament*, pp. 105–06.

20. Ibid., p. 107.

adduced. We should, of course, observe that they are primarily negative arguments, or arguments from silence. However, we do not expect such silences, given the dating required by form critics and their stress on the *Sitz im Leben*. The point is that the arguments for later dating are not persuasive; indeed, the arguments for pre–A.D. 70 dates for the Gospels are sufficiently strong to place the burden of proof on those who would claim later dates.[21] Robinson even goes as far as to suggest a rough chronology:

1. Formation of stories- and sayings-collections ("P," "Q," "L," "M"): 30s and 40s+
2. Formation of "proto-gospels": 40s and 50s+
3. Formation of our Synoptic Gospels: 50–60+[22]

The Oral Tradition
The Form-Critical View

We must next ask about the preservation of the traditions regarding Jesus during the period between the occurrence of the event and the writing of the Gospels. The standard form-critical account tended to assume that the early church was not greatly concerned about exact preservation. This affected the accuracy of the later oral tradition in two ways: (1) Accidental alterations occurred because the early Christian community was not diligent in attempting to preserve word-for-word accounts of what the Lord had said and done. Such alteration happens freely and naturally in the transmission of oral tradition. (2) The community had no great compunctions about rather freely altering the tradition and even making creative additions to it. Analogies were frequently drawn to present-day rumors and games in which a message is successively whispered from one participant to the next.

The Scandinavian School

A sharply opposed alternative came on the scene with the theories of Harald Riesenfeld, Birger Gerhardsson, and the so-

21. Ibid., pp. 30, 92.
22. Ibid., p. 107.

called Scandinavian school. Peter Davids has likened their challenge to the Viking invasions which struck fear into the heart of European culture.[23] The first publication enunciating this new approach was Riesenfeld's *Gospel Tradition and Its Beginnings*. This was followed by a number of publications by his pupil Gerhardsson: *Memory and Manuscript, Tradition and Transmission in Early Christianity*, and *The Origins of the Gospel Traditions*.

What these men have attempted to do is to evaluate the transmission of the tradition from the perspective of its Jewish milieu. It does not make sense to try to reconstruct the process from the perspective of a different time and culture, as many critics have attempted to do. The Scandinavians observe that the letters of Paul and certain other New Testament writings assume a familiarity on the part of their readers with certain teachings of Jesus. This is seen, for example, in the fact that there are countless allusions to the sayings of Jesus, but no exact citations. Riesenfeld writes, "The sayings of Jesus, and hence the tradition about Jesus, were presumed to be already known, but this tradition was not cited in its verbal form."[24] Indeed, the Epistle of James contains four of the eight beatitudes found in Matthew, and in the same order.[25]

Riesenfeld also observed that the primitive Christian community used the same terminology for the process of tradition as was found within Judaism. Thus an examination of the way in which the Jewish community transmitted the tradition should help us understand what happened in early Christianity as well. Riesenfeld describes the process within the Jewish community:

> The situation as here conceived is not the vague diffusion of narratives, sagas, or anecdotes, as we find it in folk-lore, but the rigidly controlled transmission of matter from one who has the mastery of it to another who has been specially chosen to learn it. The bearer of the tradition and the teacher (*rabbi*) watched over its memorizing by his approved pupils (*talmīd*) and what

23. Peter Davids, "The Gospel and Jewish Tradition: Twenty Years After Gerhardsson," in *Gospel Perspectives*, ed. R. T. France and David Wenham, 6 vols. (Sheffield: JSOT, 1980–1986), vol. 1, p. 75.

24. Harald Riesenfeld, *The Gospel Tradition and Its Beginnings: A Study in the Limits of "Formgeschichte"* (London: A. R. Mowbray, 1957), pp. 14–15.

25. Ibid., p. 15.

was passed on in this way was, in the matter both of content and form, a fixed body of material.[26]

The words of the rabbi were regarded as holy, and the ideal pupil was one who never lost one iota of the tradition. This means that the content, and for that matter the form as well, were no less fixed and accurate for being oral in nature than if they had been written. Gerhardsson has described at great length how this oral tradition was preserved and transmitted within the rabbinical schools.[27]

This was the way in which the Jewish tradition was passed on in New Testament times. The next step in the argument is to contend that a similar process was at work in the preservation and transmission of the New Testament tradition. We noted above the Scandinavian school's observation that the Christian community used the same terminology for the tradition as did the Jewish community. They also make the point that Jesus taught his disciples, giving them instruction, not mere preaching, and in this he resembled the rabbis. "And this implies that Jesus made his disciples, and above all the Twelve, learn, and furthermore that he made them learn by heart." It is worth observing that the form of his teachings was such as to facilitate transmission.[28] We come to the conclusion that the early church's tradition goes back to Jesus himself. Only on such a basis could the tradition about Jesus have already possessed the character of Holy Word in the first age of the church.[29]

Objections to the Scandinavian Approach

It should not be surprising that such a radical criticism, striking at the very foundations of the form-critical conclusions which constituted the consensus of the time, received a considerable amount of negative response. Among the objections, two major groupings can be observed:

1. Some persons, especially some Jewish scholars, have contested applying studies of the practices of the rabbinic schools

26. Ibid., pp. 17–18.
27. Birger Gerhardsson, *Memory and Manuscript: Oral Tradition and Written Transmission in Rabbinic Judaism and Early Christianity* (Lund: C. W. K. Gleerup, 1961), pp. 93–170.
28. Riesenfeld, *Gospel Tradition*, pp. 24–25.
29. Ibid., p. 23.

in the second century back into an earlier period, and particularly the period prior to the Jewish war. Most notably Jacob Neusner has argued that the war introduced radical changes into Judaism. The practices the Scandinavians describe are almost entirely those of second- and third-century Pharisaism, which became fairly uniform after the destruction of the temple and of rival Jewish sects in the year A.D. 70.[30]

2. Even if we are justified in extending later rabbinic practice back into the period prior to A.D. 70, it is questionable whether Jesus used typical rabbinic procedures. After all, the contrast between his teaching and that of the scribes was conspicuous. Further, he was an itinerant preacher, identified more as a prophet than a teacher, and with an uneducated group of followers. This certainly did not accord with the typical picture of a rabbi and his pupils.[31] Moreover, Gerhardsson's account focused on the Jewish community's handling of the *Halakah*, the legal traditions of the scribes. Most of Jesus' teachings, however, would be more properly classified as *Haggadah*, less formal instructional material which would not have been subject to the same strict controls.[32] Finally, there is indication of considerable flexibility with and adaptation of the tradition by the early church. This scarcely fits with the picture of verbatim memorization and repetition of the message.[33]

It appears that Riesenfeld and Gerhardsson may, at least initially, have overstated their case. Yet some strong effects of their basic argument are not so easily disposed of as its critics have seemed to think. For one thing, although the evidence cited was primarily from the second century and later, it seems unlikely that such a practice would simply have arisen without antecedents.[34] Further, Gerhardsson responds that there was in

30. Morton Smith, "A Comparison of Early Christian and Early Rabbinic Tradition," *Journal of Biblical Literature* 82 (1963): 169–76; Jacob Neusner, *From Politics to Piety: The Emergence of Pharisaic Judaism* (Englewood Cliffs, N.J.: Prentice-Hall, 1973), pp. 92–95, and *Early Rabbinic Judaism* (Leiden: Brill, 1975), pp. 77–99.

31. C. K. Barrett, review of *Memory and Manuscript* by Birger Gerhardsson, *Journal of Theological Studies* 14 (1963): 445–49.

32. France, *Evidence*, p. 108.

33. W. D. Davies, "Reflections on a Scandinavian Approach to the Gospel Tradition," in *Neotestamentica et Patristica: Eine Freundesgabe, Herrn Professor Dr. Oscar Cullmann zu seinem 60. Geburtstag überreicht* (Leiden: Brill, 1962), pp. 14–34.

34. I. Howard Marshall, *I Believe in the Historical Jesus* (Grand Rapids: Eerdmans, 1977), pp. 195–96.

antiquity a general conservatism regarding pedagogical methodology.[35] He contends as well that "most of the characteristic features of Rabbinic pedagogics have a long history, *which can be traced far back into Old Testament times.*"[36] Such considerations cause even W. D. Davies, who had written a critical review, to comment in an admiring fashion:

> By bringing to bear the usages of contemporary Judaism, in a fresh and comprehensive manner, on the transmission of the Gospel Tradition, [the Scandinavian scholars] have forcibly compelled the recognition of the structural parallelism between much in Primitive Christianity and Pharisaic Judaism. This means, in our judgement, that they have made it far more historically probable and reasonably credible, over against the skepticism of much Form-Criticism, that in the Gospels we are within hearing of the authentic voice and within sight of the authentic activity of Jesus of Nazareth, however much muffled and obscured these may be by the process of transmission.[37]

Further Support for the Scandinavian Approach

The second main point of criticism, namely that the parallel between Jesus' teaching and that of the Jewish rabbis is unfounded, seems to be the stronger argument against the Scandinavian approach. There are, however, two indications that the Scandinavian challenge to the form-critical consensus is not to be so easily overthrown.

The first is the work of the German scholar Rainer Riesner, who studied the varieties of education in ancient Israel and her neighbors. He notes that memorization was a popular pedagogical method in the parental home, the synagogue, the elementary school, and the recollection of the tradition. Riesner cites Hieronymus and Eusebius to the effect that some Jews could perform astonishing feats of memory, reciting the lists of names in Chronicles forwards and backwards, and even mastering the Torah and the Prophets by rote.[38]

---

35. Birger Gerhardsson, *Tradition and Transmission in Early Christianity* (Lund: C. W. K. Gleerup, 1964), pp. 14–15.

36. Ibid., p. 15.

37. Davies, "Reflections," pp. 33–34.

38. Rainer Riesner, "Jüdische Elementarbildung und Evangelienüberlieferung," in *Gospel Perspectives*, ed. France and Wenham, vol. 1, pp. 211–18.

Riesner poses the question of whether there was a pre-Easter tradition about Jesus in which memorization played a role. He lists a number of considerations that have led him to answer this question in the affirmative:[39]

1. Nazareth had its own synagogue in which the Old Testament writings could be studied and a thorough knowledge of the Scriptures could be acquired. This entailed memorization of significant amounts of the Old Testament.

2. The degree of basic education which the Jewish child received depended upon the religious interest in the home, and Jesus came from a very devout family. Indeed, Riesner characterizes the twelve-year-old Jesus' interacting with the teachers in the temple not as a "wonderful" event, but as a sign of a good basic education.

3. Jesus' claim for himself must be described as messianic. His hearers simply could not have forgotten the words of someone who was, or could have been, the Messiah.

4. Much of Jesus' teaching utilized short, penetrating words and literary devices such as imagery, hyperbole, contrast, parallelism, rhythm, and rhyme. These devices were consciously crafted by Jesus to provide memorable teaching summaries which he repeated on various occasions.

5. Formulas such as "Truly, I say to you," and "Hear!" which introduce special teaching summaries, seem to enjoin memorization. The call to salvation includes the imperative, "Learn from me!"

6. Jesus assigned the narrow circle of disciples to learn his teaching and commissioned them to transmit his authentic words. This required instruction in the most important teaching summaries.

7. Since a pre-Easter beginning of the Jesus tradition has been established on various grounds, Riesner declares that one may with Riesenfeld and Gerhardsson "place a greater confidence in the dependability of the synoptic tradition than has been possible since the beginning of the 'form-critical school.'"[40]

---

39. Ibid., pp. 218–20. A much more detailed argument is presented in his dissertation, *Jesus als Lehrer: Eine Untersuchung zum Ursprung der Evangelien-Überlieferung* (Tübingen: J. C. B. Mohr [Paul Siebeck], 1984), and summarized on pp. 499–502.

40. Riesner, "Jüdische Elementarbildung," p. 220.

This emphatic commitment to the dependability of the tradition and endorsement of Riesenfeld's and Gerhardsson's work is repeated in the concluding words of his dissertation: "One may then interrogate the synoptic tradition with the justifiable hope that it can give us more information regarding who Jesus was and what he wanted."[41]

Here then is broad confirmation of the conception that processes at work during the period of Jesus' ministry and until the writing of the Gospels helped to guarantee accuracy. Riesner's general contention is supported by two other German dissertations that focus respectively on the general conservatism of tradition and the role Christian "teachers" played in preserving it.[42]

The other field of investigation bearing upon this issue is anthropological studies of societies where oral preservation of tradition is practiced extensively. These studies represent a mediating position between classical form criticism and the Scandinavian school, although they appear to be considerably closer to the latter. A certain amount of caution must be exercised in the employment of such materials, since they reflect our time rather than the biblical period. It should be noted, however, that they are in many ways closer to the cultural situation prevailing in the early church than are some of the settings frequently appealed to as parallels.

One of the most useful of these studies was done by the Harvard anthropologist Albert B. Lord. Lord studied Yugoslavian folksingers who had memorized epic stories of up to a hundred thousand words in length. The plot, characters, main events, and virtually all of the details remained the same each time the story was told or sung. Members of the community were sufficiently familiar with the stories to be able to correct a singer who erred in any significant way. The wording might change slightly, but in ways not unlike the variations in the three Synoptic Gospels. Lord sums up his findings:

> When we look back over these examples of transmission, we are, I believe, struck by the conservativeness of the tradition. The basic story is carefully preserved. Moreover, the changes fall into cer-

---

41. Riesner, *Jesus als Lehrer*, p. 502.
42. G. Müller, *Der Traditionsprozess im Neuen Testament* (Freiburg: Herder, 1982); and A. F. Zimmermann, *Die urchristlichen Lehrer* (Tübingen: Mohr, 1984).

tain clear categories, of which the following emerge: (1) saying the same thing in fewer or more lines, because of singers' methods of line composition and of linking lines together, (2) expansion of ornamentation, adding of details of description (that may not be without significance), (3) changes of order in a sequence (this may arise from a different sense of balance on the part of the learner, or even from what might be called a chiastic arrangement where one singer reverses the order given by the other), (4) addition of material not in a given text of the teacher, but found in texts of other singers in the district, (5) omission of material, and (6) sub-stitution of one theme for another, in a story held together by inner tensions.[43]

Here is a situation in which there are great fidelity to the content and yet allowance for variations which are incidental to the meaning. This seems to fit well with the view that while Scripture preserves accuracy in its accounts, yet there is freedom in the forms of expression.

The study by Lord is not an isolated case. Another significant study was done by Jan Vansina on African oral cultures, especially in the Congo (now Zaire). He found that texts of a religious and ritual nature were carefully memorized and recited, usually by specialists (priests and sorcerers). The people believed that any alteration could lead to serious supernatural sanctions.[44]

Christian Prophets and the Formation of the Tradition

One additional consideration which deserves at least brief treatment is the role of Christian prophets in the early church with respect to the formation of the tradition. Certain more rad-ical form and redaction critics, such as Rudolf Bultmann and Norman Perrin, maintained that certain "prophets" were active within the early church, delivering messages purportedly re-vealed by the risen Lord, and that the church incorporated these messages into the tradition as if they had been spoken by Jesus

---

43. Albert B. Lord, *The Singer of Tales* (Cambridge, Mass.: Harvard University Press, 1960), p. 123.

44. Jan Vansina, *Oral Tradition: A Study in Historical Methodology* (London: Routledge and Kegan Paul, 1965). My colleague Herbert Klem knows of African tellers of tales who can recite from memory for two days at a time.

during his time of earthly ministry. Bultmann says, for example, "The Church drew no distinction between such utterances by Christian prophets and the sayings of Jesus in the tradition, for the reason that even the dominical sayings in the tradition were not the pronouncements of a past authority, but sayings of the risen Lord, who is always a contemporary for the Church."[45] Perrin makes a statement virtually identical in its effect: "The early Church made no attempt to distinguish between the words the earthly Jesus had spoken and those spoken by the risen Lord through a prophet in the community."[46]

It is not only the more radical critics who have espoused such a theory, however. Gerald Hawthorne argued for it in a paper presented to the Society of Biblical Literature's seminar on Christian prophecy.[47] Ralph Martin and E. Earle Ellis also appear to follow a somewhat similar line of argument.[48]

Before proceeding to evaluate this thesis, it is important that we define exactly what the issue is. We are not asking whether the church and the Gospel writers may have edited Jesus' sayings, paraphrasing, reordering, abbreviating, and expanding them. We are not questioning whether the Lord after his ascension continued to give revelations which are now recorded in Scripture, for example, the Pauline Epistles. Nor are we even questioning whether the Lord may have revealed to a writer something which he had actually said during his earthly ministry, but which had not been preserved in the tradition. The question is whether something spoken by a prophet is reported as having been spoken by the earthly Jesus, even though this was not the case. There are several reasons why we must answer this last question in the negative:

1. There is no biblical precedent, as far as we can tell. The one place where a biblical writer reports the words of the ascended Lord directly to his people is in the letters to the seven churches

---

45. Rudolf Bultmann, *The History of the Synoptic Tradition*, rev. ed. (New York: Harper and Row, 1976), pp. 127–28.

46. Norman Perrin, *Rediscovering the Teaching of Jesus* (New York: Harper and Row, 1967), p. 15.

47. Gerald Hawthorne, "Christian Prophecy and the Sayings of Jesus: Evidence of and Criteria for," *Society of Biblical Literature 1975 Seminar Papers*, 2 vols. (Missoula, Mont.: Scholars, 1975), vol. 2, pp. 174–78.

48. Ralph P. Martin, *New Testament Foundations: A Guide for Christian Students*, vol. 1, *The Four Gospels* (Grand Rapids: Eerdmans, 1975), p. 159; E. Earle Ellis, *Prophecy and Hermeneutic in Early Christianity: New Testament Essays* (Grand Rapids: Eerdmans, 1978).

in Revelation 2–3. There is no suggestion, however, that Jesus had uttered these words during his earthly life.

Further, there is an argument from silence. If indeed the church did attribute to the earthly Jesus the messages given by the ascended Lord through prophets, is it not strange that we find no reference in the records of his earthly ministry to some of the most troublesome problems the early church had to face, such as the questions of speaking in tongues, eating meat offered to idols, and the place of circumcision?[49]

2. It is unlikely that the church would have accepted the sayings of prophets as sayings of Jesus. Prophecies in the New Testament were not anonymous, but were clearly tied to the persons who had uttered them. Further, although there were prophets in the early church, apostolic tradition was considered to possess higher authority than prophetic inspiration. Thus Paul emphasizes that all prophecy has to be evaluated (1 Cor. 14:29–33).[50]

3. Finally, it appears that the case for a creative role by Christian prophets is lacking any real evidence. David Aune, in a highly regarded treatment of early Christian prophecy, says of this particular contention, "In spite of the theological attractiveness of the theory, however, the historical evidence in support of the theory lies largely in the creative imagination of scholars."[51] David Hill's verdict is similarly negative: "Indeed, the evidence produced and repeated in support of the contention that the Christian prophets played a creative role in respect of sayings later attributed to the earthly Jesus proves, on examination, to be lacking in substance and authority."[52]

Criteria of Authenticity

What we have been advancing are in a sense rebuttals of (or at least alternatives to) the variety of form criticism which casts serious doubt upon the historical reliability of the Gospel accounts of Jesus. This might be regarded by some as sufficient, so that we

---

49. Craig Blomberg, *The Historical Reliability of the Gospels* (Downers Grove, Ill.: Inter-Varsity, 1987), pp. 31–32.

50. F. Neugebauer, "Geistsprüche und Jesuslogien," *Zeitschrift für die neutestamentliche Wissenschaft* 53 (1962): 218–28.

51. David E. Aune, *Prophecy in Early Christianity and the Ancient Mediterranean World* (Grand Rapids: Eerdmans, 1983), p. 245.

52. David Hill, "On the Evidence for the Creative Role of Christian Prophets," *New Testament Studies* 20.3 (April 1974): 272.

might rest our case here. We may, however, go further and argue that in addition to neutralizing the negative considerations through evidence for the general reliability of the Gospels, we can also cite evidence which will help to demonstrate the authenticity of specific biblical statements attributed to Jesus, that is to say, to demonstrate that they indeed do go back to him. By doing so, we will have doubly strong confirmation of our hypothesis and doubly strong justification for our use of these materials when we attempt to reconstruct Jesus' self-understanding.

To this end, a number of criteria of authenticity have been developed. Some of them originated with the early, more radical form critics, such as Bultmann. Others have been developed by more conservative scholars or, as France prefers to term them, the historicists.[53] How one regards these criteria will depend on where one places the burden of proof. Those who hold that the Gospels are not to be regarded as historically dependable unless proven to be so, consider the presence of the criteria as a requisite of historicity, and their absence as disproof of historicity. Those, on the other hand, who see the burden of proof as lying upon those who doubt the historicity of the Gospels consider the presence of the criteria as confirmation of historicity, but they do not view absence as disproof. On the basis of the general considerations we have adduced thus far, we will consider their presence to be positive evidences of authenticity.

Multiple Attestation or Multiple Forms

While the lists of the criteria of authenticity and the emphases upon specific items on those lists vary, there are certain common factors. Multiple attestation is perhaps the most frequently cited criterion; in fact, it is widely used in historical study in general quite apart from Gospel research. The principle here is simply that where more than one source essentially agree with one another, the statements can be accorded a high degree of certainty, especially if their mutual independence can be established. Essentially, this is an issue of source and literary criticism. If, for example, we consider the primary sources of the Gospels to be Mark; "Q," or the portions common to Matthew and Luke, but not found in Mark; "M," the portions unique to Matthew; "L," the

---

53. R. T. France, "The Authenticity of the Sayings of Jesus," in *History, Criticism and Faith*, ed. Colin Brown (Downers Grove, Ill.: Inter-Varsity, 1976), p. 126.

materials unique to Luke; and the Gospel of John, the presence of a passage or saying in two or more of these sources would be considered a sign of authenticity.

There are, of course, some significant criticisms which have been leveled at this criterion. One is that it presupposes a particular solution to the efforts of source criticism or, more precisely, to the Synoptic Problem and the problem of the relationship of the fourth Gospel to the other three. That solution is not unshakable and has been seriously challenged.[54] Just as the second course of a masonry wall can be weaker but not stronger than the course upon which it rests, so this criterion's strength depends upon the solidity of its solution to the problems of source criticism.

Another difficulty is that one may be justified in saying that a particular statement is found at a very early or even the earliest level of the tradition, but the step from there to declaring that it is an authentic saying of Jesus is an inference. While the inference may be valid, it nonetheless requires an additional premise, namely, "the earliest tradition is the authentic sayings of Jesus."[55] In all likelihood, that premise should be qualified as a statement of probability rather than certainty.

Closely related to multiple attestation, and treated either as a similar subpoint of a larger category or as a similar principle, is the criterion of multiple forms.[56] Here the argument is that the presence of a given saying or motif within different classes of Gospel material, as identified by the form critics, argues for its authenticity. While this criterion is somewhat more difficult to apply than is multiple attestation proper, it does prove a valuable supplement. The occasional problem of establishing that different written sources do not go back to a common source is usually avoided when we are dealing with different forms.

Dissimilarity or Discontinuity

A second principle, virtually universally cited, but variously evaluated, is that of dissimilarity or discontinuity. This was the one criterion identified by such radical form critics as Bultmann and Perrin: a statement attributed to Jesus can be considered

---

54. See, e.g., William R. Farmer, *The Synoptic Problem: A Critical Analysis* (New York: Macmillan, 1964).

55. Perrin, *Rediscovering the Teaching of Jesus*, 1976 ed., p. 46.

56. C. H. Dodd, *History and the Gospel* (New York: Scribner, 1938), pp. 86–103.

authentic when it is shown to differ significantly from anything which can be found either in Judaism or in the early church. While this criterion is generally applied to the content of Jesus' teaching, it may also be applied to form, to attitudes, and even to the whole concept of the Gospels as a distinctive genre.[57]

Certain cautions need to be observed. In particular, dissimilarity should not be viewed as an indispensable or the sole criterion. If it were, the only teaching of Jesus that we could accept as authentic would have to be totally novel and unique. That, however, conflicts with the fact that Jesus was a Jew raised in the Hebrew faith, and that he claimed to have come not to destroy the law, but to fulfil it. It also ignores or contradicts the fact that the church claimed to have derived its teaching from Jesus and to be seeking to preserve and follow that teaching. Both of these considerations create an a priori presumption against there being much uniqueness in Jesus' teaching.

It should also be noted that the efficacy of dissimilarity rests on our ability to determine with considerable certainty the content and nature of the teaching of Judaism and of early Christianity.[58] Any uncertainty here multiplies as we apply the criterion.

Probably the most sustained and penetrating criticism of the criterion of dissimilarity is that by Morna Hooker.[59] When closely examined, however, her critique will be seen to apply to the misuse or overextension of this principle. A proper use of the principle seems to parallel the principle of the textual critics that the more difficult reading is probably the correct one. The idea behind the criterion of dissimilarity is that for something that was actually foreign to either the background or the current belief of the early Christian community to have been preserved in the oral tradition must mean that it was recognized as authentically from Jesus.

Palestinian Environment

A third criterion frequently employed is a Palestinian environment, including the Aramaic language. If a saying attributed to Jesus can be shown to rest upon an Aramaic expression, or if

57. René Latourelle, *Finding Jesus Through the Gospels: History and Hermeneutics* (New York: Alba, 1979), p. 224.

58. Marshall, *I Believe in the Historical Jesus*, pp. 201–02.

59. Morna Hooker, "On Using the Wrong Tool," *Theology* 75 (1972): 570–81; and "Christology and Methodology," *New Testament Studies* 17.4 (July 1971): 480–88.

a concept or event can be shown to reflect early first-century Palestine, it is not necessary nor advisable to ascribe it to a later Hellenistic setting.[60] Application of this criterion can sometimes be quite straightforward. For example, a saying of Jesus may be seen to represent an Aramaic original because it reflects a Semitic parallelism or rests upon a pun in Aramaic that does not appear in the Greek language.[61] By contrast, a general congruence with first-century Palestine is less clearly demonstrated, and frequently depends upon the results of archaeology.

Here again a modicum of caution must be employed, for evidence of an Aramaic original does not guarantee that a saying came from Jesus, but only from someone familiar with Aramaic. There is, however, a greater presumption of authenticity than would otherwise be the case.

Coherence

Coherence is another criterion listed in many discussions of authenticity. Once we have established the authenticity of certain sayings by the use of other criteria, related sayings can also be viewed as authentic. The more radical critics frequently focus on sayings authenticated by the criterion of dissimilarity.[62] Most of the conservative (historicist) critics concentrate on "core" sayings substantiated by multiple attestation.[63]

There is not always great clarity about the meaning of the term *coherence*. In some cases, it seems to mean noncontradiction of previously authenticated sayings.[64] In other cases, it is used to refer to positive interfacing and even interlocking of the concepts.[65] To the extent that the meaning is the latter, coherence proper, rather than mere logical consistency, the value of the criterion is enhanced. Whenever it is generalized to mean conformity with a central or basic teaching of Jesus, such as the kingdom of God, the criterion of coherence tends to lose its utility, along with its specificity.[66]

60. Blomberg, *Historical Reliability*, p. 247.
61. Robert Stein, "The 'Criteria' for Authenticity," in *Gospel Perspectives*, ed. France and Wenham, vol. 1, pp. 234–35.
62. Perrin, *Rediscovering the Teaching of Jesus*, pp. 43–45.
63. Blomberg, *Historical Reliability*, p. 248.
64. Marshall, *I Believe in the Historical Jesus*, p. 205.
65. Latourelle, *Finding Jesus*, p. 227.
66. Ibid., p. 228.

Unintentionality

The basic thought behind the criterion of unintentionality, which is also known by several other names, is that references to matters that are not part of the basic intention and purpose of the writer or of the early church are probably authentic. For example, I. Howard Marshall points out that the major thrust of the early church was to emphasize the supernatural origin and character of Jesus, yet there are places where his humanity unmistakably shines through. This argues for the authenticity of what is there reported or described.[67] There also are situations where what is reported not only does not aid the express purpose of the writing, but may even militate against it. C. F. D. Moule points to the picture of Jesus' relationship to women.[68] That as a young unmarried man Jesus moved freely among women of all sorts, including the disreputable, does not seem to fit with what the church wanted to stress. Numerous other examples could be cited as well.

Causal Effect

Causal effect is another criterion which is known by various names. Marshall speaks of "traditional continuity,"[69] and René Latourelle of "necessary explanation," which he says is the special application to history of the general principle of sufficient reason.[70] By this is meant simply that there must have been a cause sufficient in effect to account for the presence of each part of the tradition. There must have been something to produce it. What, for example, could account for the report that, following the multiplication of loaves, Jesus was thought to be a great prophet, perhaps even the Prophet for whom the nation had been waiting, and the people wanted to make him king? Why did the feeding of the multitude become a decisive event for the disciples? And why was it given such great significance in the tradition? The extraordinary reaction to the event calls for acknowledgment of the reliability of the account.[71] If we do not

---

67. Marshall, *I Believe in the Historical Jesus*, pp. 205–06.
68. C. F. D. Moule, *The Phenomenon of the New Testament* (Naperville, Ill.: Allenson, 1967), pp. 63, 65.
69. Marshall, *I Believe in the Historical Jesus*, pp. 207–11.
70. Latourelle, *Finding Jesus*, pp. 229–32.
71. Ibid., pp. 231–32.

assume that the influence of Jesus was what led to the origin of this tradition, then we are forced to maintain that Jesus' influence was minimal and, like a nuclear reaction, led to the release of energy far greater than its own. But one must then ask what forces could have been present in the situation to lead to such a reaction. Marshall concludes that "historical study has not produced any plausible answers to this question."[72]

When we apply the various criteria we have examined, we find that there is a considerable basis for confidence in the accounts which we have in the Gospels. It is not necessary for a particular account to satisfy more than one of these criteria. Some accounts, however, satisfy several and thus carry even greater probability.

72. Marshall, *I Believe in the Historical Jesus*, p. 208.

16

The Reliability of the Historical Evidence for Jesus. (2) The Gospel of John

Of all the problems concerning the historicity of the Gospels, probably the largest and most vexing over the years has been the problem of the Gospel According to John or, as it has been popularly referred to in recent years, the fourth Gospel. That designation is, as John A. T. Robinson has pointed out, something of an affectation that is symptomatic of a larger set of issues or, more correctly, a different mind-set. He notes that there is no tendency among scholars to refer to "the first Gospel," or to the other Synoptic Gospels by number rather than by traditionally assigned author, even though there is no greater agreement among them that Matthew wrote the first Gospel than that John wrote the fourth Gospel; in fact, there is

409

probably even less.[1] Without prejudicing the case, the name writers and speakers use to refer to this particular Gospel may well be a good clue to their attitude toward it.

The "New Look" on the Fourth Gospel

For a long time there was a consensus that the Gospel traditionally attributed to Johannine authorship was not to be regarded as of much historical value. In part this was due to the fact of the author's rather obvious theological interest. One of the more extreme early statements was that of David Strauss, who asserted that the strongly theological orientation indicates that this Gospel is almost completely myth and not history.[2] This view has been perpetuated in the strong distinction made in form and redaction criticism between the Jesus of history and the Christ of faith, between event and interpretation, fact and symbolism. The consensus about John's Gospel was so strong that in 1957, when Robinson presented a paper on "The New Look on the Fourth Gospel," he could speak of what he termed "critical orthodoxy" or "the old look" in studies of the fourth Gospel.[3] This perspective had been so widely accepted that it was considered virtually unscholarly to deviate from it. Robinson stated that the old look in studies of the fourth Gospel rested upon five presuppositions:

1. The author is dependent upon sources, including, for the most part, one or more of the Synoptics.
2. The background of the author is other than that of the events and teachings which he purports to record.
3. He is not to be seriously regarded as a witness to the Jesus of history, but only to the Christ of faith.
4. He represents the end term of theological development in first-century Christianity.
5. He is not the apostle John, nor a direct eyewitness of the events reported.[4]

1. John A. T. Robinson, *Can We Trust the New Testament?* (Grand Rapids: Eerdmans, 1977), p. 26.
2. David F. Strauss, *Life of Jesus, Critically Examined* (New York: Macmillan, 1892).
3. John A. T. Robinson, *Twelve New Testament Studies* (Naperville, Ill.: Allenson, 1962), pp. 94–106.
4. Ibid., p. 95.

Robinson contrasted this critical orthodoxy with what he called the "new look," which was prepared to rethink the nearly unanimous opinion on the fourth Gospel. He noted that the presuppositions ruled out as impertinent certain questions which, if one were to ask them, yield answers which make a great deal of good sense.[5] When Robinson presented his paper, he spoke of what seemed to him to be straws in the wind, but which he was inclined to take seriously, because all of the straws were blowing in the same direction.[6] In actuality, the number of straws has been increasing, so that the old thinking can no longer be simply accepted uncritically. Robinson was not the first to raise anew the question of the historicity of the fourth Gospel. In the Sarum Lectures at Oxford University in 1954–1955, which in 1963 were expanded into a book entitled *Historical Tradition in the Fourth Gospel*, C. H. Dodd had spoken of the new situation, describing the change in terms much like those used by Robinson.[7] This was certainly one of the straws in the wind of which Robinson spoke.

Why is the question of the historicity of John so important? Craig Blomberg, after arguing at length and in a variety of ways for the historical reliability of the Gospels, observes that there are obvious differences between John and the Synoptics. "As a result, a viable case for the historical reliability of the Synoptics does not automatically apply to the Gospel of John as well."[8] Making a case for John is important, because of all four Gospels John is the most concerned with theology, and especially with Christology. It is therefore imperative that we determine the extent to which this Gospel gives us reliable information about the historical Jesus which we can use to construct our Christology.

The Relationship of John's Gospel to the Synoptics

The Nature of the Problem

One of the primary issues which need to be investigated to determine some sort of answer to the question of the historical

5. Ibid., p. 96.
6. Ibid., p. 94.
7. C. H. Dodd, *Historical Tradition in the Fourth Gospel* (Cambridge: Cambridge University Press, 1963).
8. Craig Blomberg, *The Historical Reliability of the Gospels* (Downers Grove, Ill.: Inter-Varsity, 1987), p. 153.

reliability of the fourth Gospel is its relationship to the Synoptic Gospels. This issue has attracted a great deal of attention. We have observed that the first of the presuppositions which Robinson recognized in the old look was that the author of this Gospel relied upon sources, including one or more of the Synoptic Gospels, for his material. Here we find a dilemma of sorts. On the one hand, if John had one or more of the Synoptics before him, the differences must be seen as alterations from the basic tradition and the additions as imaginative embellishments. On the other hand, if John worked independently and the differences from the Synoptics are substantial, the historical reliability of John is called into question. For by the law of noncontradiction, if we assume the reliability of the Synoptics, any contradiction between John and them is an indication of error or falsehood on John's part. Ideally, then, the evidence most conducive to a conclusion of the historical reliability of John would be that his material was independent of, but harmonious with, that of the Synoptic Gospels.

We turn first to the question of literary dependence or independence. In 1938, Percival Gardner-Smith published a small book which in many ways anticipated the new look in studies of the fourth Gospel.[9] By comparing John and the Synoptics for similarities and differences, he challenged on purely literary grounds the commonly accepted theory of dependence. He noted that the earlier studies had emphasized the correspondences and then tried to explain the divergences. He proposed, instead, to study the similarities and dissimilarities simultaneously. As a result of his investigation he concluded that John may well provide an "independent authority" for the life of Jesus. He observed: "If in the Fourth Gospel we have a survival of a type of first century Christianity which owed nothing to synoptic developments, and which originated in quite a different intellectual atmosphere, its historical value may be very great indeed."[10]

Dodd believed that Gardner-Smith's book had marked the turn of the tide; it "crystallized the doubts of many, and has

9. Percival Gardner-Smith, *Saint John and the Synoptic Gospels* (Cambridge: Cambridge University Press, 1938).

10. Ibid., pp. 96–97.

exerted an influence out of proportion to its size."[11] But if Gardner-Smith's book marked the turn of the tide, Dodd's accelerated the tide by doing the work that forcefully undermined the assumption of John's dependence upon the Synoptics.

Dodd's approach is to examine the passages where John refers to an incident also mentioned in the Synoptics, and then, comparing the different accounts in detail, to consider the possibilities of Johannine dependence upon the Synoptics. He examines such incidents as the anointing of Jesus, the feeding of the multitude, the cleansing of the temple, the entry into Jerusalem, the arrest and trial, as well as the sayings of Jesus common to the Synoptics and to John. In each case he concludes that it is very unlikely that John would have extracted from the different Synoptics and then combined just those details which he used to construct his own version of the event. Rather, it seems much more likely that John was working with an independent tradition. Robinson refers to Dodd's work as "a massive demonstration of the greater probability that the Johannine material rested on tradition independent of and often more primitive than that of the Synoptic Gospels."[12]

There is a negative aspect to Dodd's case as well. He looks closely at features of the Synoptic record which John does not include, but which we might expect would have been included had he been working directly from the Synoptics. Among these features are the darkness at the crucifixion, the rending of the temple veil, and the confession by the centurion that Jesus was the Son of God. All of these elements, found in Mark, would have suited John's symbolism well. Further, in light of John's liking for the "I am" (ἐγώ εἰμι) sayings of Jesus, it is surprising that he did not include Jesus' declaration at the climax of the trial before the high priest (Mark 14:62) or his self-identification at the moment of reunion in the upper room (Luke 24:39). The absence of what one would expect John to include if he were working with the Synoptic Gospels before him constitutes a confirming evidence of John's independence of the Synoptics, and thus of his use of a separate historical source, which may well be as reliable as (or more so than) the sources of the Synoptics.

11. Dodd, *Historical Tradition*, p. 8 n. 2.
12. John A. T. Robinson, *The Priority of John* (London: SCM, 1985), p. 12.

Robinson gives much the same sort of argument in his consideration of the priority of John.[13]

The case argued by Dodd made quite a strong impression upon the world of New Testament scholarship. One notable defense of the classic position of John's dependence upon Mark, his probable dependence upon Luke, and possible dependence even upon Matthew, appears in C. K. Barrett's commentary on John, which was issued in 1955.[14] By the time of the second edition (1978), however, although he still sticks to his guns, he is in the minority, according to Robinson, and very much aware that he is on the defensive. Now it is John's dependence on the Synoptics that must be established. The consensus has shifted, and the case for dependence must now be argued against the odds.[15] Of course, one must bear in mind that the current view is still only a presumption, as in the presumption of innocence of the accused in a court trial. It is now presumed by many scholars that John, unless proven otherwise, is independent of the Synoptic Gospels. The burden of proof has shifted. This should not be an excuse for prejudice, or for prejudgment. We must continue to explore the evidence. Whether it is as strong and compelling as the advocates of the new look hold, it is sufficiently strong to require some reexamination of the presuppositions.

We should not underestimate the importance of this issue. Maintaining that this is the most crucial of the five presuppositions which Robinson identified with the old look on John, Stephen Smalley says, "Once it is allowed that John to any extent depends on the synoptic Gospels, it follows that the only way to account for the differences between the synoptic and the Johannine traditions when they are in conflict is to say that the fourth evangelist has altered the material to suit his own purposes." And then the four other presuppositions follow as well.[16]

The Differences Between John's Gospel and the Synoptics

We must now consider the other major aspect of the problem of the relationship between John's Gospel and the Synoptics,

13. Ibid., pp. 158–342.
14. C. K. Barrett, *The Gospel According to St. John* (New York: Macmillan, 1955); 2d ed. (Philadelphia: Westminster, 1978).
15. Robinson, *Priority*, p. 11.
16. Stephen S. Smalley, *John: Evangelist and Interpreter* (Exeter: Paternoster, 1978), p. 12.

namely their differences. If Gardner-Smith, Dodd, Robinson, and Smalley are correct, the fourth Gospel rests upon sources independent of those of the Synoptic Gospels. If this is the case, then John should supplement what we have in the Synoptics. And if we proceed on the assumption that they are historically reliable, he should not contradict them.[17] We must therefore examine the dissimilarities to see whether John is complementary or contradictory to the Synoptics.

Blomberg has listed five major areas in which John's Gospel differs from the other three:[18]

1. *Selection of material.* Some of the most significant accounts in the Synoptics do not appear in John: an explicit statement of Jesus' baptism, the commissioning of the twelve apostles, the transfiguration, the institution of the Lord's Supper, the exorcisms, and the parables. Conversely, John includes material not found in the others: Jesus' first miracle in Cana, the raising of Lazarus, Jesus' early ministry in Judea and Samaria, and his extended discourses both public, in the temple and the synagogues, and private, in meetings with both his disciples and his opponents.

2. *Theology.* John is the only Evangelist to clearly identify Jesus as divine. Further, the Synoptists seem to depict a gradual development of Jesus' own messianic consciousness, together with the disciples' apparent blindness to his identity until the declaration by Peter (Mark 8:27–30). In John's opening chapter, however, John the Baptist, Andrew, Philip, and Nathanael all confess Jesus to be the Christ; and Jesus later reinforces this conviction with his self-designations, including even the "I am" of the Old Testament (John 8:58). In addition, in John eternal life is pictured as being present rather than future; John the Baptist denies being Elijah, even though the Synoptics say that he

---

17. Robinson (*Twelve New Testament Studies*, p. 96) has pointed out that while the twentieth-century critics have used the fourth Gospel's supposed dependence upon the Synoptics to discredit its historical reliability, in the nineteenth century it was its independence that was thought to count against it. How could John be reliable when his picture was so different from the Jesus of history presented by the Synoptists?

18. Blomberg, *Historical Reliability*, pp. 153–56.

was; and the time and nature of the coming of the Holy Spirit, privately and before the ascension (John 20:22), are different from the accounts given by the Synoptists.

3. *Chronology.* Whereas the Synoptics seem to indicate that the ministry of Jesus lasted only one year, John refers to three Passovers. There are major discrepancies regarding the chronology of the last twenty-four hours of Jesus' life as well. And certain events seem to have been transposed, such as the cleansing of the temple, which in the Synoptics occurs in the last week of Jesus' ministry, but in John takes place in its early days.

4. *Historical facts.* John, who has no account of Jesus' nativity, was apparently unaware of the birth in Bethlehem, for he reports that some Jews rejected Jesus on the grounds that the Christ was to come not from Galilee, but from Bethlehem (7:41–42). John also appears to be guilty of a serious anachronism when he tells of the Jews' being put out of the synagogue for believing in Jesus (9:22), a policy not established until the end of the first century.

5. *Style.* Whereas in the Synoptics Jesus' words are readily discernible, it is sometimes difficult to distinguish Jesus' teaching from John's interpretation, as in the conversation with Nicodemus (John 3). In John, moreover, Jesus speaks in extended discourses rather than the short proverbial sayings found in the Synoptics.

These problems deserve treatment and response. We will not attempt to deal with all of them, for that is an undertaking well beyond the scope of this book. We will, however, make some selected observations.

1. It appears that the difference in the selection of materials is the least of our problems—there is no indication of contradiction. The author of John's Gospel notes that he selected from among the multitude of things that Jesus had said and done, and that the material at his disposal was much larger than he could include (20:30; 21:25). The differences in the materials selected for inclusion in the respective Gospels seem to be well within the range which one finds in other accounts of the same general topic by various historians.[19] Sometimes it appears that

19. For a discussion of this sort of selectivity among historians see Martin Hengel, *Acts and the History of Earliest Christianity* (Philadelphia: Fortress, 1979), pp. 3–34.

the critics are requiring of first-century materials the sort of precision expected in the twentieth century, but here they may be demanding something not required of ordinary twentieth-century journalism:

> There is a world—I do not say a world in which all scholars live but one at any rate into which all of them sometimes stray, and which some of them seem permanently to inhabit—which is not the world in which I live. In my world, if *The Times* and *The Telegraph* both tell one story in somewhat different terms, nobody concludes that one of them must have copied the other, nor that the variations in the story have some esoteric significance. But in that world of which I am speaking this would be taken for granted. There, no story is ever derived from facts but always from somebody else's version of the same story.[20]

2. The theological differences are more troublesome. We should, however, note that they may represent differing emphases rather than contradictory affirmations. It is true that John emphasizes the deity of Christ, but he certainly does not deny or neglect the humanity. Indeed, the culminating statement of the prologue, "And the Word became flesh and dwelt among us . . . " (1:14), is as strong a declaration of the incarnation of the divine Word in genuine humanity as one can find anywhere in the Bible.

And what of the differences regarding the disciples' consciousness of Jesus' messiahship? The problem is severe only if we feel that the Synoptic Gospels' accounts preclude any awareness by the disciples prior to Peter's confession. Further, in view of the disciples' tendency to oscillation and even retreat from what they had seemingly believed (as at the crucifixion and immediately thereafter), the silence of the Synoptics should not be taken as evidence that the disciples lacked belief. That in John 4:25–26 Jesus identifies himself as the Messiah to the Samaritan woman, but in Mark 8:30 (immediately after Peter's confession) charges his disciples to tell no one about him, may be due to the fact that as a Samaritan she did not have the political expectations of the Messiah that the Jews had.

---

20. A. H. N. Green-Armytage, *John Who Saw: A Layman's Essay on the Authorship of the Fourth Gospel* (London: Faber and Faber, 1952), p. 12.

It appears that what John has done is to make explicit that which is implicit in the Synoptic Gospels. While the Synoptics, unlike John, do not report the direct claims of Jesus, there are certainly implied claims in what he says there. Royce Gruenler says, "I honestly cannot say that I find a single explicit christological utterance of Jesus in the Gospels, including the Gospel of John, that is generically inappropriate to his implicit claims arrived at by the criterion of dissimilarity."[21]

3. It is ironic that the relationship of John's overall chronology to that of the Synoptics is raised as a problem for the fourth Gospel, since many scholars who compare John with the other three find John's chronology easier to defend. A ministry of two to three years seems to fit the overall activities of Jesus better than does one of only a year. We should note, however, that the Synoptics do not limit the ministry to one year; they simply do not refer to three Passovers, as does John.

In fact, the Synoptics show relatively little interest in time, place, and sequence, whereas there are many chronological references in John. Some have even argued that John's Gospel is organized on a more strictly chronological basis than are the Synoptics, which rely more on topical arrangements.[22] The Synoptics do, however, hint or seem implicitly to require that Jesus had visited Judea prior to the events at the close of his life. How, for example, had Jesus come to know Mary, Martha, and Lazarus, at whose home he stayed in Bethany? Why should the scribes and Pharisees react so vigorously against Jesus' ministry if he had never visited Jerusalem before? And to what occasions was Jesus referring when he lamented over Jerusalem in Matthew 23:37: "How often would I have gathered your children together as a hen gathers her brood under her wings, and you would not!" These and several other references appear to require previous ministries by Jesus in Judea.

The specifics here are too numerous to begin to treat in a work of this size. We should note, however, that there seems to be no good reason why there could not have been two cleansings of the temple, one at the beginning of Jesus' ministry and

21. Royce Gordon Gruenler, *New Approaches to Jesus and the Gospels: A Phenomenological and Exegetical Study of Synoptic Christology* (Grand Rapids: Baker, 1982), p. 15.

22. Blomberg, *Historical Reliability*, p. 169.

the other at the end. This is quite likely in view of the fact that the details of the two accounts vary considerably.

4. Some of the supposed historical discrepancies can be resolved relatively easily. That Jesus' birthplace was in Galilee, not Bethlehem, is an error reported by John, not affirmed by him. It is not surprising that the people of Jerusalem should be ignorant of the birthplace of a thirty-year-old man who had lived in Nazareth virtually all his life and whose parents were from Nazareth. John simply reports their error, just as he reports, without endorsement or correction, their statement (7:52) that there was no prophecy of a prophet coming from Galilee, which was clearly mistaken in light of Isaiah 9:1–2.

Just as easily resolved is the alleged conflict between the Synoptics and John over whether Jesus' arrest was caused by the (second) cleansing of the temple (Mark 11:18) or by his raising of Lazarus (John 11:45–48). There would be a discrepancy only if one of the accounts had claimed to report the sole cause, or if we were to assume that an event can have only one cause.

Perhaps the most serious problem pertains to the apparent expulsion of Christians from the synagogue, referred to in 9:22 as well as in 12:42 and 16:2 (note, however, that the last is a reference to the future). It is alleged that John is here referring to a practice involving the *birkat ha-minim* ("Prayer Against the Heretics"), which was introduced about A.D. 85–90. This is the twelfth of the Eighteen Benedictions, the principal supplicatory prayer of the Jewish liturgy. All those who failed to pray this benediction or at least say Amen to it could supposedly be identified as followers of Christ and cast out of the synagogue. There are varying opinions as to whether this entailed nothing more than expulsion from the synagogue itself[23] or a permanent banning from the heritage of Israel.[24] The most significant work on this subject has been done by the Jewish scholar Reuven Kimelman. He has three objections to the argument that associates the *birkat ha-minim* with John 9:22: (1) nothing in the

---

23. Lawrence Schiffman, "At the Crossroad: Tannaitic Perspectives on the Jewish-Christian Schism," in *Jewish and Christian Self-Definition*, vol. 2, *Aspects of Judaism in the Graeco-Roman Period*, ed. E. P. Sanders, A. J. Baumgarten, and Alan Mendelson (Philadelphia: Fortress, 1981), p. 150.

24. F. J. Moloney, "The Fourth Gospel's Presentation of Jesus as 'the Christ' and J. A. T. Robinson's *Redating*," *Downside Review* 95 (1977): 241.

context of this passage or of 12:42 and 16:2 suggests that the practice here in view extended beyond Jerusalem; (2) the word ἀποσυνάγωγος which is used in these passages to describe the practice, does not occur in any later discussions of the more extreme form of exclusion; and (3) the early nonbiblical sources do not indicate that the *birkat* ever was used specifically to identify the followers of Jesus.[25]

5. Much of the issue of style centers on Jesus' extended discourses found in John's Gospel, which are unlike his manner of speaking in the Synoptics. Is this evidence that John invented these discourses, writing them in the very style he used in the narratives? Blomberg offers eight considerations for answering this question in the negative:[26]

a. One need not hold that the discourses present the actual words (*ipsissima verba*) of Jesus, but only faithful summaries and interpretive paraphrases (*ipsissima vox*).

b. It is not true that the discourses are stylistically indistinguishable from John's narrative elsewhere. H. R. Reynolds has compiled a list of over 145 words which appear in the discourses but not in the narratives. Many of these words are general enough that one would expect to find them in narrative as well as discourse.[27]

c. To some extent, John's style may have been inspired by Jesus. In at least one Q passage (Matt. 11:25–27; Luke 10:21–22), Jesus uses language which is almost identical to that of the discourses in John.

d. Much of John's homiletic or sermonic style for Jesus' teaching may reflect the way in which that teaching was used in preaching or liturgical contexts in the early church.

e. John emphasized Jesus' teaching regarding the role of the Holy Spirit in enabling the disciples to remember what he said, as well as in guiding them into new truth (14:26; 15:26; 16:12–13). This means that John believed that the Spirit pre-

---

25. Reuven Kimelman, "*Birkat Ha-Minim* and the Lack of Evidence for an Anti-Christian Jewish Prayer in Late Antiquity," in *Aspects of Judaism*, ed. Sanders et al., pp. 226–44.

26. Blomberg, *Historical Reliability*, pp. 183–84.

27. H. R. Reynolds, *The Gospel of St. John*, 2 vols. (New York: Funk and Wagnalls, 1906), vol. 1, pp. cxxiii–cxxv.

served the tradition and the memories of the eyewitnesses from error. John also is the only Evangelist to report repeatedly that the disciples did not initially understand a saying of Jesus but later came to understand it. He took pains to retain what Jesus had said, even when not initially understood. He did not confuse the words of the earthly Christ with later understanding, no matter how inspired.[28]

f. Some of the differences between Jesus' words in John's Gospel and in the Synoptics may well stem from different contexts. For example, the private farewell address to the disciples and the more formal teaching in the temple and synagogues, which we find in John, called for a style quite different from that of the informal addresses to crowds in the open air.

g. The dichotomy of brief speeches in the Synoptics and extended discourses in John does not hold, for both types are found in both sources, although to differing degrees. Mark devotes an entire chapter (13) to an eschatological discourse, while Matthew contains five extended discourses (chs. 5–7, 10, 13, 18, 24–25).

h. Recent studies show that the discourses have a tightly knit unity, negating the idea that they are a conglomeration of a few historical sayings of Jesus that were fastened together by creative additions by the Evangelist himself.

Positive Evidences for the Historicity of John's Gospel

In discussing the relationship between the fourth Gospel and the Synoptics, we observed that there are enough significant differences to argue that in John's Gospel we have an independent historical tradition. We also examined the differences to see whether they are so great as to require us to hold that the two traditions are contradictory rather than complementary. We will now investigate two types of positive evidence for the historical dependability of this fourth Gospel, namely, indications of a

---

28. See D. A. Carson, "Historical Tradition in the Fourth Gospel: After Dodd, What?" in *Gospel Perspectives*, ed. R. T. France and David Wenham, 6 vols. (Sheffield: JSOT, 1980–1986), vol. 2, pp. 121–22.

first-century Jewish background, and archaeological confirmations of its topography.

The First-Century Jewish Background

It has been commonplace in some circles to consider John to be a thoroughly Hellenistic Gospel. Adolf von Harnack, for example, referred to it as "the acute hellenization of Christianity."[29] Benjamin Bacon entitled one of his studies of John *The Gospel of the Hellenists,*[30] and E. F. Scott refers to the interpretation that in John "the Messianic idea is replaced by that of the Logos."[31] This interpretation holds that the book was written under the influence of Hellenism, and therefore is geographically removed from the simple world of Galilean fishermen and even Palestinian Judaism prior to the Jewish war; but more than that, it is conceptually removed from that setting. Indeed, this argues that John is temporally separated as well, reflecting a later period of Hellenistic influence rather than the early period of Jewish influence upon the church. All of these considerations argue that this Gospel does not represent a genuine or authentic tradition regarding Jesus.

A number of factors have contributed to the breakdown of this conception. One of the most influential was the discovery of the Dead Sea Scrolls in 1947. The pre-Christian Palestinian community which produced them represented a first-century Judaism far different from Pharisaic Judaism, and the documents show some interesting parallels to John's Gospel, not only in language and terminology, but more importantly in ideas.

Literary parallels are found especially in the *Manual of Discipline*. In ways quite similar to John, for example, the very opening column of this document refers to "practicing truth" and loving the "sons of light" while rejecting the "sons of darkness." Both the *Manual* and John also associate the concept of knowledge with the existence and action of God and human relationship to him.[32]

---

29. Quoted in Robinson, *Priority*, p. 38.

30. Benjamin W. Bacon, *The Gospel of the Hellenists*, ed. Carl H. Kraehling (New York: Holt, 1933).

31. E. F. Scott, *The Fourth Gospel: Its Purpose and Theology* (Edinburgh: T. & T. Clark, 1943), p. 6.

32. Smalley, *John*, p. 33; cf. 1QS3.15 with John 1:2.

More significant, however, than these terminological resemblances is the presence on a deeper level of what Raymond Brown has labeled a "modified dualism" which pervades both.[33] The Qumran documents give testimony of an ongoing struggle between truth and perversity, light and darkness, good and evil, which involves all human beings, and in which each side is ruled by the appropriate spirit. There are significant differences, however, between this dualism and that of second-century Greek Gnosticism. For one thing, it is not pictured as a struggle between equal forces, in which the outcome is in doubt. As fierce as the struggle may be, God will win out, and soon. Beyond that, however, there is a difference in the nature of this dualism. The Greek dualism is a conflict between powers or forces, and may be described as physical and substantial. The dualism of the Dead Sea Scrolls, on the other hand, is ethical. It is the forces of good and evil that are opposed.[34]

The parallel to John's Gospel is not difficult to see. As Smalley puts it, "We are not far here from the world of John."[35] A similar dualism runs through his writing. There is the opposition of light and darkness, good and evil (John 12:35–36). The final outcome will be the victory of God, and this involves a judgment which has already begun (3:18–21).

This dualism divides the human race. While the influence of the evil spirit is present even in those who are primarily sons of light, in the Scrolls there is a definite separation between those who are sons of light and those who are sons of darkness. John also has a clear separation between those who are in the right and those who are not, but in his thought the former are distinguished primarily by their relationship to Christ. Thus Jesus refers to his sheep, his disciples, true worshipers.[36]

Some scholars have argued that the Qumran community had a strong influence upon or even a direct connection with the author of the fourth Gospel, possibly through John the Baptist. What we need to observe here is simply that there is evidence

33. Raymond E. Brown, "The Qumran Scrolls and the Johannine Gospel and Epistles," in Raymond E. Brown, *New Testament Essays* (Milwaukee: Bruce, 1965), pp. 105–20.
34. Smalley, *John*, p. 32.
35. Ibid.
36. Leon Morris, *Studies in the Fourth Gospel* (Grand Rapids: Eerdmans, 1969), p. 330.

that concepts of the type found in John's Gospel were current in first-century Palestine in a community that was thoroughly Jewish. It is important not to overstate the nature and significance of the relationship between the fourth Gospel and the Dead Sea Scrolls. F. F. Bruce warns, "It would be wise to remember that practically every new discovery in the field of Near Eastern religion of the closing years B.C. and early years A.D. has been hailed in its time as the solution to 'the problem of the Fourth Gospel.'" Nonetheless, he continues, "the affinities with Qumran certainly provide additional evidence for the Hebraic foundation of the Fourth Gospel."[37] Wilhelm Michaelis has put it even more strongly: "It may now be said that the Palestinian character of the Gospel of John has become so clear that attempts to prove another provenance should really cease."[38] On the other hand, we should bear in mind Robinson's cautionary note that this has been merely a negative clearing of the ground: "The most that this shift has shown is that the Gospel *need* not be so Hellenistic or so late as was formerly supposed."[39]

Archaeological Confirmation of Topographical References

It is of interest that John has more geographical and topographical references than do the Synoptic Gospels. These references have been interpreted in differing ways. Some scholars have understood them as having a symbolic or theological significance to the author. R. H. Lightfoot, for example, argued that John regarded Galilee as signifying acceptance of Jesus and Judea as signifying rejection.[40] This is difficult to fit with the actual facts of his ministry, however, for it was in Galilee that Jesus observed that a prophet has no honor in his own country (John 4:43–44). It was considerations such as this that led W. D. Davies to say, "Only by a *tour de force* can Judea be

---

37. F. F. Bruce, "The Dead Sea Scrolls and Early Christianity," *Bulletin of the John Rylands Library* 49 (Autumn 1966): 81.

38. Wilhelm Michaelis, *Einleitung in das Neue Testament: Die Entstehung, Sammlung und Überlieferung der Schriften des Neuen Testaments* (Bern: Berchteld Haller, 1961), p. 123—quoted and translated in C. K. Barrett, *The Gospel of John and Judaism* (Philadelphia: Fortress, 1975), p. 8.

39. Robinson, *Priority*, p. 45.

40. R. H. Lightfoot, *Locality and Doctrine in the Gospels* (New York: Harper, 1938), pp. 144–46.

made a symbol of the rejection, and Galilee and Samaria a symbol of the acceptance of the gospel."[41] Dodd was even more emphatic: "All attempts that have been made to extract a profound symbolical meaning out of the names . . . are hopelessly fanciful; and there is no reason to suppose that a fictitious topography would in any way assist the appeal of the gospel to an Ephesian public."[42]

C. H. H. Scobie opts for a different type of interpretation, saying that the references in the fourth Gospel to Cana and Bethsaida suggest "the existence there of Johannine communities, jealously preserving their own traditions and regarding Capernaum as a rival," which is therefore in this Gospel "played down in a remarkable way."[43] Robinson, however, points out that this simply is not true. In John, Jesus makes two visits to Cana, none to Bethsaida (as compared with two in Mark); and Capernaum, supposed by Scobie to be a rival city because of the existence of a Petrine community there, is mentioned more times in John than in any other Gospel. Robinson believes that Scobie has allowed the valid insights of form and redaction criticism to run wild and distort matters out of proportion.[44]

Robinson, together with Smalley and a number of others, sees the topographical references as evidence of the historical reliability of John's Gospel. Their extent indicates an unusual degree of interest in such matters. It is interesting to compare these references in John with those in Luke, who, as is generally known, is very precise when he is familiar with the territory, as in the Book of Acts. In the chapters of his Gospel that deal with the Galilean ministry, however, and in the long central section (9:51–18:14), he is very vague and unspecific. To introduce his account of a visit Jesus made to the home of Mary and Martha, Luke simply says, "Now as they [Jesus and his companions] went on their way, he entered a village" (10:38). The writer gives us no idea of its name, location, or the reason Jesus went there.

41. W. D. Davies, *The Gospel and the Land: Early Christianity and Jewish Territorial Doctrine* (Berkeley: University of California Press, 1974), p. 329.

42. C. H. Dodd, *Interpretation of the Fourth Gospel* (Cambridge: Cambridge University Press, 1953), pp. 452–53.

43. C. H. H. Scobie, "Johannine Geography," *Studies in Religion/Sciences Religieuses* 11 (1982): 82.

44. Robinson, *Priority*, p. 50.

By way of contrast note how specific John is in 11:1–12:1, where he refers to the same place: he names it, tells us that it was about two miles from Jerusalem (11:18), and informs us why Jesus went there on two different occasions, and from where, and, in the case of the second visit, exactly when—six days before the Passover. Robinson's comment here is apt: "It is hard to believe that such detail is put in purely for symbolic purposes or that it does not rest upon genuine memory."[45]

This is not an isolated case. Recent archaeological study has tended to support the view that the Gospel of John reflects a tradition which knew Palestine intimately. It is evidently the work of someone who was familiar with the places in which the story is set.[46]

There have, to be sure, been some difficulties. Two are mentioned by Robinson and Smalley, the former referring to them as matters which "require more critical scrutiny."[47] Until 1878, there was, outside John's Gospel (5:2), no knowledge of the pool of Bethesda. Some felt that the reference to five porticoes was allegorical or symbolic, and that John had invented them to provide a setting for the healing of the man who had been ill for thirty-eight years. In the first stage of excavation, two large pools were discovered, over which a Byzantine church had once been erected. These were thought by many to be the pools in question. Later excavations, however, convinced the White Fathers, who were conducting the work, that shallower pools to the east are the actual site.[48] Robinson even suggests an explanation of the stirring of the waters (v. 7, but not v. 4, which is textually suspect): an intermittent siphon spring. Although we know of no such springs in the Bethesda area, Josephus reports that there was one. Both Robinson and Smalley place a great deal of emphasis upon such archaeological data. Robinson says, "So John's account is impressively confirmed, even though again it is not possible to verify the porticos by sight."[49] Smalley agrees: "Here is impressive support for the historicity of the tradition in

45. Ibid., p. 53.
46. Ibid.; see also W. F. Albright, *The Archaeology of Palestine*, rev. ed. (Baltimore: Penguin, 1956), pp. 242–49.
47. Robinson, *Priority*, p. 53.
48. Smalley, *John*, pp. 35–36.
49. Robinson, *Priority*, p. 59.

John 5. If Bethesda indeed existed, we need not assume that John is being imaginative when he locates this sign at the pool."[50]

The other major site which has come in for a considerable amount of attention is what John calls The Pavement, or in Aramaic, Gabbatha (19:13). Some have thought that this refers to a large area of Roman paving which was near the Antonia fortress and is found today under the Ecce Homo Convent. This, however, is probably not the location. A more likely site is Herod's palace.[51] It appears from archaeological evidence that the palace, like the temple, was built on a very large raised platform.[52] Unfortunately, both palace and platform have been destroyed. The pavement found at the site of the Antonia, although probably not the pavement in question, gives an indication of what it was like.

Was the Author an Eyewitness?

Was the author of the Gospel of John an eyewitness to some (or perhaps even all) of the events that he narrates? If so, this would add considerably to our presumption of the historical reliability of the text. One way to deal with this issue is to examine closely the writing, to see whether we can detect the type of phenomena which would tend to be present if the author were an eyewitness, but probably would be absent if he were not. While space forbids an exhaustive listing of such items, we will mention a few.[53]

1. *The notices of the day (1:29, 35, 43), time of day (18:28; 20:19), or even the hour (1:39; 4:6, 52; 19:14).* These are references where no symbolic meaning seems possible.
2. *Nathanael's use of the title "King of Israel" (1:49).* This title is not likely to have been used after the fall of Jerusalem.
3. *The inclusion of small, sometimes seemingly irrelevant data.* An example is in 2:12, where Jesus is reported as going with his mother, brothers, and disciples to Caper-

50. Smalley, *John*, p. 36.
51. Robinson, *Priority*, p. 267.
52. Ibid.
53. Many of these references are taken from Morris, *Studies in the Fourth Gospel*, pp. 139–214.

naum. This detail has no real connection with what precedes or follows. It is unlikely to have been included unless an eyewitness recalled that it occurred at this point.

4. *The reports of a change in the disciples' understanding of something which had been said (2:17, 22).* This is the type of item that an observer would be likely to know and remember.

5. *The reference in 2:20 to the length of time that the temple had been under construction—forty-six years.* This figure fits exactly the date of the beginning of Jesus' ministry, when he cleansed the temple for the first time. The construction took a total of eighty-four years—the temple was begun in 20–19 B.C., completed in A.D. 64, and destroyed in 70. For a writer late in the first century or early in the second century to have come up with the correct figure would have taken considerable research. And in that case it seems unlikely that this detail would have been slipped in so casually.

6. *The mention of Philip and Andrew in the account of the feeding of the five thousand.* John is the only one of the four Evangelists to mention these names in connection with that event. Since Philip was from the area of Bethsaida and presumably knew the neighborhood, he was the logical person to ask where bread could be bought.

These are only samples of the numerous items that could be cited. To be sure, some of them argue only for an early and reliable tradition, not necessarily for an eyewitness, but the best explanation that can be offered for the cumulative evidence is that it reflects the observations of an eyewitness. A good case can be made that the author is, as tradition says, John the son of Zebedee.[54] We cannot go any further into the argument here, however, for it rests on substantially different grounds.

54. For recent defenses of this position see Morris, *Studies in the Fourth Gospel*, pp. 215–92; and F. F. Bruce, *The Gospel of John: Introduction, Exposition and Notes* (Grand Rapids: Eerdmans, 1983), pp. 1–6. The classic presentation of the case is Brooke Foss Westcott, *The Gospel According to St. John: The Authorized Version with Introduction and Notes* (Grand Rapids: Eerdmans, 1950), pp. v–xxxii.

We have sought in this chapter to argue that the Gospel of John, no less than the Synoptic Gospels, gives us reliable historical data about Jesus, and thus may be used as a source for our Christology. We have both offered criticism of the contrary positions and given positive evidence of the reliability of this book. The extent to which the issues interlock is noteworthy. For example, when the case for the dependence of John upon the Synoptics is set aside, then the argument that this Gospel must necessarily be quite late is undercut. And with that comes greater credibility for the contention that the author was an eyewitness to the events described. And the very nature of his descriptions supports this thesis. While we will have to examine each passage carefully before using it to help construct our Christology, there is no strong reason not to proceed on the assumption of the historical reliability of the Gospel of John.

17

Jesus' Testimony to His Deity

We must deal now with an issue of great importance, namely, does the Bible teach that Jesus was divine in nature? We begin with this aspect of Christology because there is no doubt that it is the part of the traditional formulation that has been most under dispute in the past century. To be sure, there have been disputes about the humanity of Jesus. These disputes, however, which were set off primarily by two modern tendencies, centered more on its significance than on the fact itself. The first tendency was a denial of the epistemological significance of Jesus' humanity; that is, it was maintained that we cannot learn much that is of importance for faith from the materials dealing with the historical Jesus. This tendency is found in the thought of Karl Barth, but even more markedly in the writings of Rudolf Bultmann. The second is the popular tendency not to take seri-

431

ously the humanity of Jesus, to be skeptical regarding the possibility of his really being like us. But this is almost more a denial in practice than in theory. Indeed, the one thing of which most theologians and New Testament scholars in this century have been certain is that Jesus was fully human, whether we can know much about his earthly life or not. From the standpoint of technical theology, it is the deity of Jesus which has been in dispute, and which needs justification. The question may and should be treated in two respects: Jesus' own self-consciousness, and the teaching of the New Testament writers regarding him. We turn first to the question of Jesus' self-consciousness, or who and what he understood himself to be.

The Nature of Self-Awareness

It may be well to note first a distinction which Raymond Brown has developed between self-consciousness and self-knowledge.[1] He suggests that in a number of areas of human knowledge, such as artistic matters or perception of one's own self, there may be a vivid awareness of something long before there is a "reasonably adequate way to express that consciousness."[2] This awareness is rather intuitive in nature. Thus, Jesus may have had a consciousness of aspects of his nature long before he was able to give adequate formulation and expression to them in overt language. He may never have used in regard to himself particular terms which the church later used, and yet he may have experienced the characteristics delineated by those terms. This idea is based at least in part upon our understanding of Jesus' humanity.[3] If his growing "in wisdom and in stature, and in favor with God and man" (Luke 2:52) included growth in theological understanding, then perhaps at some point in his life Jesus could not have expounded the Trinity even though he had already experienced his unique relationship to the Father.

A moment's thought will reveal that the distinction between direct knowledge and an interpretative, reflective understanding

---

1. Raymond E. Brown, *Jesus, God and Man: Modern Biblical Reflections* (Milwaukee: Bruce, 1967), p. 93.
2. Ibid., p. 94.
3. Ibid., p. 95.

of it exists in other areas as well. For example, a person may grow up speaking virtually flawless English, but have no real knowledge of the rules of grammar or even an awareness that there is such a thing as grammar. The reason is that infants do not learn language by memorizing rules of grammar and then making their usage of words accord with those rules, but by repeating language as they hear it spoken. Children growing up in a home in which excellent English is spoken will use correct grammar without realizing that they are doing so. Indeed, for many Americans the first real awareness that there is such a thing as English grammar comes when they begin studying another language. Similarly, there are people who can play music by ear without being able to read a note.

Having reflected on the nature of self-awareness, Brown says that the question "Did Jesus know that he was God?" is "so badly phrased that it cannot be answered and should not be posed."[4] His reason for this assertion is that to the Jews of Jesus' time the word *God* applied to the Father in heaven. It was only later, in the last third of the first century, that the necessity of giving proper honor to Jesus forced believers to broaden the concept of God. It is certain that Jesus did not think of himself as being the Father in heaven to whom he prayed.[5] He had, however, an intuitive knowledge of himself and his unique status and role. It is important to note that Brown's certainty here rests upon a particular assumption on the issue of kenosis. The truth within his contention may, however, be more safely put by saying that in the initial stages of his life Jesus, while sensing his uniqueness, certainly did not confuse himself with the Father in heaven. This allows for the possibility of a more theologically sophisticated self-knowledge at later stages of Jesus' life.

Jesus' Implicit Claims

What all of this means is that we must try to get behind the explicit claims of Jesus, to attempt to read his mind as it were, in order to see how he regarded himself. There have been some fruitful studies done in this area in recent years. We will initially

4. Ibid., p. 86.
5. Ibid., p. 87.

be looking only for indications that Jesus was conscious of having a unique status, role, and relationship to the Father.

Amen

One of the indications that Jesus was conscious of being unique is his use of the word ἀμήν ("Amen," "truly") in connection with his sayings. This term was used in the Old Testament by both the individual and the community as a response indicating that a particular word was valid and binding upon them. Thus it means that which is sure and valid.[6] This usage continued and expanded in the Christian community as a response to prayers and to the divine Word. It was Jesus who most fully developed the term, however, with the use of Amen before his sayings. The application of this expression to one's own sayings is what is unusual here. Heinrich Schlier comments: "The point of the Amen before Jesus' own sayings is . . . to show that as such they are reliable and true, and that they are so as and because Jesus himself in his Amen acknowledges them to be His own sayings and thus makes them valid."[7] Reginald Fuller puts it similarly: "In this 'Amen,' Jesus pledges his whole person behind the truth of his proclamation."[8]

Note what is being said here: Jesus' usage of the term *Amen* lays an implicit claim to the validity and authority of his words precisely because he was speaking them. While it might be considered an overstatement to say that he felt that his speaking gave to his words the same authority that God had given to the words spoken through the prophets, there is a strong element here of Jesus' self-consciousness. Schlier says that all of the sayings prefixed by an Amen have to do with the history of the kingdom of God as bound up with Jesus' own person. "Thus in the ἀμήν preceding the λέγω ὑμῖν of Jesus we have the whole of Christology *in nuce*. The one who accepts His word as true and certain is also the one who acknowledges and affirms it in his own life and thus causes it, as fulfilled by him, to become a demand to others."[9]

6. Heinrich Schlier, ἀμήν, in *Theological Dictionary of the New Testament*, ed. Gerhard Kittel and Gerhard Friedrich, trans. Geoffrey W. Bromiley, 10 vols. (Grand Rapids: Eerdmans, 1964–1976), vol. 1, p. 335.

7. Ibid., p. 338.

8. Reginald H. Fuller, *The Foundations of New Testament Christology* (New York: Scribner, 1965), p. 104.

9. Schlier, ἀμήν, p. 338.

Schlier's treatment suffers somewhat from the brevity inherent in a dictionary article. Joachim Jeremias has treated the usage of Amen at greater length. He concludes both that Jesus' usage of the term is unique, and that the authenticity of the words which it introduces can be established on other grounds as well. Thus in the use of Amen by Jesus we have evidence of, if not the *ipsissima verba*, at least the *ipsissima vox* of Jesus.[10] Victor Hasler and Klaus Berger have disputed this contention. They point out that in the Old Testament the usage of Amen is in response to the words of another, whereas here it is used to introduce and validate one's own sayings. They then try to show that these sayings do not go back to Jesus, but are to be ascribed to prophets speaking in the name of Jesus to the church. Their effort follows two lines: they seek to find parallels in Judaism to these sayings (thus negating the principle of dissimilarity), and they seek to show how the change in usage could have arisen within the early church.[11] The arguments of Hasler and Berger have some very significant flaws, however, so that the contentions of Jeremias and Schlier stand intact.[12]

Abba

A second term which has received considerable attention is the expression Ἀββά, which Jesus uses in addressing the Father (Mark 14:36). Jeremias observes that this Aramaic term, used within intimate family relationships, has no parallels in the terms used in Jewish prayers for addressing God. He concludes that this is an authentic word of Jesus, expressing his own intimate relationship with the Father, into which he also led his followers (see Rom. 8:15; Gal. 4:6). Jeremias offers a wealth of linguistic evidence in support of his contention.[13] New Testament scholars have been more willing to accept this argument than

10. Joachim Jeremias, "Characteristics of the *ipsissima vox Jesu*," in *The Prayers of Jesus* (Naperville, Ill.: Allenson, 1967), pp. 108–15.

11. Victor A. Hasler, *Amen: Redaktionsgeschichtliche Untersuchung zur Einführungsformel der Herrenworte "Wahrlich ich sage euch"* (Zurich: Gotthelf, 1969); Klaus Berger, *Die Amen-Worte Jesu* (Berlin: deGruyter, 1970).

12. For a brief but cogent summary of these flaws, see I. Howard Marshall, *The Origins of New Testament Christology* (Downers Grove, Ill.: Inter-Varsity, 1977), pp. 58–59 n. 9.

13. Jeremias, "Abba," in *Prayers of Jesus*, pp. 11–65; see also his *New Testament Theology* (New York: Scribner, 1971), vol. 1, pp. 61–68.

that relating to the use of Amen. Though Hans Conzelmann has challenged the inferences drawn from the use of *Abba,* his objections are themselves more questionable than the argument which he is criticizing.[14]

The significance of Jesus' usage of *Abba* has had various interpretations. Brown feels that Jesus' promise to enable others also to know the Father in an intimate way modifies the extent to which we should regard *Abba* as implying uniqueness for Jesus.[15] It is noteworthy, however, that John restricts the use of *huios tou theou* ("Son of God") to Jesus himself, referring to believers as *tekna* ("children"), while Paul speaks of Christians as adoptive sons. Although, as Brown points out, it is not possible to prove scientifically that such a distinction existed in Jesus' own words and promises,[16] it is significant that what presumably represent two traditions interpret Jesus' overall teaching on the subject as involving some distinction. Accordingly, I. Howard Marshall says with regard to the arguments from *Abba* and Amen: "We may therefore with all due caution accept that in these two words *amen* and *abba* we have indirect indications of Jesus' consciousness of his unique position."[17]

Ego de Lego

The sense of personal authority evidently felt and displayed by Jesus is seen especially in his ἐγὼ δὲ λέγω ("but *I* say") statements. These are somewhat more easily appealed to because of the acknowledged authenticity of the sayings which they introduce. Ernst Käsemann, for example, says, "All exegesis is agreed that the authenticity of the first, second and fourth antitheses in the Sermon on the Mount [Matt. 5:22, 28, 34] cannot be doubted."[18] He finds these to be among the most astonishing

---

14. Hans Conzelmann, *An Outline of the Theology of the New Testament* (New York: Harper and Row, 1969), pp. 103–05. See Marshall's criticism in *Origins,* p. 59 n. 11.

15. Brown, *Jesus,* pp. 88–89. Brown's objection rests in part upon his contention that *Abba* was the term which Jesus taught his disciples to use in addressing the Father, Luke 11:2–4 being the original form of the Lord's Prayer. It would seem, however, that Brown's theory is, if anything, more difficult to verify than is the contention he is opposing, since the Greek text here does not give *Abba* as a transliteration of what Jesus supposedly said originally.

16. Ibid., pp. 89–90.

17. Marshall, *Origins,* p. 46.

18. Ernst Käsemann, "The Problem of the Historical Jesus," in Ernst Käsemann, *Essays on New Testament Themes* (Naperville, Ill.: Allenson, 1964), p. 37.

words anywhere in Scripture. The form of Jesus' explanations is similar to what a rabbi would have used in giving the sense of Scripture. Käsemann, however, sees a very significant contrast in Jesus' introductory phrase:

> The determining factor, however, is that the words *ego de lego* embody a claim to an authority which rivals and challenges that of Moses. But anyone who claims an authority rivalling and challenging Moses has *ipso facto* set himself above Moses; he has ceased to be a rabbi, for a rabbi's authority only comes to him as derived from Moses. . . . To this there are no Jewish parallels, nor indeed can there be. For the Jew who does what is done here has cut himself off from the community of Judaism—or else he brings the Messianic Torah and is therefore the Messiah.[19]

Käsemann sees in Jesus an attitude completely different from that of the rabbis, namely, "immediate assurance of knowing and proclaiming the will of God."[20] He maintains that Jesus was different, too, from any of the prophets, for he set himself against the law of Moses, thus elevating himself to a position above that of mere humans and even of the major leader of the people of Israel in the Old Testament.

Strong objection has been made to Käsemann's interpretation of what Jesus was doing in the *ego de lego* statements. It can well be argued that Jesus was not opposing himself and his teachings to Moses and the law per se. Indeed, such would be a strange thing for the Messiah to do. Rather, Jesus was opposing the scribal interpretations which had been overlaid upon the law. When the alleged antitheses to the law of Moses are closely examined, they are found not to be in contradiction to it at all. For example, in some cases Jesus was heightening the demands of the law by requiring its application not only to outward acts, but also to inward thoughts and motives (Matt. 5:21–22, 27–28, 33–37, and 43–48). Seen this way, Jesus' statements actually strengthen the law of Moses by increasing its requirements. It is not its necessity but its sufficiency that is at stake here. Moreover, instead of being contrary to the law, Jesus' justification of his disciples' plucking corn on the Sabbath was actually based upon what had been

19. Ibid.
20. Ibid.

allowed in the Old Testament, as seen in an episode involving David.[21] It is not, then, either Jesus or Moses, but both Jesus and Moses. Even Jesus' statement on divorce (Matt. 5:31–32; Mark 10:11–12; and Luke 16:18) does not really oppose Moses. Rather, it puts divorce into its proper context as a concession to human weakness. The basis for this interpretation of divorce is not merely Jesus' own authority, but Genesis 1:27. Similarly, where Jesus seems to be contradicting or suspending the rules of revenge (Matt. 5:38–42), there really is no contradiction, since the purpose of the law was not to insist that revenge be taken, but to set limits upon it (i.e., the law did not say that an eye must be taken for an eye, but that no more could be taken or done).

It appears from these considerations that Käsemann has perhaps stated his argument a bit too strongly. Yet there is value in what he has said, and with some modification it is still a serviceable set of observations. Marshall suggests a restatement somewhat as follows:

1. In the time of Jesus, the Jews came to associate the Mosaic law and the scribal interpretations of it so closely that an attack upon the latter was perceived as an attack upon the former as well. Thus Jesus' opposition to certain scribal interpretations was viewed as being a contradiction of the law, and the Jews responded by raising the issue of authority.
2. Jesus claimed to know the will of God which underlay the law, and thus to declare authoritatively its true meaning or interpretation. In so doing, he did not cite prophetic inspiration or give the traditional "Thus says the Lord." He gave the impression of speaking on his own authority. In short, "he thus spoke as if he were God."[22]

Jesus' Attitude Toward Future Teachers and Authorities

We have seen Jesus' attitude regarding the authority of what and who had preceded him. It is also helpful to note his attitude

21. C. E. B. Cranfield, *The Gospel According to St. Mark*, 2d ed. (New York: Cambridge University Press, 1963), p. 115.
22. Marshall, *Origins*, pp. 49–50.

toward future teachers and authorities. Here we should bear in mind the attitudes and statements of the prophets and of John the Baptist. They did not regard themselves as the final step of the process or the pinnacle of the edifice of authority. With varying degrees of explicitness, becoming most prominent in John the Baptist, they anticipated the coming of an ultimate prophet or authority. With Jesus there are no anticipations of this type, however.[23] The impression one obtains is that Jesus did not expect his words to be supplanted, or even supplemented or interpreted. Even the Son of man, in the event that Jesus' self-consciousness drew some sort of distinction between himself and that apocalyptic figure, would not be a further authority upon earth, since the Son of man is connected only with future judgment.[24]

Jesus' Understanding of His Own Authority

Jesus' attitude toward other authorities past and future raises for us the question of his understanding of his own authority. His self-perception can be seen both in his actions and in his teachings. One of the things that brought him into disfavor with the Pharisees was his overt claim to forgive sins. This surely was blasphemy, since only God has the right to forgive sins. Beyond that, however, his fellowship with sinners brought criticism upon him. This was an implicit acceptance rather than condemnation of sinners and their sins. Marshall describes Jesus' actions and sayings as being "beyond critical cavil."[25] As Ernst Fuchs and others have observed, the implication was that he was acting in the place of God.[26] To do what he did (e.g., eat with sinners) would usually not be interpreted as an act of self-assumed divinity, but as sinful behavior; and this was the interpretation which the scribes and Pharisees placed upon it.

Jesus' Teaching About the Kingdom of God

Similarly presumptuous was Jesus' teaching about the kingdom of God, in which he explained the conditions of inclusion

23. C. F. D. Moule, *The Phenomenon of the New Testament* (Naperville, Ill.: Allenson, 1967), pp. 68–69.
24. Marshall, *Origins*, p. 51.
25. Ibid., p. 50.
26. Ernst Fuchs, *Studies of the Historical Jesus* (Naperville, Ill.: Allenson, 1964), pp. 20–21.

or exclusion, and the role which he played in defining those conditions and in serving as the actual way of entry into the kingdom. In the scene of final judgment, he is not only the judge, but also, by his own self-description, the king.[27] And not only did he consider the wonders which he performed the signs of the presence or the coming of the kingdom (Matt. 12:28; Luke 11:20), but he made a positive response to himself the one real condition for entering the kingdom (Matt. 7:21–27; Luke 6:46–49; 22:28–30; 23:42–43). Marshall is careful to stress the authenticity of these passages that suggest Jesus' uniqueness:

> The significance of all this is that it points not merely to a sense of authority on the part of Jesus but to a position of uniqueness. He stands alone; he has no equals. It might be objected that this is precisely the picture of him that we might expect from Christian tradition, but in fact we have built our case above purely on material that passes radical criteria for authenticity, and we have not used the vast amount of corroborative evidence that could be said to stand under suspicion when radical tests are applied.[28]

Jesus' Application of the Old Testament to Himself

Some other aspects of Jesus' action and teaching bear further examination. One of these is his use of the Old Testament, especially his interpretation of it and his application of some of its statements about God to himself. The judgment scene in Matthew 25 contains imagery which R. T. France says "clearly echoes the theophanic language of e.g. Daniel 7:9f.; Joel 3:1–12 (Heb. 4:1–12); and Zechariah 14:5."[29] This is a fairly frequent practice on Jesus' part. In Matthew 21:16 he applies to himself the children's praise of God in Psalm 8:1–2. The reference in Luke 19:10 to his mission to seek and save the lost is evidently

27. R. T. France, "The Uniqueness of Christ," *The Churchman* 95.3 (1981): 206.
28. Marshall, *Origins*, pp. 50–51 (the quotation is from p. 51). For discussions of the authenticity of Luke 6:46, see Rudolf Bultmann, *The History of the Synoptic Tradition*, rev. ed. (New York: Harper and Row, 1968), pp. 128, 151. On Luke 12:32 see Joachim Jeremias, ποιμήν, ἀρχιποίμην, ποιμαίνω, ποίμνη, ποίμνιον," in *Theological Dictionary of the New Testament*, ed. Kittel and Friedrich, vol. 6, p. 501 and n. 20. On Luke 22:29–30 see Carsten Colpe, "ὁ υἱὸς τοῦ ἀνθρώπου, in *Theological Dictionary of the New Testament*, vol. 8, pp. 447–48.
29. France, "Uniqueness," p. 206.

an allusion to the divine shepherd of Ezekiel 34:16, 22. The stone of stumbling mentioned in Isaiah 8:14–15 Jesus identifies with himself in Luke 20:18a. He applies to John the Baptist the prophecies of Malachi (3:1; 4:5–6) about a messenger who will serve as a forerunner of God's coming in judgment. And Jesus' characterization of his own words as permanent and indestructible (Mark 13:31) is comparable to what is said about God's Word in Isaiah 40:8. France is impressed both by the way in which Jesus conveyed these ideas and by the implications for critics:

> Such tendencies of language (and more could and should be added if time allowed) are the more impressive because they are so unobtrusive. They are evidence, not of a crusade by Jesus to establish his claim to a special status, but of an assumption of a special relationship with God which does not need to be defended. It is a staggering assumption in the setting of first-century Judaism, and yet it pervades much of the teaching and activity of Jesus. A critical approach to Jesus' sayings would need to be designed with the specific intention of excluding all such claims if it was to succeed in dismissing all such language from the authentic teaching of Jesus, and even then it would not have an easy task![30]

The Parables

One set of data is so extensive and significant as to deserve separate treatment, namely, Jesus' self-consciousness as revealed in the parables. There are at least two reasons why this is a particularly important area to investigate. On the one hand, the parables constitute a major portion of and a favorite means in Jesus' teaching ministry. Secondly, the parables are among the materials most widely regarded as authentic, and thus are eminently usable in a study of the type which we are undertaking here.

Philip Payne has given a great deal of attention to the parables. In addition to his doctoral dissertation on the parables, he has authored an article on their authenticity; the appendix to this essay deals with the christological significance of Jesus'

30. Ibid., p. 207.

teachings in the parables.[31] It is in an article entitled "Jesus' Implicit Claim to Deity in His Parables," however, that he has addressed these issues most directly and extensively.

In agreement with Jeremias,[32] Payne holds that the parables of Jesus compel their audience to come to a decision about his person and mission. In that sense they are christological. But while it has long been recognized that Jesus depicts himself and his ministry through the parables, two factors have generally been overlooked. The first is the uniqueness of Jesus' references to himself. They are without parallel in the vast collection of rabbinic parabolic teaching. No other rabbi depicts himself through his parables. This in itself is a confirmation of the authenticity of the parables: they fulfil the criterion of dissimi-larity.[33] The other factor which has frequently been overlooked, but is crucial for our purposes here, is that in the majority of the parables Jesus depicts himself through images which in the Old Testament refer to God. While these images occasionally allude to other objects, in most cases they picture God.[34]

Payne suggests two key questions to ask in assessing whether a parable of Jesus may have conveyed an implicit claim to deity:

1. Is the image commonly used in the Old Testament or in later writings from around the time of Jesus to depict God?
2. Do the actions or qualities of the figure in the parable resemble those of Jesus?

If the answer to both of these questions for any given parable is in the affirmative, then "the possibility must be considered that Jesus was making an implicit claim to deity."[35] This possibility becomes more probable as we see a pattern emerging in which Jesus frequently depicts himself through images which in the Old Testament represent God. Payne finds ten such images in

31. Philip B. Payne, "The Authenticity of the Parables of Jesus," in *Gospel Perspectives*, ed. R. T. France and David Wenham, 6 vols. (Sheffield: JSOT, 1980–1986), vol. 2, pp. 338–41.

32. Joachim Jeremias, *The Parables of Jesus*, 2d ed. (London: SCM, 1972), p. 230.

33. Philip B. Payne, "Jesus' Implicit Claim to Deity in His Parables," *Trinity Journal*, n.s. 2.1 (Spring 1981): 3.

34. Ibid.

35. Ibid.

twenty of Jesus' parables. We will concentrate on three of those figures.

1. *The sower.* God in his messianic activity is often depicted as a sower (Isa. 61:11; Jer. 31:27; Ezek. 36:8–9; Hos. 2:21–23; Zech. 10:9) or a planter (Exod. 15:17; 2 Sam. 7:10; Isa. 60:21; 61:3; Jer. 24:6–7; 31:28; 32:41; Ezek. 17:22–23; Amos 9:15). Some of his works that are not specifically messianic are similarly described as planting (Num. 24:6; Pss. 80:8, 15; 94:9; 104:16; Isa. 5:2, 7; Jer. 2:21; 11:17; 12:2; 18:9; 24:6; 42:10; 45:4). In addition, this figure appears frequently in later Jewish literature. When used in a setting dealing with human destiny, it almost invariably refers to God.

No fewer than four parables speak of a sower, whether directly or implicitly: the parables of the sower (Matt. 13:3–8; Mark 4:3–8; Luke 8:5–8); the seed growing secretly (Mark 4:26–29); the mustard seed (Matt. 13:31–32; Mark 4:30–32; Luke 13:18–19); and the tares (Matt. 13:24–30). The basic thrust of the parable of the sower (or the soils) seems to be that response to Jesus' word is crucial. The parallel between Matthew 13:1 and 13:3 apparently associates Jesus with the sower, and Jesus himself draws that conclusion at the end of this group of parables (v. 37).

The parable of the mustard seed points to the seeming insignificance of the kingdom proclaimed in the teaching and preaching of Jesus. There are two indications that the kingdom of God is in view here. In each of the three Gospels there is an introductory indication to that effect. For example, Mark asks, "With what can we compare the kingdom of God?" In addition, each concludes by quoting Ezekiel 17:23, which speaks of the Lord God's planting a cedar on the mountain height of Israel, representing the future kingdom that he would raise up. This is also the work of the Son of man, who, as we assume, is to be identified with Jesus. The argument here for associating Jesus with the sower is that the sower mentioned in the parables of the seed growing secretly and of the tares, and implied in the parable of the mustard seed, performs a role analogous to Jesus' inauguration of the kingdom.[36]

2. *The shepherd.* God is depicted as a shepherd in several Old Testament passages (Gen. 49:24; Pss. 23; 28:9; 80:1; Isa. 40:11; Jer. 23:3; 31:10; Ezek. 34:10–22, 31; Zech. 9:16; 11:7–10). The

36. Ibid., p. 5.

The Construction of a Contemporary Incarnational Christology

basic picture, seen most clearly in Ezekiel 34, is of God as the shepherd who seeks the sheep that have gone astray and are lost.

The parables in which Jesus uses this imagery are the lost sheep (Matt. 18:12–14; Luke 15:4–7), the good shepherd (John 10:1–5), and the hireling (John 10:11–13). While the two tellings of the parable of the lost sheep do not explicitly state that Jesus is the shepherd, the context tends to sustain this identification. In Luke 15 Jesus tells the parable to defend his reception of repentant sinners, and in Matthew 18 to justify his welcoming of children. While it could of course be argued that the parable refers to God's seeking the lost, in Luke 19:10 Jesus explicitly describes himself as having come to seek and save the lost, quoting Ezekiel 34:16 and applying it to himself. Further, in the parables of the good shepherd and the hireling, Jesus does depict himself as the shepherd.[37] He does so by contrasting himself with those who are not good shepherds, namely, the thief, the stranger, and the hireling. He is in fact contrasting his ministry with that of other religious leaders. What we have here is parallel to Ezekiel 34 and Zechariah 11, where Israel's thieving shepherds (Ezek. 34:2–10; Zech. 11:5–6, 8, 16–17) are contrasted with God, the good shepherd (Ezek. 34:11–22; Zech. 11:7–10).

Thus Jesus on several occasions described himself as the good shepherd, evidently having in mind the imagery of Ezekiel 34. He depicts himself as performing the same acts the good shepherd, God, performs in the Old Testament: searching for the scattered sheep and bringing them back (Ezek. 34:11–13, 16, 22; the parable of the lost sheep); leading them into good pastureland, feeding them, and being a good shepherd to them (Ezek. 34:13–15, 31; the parable of the good shepherd); caring for them and protecting them from prey (Ezek. 34:15, 22; the parable of the hireling); and judging the flock, separating the sheep from the goats (Ezek. 34:17–22; Matt. 25:31–33). Payne's summary is appropriate: "Jesus depicts himself in these parables as the shepherd of Ezek. 34:11–22, and in so doing implicitly claims to be God."[38]

3. *The bridegroom.* There are a number of Old Testament passages which describe God as being a bridegroom, with Israel

---

37. Regarding the authenticity of these parables, see Raymond E. Brown, *The Gospel According to John*, 2 vols. (Garden City, N.Y.: Doubleday, 1966, 1970), vol. 1, pp. 390–91, 395–96.

38. Payne, "Jesus' Implicit Claim," p. 11.

being his bride (Isa. 54:4–8; 62:4–5; Jer. 2:2; 3:1–14; 31:32; Ezek. 16:8–14; 23:4–5; Hos. 2:1–3:1). There are similar allusions to this relationship in a number of other passages. The image is present as well within the rabbis' teaching. "Wholly along the lines of the OT the Rabbis extolled the conclusion of the covenant at Sinai as the marriage of Yahweh with Israel. The Torah is the marriage contract. Moses is the friend of the bridegroom and Yahweh comes to Israel as a bridegroom to his bride. . . . In Jewish eschatological expectation, God is the one who renews the marriage bond with his people."[39]

Jesus told three parables involving a bridegroom: the parable of the bridegroom (Matt. 9:15; Mark 2:19–20; Luke 5:34–35); the parable of the wedding feast (Matt. 22:1–14); and the parable of the ten virgins (Matt. 25:1–13). In the first, as in several of his other parables, Jesus is defending his actions and those of his disciples. In answer to criticism that they do not fast, he pictures himself as the bridegroom and points out that the wedding guests surely are not to fast when he is with them. In the second, he is the bridegroom to whose feast the people in the streets are invited after the original invitees fail to show. In the third, he is the bridegroom who is to come and for whom the virgins are to be watchful. This seems to be a rather clear case of Jesus' changing the application of Old Testament symbolism: he himself now takes the role played by God in the Old Testament. Ethelbert Stauffer puts it in unqualified fashion: "In the NT Christ takes the place of God as the heavenly Bridegroom. According to Mt. 22:1ff. He is the King's Son for whom the βασιλεύς holds the great wedding feast (ἐποίησεν γά–μους). Again, the image can hardly be accidental. Jesus often speaks of the Messianic feast."[40]

The question of the interpretation of these passages still must be faced, however. Could not Jesus be claiming simply to be a prophet like the Old Testament prophets? For, like them, he spoke on behalf of God and did his work. There are some crucial differences, however, as Payne points out. First, although the Old Testament prophets sometimes spoke in parables, none of them consistently applied to himself the symbols for God.

---

39. Ethelbert Stauffer, γαμέω, γάμος, in *Theological Dictionary of the New Testament*, ed. Kittel and Friedrich, vol. 1, pp. 653–54.
40. Ibid., p. 655.

Second, none of the prophets claimed God's specific preroga-tives, such as forgiving sins and dividing those who will enter the kingdom from those who will not. Third, Jesus' parables do not speak merely of what Jesus does or will do, but of what he is. We find him referring to himself as the bridegroom, the shep-herd, the sower. It is not merely function, but status that is involved. A functional Christology, then, cannot fully fit the pic-ture of Jesus that is drawn in the parables.

As we suggested earlier, Payne deals with a larger number of parables and images than we have treated here. He summarizes his findings in a tabular form, which, while it may at times over-state the case by utilization of passages where the reference is somewhat obscure, nonetheless sets forth with considerable force the cumulative effect of the parabolic images Jesus used to refer to himself. The "conclusion is of vital relevance to the current debate on the deity of Jesus. Did he really understand himself to be deity? Here in the parables, the most assuredly authentic of all the traditions about Jesus, is a clear, implicit affirmation of Jesus' self-understanding as deity. His sense of identification with God was so deep that to depict himself he consistently gravitated to imagery and symbols which in the OT typically depict God."[41]

Jesus' Assumption of the Role of Yahweh

We have noted some passages where Jesus applies to himself Old Testament statements and imagery that refer to God. We need now to note especially those passages in which he assumes the role of Yahweh. Having thoroughly studied these passages in his doctoral dissertation on Jesus and the Old Testament, R. T. France concludes, "The relevant quotations are not numer-ous, nor is the implication always clear, but the cumulative effect is to present a striking and daring claim."[42] France classi-fies these passages as nonpredictive, messianic, and predictive of the coming and judgment of Yahweh.

The first of the nonpredictive passages is Mark 13:31 (Matt. 24:35; Luke 21:33). While there is no verbal parallel, the saying recalls Isaiah 40:8. In each case the permanence of a word is

41. Payne, "Jesus' Implicit Claim," p. 11.
42. R. T. France, *Jesus and the Old Testament: His Application of Old Testament Passages to Himself and His Mission* (Downers Grove, Ill.: Inter-Varsity, 1971), p. 151.

contrasted with the nonpermanence of the natural order. Isaiah says that the Word of Yahweh, unlike grass and flowers, will endure forever. In taking over this idea, Jesus substitutes his own word for that of Yahweh, and makes the statement stronger by replacing Isaiah's reference to grass and flowers with "heaven and earth." France points out that even if the allusion to Isaiah 40:8 is doubted, similar statements in Psalm 119:89, 160, and Jesus' own words in Matthew 5:18 and Luke 16:17 show that the permanence of the Word of God was a common idea.

A second nonpredictive passage is Matthew 21:16, which is a quotation of Psalm 8:3 (v. 2 in the English translation). Jesus had just cleansed the temple and received the messianic salutation from the children. The chief priests and teachers of the law became indignant at what the children were saying. Jesus, however, not only did not restrain nor criticize them, but quoted Psalm 8, which says that God has ordained the praise of children. The force of Jesus' argument depends upon his applying this statement to himself. France says, "Unless he is here setting himself in the place of Yahweh, the argument is a *non sequitur.*"[43]

Luke 10:19, where Jesus says he has given his followers power over the enemy, may be an allusion to Psalm 91:13. This is suggested not only by the details, but also by the shared idea of protection given to the faithful. (A possible allusion to Deut. 8:15 is less likely because of both the wording and the context.) In Luke it is Jesus, not Yahweh, who gives immunity to his followers.

Luke 20:18 alludes to Isaiah 8:14–15, where Yahweh is described as a stone of offense and rock of stumbling to Israel; many will stumble thereon, fall, and be broken. Jesus applies the analogy to himself, stating that he is the head cornerstone; and those who reject him will find him to be the stumbling block, and they will be broken. Our response to him will reap the same results as will our response to Yahweh.

In the second group of passages France examines, there is a close association, amounting to a virtual identification between the Messiah and Yahweh. The passages in view include Daniel 7:13–14 (cf. Matt. 24:30; 26:64); Zechariah 12:10 (cf. John 19:37); and Zechariah 13:7 (cf. Matt. 26:31).

More impressive, however, is the third group, which consists

43. Ibid., p. 152.

of predictions of the coming and judgment of Yahweh. The first cluster of passages here is Mark 9:12–13 (Matt. 17:11–12); Matthew 11:10 (Luke 7:27); and Matthew 11:14. These are references to Malachi 3:1 and 4:5–6, which predict that Elijah will come as the forerunner of Yahweh. Jesus identified John the Baptist as Elijah. But John the Baptist had come as a forerunner for Jesus. France reasons: "The implication is as clear as it is startling: the reference to [4:5–6] implies that the 'day of Yahweh' is at least imminent, if not already present in the work of Jesus; that to 3:1 can hardly imply less than that the coming of Jesus is the coming of Yahweh for judgment."[44]

In Luke 19:10 ("For the Son of man came to seek and to save the lost") Jesus alludes to Ezekiel 34:16, 22. While in the latter part of the chapter Ezekiel introduces a messianic shepherd (David), in the earlier verses Yahweh himself speaks of what he will do for his sheep; it is to these verses that Jesus alludes. Thus Jesus is identifying himself with Yahweh's promises of what he will do for his people.

Matthew 13:41 is an allusion to Zephaniah 1:3. In the Old Testament passage, Yahweh says that he will sweep away "the stumbling blocks with the wicked" (BV). Jesus says that he will send out his angels to gather and burn "the stumbling-blocks and those practicing lawlessness" (BV).

In both Matthew 19:28 and 25:31–46, Jesus alludes to Daniel 7. In Daniel 7:9 the Ancient of Days sits upon a throne. Jesus takes upon himself the role of the Ancient of Days, sitting upon his "glorious throne." Furthermore, just as Daniel depicts a court scene with the Ancient of Days as the judge, so Jesus depicts a court scene with himself as the judge.

Matthew 25:31 seems to be an allusion to Zechariah 14:5, "Then the LORD your God will come, and all the holy ones with him [Heb., you]." The second-person reading at the end of this verse may well be corrupt; if so, the allusion is even stronger. But on either reading the parallel is striking. Just as Zechariah pictures Yahweh coming with his holy ones on the day of judgment, so Jesus pictures himself coming with his angelic retinue to judge and save.

The final reference is Matthew 25:32, which is reminiscent of Joel 4:1–12 (Eng. trans., 3:1–12). The gathering of the nations to

44. Ibid., p. 157.

be judged is found in both passages. While Daniel 7:13–14 refers to the Son of man's dominion over all the nations, it does not refer, at least explicitly, to his judging them; so it is likely that both Joel 4 and Daniel 7 lie behind Matthew 25:31–46. In any event, Jesus here assigns Yahweh's role as judge to himself.

Having thoroughly examined the various references we have but briefly surveyed, France summarizes his findings:

> The passages considered in this section add up to the conclusion that, pre-eminently in his expectation of the central role in the final judgment, but also with reference to his work on earth, Jesus did not scruple to apply to himself and his work words and ideas which the Old Testament used to describe the attributes and work of Yahweh. The number of such cases is not large, and the implication seldom made obvious in Jesus' words, but the remarkable fact is that this transfer could be made without comment and without argument; its validity is assumed.
>
> If even a few of these sayings are genuine (and we see no reason to question most of them), this aspect of Jesus' use of the Old Testament goes to confirm what other parts of his teaching suggest, that he thought of his work as the work of God, his coming as the coming of God, and himself as closely related to God in a relationship which was more than merely functional. That the Messiah would be God's agent and representative would be no very new idea. But Jesus seems to have gone further, and suggested not only that he had come to do the work of God, but that he and his Father were one.[45]

The Phenomenology of Jesus' Words and Actions

One additional type of approach to Jesus' self-awareness is a bit more difficult to label, but might be termed the phenomenology of Jesus' words and actions. It cuts across several types of data which we previously examined and presses more specifically the question of what kind of self-conception underlay the picture of Jesus in the Synoptics.

One person who has developed this approach most fully is Royce Gruenler. Gruenler is a New Testament scholar who abandoned the conservative or evangelical position to adopt process theology and then returned to evangelicalism as a result of his

---

45. Ibid., p. 159.

scholarly studies. He attempts to apply Ludwig Wittgenstein's philosophy of ordinary language to the core sayings of Jesus, those which even as radical a critic as Norman Perrin would accept as authentic. Focusing on the "language game" that is involved in making the types of statements that Jesus does about himself, Gruenler seeks to determine what kind of person makes such claims. While we may have some reservations about the specifics of the method which Gruenler adopts and the solidity of the conclusions which he draws, we must credit him with a worthy attempt to develop a new approach to Gospel criticism and New Testament Christology by applying a method not ordinarily used in quite so self-conscious a fashion.

Gruenler's method rests upon the assumption, now popular in psychology, that we communicate far more than we realize. A former colleague of mine who taught in the area of pastoral care, a man of unusual insight and good sense, made the profound statement, "You cannot not communicate." A skilled observer who spends time listening and watching (which, after all, is how we learn) can often gain quite a bit of insight into another person's self-conception. The way we speak, stand, use our eyes, and many other such factors tell a great deal, for example, about our self-confidence, security, and trust in other people.

Writing from the perspective of analytic philosophy rather than psychology, Wittgenstein makes much the same point. Too often language is discussed as if it were merely the use of symbols to refer to objective things, which are the third factors (i.e., in addition to the speaker and the words) in the process of verbal communication. According to such an understanding, one communicates about oneself only when one speaks about oneself. But language is far more than the assertion or denial of lifeless facts. Rather, as Gruenler puts it, "a person indwells his words when he speaks and acts, and without that indwelling no meaning or understanding is possible."[46] There is an element of intention in the statements that we make. Consider as evidence the difference between third-person and first-person statements that incorporate someone's belief. It is possible to say of someone else, "He believes falsely that. . . . " It is not possible to say,

46. Royce Gordon Gruenler, *New Approaches to Jesus and the Gospels: A Phenomenological and Exegetical Study of Synoptic Christology* (Grand Rapids: Baker, 1982), p. 21.

however, "I believe falsely that. . . . " We cannot affirm that a belief is false and at the same time accept it as true; conversely, to affirm that we believe something is to affirm that it is true. Thus there is a dimension of intentionality in a first-person statement which makes it more than a mere descriptive statement. Gruenler holds that biblical exegesis has too often concerned itself with the words of Jesus, and not sufficiently with Jesus as the author of those words.[47] In addition, Gruenler maintains that people speak and act consistently. If we are able to identify the underlying self-conception of Jesus from the undisputed materials, we should be able to use the principle of coherence to test some of the disputed material.[48]

It perhaps is important to state again what Gruenler is attempting to do. He works initially with the core sayings, those sayings attributed to Jesus which even radical criticism acknowledges to be authentic. He selects as representative of radical criticism Norman Perrin's *Rediscovering the Teaching of Jesus*, which, utilizing dissimilarity as its primary criterion, accepts as genuine a collection of sayings which are quite novel when compared with Judaism.[49] Gruenler's major complaint with radical criticism is at this point not its selection of sayings, but its treatment or interpretation of those sayings. It treats them only in terms of what Jesus said, and neglects what they reveal about Jesus himself. Gruenler notes that Perrin's book deals with rediscovering Jesus' teaching, not with rediscovering Jesus.[50] He also points out James Robinson's distinction between the understanding of existence which emerges from the study of Jesus' activity, and Jesus' self-understanding of that activity. Robinson pursues the former and abandons the latter.[51]

Gruenler then proceeds to examine in some detail all of the core passages. As he does so, it becomes apparent that Jesus was indeed making some audacious claims for himself, or at least had some remarkable conceptions of himself, which involved fulfilling the role which only God can fulfil. Even Perrin has to

47. Ibid., p. 22.
48. Ibid., pp. 24–25.
49. Norman Perrin, *Rediscovering the Teaching of Jesus* (New York: Harper and Row, 1967).
50. Gruenler, *New Approaches*, p. 36.
51. Ibid., p. 39; James M. Robinson, "The Recent Debate on the 'New Quest,'" *Journal of Bible and Religion* 30 (July 1962): 202.

acknowledge this phenomenon: "Each of the major elements of [Jesus'] teaching . . . contains a surprising aspect of uniqueness, of boldness, of audacity. . . . He is acting, and implicitly claiming to act, as I once heard Ernst Fuchs express it in a class at the 'Kirchliche Hochschule' in Berlin, *'Als ob er an die Stelle Gottes stünde'* (as if he stood in the very place of God himself)."[52] Here is a straightforward statement that would seem to compel one to draw the conclusion that Jesus thought of himself as being equal with God and having the right to exercise the same authority as God. This Perrin does not do, however. Instead, he moves to a more impersonal statement concentrating on the message about the kingdom rather than on the one proclaiming it:

> What is true of the address of God [*abba*] is true of the totality of the message of Jesus: it implies a claim for his person and it reflects his authority. But if we concentrate our attention upon that implication and build greatly upon that authority then we are doing violence to the message itself. The authority of that message was derived from the reality of the kingdom it proclaimed, not from the person of the proclaimer. However true it may be to say that the person cannot be separated from his words, it is also true that the authority of the historical Jesus was the authority of the proclamation, not that of the proclaimer.[53]

It does appear that violence is being done to the message, but that it is Perrin who is inflicting that violence. For the conclusion that we would expect to be drawn is rejected or at least deflected. Apparently there are factors at work which lead Perrin in this other direction. Gruenler identifies the problem as being the cardinal sin (from the standpoint of analytic philosophy) of committing a category error, in this case, of moving from person language to thing language.[54] Whether or not we analyze the flaw in precisely this way, it does appear to involve one or more suppressed premises, thus constituting an enthymeme. In the final analysis, a presupposition that is for all practical purposes a prejudice is at work here, dictating Perrin's conclusion.

---

52. Norman Perrin, *A Modern Pilgrimage in New Testament Christology* (Philadelphia: Fortress, 1974), pp. 51–52.
53. Ibid., p. 53.
54. Gruenler, *New Approaches*, p. 75.

To summarize the thrust of Gruenler's argument: Even if we restrict ourselves to those core sayings which the most radical New Testament critical scholars consider to be authentic words of Jesus, there is abundant evidence that Jesus thought of himself, or at least experienced himself, as being of equal status with God and having the right to perform the functions that only God can appropriately do. In addition, Gruenler goes on to point out that some of the other sayings which involve more directly overt or explicit claims to deity are not only consistent, but also coherent with the implicit claims in the core sayings. That is to say, they are sufficiently similar both in content and in tone that we can conclude that they come from the same person. Thus Gruenler argues, on the basis of the criterion of coherence, that it is not necessary to attribute the more explicit statements to the church's interpretive theologizing, but they also can be treated as authentic sayings of Jesus.[55] While I have some reservations about Gruenler's method[56] and would apply it somewhat more cautiously and tentatively, I believe that the basic insights which he offers are valid and do not depend solely upon his specific approach.

We have examined several approaches to the issue of Jesus' self-understanding. We noted that they converge toward a view which says that Jesus experienced himself as having the right to act as God and do those things which ordinarily only God does. Alternative interpretations of specific biblical passages may well lead us to reject any of these approaches individually. In the final analysis, however, the sheer number and diversity of considerations produce a conclusion that is as difficult to avoid as is every stone in an avalanche.

55. Ibid., pp. 77–108.
56. I would state my reservations as follows:
   a. Care should be taken to define the phenomenology of persons in such a way as to guarantee a genuinely cross-cultural understanding.
   b. The explanation of intentionality should take account of the insights of Sigmund Freud and others regarding the unconscious.
   c. Clarity needs to be achieved regarding the extent to which presuppositions play a role in linguistic analysis.
   d. The basis of preference for the Wittgensteinian versus the Husserlian phenomenology of personal communication should be enunciated more clearly. Presumably, Gruenler believes that the former can account for more of the data with less distortion than can the latter.

18

The New Testament Witness Regarding Jesus' Deity

We turn now to the issue of whether the New Testament teaches that Jesus was divine. This may seem to be a superfluous question after our discussion of Jesus' self-understanding. In reality, however, that is not the case. It is quite possible that while Jesus understood himself to be divine, even his closest disciples may not have fully comprehended. For, as we have seen in the preceding chapter, Jesus' claims were largely implicit in nature. Moreover, on more than one occasion Jesus made quite explicit claims with respect to the matter of his crucifixion and resurrection, and yet his disciples failed to understand or believe, so that the crucifixion took them largely by surprise. It

455

would not be surprising, then, if they failed to discern his deity immediately.

Both Jesus' claims and the disciples' difficulty in comprehending them must be seen in the light of the Jews' strong monotheism. The oneness of God was the most basic feature of their belief. It is difficult for us to fully comprehend the problem anyone in that setting would have encountered in coming to understand and accept as divine someone other than and in addition to the heavenly Father. As R. T. France puts it, "Perhaps only those who have lived in a non-Christian monotheistic culture (e.g. Islamic) can fully appreciate the significance of this fact."[1] The intense monotheism may help to account for the relative scarcity of texts in the New Testament which say in so many words, "Jesus is God." Just as statements by Jesus of his own divinity are extremely rare, so statements by the New Testament authors to this effect are much fewer in number than one might expect to find.

There are several approaches which we might take in exploring the subject. To do justice to all of them would of course require a complete book. We will first examine briefly those references which seem to indicate that Jesus is not God, those that are unclear about whether he is God, and those that appear to teach that he is God. Then we will ask whether the later New Testament affirmations of Jesus' deity are an overlay of foreign theological conceptions upon a basically simple picture of Jesus or an explicit expression of an idea that was implicitly present early on. We will investigate early teachings and behavior implying belief in Jesus' divinity. Finally, we will examine a classic christological passage, Philippians 2:6–11.

The Varied Testimony

Passages Seemingly Denying Jesus' Deity

When we look at the passages which seem to bear directly upon the question of whether Jesus is God, we must note first that there are some which appear to count on the negative side. One of the best known is Mark 10:17–18, where a man addresses Jesus as "Good Teacher," and Jesus replies, "Why do you call me

---

1. R. T. France, "The Uniqueness of Christ," *The Churchman* 95.3 (1981): 204–05.

good? No one is good but God alone." A common patristic interpretation held that Jesus is not here denying his divinity or his
goodness, but trying to help the man draw the conclusion that
Jesus is God. Another such passage is Jesus' cry on the cross,
"My God, my God, why hast thou forsaken me?" (Matt. 27:46;
Mark 15:34). The argument that this indicates a distinction
between Jesus and the Father is somewhat weakened by the fact
that he is repeating the words of Psalm 22:1. No such consideration, however, applies to John 20:17, where Jesus says to Mary
Magdalene, "I am ascending to my Father and your Father, to
my God and your God."

These three statements are reported as coming from Jesus. As
such, they are subject to debate over whether they are his
authentic words and truly represent his self-understanding, or
whether they are interpretations by the Gospel writers. Thus
they may or may not be a suitable topic for discussion in this
chapter. More directly pertinent are those passages in which the
Scripture writer seems to distinguish between Jesus and God.
One of the most significant is Ephesians 1:17, which speaks of
"the God of our Lord Jesus Christ, the Father of glory." In
1 Corinthians 8:6 Paul distinguishes between the "one God, the
Father," and the "one Lord, Jesus Christ." A distinction is drawn
between one Spirit, one Lord, and one God and Father of us all
in Ephesians 4:4–6 and 1 Corinthians 12:4–6. Similarly, 1 Timothy 2:5 distinguishes between the "one God" and the "one
mediator between God and men, the man Christ Jesus." It is
clear that the author in each case is distinguishing Jesus from
the Father. Whether that distinction means they are mutually
exclusive is a question that will have to be addressed.

Texts Ambiguous Regarding Jesus' Deity

There are, secondly, several texts in which the witness to
Jesus' deity is unclear or ambiguous. The uncertainty is of two
types: textual (how the Greek text should read) and syntactical
(how it should be translated). Among the textually disputed passages is Galatians 2:20, where the dispute is between the reading τοῦ θεοῦ καὶ Χριστοῦ ("God and Christ") and the more commonly accepted τοῦ υἱοῦ τοῦ θεοῦ ("the Son of God"). In Acts
20:28 we find the variant reading ἐκκλησίαν τοῦ κυρίου ("church
of the Lord") and the more common τοῦ θεοῦ ("of God"). In John

1:18 some manuscripts have ὁ μονογενὴς υἱὸς θεοῦ ("the only Son of God") rather than μονογενὴς θεός ("the only God"). Textual criticism is a highly developed science practiced by specialists, and space does not here permit a full treatment of the textual issues. I am inclined to find more likely the reading which favors the affirmation of deity in the second and third instances, although varied possibilities for translation make the second instance more problematic; in the first instance I lean toward the reading which does not affirm the deity of Jesus.

The passages where the syntax makes the translation or the interpretation problematic are more numerous. Among them are Romans 9:5; Colossians 2:2; 2 Thessalonians 1:12; Titus 2:13; 2 Peter 1:1; and 1 John 5:20. Limitations of space forbid complete discussion of each of these passages. Basically I concur with the judgment of Raymond Brown, who concludes that all except Colossians 2:2 and 2 Thessalonians 1:12 are probably calling Jesus God, as does one of the textually questionable passages, namely, John 1:18.[2] Brown chastises Rudolf Bultmann and Vincent Taylor for neglecting these five probable affirmations of Jesus' deity:

> As we have insisted, the textual or grammatical probabilities favor the interpretation that these five passages call Jesus God. In one or the other instance the interpretation may be wrong, but simply to write off all five as unconvincing and therefore unimportant for the discussion is not good method. It would be foolish to develop a theory about the New Testament use of "God" for Jesus that would depend for a key point on one of these five texts, but it would be just as foolish to develop a theory that would be invalid if Jesus is really called God in several of these instances. In all that follows we intend to take these five instances seriously.[3]

Clear Statements of Jesus' Deity

We come now to three instances where the biblical writer speaks quite clearly and unequivocally of Jesus as God. Probably the most useful of these is Hebrews 1:8–9, which, quoting from

2. For a detailed discussion of these passages see Raymond E. Brown, *Jesus, God and Man: Modern Biblical Reflections* (Milwaukee: Bruce, 1967), pp. 13–23.
3. Ibid., p. 29n.

Psalm 45:6–7, is presented as what God says to the Son: "But of the Son he says, 'Thy throne, O God, is for ever and ever, the righteous scepter is the scepter of thy kingdom. Thou hast loved righteousness and hated lawlessness; therefore, God, thy God, has anointed thee with the oil of gladness.'" Some, taking the word θεός in verse 8 as being in the nominative rather than the vocative, have translated, "God is thy throne for ever and ever." This, however, is a most unlikely interpretation, because the preceding verse in the Septuagint translation of the psalm which is being quoted begins, "Thy weapons, O Mighty One, are sharpened," and the nature of Hebrew parallelism is such as to require the rendering, "Thy throne, O God." Further, the parallelism extends to the next line of the psalm, "the righteous scepter is the scepter of thy kingdom." All of this suggests that "throne" rather than "God" is the subject of the clause in question.[4] Oscar Cullmann holds that in Hebrews 1:9 "the word 'God' as the subject refers to the Father; as the object (in the vocative) to the Son: 'Thy God (the Father) has anointed thee, O God (the Son).'"[5] The use of parallelism throughout this passage suggests that the juxtaposition of the two occurrences of ὁ θεός here should be interpreted as entailing a recurrence of the vocative rather than an apposition of the nominative subject, since the point of quoting the psalm seems to be to emphasize the Father's addressing the Son. Cullmann's verdict on the entire passage is categorical: "Hebrews unequivocally applies the title 'God' to Jesus. . . . With this twofold use of the word 'God' Hebrews, like the Gospel of John, thus bears witness to the paradox of all Christology."[6]

The second unambiguous passage is John 1:1, "In the beginning was the Word, and the Word was with God, and the Word was God." Some debate has centered upon the anarthrous use of θεός in the third line: καὶ θεὸς ἦν ὁ λόγος. Some have explained this by invoking the rule that when predicate nouns precede the subject of the sentence, they often lack the definite article; this serves to distinguish them from the subject. While it

---

4. Ibid., p. 24.

5. Oscar Cullmann, *The Christology of the New Testament* (Philadelphia: Westminster, 1959), p. 310.

6. Ibid., pp. 310–11. By "paradox" Cullmann means that here, as in John 1:1, Jesus Christ is presented as both "God" and "with God."

indeed is probable that θεός is the predicate here, Brown maintains that the rule does not necessarily hold for statements in which the subject is equated with the predicate noun. Examples are to be found in the "I am" sayings in John 11:25 and 14:6, where predicate nouns appear with the definite article.[7] Note, however, that these examples are not strictly the same as the instance under consideration. They are found in sentences with a normal word order; that is, the subject comes first. But in John 1:1 the predicate comes first. To follow through on the idea that an anarthrous noun suggests "of the quality of," some translators, such as James Moffatt, have rendered the statement, "The Word was divine." This, however, could also have been more unambiguously rendered by the adjective θεῖος, which is used elsewhere in the New Testament (Acts 17:29; 2 Peter 1:3).

We must utilize a little logical analysis to try to determine what prompted John's fairly unusual syntax. In an Indo-European language like New Testament Greek, there are at least three usages of the simple copula. One is the "is" of inclusion, where the subject is said to be a member of a class. One is the "is" of predication or of attribution, where a particular quality is predicated of the subject by use of an adjective. The final use is the "is" of identity, where the subject is equated with the predicate. This is, in the terminology of logic, a double A-type proposition where "All X is Y" and "All Y is X." Such propositions are invertible; in other words, there really is no subject and predicate, only nouns in the first and second position. The predicate nominative in English begins to approximate this usage, which John seems to have had in view.

Another consideration is the unusual word order and the anarthrous usage of θεός. Because all other possible meanings could have been conveyed in some other way, it appears likely that John's purpose is to put the emphasis upon "God." It is as if John is saying, "*God* is what the Word was." Again it seems that we have here a statement of identity. On the other hand, by placing it in such close proximity to "the Word was with God," John indicates that it is not merely a statement of identity. Something more is involved. But regardless of how we interpret the grammatical construction of 1:1, it is clear that the author

---

7. Brown, *Jesus, God and Man*, p. 26.

who wrote the end of the prologue ("No one has ever seen God; the only Son [or God], who is in the bosom of the Father, he has made him known," 1:18) and presumably also 20:28 would not be here asserting that Jesus was somehow less than God the Father.

The final passage is John 20:28, in which Thomas is reported to have uttered the exclamation, "My Lord and my God!" Nowhere in the New Testament is Jesus more clearly identified as God. Following the resurrection of Jesus the disciple who had been most skeptical gives utterance to the most complete expression of conviction of the divine status of Jesus, an expression that parallels Psalm 35:23, where the psalmist exclaims, "My God and my Lord."

We have seen that there are three clear instances and five probable instances of Jesus' being called "God" in the New Testament. It is probably worth noting, however, that they tend to be found in the later books of the New Testament, although Romans 9:5 is from one of the very earliest books. We should also bear in mind that John A. T. Robinson's work on the dating of the New Testament books, and especially the Gospel of John, qualifies this assertion. In general, however, we probably are safe in saying that the explicit references to Jesus as God tend to come from later developments in the tradition. Yet it is also noteworthy that at least four of them occur in doxologies or in formulaic statements of faith, and that Hebrews 1 is quoting a psalm. Such formulas were frequently used and psalms were often sung by the Christian communities in worship.[8] It is possible, then, that these texts reflect a usage in the community that goes further back than the books in which they appear.

The Evolutionary Hypothesis
The Theory of Stages in New Testament Christology

We must now come to grips with the evolutionary hypothesis regarding the rise of New Testament Christology. This hypothesis is a phenomenon of modern Christologies growing out of or at least influenced by the "history of religions" school. Probably the first to give this theory formative expression was Wilhelm

---

8. Ibid., p. 35.

Bousset.[9] He was a rationalist in that he attempted to give an explanation of the New Testament phenomena without any recourse to supernatural causes. In particular, he was a member of the "history of religions" school, which concentrated upon studying early Christianity against its cultural background, maintaining that most of its ideas derived from the current environment. The Christian "third day" motif, for example, was allegedly based on the folk belief that it is on the third day after death that the soul leaves the body.

Bousset was particularly interested in the study of Christology. He emphasized that between the time of Jesus and Paul there arose not only the primitive Jewish church in Palestine, but also Hellenistic Jewish-Christian communities in such places as Antioch, Tarsus, and Damascus. Thus, when Paul received the tradition, it had already been touched by Gentile Christians, whose thinking was open to and had absorbed some pagan influences. So Paul, a Jew, received a version of Christianity which included mixtures of Hellenism.

The theory devised by Bousset received considerable attention and was further refined. Relatively recently, Ferdinand Hahn, a pupil of Günther Bornkamm's, gave it an extensive elaboration and advancement.[10] He followed Oscar Cullmann's procedure of studying the various titles for Jesus. In doing so, he worked with a scheme that posited three stages between Jesus and Paul:

1. *The Palestinian Jewish church.* At first the church was Aramaic-speaking and centered in Jerusalem.
2. *The Hellenistic Jewish church.* In time the church turned to some extent to the Greek language, used the Septuagint, and became more open to Hellenistic ideas.
3. *The Hellenistic Gentile church.* Finally, the church was predominantly Gentile, definitely Greek-speaking, and much more influenced by pagan concepts.

Hahn maintains, then, that the Hellenistic influence did not first come upon the church when it became predominantly Gentile

9. Wilhelm Bousset, *Kyrios Christos: A History of the Belief in Christ from the Beginnings of Christianity to Irenaeus* (Nashville: Abingdon, 1970).

10. Ferdinand Hahn, *The Titles of Jesus in Christology: Their History in Early Christianity*, trans. Harold Knight and George Ogg (New York: World, 1969).

in makeup—the Hellenistic influence was already present in the Jewish period. Hahn is also careful to avoid making any geographical associations with the three stages. The measure of each stage is not geographical distance from Jerusalem, but rather the respective degrees of Jewish and non-Jewish influence. He believes that he has here an apt framework for studying the development of Christology. Working with massive amounts of detailed material, his method is to show the changes in meaning that each title of Jesus underwent as it moved from one stage to another. "He thus attempts to repeat the work of Bousset in a more refined manner."[11]

Criticism of the Evolutionary View

Because we have presented the evolutionary thesis at some length, a response in a few sentences will not be possible. As I. Howard Marshall says, "It shows the typical German quality of thoroughness, and whoever disagrees with its conclusions must discuss the evidence in equal detail; it will not do simply to quote Cullmann on the other side!"[12] It will not, of course, be possible to undertake a lengthy criticism here. What we will do is point our attention to two endeavors by New Testament scholars which respond to this hypothesis with appropriate detail. One strategy is to challenge the scheme of the three stages itself, showing that it does not fit the actual data. The other is to show that ideas that supposedly arose as the tradition evolved were actually latent at the very beginning of the Christian movement.

A natural first step in attempting to evaluate the evolutionary view is to see whether a distinction can be found between Palestinian Judaism and Diaspora Judaism. It is, of course, possible to draw such a distinction, with the former being a more traditional outlook, and the latter more open to influence from the pagan environment. The distinction is not hard and fast, however; there are many ideas which we cannot identify as necessarily having originated in Palestine, or as necessarily having originated in the Diaspora. In a massive and detailed study Martin Hengel has shown that there was considerable Hellenistic influence upon Judaism in the period up to 150 B.C. He

11. I. Howard Marshall, *The Origins of New Testament Christology* (Downers Grove, Ill.: Inter-Varsity, 1977), p. 25.
12. Ibid., p. 24.

speaks of Jewish "Hellenists" who between 175 and 164 "attempted to dissolve Judaism completely into Hellenistic civilization, but failed because of their own lack of unity and the political obtuseness of Antiochus IV."[13] In fact, doubt has been shed upon the conventional wisdom that the earliest church must have spoken Aramaic rather than Greek.[14]

If we cannot draw an ideologically significant distinction between Palestinian and Hellenistic Judaism, it seems unlikely that we can draw such a distinction within Christianity. To be sure, there is a distinction between Hebrews and Hellenists in the early church (Acts 6:1). The usual explanation has been that members of the former group used Aramaic in their worship, were of Palestinian origin, and adhered to traditional Jewish culture; members of the latter group used Greek in their worship, stemmed from the Dispersion, and were more Hellenistic in culture.[15] However, Marshall points out that several qualifications must be attached to this conception:[16]

1. The linguistic and cultural differences were not absolute; that is to say, the two groups were not separated by clear-cut characteristics.
2. The terminology is used loosely. Paul appears to have characterized as "Hebrews" some people to whom Luke would probably not have applied the term. Paul seems to have based his definition of "Hebrew" less upon language than upon Jewish descent and customs. Another matter to consider is how Luke would have classified Paul and Barnabas, who were equally at home in both worlds.
3. Hellenists living in Jerusalem were part of the church from a very early date. There may well have been no time when the church was without Greek-speaking Christians.[17]
4. Although there apparently were differences over the continuing role of the law and the status of Gentiles, it is

13. Martin Hengel, *Judaism and Hellenism: Studies in Their Encounter in Palestine During the Early Hellenistic Period*, 2 vols. (Philadelphia: Fortress, 1974), vol. 1, p. 255.

14. See, e.g., J. N. Sevenster, *Do You Know Greek? How Much Greek Could the First Jewish Christians Have Known?* (Leiden: Brill, 1968).

15. F. F. Bruce, *The Book of the Acts*, rev. ed. (Grand Rapids: Eerdmans, 1988), pp. 127–28.

16. Marshall, *Origins*, pp. 37–38.

17. C. H. Dodd, *According to the Scriptures* (London: Nisbet, 1953), p. 118 n. 1.

doubtful whether any similar differences existed in matters of Christology. The juxtaposition of the two groups from the beginning rules out the theory of stages in christological thinking.

If, however, it is not possible to find ideological distinctions between the two varieties of Jewish Christianity, is it possible to draw a distinction between Jewish and Gentile Christianity? It is questionable whether there were any purely Jewish churches prior to Paul's missionary activity, and the churches which he founded certainly comprised mixtures of Jewish and Gentile Christians. The teams which carried on evangelism among the Gentiles were largely Jewish, but also included Gentiles.[18] Marshall maintains that "we are still moving within the Jewish Christian orbit, and all that we have established is that, as the Jewish Christian church began to move out to the Gentiles, it began to broaden its theological horizons."[19]

But may it be possible to distinguish, on the basis of geography and history, between a primitive church in Jerusalem, which was largely traditionally Jewish in its outlook, and a more Hellenistic church in Antioch, which came later and conducted the Gentile mission? As appealing as this hypothesis would be as a basis for the evolutionary view of Christology, it must fail because of the lack of time. Paul wrote his earliest epistles within about twenty years of the end of Christ's life and the events of Pentecost. The Gentile mission at Antioch dates from no more than fifteen years after the crucifixion, and Hengel thinks the time span should be reduced to no more than five years.[20] This simply does not allow for the changes required by the evolutionary theory.

We must conclude that the theory and its analytical apparatus are not satisfactory and usable. Marshall summarizes: "It follows that the three-stage scheme of development has been shown to be an inexact means of plotting Christological thought. Not only

18. E. Earle Ellis, "'Those of the Circumcision' and the Early Gentile Mission," *Studia Evangelica* 4 (1968): 390–99.

19. Marshall, *Origins*, p. 39.

20. Martin Hengel, "Christologie und Neutestamentliche Chronologie," in *Neues Testament und Geschichte: Historisches Geschehen und Deutung im Neuen Testament. Oscar Cullmann zum 70. Geburtstag*, ed. Heinrich Baltensweiler and Bo Reicke (Zurich: Theologischer; Tübingen: J. C. B. Mohr, 1972), pp. 63–64.

are the boundaries between the three areas of thought too fluid, but the very existence of the third stage at this early date has been called into question."[21] He also finds that the argument rests upon circular reasoning; it tries to force the New Testament evidence into a straitjacket into which it was not designed to fit.[22] Similarly, Werner Kümmel finds that the theology of the Hellenistic Jewish and Gentile churches cannot be distinguished, nor can that of the earliest church and the Hellenistic church.[23] Cullmann says that we must "completely discard the rigid scheme, Judaistic original Church—Hellenistic Christianity. . . . Not only do we lack the texts which would allow us to fix the boundary lines, but, more important, it has been demonstrated that such an abrupt contrast does not exist at all."[24]

The Developmental Interpretation

We now need to explore in a somewhat different way the issue of whether the conception of Jesus as divine evolved from an earlier, simpler form of belief. This is the question posed by the "history of religions" school, as we have seen. In its crudest form their position is that the church, under the influence of outside philosophies such as Gnosticism, came to interpret the simple rabbi, Jesus of Nazareth, in an increasingly supernatural way. We observed that there are two ways of refuting this hypothesis. One is to challenge the basic scheme, namely the view that there were stages in the life of the early church, Palestinian Jewish, Diaspora Jewish, and Hellenistic Gentile. This we have done. Now we will establish that christological ideas which supposedly arose as the tradition evolved were actually present quite early in time.

C. F. D. Moule has described and contrasted what he calls the evolutionary and the developmental views of Christology. The former is reminiscent of biological evolution in that mutations occur from which emerge forms radically different from the original; in other words, new species of ideas appear. This is the "history of religions" approach to Christology. The other approach is

21. Marshall, *Origins*, p. 40.
22. Ibid., p. 41.
23. Werner G. Kümmel, *Theology of the New Testament According to Its Major Witnesses* (Nashville: Abingdon, 1974), pp. 105–06, 118–19.
24. Cullmann, *Christology*, p. 323.

what Moule terms the developmental. Instead of radically different or novel forms, there is a gradual unfolding of what was latent or implicitly present from the beginning. The biological parallel here is the growth of a given member of a species from birth to maturity.[25] When applied to Christology, the developmental approach tends

> to explain all the various estimates of Jesus reflected in the New Testament as, in essence, only attempts to describe what was already there from the beginning. They are not successive additions of something new, but only the drawing out and articulating of what is there. They represent various stages in the development of perception, but they do not represent the accretion of any alien factors that were not inherent from the beginning: they are analogous not so much to the emergence of a new species, as to the unfolding (if you like) of flower from bud and the growth of fruit from the flower. Moreover, when once one assumes that the changes are, in the main, changes only in perception, one is at the same time acknowledging that it may not be possible, *a priori*, to arrange such changes in any firm chronological order. In evolution, the more complex species generally belong to a later stage than the more simple; but in development, there is nothing to prevent a profoundly perceptive estimate occurring at an early stage, and a more superficial one at a later stage: degrees of perception will depend upon individual persons and upon circumstances which it may be impossible to identify in any intelligibly chronological sequence.[26]

Moule's first step is an investigation of several of the christological titles. This has become a very common approach to doing Christology. He attempts to show that such expressions as "Son of man" and "Son of God" either go back to Jesus' own usage or appeared very early in the church. As important as is that part of his investigation, we will here concern ourselves primarily with certain practices and implicit beliefs of the early Christians.

The Corporate Christ

Our first consideration is what Moule calls the "corporate

---

25. C. F. D. Moule, *The Origin of Christology* (Cambridge: Cambridge University Press, 1977), pp. 1–2.
26. Ibid., pp. 2–3.

Christ." There are a large number of passages in the writings of Paul and, for the purposes of our argument, in his early and undisputed letters, where the believer is referred to as being incorporated "in Christ." A very high percentage of such references in the New Testament are found in Paul. To be sure, many of his "in Christ" references are simply cases of instrumentality or agency which in no way suggest incorporation of the believer in Christ.[27] There are also, to be sure, a number of references in which Christ is said to be in the believer. One might therefore conclude that what is in view is not incorporation but merely "mutual interpenetration of two individuals in intimate relationship."[28] It is significant, however, that references to the believer's being "in Christ" are far more frequent than references to Christ in the believer, and that in the latter case "there is a strong tendency to speak in terms only of Christ's *activity*, rather than *existence*, in us."[29] (The reverse is true of references about the believer and the Spirit, where the prevalent expression is that the Spirit is in the believer.) In addition to the direct statements regarding the believer's being in Christ, there are the figures of the church as the body and temple of Christ, which imply quite the same thing.

We must now interpret these data. Of what kind of person would it be said that another individual is "in him," indeed, that large numbers of people are in him, as if they are somehow incorporated into him? There is no evidence that this concept was borrowed or adopted from nonreligious culture. It is true that classical Greek (e.g., Sophocles' *Oedipus Tyrannus*) has expressions like "We are in you," but this is only a verbal parallel meaning something like "We are in your hands" rather than "We are incorporate in you."[30] There is also, in some non-Christian thought, the concept of being "in Adam," but this points simply to membership in the human race. Jewish thinkers regarded certain patriarchal figures as symbols of their people, but nowhere is it said that the people are "in" Abraham, David, or Hezekiah. In Greek thought, even the disciples of Socrates, devoted follow-

27. C. F. D. Moule, *The Phenomenon of the New Testament* (Naperville, Ill.: Allenson, 1967), pp. 22–23.
28. Ibid., p. 24.
29. Ibid., p. 25.
30. Ibid., p. 39.

ers though they were, are not said to be in him, nor is there any such usage regarding the emperor.[31]

The question, then, is how this bold conception could have come into being. As Moule puts it, "[The early Christians] began to regard the Rabbi, whom some of them had known personally, whom all of them knew of as a recently executed victim of injustice, as the body in which they were limbs. Can you conceive of Paul speaking of himself as 'in Gamaliel'? Whence, then, sprang this most unlikely sense?"[32]

When Paul characterized believers as being incorporated in Christ, he was saying that their very existence was related to, indeed depended on, a rabbi who had died some years before. Moule describes the implications of this understanding: "And this means, in effect, that Paul was led to conceive of Christ as any theist conceives of God: personal, indeed, but transcending the individual category. Christ is like the omnipresent deity 'in whom we live and move and have our being'—to quote the tag from Acts 17:28 which is generally traced to Epimenides."[33]

Moule points out that the usage in other New Testament writers is slightly different from that in Paul; in particular, they view Jesus more individualistically than does Paul. Yet, Moule continues, they see Jesus as more than

> merely an exalted individual human being: even they make it clear that they know him as uniquely close to God and (so to speak) one with the Creator in a way in which no mere created human being can be. And, more than this, these writers also assume, as universally recognized and accepted among Christians, aspects of Christian experience which require and imply, even if they do not make explicit, that more than individuality which is explicit in Paul.
>
> Putting all these phenomena together, we shall be presented with evidence of a consistently 'high' Christology from the very earliest datable periods of the Church's life, endorsing quite independently the conclusions to which, as it seems to me, the critical study of the titles of Jesus also points.[34]

31. Ibid., p. 40.
32. Ibid., p. 41.
33. Moule, *Origin*, p. 95.
34. Ibid., p. 96.

Worship of Jesus

Another indication that the earliest Christians regarded Jesus as divine is their worship of him. Though the belief may not yet have been enunciated in a formal doctrine, there are various evidences that such a belief was held tacitly, that Jesus was thought worthy of worship.

One evidence that Jesus was worshiped early on is the doxologies which refer to him. There are three which definitely name him: Romans 9:5; 2 Peter 3:18; Revelation 1:5b–6. Two others are debatable. Hebrews 13:20–21 probably does not refer to Jesus, but 2 Timothy 4:18 ("The Lord will rescue me from every evil and save me for his heavenly kingdom. To him be the glory for ever and ever. Amen.") probably does. Here the issue is whether "the Lord" refers to the Father or to Christ. The key to interpretation of the passage appears to be the description of the Lord as the "righteous judge" (v. 8). The righteous judge is Jesus, because verse 1 refers to his judging the living and the dead. In addition, this verse speaks of Christ's appearing and kingdom, which suggests that "his heavenly kingdom" in verse 18 is a reference to Christ's kingdom. There also are two doxologies in Revelation (5:13; 7:10) which are addressed to both the Father and the Son.[35] It should be noted, however, that most of the doxologies we have cited come from relatively late New Testament writings.

A second major evidence of early worship of Christ is the prayers addressed to him. The Book of Acts contains one such prayer, Stephen's as he was being martyred (Acts 7:59–60). One might argue that this was simply a request for forgiveness for his executioners. The first part of the prayer, however, the request for Jesus to receive his spirit, was not the sort of petition one would direct to another human. It is striking that Stephen has just declared that he sees the Lord (vv. 55–56), who has died, been resurrected, and ascended.

A rather indirect indication of early prayer to Jesus is the use of the expression *Maranatha* in 1 Corinthians 16:22. This is Aramaic for "Our Lord, come!" It certainly has to be treated as a prayer, one which was by this time sufficiently established to be

---

35. Arthur W. Wainwright, *The Trinity in the New Testament* (London: SPCK, 1962), pp. 94–95.

familiar to Paul's readers. Indeed, France contends that this argues for a very early date:

> The use of the Aramaic formula of prayer to Jesus, *Maranatha* ("Our Lord, come"), in I Corinthians 16:22 when writing to a Greek church can only indicate that this formula, like such foreign expressions as "Hosanna" and "Hallelujah" today, was hallowed by long usage. When it originated in the Aramaic-speaking church can only be guessed at, but to be familiar in Corinth in the 50s it is likely to date from the very early days of the Jerusalem church; in that case Jesus, not long after his death, was being "called upon" by Christians from his own cultural background.[36]

Although the circumstances of the prayer's origination are somewhat unclear, Paul's use of the expression is a significant consideration,[37] and appears to count on the side of an early worship of Jesus.

There is in Paul's writings at least one other likely instance of petitionary prayer addressed to Jesus, namely, 2 Corinthians 12:8. Paul tells us that he asked the Lord three times to remove his thorn in the flesh. That this prayer was directed to Jesus is clear from verse 9: having received the Lord's reply, "My power is made perfect in weakness," Paul will in the future gladly boast of his own weakness, "that the power of Christ may rest upon me."

Finally, three benedictions in Paul's earliest writings invoke Jesus: 1 Thessalonians 3:11–12; 2 Thessalonians 3:5; and 3:16. The first of these speaks of both God the Father and "our Lord Jesus." The other two are directed to "the Lord." Since the expression "the Lord Christ" appears three times in this chapter (vv. 6, 12, 18), it appears likely that the reference here is to Christ.[38]

Arthur Wainwright holds that "the readiness of first-century Christians to pray to Christ is strong evidence of their belief in his divinity. But it is not absolutely conclusive, for in Judaism prayers were offered to others besides God."[39] Many Jews, for

---

36. R. T. France, "The Worship of Jesus: A Neglected Factor in Christological Debate?" in *Christ the Lord: Studies in Christology Presented to Donald Guthrie*, ed. Harold H. Rowdon (Downers Grove, Ill.: Inter-Varsity, 1982), p. 30.

37. Wainwright, *Trinity*, pp. 85–86.

38. Ibid., p. 98.

39. Ibid., p. 100.

instance, prayed to angels to intercede for them, but the prayers to Christ cited here are not merely requests for intercession. The fact that Christ is addressed as if he had the ability to answer prayer in his own right as did the Father "suggests that his followers ranked him with the Father."[40] Richard Bauckham, however, is not willing to concede this much. He shows that in the apocalyptic tradition of early Christianity a definite line was drawn between God, who was worshiped, and angels, who were not to be. While Jesus may not have been equally ranked, he was, Bauckham acknowledges, regularly placed on the side of the line with the Father.[41]

In summarizing the worship of Jesus by the early Christians, France notes that behind all the theological terms and titles is the worship of the carpenter, "a phenomenon sufficiently arresting to require explanation, even if they had never progressed to the stage of openly calling him 'God.'"[42] Such worship would have been a difficult option for pious Jews in view of their own monotheistic inclinations, the hostility of their fellow Jews, and the ridicule of Gentiles. "Men do not gratuitously court such opposition and ridicule merely out of a dispassionate search for a new religious ideology. There must have been an irresistible compulsion, so that they could do no other. It is the task of our Christology, as it was of theirs, to account adequately for this compulsion."[43]

Jesus and Judgment

We come now to examine the biblical testimony regarding Jesus as judge. It can be demonstrated from the Old Testament and from other Hebrew literature that judging was quite clearly a role performed by God and uniquely reserved to him. There were, of course, different aspects of judging: the daily task of administrative justice, which was often performed by human agents; the judgment upon nations by conquerors, often unwitting servants of the Lord; the judgment at the coming day of the

40. Ibid., p. 101.
41. Richard J. Bauckham, "The Worship of Jesus in Apocalyptic Christianity," *New Testament Studies* 27.3 (April 1981): 322–41.
42. France, "Worship," p. 35.
43. Ibid.

Lord; and the judgment pronounced upon the inner attitude of the individual. The first two could be delegated by God to human agents, and frequently were. The latter two Scripture assigned to God alone.[44]

The judgment to occur on the day of the Lord is of particular interest to us here. Whereas the people of Israel apparently believed that they would win a decisive victory over their enemies on that day, Amos warned them that it would be a day of punishment, bringing darkness rather than light (Amos 5:18). It would entail the vindication not of God's people, but of his justice. Isaiah 2:12 stressed that it would bring low all who are proud and haughty. Joel described it as the great and terrible day of the Lord, an event involving cosmic disturbances (Joel 2:30–32). Malachi described it as a day of judgment and punishment which will inaugurate a period of peace and blessedness (Mal. 4:1–5). Although the righteous will tread down the wicked on that day, they will not be the ones who execute judgment. Rather, that will be done by Jehovah alone (3:5).

We observed in the preceding chapter Jesus' taking upon himself certain prerogatives of God, one of which was judgment. Here we must examine what the earliest New Testament writings, that is, those that appeared before the doctrine of the deity of Jesus Christ was formally articulated, have to say on this matter of judgment. Most pertinent to our inquiry are the earliest writings of Paul. Twice in 1 Thessalonians Paul speaks of the coming of the Lord Jesus Christ. In 3:13 he speaks of the Lord's coming with his saints. In 5:23b Paul prays that the soul and body and spirit of his readers may be kept blameless at this coming. Both of these passages refer to the coming of Jesus in judgment, as is made clear by the emphasis upon the need for blamelessness and holiness. This is made still clearer in 2 Thessalonians 1:7–10, where Jesus is depicted as coming with his angels to render vengeance on the wicked and to be glorified in his saints. And in 1 Corinthians 4:4–5 Paul speaks of the Lord as judging, bringing to light both the evil of our hearts and the praiseworthy matters. While the immediate context does not make clear that Jesus Christ is in view, the day of judgment is

---

44. Wainwright, *Trinity*, p. 106.

called "the day of the Lord Jesus" in 1 Corinthians 5:5, and the phrase "the day of our Lord Jesus Christ" appears in 1:8. In 2 Corinthians Paul again speaks of "the day of the Lord Jesus" (1:14), and states that "we must all appear before the judgment seat of Christ, so that each one may receive good or evil, according to what he has done in the body" (5:10).

Paul says little about the final judgment in his later writings. This is of special interest and significance for our purposes here. As Wainwright observes,

> It has often been contended that Paul's high Christology was developed in the later epistles, in which Christ is portrayed as the author and goal of all things. But in the earlier epistles Paul describes Christ as the judge, and this is the mark of a developed Christology. Paul had already accepted a high Christology in the earlier writings, for a high Christology was taught by Jesus himself and handed down by the early Church, the Christology which spoke of Christ as the judge.[45]

Divine Preexistence (Phil. 2:6–11)

There are other passages which speak more directly of Jesus' deity without explicitly calling him God. One which is of especial importance, since it seems to introduce the idea of divine preexistence, is Philippians 2:6–11. This interpretation is not universal, however. A rather influential alternative interpretation is that of James Dunn. He freely acknowledges that *"Phil. 2:6–11 certainly seems on the face of it to be a straightforward statement contrasting Christ's pre-existent glory and post-crucifixion exaltation with his earthly humiliation."*[46] Having acknowledged this, however, he argues that this straightforward interpretation rests on the assumption that Christ's preexistence was taken for granted by Paul's readers; it was, then, not a conclusion from the available data, but a presupposition already accepted. Dunn questions this assumption and the traditional interpretation to which it has led.

---

45. Ibid., p. 24.
46. James D. G. Dunn, *Christology in the Making: A New Testament Inquiry into the Origins of the Doctrine of the Incarnation* (Philadelphia: Westminster, 1980), p. 114.

Dunn's argument, which is fairly involved, includes two major steps. In his view the key question in determining what interpretation to give to a passage is the background that was presupposed by the writer and would have been understood by the readers. He is aware that there is a great deal of disagreement and even controversy over the background of Philippians 2:6–11. Among the issues are whether it is a hymn and, if so, whether it originated with Paul or elsewhere.[47] Rebutting at length the Bultmannian hypothesis that it is of Gnostic origin, Dunn argues that it originated with Paul and is therefore to be understood in the light of what Paul has written elsewhere. On the basis of several other passages which he has already examined, Dunn concludes that a Christology incorporating the imagery of the second Adam was a prevalent and even a dominant theme in that culture, and thus a very likely background for Philippians 2:

> In brief, the most informative and probable background in my judgment is the one we have been sketching in throughout this chapter—that of the Adam christology which was widely current in the Christianity of the 40s and 50s. It seems to me that Phil. 2.6–11 is best understood as an expression of Adam christology, one of the fullest expressions that we still possess. We have already seen how *widespread* was this Adam christology in the period before Paul wrote his letters—a fact not usually appreciated by those who offer alternative exegeses of the hymn.[48]

To bolster his contention, Dunn observes that the imagery developed in Philippians fits well the details of Genesis 1–3.[49] He points, for example, to two sets of contrasts in the Pauline passage: between "the form of God" and "the form of a servant" (between what Jesus was and what he accepted), and between "equality with God" and "likeness to man." What we surely have here is a contrast with the situation of the first Adam, who was in God's image but chose a life of slavery by his sin, and who sought to be equal with God rather than accept the status that God had given him. This imagery is so obviously drawn from

47. Ibid., pp. 98–113.
48. Ibid., pp. 114–15.
49. Ibid., p. 115.

Genesis 1–3 and from the Adam theology which Paul has expounded elsewhere that we must find it to be the basis of Philippians 2.[50]

The other major element in Dunn's argument is the identification of the μορφή ("form of God") of Philippians 2:6 with the "image of God" in Genesis 1. Though "image" was usually translated by the Greek εἰκών, part of Dunn's contention here is that εἰκών and μορφή are to be regarded as synonyms.[51] The reference in verse 6, then, is not to a preexistent possession of the divine nature, but to Jesus' possession of the image of God that Adam had and that presumably all humans have. Thus no preexistence is involved and, for that matter, perhaps no deity either. Paul has in view two stages in Jesus' humanity: his possessing the image of God and taking the role of a servant.

Dunn's argument deserves much more complete exposition than we can give it here. We will, however, evaluate its leading features. His interpretation of Philippians 2:6–11 in light of the theme of the second Adam must be called into question. There is no reference to Adam within the passage. Yet Dunn sees this theme as so pervasive of Paul's thought that he finds it here also.[52] But is it really that widespread? Explicit reference is made to this theme in only two passages: Romans 5 and 1 Corinthians 15. It is only through a process not unlike that followed with respect to Philippians 2 that Dunn finds an Adam Christology in Romans 1:18–25; 3:23; 7:7–11; 8:3, 19–22; 2 Corinthians 5:21; and Galatians 4:4. Since this is the case, he is in real danger of engaging in eisegesis rather than exegesis. Moreover, given the cumulative nature of Dunn's argument, in which each proposition depends upon preceding ones, it is of some interest to note the recurrent use of phrases like "it is probable that," "it is just possible that," "it is likely that," "best understood as," and "presumably it is because."[53] In such a series of individual statements of probability, the probability of the whole argument diminishes with the addition of each new element. The conclusion seems considerably less solid than Dunn is willing to concede.

---

50. Ibid., pp. 116–17.
51. Ibid., p. 115.
52. Ibid., pp. 101–13, 115.
53. There are at least six instances of such expressions in 2½ pages.

Even if Dunn is correct in seeing the theme of the second Adam in Philippians 2:6–11, that does not rule out a reference to preexistence and a genuinely divine nature here. For certainly it was not the human nature of Jesus that was preexistent. The larger issue concerns the status of μορφή, which in large measure turns upon our lexicographical source. If we consult a lexicon dealing with the standard philosophical literature of the classical Greek period, we find a definition in terms of essence, which favors the concept of substantial or essential deity.[54] It seems more appropriate to examine the Septuagint usage, since Paul and his readers would be likelier to have been familiar with that.[55] Here the results are rather interesting. Ralph Martin, following a number of others, concludes that the two terms μορφή and εἰκών are used interchangeably and are therefore nearly synonymous.[56] If, however, Philippians 2:6 is to be identified with Genesis 1:26–27, it would seem that the Hebrew words dĕmût ("likeness") and ṣelem ("image") would have to be identified with μορφή. The Septuagint, however, never uses μορφή to translate dĕmût and only once to translate ṣelem (Dan. 3:19). It is also used to translate four other words. On the other hand, εἰκών is used to translate five Hebrew words, ṣelem being the most common (it translates dĕmût only once).[57]

Beyond this, however, we must ask about the relationship of μορφή in Philippians 2:6 to "equality with God" and "the form of a servant." It appears that there are both a positive parallelism with "equality with God," thus making "the form of God" a strong statement of deity, and an adversative parallelism with "the form of a servant," thus forming a contrast. D. F. Hudson says, "There is a clear pairing of 'the divine nature' and 'the nature of a slave,' and any fair exegesis of the passage which

54. Johannes Behm, μορφή, in *Theological Dictionary of the New Testament*, ed. Gerhard Kittel and Gerhard Friedrich, trans. Geoffrey W. Bromiley, 10 vols. (Grand Rapids: Eerdmans, 1964–1976), vol. 4, p. 752.

55. Paul Feinberg, "The Kenosis and Christology: An Exegetical-Theological Analysis of Phil. 2:6–11," *Trinity Journal*, n.s. 1.1 (Spring 1980): 29.

56. Ralph P. Martin, *Carmen Christi: Philippians 2:5–11 in Recent Interpretation and in the Setting of Early Christian Worship* (Cambridge: Cambridge University Press, 1967), pp. 102–20.

57. Feinberg, "Kenosis," p. 29; Robert B. Strimple, "Philippians 2:5–11 in Recent Studies: Some Exegetical Conclusions," *Westminster Theological Journal* 41.2 (Spring 1979): 260; D. H. Wallace, "A Note on μορφή," *Theologische Zeitschrift* 22.1 (Jan.–Feb. 1966): 21.

tries to avoid the full force of the first, cannot lay any weight on the second."[58] Such an interpretation would, in other words, tend towards Docetism.

There is one other consideration, also of internal import. It is allied to and elaborates our last comment. Marshall says that the recapitulatory phrase, "and being found in form as man" (v. 8), "is very odd if it refers to a person who had never been anything else but a man; again the *contrast* clearly expressed between 'being in the form of God' and 'becoming in the form of men' is extremely odd if the contrast is between two stages in the career of a man."[59]

In light of the foregoing, we find that the traditional interpretation better accounts for the phenomena of the passage, and with less distortion, than do the alternative positions which see in "the form of God" a reference to the image of God in a Jesus who need not be more than human.

We have come now to the end of our investigation of the New Testament witness regarding Jesus' deity. It is probably worth drawing and elaborating upon the distinction between what we might call arguments in which the evidence is added and those in which it is multiplied. In the former case, evidence of various kinds would serve to establish the hypothesis, and the force of each is independent of the others. This is the type of evidence that has been appealed to here. If we have six texts, each of which has a 75 percent probability of being correctly interpreted as teaching the deity of Christ, then, taking them all together, we have a very high probability, unless of course additional texts are adduced which have a probability of teaching that he was not divine. On the other hand, an argument like that of Dunn is like a chain with many links. If any one breaks, the entire chain breaks. Here, if there are six links, each of which has a 75 percent probability of teaching a certain thing, the probability of the whole is less than 18 percent.

Because our argument has been cumulative (i.e., one of addition), we conclude that there is adequate New Testament evi-

---

58. D. F. Hudson, "A Further Note on Philippians ii: 6–11," *Expository Times* 77.1 (Oct. 1965): 29.

59. I. Howard Marshall, "Incarnational Christology in the New Testament," in *Christ the Lord*, ed. Rowdon, p. 6.

dence for the deity of Jesus. That there is not more is not surprising in view of the strong monotheism of the Jews. And finally, unlike those who maintain that there was an evolution, due to outside influences, from a simple human Jesus to the concept of the divine Christ, we find, with Moule and others, that this concept was initially present implicitly and developed in time to an overt and explicit statement.

19

The Uniqueness of Christ: The Resurrection

We noted in our chapter on universalist Christology the contention by theologians like John Hick and Paul Knitter that there is no essential difference between Jesus and other great religious leaders. Thus, any of them may be regarded as equally proper objects of worship and devotion. This facilitates a more tolerant view toward other religions and indeed other cultures. We must now examine that contention more carefully.

Are there characteristics of the person and work of Jesus that set him apart from the leaders of other great world religions, and, for that matter, from the other giants of the Judeo-Christian faith, both in biblical times and since then? It is our contention that such is indeed the case. One of the most significant, probably the most significant of Jesus' distinctive marks, is his resurrection. The position we will take is that the resurrection was an actual occurrence in which Jesus Christ rose bodily from the dead, and that this sets him apart as clearly unique among all human beings who have ever lived.

Several aspects of this matter need to be dealt with. There must first be a consideration of the question of the possibility of miracles. That involves examination of the philosophical issue of the relationship between miracles (or claimed miracles) and natural law. We shall then evaluate the historical evidence for the alleged resurrection of Jesus Christ. Finally, we will need to look at the alternative explanations of the phenomena on which the belief in the resurrection is based.

The Philosophical Issue

Some discussion of the resurrection proceeds as if one could merely by citing historical evidence settle the question of whether Jesus did or did not rise from the dead. Yet, as we shall see, how those historical data are interpreted depends upon the prior conceptions we bring to them. It may be that in some cases the standards which an event must satisfy to be considered actual are such as to virtually eliminate miracles a priori. These prior conceptions are therefore in need of some examination.

By their very definition, miracles are unusual or rare occurrences; they are contrary to the way in which we customarily experience nature. The question is whether we should regard them as statistical anomalies, or deny them altogether because they are opposed to a regularity in the universe that is somehow necessary. In other words, the relationship of miracles to natural law is the real underlying issue.

David Hume's Treatment of Miracles

Probably the most influential or at least the most widely cited treatment of the possibility of miracles is David Hume's essay "Of Miracles" in *An Enquiry Concerning Human Understanding* (Section X). Although introducing variations, many contemporary treatments come back to his basic approach.

In part 1, the main thrust of Hume's argument is that in conducting an inquiry, and especially any historical inquiry, "a wise man . . . proportions his belief to the evidences."[1] A belief founded upon the evidence of infallible past experience can serve as a full proof of future experience. We do not always or even generally work with infallible evidence, however. More often, it is necessary to work with probabilities. We must weigh the experiences counting on either side of an issue.[2]

Hume was, of course, a thoroughgoing empiricist, and in many ways the person who most fully and finally developed the eighteenth-century version of the experiential theory of knowledge. Even in his appeal to witnesses he seeks to abide by the principle of reliance upon experience. The reason we consider their testimonies is that we have observed human reliability and veracity. We have discovered by experience the tenaciousness of memory (at least to a certain degree), the inclination of humans to truth and a principle of probity, and their sensibility to shame when they are detected in a falsehood. We therefore range the witnesses on opposite sides of an issue, considering which side is attended by the greater number of "experiments," and in effect subtracting the testimony on the minority side from that on the majority.[3] In a sense, however, Hume is not advocating merely counting the witnesses but weighing them. Contrary evidence may come not only through witnesses on the opposing side, but also when the witnesses on either side contradict each other, when they are few or of doubtful character, when they have a self-interest in what they affirm, and when they deliver their testimony with hesitation or, on the contrary, with too violent asseverations.[4]

In a situation of probability, there are evidences on both sides of the issue, but a sufficient preponderance on one so that we feel justified in giving it preference. We have a relative confidence; that is, our degree of conviction is less than if there were no contrary considerations. For ordinary types of issues, it is simply a question of which side has the weightier evidence.

But what of the more unusual sort of experience? How are

---

1. David Hume, *An Enquiry Concerning Human Understanding* (LaSalle, Ill.: Open Court, 1949), p. 122.
2. Ibid.
3. Ibid., p. 123.
4. Ibid., p. 124.

these cases to be handled? Here another principle enters. Hume says, "In that case, the evidence, resulting from the testimony, admits of a diminution, more or less, in proportion as the fact is more or less unusual."[5] In the case of an event which has seldom been observed, we have "a contest of two opposite experiences; of which the one destroys the other, as far as its force goes, and the superior can only operate on the mind by the force which remains."[6]

This situation is even more accentuated when the event under consideration is not merely unusual, but actually marvelous or miraculous. No matter how strong and impressive the testimony may be, we must reckon with the fact that it is for a miracle, which Hume defines as "a violation of the laws of nature." This places matters in a very different light: "as a firm and unalterable experience has established these laws, the proof against a miracle, from the very nature of the fact, is as entire as any argument from experience can possibly be imagined."[7] There is a uniform experience against the kind of events termed miracles, and this constitutes a direct and full proof which cannot be destroyed. From these considerations Hume concludes "that no testimony is sufficient to establish a miracle, unless the testimony be of such a kind, that its falsehood would be more miraculous, than the fact, which it endeavours to establish; and even in that case, there is a mutual destruction of arguments."[8]

This is Hume's main argument dealing with the status of claims for miracles. In part 2 of his essay he adduces several subsidiary arguments relating to whether any miracles have actually occurred. These arguments are, in effect, objections to the credibility of the testimonies for miracles:

1. There is not, in all of history, any miracle sufficiently attested by a large enough number of witnesses.
2. The wondrous provokes curiosity and gossip, and even religious persons are given to telling falsehoods to promote that which they believe to be true.
3. Claims of miracles come principally from ignorant and barbarous nations.

5. Ibid.
6. Ibid., p. 125.
7. Ibid., p. 126.
8. Ibid., pp. 127–28.

4. Many religions claim that there have been miracles, and that these wonders were performed by their god. Each of these claims, however, constitutes an argument against the truth of the others. Thus there is a mutually negating effect by the various witnesses.[9]

Antony Flew's Version of Hume's Argument

Because Hume wrote in the eighteenth century, our citing his position may seem like beating a dead horse or setting up a straw man. Before such a conclusion is drawn, however, it is worth noting that Hume's arguments are still being employed to a considerable extent. Indeed, Antony Flew, one of the leading contemporary critics of the biblical miracles, actually presents a strengthened form of Hume's position. Hume suggested that no amount of evidence that a given miraculous event actually happened can ever be stronger than the evidence supporting a law of nature. Thus the event could not and consequently did not happen. Adopting and defending this argument, Flew adds that since each alleged miracle is particular and often singular and in the past tense, it can no longer be directly examined by an inquirer, whereas the law of nature is a general nomological statement. In theory, though not necessarily in practice, it can be tested at any time by any person.[10]

Response to Hume and Flew

What shall we say to such a position? It appears that we have here a case of stipulative definition: the law of nature is stated in such a way that there cannot be any negative evidence. But if such is the case, the issue is settled in advance. In effect, what is being said is that if A is followed by B ten thousand times, and then we have a case where A is not followed by B, the proportion between the occurrence and nonoccurrence of B after A is not 10,000 to 1. Rather, the claimed exception is eliminated, so that the ratio is 10,000 to 0. That being the case, there is no way in which a law can ever be overturned or reversed. This amounts to arguing in a circle. C. S. Lewis put it clearly when he said,

9. Ibid., pp. 128–45.
10. Antony Flew, *Hume's Philosophy of Belief* (London: Routledge and Kegan Paul, 1961), pp. 207–08.

"Unfortunately, we know the experience against [miracles] to be uniform only if we know that all reports of them are false. And we can know all the reports to be false only if we know already that miracles have never occurred. In fact, we are arguing in a circle."[11]

A similar difficulty attends the empirical epistemology which Hume developed. He questioned the concept of cause, noting that it is not really found within our experience. What we have is a constant conjunction of events, but no necessary connection between them. From a repeated sequence of events (e.g., one pool ball strikes another, which then rolls away) we deduce the idea that A causes B, whereas we should correctly say only that A has always been followed by B. What we come to have is a concept of constant conjunction. The idea of cause, as some necessity or force, has been replaced by a psychological disposition, as it were, which expects that A, when it occurs, will be followed by B.

What seems to have happened in Hume's reasoning, and in that of Flew as well, is that this psychological disposition of anticipation has hardened into a necessity. After many instances of A's being followed by B, one anticipates B whenever A occurs, and will be surprised, perhaps very surprised, if B does not follow. What we have here, in effect, is the notion that A must result in B; that is, not-B cannot follow. Any apparent case of non-B after A must be a mistake.

But this is at odds with the predominant present-day view on natural laws. There has been a shift from thinking of them as absolute rules controlling and governing the universe to regarding them as statistical observations. In the era of Newtonian physics, natural laws were thought of as absolute, causing and controlling what happens and what can happen. With the advent of twentieth-century quantum physics, however, this has changed, so that many scientists regard these laws not as absolute, but as statistical. They describe what ordinarily occurs. This means that events that are violations of natural laws can occur; unexplainable in terms of natural laws, such events are regarded as nonrepeatable exceptions to those laws.[12] The German physicist Werner

11. C. S. Lewis, *Miracles* (New York: Macmillan, 1947), p. 105.
12. Richard Swinburne, *The Concept of Miracle* (London: Macmillan, 1970), pp. 3, 27–32.

Schaaffs states that "even the physicist must officially concede the possibility of intervention by God."[13]

Finally, Hume's position seems to exclude by definition the possibility of any intervention or effect within the natural world from some supernatural realm. Natural science formulates laws that describe the normal, customary events within the realm of nature. But what if there is something outside which can exert an influence on nature? That cannot be plotted by natural science.

Apparently aware of this consideration, Flew points out that it involves assuming the existence of a god so that a miraculous occurrence would be plausible. To make such an assumption requires that one "must already be in possession either of a rich revelation or an unusually abundant natural theology."[14] But is this assumption really necessary? A truly historical approach would begin not with the assumption that God exists or does not exist, that miracles have occurred or have not occurred, but merely with an openness to either possibility. We would begin, then, either with no presupposition, or with two opposed presuppositions, with an aim to seeing which of the two can account for a larger amount of the data with less distortion.[15]

There are numerous other objections to the approach of Hume and Flew, such as the misleading statements in part 2 of Hume's essay on miracles[16] and the narrowness of his treatment of research into past events.[17] But enough has been said herein to establish the arbitrary and a priori nature of their argument against miracles.

Historical Evidences

At the beginning of our investigation, we need to note that there is no direct historical evidence for the resurrection as such; there is no claim that any human witnessed the actual event. Rather, the evidence is indirect: the empty tomb and the appearances of Jesus following his crucifixion and burial. There

13. Werner Schaaffs, *Theology, Physics, and Miracles* (Washington: Canon, 1974), p. 66.

14. Antony Flew, in Gary R. Habermas and Antony Flew, *Did Jesus Rise from the Dead? The Resurrection Debate*, ed. Terry L. Miethe (San Francisco: Harper and Row, 1987), p. 7.

15. Habermas, in *Did Jesus Rise from the Dead?* p. 17.

16. Swinburne, *Concept of Miracle*, pp. 15–18.

17. Ibid., pp. 33–37.

are also the significant change in the apostles and the accompanying rise and growth of the fledgling movement of Christianity.

The Empty Tomb

An important first step is to establish Jesus' death and burial. This is foundational to the testimony of the empty tomb, because if Jesus died and was buried and that fact was generally known, the location of his tomb would have been well known to Jew and Christian alike. So the tomb would have had to be empty at the time that the Christian preaching of the resurrection occurred.[18] There are several indications of the reliability and historicity of the burial accounts.

Paul speaks of the burial in 1 Corinthians 15:4. This account represents a very early tradition, for Paul was in Jerusalem approximately six years after the event and conferred with Peter and James. He says in verse 11 that all the apostles preach what he has written here, which upon close inspection appears to be a summary of the sermons in Acts, which must themselves be very early material. Thus it appears that we have a very ancient tradition reflected here.

Further, the scriptural account gives no indication of inclusion of legendary material. Even Rudolf Bultmann, prone as he was to find legend and myth, said of the burial narrative in Mark 15: "This is an historical account which creates no impression of being a legend apart from the women who appear again as witnesses in v. 47, and vv. 44, 45 which Matthew and Luke in all probability did not have in their Mark."[19] Vincent Taylor considers Bultmann's comment "a notable understatement," and affirms, "The narrative belongs to the best tradition."[20]

We should also note that we here have an agreement by more than one tradition. If, as was argued in chapter 16, John's Gospel represents a distinct tradition independent of the Synoptic Gospels, then the agreement between Mark and John is a source of confirmation. The naming of Joseph of Arimathea and the

---

18. William Lane Craig, *Knowing the Truth About the Resurrection* (Ann Arbor: Servant, 1988), p. 64.

19. Rudolf Bultmann, *The History of the Synoptic Tradition*, rev. ed. (New York: Harper and Row, 1968), p. 274.

20. Vincent Taylor, *The Gospel According to St. Mark*, 2d ed. (London: Macmillan, 1966), p. 599.

fact that the description of the tomb agrees with what we know of tombs from that time and culture are additional confirmations that we have a historical account here. Furthermore, it was customary in that time to preserve carefully the graves of Jewish holy men. It is unlikely that the grave of Jesus would not have been carefully noted and observed.[21]

We now turn to the empty tomb itself. It is important to note that several powerful arguments employing the criteria of form criticism indicate that the tradition of the empty tomb is early and reliable:[22]

1. The story is present in all four of the Gospels and in at least three of the sources: Mark, M (special Matthew), and John. The convergence of these sources is impressive.

2. Numerous Semitisms and references to Semitic customs argue that the accounts of the empty tomb are early and originated in a Palestinian setting. Some of these Semitisms are: "on the first day of the week" (Mark 16:2); "an angel of the Lord" (Matt. 28:2); "answering, said" (Matt. 28:5 lit.); and "bowed their faces to the ground" (Luke 24:5).[23]

3. One further evidence of historicity, though not necessarily of early origin, is the fact that women are mentioned as witnesses to the empty tomb. The testimony of women was not admissible in Jewish courts of law.[24] It seems extremely unlikely that the early church, if it made up the account, would have presented women as the primary witnesses.

4. The critical principle that the Gospels reflect in part the *Sitz im Leben* of the early church seems to be violated by the fact that the disciples, the leaders of the early church, are not shown in a very favorable light here. Instead of

21. Joachim Jeremias, *Heiligengräber in Jesu Umwelt* (Göttingen: Vandenhoeck & Ruprecht, 1958).

22. Robert Stein, "Was the Tomb Really Empty?" *Journal of the Evangelical Theological Society* 20.1 (March 1977): 25–28.

23. For a more complete discussion of the Semitisms in these accounts, see E. L. Bode, *The First Easter Morning* (Rome: Biblical Institute, 1970), pp. 6, 58, 71.

24. C. F. D. Moule, ed., *The Significance of the Message of the Resurrection for Faith in Jesus Christ* (London: SCM, 1968), p. 9.

being the first witnesses of the empty tomb, they are in hiding. It is difficult to explain this portrayal of the disciples if the account was fabricated to meet the needs of the early church, which presumably included establishing the authority of its leaders.

5. The disciples' proclamation of the resurrection, coming as soon as it did after the crucifixion, and occurring in Jerusalem, is difficult to explain if the tomb was not indeed empty. Certainly all that would have been necessary to refute the claim and to vanquish Christianity as a religion and a way of life would have been to simply point out the tomb, still closed and sealed. A more radical step, but certainly effective, would have been to exhume the body and display it to the populace. Neither of these steps was taken, presumably because the tomb was indeed empty at this time. Certainly, if the tomb had not been empty, the disciples would not have been so bold as to make this claim in the very locale where the events of Jesus' arrest, trial, crucifixion, and burial were well known. And the disciples would certainly have known if the tomb was empty or not. It would have been peculiar at best had they proceeded to preach something they obviously knew to be false.

6. The nature of the Jewish polemic against Christianity also presupposes the empty tomb. Matthew tells us the response made by the Jews: the disciples had come and stolen the body. Rather than denying that the tomb was empty, the Jews found it necessary to offer an explanation of its being empty. Indeed, Matthew gives indication that this explanation was still being circulated at the time of his writing: "and this story has been spread among the Jews to this day" (28:15). The best explanation for the polemic's taking the particular form which it did is that the tomb was empty, and the Jewish leaders knew that to be the case.

7. In our discussion of Jesus' burial, we noted the Jewish practice of venerating the graves or burial places of holy men. This custom plays a part here as well. For there would surely have been some veneration of the burial place if Jesus' body still lay there. The absence of any

such account is another testimony to the fact that the
tomb was empty.[25]

8. That the tomb is referred to as that of Joseph of
Arimathea helps give it definite identification. It was not
merely some tomb somewhere. The possibility of mistak-
ing some empty tomb for that in which Jesus had been
laid was virtually eliminated by this specification. Clearly,
the disciples were willing and perhaps even eager to have
the place of the burial positively identified.

There is additional significance to the mention of
Joseph of Arimathea, namely the support it lends to the
historicity of the account. Had this been a fabricated
account, it seems unlikely that a major role would have
been accorded to someone who occupies no significant
place in the later life of the church. It is difficult to see
how the mention of Joseph can be correlated with the
Sitz im Leben of the church. It is noteworthy that some
critics who reject the account of the empty tomb as a late
apologetical construction acknowledge the historical
connection of Joseph of Arimathea with Jesus' burial.

Much is sometimes made of the fact that Paul does not specifically mention the empty tomb. Might this be an indication that
this element of the tradition was unknown to him because it arose
at a later point? It is true that Paul does not mention the empty
tomb in 1 Corinthians 15, where it would have been a clinching
evidence to those who denied the reality of the resurrection. Some
additional observations need to be made, however, lest we draw
the conclusion that the empty tomb was unknown to Paul.[26]

We need to note that the verbs which Paul uses of the resurrection of Jesus are such as to imply the empty tomb. Although
Hans Grass complains that Paul really should have said καὶ ὅτι
ἐγήγερται ἐκ τοῦ τάφου ("and that he was raised from the grave")
in 1 Corinthians 15:4, it is significant that he does use ἐκ νεκρῶν
ἐγήγερται ("was raised from the dead") in verse 12. The primary
meaning of the verb is "to awaken," which is used here against

25. James D. G. Dunn, *Jesus and the Spirit* (London: SCM, 1975), p. 90.
26. Hans Grass, *Ostergeschehen und Osterberichte*, 4th rev. ed. (Göttingen: Vandenhoeck & Ruprecht, 1970), p. 146.

the background of speaking of death as sleep. Together with ἀνιστάναι, with which it is synonymous, it can mean "to raise upright." It can also have the meaning "to draw out of," as out of a hole.[27] Paul's choice of verb would seem to mean little if he was referring only to some revival of the spirit which did not involve the resurrection of the body. Indeed, as William Lane Craig puts it, if today we were told that someone had died, was buried, and then rose from the dead, "*only* a theologian would think to ask, 'But was his body still in the grave?'"[28]

It is worth noting at this point that the Jews' idea of resurrection was very physical in nature. They would not have drawn a distinction between a resurrection and an emptying of the tomb in which the body had been laid. Earle Ellis comments: "It is very unlikely that the earliest Palestinian Christians could conceive of any distinction between resurrection and physical, 'grave-emptying' resurrection. To them an *anastasis* (resurrection) without an empty grave would have been about as meaningful as a square circle."[29]

We also should take note of the fact that Paul's testimony here reflects a very early tradition, since he was in Jerusalem no more than six years after the events had taken place. Thus he was told of the empty tomb too soon after the fact for any legend to have grown. Indeed, it seems quite likely that in 1 Corinthians 15:3–5 he is quoting an early confession of the church, probably to be dated before A.D. 40, which specifically stated that Jesus died, was buried, and rose on the third day.[30]

The empty tomb is one of the less severely contested points in the issue of the resurrection, but it is important to establish nonetheless. Rudolf Schnackenburg comments, "Most exegetes accept the historicity of the empty tomb, so that this question is not the decisive point in the discussion about the resurrection."[31]

27. Albrecht Oepke, ἀνίστημι, ἐξανίστημι, ἀνάστασις, ἐξανάστασις, in *Theological Dictionary of the New Testament*, ed. Gerhard Kittel and Gerhard Friedrich, trans. Geoffrey W. Bromiley, 10 vols. (Grand Rapids: Eerdmans, 1964–1976), vol. 1, pp. 368–72; idem, ἐγείρω, ἔγερσις, ἐξεγείρω, γρηγορέω (ἀγρυπνέω), in vol. 2, pp. 333–39.

28. William Lane Craig, *Assessing the New Testament Evidence for the Historicity of the Resurrection of Jesus* (Lewiston, N.Y.: Edwin Mellen, 1989), p. 91.

29. E. Earle Ellis, ed., *The Gospel of Luke* (Greenwood, S.C.: Attic, 1974), p. 273.

30. Reginald H. Fuller, *The Formation of the Resurrection Narratives* (New York: Macmillan, 1971), p. 10; and Bode, *First Easter Morning*, pp. 91–93.

31. Rudolf Schnackenburg, personal letter, 21 Sept. 1979, quoted in Craig, *Assessing*, p. 374.

Jacob Kremer says, "By far, most exegetes hold firmly . . . to the reliability of the biblical statements about the empty tomb." He lists twenty-eight prominent scholars who accept the biblical account: Blank, Blinzler, Bode, von Campenhausen, Delorme, Dhanis, Grundmann, Hengel, Lehmann, Léon-Dufour, Lichtenstein, Manek, Martini, Mussner, Nauck, Rengstorf, Ruckstuhl, Schenke, Schmitt, K. Schubert, Schwank, Schweizer, Seidensticker, Strobel, Stuhlmacher, Trilling, Vögtle, and Wilckens.[32] Craig adds Kremer's name to the list, as well as seventeen others: Benoit, Brown, Clark, Dunn, Ellis, Gundry, Hooke, Jeremias, Klappert, Ladd, Lane, Marshall, Moule, Perry, J. A. T. Robinson, Schnackenburg, and Vermes.[33] On the basis of the foregoing considerations, we feel confident in asserting that one who utilizes the methods of modern critical scholarship may conclude that Jesus of Nazareth did indeed die, that he was buried, and that the tomb in which he had been buried was subsequently empty.

The Appearances of Jesus

The Pauline Testimony

The second line of argument concerns the appearances of Jesus to various persons. Records of these appearances, which began on the morning of the third day and continued for some weeks before ending suddenly, can be found in both Paul's testimony and the Gospels. In some ways the most impressive evidence historically is Paul's account in 1 Corinthians 15:3–8:

> For I delivered to you as of first importance what I also received, that Christ died for our sins in accordance with the scriptures, that he was buried, that he was raised on the third day in accordance with the scriptures, and that he appeared to Cephas, then to the twelve. Then he appeared to more than five hundred brethren at one time, most of whom are still alive, though some have fallen asleep. Then he appeared to James, then to all the apostles. Last of all, as to one untimely born, he appeared also to me.

We have already noted that Paul's testimony here reflects an early tradition, information he acquired during his visit with

32. Jacob Kremer, *Die Osterevangelien—Geschichten um Geschichte* (Stuttgart: Katholisches Bibelwerk, 1977), pp. 49–50.
33. Craig, *Assessing,* pp. 373–74 n. 29.

Peter and James probably within six years of the purported events. That so little time had elapsed, and that he consulted with at least two of those mentioned on this list, are powerful arguments for the reliability of the testimony preserved here. A number of characteristics of this passage argue that it represents pre-Pauline, traditional material: the use of the technical terms *delivered* and *received*, the parallelism and somewhat stylized content, the proper names of Cephas and James, the non-Pauline words, and the hints of an Aramaic original.[34] Because this passage reflects a visit within six years of the events and a formula which was already in use in the church, it may take us back almost to the events themselves.

Further, the recounting of an appearance to as large a number as five hundred, most of whom were said to be alive at the time of Paul's writing, is impressive. It seems strange that this is the only mention we have of that appearance, but that may be because it took place in Galilee.[35] Paul's comment that most were still alive indicates that he had personal knowledge of many of the people involved. So it is extremely difficult to dismiss this incident as a mere legend. C. H. Dodd says, "There can hardly be any purpose in mentioning the fact that most of the 500 are still alive, unless Paul is saying, in effect, 'the witnesses are there to be questioned.'"[36] Believing that Paul could never have made this statement if the event had not actually occurred, Craig says, "Therefore, it is nearly indisputable that this appearance took place."[37]

Of further significance is Paul's claim that he also had seen the Lord. We know that this was no peripheral or incidental experience, for in addition to Luke's account (Acts 9:1–9), Paul himself on two occasions retells the story of his conversion (Acts 22:3–16 and 26:9–23). He also refers to it several times in the Epistles (1 Cor. 9:1; 15:8; Gal. 1:15–16), indicating the profound change made in his life by the appearance of Christ to him and the accompanying call to service.

34. Habermas, in *Did Jesus Rise from the Dead?* p. 23. For more complete discussion see Joachim Jeremias, *The Eucharistic Words of Jesus* (London: SCM, 1966), pp. 101–03; and Fuller, *Formation of the Resurrection Narratives*, ch. 2.

35. Craig, *Assessing*, p. 379.

36. C. H. Dodd, "The Appearances of the Risen Christ: An Essay in Form-Criticism of the Gospels," in *More New Testament Studies* (Grand Rapids: Eerdmans, 1968), p. 128.

37. Craig, *Knowing the Truth*, p. 90.

The Gospel Accounts

In addition to the Pauline testimony the Gospels have several accounts of Jesus' appearing after his death. The large number of reports is impressive, as is the variety of settings in which his postresurrection appearances occurred. Many of the persons to whom he appeared were still alive, or at least their immediate disciples were still alive at the time of the writing and circulation of the Gospel accounts. Certainly, if the Gospels' interpretation of these events as appearances of a resurrected Jesus Christ differed in any significant way from what had actually happened, there would have been some protest or correction.

It is worth noting that the Gospel accounts of Jesus' post-resurrection appearances have a number of characteristics which help substantiate their veridical nature. One is that they speak of his appearances to women. As noted earlier, this is a most unlikely feature to have included if the writers' aim was to secure belief, since the testimony of women was not admissible in Jewish courts of law. That women are reported to have been the first to witness the risen Christ is a powerful argument for the reliability of the account. Had this story been created or fabricated, the first testimony to the resurrection would have been given by a man, and preferably one of the prominent disciples.

Dodd points out that a number of the postresurrection passages give indication of being very early in their origin. He sees this particularly in Matthew 28:8–10, 16–20; John 20:19–21; and, to a lesser extent, Luke 24:36–49.[38] It is also notable that the various accounts of Jesus' appearances do not display qualities markedly different from the other narratives in the Gospels. In particular, there is an impressive freedom from the myth which some critics have claimed is present. Dodd summarizes the results of his extensive investigation:

> It has been not unusual to apply the term "myth" somewhat loosely to the resurrection-narratives of the gospels as a whole. The foregoing investigation will have shown that, so far as the narratives of the appearances of the risen Christ are concerned, form-criticism offers no ground to justify the use of the term. The more circumstantial narratives certainly include traits properly described as legendary, but "legend" and "myth" are different categories, and

---

38. Dodd, "Appearances," pp. 103–07, 111–13.

should not be confused. *Formally*, there is nothing to distinguish the narratives we have been examining from the "Paradigms" and other concise narratives on the one hand, and the "*Novellen,*" or "Tales," on the other, which occur in other parts of the gospels, and they merit the same degree of critical consideration, not only in their aspect as witnesses to the faith of the early Church, but also as ostensible records of things that happened.[39]

We should note briefly the tendency of some scholars to dismiss the postresurrection accounts as legends (by which they mean unhistorical accretions upon the facts). They assume that the process of oral transmission produced the growth of legends which appear in the Gospels just as in extrabiblical accounts. A most compelling counterargument is the relatively brief period of time available for the growth of the tradition. We have already noted this factor several times in relationship to the earliness of Paul's testimony. It also relates to the Gospels. We need not repeat here our discussion of the dating of the Gospels (see pp. 388–93). It should be recalled, however, that the trend has been toward considerably earlier dates than were held at the beginning of this century. Thus the plausibility of the argument that the Gospels contain legends has faded. One hundred fifty years ago, Julius Müller challenged David Strauss and his confederates to name a parallel situation where legend has taken hold both in the very region where the events occurred and within a period as brief as thirty years, that is, while eyewitnesses were still alive.[40] That challenge has never been accepted.

Some conceptions die hard, however, so it is worth noting the status of the historical material available to the Gospel student. A. N. Sherwin-White, a historian who focuses on Roman times, has compared the Gospel materials with those usually utilized by researchers into Roman history. They frequently work with sources one or two generations removed from the events, yet are

39. Ibid., p. 133. In a footnote Dodd points out that the term *legend*, as a formal category, does not entail any judgment about the truth of a story, but refers merely to the manner of telling.

40. Julius Müller, *The Theory of Myths, in Its Application to the Gospel History, Examined and Confuted* (London: John Chapman, 1844), pp. 26–29. Appropriate here is Vincent Taylor's oft-quoted remark that if some of the New Testament critics are right, the disciples "must all have been translated into heaven immediately after the Resurrection" (*The Formation of the Gospel Tradition*, 2d ed. [London: Macmillan, 1935], p. 41).

able to reconstruct what occurred. New Testament critics do not realize what invaluable resources they have available to them. There simply was not enough time for legends to have accumulated before the New Testament documents were written. If the New Testament incorporated legends, they must have grown at an "unbelievable" rate, says Sherwin-White. He points to the writing of the Greek historian Herodotus. Even two generations were insufficient in his case for legends to grow and wipe out the foundation of historical fact.[41] Craig points out that if we allow for the usual length of time it takes for legends to grow, we would be in the second century, where the apocryphal gospels are to be found. He comments, "These are the legendary accounts sought by the critics."[42]

Two problems in particular need to be examined before we can leave the question of the Gospel accounts and their witness to the postresurrection appearances. One is the apparent silence of Mark; the other is the seeming lack of agreement among the several Gospels. The problem of Mark is of special importance because standard source-critical theory regarding the Gospels has tended to view Mark as the earliest and most basic of the sources. A record in Mark of postresurrection appearances would be a strong consideration in favor of the historical reliability of the claim. It is now nearly universally agreed that the longer ending of Mark, 16:9–20, does not belong there, not being found in the earliest and best manuscripts. It is clear, however, that the resurrection is important to Mark, for it is mentioned in 8:31; and 9:9, 31. It would seem strange, therefore, if he said nothing about it at the close of his book. As it stands, the Gospel of Mark ends quite abruptly at 16:8; so many scholars believe that originally there was a different ending which probably referred to appearances by Jesus, but which was lost very early, and therefore is not found in any of our manuscripts. We probably cannot determine the answer to this puzzle. Whatever the case, we should view the lack of references in Mark as the absence of a positive consideration in regard to Jesus' resurrection rather than as the presence of a negative consideration.

41. A. N. Sherwin-White, *Roman Society and Roman Law in the New Testament* (London: Clarendon, 1963), pp. 188–91.
42. Craig, *Knowing the Truth*, p. 96.

When we compare the several Gospels with one another, we do find positive evidence. Luke 24:36–43 and John 20:19–20 recount the same event, the appearance of Jesus to the eleven disciples. Since these accounts are independent of one another, their agreement is an indication of historical credibility. While critics may object that there should be more of this type of agreement, only one instance is really necessary to make the point. One genuinely credible appearance is proof enough of the resurrection.

The difficulty becomes more acute, however, when the issue is not the lack of correspondence, but the seeming lack of consistency, or even actual contradiction, between two or more of the Gospels. Contradiction between witnesses in a courtroom setting is a means of breaking down the effectiveness of testimony; the same potential situation exists here as well. George Ladd, who devoted quite a lot of attention to this problem, notes that a certain amount of the apparent inconsistency is simply the normal type of variation one finds among different authors; they are, after all, addressing somewhat different audiences and writing from somewhat different perspectives. Examples here would be the variations in names.[43] Other instances are more serious, however.

Limitations of space prevent our going into all of the seeming inconsistencies.[44] One which has been especially troublesome, however, and therefore requires treatment, is the locale of the appearances. What is striking is that while Matthew and John record appearances both in Judea and in Galilee, Luke seems to know nothing of the Galilean appearances. All of the appearances of Jesus which Luke reports take place in Jerusalem. It should be noted that Luke throughout his writing has a special interest in and concentration upon Jerusalem. The purpose of Acts is to show how a little group of Jewish believers from the capital city of Judaism extended themselves throughout the Roman Empire until a group of Gentile believers was established in Rome itself. Thus Luke devotes some five-and-a-half chapters (21:17–26:32) to Paul's last experience in Jerusalem and its aftermath, even though no new churches were founded at that time and no new teachings given.

43. George E. Ladd, *I Believe in the Resurrection of Jesus* (Grand Rapids: Eerdmans, 1975), p. 84.
44. For a discussion of the major problems see Ladd, *I Believe,* pp. 84–90.

Many contemporary scholars feel it necessary to choose between Jerusalem and Galilee as the site of Jesus' postresurrection appearances. Dodd, however, appears to have held that both locales can be maintained.[45] C. F. D. Moule suggests that there is a case for both traditions.[46] Extensive efforts have been undertaken to harmonize the several appearances in terms of both time and location. Here, as in so many other endeavors, the presuppositions one brings to the task go a long way toward determining the conclusions. In general, the suggested harmonizations have solved more problems than they have created, so that we need not reject the accounts because of seeming inconsistencies.[47]

The Rise of Easter Faith

One further consideration requires attention as we seek to answer this question of the reality of the resurrection of Jesus. It is generally acknowledged that at the crucifixion and immediately afterwards the disciples were a discouraged, disheartened group. They had fled when Jesus was taken away to trial, and their chief actually denied any acquaintance with him. Yet, somehow, from that defeated little handful of followers, the powerful movement of Christianity arose. Somehow their timidity and fear was metamorphosed into boldness and aggressive belief and commitment. What could account for such a change?

It is now rather widely acknowledged that at the very center of the apostles' teaching and preaching was belief in the resurrection of Jesus. Even Bultmann, although he denied the reality of the resurrection, conceded the disciples' belief in it,[48] and similar judgments have been made by Günther Bornkamm[49] and Gerhard Koch.[50] This, however, avoids the crucial issue only temporarily. Belief in the resurrection of Jesus may be what led

45. C. H. Dodd, *The Founder of Christianity* (New York: Macmillan, 1970), pp. 167–72.

46. C. F. D. Moule, "The Ascension—Acts i.9," *Expository Times* 68.7 (April 1957): 207.

47. See Ladd, *I Believe*, pp. 91–93, and Michael C. Perry, *The Easter Enigma* (London: Faber and Faber, 1959), pp. 65–71, for two independently constructed but strikingly similar schemes.

48. Rudolf Bultmann, "The New Testament and Mythology," in Rudolf Bultmann et al., *Kerygma and Myth: A Theological Debate*, ed. Hans Werner Bartsch (New York: Harper and Row, 1961), p. 42.

49. Günther Bornkamm, *Jesus of Nazareth* (New York: Harper, 1960), pp. 180–86.

50. Gerhard Koch, *Die Auferstehung Jesu Christ* (Tübingen: J. C. B. Mohr, 1959), p. 25.

to the rise of Christianity, but what led to that belief? As Reginald Fuller put it, even the most skeptical critic must posit some unknown x which gave impetus to the movement, but what was that x?[51] According to Craig, if one does not allow the possibility of the resurrection of Jesus, the belief must stem either from pagan or Jewish influences.[52]

In the heyday of the "history of religions" school, it was popular to maintain that the resurrection is parallel to certain ideas in various pagan religions. This belief within Christianity, then, was adopted or copied from paganism. In recent years that hypothesis has been largely abandoned by biblical critics. There are two reasons why this is so: (1) the resemblance between the creation account in Christianity and in other religions, which was the centerpiece in the hypothesis of interreligious influence, has been shown to be slight and strained at best; and (2) no direct connection has been established between Christianity and pagan religions.[53]

It must therefore be from Jewish sources that the doctrine of Jesus' resurrection came. At first glance, this seems a fruitful direction in which to turn, for there was a definite belief in resurrection within Jewish thought. The Old Testament prophetic books mention it three times (Isa. 26:19; Ezek. 37; Dan. 12:2). And the literature of the intertestamental period witnesses to a growing belief in resurrection. In Jesus' time the Pharisees held to this view, a point which separated them from the Sadducees. There are, however, two major points of difference between the Jewish understanding of resurrection and what the followers of Jesus taught about him. The Jews believed that the resurrection would occur at the end of history, not within it. They also saw it as involving all people, not just a specific individual. In other words, they believed in what Christians today term the final, general resurrection, but had no place for an isolated individual case apart from that event. Joachim Jeremias says, "Nowhere does one find in the literature anything comparable to the resurrection of Jesus."[54]

---

51. Fuller, *Resurrection Narratives*, p. 2.
52. Craig, *Knowing the Truth*, p. 117.
53. Walter Künneth, *The Theology of the Resurrection* (St. Louis: Concordia, 1965), pp. 50–63.
54. Joachim Jeremias, "Die älteste Schicht der Osterüberlieferung," in *Resurrexit*, ed. Edouard Dhanis (Rome: Libreria Editrice Vaticana, 1974), p. 194.

So the two candidates for the role of the mysterious x which caused the rise of Easter faith have failed, and we still are confronted with the mystery. It would seem that the best and in many ways the only viable explanation is that Jesus really did rise from the dead. Accordingly, Moule issues a challenge to skeptics: "If the coming into existence of the Nazarenes, a phenomenon undeniably attested by the New Testament, rips a great hole in history, a hole of the size and shape of the Resurrection, what does the secular historian propose to stop it up with? . . . The birth and rapid rise of the Christian Church . . . *remain an unsolved enigma for any historian who refuses to take seriously the only explanation offered by the Church itself.*"[55]

Alternative Explanations

We must now look at some alternative explanations which have been propounded to account for the evidence on some basis other than the actual resurrection of Christ. These explanations have gone through a complete cycle. At an earlier period, when there was relatively little dispute about the historical reliability of the biblical materials, alternatives to the conclusion of the resurrection were introduced. Then, however, during the period of greatest skepticism about the Scripture, in the heyday of biblical criticism, it appeared that such alternatives were unnecessary, for the evidence they sought to explain was no longer thought to be genuine. With an increased belief in the reliability of the New Testament documents, however, those who for whatever reason cannot accept the resurrection once again feel a need for alternative explanations. Thus, some of the explanations have been revived, and it may be anticipated that others will come into renewed favor. While some of them have been effectively refuted in the past, they are worth examining again because some persons, unfamiliar with the history of the discussion of the resurrection, may think them valid, and because the nuanced form in which a theory may be presented is not always recognized as a reworking of an old explanation.

55. C. F. D. Moule, *The Phenomenon of the New Testament* (Naperville, Ill.: Allenson, 1967), pp. 3, 13.

The Theft Theory

The theft theory, which is also called the conspiracy theory, is the most ancient of alternative explanations, having been propounded by the Jews within the New Testament period itself. It was proposed by Celsus in the late second century, and responded to by Origen. Eusebius, the church historian, also rebutted it. In more modern times it was advocated by the deists and given special prominence by Hermann Reimarus.[56] According to this view, the disciples stole the body from the tomb and hid it, then proclaimed that Jesus was risen. It is notable, is it not, say the advocates of this view, that there is no claim of Jesus' ever having appeared to an unbeliever?

The theft theory has been criticized effectively on two sets of grounds: moral and physical. The disciples were persons of such moral character that the deliberate promulgation of a hoax seems unlikely. Further, it seems incredible that they, who had been frightened and cowardly at the capture of Jesus, would now preach emphatically what they knew to be a lie, and even risk their lives, eventually dying martyrs' deaths according to tradition.[57] The physical considerations relate to the difficulties of moving the stone and removing the body so quietly that the sleeping guards were not awakened, or else somehow overcoming the armed guards. Indeed, that professional soldiers would all fall asleep on such an important assignment, where their jobs and even their lives depended upon their staying awake and warding off intruders, seems incredible.

The Survival Theory

Also known as the swoon theory or the apparent-death hypothesis, the survival theory maintains that Jesus was alive after the crucifixion and burial, not because he died and was resurrected, but because he never really died. Heinrich Paulus propounded this view in 1828.[58] David Strauss, although he did not himself hold to the resurrection, rejected this theory as

56. Hermann S. Reimarus, *Fragments,* trans. Ralph S. Fraser, Lives of Jesus Series (London: SCM, 1971), pp. 172, 212.

57. Eusebius *Demonstratio evangelica* 3.4–5; William Paley, *A View of the Evidences of Christianity,* 2 vols., 5th ed. (Farnborough, England: Gregg, 1970).

58. Heinrich E. G. Paulus, *Das Leben Jesu als Grundlage einer reinen Geschichte des Urchristentums,* 2 vols. (Heidelberg: C. F. Winter, 1828).

untenable.[59] In more recent years, Hugh Schonfield presented a modified form of the theory.[60]

According to this view, Jesus did not die on the cross; he merely lapsed into unconsciousness and into such a low state of physical activity that he was thought to be dead. In Schonfield's version, his cry, "I thirst," was a signal for someone to pass him a sponge containing a drug which induced this cataleptic state. In the cool of the tomb he revived, then made his way out, appeared to his disciples, and was proclaimed to be risen from the dead. (In Schonfield's rendering of the story, however, a miscalculation resulted in his actual death soon after he regained consciousness.)

The survival theory also presents severe problems, both moral and physical. The moral difficulty is that it makes Jesus a deceiver and charlatan. How someone who taught the sublime ethical truths he did and displayed the moral qualities he did could engage in such a ruse is difficult to understand, and why anyone would follow the teachings of such a person is even less comprehensible. But the physical difficulties are overwhelming as well. Given the description of the crucifixion, and especially the spear thrust into Jesus' side, it is difficult to believe that anyone could have survived this experience. And if he did, how could he then survive in the tomb without medical care? And how could he, in his weakened condition, remove the stone to gain egress from the tomb? Even supposing all of this were possible, would a person in his condition be able to inspire the disciples to believe in his resurrection and to go out to preach it? All in all, the theory is more incredible than the alternative.

The Wrong-Tomb Theory

The best-known expression of the wrong-tomb theory is that of Kirsopp Lake.[61] According to Lake, the women made a mistake and went to the wrong tomb. Since there probably were a number of similar tombs in the burial area, this should not be thought surprising. Realizing the women's error, a young man at the site

59. David F. Strauss, *A New Life of Jesus*, 2 vols., 2d ed. (London: Williams and Norgate, 1869), vol. 1, pp. 408–12.

60. Hugh Schonfield, *The Passover Plot* (New York: Bernard Geis, 1965), pp. 165–82.

61. Kirsopp Lake, *The Historical Evidence for the Resurrection of Jesus Christ* (London: Williams and Norgate, 1907), pp. 247–79.

said to them, "You are seeking Jesus. He is not here." Frightened, they fled. When the "appearances" occurred, the story circulated that the women had found the empty tomb of Jesus. The tomb which the women found was indeed empty, for it always had been. It simply was not the tomb in which Jesus had been buried.

There are several problems with the wrong-tomb theory. One is that it is unlikely the women would have made such an error. They had carefully made note of the tomb, so that they would be able to return (Luke 23:55). Further, not only would the women have made this mistake, but so would the men who came to check the story. That no one ever detected the error seems unlikely if the body still lay in its tomb. Equally unlikely is that the account of the resurrection would have arisen if the religious rulers could have refuted it simply by going to Jesus' tomb and displaying the body. Finally, Lake is very selective in his quotation of the "young man" at the tomb: he cites the words, "He is not here," while passing over, "He is risen."

The Subjective-Vision or Hallucination Theory

The three theories we have examined are attempts to deal with one aspect of the evidence, namely, the empty tomb. Two other theories have been propounded to account for the appearances of Jesus. The first is that the disciples experienced subjective visions or hallucinations. An emphatic advocate of this view was Johannes Weiss. According to this view, the disciples did not actually see a risen Christ, but rather, out of their unfulfilled hopes and their disappointment, they had visions of him. These visions were not so much the basis of their faith as the product of it.[62]

There are several significant psychological objections to this view. For the disciples in their depressed state of mind, in which they did not expect to see Jesus, to have had visions or hallucinations of him is contrary to what we today know of hallucinations, as are the facts that the phenomenon was experienced by more than one person at a time, and in one case by as many as five hundred, in varied settings, over a period of forty days, and then ceased suddenly and finally.[63]

---

62. Johannes Weiss, *Earliest Christianity*, 2 vols. (New York: Harper, 1959), vol. 1, p. 30.
63. William Milligan, *The Resurrection of Our Lord* (New York: Macmillan, 1927), pp. 81–114; Wolfhart Pannenberg, *Jesus—God and Man* (Philadelphia: Westminster, 1968), pp. 95–97.

The Objective-Vision Theory

The objective-vision theory denies that the resurrected Jesus made a bodily appearance to his disciples; rather, he sent them a visual representation of himself as a message. Michael Perry, for example, holds that Jesus experienced a spiritual resurrection and then sent a telepathic vision back to the disciples which caused them to "project an apparition of his body as they had known it."[64] Perry appeals to parapsychology to explain this phenomenon. In regard to the empty tomb he maintains that the body of Jesus was withdrawn therefrom rather than resurrected.

Here the major problem seems to be a moral one. Jesus and God in effect deceived the disciples or allowed them to deceive themselves. In addition, the objective-vision theory runs contrary to the accounts we have and the seeming corporeality of Jesus (Matt. 28:9; John 20:17, 27). There are also problems with the appeal to parapsychology, which is insufficiently developed as a science to be of much help. What parapsychology does suggest in this area, however—that telepathic visions of a dead person may be experienced by people who do not know the individual is dead—certainly does not fit the disciples' situation.

We are faced, then, with both the philosophical possibility that miracles can occur and rather significant historical evidence that Jesus indeed was bodily resurrected.[65] None of the theories which have been formed to account for the empty tomb and the appearances seems adequate, nor does any combination of them. We are forced to conclude that the most reasonable explanation is that Jesus did indeed come back to life again in a bodily resurrection.

64. Perry, *Easter Enigma*, p. 195.
65. Readers will note that I have made no mention of the Shroud of Turin as a historical evidence of the resurrection. This would constitute an example of a kind of evidence, physical traces, which Swinburne says Hume ignores in his treatment of miracles (*Concept of Miracle*, p. 33). I am aware that a number of evangelical apologists, notably Gary Habermas (in *Did Jesus Rise from the Dead?* pp. 27–28) and William Lane Craig (*Knowing the Truth*, pp. 57–61), place considerable stock in this argument, but I have two reasons for not using it. First, the evidence appears to me to be insufficiently clear at this time; and second, it is not necessary nor expedient to appeal to all the evidence. Our discussion has been limited to areas where the methodological assumptions of those who disagree can be either accepted or clearly challenged. In the case of the shroud there are methodological issues related to dating which go beyond the scope of this volume.

20

The Metaphysical Basis of the Incarnation

One of the tasks of systematic theology is to restate theology in a form which is fitting to the current period of the church. This involves finding a medium or a set of concepts which will make the message intelligible to persons of the present age. In the particular case at hand, we will try to construct a defensible metaphysic or theory of the general nature of reality that can be employed to express the idea of incarnation suitably.

Our development of a metaphysical basis for the doctrine of incarnation will follow several steps. The first will be brief sketches of the metaphysics of the earliest Christians and of Chalcedon. This will involve a reprise of some of the issues discussed in our chapter on functional Christology (ch. 9). We will then inquire regarding the nature of metaphysics. That will be followed by a brief examination of the necessity of doing and the

507

criteria for evaluating metaphysics. We will then sketch a general metaphysic within which we will in subsequent chapters develop a specific understanding of the incarnation.

The Metaphysics of Early Christianity

The Metaphysics of the Earliest Christians

For some time it has been fairly customary to hold that the earliest Christians thought of Jesus primarily in functional rather than ontological categories, that is, in terms of what he did rather than what he was.[1] This is natural, for the primary concern of those Jewish Christians was soteriological or redemptive; Jesus had freed them from the human predicament of sin and separation from God. Richard Longenecker sees the early view of Jesus as having developed sequentially. Being by temperament more interested in the dynamic and historical than the static and speculative, the Hebrew Christians had an "initial appreciation of Jesus in terms of his redemptive activity" and then came to a "subsequent understanding of him in terms of his character or essential nature," even though ontological categories had been inherent in their functional thought.[2] R. T. France is reluctant, however, to put it in quite that fashion. To be sure, what was first perceived functionally was then necessarily worked out in ontological terms, since the idea of a man exercising divine functions would have soon stirred the Jews to consider its impact upon their radical monotheism. But while there was a chronological sequence, France emphasizes the complementary character of the functional and ontological: neither can long exist in isolation from the other. In light of this, "it is perhaps unrealistic to speak in terms of a linear progression from one to another."[3] There is little difference, however, between France's position and that of Longenecker, who, when speaking of the Jerusalem Christians' functional conceptions of

1. Oscar Cullmann, *The Christology of the New Testament* (Philadelphia: Westminster, 1959), p. 326.
2. Richard N. Longenecker, *The Christology of Early Jewish Christianity* (Naperville, Ill.: Allenson, 1970), pp. 134–35.
3. R. T. France, "The Worship of Jesus: A Neglected Factor in Christological Debate?" in *Christ the Lord: Studies in Christology Presented to Donald Guthrie*, ed. Harold H. Rowdon (Downers Grove, Ill.: Inter-Varsity, 1982), p. 34.

Jesus, notes that ontological categories were "inherent in the substratum of their thought."[4] Both are agreed that the functional understanding presupposed an ontological basis.

Reginald Fuller likewise does not agree with the contention that the New Testament Christology is purely functional. It is true that there is a great deal of the functional there. Holding to a modified form of the theory of stages in the early church (see pp. 461–63), he acknowledges that especially in the Palestinian and Hellenistic Jewish stages the references to Jesus were primarily functional, either in terms of what he would do or of what God did through him (Fuller's explanations are at times somewhat strained here).[5] In what he calls the "Gentile mission," however, ontic statements began to emerge. Holding to the traditional interpretation of Philippians 2, he notes that in the preexistent state Christ is not pictured as doing anything, but as *being* (ὑπάρχων) "in the *form* (μορφή, denoting not merely function but mode of existence) of God."[6] The Son then takes the form of a man. This, says Fuller, is not merely the function of a man, but "he *is* man, ontically so, prior to his functional activity."[7] Similarly, at his exaltation he does not merely function as *Kyrios*, but is given the name, denoting the being of God himself.[8] Fuller is aware of the charge that this is merely the translation into Greek terms of what the earlier functional Christologies were asserting. He comments: "This is true, but it is not the whole truth. For it is not just a quirk of the Greek mind, but a universal human apperception, that action implies prior being—even if, as is also true, being is only apprehended in action. Such ontic reflection about Yahweh is found even in the OT, e.g., 'I AM' (Exodus and Deutero-Isaiah)."[9]

This last observation is a particularly interesting one. It would be a profitable endeavor to compile the ontic statements that appear in the Old Testament. This would be a suitable test of the purity of the conceptions regarding the difference

4. Longenecker, *Christology*, p. 134.
5. Reginald H. Fuller, *The Foundations of New Testament Christology* (New York: Scribner, 1965), pp. 247–48.
6. Ibid., p. 248.
7. Ibid.
8. Ibid.
9. Ibid., pp. 248–49.

between the Hebrew and Greek mentalities. At any rate, Fuller's comment suggests that conceptions about who and what Jesus was did develop within the New Testament period, and they did not represent the importation of something foreign to the discussion. Rather, they were the explicit enunciations of what was already implicit in early Christian belief. As Longenecker points out with respect to our awareness of reality and its significance, "It is an axiom of human experience that the underlying conviction precedes any adequate or precise expression."[10] He then summarizes his findings as they bear upon the issue we are considering:

1. While the earliest Jewish Christians' Christology was primarily functional, "it presupposed and carried in substratum ontological commitments."
2. Although there was extensive development, even within the Jewish Christian circle, that development was "of the nature of explication and not deviation."
3. The proclamation of Christ in the Gentile mission was "in essentials not unfaithful to the earlier preaching."
4. There was a more than merely implicit continuity between Jesus' self-consciousness, the earliest Jewish convictions regarding Jesus, and Paul's affirmation in the Gentile mission.[11]

Could the church have remained with a simple functional Christology which discussed only what Jesus had done, and not who and what he was? This seems unlikely. For a function cannot be separated from the subject doing the functioning. Inevitably, the question must be raised, "What sort of being could act on behalf of God to forgive sins?" Certainly a tree could not, a dog could not, and for that matter a human being could not do so. Of course, we humans can announce to others that God has forgiven them, but that is not what Jesus did. He claimed to forgive sins himself. It is also true that we as humans have a certain amount of prerogative to forgive sins, namely, those sins which have been committed against us; but it is only that dimension of sin that we can forgive. Insofar as sin, the

10. Longenecker, *Christology*, p. 155.
11. Ibid.

breaking of God's laws, is also against him, we are unable to forgive it. Inevitably the question must arise, "Who is this, that he can forgive sins?" And in fact the Jewish leaders did raise that question (Mark 2:7; Luke 5:21).

A function cannot be free-floating. If it were, it would be like the grin of the Cheshire cat in *Alice in Wonderland*. Sitting in a tree, the cat gradually faded away, leaving only its grin. But a grin without a face is an absurdity. Similarly, a function without a person to perform it is meaningless.

Perhaps we should note the breadth of the issue. Fuller points out that the Hebrews were not as nonmetaphysical as is sometimes thought. In speaking of the Hebrew mentality in general rather than restricting the discussion to whether the first Christians thought ontologically (or at least ontically) about Jesus, the New Testament Christologists have, by implication, broadened the issue of functional versus ontological from Christology to theology proper. To the extent that the argument is that the first Christians could not have thought of Christ ontologically because the Hebrews simply did not think ontologically about anything, evidence for ontological thinking about God will count against the thesis of a purely functional Christology.

And there are, indeed, indications that the people of Israel saw what God did as being very closely tied to who and what he was, and that they understood the latter to be the basis and cause of the former. A few illustrations will help. Through the narratives of the plagues of Egypt runs the theme, "that you may know that I am the LORD" (e.g., Exod. 10:2; 12:12). This is not surprising, for it fits nicely with what God told Moses when he called him to free the people of Israel (Exod. 3:14). A second major example is found in the narrative of the contest between Elijah and the priests of Baal on Mount Carmel. The test was to see whether Yahweh or Baal was God. Only the true God would be able to act when called on (1 Kings 18:24, 36–37). When the priests of Baal proved unsuccessful and then God sent a consuming fire, the people cried out: "The LORD, he is God; the LORD, he is God" (v. 39). The functional had powerful implications for the ontological.

Similar indications are found in the Psalms. Here there is great extolling of God for what he has done. In numerous cases, however, the psalmist praises God for what he is, which is revealed to us by what he has done. For example, Psalm 47:2 says, "The LORD . . . is . . . a great king over all the earth." Psalm 93:1–2 reads, "The LORD reigns; he is robed in majesty; the LORD is robed, he is girded with strength. Yea, the world is established; it shall never be moved; thy throne is established from of old; thou art from everlasting." In Psalm 147, in the midst of reciting the mighty works that God does, the psalmist exclaims, "Great is our LORD, and abundant in power; his understanding is beyond measure" (v. 5). Not only the greatness of God (his natural attributes), but also the goodness of God (his moral attributes), is seen in what God does. The righteousness of God (Ps. 5:8) is seen in his blessing the righteous (v. 12).

The argument that we have been pursuing does not depend upon form criticism, for we are not seeking to determine exactly what occurred historically, but the nature of Hebrew thinking, which certainly was part of the tradition of Old Testament Israel. Enough examples have been cited to demonstrate that the Hebrew people were not incapable of metaphysical thinking, at least when God was involved. And presumably the same could be said with respect to Christ. What would cause difficulty for the Jewish Christians was the conflict between belief in his deity and their strong monotheism.

Let us summarize what has been said thus far. The Hebrews were not incapable of thinking about things metaphysically. That was not their primary concern, however. It is probably significant to observe that there was no guild of philosophers in Israel. There were prophets, and there were priests, and these two groups were the formers of opinion and convention. There were, however, no persons who spent their time reflecting on the ultimate questions about the nature of reality. Nonetheless, it appears that the earliest Christians did have conceptions of Jesus which implicitly included his deity. At a substratum below conscious awareness, to paraphrase Longenecker, they thought of him not only as doing what God did, but as being the kind of person who was capable of divine actions, that is, someone who himself was deity. For a variety of reasons, this preconception about Jesus did not come to consciousness and to discursive discussion. At somewhat later stages, however, as in the writings of Paul, what had been implicit within the earlier belief became explicit. These writings were not, however, formal and systematic treatments of the metaphysical questions. They were, as Fuller puts it, "ontic" but not yet "ontological" statements.

The Metaphysics of Chalcedon

As time went on, additional questions were being asked. One of the contributing factors was the spread of the Christian movement into cultures which were by nature more inquiring and more theoretical in their thinking, particularly that of the Greeks. Another factor was simply the elapsing of time with the consequent maturing of Christian thought. Christians were able to build upon the knowledge they had acquired regarding the nature of things. A shift took place from ontic to ontological thinking. The question "What does that mean?" was being posed in regard to all that was believed, affirmed, and proclaimed. It is one thing to say that Jesus is God and that he is man. What, however, does that mean? On the one hand, what does it mean for the doctrine of God; and what precisely is the relationship between Jesus and God the heavenly Father? Beyond that, however, other questions were being asked, "What does it mean for one person to be both human and divine? How can this be? What is the nature of the two affirmations being made, and how do they relate to one another?" These were not easy questions to answer, but they needed to be answered if the credibility of Christianity was to be maintained. Furthermore, they had to be discussed on a level to which people were not accustomed.

It will probably be helpful to distinguish two meanings of the word *metaphysics*, which correspond roughly to what Fuller calls "ontic" and "ontological" statements respectively. In one sense, metaphysics encompasses any statement about the nature of reality, such as "reality is essentially mental." The technical elaboration of such statements, the probing of their meaning, is metaphysics in the second sense. Any Christian sitting in a worship service in a church sanctuary and believing that there is a transcendent God has a metaphysic. Very few if any of the persons in the congregation do genuine metaphysical thinking about that tenet, however, working out in detail what the nature of God is like, how he is related to the world and its laws, whether he is a single simple substance, and so forth. It is this latter attempt to give the general belief some specific content and interpretation that constitutes "scientific theistic metaphysics." There are several conceptual schemes within which one can pursue this endeavor. For example, one can think of God in the categories of Thomism or Neo-Thomism, using basically an Aristotelian framework. Or one can think about him, equally theistically, in existentialist categories.

To a large extent, the attempts to clothe the bones of a doctrinal belief with flesh are also attempts to give it a concrete expression at a particular time and place in the historical and cultural universe. This is what the theologians of Nicea and Chalcedon and the other councils of that period were doing. They attempted to explain or expound in Greek metaphysical categories the doctrine of the incarnation of the divine-human person. As Fuller puts it, "If the church was to preserve and to proclaim the gospel in the Graeco-Roman world, it had to answer [ontological questions] in terms of an ontology which was intelligible to that world. Its answer to these questions was the doctrines of the Trinity and the Incarnation."[12] What the church did was to take the ontic language of the New Testament, words like θεός, πατήρ, μονογενής, υἱός, σάρξ, and ἄνθρωπος ("God," "Father," "only begotten," "Son," "flesh," and "human"), and explain them in ontological language derived either from Greek philosophy (οὐσία, ὁμοούσιος, φύσις, ὑπόστασις) or Latin (*substantia, consubstantialis, natura,* and *persona).*

We should not, of course, assume that the ontological terms were understood in precisely the same sense by the users of Latin and by those who worked in Greek. For that matter, we should not assume that all persons involved in the discussion had a common understanding of each Greek or Latin term. Some discussions of Greek philosophy assume a monolithic character which belies the history of Greek philosophy, as any student of ancient philosophy knows. There were numerous streams, traditions, nuances of meaning, the two largest clusters being the Platonic and the Aristotelian. In general, however, we can discern some common understandings of the terms in the overall culture.

We need to recognize the appropriateness of what the church did in defining its Christology through the particular metaphysic

12. Fuller, *Foundations,* p. 249.

of its time. It was not doing something illegitimate in stating the message in nonbiblical terms. Sometimes biblical theologians object to the use of any nonbiblical terms or concepts, forgetting of course that on the level of analysis they themselves use many nonbiblical terms. As someone has said, it is amazing how few times the term *Heilsgeschichte* appears in the biblical text (to say nothing of redaction, trajectories, or even Q and Logia). In addition, the objection to nonbiblical concepts assumes that the present-day interpreter of the Bible does so in a sort of ideologically pure fashion, whereas in actuality all of us interpret the Bible (and the historical tradition) from the perspective of our own current presuppositions. It is therefore infelicitous for us to criticize the Chalcedonian fathers for doing their theology from the perspective of fifth-century Greek thought and at the same time fail to recognize our own ideological perspective. Indeed, there is reason to believe that at least a part of the "Hebrew mentality" that has been found in the Bible is twentieth-century pragmatism, existentialism, and other ideologies read into the text by uncritical exegetes and theologians. The task of systematic theology is to interpret the content of biblical revelation anew for each generation, and to do so using terms and concepts appropriate for that era. The conservative theologian insists that during this process special care be exercised to preserve the essence or the basic content of the original revelation.

We may well need to do for our generation what the Chalcedonian theologians did for theirs. This will mean a more current contextualization of the message rather than a decontextualization, which is probably impossible. Fuller is one New Testament theologian who has seen the limits of biblical theology and the necessity of systematic theology. He writes regarding the early creeds of the church:

> We must recognize the validity of this achievement of the church of the first five centuries within the terms in which it operated. It is sheer biblicism to maintain that the church should merely repeat "what the Bible says"—about Christology as about everything else. The church has to proclaim the gospel *into* the contemporary situation. And that is precisely what the Nicene Creed and the Chalcedonian formula were trying to do. "The Definition of Chalcedon was the only way in which the fifth-century fathers,

in their day, and with their conceptual apparatus, could have faithfully credalized the New Testament witness to Christ."[13]

Before we too quickly dismiss the Nicene and Chalcedonian formulations, we should note that they are fifteen to sixteen centuries closer to the New Testament than we are, and to some extent the tradition in which they stand is closer to that of the New Testament writers. For with all of the varieties of Greek thought and all of the development that had taken place in the three to four centuries since the New Testament, some of the marks of what may be called classical culture still prevailed, such as a certain view of the universe or of the nature of and tests for truth. It may therefore be that fourth- and fifth-century Christians understood somewhat better than do we, despite the progress in methods of biblical interpretation, certain facets of the meaning of the biblical message. So we must ask several questions: What are the essentials affirmed in the Scripture? To what extent is the Greek culture that became available as a vehicle of the revelation actually incorporated into or endorsed by the revelation? and To what degree, then, is the form as well as the content normative?

In selecting a contemporary medium for reexpression of the message, we must be certain that there is minimum distortion of the concepts. And since we are doing systematic theology, we will need to choose our set of thought forms for their ability to convey the whole gamut of biblical concepts, not merely those of Christology. It will not do to have one metaphysic for the exposition of the doctrine of God and another for the doctrine of the person of Christ.

The Nature of Metaphysics

We must now attempt to gain a general overview of metaphysics. We have suggested that metaphysics is the search for ultimate principles that explain the nature of what we apprehend to be reality. A number of positions are possible, and there

13. Ibid., pp. 249–50. The quotation at the end of the paragraph is from Hugh Williams Montefiore, "Towards a Christology for Today," in *Soundings: Essays Concerning Christian Understanding*, ed. A. R. Vidler (Cambridge: Cambridge University Press, 1962), p. 160.

is occasional overlap between them. All of them focus on a few basic issues:

1. *The status of the perceivable world.* Presumably all of us would acknowledge that through our senses we are aware of a set of entities surrounding us. While some would deny the objective reality of these entities, and thus the objective validity of sense perceptions, most would be in this case commonsense realists, holding that the entities have some real existence. The crucial question is whether this system, nature, is the whole of what there is and self-sufficient, or whether there is something else or something more, that is, something *super*natural. The two opposed views, then, are naturalism and supernaturalism. In practice, however, the issues are more complex than this. For that which is more than nature may not be merely outside or beyond or above it. It may also be within it. This is the position, for example, of various types of emergent evolutionism (the theory that new entities are arising from creative forces within the evolutionary process), as well as of certain views that see God as entirely immanent within nature, which begin to approach or actually merge into pantheism.
2. *The unity or multiplicity of reality.* Another key question is whether all reality can be reduced to one type or one level. Is there in actuality a qualitative difference between what may seem to be two different types of reality, or are they merely two manifestations of the same thing? The issue here is really monism versus dualism.
3. *The nature (or dominant nature) of reality.* Our view of the nature of reality depends in part on whether we believe it has more than one aspect or component. Where reality is believed to be of one type, we have either absolute idealism or absolute materialism (sometimes called reductionism). Where reality is believed to be of two types, but one is dependent upon or derived from the other, we have either realistic idealism or epiphenomenalism.

It should be now be apparent that there is a considerable complexity of positions. We may simplify somewhat by examining the different meanings of two key terms, idealism and realism, which have often been seen as opposed to one another.

In a now classic article, Arthur Lovejoy described several different emphases within the pragmatic movement, each of which could be developed into a basic philosophy.[14] Hence two "pragmatists" might have quite different overall conceptions, and some who would identify themselves as pragmatists might be claimed by some other schools of thought as well. While there is not quite this wide variety of idealisms, there are several types. They have been classified and described quite accurately and concisely by Edgar Sheffield Brightman, who was himself an adherent of Lotzean idealism:

1. Platonic idealism holds that value is objective, its origin and meaning being more than human.
2. Berkeleian idealism maintains that reality is mental. There is no reality that is not mental, and anything seemingly nonmental is that in appearance only.
3. Hegelian idealism emphasizes that reality is organic. All of reality is interconnected, and the reality of the whole exceeds that of the parts in the sense of having properties which the individual components do not.
4. Lotzean idealism affirms that reality is personal. Only persons or selves are ultimately real.[15]

According to this classification system, any philosophy is to be termed an idealism if it affirms one or more of these tenets. There may be combinations. For example, the Hegelian or organic view (what is usually termed absolute idealism) also affirms that reality is mental, although this affirmation differs somewhat from the Berkeleian position. In Hegelianism all of reality is indeed mental; but the mind that is doing the thinking, and whose thoughts make up the individual entities and occurrences of our world, is not some individual mind, but the mind which constitutes the whole. Much confusion can be avoided, however,

---

14. Arthur O. Lovejoy, "The Thirteen Pragmatisms," *Journal of Philosophy* 5 (16 Jan. 1908): 29–39; the article was reprinted in Walter G. Muelder and Laurence Sears, eds., *The Development of American Philosophy* (Boston: Houghton Mifflin, 1940), pp. 404–10.

15. Edgar Sheffield Brightman, "The Definition of Idealism," *Journal of Philosophy* 30 (1933): 429–35.

by keeping Brightman's schematism in mind. Frequently, references to "idealism" have in view one of his four classes. In the nineteenth and early twentieth century, for example, idealism usually meant Hegelian idealism.

Realism is also a complex variety of conceptions. What all of them emphasize, as over against idealism, and especially Berkeleian idealism, is the actuality of the physical world and of physical objects. The more technical versions of realism emphasize that material objects exist independently of anyone's perceiving them. We might briefly distinguish four basic types of realism:

1. Naive realism is probably the view of the vast majority of persons in the Western world. They eat, kick, sit on, and do all sorts of other things to physical objects as though they are real, without giving a second thought (or perhaps even a first thought) to the matter.

2. Commonsense realism is the Scottish realism introduced into American thought by John Witherspoon and James McCosh, both presidents of Princeton University. Representing commonsense views of God and the world, and emphasizing a dualism between the two, it had little relation to modern realism.

3. New realism arose as a protest against the idealist conception that the existence of an object depends upon its being perceived. The new realists also insisted that in perception we directly know the object; that is, knowledge of the object is not mediated to us through an idea which functions as a kind of third entity between the subject and the object of knowledge.

4. Critical realism saw the view of the new realists as naive realism. The critical realists emphasized an epistemological dualism involving material objects and ideas. We know the ideas directly, and the material objects are then inferred from them. In many ways, critical realism is compatible with and overlaps certain types of idealism.

Increasingly, realism came to be distinguished by its epistemological concerns. It was, however, first and primarily a metaphysic, or a theory of reality, from which its theory of knowledge followed.[16] William Montague has distinguished three types of realism, using a morphology analogous in many ways to Brightman's classifications of idealism:

1. Existential or particularistic realism maintains that at least some of the *particulars* of which we are conscious exist even when we are not conscious of them, that is, their existence is independent of their being perceived or thought.
2. Subsistential realism holds that at least some of the *essences* or *universals* of which we are conscious subsist even when we are not conscious of them.
3. Presentative realism affirms that at least some of the particulars as well as the universals that are real are apprehended directly rather than indirectly through copies or mental images.[17]

We have alluded to the areas of overlap or commonality between realism and idealism. It is interesting to note that both Platonic idealism and subsistential realism claim Plato and his philosophy as their own. In addition, a view which holds to the objectivity of values, and stresses the importance of the personal, while insisting that material objects have reality independently of any human consciousness of them, can, depending upon one's emphasis, be termed either realism or idealism. Platonic and Lotzean idealism is quite compatible in many ways with critical realism. And, as we shall see, it is also compatible with biblically revealed theism.

The Necessity of Doing Metaphysics

We must ask ourselves at this point whether it is really necessary to engage in this type of metaphysical activity, that is, to have a metaphysic in the second or more technical sense. Here a

16. It is, in my judgment, extremely difficult to separate metaphysics and epistemology, and to assign priority to one over the other. To arrive at a conclusion about the nature of what is known, one must have a conception of how knowledge is gained. Conversely, in order to know how we know, there must be some conception of the nature of the objects known.

17. William P. Montague, "The Story of American Realism," in Muelder and Sears, *Development of American Philosophy*, pp. 421–24.

parallel in another field may help us to focus more insightfully upon the issue.

In a sense, all functioning adults, and for that matter children old enough to manage their own financial dealings, have a theory of economics. It may not be very well worked out, and may in fact be almost entirely implicit, but there is a theory nonetheless. Financial dealings are based upon one's understanding of concepts like value and exchange. Inflation is somewhere, at least crudely, factored into decisions about whether and what to purchase.

When, however, we become more reflective about the earning and expending of money, we begin to realize that there are complicating factors, and our thoughts necessarily range into ever-broader contexts. For example, if we work for a small manufacturer, and sales have not been good, the chances for a substantial wage increase are not favorable; indeed, the potential for continuing employment may even be in jeopardy. New competitors entering the field, or a competitor's introducing a lower-priced product of equal quality, or a comparably priced product of superior quality, will certainly also alter our employer's potential for profit. Eventually we may even become sophisticated enough to decide on the purchase of a larger home only after studying the impact which the exchange rates of international currency will have upon our earnings. This may in turn require making a choice among macroeconomic theories. Thus the increasing sophistication of the decisions involved in everyday living will result in our asking broader and broader economic questions.

In similar fashion, the increasingly penetrating questions that grow out of practical life situations lead us to hypotheses of expanding inclusiveness, and ultimately we begin to ask about the nature of reality or of the world. Indeed, the economic inquiry that we just described will eventually reach that point. It all depends on how far we are inclined to go in seeking answers to our questions.

Stephen Pepper has described the process of expanding the range of our concerns and inquiries as "structural corroboration." This he contrasts with "duplicative corroboration," where, either through observation or experimentation, one tests a particular hypothesis repeatedly, or several persons add their experiences together. Duplicative corroboration lends itself to scientific-type situations where the hypothesis can be put to a test. Suppose, says Pepper, we wish to assess the strength of a chair. Duplicative corroboration would consist of sitting in the chair, and having a number of persons do so, to see whether it actually supports the weight. Structural corroboration, on the other hand, is more inferential. We would in this case take into consideration the type and strength of the wood, the glue and nails used, the reputation of the manufacturer, and any signs of wear which suggest that the chair has been sat on numerous times in the past.[18] Employing this evidence entails a set of hypothetical connections, mostly causal.[19]

Increasing the reliability of a crude hypothesis usually involves giving it greater precision and greater scope. Unless one extends the scope of the hypothesis, it is vulnerable to contradiction by other possible considerations. For example, the signs of wear may have been caused by a very small person who often sat in the chair. In that case, they are not proofs of the strength of the chair. To insure a hypothesis against being derailed by similar considerations, there is a continuous drive toward giving it a greater inclusiveness:

> It thus has become clear that, in the pursuit of reliability, structural corroboration does not stop until it reaches unlimited scope. For as long as there are outlying facts which might not corroborate the facts already organized by the structural hypothesis, so long will the reliability of that hypothesis be questioned. The ideal structural hypothesis, therefore, is one that all facts will corroborate, a hypothesis of unlimited scope. Such a hypothesis is a world hypothesis.[20]

There are, to be sure, those who insist that the duplicative approach is the only proper type of corroboration, the most notable among them being the logical positivists. Their view, which Pepper terms a "conventionalistic hypothesis," has no real value, only utility and beauty.[21] For positivists who claim that

18. Stephen C. Pepper, *World Hypotheses* (Berkeley: University of California Press, 1970), pp. 47–51.
19. Ibid., p. 75.
20. Ibid., p. 77.
21. Ibid., pp. 74, 82–83.

their view has real cognitive value are either being dogmatic, or becoming metaphysicians, and thus they are in effect denying positivism.[22]

The Criteria for Evaluating Metaphysics

Now another major issue arises. How do we go about comparing and evaluating worldviews? There was an extended period in the twentieth century when all proposed answers to this question were regarded as vacuous. It was believed that all-inclusive or synoptic statements could not be meaningful, and therefore there was no way of evaluating their truthfulness. Even Pepper, who argues for the necessity of worldviews, seems to suggest that there may be a number of worldviews which are all equally adequate (he may, however, be speaking only of the evidence as known).[23]

I have found particularly helpful Frederick Ferré's criteria for grading worldviews. He asks whether it is possible to evaluate worldviews, and concludes despite widespread protests that it is possible.[24] He then adapts Charles Morris's semiotic (general theory of signs). Morris speaks of three dimensions of meaning. There is the relationship between the signs within a language system. This dimension is called syntactics. There is secondly the relationship between a sign and that which it signifies; this is semantics. Finally, there is the relationship between the sign and its knower or interpreter; this is pragmatics.[25] The pragmatic dimension of a sign is the degree to which it influences the knower, or, in the case of a worldview, the degree to which one can live by the worldview of which that sign (individual concept) is a part.

The syntactic dimension is the internal relationships between signs. Here there are two criteria for grading worldviews. Consistency is the lack of internal contradiction between different concepts. This is at best a negative test, but an important one, for

22. Ibid., pp. 64–70, 73–74.
23. Ibid., pp. 98–100.
24. Frederick Ferré, *Language, Logic, and God* (New York: Harper and Row, 1961), p. 148.
25. Charles W. Morris, *Foundations of the Theory of Signs* (Chicago: University of Chicago, 1938), pp. 1–9.

in the final analysis we are incapable of believing that which is internally contradictory, and we are certainly unable to communicate it to others. Yet two (or more) concepts or propositions may be free of contradiction simply because they are unrelated. Being drawn from different universes of discourse, they cannot conflict. Thus the second internal criterion, coherence, is necessary. To the extent that concepts are interrelated and contribute to one another, they are the more likely to agree with reality. Both of these criteria, however, could be present in a well-written fairy tale. The absence of consistency and coherence would tend to falsify, but their presence does not necessarily verify.

A second pair of criteria must therefore be considered. These are external criteria dealing with the semantic dimension of meaning, the relationship of a sign or a set of signs to the world as experienced. One of these criteria is applicability, the measure of the ability of a metaphysical system to depict or portray accurately some aspect of the experienced world. In other words, does the system ring true to experience? Yet presumably all worldviews are applicable to some segment of experience. If this were not so, they would not be believed and adhered to by anyone. Adequacy is the measure of the ability of a worldview to account for or give an intelligible rendition of the widest possible sweep of experience. If a particular worldview describes a wider span of reality as we experience it than do other worldviews, then it is entitled to be graded higher than its competitors.

A Theistic Metaphysical Scheme

We may now begin to sketch an overall metaphysical scheme consistent with and indeed derived (at least implicitly) from the biblical revelation, a scheme which can be utilized as a basis for developing an incarnational Christology for today. It will not be our primary task in this chapter or elsewhere in this work to demonstrate the truth of the Christian worldview by using the criteria delineated above. That is more the task of apologetics than of theology. It is sufficient for us to show how one would go about vindicating the adoption of this particular worldview, and to indicate how this metaphysic alleviates the conceptual difficulties of the doctrine of the incarnation.

There is a fundamental dimension of the Christian worldview which has much in common with certain types of idealism, especially objective and personalistic idealisms. That is the affirmation that the most basic fact about reality is the spiritual (idealists use the term *mental*). The Supreme Being, the source of all that is, the one unoriginated and independent entity in the entire universe is a spirit, God, the infinite Spirit. Everything else, including the material universe and all other selves or spiritual beings, derives from him through the act of creation. This was a voluntary act of God by which, without the use of preexisting materials, he brought into existence everything that is. In terms of the first set of categories that we sketched above (p. 517), we have here a supernaturalism rather than a naturalism. While not denying either the reality or the value of nature and the created world, this view affirms that all that is other than God is, both as to origin and nature (existence and essence), derived from him, dependent upon him, and subject to his ultimate control and direction.

On the issue of simplicity or duality of reality, Christian theism gives a somewhat paradoxical answer—contingent dualism. For there was a time when monism of a spiritual type obtained. There was a point, before creation, when God—Father, Son, and Holy Spirit—was all that there was, and it had always been so. There never was a time when this Triune God did not exist, but there was an eternity before anything else came to be. Then, however, God created, bringing into existence the material world. At that point reality became dualistic. This is a contingent dualism, however, for although God exists necessarily (i.e., he cannot not exist), all of the creation exists only contingently. It could cease to exist, and would, were it not for God's continued willing of its existence and his continued action to keep it in existence. Not only physical objects but values as well are derived from God. He is the creator and sustainer of values. He supports them, not by an arbitrary decision that certain values shall be approved (or "good") and others disapproved (or "bad"), but rather as an expression of his very nature. Truth is a good, not because that is what God decided from among a number of options, but because his very nature is truth, and he has commanded humans to be as he is (Lev. 19:35–37).

The biblical metaphysic, at least as we construct it, is also a type of idealism having common grounds with realism, particularly critical realism. This form of idealism has sometimes been termed "objective idealism," which H. B. Acton defines as "idealism that is antinaturalist without being antirealist."[26] The genuineness and goodness of the creation are underscored in Genesis 1, especially the account of God's surveying his work after several steps in the process and seeing that it was good (vv. 12, 18, 21, 25, 31). Nature, although created by and dependent upon God, is not simply a part or aspect of him. It is other than him, distinct from him.

The key to understanding this whole scheme is to realize the special status and role of persons. For the supreme person or self, God, completed his creative work by bringing into existence finite persons, that is, humans. That they are the crowning element in his creation is indicated by several considerations: (1) they alone are spoken of as created in his own image and likeness (Gen. 1:26–27); (2) it is only after they are created that God pronounces the creation not merely good, but *very* good (v. 31)— although it could be argued that it is not the creation of humans but the completion of creation that brings out this higher assessment, the fact is that the creation is incomplete without humans; (3) only humans seem to have interaction and communion with God; (4) human need is presented as the reason for the incarnation; and (5) Jesus placed a higher value on humans than on other creatures (Matt. 10:31). Persons, then, are the key to understanding the whole of reality.

The significance of human persons can scarcely be overstated. For although they share with the rest of the creatures the fundamental qualities of creaturehood, namely finiteness and the various limitations which that entails, they are uniquely like God. The full signification of the image of God is not elaborated in Scripture. It certainly seems to involve the qualities of personhood, in particular the ability to relate meaningfully to and interact with other persons, including God. It also evidently involves to a limited extent the moral qualities which God manifests, such as love, mercy, and patience. If this were not the case, it would make no sense for him to command us to be like him. To be noted as well is that this complex of characteristics which constitutes the image of God and distinguishes humanity

26. H. B. Acton, "Idealism," in *The Encyclopedia of Philosophy*, ed. Paul Edwards, 8 vols. (New York: Macmillan, 1967), vol. 4, p. 110.

as a species is more significant than the variations which separate them or distinguish them from one another. The image of God is universal; it is present in all humans regardless of race, nationality, gender, and age. We also know that it remained, although in a somewhat impaired form, even after sin entered the human race at the time of the fall in the Garden of Eden, for God later prohibited murder on the grounds that humans are made in the divine image (Gen. 9:6).

The disruption of the creation because of human disobedience is a major factor in our metaphysical scheme. Sin, which can be either active transgression of God's laws or passive failure to fulfil his will, ruptured the close fellowship which God and his highest creature had with one another. As a result of sin, there is an obscuration of the human understanding; and this obscuration, as Emil Brunner put it, is greatest in those areas where our relationship with God is most directly involved.[27] The effect is more than merely intellectual, however. The emotions, the will, the entire person, are oriented away from loving God and doing his will. This condition must be overcome if there is to be the sort of relationship with God for which the human was originally intended.

The debilitating effect of sin extends not only to the human, but to the entirety of the creation. In Genesis 3 God pronounces curses which are manifested at least in part in disruptions of the normal conditions of nature. In addition, Paul speaks of the whole creation's groaning and travailing, waiting for deliverance from the bondage to which it has been subjected (Rom. 8:18–25). Part of the events of the last days will be the renewal of the creation.

Another significant feature of our metaphysical scheme is God's continued relationship to and his care and direction of the creation. Although God is high above and beyond this universe, he is also immanent within it. Particularly through the mediation of the Holy Spirit, the Triune God is present and active here. He has not totally lost contact with any human being. And in the case of the believer, the Holy Spirit in some mysterious sense inhabits the person. Despite the activities of ungodly per-

27. H. Emil Brunner, *Revelation and Reason* (Philadelphia: Westminster, 1946), p. 383.

sons, God is providentially at work directing history so that his plans are fulfilled. History is moving toward a goal. It is linear in that sense. It is not moving in cycles.

We have examined the overall metaphysical scheme of Christian theism. Now we need to look briefly at the components of reality. The classical tradition had a concept of substance. There were widely differing understandings of this concept, so any characterization will be a gross oversimplification.[28] Nonetheless, it is clear that for a long period Western philosophy held the general idea that everything has a substance, a sort of underlying substratum, to which various attributes or accidents attach or adhere. The accidents might change, without affecting the substance. Thus a person might grow taller, older, and grayer, but still be the same human being; and a metal might change size and shape, but still be the same substance. It was common in the Western theological tradition to speak of material and spiritual substances.

In some ways, this scheme has been rendered problematic by Einsteinian physics. For we now understand that the material world is not as solid as we once thought. Matter now is understood as consisting of minute electrical charges in orbit around nuclei containing charges of opposite polarity—at least that is what we think is the case. And matter is not as fixed as we once thought either. Matter and energy are now understood to be convertible. Matter, if accelerated to the speed of light, becomes energy.

In many ways, the universe is now thought of as basically dynamic rather than static in character. This observation has led some, such as the process theologians, to consider all things to be in flux. This seems to be an unnecessarily extreme adjustment. For there needs to be some underlying basis of continuity in all that is in process. Yet at the same time there needs to be an understanding that God is not the static, unmoving, unfeeling being that he was thought to be by the classical theological tradition dominant in the Middle Ages. We will develop this concept later on (pp. 541–44). At this point we need merely

---

28. The reader is reminded of the caveat regarding the phrase *the Greek idea of___*. One essay question on the metaphysics section of the author's M.A. comprehensive examination at the University of Chicago involved tracing the history of the concept of substance in Western philosophy.

observe that the clash between a dynamic, acting, responding creation and an objective, eternal, unchanging God is not so great as might be thought.

We have said that the most significant aspects of reality are persons, selves, subjects. This means that we should think of ourselves not so much as substances with attributes, but as subjects who display certain characteristics. These characteristics should not be thought of as some sort of external predicates added to a substance, but as discernible qualities of the person; they are ways of understanding and thus of describing the individual. In a sense, we are not even subjects with attributes attached, but the whole set of qualities which go to make up what we are, including both past and future qualities and all of our thoughts, actions, experiences, and relationships. This does not mean, however, that we are simply a bundle of predicates. What must be stressed is that each of us is a person, a subject; and everything we are, have been, and will be, is part of that person.

In some ways this approach is closer to the classic view of Plato than to that of Aristotle. Unlike the substance-attribute schematism of Aristotle, Plato's view saw each individual existent as an instantiation of a form or idea. Each individual horse, for example, was a particular instance of the form of "horseness." It participated in or reflected the idea of horse.[29] Difficulties, of course, arise for Platonism because it seems that a particular may participate in more than one form (e.g., horseness, blackness), and the relationship of the particular to these forms is unclear at best. A possible way out of these difficulties is to think of each human person as the instantiation of a form of which there is and can be only one instance.[30] Thus I am the instantiation of the form or concept of Millard J. Erickson. This is a concept which God holds and which he has used as the pattern for creating me, bringing me into life, and directing the events of my

---

29. The idea of horseness is not a horse, nor is the idea of redness red. Rather than possessing the qualities of its particulars, the form or idea is like a formula specifying those qualities, just as the mathematical formula for a curve is not itself curved, nor is the chemical symbol NaCl salty. The author has expounded this interpretation in "Platonic Forms and Self-Predication: A Critical Examination of Gregory Vlastos' Interpretation of the 'Third Man' Argument in the *Parmenides*" (master's thesis, University of Chicago, 1958).

30. Identical twins may pose a difficulty until one realizes that each person is the whole set of qualities and experiences he or she will ever have.

life. There are obvious parallels here to Gottfried von Leibniz's view that from the realm of essences God chooses certain individuals to actualize or bring into the realm of existence.

Viewing the person or the subject as the individuating factor may work in the case of humans, but what of nonpersonal members of the creation, including the inanimate? Here we may speak of each creature as being the set of qualities and the history which it has, but what gives it identity metaphysically? What separates each sparrow or sheep from all the others? The concept of subject or person certainly does not apply in such cases. Could it not be that God's knowledge of each individual creature, his thinking specifically of it rather than any other, gives it metaphysical identity and coherence?

A rather crude illustration may be of some help here. It is not necessarily the case that all portions of a computer file are entered in contiguous sectors on the floppy disk. Since there may already be some other files on the disk, and still others may have been erased earlier, portions of the file in question may, because of constraints of space, be entered in scattered locations. The computer, however, can pull the bits and bytes together and present them as a coherent file. In the same way, the mind of God knows, records, and can pull together into a coherent whole the various qualities of each individual thing. Consider the references to God's will for the individual sparrow (Matt. 10:29) and his knowledge of each of his sheep (John 10:14).

We need to be careful in our thinking at this point. For we are not saying that the impersonal members of the creation exist only as thoughts in the mind of God. Nor are we saying that they would not exist if neither he nor anyone else were conscious of them (although quite possibly God cannot not be conscious of everything). What we are saying is that the locus of their identity, that which causes the whole set of predicates that constitute each individual to cohere, is the concept in the mind of God. That concept is instantiated in the impersonal creature. Thus our metaphysical scheme can accommodate each and every member of the creation.

The Logic of the Incarnation (1)

The Nature of the Issue

As usually understood in orthodox theology, the doctrine of the incarnation involves the idea of Jesus as both fully God and fully man, possessing all of the attributes of each. This appears to be a logical contradiction of very great proportions. It seems to affirm that one person has diametrically opposite qualities at the same time and in the same respect. Jesus is infinite and finite at the same time and in the same respect. He is omniscient, knowing all things; and yet he is unaware of some truths and has a finite intelligence quotient. He is omnipresent, being everywhere, and yet limited to the location occupied by a human body. He is able to do anything, yet has limits upon his physical strength and other capabilities. There often is a moral or spiritual factor complicating this analysis as well. God is perfect and sinless, and indeed cannot be tempted, according to James 1:13.

531

Humans, however, all sin, or at least all are tempted, according to 1 Corinthians 10:13. The idea of a genuine incarnation therefore violates one of the most basic laws of logic and consequently would seem to be an impossibility.[1]

Some Classic Responses

Faced with this difficulty, theologians have developed a number of responses, some of which have taken on virtually classic form. All of these responses have been treated to some degree in earlier parts of this writing, so only the most basic of treatments will be given here.

Docetism, probably the earliest of these attempts, solved the problem by denying the reality of one factor or component, the human. It maintained that while the deity of Christ was genuine, the humanity was only apparent. Jesus seemed (δοκέω in Greek) to be human, but his humanity was something of a phantom. He did not really assume physical human nature, nor did his psyche have the limitations that are common to humanity. When he seemed not to know certain matters, he was only pretending.

The second major attempt to respond to the problem is Adoptionism. This approach regards Jesus as fundamentally a human being who at some point in his life was favored by God to the point of being received into a special status and relationship with him which are not true of any other human being. In some sense, Jesus became the Son of God. In general, the concept of preexistence is foreign to Adoptionism.

A third approach is that known as kenotic Christology. This takes its name from Philippians 2:1–11, and especially verse 7, which says that Jesus emptied himself" (ἐκένωσεν in Greek). There are varying degrees of this view, but all approach the logical problem of the incarnation with the idea that in the process of becoming a human, the Second Person of the Trinity divested himself of some qualities of deity, those incompatible with being human, so that it was possible to be genuinely human.

The fourth approach includes all those Christologies which conceive of the deity of Christ in some dynamic fashion rather

---

1. Thomas V. Morris, *The Logic of God Incarnate* (Ithaca, N.Y.: Cornell University Press, 1986), pp. 17–24.

than in traditional terms of his "nature." One of these, very widespread in influence, is functional Christology, which stresses what Jesus did rather than what he was, and sees him as acting on behalf of God, but not actually possessing the qualities of deity. Something of a variation is the introduction of the concept of inspiration into the discussion. Donald Baillie and John Hick, for example, hold that God was at work in the man Jesus in a dynamic way, perhaps not unlike his activity in the lives of believing Christians.[2] "God was in Christ" is a better way of thinking of the incarnation than is "Christ was God." There is in this view, then, no problem over Jesus' supposed two natures, because Jesus was not metaphysically God. Indeed, this view may not even involve itself with the matter of "nature" at all.

These are the four basic types of attempts to maintain in some way or to some degree both parts of the paradox. There are, of course, many for whom the incarnation really is not a problem, for they do not hold to both the deity and humanity of Jesus. They usually have collapsed the tension by rejecting the deity. Of the solutions sketched above, some are not available to us in light of the conclusions we arrived at earlier. The most promising possibility appears to lie in some variation of kenotic Christology carefully defined. Certain varieties of it are not feasible for the ideology we previously developed, so we will advocate here a carefully nuanced position. In doing so, we are conscious that the paradox will probably never be eliminated in this life, but that there are ways in which it can be alleviated.

A Recent One-Nature Model

Before we move on to a constructive treatment, there is one recent approach which because of its creativity and novelty on the one hand, and its avowed determination to retain the full deity and full humanity of Jesus on the other, is worthy of a special examination. In an attempt to preserve both of these elements and yet to avoid falling into logical contradictions, Ronald

2. Donald M. Baillie, God Was in Christ: An Essay on Incarnation and Atonement (New York: Scribner, 1948), pp. 106–32; John Hick, "An Inspiration Christology for a Religiously Plural World," in Encountering Jesus: A Debate on Christology, ed. Stephen T. Davis (Atlanta: John Knox, 1988), pp. 5–22, 32–38.

Leigh has propounded a view of Jesus as possessing one nature, both divine and human.

Leigh believes that his model is simply the most logical and hermeneutically sound treatment of the biblical data. Examining the doctrine that Jesus had two natures, Leigh concludes that it is logically contradictory and thus cannot be rationally maintained. He defines "nature" as that set of characteristics which an individual must have in order to be included in its class.[3] It is not possible, he argues, for an individual to have more than one nature:

> Suppose that nearly all individuals have been classified according to their characteristics. Then an individual is found whose one set of characteristics includes characteristics from two previously established classifications. Even in such a case it would not be appropriate to say that that unique individual has two natures. Every individual is what it is. What it is, its nature, is its set of essential characteristics. Certainly this individual has a unique set of characteristics which include characteristics not previously found together in a single individual. But that does not change the fact that it has one set rather than two sets of characteristics.[4]

Leigh insists that the idea of two natures is not required by Scripture. The New Testament refers to Jesus as God, and it also refers to him as man, but it never explicitly says that he has two natures. This is one way of thinking of him, but it is not the only way. It is an approach which a number of theologians have followed, but anyone who sets out to defend it must be aware that it is merely a theory which past theologians have held, not a view explicitly stated in the Bible.[5]

The problem for any view which maintains that the one person Jesus was both divine and human is, of course, the seemingly contradictory character of such a person. Orthodox theologians have sometimes sought to handle this problem by referring to the relationship of the two sets of traits, limited and unlimited, as an antinomy. This will not do, however, according

---

3. Ronald W. Leigh, "Jesus: The One-natured God-Man," *Christian Scholar's Review* 11.2 (1982): 125.
4. Ibid., pp. 125–26.
5. Ibid., pp. 130–31.

to Leigh. To introduce the idea of an antinomy is neither desirable nor necessary. It is not desirable because it conflicts with the epistemology of evangelical theologians and apologists, who have usually appealed strongly to the law of contradiction as a major test for truth.[6] In addition, it is not necessary, for the New Testament never speaks of the nature of Jesus as an antinomy. While Paul occasionally speaks of "the mystery of Christ," he does not use this term with respect to Jesus' nature, and by "mystery" he does not mean "antinomy."[7]

All of these considerations raise the suspicion that it is best not to think of Jesus as having two natures, but only one. Is it possible, Leigh asks, for one individual to fall properly into two classifications? He affirms that it is. As an analogy, he cites the chair desk, which has sufficient characteristics of a chair and sufficient characteristics of a desk to justify including it in both classifications at once. The most appropriate designation for this piece of furniture, however, is neither chair nor desk, but chair desk. This is a whole new classification. Yet it should be noted that this new classification is not a genuine *tertium quid*. It includes rather than excludes the qualities of the other two classes. The chair desk has whatever essential qualities are necessary for an object to be properly called a chair, and also whatever essential qualities are necessary for an object to be called a desk, even though it is not exactly identical in its essence to all other desks or to all other chairs. There is a consistency between the two classes which is crucial: "The characteristics which qualify it as a desk do not disqualify it from being a chair, and the characteristics which qualify it as a chair do not disqualify it from being a desk."[8]

This is analogous to how Jesus Christ is to be understood. He falls into two classifications at once. It is appropriate to speak of him as God, including him in the classification of deity, because he possesses the characteristics essential to being called God; and it is appropriate to call him man, and include him in the classification of humanity, for he possesses all of the quali-

6. Ibid., pp. 128–30.
7. Ibid., p. 130.
8. Ibid., pp. 131–32.

ties necessary for inclusion therein. Yet he is not some *tertium quid* which is neither God nor human. These are two classes which to some extent overlap. The doctrine of the image of God is of great importance here, because it establishes that these two classifications are not totally dissimilar. Just as there is some commonality between desks and chairs that one would not find between desks and stockings, for example, so there is essential similarity between God and human.[9]

The one-nature approach involves distinguishing the essential from nonessential characteristics of God, as well as of humanity. Leigh says that Jesus was "like the Father *in areas essential to deity* but unlike the Father in some areas nonessential to deity, and like fallen man *in areas essential to humanity* but unlike fallen man in some areas nonessential to humanity."[10] Like the Father, he was uncreated spirit, holy, and personal, but whereas the Father is unembodied, omniscient, and omnipotent, he was embodied, nearly omniscient, and nearly omnipotent. Like fallen humanity, he was personal and embodied; but he was not created spirit, sinful, nearly ignorant, or nearly impotent.[11]

Leigh believes that the problem with the two-nature model lies in a step within its theological-hermeneutical procedure. Specifically, it involves "adopting a predetermined idea of the nature of God and therefore a certain nature for Jesus." Instead, one should note all of the New Testament statements about Jesus, and then correlate and integrate them to form "a view of the nature of Jesus based on all the data."[12] Included in this argument is the suggestion of some essential differences between the members of the Trinity. For example, Leigh points out not only that Jesus, unlike the Father, did not know the time of his second coming, but that the biblical texts imply that the Holy Spirit did not either. Thus, "the ignorance of Jesus about the timing of his return is not necessarily a result of the Incarnation since the Holy Spirit appears to have the same limitation without an Incarnation."[13]

9. Ibid., pp. 132–34.
10. Ibid., p. 135.
11. Ibid.
12. Ibid.
13. Ibid., p. 136.

We have here a genuinely creative attempt to deal with the problems of incarnation. Although advocating the idea that Jesus had a single nature, Leigh takes great pains to point out that Jesus must be thought of as fully God and fully human. Leigh is attempting to preserve the doctrine of incarnation in the orthodox sense. We include his view here because he introduces concepts which are helpful in understanding the incarnation correctly, yet we must also note that he states his overall position in a way which can be improved upon.

On the positive side, Leigh's concept that Jesus was unlike fallen humanity in some areas nonessential to humanity needs to be retained, and the caution against bringing an abstract definition of deity to the discussion is also helpful. We will utilize later (pp. 544–45) the emphasis upon the image of God in humans as a linking factor making the incarnation possible. Similarly, Leigh's unwillingness to fall back quickly and easily upon antinomy as the solution to the logical problem is commendable.

On the negative side, Leigh seems to present us with a stipulative definition. He understands the concepts of individual, nature, and classification in such a way that an individual having more than one nature is, for all practical purposes, a self-contradictory concept. He fails to distinguish between what Thomas Morris calls a kind-nature and an individual-nature.[14] A further difficulty is that Leigh apparently holds that Jesus possesses his nature (which Morris chooses to call Incarnality) essentially. However, since Jesus has his human properties only contingently, and since his humanity is part of his one nature, he must possess his one nature of Incarnality nonessentially. There is, in other words, a contradiction within Leigh's view.[15] One clue to this is his statement, "In the beginning, the second person of the triune Godhead was divine but not human."[16] In a sense, any orthodox incarnational Christology which holds to the preexistence of the Logos must make a statement of this type. Making such a statement is very difficult, however, for a view which cannot say that Jesus added human nature to his

14. Morris, *Logic*, p. 39.
15. Ibid., pp. 42–43.
16. Leigh, "Jesus," p. 133.

divine nature. Leigh must posit an alteration in Jesus' essential nature from exclusively divine to "one-natured God-man."

Leigh attempts to solve the problem of the apparent contradiction between the infinite attributes of deity and the finite attributes of humanity by recourse to the distinction between essential and nonessential attributes. Those nonessential attributes of deity which are incompatible with humanity, such as omnipresence, omnipotence, and omniscience, were not possessed by Jesus Christ. One way of working out this idea is by appealing to some form of kenotic Christology, according to which Jesus gave up the nonessential attributes of deity, while retaining the essential attributes. Leigh chooses not to follow this path, however, but to go a somewhat different route. He argues that there are, in effect, significant differences between the members of the Trinity. For example, only the Father has omniscience; the Son and the Spirit do not.

Now, to be sure, there are some differences which distinguish the three members of the Trinity as separate persons. Usually, however, these differences are seen as involving function rather than power. It is one thing to say that both the Father and the Son have omniscience, but that the Son does not exercise this attribute. It is quite another to say that the Son lacks such an attribute. While space does not permit us to explore all of the ramifications of the issue, it is highly questionable whether, given such an understanding of the Trinity, we could say that the three are of the same essence. For that matter, to consider Jesus Christ to be nearly omniscient and nearly omnipotent, whereas God the Father is omniscient and omnipotent, and fallen humanity is nearly ignorant and nearly impotent,[17] raises the question of whether Jesus is coessential with either God or humanity. While Leigh has carefully distanced himself from the classic version of Monophysitism, it appears that he may not have avoided some of the problems that attached to it. Despite the positive qualities that we have observed, it seems to us that the difficulties in Leigh's view are too great to warrant adopting it. We must therefore turn elsewhere while retaining its best insights.

---

17. Ibid., p. 135. It should be pointed out that Leigh places question marks after "nearly omniscient" and "nearly omnipotent."

Theological Components of an Incarnational Model for Today

There are several themes or elements which must go into the formulation of an incarnational model for today. Because, as we have contended earlier in this work and elsewhere, theology is organic, we must incorporate conclusions reached in various other doctrinal areas. The several factors will gradually fit together to form a viable understanding of the incarnation.

God and Creation

When God created, he genuinely created. Unlike the demiurge of Plato and others, God did not work with and from existing material, with its inherent characteristics and limitations. There was nothing external to him, no other givens with which he could work. He is, of course, limited by the laws of logic, but they are not external to or independent of him. They are, in fact, the very way in which his person is ordered and the patterns of his thought. They became, then, the organizational principles and structures of the creation which he originated. Thus the creation, although not part of him, or an outflow from him, is nonetheless like him, in the sense that it reflects the pattern of his nature. It is like him in the way in which a painting is like the artist. It may be very different in appearance, but it reflects some aspects of the artist's nature, perhaps some that are very deeply hidden from view and thus not widely recognized by others (and perhaps not even by the artist). What the painting is results from what the artist is. Of course, given the complexity, freedom, and creativity of the artist, the paintings produced may vary greatly. Nonetheless, there are characteristics of technique which will enable the art expert to identify a genuine work of a particular artist (such judgments, of course, are necessary only in the case of celebrated artists).

Sometimes theologians and lay people, especially those with a bit of an existential orientation or flair, tend to think of God not only as beyond the bounds of logic, but also as perhaps essentially paradoxical. Often this notion comes from observing that human beings, who presumably are the members of the creation that most closely resemble God, do not lend themselves to systematic, rational analysis. This must, it is reasoned, be true of God as well.

Is this an accurate view, however? Can we conclude, on the basis of thinking and behavior which often enough seem incomprehensible and contrary to logic, that humans are not rational or, more correctly, that there are no rational explanations of their thinking and behavior? Our knowledge of human personality, thinking, emotions, and actions has been growing slowly. We have, however, begun to discover some of the laws which contribute to human behavior. At least on a group basis, a certain amount of predictability is possible. Research done at the University of Minnesota on identical twins separated early in life indicates that heredity may have much more influence than some scholars, especially behavioral scientists, have been inclined to admit.

We ought to note, however, that if Emil Brunner's Rule of Proximity applies here,[18] human beings in their present empirical state are further from their original condition than is any other part of the creation. Thus the physical universe, with its orderliness and rational structure, may well be a better indication of the essential nature of God. So then, we may look to the nature of nature, so to speak, for clues to the divine nature.

It is clear that God can relate to a universe which came from his creative activity and is at least homologous to him. What all of this means for our purposes is that in entering the world through the incarnation he was not entering something foreign in nature to him. There was a sort of receptivity of the creation to its master, as it were. That which by its character obeys the Lord's will is certainly quite capable of becoming a vehicle for his redemptive activity.

We should also mention God's immanence within the world. We will not go into the biblical treatment of that subject, since the reader may consult any standard systematic theology for information.[19] It is sufficient to observe here that the Bible witnesses to the continued influential presence and activity of God within the creation. God's constantly inhabiting his creation is

18. This is the idea that the effect of the fall upon creation and upon perception of the truth is greatest in those areas where the relationship between God and humans is most directly involved, and least where that relationship is not at all in view; see H. Emil Brunner, *Revelation and Reason* (Philadelphia: Westminster, 1946), pp. 382–84; idem, *Man in Revolt* (Philadelphia: Westminster, 1947), p. 544.

19. See, e.g., Millard J. Erickson, *Christian Theology* (Grand Rapids: Baker, 1986), pp. 302–03.

an additional indication that he has invested it with qualities which make it "hospitable" to his presence, and potentially so on a much more intensive and continuous basis.

The Dynamic Character of God

One factor which seems to work against the traditional view of the incarnation has been countered by process theology. God, especially in the theological tradition influenced by Greek philosophy, is understood as unchanging and seemingly static. He is perfect and therefore cannot develop or grow. He cannot have any new experiences or discover anything he did not already know. He cannot really be affected by anything external to him. The creation, however, is otherwise. Here the beginning of life, growth and development, and death or termination of existence are commonplace parts of reality. There are not only variations in the individual members of the creation within their lifetime, but also changes or developments within the whole. New species arise, and others cease to exist.

There is a specific problem for the incarnation here. It can be seen in Luke's statement about Jesus' development: he "increased in wisdom and in stature, and in favor with God and man" (2:52). This has usually been interpreted to mean that Jesus grew not only physically, but also intellectually, socially, and spiritually. Here the problem is not simply the difference between omniscience and ignorance, but the alteration of Jesus' state. Could a divine being really develop in knowledge?

Closely allied to this consideration is the idea of divine impassibility. This is the concept that God is unmoved by what happens within his world. He is not frustrated nor elated by what occurs. On the other hand, humans are very susceptible to suffering, both physically and psychologically. How could Jesus have been both God, with his impassibility, and human, with all the passions human nature entails?

We are now coming to realize, however, that God is not as impassible and static as has at times been thought. These conceptions derive more from Greek philosophy than from biblical revelation. God, to be sure, is perfect and complete, so he cannot develop in the sense of growing toward perfection or eliminating imperfection. On the other hand, there is biblical testimony to a very active, dynamic God, who effects real changes in things.[20] Many of the psalms, for example, are powerful doxologies to God for what he has done. The people of Israel celebrated the "mighty deeds" of Jehovah in creating, sustaining, and saving them. The history of Israel is a record of dynamic activity by God.

Some important distinctions need to be drawn here, lest we fall into some of the same types of misunderstanding and even apparent contradiction which we have been trying to avoid. Both God and his universe are dynamic, but in different ways. As a matter of fact, it is more proper to use the term *dynamic* in reference to God than to the creation, because the universe is only derivatively dynamic, drawing its energy from him, whereas he is originatively dynamic. The universe is developmentally dynamic, whereas God is nondevelopmentally dynamic. He is active externally and alive internally, but that in no way changes his essence, status, or quality.

Confusion may in part be avoided by distinguishing between "static" and "stable." The assumption is that if God does not change, he must be static, unmoving, fixed. That does not necessarily follow, however. There is a dynamic, constant activity that neither increases nor diminishes. This we call stable activity. A generator might (at least in theory) continuously produce electricity without ever varying the voltage or the amperage, and without ever stopping and starting up again. There would, of course, be continual changes of polarity, since we are dealing here with alternating current. The voltage at a given pole would move from maximum positive to maximum negative some sixty times per second, but this would for all practical purposes not produce a change in output. In a similar manner God is continuously active, even though there is no change in his character. (Actually, stable energy is generally the most useful; wide fluctuations in output are frequently inefficient.)

The idea that God is quite impassive or unaffected by what goes on in the world is as questionable as the notion that he is static. When we look closely at the biblical picture of God, especially as developed in the Old Testament, we see considerable

20. See, e.g., Bruce A. Ware, "An Evangelical Reformulation of the Doctrine of the Immutability of God," *Journal of the Evangelical Theological Society* 29.4 (Dec. 1986): 431–46.

"passion" or emotion there.[21] It must be borne in mind that many of the incidental dimensions of the picture are anthropomorphisms or, more correctly, anthropopathisms. Nonetheless, something genuine is represented under these figures. We have a God who grieves and sorrows, becomes angry, and feels compassion.

And what of the specific case of the crucifixion? It is sometimes supposed that the suffering of Jesus was experienced only by his human nature, and the anguish expressed ("my God, my God," rather than "my Father, my Father") was that of a human. Are we to conclude that God the Father did not, indeed could not, participate in the suffering of Jesus? I would propose that God experiences vicariously the suffering of all of his children, and especially experienced the suffering of Jesus, with whom he had a uniquely close relationship (John 17:22–23). What human parents do not share in the suffering of a child whom they truly love? Thus our picture of a God who feels is intensified and underscored in the biblical record of the suffering of Jesus. And a God who feels the pain of his people is certainly congruous with the concept of incarnation.

The affinity that we have seen exists between God and his people helps to allay the objection that the created world does not move in the same patterns and at the same speed as does God. A useful analogy here is the invention of the synchromesh transmission. Many persons today have never driven a car with a manual transmission, and of those who have, only a handful have experienced one that did not have synchronizers. In early transmissions, one problem was that the gears which were to be engaged with one another rotated at very different speeds. In order to minimize this problem, a technique known as double clutching was utilized. The clutch would be depressed, and the gearshift moved to neutral. The clutch would then be released briefly and then depressed again as the gearshift was moved to the desired position. That had the effect of adjusting the speed of rotation so that the gears would not clash too severely. The synchromesh transmission handled that problem automatically. In like manner, God's affinity with the creation allows them to

---

21. Ibid., pp. 444–46.

move at similar speeds, so to speak. That the creation is of his own making rather than a given forced upon him means that God does not clash with the general characteristics of the universe. There is harmony instead, so that incarnation is a genuine possibility.

The Image of God

The action of God in becoming incarnate should not be viewed simply in terms of the infinite meeting the finite. Keep in mind that God did not become incarnate within just any part of the creation. The situation would have been very different if the Second Person of the Trinity had become incarnate in a tree, a slug, or even a horse or a dog. There the clash of levels of reality would have been severe. What he did instead was to become united with a specimen of the one creature that had been made in his own image and likeness. In other words, there was a natural likeness or affinity between God and the human person in whom he became incarnate. There was a type of fit of the one for the other.

We do not know all that the image of God in the human involved. It certainly included the fact of personality: God and all humans are persons. Some have sought to argue that the image of God does not involve intrinsic qualities (i.e., they deny the structural or substantive view) and propose instead that the image of God is the relationship (actual or potential) between the human and God. That, however, evades the question of why humans can have this relationship, which none of the other creatures experience, and whether there might not be something within the constitution of the human which makes it possible. In other words, those who maintain that the image of God is basically a matter of relationship encounter the same type of difficulties which beset functional Christology, with which their view has much in common. Humans are capable of acting on behalf of God, of exercising dominion for him over his creation. Since humans can do this, they obviously have within them many of the qualities found in God. They are, then, not as foreign to God as might otherwise be thought on purely a priori grounds.

A closely allied consideration stems from the doctrines of sin and salvation. Holiness is defined as being like God himself; sin, on the other hand, is that which separates one from God. This was seen clearly in the Garden of Eden, where, after the fall, a series of curses was pronounced, and the man and the woman were thrust from God's presence. Death became their end. In the law, sin is seen as failure to conform to God's nature as expressed in his revelation preserved in the law. Thus sin is departure from the true destiny and nature God originally intended for humans; it is a distancing of oneself from God and his moral likeness.

Salvation represents the reversal of this situation. It is restoration to the status of rightness before God; but more than that, it is reception, in a gradual fashion, of the holiness of or a likeness to God. This process is called sanctification. In the Old Testament, sanctification involved setting persons, places, and objects apart uniquely for God's use; similarly, sanctification in the New Testament entails assimilation of the moral qualities of God. In partial measure, Christians are to display the love, mercy, compassion, and integrity that God displays. The state to which the believer is restored is indicative of what the human was intended to be and is the purest representation of human nature. This is what Paul seems to be saying in 2 Corinthians 3:18: "And we all, with unveiled face, beholding the glory of the Lord, are being changed into his likeness from one degree of glory to another; for this comes from the Lord who is the Spirit."

What all of this means is that divine and human nature are not directly and categorically opposed. In logical analysis, the difference is not like that between an A statement ("All X is Y") and an E statement ("No X is Y"), nor is it even like that between an A statement and an O statement ("Some X is not Y"). It is more like that between an A statement and an I statement ("Some X is Y"). The subject of the latter is included within the subject of the former, although not vice versa. So the difference between the knowledge God possesses and that which humans possess is quite unlike the difference between God's knowledge and that of a stone, for example. Similarly, the difference between divine love and the love of which humans may be capable is quite unlike the difference between God and a demon or Satan himself.

The Sinlessness of Christ

In addition to becoming incarnate in a creation which was modeled after his own pattern of thought and personality, and in a member of that creation who was made in his own image and likeness, God became incarnate in a human who was free from sin.[22] One of the problems of the incarnation has been the question of how a perfectly holy God could become united with sinful human nature. On the other hand, if he did not take upon himself the depravity of fallen humanity, was the incarnation complete, and could the redemptive work of Christ be fully effective?

To some extent, the doctrine of the virgin birth, or at least the virgin conception, deals with this problem, or at least the first aspect of it. Some have even believed that the mutual exclusivity of divine holiness and sinful human nature was the reason for the virgin birth.[23] The transmission of Adam's sin is believed to have been broken by removing the human father. This seems to imply either that women do not have original sin, or at least that they do not transmit it to the next generation. This idea, however, seems to be without any firm biblical support, and is at best a very odd conception. Traditional Roman Catholic theology takes the argument one step further and eliminates the sin of Mary by means of the immaculate conception, which in effect carries the virgin birth back an additional generation, again without adequate biblical testimony. Whatever the means, it does seem that what Mary contributed to the union was sanctified or purified in advance of the actual conception/incarnation. It may be that, contrary to traditional thinking, Mary did not even contribute an ovum, with the Holy Spirit instead producing and implanting a fertilized ovum. In any event, the angel told Mary that because the Holy Spirit would come upon her and the power of the Most High would overshadow her, the child to be born would be called "holy" (Luke 1:35). Furthermore, Jesus did not commit any sin

22. The way in which this and several other statements in this section are cast could be interpreted as implying that Jesus existed as a human being prior to the incarnation. Such a notion, which would be a species of Adoptionism, is not intended. Rather, we are attempting to avoid the idea that the humanity of Jesus was impersonal. The incarnation took place in a definite and specific and complete human being, Jesus, but that human being did not exist prior to the incarnation.

23. James Orr, *The Virgin Birth of Christ* (New York: Scribner, 1907), pp. 190–201.

after his conception and birth (Heb. 4:15). This is supported by Paul's statement that God "made him to be sin who knew no sin" (2 Cor. 5:21). Here apparently was the only human free from sin.

Since Jesus was sinless, he alone (except for Adam and Eve prior to the fall) was human in the true and fullest sense. The sin which we find in ourselves, which is so opposed to the nature of God and thus would have been an obstacle to incarnation, was not present in him. That God united with sinless humanity indicates that the seeming incommensurability between human nature and divine nature is not inherent in human nature. We must remember that the empirical human nature with which we deal is distorted. It is possible that even some of the limitations of human nature which are not so obviously spiritual and moral were introduced or increased as the result of sin. For example, although human intelligence is presumably inherently limited, it may be that sin limits our intelligence and its functioning further, hampering our understanding, especially insight into spiritual matters.

The time has come to recapitulate our argument. We have sought to show that the difference between the human nature of Jesus and the divine nature, although it is both quantitative and qualitative, is not what Søren Kierkegaard in another context called an "infinite qualitative distinction." There is some affinity between the two, because the creation was structured in accord with laws reflecting the very nature of God, humans were made in the image and likeness of God, and the particular human nature of Jesus was sinless. We have used illustrations from the physical and logical realms, which we will now supplement with an analogy taken from the area of the life sciences.

If there were a fundamental antithesis between the humanity and the deity of Christ, incarnation would not be possible. The deity, for example, being by its very nature opposed to sin, could not unite with anything spiritually or morally imperfect. There would be a repulsion or rejection of it. The situation is parallel to what occurs in an organ transplant. The body is designed to repel foreign objects. Thus, if one gets a wood sliver in a finger, the sore festers and the sliver is ejected. This is part of the immune system, whereby the body protects itself from infections and other ills. Unfortunately, however, this same immune system regards an organ which has been transplanted into the body as a foreign object and thus a threat. So immunosuppressive drugs must be administered to prevent rejection. To the degree that there is genetic similarity between the donor and the recipient, this problem diminishes. Frequently a close relative is sought as the donor. The ideal situation is identical twins; having the same genetic makeup, they can exchange organs with only a minimal risk of rejection. The host body regards the new organ as its own and treats it that way.

The point of the argument in the last several pages is that there is considerable genetic similarity, as it were, between the deity and the humanity of Jesus. It is not merely that God united with a part of the creation, or even with a human being. He united with a specific member of the human race who was made in the image of God and free from sin. To judge the possibility of incarnation by appraising empirical human nature (which in turn is being done by fallen human nature) may be as unwise as utilizing information regarding organ transplants between total strangers from different parts of the world to judge the possible success of an organ transplant from one's parent.

Divine Self-Limitation

Some of the discussion of the difficulty of the infinite God's becoming incarnate in a finite person centers upon that very infinity, and seems to assume that he must remain or function as infinite. This means, in other words, that the infinity of God must necessarily be exercised, and that infinity does not include the ability to be or become or act as something less than infinite. But is this the case? May not the incarnation be a matter of divine self-limitation, freely chosen and appropriate to deity?

It will be helpful to examine briefly God's conduct in other relationships. Although God, by his own nature, is free and not obligated to anyone or anything, he has chosen to take on various obligations, thus in effect curtailing severely his freedom and sovereignty. For example, was God required to provide redemption for lost humanity? No, for he had warned them of the consequences of sin, and would have been quite within his rights to exact the punishment they deserved. He did not have to act mercifully. He chose to do so, however, and pledged and promised that he would provide redemption. Once he did that, once he entered into a covenant with humanity, he was obliged to fulfil it (Heb. 6:17–18). Every promise, every covenant which God made, was a limitation upon his freedom. For that matter, creation was a limitation upon his freedom, for now there existed realities other than himself, and he could never undo the fact that he had created. Nor, for that matter, could he simply wipe out his creation, if doing so would contradict his nature. Such circumstances are not to be thought of as in conflict with his sovereignty and freedom, however, since they were freely chosen in the first place.

The incarnation can be thought of along those lines. While giving up the divine nature would be a surrender of deity, and even giving up certain of its attributes might well be, a voluntary decision to restrict the independent exercise of some divine attributes is not necessarily a forfeiture of deity. The limitations accepted in the incarnation are like those accepted in the promises and covenants made by God. They do not diminish what he is or even in one sense what he can do, but they do limit the conditions under which he can exercise his capabilities.

For example, the divine ability to be everywhere (or omnipresence, as theologians prefer) was not lost by the Second Person of the Trinity. In that sense, what he was did not diminish. He did, however, limit himself to exercising that power only in connection with the restrictions imposed by a human body, which meant that he could be in only one physical location at a time. He made a voluntary decision to limit the exercise of his omnipresence for a certain period of time. This is not to imply that he could have overridden the decision at any moment. He had willed that from approximately 4 B.C. to A.D. 29 he would not have the free use of his omnipresence. It was not that he was pretending that he could not use it; he really could not. In like manner, when Jesus asked how long a child had suffered from a disease, or when he professed that he did not know the time of his second coming, he was not pretending. He had chosen to subject his omniscience to the veiling or cloaking effect of humanity. For the time being, he gave up his intuitive knowledge of many of the things which God knows, and in many cases he had to learn the truth through sense experience instead.

The character of the limitation Jesus voluntarily took on needs to be looked at more closely. The distinction between "nature" and "conditions" is worth pursuing. What we are saying is that his basic powers were not lost, but only the ability to exercise them. I am reminded of a picnic to which my wife and I were invited when our youngest daughter was in junior high school. Included among the activities was a softball game. There was one unusual feature of the rules that day. The young people were permitted to bat in their normal fashion, but as a means of equalizing the competition, the parents were placed under a handicap. Right-handed batters had to bat left-handed, and vice versa (switch-hitters, of course, had a great day). Now one's ability as a right-handed batter was not diminished, but it could not be exercised because of the requirement to bat from the left-handed-batter's box. Although one was still able to bat right-handed, one was not allowed to in that particular game, and thus could not bat with the usual effectiveness. In a sense, the limitation was not ultimately physical, for it resulted from a moral limitation: conscience compelled us to tell the truth about how we normally batted.

This is in some ways roughly parallel to what happened in the incarnation. Jesus did not give up the qualities of God, but gave up the privilege of exercising them. Perhaps, at least for part of his life, he even gave up the consciousness that he had such capabilities and had exercised them with the Father and the Holy Spirit prior to the incarnation.

22

The Logic of the Incarnation (2)

Kenotic Variations Relevant to a Modern Incarnational Christology

The reader will have surmised that the view we have been introducing is a species of kenotic theology, but rather different from that which one usually encounters. To clarify what we are asserting (and also what we are not asserting), we will need to look somewhat more closely at the nature of kenosis. We will

551

then try to explain somewhat more definitely what was involved metaphysically in the incarnation.

The Nature of Kenotic Christology

The classic passage on which kenotic Christologies have usually been based is of course Philippians 2:1–11. In addition, Jesus' asking the Father to glorify him with the glory which he formerly had (John 17:5), but presumably did not have at the time of this prayer, is often understood to be a subsidiary text. To a considerable extent, the passage in Philippians is not subjected to intensive literal exegesis; that is, theologians do not attempt to extract from the text an explanation of what "emptying himself" means, in what it consisted, and how it was accomplished. Rather, the pivotal Greek word (κενόω) is used to name a theory which does some speculation about the nature of Jesus' earthly state.

We discussed in chapter 3 the form of kenotic Christology which became quite popular in the nineteenth century. There had, of course, been some allusions in early Christology to the divine self-emptying, but it seems unlikely that any of them were explicitly kenotic. Probably the closest was Apollinarius's comment that "Incarnation is self-emptying."[1]

The most complete or purest form of kenotic Christology holds that what the Second Person of the Trinity did was to actually give up the attributes of divinity. He set them aside for the period of the incarnation. This action, however, did not endanger the deity of Christ. He was still God, but without the attributes of God. This, however, seems a bit difficult to maintain, given today's understanding of attributes and properties. One could perhaps argue that the divine substance was retained, but without certain attributes which distinguish God from humanity. It is hard to know what this means, however. What is a divine being that does not have the attributes of divinity? Rather than incarnation, there seems to be a virtual transmutation of deity into humanity. Donald Baillie says, "For though the Son of God keeps His personal identity in becoming the subject of the human

---

1. John M. Creed, *The Divinity of Jesus Christ: A Study in the History of Christian Doctrine Since Kant* (London: Collins, 1964), p. 77; Donald M. Baillie, *God Was in Christ: An Essay on Incarnation and Atonement* (New York: Scribner, 1948), p. 94.

attributes which He assumes, He has divested Himself of the *distinctly divine* attributes; which would imply, if language means anything, that in becoming human He ceased to be divine."[2]

Kenosis of Relational Attributes (Gottfried Thomasius)

Because of these difficulties, modified versions of kenotic Christology have been proposed, usually contending that the Second Person of the Trinity did not lay aside all the attributes of divinity, but only certain ones which would be incompatible with humanity. Gottfried Thomasius, for example, held that Christ gave up the relational attributes only. He retained the immanent attributes, those which he has in and of himself, such as love, truth, and holiness, while divesting himself of those which have to do with his relationship to the creation, namely, omnipotence, omniscience, and omnipresence.[3] This division, it will be noted, is similar to the dichotomy between moral and natural attributes. It was Thomasius's view that Christ became in a certain sense as he was before the creation took place, when there was no everywhere for his presence to occupy, and there was nothing against which his power could be measured. Yet this view is not fully satisfactory either, for the relational attributes are applications, as it were, of the more absolute or immanent attributes. God's omniscience is, so to speak, his absolute wisdom and knowledge as it relates to the truth of the creation; and his omnipresence is his immensity as it relates to the creation.[4]

Kenosis of Accidental Attributes (Stephen Davis)

One other variation of the kenosis theme is that of Stephen Davis, who distinguishes between essential and accidental attributes. Accidental attributes are those which I can change without altering who I am, such as the length of my hair, or the fact that I am sitting rather than standing. Essential attributes or properties are those which all members of a group or a class

2. Baillie, *God Was in Christ*, p. 96.

3. Gottfried Thomasius, "Christ's Person and Work," in *God and Incarnation in Mid-Nineteenth Century German Theology*, ed. Claude Welch (New York: Oxford University Press, 1965), pp. 46–56.

4. Augustus H. Strong, *Systematic Theology* (Westwood, N.J.: Revell, 1963), p. 702.

must have to qualify as members of that group (every circle, e.g., is an enclosed geometrical figure with all points equidistant from the center).[5] We must distinguish between those attributes of God which are essential attributes of deity, and those which are accidental, and similarly with the attributes of humanity. Davis introduces two lists of properties, belonging to God and human beings respectively:

God	Human Beings
1. Being necessary	1' Being contingent
2. Living forever	2' Living only for a finite time
3. Being omnipotent	3' Being nonomnipotent
4. Being omniscient	4' Being nonomniscient
5. Being incorporeal	5' Being corporeal

Davis observes that if each of these properties is an essential property either of God or of human beings, and if the classical doctrine says that Jesus Christ must have all of these qualities simultaneously, and if it is logically impossible for any being simultaneously to have all the properties in both sets, then the traditional doctrine is indeed incoherent. The contention made by John Hick and others that the doctrine is incoherent rests upon the assumption that each of the properties listed is essential either to God or to humans. This assumption Davis is not quite ready to grant.[6]

Davis then draws a crucial distinction, for which he gives some credit to Thomas Morris, between being *truly human* and being *merely human* (i.e., being human without being divine), and between being *truly divine* and being *divine simpliciter* (i.e., being divine without being human). Perhaps, he says, properties 1–5 are essential properties of being *divine simpliciter* and properties 1'–5' are essential properties of being *merely human.*[7] What happened in the incarnation is that God gave up any divine attributes inconsistent with being human, which would necessarily be accidental, while he retained all essential divine

---

5. Stephen T. Davis, "Jesus Christ: Savior or Guru?" in *Encountering Jesus: A Debate on Christology*, ed. Stephen T. Davis (Atlanta: John Knox, 1988), pp. 50–51.

6. Ibid., p. 51.

7. Ibid., pp. 51–52.

attributes. Similarly, he did not assume any human attributes inconsistent with being divine, which would necessarily be accidental, while he assumed those attributes which are essential to humanity. Davis says, correctly, "The whole picture depends on there not being any essential divine properties that a human being cannot have and on there not being any essential human attributes that God cannot have."[8]

Some problems arise from the fact that this scheme proceeds almost analytically. For example, the definition of essential divine qualities appears to be whatever divine qualities are not incompatible with being human. Moreover, we seem to face a dilemma: either we have to say that divinity simpliciter is different from true divinity; or, if it is not, we have to explain how the essential attributes of divinity simpliciter could be truly essential and yet, unlike those of true divinity, given up when God became joined to a human being. These issues need to be addressed.

Elements of a Modern Incarnational Christology

Kenosis by Addition

Although there are shortcomings, the basic concept with which Davis is working is a very helpful one, and his approach is in certain ways quite similar to what I am proposing. Rather than suggest that God gave up certain attributes of divinity as well as certain attributes of humanity in becoming incarnate (for this is a sort of double kenosis), I prefer to emphasize that what he did in the incarnation was to add something to each nature, namely, the attributes of the other nature. Thus I would interpret the participle λαβών ("taking") in Philippians 2:7 as an instrumental participle, so that it should be rendered, "He emptied himself by taking the form of a servant." The context seems to indicate that what he emptied himself of was his glory, nothing being said about giving up any attributes of deity, either essential or accidental. He retained the μορφή of God, but added to it the form of a servant. He still had divine attributes, but they now were exercised in connection with the humanity which he had assumed.

8. Ibid., p. 52.

Deity and Humanity in Abstraction and in Incarnation

The approach we are advocating agrees with Davis's position in emphasizing the difference between being God in abstraction and being God in incarnation, and between being human in abstraction and being human in incarnation. In incarnation the same qualities are present, not having been lost, but their manifestation and function are different. An imperfect analogy is the difference between the status of sodium atoms or chlorine atoms in the free state and in combination to form common table salt. The qualities of the compound are quite different from those of either of the elements making it up. The analogy should not be pressed too far, however. We are not suggesting that Jesus' humanity and deity formed a union like that of a chemical compound, but only that the illustration may be of some general help to us.

We are suggesting that the two sets of qualities which the one subject or self, Jesus, possessed functioned together in such a way that the manifestation of each now was different from the manifestation of either one alone. We have tended to emphasize the limitation of the divine by the presence of the human, but we ought also to emphasize equally the limitation (which is actually an elevation) of the human by the divine. The divine prevents the human from being merely human. Pertinent here is our earlier suggestion (p. 545) that the two natures are not to be thought of as opposed, but as partial and complete versions of the same thing. We drew this conclusion from the image and likeness of God in the human, and the fact that the human is called upon to emulate the qualities of God.

It may be that we need to distinguish between active and latent attributes. Abstract deity, that is, deity which has not become united with humanity, possesses all of its attributes actively. God is actually able to do all things, and he actually knows all things. In incarnation, however, these attributes became latent. God's knowledge of all things may have been limited in actual exercise by his consciousness' being related to a human personality and particularly to a human brain. Similarly, abstract humanity, or what Morris terms "mere humanity," has certain active characteristics, such as having come into being at a particular point in time and being contingent.[9] Incarnate humanity, however, has these qualities only latently, so that such a person may have had a preexistence from all eternity, but of course not as a human.

Part of the problem comes from our formulating our understanding of humanity through an empirical examination of humans as we find them. As John Macquarrie has said, "We discuss the divinity and even the humanity of Christ in terms of ready-made ideas of God and man that we bring with us, without allowing these to be corrected or even drastically changed by what we learn about God and man in and through the incarnation."[10] Apart from being sinful or modified specimens, all the humans we examine are also instances of abstract humanity. Finding a certain characteristic in each instance of human being that we encounter, we may conclude that this is an essential characteristic, a characteristic without which the person would not be human. That does not follow, however. Morris points out one characteristic that we find universally among persons—they live on the earth. That, however, need not be the case. One can conceive of persons living on a space platform or perhaps inhabiting another planet without thereby losing their humanity.[11] Similarly, all human beings whom we have ever known have had limitations upon their knowledge. That, however, does not establish what a human being would be like in an incarnational union with a divine nature. Herbert McCabe says, "A human person just is a person with a human nature, and it makes absolutely no difference to the logic of this whether the same person does or does not exist from eternity as divine."[12]

One might respond at this point that whereas a lesser entity can coexist with a greater of which it is a part, the problem is not quite the same when we are dealing with not merely a greater degree of the same thing, but an infinitely greater. Do we not face here the problem, perhaps in a somewhat different way, of the

9. Thomas V. Morris, *The Logic of God Incarnate* (Ithaca, N.Y.: Cornell University Press, 1986), p. 65.

10. John Macquarrie, "The Humility of God," in *The Myth/Truth of God Incarnate*, ed. Durstan R. McDonald (Wilton, Conn.: Morehouse-Barlow, 1979), p. 13.

11. Morris, *Logic*, p. 63.

12. Herbert McCabe and Maurice Wiles, "The Incarnation: An Exchange," *New Blackfriars* 58 (Dec. 1977): 552.

incommensurability of finite and infinite? We must recall, however, our earlier observation regarding divine self-limitation (pp. 548–50). It seems impossible, for example, that a God who has the power of life and death could ever be in a situation where he cannot take someone's life. Yet if he voluntarily promises not to take a life, he must abide by his word. Similarly, the decision to so connect the attributes of the divine nature with the human that they could not be exercised apart from it, and apart from dependence upon the Father, was a choice made freely which imposed real limitations upon the subject who made it.

What we have been saying is close to the view of Thomas Morris, who holds what he terms the "two minds" theory of the incarnation. Christ had two minds: (1) a fully divine mind, which possessed all of the attributes of God and had access to the human mind; and (2) the human mind, which was limited by the sorts of ignorance found in human beings and lacked access to what was within the divine mind, except for what the divine mind allowed it on occasion to have.[13] While Morris's basic statement is accompanied by some problems, particularly a tendency toward Nestorianism, it has the virtue of emphasizing that the divine Logos did not give up anything of what he was and had, but added to it the mind of the human, and thus restricted somewhat the conditions under which his divine qualities could be exercised. A difficult question for Morris's fully developed view is whether the one person could function only on the basis of the human mind (and such access to the divine mind as it allowed). If that is the case, it appears either that the one person was a human, not a divine-human person, or that there were two persons. The latter alternative seems almost to be implied by the suggestion that the divine mind allowed the human mind to have access to it.

Omniscience and the Unconscious

A better understanding draws upon one of the insights which Morris offers in his unusually penetrating analysis. Jesus was a divine-human person who had both a complete human nature and a complete divine nature. That is to say, he possessed all of the qualities found in pure deity and all of those found in gen-

---

13. Morris, *Logic*, p. 103.

uine humanity. In the course of his development, he gradually became aware of his divine aspect. The exhaustive knowledge of all truth which the deity of Christ possessed (his omniscience) was in his unconscious. He therefore, just like anyone else, had to grow in knowledge of the subjects that a Jewish boy of that time would learn. The infinite knowledge possessed by his deity was accessible to him, not when his divine nature permitted access, as Morris suggests, but when the Father permitted access. The Son had chosen to live in dependence upon the Father, and this was one dimension of that dependence or subordination. Presumably the access the Father allowed was selective; that is to say, the whole of divine knowledge did not come pouring in during moments of illumination. This particular model has the advantage of tying the persons of the Trinity together more closely than do some other views.

To explore a bit what we mean when we speak of Jesus' possession of the divine attribute of omniscience, let us look at our experience of our own unconscious. We do not know, of course, exactly what the consciousness of the divine-human person was like, nor its relationship to that of which it was unconscious. To the extent that our earlier contentions regarding the difference between Jesus and us are accepted, we will be unsure of the exact nature of his consciousness. Yet we are probably safe in assuming that there is enough commonality on this point between Jesus and us that we may trust the analogy of our own experience.

I learned in high-school trigonometry that the square of the hypotenuse of a right triangle is equal to the sum of the squares of the two other sides. I seldom think about that fact. Yet when I do, I can readily call it into my consciousness from what Sigmund Freud called the preconscious. There are other mathematical facts which I may have somewhat greater difficulty in bringing to consciousness, however. I struggled before recalling the formula for the volume of a cone, for example. Some of the axioms of geometry come back when least expected. Sometimes a language learned years earlier comes flashing back, as those whose Greek and Hebrew have grown somewhat rusty can testify. The truly unconscious may be recoverable only under the influence of psychoanalysis, drugs, or hypnotism. Now, we must ask, do we "know" those things of which we are not conscious but may be able to recall through exerted effort? They are not facts that we learn when they come to consciousness, for they were there all along. I would contend that in similar fashion, Jesus was omniscient, but was not conscious of all that he knew.

Omnipotence as Latent Power

It may well be that the omnipotence of Christ during his incarnation can be handled in a like manner, or that it was dependent upon his limited consciousness. Morris suggests that Jesus retained his omnipotence, but did not exercise it because he was unaware that he could do all things. This, however, would mean that he never failed at anything he attempted, for he would never have reached the limitation of his power. Moreover, being a normal boy, he undoubtedly engaged in some competitive games or sports where physical strength was a factor. In the process of exerting maximum effort, would he not have unleashed unlimited power without realizing he was doing so? This does not seem to be a viable way of understanding the limitation of his power.

I believe that it is more consonant with the biblical picture to conceive of Jesus as possessing the ability to do all things, but having that ability latently. He possessed and exercised it in connection with the presence of a fully human nature. His ability to actively exert unlimited power depended upon the Father. Throughout much of his life he was probably not fully aware of possessing this power.

Omnipresence and the Limitation of Corporeality

One especially troublesome issue is that of omnipresence. It is probably significant that Morris dismisses this attribute with a mere two sentences. Having defined it as "being present everywhere in virtue of knowledge of and power over every spatially located object," he states that divesting oneself of omnipresence would be a matter of divesting oneself of the requisite knowledge or power.[14] This definition appears to be stipulative: he frames it in such a way as to make it fit the purpose he has in mind. But this does not appear to be what theologians have meant by "omnipresence." They have generally understood it to

14. Ibid., p. 91.

mean a genuine *presence with* all objects, not merely knowledge of them or power over them. This, in turn, is related to the biblical witness that God is actually present with us, not that he merely knows us. There is a difference, for example, between David's testimony in Psalm 139:7–12 to God's presence with him and his testimony regarding God's knowledge of him in the remainder of the psalm. Jeremiah also sees God as filling the whole of heaven and earth (Jer. 23:23–24).

Omnipresence is the attribute where the necessity of limitation involved in the incarnation is perhaps clearest. As God, Jesus had the capability of being everywhere. Yet, for the period of his earthly incarnation, he limited himself to the restrictions in location which having a physical human body entailed. He had possessed the capability of active omnipresence: being pure spirit, he was not limited to any particular place and time. But as part of the decision to become incarnate, he also decided not to exercise that capability, or to make it latent, for a period of time.

Temptation and Sin

An additional problem, and perhaps in some ways the most difficult, is that of the temptation of Jesus. For whereas the other matters we have examined pertain to the natural attributes of God, Jesus' temptation relates to a major moral attribute of God, his holiness. Not only are the general statements of the Bible about the goodness and righteousness of God at stake, but the specific statement of James 1:13 is in jeopardy: "God cannot be tempted with evil." Compounding the difficulty is the fact that, for the most part, those who hold that Christ laid aside the natural attributes of God in the incarnation do not believe that he divested himself of the moral attributes as well.

There seem to be clear indications that Jesus was indeed genuinely tempted. Most direct is the narrative of the temptations at the initiation of his ministry (Matt. 4:1–11; Mark 1:12–13; Luke 4:1–13). In addition, we have the direct statement of Hebrews 4:15 that in Jesus we have "one who in every respect has been tempted as we are, yet without sin." This seems to be a clear statement of the genuineness of Jesus' temptation. But what does it mean? Does it mean that he was tempted, but there was no real possibility of his sinning? If that were the case, however, in what sense and to what sin was he tempted? Further, how are we to interpret the statement by the author of Hebrews that Jesus has been tempted "in every respect . . . as we are"? Does this mean simply that his temptation covered the whole range of activities that could be considered sin, or does it also suggest that like us he could have yielded to the temptation? The thrust of the passage is that he is able to intercede for us because he has completely identified with us; this seems to imply that his temptation included not only the whole range of sin, but the real possibility of sinning.

One way to avoid this difficulty is to distinguish between the *epistemic* possibility of sin and, more broadly, the logical or metaphysical possibility. On such grounds, it was really possible for Jesus to decide to sin, but the divine nature precluded his actually doing so. As long as his divine nature did not preclude his thinking that he could perform the sin, there was genuine temptation.[15] This does not minimize the value of his resisting. He chose not to sin, thus never encountering the fact that he could not have sinned.

Morris comments, "Perhaps [Jesus'] divine property of being necessarily good, although it rendered impossible his having decided or having done otherwise than he did with respect to resisting temptation, as a matter of fact played no causal role in his doing as he did."[16] Here we have something of a change from the earlier distinction of epistemic and metaphysical possibility. For in that case the illustration of a man who, not knowing that the door is locked, freely decides not to try to leave a room, is applicable. Here, however, it is impossible even to decide to do the act. This has the advantage of recognizing that sin is not a matter simply of external acts, but also of attitudes and thoughts, as Jesus made clear (Matt. 5:21–22, 27–28). There is a problem, however, as to whether the temptation was genuine.

A somewhat different way to approach Jesus' temptation is to distinguish between the possibility of what could occur and the likelihood of what would occur. The view that it was impossible for Jesus to sin seems to say that there is no set of conditions under which he could have sinned, whereas the view that it was

15. Ibid., pp. 147–50.
16. Ibid., p. 152.

unlikely says that there are conditions under which he could have sinned, but that it was certain those conditions would not all be fulfilled. Thus Jesus really could have decided to cast himself down from the temple pinnacle, but it was certain that he would not.

In evaluating the temptation, it is important to bear three things in mind. First, Jesus' humanity was different from ours in one important respect. Whereas we begin life with a corrupt nature and continue to experience its lingering effects, he was free from original sin. Second, he lived under the limitations of humanity. Just as his omniscience did not overwhelm his limited human knowledge with information, so also the holiness of his divine nature did not preclude a real struggle as to whether to succumb to temptation. Third, he had a uniquely close relationship to the Father. Being united with the divine nature, he experienced influences which helped guarantee that he would not sin. Just as his omniscience at points infilled his limited human knowledge, so the incarnation meant that his contact with the holiness of deity was closer than ours. This helped insure that he would not turn from the path he had chosen. The writer to the Hebrews says, "For the joy that was set before him [Jesus] endured the cross, despising the shame, and is seated at the right hand of the throne of God" (12:2).

Since we have concluded that Jesus could have sinned, we must at this point ask what precisely would have been entailed in that event. Here we lack any clear statements (or even intimations) of Scripture. We may be tempted to say that since Jesus would not have sinned, we need not ask what would have occurred if he had. This, however, hardly seems fully honest. Although we are reduced virtually to speculation, we must consider some type of answer.

Certainly God cannot sin, and indeed cannot even be tempted. Thus, if Jesus were to have sinned, his deity could not have been involved. Unless we are to adopt some form of Nestorianism, the conclusion seems to be that the incarnation would have terminated short of the actual sin. At the very brink of the decision to sin, where that decision had not yet taken place, but the Father knew it was about to be made, the Second Person of the Trinity would have left the human nature of Jesus, dissolving the incarnation. Quite possibly, to sever the union should such a situation arise was a preincarnate decision of the Second Person of the Trinity, which was made as part of the decision to become incarnate and accept the limitations of such a state. We would have here, then, something of a limitation upon the limitation, as it were. Had the Logos departed, Jesus would not have died. That would have been the case only if the person had been merely divine, only the Logos, as various forms of Apollinarianism required. Rather, Jesus would have survived, but would have "slumped" to mere humanity, and sinful mere humanity at that.

Jesus' Death

A final problem for consideration is the question of Jesus' death. How could he die, since he was divine, and since God, being eternal (without beginning and end) and uncaused (or the cause of his own existence), exists necessarily, not merely contingently? Supposedly, then, Jesus could not have died.

We must ask, first, what death is, and that in turn will raise the question of what human nature is. Death, physical death, is the cessation of life in the bodily condition. Clearly, someone or something existing in a bodily form is a prerequisite here. Since God, being pure spirit, does not have a body, he cannot die, at least not a physical death. In the case of living creatures lower than humans, death is the termination of existence. The entity ceases to exist as a living being. What is the case for humans, however?

In an earlier period, when human nature was thought of dualistically (i.e., as involving a physical aspect, the body, and an immaterial aspect, the soul and/or spirit), physical death was frequently described as the separation of the body and soul. This may still be a useful way to conceive of death, but in recent years there has been a growing emphasis upon the unity of the person. To the extent that this concept tries to take full account of the biblical testimony, however, a problem arises. The Bible contains a teaching of an intermediate state, a state of conscious existence between death and the resurrection. One model which attempts to take this teaching seriously is contingent monism. According to this view, the human is capable of existing in either a materialized or an immaterialized state. A parallel is the current understanding of reality, according to which matter and energy are convertible. Similarly, the human person can go from the embodied or materialized state (physical life) through physical death to the intermediate state (immaterialized state). Then, at the resurrection there will be a resumption of the materialized state, although with a different kind of body and in a quite different condition. "Death" is the word for the first of these transitions, "resurrection" for the second.

In a sense, contingent monism holds that humans do not really die. They simply undergo transition from one state to another. This is not extinction or the end of life, but only the end of one kind of life. It is, to a limited extent, a transition to certain aspects of the type of existence which is true of God at all times. It involves leaving behind one aspect of the human nature, but only temporarily. Although the human will never return to the exact form of bodily existence experienced before death, the new bodily existence will have some point of continuity with the old.

We have here another of those situations where it will be useful to distinguish true humanity from mere humanity. Certainly, every human we have ever known was embodied or materialized or reified. That, however, does not establish that an embodied or materialized state is somehow an essential attribute of humanity. Given this understanding, death is not a real problem for the deity of Christ, for it is simply a transferring of the person to a condition even more like abstract deity; and thus the death of Christ becomes, if anything, easier to maintain.

Views of the Continuing Incarnation

Another potentially helpful issue for our consideration is the status of Jesus' incarnation since his ascension to the presence of the Father. To what extent are the limitations imposed by the incarnation, as observed in Jesus' life here on earth, still present? Here we lack some of the data which we would like to have, for the biblical revelation is not as complete on this subject as we might wish. So we will need to draw logical inferences from the few data that we do have.

Semiphysical Resurrection

A major issue is the character of the glorified body of Christ. It is notable how little treatment has been given by evangelical and orthodox theologians to this topic and related matters such as the nature and time of the exaltation, and the significance of the ascension. Most systematic theologies deal with Christ's glorified body very lightly if at all, and most biblical theologies proceed on the assumption that it is beyond their scope.

One rather commonly held view is that the body of Jesus in the resurrection is identical with that which he has had since the ascension. The ascension, in other words, effected no real change in the resurrection body. The characteristics of Jesus' body during the forty days between resurrection and ascension may therefore be taken as clues to the nature of his present body. In addition, since he is the "first fruits" of the resurrection, his resurrection body and ours are identical. Thus the argument is sometimes worked in both directions. The description of Christ's resurrection body and its characteristics is taken as indicative of our resurrection bodies,[17] and Paul's discussion of the believer's resurrection body is taken as indicative of what Jesus' resurrection body must have been like.[18]

The resurrection body of Christ possessed many of the characteristics of the earthly body, but with some significant differences. He was physically perceived by the eyewitnesses, and he could eat, and did so.[19] Indeed, Norman Geisler maintains that Jesus ate at least four times in his resurrection body, which was "capable of assimilating physical food."[20] In this respect, his resurrection body was similar to that of believers, of which Geisler says, "While the resurrection body may not have the necessity to eat, it does have the ability to eat. Eating in heaven will be a joy without being a need."[21] Further, Jesus' resurrection body was composed of molecules and occupied space.[22] At the same time there were changes, for he was now capable of entering and leaving rooms whose doors were locked.[23] That in some cases

17. Gordon R. Lewis and Bruce A. Demarest, *Integrative Theology*, 2 vols. (Grand Rapids: Zondervan, 1987, 1990), vol. 2, p. 470.

18. Ibid., p. 464; Louis Berkhof, *Systematic Theology* (Grand Rapids: Eerdmans, 1941), p. 346.

19. Lewis and Demarest, *Integrative Theology*, vol. 2, p. 465.

20. Norman L. Geisler, *The Battle for the Resurrection* (Nashville: Thomas Nelson, 1989), p. 122.

21. Ibid.

22. Ibid., p. 121; Lewis and Demarest, *Integrative Theology*, vol. 2, pp. 471–72.

23. Lewis and Demarest, *Integrative Theology*, vol. 2, p. 465; Berkhof, *Systematic Theology*, p. 346.

Jesus was not immediately recognized by people who presumably knew him is further indication of the changes that had taken place in the resurrection.[24]

There is little real argumentation for the central points of this general position. For example, Gordon Lewis and Bruce Demarest affirm, "A spiritual body is a resurrected physical body with greater capacities as an instrument of the spirit."[25] They also say, in regard to the ascension, "Jesus' transformation to a glorified 'state' had already occurred at his resurrection."[26] In each case the statement is simply asserted without any supporting argumentation.

Such a view entails several difficulties, however. One is that the appearances of the resurrected (but not yet ascended) Christ are not consistent with the appearance of the ascended Christ to Saul of Tarsus, which seemed to involve less specific physical perception. Another difficulty is the questions that arise from the contention that Jesus actually ate fish: Did the molecules enter into his digestive system? Did they provide nourishment? Did they produce new body cells? If our resurrection bodies in heaven will be capable of being nourished, will they also be capable of becoming malnourished? If so, what type of imperishable bodies are they? Further, if the final, glorified body of Jesus had visible nail prints and an unhealed wound into which one could thrust his hand, what is the status of such wounds now? Have they healed? If wounds and injuries from this life persist into the next life, will there really be perfected bodies, or will, for example, amputees be missing their limbs throughout eternity?

A further problem of the view we have been discussing is its stress on location in space and time. For instance, there is a general insistence that heaven is not merely a state, but also a place. Thus Jesus in his ascension actually passed through space en route to heaven. But if, as is presumed, space and time came into existence at the creation, "where" was the Trinity prior to that event? And is it really possible to speak of the location of a spirit? This problem is sometimes recognized in connection with

24. Berkhof, *Systematic Theology*, p. 346.
25. Lewis and Demarest, *Integrative Theology*, vol. 2, p. 465.
26. Ibid., p. 472.

Jesus' sitting at the right hand of the Father, although the implications are usually not drawn. And what of the intermediate state? If individuals who have died are somehow in a disembodied condition, how can they have location? This spatiotemporal emphasis seems to lead to an overly physical view of the resurrection, a view countered by both the promises of the perfection to come (Rev. 21:4) and the few hints we are given regarding the nature of the resurrection existence (e.g., Luke 20:34–38). An alternative would be either to abandon the stress on location in space and time, and with it the stress on a literal physical body, or to conceive of "place" in a fashion consistent with a spirit's being "located" there.

Jesus' Resurrection Body as a Corporeal Revelation

More subtle and nuanced is the view of George Ladd. It is particularly significant because it advances many of the arguments of the previous view in a refined fashion, yet recognizes certain difficulties and attempts to deal with them in a creative way. His overall position can be summarized in several basic tenets:

1. *The resurrection body of Christ and his final, glorified body are the same.* The conditions which pertained between the resurrection and the ascension are therefore the conditions in which he functions at present and will for all eternity. The major arguments which Ladd advances in support of this thesis are the unusual qualities which the body of Jesus possessed after (but not before) the resurrection. Particularly in view is the ability to leave the sealed tomb and to appear and disappear at will, passing through solid objects if necessary. The episode involving the two disciples in Emmaus is the primary case of his disappearance at will, although Ladd assumes a similar disappearance from the meeting with the disciples in Jerusalem on that same Sunday evening.[27] The record of Jesus' appearances to the disciples when behind closed and presumably locked doors is equally forceful evidence. Ladd concludes, "He possessed a real body, but also powers never before heard of—of being able to appear and disappear at will to the human senses."[28]

---

27. George E. Ladd, *I Believe in the Resurrection of Jesus* (Grand Rapids: Eerdmans, 1975), pp. 96–99.
28. Ibid., p. 99.

There are two weaknesses in Ladd's position. The first is that although the unusual occurrences argue for a changed body, that is not the only possible conclusion. They do not require bodily transformation, only miraculous activity. So, for example, Philip was caught away by the Spirit from the presence of the Ethiopian (Acts 8:39–40). The escape of Jesus through the crowd that intended to kill him may also have been of this nature (Luke 4:28–30).

More significant, however, is the failure to establish that Jesus' resurrection body, which was different from his predeath body, was the final form he would have following the ascension. Ladd is aware of the "striking difference" between the form of Jesus' appearance to Saul on the Damascus road and the postresurrection appearances recorded in the Gospels.[29] We will look more closely later at Ladd's explanation of the difference (see pp. 571–72); here we need observe merely that he rejects any differentiation between the resurrection body and the ascension body. While it has been suggested that "during the forty days, [Jesus] was in a different mode of existence which involved a different body than after his ascension when he returned to the world of God and became a 'life-giving Spirit,'" Ladd's response to this hypothesis is quick and categorical: "However, the logic of what we found thus far in the witness of both the Gospels and Paul suggests that *the resurrection of Jesus was his exaltation.* At his resurrection he entered the invisible world of God."[30] We must point out, however, that the only evidence Ladd has presented is the unusual powers of Jesus' resurrection body as compared with his earthly body and the biblical description of the resurrection body of the believer.

2. *The resurrection bodies of believers and the body which Jesus had on earth after his resurrection are of the same order.* Therefore whatever the Bible teaches about the one can be correctly predicated of the other as well. This contention rests entirely upon 1 Corinthians 15:20–23, where Paul speaks of Christ as the first fruits of those who have fallen asleep. Ladd's interpretation of verse 23 is pivotal: "That is to say: *the resurrection body of Jesus was of the same order as the resurrection bodies of the saints at the*

29. Ibid., p. 126.
30. Ibid., p. 127.

end of the age. Both Jesus and the saints have a 'spiritual body.' Both Jesus and the saints have a glorified body."[31] This appears, however, to be extracting more from the text than can be found therein. Without considering that great cosmic changes will presumably take place at the time of Jesus' second coming and the consequent resurrection of believers, Ladd simply asserts the equivalence of Jesus' resurrection body and that of the believer. But if this is the case, Ladd must be prepared to explain away some of the activities of Christ during the forty days.

3. *Jesus' postresurrection appearances in the Gospels are semi-physical in nature.* While this term is not used by Ladd, it seems applicable in view of the two sets of phenomena which are reported there. On the one hand, we have the miraculous appearances and disappearances. On the other hand, we have several indications of a real body: Thomas was invited to see and touch the nail prints and to thrust his hand into the wound in Jesus' side (John 20:24–29); the same invitation was extended to the Eleven (Luke 24:36–39); Jesus then said, "A spirit has not flesh and bones as you see that I have" (v. 39); and he took a piece of fish and ate it (vv. 42–43). In some respects it seemed that Jesus had a normal human body, for he could eat and be touched; yet he was not subject to the limitations imposed by the laws of physics, so that he could pass through walls and vanish from sight. It was therefore a "real," but not a "physical" body (Ladd reserves the use of the latter term for the body as we now have it, i.e., subject to decay and death).[32]

Ladd is faced with two choices at this point. One is simply to declare that what the disciples saw was the final, glorified body of Christ. This Ladd does not choose to do, his only reason being that the evidence concerning the resurrection body of the believer (which, it will be remembered, Ladd maintains is of the same order as that of Christ) suggests a very different sort of body.[33] On the other hand, C. K. Barrett speaks of "the mysterious power of the risen Jesus, who was at once sufficiently corporeal to show his wounds and sufficiently immaterial to pass through closed doors."[34] In such a view, presumably the final,

---

31. Ibid., pp. 123–24.
32. Ibid., pp. 99, 103 n. 23.
33. Ibid., pp. 114–17.
34. C. K. Barrett, *The Gospel According to St. John* (New York: Macmillan, 1955), p. 472.

glorified body of Jesus is "semiphysical," and so also will be the believer's resurrection body.

The alternative for Ladd is to maintain that what the disciples saw was not Jesus' final, glorified body, but that he manifested himself in a fashion that would convince them of the reality of his bodily resurrection. So Ladd comments regarding Jesus' invitation to the disciples to see and touch his wounds: "These words need not be taken to be a description of the actual material composition of Jesus' body, but are intended as a proof of Jesus' corporeity." Similarly, he says of Jesus' eating of the piece of fish, "This again need be nothing more than evidence that Jesus' presence was in tangible, visible, bodily form."[35]

What, then, did happen in the appearances? Ladd sets this question against the background of what happened in the resurrection: "Jesus' dead body was raised into the immortal, eternal life of the world of God, which is invisible to mortal eyes, unless it makes itself visible. The appearances, then, were condescensions of the risen, exalted Lord by which he convinced his disciples that he was no longer dead."[36]

The issue is faced again when Ladd discusses the difference between the appearance to Paul (actually still Saul of Tarsus) and the appearances recounted in the Gospels. He readily acknowledges the difficulty: "In the Gospels, Jesus has a far more flesh-like body which can be not only heard with the ears but also observed with the eyes and felt with the hands. We would not gloss over the difference between Paul and the Gospels; it is real and striking."[37] Scholars have various ways of dealing with this problem. Some regard the emphasis on the physical as a product of the church's theologizing which appeared in the later strata of the tradition.[38] Wolfhart Pannenberg holds that all of the appearances were of the same nature as the appearance to Paul, which he calls an objective vision, and that the disciples' understanding this "completely alien reality" to be an encounter with someone who had been raised from the dead "can only be explained from the presuppo-

35. Ladd, *I Believe*, p. 98.
36. Ibid., p. 101.
37. Ibid., p. 126.
38. Leonhard Goppelt, *Apostolic and Post-Apostolic Times* (New York: Harper and Row, 1970), p. 19.

sition of a particular form of the apocalyptic expectation of the resurrection of the dead."[39]

Ladd goes partway with Pannenberg, but not all the way. The appearances in the Gospels and to Paul were of different kinds. To the disciples Jesus revealed himself in apparent corporeal form. This was a case of the invisible glorified Jesus' making himself visible (as well as audible and tangible) to his disciples. Ladd argues: "Speaking from the theological point of view, if Jesus had actually entered a new realm of existence at his resurrection, there remains no reason to deny the possibility that he could appear to his disciples in completely human form, as the Gospel witness said he did. We are here dealing with a realm of existence unknown to us. If so, such appearances were condescensions of the risen, exalted Jesus to the obtuseness and unbelief of his disciples."[40]

4. *The ascension really added nothing to the exaltation of Jesus, which was fully accomplished at the resurrection.* The purpose of the ascension was simply to signify the end of the appearances.[41] Ladd holds that the resurrection and the exaltation are equated in numerous New Testament passages, such as Acts 2:32–33; 5:30–31; Colossians 3:1; and Hebrews 1:3, 13; 8:1; 10:12; and 12:2. He acknowledges that the resurrection does not appear in several of these texts. Indeed, they refer more frequently to Jesus' being at the right hand of the Father, certainly an allusion to the ascension. One would expect the inference that the ascension constitutes the exaltation, or at least its completion. Yet, paradoxically, Ladd concludes that the resurrection should be identified with the exaltation. This leaves the ascension with only a revelatory significance.

Although his view is somewhat ambiguous, William Lane Craig also appears to believe that Jesus took on his final, glorified form at the resurrection. He says that Jesus' appearances were "appearances in the visible realm out of the invisible."[42] We can only speculate about the nature of this invisible realm,

39. Wolfhart Pannenberg, *Jesus—God and Man* (Philadelphia: Westminster, 1968), p. 93.
40. Ladd, *I Believe*, pp. 126–27.
41. Ibid., p. 128.
42. William Lane Craig, *Assessing the New Testament Evidence for the Historicity of the Resurrection of Jesus* (Lewiston, N.Y.: Edwin Mellen, 1989), p. 345.

which according to the Bible is inhabited by angels and demons. He does suggest, however, that the resurrection body could be "analogous to the bodies of angelic beings, who can materialize and dematerialize in the physical universe."[43] Although the Gospels do not draw an explicit comparison between the bodies of angels and Christ's resurrection body, Craig notes that "the description of Jesus's resurrection body reminds one of angelic bodies, and the latter are a useful analogue to make the former more understandable."[44]

An earlier presentation of the same view was made by W. J. Sparrow Simpson. He notes the differences between the two sets of witnesses to the resurrection body of Jesus: those that depict him as having a basically materialistic body, and those that speak of his coming and going mysteriously and not always being recognized.[45] Simpson's solution is a spiritual body which sometimes appeared in perceptible form: "If we say that our Lord being normally intangible, inaudible, invisible, existing in a purely unearthly state, did nevertheless assume solidity, and make Himself tangible, audible, visible, for evidential and instructive purposes, and so temporarily bring Himself within range of our earthly organisations, we have an explanation which does justice to all the facts, leaves the narrative intact, and removes the contradiction."[46]

A Two-Stage Exaltation

It seems to me there is a better way to deal with the issues we have been considering. Ladd's selection of evidence for the nature of the resurrection body is, in my judgment, essentially correct. Paul's discussion of the resurrection body (1 Cor. 15) suggests that it will have some point of contact with the original earthly body, but will arise from it and consequently be a completely transformed body. We are unable to understand fully its nature, for all analogies drawn from human experience fall short. Like the plant that sprouts from the seed that has been sown, it is something new that issues from the old. It is a body

43. Ibid.
44. Ibid., p. 346.
45. W. J. Sparrow Simpson, *Our Lord's Resurrection*, 2d ed. (London: Longmans, Green, 1909; Grand Rapids: Zondervan, 1964 reprint), pp. 159–62.
46. Ibid., p. 170.

that is under the control and direction of spirit rather than of the human "soul." Further, we know from Jesus' postresurrection appearances that it transcends the usual restrictions of natural laws.

Were we to stop at this point, we would encounter a variety of difficulties. The description of Jesus' body during the forty days after the resurrection differs considerably and significantly from the depictions of the final glorified bodies of Christ and of the believer. In addition, the appearance to Saul is significantly different from the appearances in the Gospels. Further, the resurrected Jesus identified himself as "flesh and bones" (Luke 24:39), but this sounds suspiciously similar to the "flesh and blood" that Paul said cannot inherit the kingdom of God (1 Cor. 15:50).[47] Thus the view which we have referred to as semiphysical resurrection is inadequate.

Ladd's view of Jesus' resurrection body as a corporeal revelation has the virtue of taking seriously the seeming contradictions between the two types of witnesses to the appearances recorded in the Gospels, and between those appearances and the manifestation to Saul of Tarsus. It also has serious shortcomings, however. We observed some of them as we expounded his view. More serious, however, is that Jesus seems to have misled his disciples. While the manner of his manifestation successfully revealed that the resurrection had been bodily rather than merely spiritual, it also led them to believe that he was still so restricted that he had palpable wounds and ate physical food. This, however, is in contradiction to what Ladd contends and Scripture reveals about the glorified body of the ascended Christ. In addition, the ascension becomes, in Ladd's scheme, a virtual sham, since Jesus was already removed from the earthly realm.

I believe that a more adequate view is what I would call two-stage exaltation. In the first stage, the resurrection body of Christ was as it appeared to the apostles. It transcended many

---

47. I am aware of the argument that "flesh and blood" is a Semitic idiom meaning "mortal human nature" and having "nothing, strictly speaking, to do with anatomy" (Craig, *Assessing*, p. 343). See, however, the contrary views of Hans Grass, *Ostergeschehen und Osterberichte*, 4th rev. ed. (Göttingen: Vandenhoeck & Ruprecht, 1970), p. 40; James M. Robinson, "Jesus from Easter to Valentinus (or to the Apostles' Creed)," *Journal of Biblical Literature* 101 (1982): 11–12; Raymond E. Brown, *The Virginal Conception and Bodily Resurrection of Jesus* (New York: Paulist, 1973), p. 87.

of the laws of nature, yet it still possessed some of the characteristics of the body of his earthly life. The ascension, however, completed the transformation. Now Christ is in a totally different realm, where space and time do not apply, although he still is active within this world. The body which he now has is the completely glorified body, free from the weaknesses and immune to the temptations of this world. What happened in two stages in the case of Christ will occur in one stage in the case of believers. At the resurrection in connection with the second coming of Christ, we will receive the glorified body, which is already present for him.

This follows rather closely the view of James Orr. Orr observed that, on the one hand, the Gospel writers take the greatest pains to point out that the resurrected body of Jesus was a true body: it bore the marks of the crucifixion and he could eat.[48] On the other hand, it was not simply a natural body. Jesus had the power to keep from being recognized and even perceived by those around him, and to transcend physical appearances.[49] Orr believed that this resurrection body must be seen in the context of an interim or transitional period:

> On *earth*, as the history shows, Jesus had a body in all natural respects, corruptibility excepted, like our own. He hungered, He thirsted, He was weary, He suffered, He died of exhaustion and wounds. In *heaven*, that body has undergone transformation; has become "the body of His glory." In comparison with the natural, it has become a spiritual—"a pneumatic"—body, assimilated to, and entirely under the control of, the spiritual nature and forces that reside in it and work through it. In the interval between the Resurrection and the Ascension its condition must be thought of as *intermediate* between these two states—no longer merely natural (the act of Resurrection itself proclaimed this), yet not fully entered into the state of glorification. It presents characters, requisite for the proof of its identity, which show that the earthly condition is still not wholly parted with. It discovers qualities and powers which reveal that the supra-terrestrial condition is already begun.[50]

48. James Orr, *The Resurrection of Jesus* (New York: Hodder and Stoughton, 1908), p. 197.
49. Ibid., pp. 198–202.
50. Ibid., p. 196.

Two-stage exaltation avoids, on the one hand, the rather grossly sensual view of the glorified body and, on the other, the view that makes Christ somewhat deceptive. In addition, it gives the ascension the importance that it deserves: the ascension constitutes the full restoration of Christ to his glory, subject only to the final revelation of his sovereignty in the second coming.

Given the view of the ascension as the second stage of the exaltation, the incarnation continues and maintains a permanent modification in the Second Person of the Trinity, but the limitations involved are greatly reduced. Now it is a glorified humanity that is in union with the deity, and such a humanity imposes even less restriction upon the functioning of the divine nature. Similarly, when we are glorified, the difference between God and us will be much less, though we will never be of the same essence as God.

Note that in evaluating the various positions on the issues we have been discussing, we must be careful not to suggest, on the basis of some similarity, that a particular position derives directly from some ancient view, say Platonism.[51] The notion of a future in which we eat merely for pleasure sounds more like the chiliasm of early church history than it does like the Bible, but that does not mean it derived from chiliasm. And even if there were derivation, that would not bear on the issue of the validity of the view. This issue must be decided by the same criteria we have so often employed: the view which accounts for a larger portion of the relevant data with less distortion than do its competitors is the one that should be adopted.

---

51. Craig, *Assessing*, pp. 157–58; Gerald O'Collins, *The Easter Jesus*, 2d ed. (London: Darton, Longman, and Todd, 1980), p. 94.

23

Jesus as the Savior of All People

We have noted in earlier chapters the objection that the orthodox doctrine of Christ makes it difficult to conceive of him as the object of faith and devotion for all peoples from all social classes. Whether as a result of his being incarnated in a male human, Jesus of Nazareth, or his having been used by the more affluent and powerful, who have invested him with their values, to exploit poorer classes and nations, he seems irrelevant to many persons. This chapter will address the question of whether Jesus can be the Savior of everyone.

Jesus and Women

It will not be possible to address in detail the relevance of Christ as Savior to each of the sociological subgroups discussed in Part 2. Consequently, we have chosen to focus upon one of them, namely, women. We have selected this particular subgroup for several reasons. For one thing, the feature that makes

577

him objectionable to some feminists simply cannot be denied. Whereas Jesus was not really from the privileged class, and his skin probably was quite dark, he definitely was male! Further, a substantial number of people today appeal to Jesus' maleness to justify various distinctions on the basis of sex. Such "discrimination" is openly advocated in a way in which the preference of white persons or First World persons or persons of relative affluence is not. Further, the ferocity with which some of the more radical feminist theologians take exception to Jesus' maleness as an inherent conflict between orthodox incarnational Christology and the interests of their group does not seem to be matched by the other social subgroups. We shall therefore examine in some detail Jesus' relationship with women, both in his teaching and in his practice. We will then look briefly at his relationship with other oppressed groups.

The Background

One can scarcely evaluate Jesus' view of women apart from its context. If we would understand his teachings and actions, we must be aware of the status of women in the society in which he lived and ministered. An acquaintance with the situation of the time will enable us to see more clearly what he was saying and doing.

To some extent, we have depended on the Mishnah for our perspective. There is some hazard in this, since the Mishnah consists of rabbinic tradition which began to be compiled after A.D. 70 and was officially promulgated about 200. The historical problem is how much we may rely upon it for knowledge of situations prior to the destruction of the temple and the fall of Jerusalem in 70. The Mishnah claims a continuity with the past, maintaining that much of what it teaches comes from the schools of Shammai, Hillel, and other pre-70 sages. This claim has been disputed by some scholars, most notably Jacob Neusner, who nonetheless concedes that from the Mishnah "we may even gain a perspective on part of pre-70 historical Pharisaism," especially the period that we are most concerned about here.[1]

---

1. Jacob Neusner, *The Rabbinic Traditions About the Pharisees Before 70* (Leiden: Brill, 1971), p. 318.

Other sources, including Josephus, have been consulted as well. He reports that, according to the law, "the woman is in all points inferior to the man."[2] Some Jewish feminists, such as Judith Plaskow, have accused Christians of drawing from such comments an unduly negative picture of the Jewish mind-set at this time in order to make Jesus' views seem more progressive.[3] We should, of course, bear in mind that Jewish writers like Plaskow, in seeking to understand the history of their religion, are not exempt from a "hermeneutics of suspicion." We should, at the same time, be careful not to universalize the views of Judaism. Elisabeth Schüssler Fiorenza, for example, develops at some length the view found in the apocryphal book of Judith, which is much more positive about women than are some of the rabbinic materials.[4] It perhaps is significant that this book did not attain canonical status.

Women in Jewish culture certainly had a place in society inferior to that of men.[5] There were neither similar privileges nor similar responsibilities of religious practice. Women could not offer sacrifice or serve as priests. It appears that this exclusion was related to menstruation and the necessity of priests' being totally free from any uncleanness.[6] Moreover, in determining whether a quorum was present for worship, women, like children and slaves, were not counted. They were separated from the men during worship, both in the temple and in the synagogue.[7] According to Josephus, their testimony was not to be accepted in a court of law, but this is a disputed opinion.[8] Social relationships and status were also different for the two sexes. Except in rare circumstances, a woman could not divorce her husband, and even then it was technically the husband who got

2. Josephus *Against Apion* 2.201.

3. Judith Plaskow, "Blaming Jews for Inventing Patriarchy," *Lilith* 7 (1980): 11–12.

4. Elisabeth Schüssler Fiorenza, *In Memory of Her: A Feminist Theological Reconstruction of Christian Origins* (New York: Crossroad, 1983), pp. 115–18.

5. For a well-balanced discussion see Leonard Swidler, *Women in Judaism: The Status of Women in Formative Judaism* (Metuchen, N.J.: Scarecrow, 1976).

6. Ben Witherington III, *Women in the Ministry of Jesus: A Study of Jesus' Attitudes to Women and Their Roles as Reflected in His Earthly Life* (Cambridge: Cambridge University Press, 1984), p. 8.

7. Leonard Swidler, "Jesus Was a Feminist," *Catholic World* 212, no. 1,270 (Jan. 1971): 178.

8. Josephus *Antiquities of the Jews* 4.8.15.

the divorce. She did not have the right to divorce him, but he had the right to divorce her. The school of Hillel, more liberal than that of Shammai, permitted a man to divorce his wife if she did anything that displeased him.[9] It would appear that, on any reckoning of the Jewish sources, women were treated as inferior and subservient to men.

Jesus' Teaching on Women

When we come to Jesus' teachings, we find an impressive interest in women and what appears to be a studied effort to include them.[10] A first instance is his teachings about adultery. In Matthew 5:28 Jesus condemns not only adultery, but even lusting after a woman, which he made tantamount to adultery. This is a significant departure from the tradition. It had been common to think of women as the temptresses against whom a man must guard himself. This theme is common in the Book of Proverbs and is carried over into the rabbinic teaching about adultery.[11] Rather than blame the woman for being seductive, however, Jesus lays the responsibility firmly upon the man.

The man's responsibility is also prominent in Jesus' discussion of divorce. Here he clearly says that a man who divorces a woman and marries another commits adultery (Matt. 19:9; Luke 16:18). Moreover, in divorcing her he causes her to commit adultery (Matt. 5:32); and the person who marries her commits adultery as well (Matt. 5:32; Luke 16:18). Further, in Mark 10:12 Jesus apparently grants the right of a woman to divorce her husband, something that was legal for Romans under their law, but not for Jews, except in the case of royal persons such as the Herods, who were more Roman than Jewish.[12]

Jesus' teaching on adultery and divorce was truly revolutionary. For the Jews never spoke of a man committing adultery against his wife, only the reverse.[13] What Jesus said implied that

9. Evelyn and Frank Stagg, *Woman in the World of Jesus* (Philadelphia: Westminster, 1978), p. 51.
10. The scope of the present volume does not permit us to justify our appeal to the various passages here cited. For a rather thorough and relatively skeptical discussion, see the treatment of these passages in Witherington.
11. Swidler, *Women in Judaism*, p. 127.
12. Stagg and Stagg, *Woman*, p. 134.
13. Witherington, *Women*, p. 27.

the woman had rights of her own which were not to be encroached upon. She was not simply an object to be used.[14] If this did not mean actual equality of the marriage partners, it certainly was a major step in that direction.

Another revelation of Jesus' conception of the worth and role of women is seen in Luke 11:27–28. While he was teaching, a woman called out, "Blessed is the womb that bore you, and the breasts that you sucked." Here was an expression, in the form of a compliment, of the common idea that the major role of women was to bear children. Jesus, however, did nothing to reinforce that conception. Instead, he said, "Blessed rather are those who hear the word of God and keep it!" This is an implicit endorsement of the right of women to be taught, something not always approved of in rabbinic circles.[15]

Also relevant is Jesus' teaching about prostitutes and the kingdom of God. In a debate with the chief priests and elders of the people (Matt. 21:23, 31–32), Jesus said that tax collectors and prostitutes would precede them into the kingdom of God. Tax collectors and prostitutes were the two most despised groups in Jewish society. Ordinarily, in the Synoptic Gospels, the expression is "tax collectors and sinners." That Jesus on this occasion altered the expression to "tax collectors and prostitutes" seems to be a deliberate effort to make clear that both sexes were included. Leonard Swidler says, "Clearly for him a woman reduced completely to a sex object is seen as the object, not of disdain, but rather of exploitation, who nevertheless is a *person*, one among those who can 'make their way into the reign of God.'"[16]

Jesus' parables are also pertinent, for it seems as if he went out of his way to include women as examples of the points he was seeking to make. The occurrence of twin parables suggests in some cases that Jesus was concerned to make clear that the lesson he was giving applied both to men and to women. In Luke 18 we have the parable of the obstinate woman, whose aggressiveness would not usually be thought of as a quality

14. Stagg and Stagg, *Woman*, p. 130.
15. Swidler, "Jesus Was a Feminist," p. 183.
16. Leonard Swidler, *Biblical Affirmations of Woman* (Philadelphia: Westminster, 1979), p. 188.

desirable in women. Her persistent plea avails, just as does the prayer of the unrighteous man, the tax collector. Similarly, in Luke 15 we have the twin parables of the man with the lost sheep and the woman with the lost coin. And in Matthew 25 the parable of the wise and foolish virgins places them in much the same role as the faithful and unfaithful stewards in the parable of the talents. In all of these instances, Jesus tacitly shows that a woman can represent the activity of God or a righteous individual equally well as can a man. C. F. Parvey comments: "Other than as a pedagogical device for repetition, there is no apparent reason for stating the same message twice except to choose examples that would make the message clearly understandable to different groups—the female and male listeners."[17]

There also are teachings in which Jesus seems to explicitly set aside or criticize the hierarchical structure of his society, and especially in relation to men and women. Fiorenza has listed three groups of such teachings:

1. Teachings on marriage and divorce, where the main intent seems to be to negate the domination of women by men (e.g., Mark 10:1–12; 12:18–27).
2. A group of afamilial sayings which speak of replacing the natural patriarchal-family bonds with a relationship to God. Those who do the will of God are brothers and sisters to each other (Matt. 10:35–39; Mark 3:32–35; 10:29–31).
3. Antidominance sayings criticizing those who try to exalt themselves (Matt. 23:2–12; Mark 9:33–37; 10:14–15; Luke 22:24–27).[18]

This last point does not mean, in the judgment of more moderate feminists, that all hierarchy is to be done away with, and especially not that of God over human beings. It is dominance of one human by another that is decried, not theistic lordship. In fact, according to Fiorenza and Rebecca Pentz, it is because

---

17. C. F. Parvey, "The Theology and Leadership of Women in the New Testament," in *Religion and Sexism: Images of Woman in the Jewish and Christian Traditions*, ed. Rosemary Radford Ruether (New York: Simon and Schuster, 1974), p. 139.

18. Fiorenza, *In Memory of Her*, pp. 143–51.

of this fatherhood that there is to be no human domination of one another.[19] For either a brother or a sister in the human community to take on the authority and power of the Father is to claim for oneself what belongs to the Father alone.

Finally, a group of Jesus' teachings concerned with the future and with judgment mention women or use feminine imagery:

1. *The queen of the South* (Matt. 12:42; Luke 11:31). Jesus declares that in the judgment two witnesses will condemn his wicked generation: the men of Nineveh, who repented at Jonah's preaching, and the queen of the South (obviously the queen of Sheba), who came from the ends of the earth to listen to Solomon. It is significant that again a feminine and a masculine example are paired. Beyond that, we should note that in the final judgment the testimony of a woman will be accepted and will be determinative. Even though some rabbis would not accept the testimony of a woman, Jesus honored this woman in a singular way.

2. *The final separation* (Matt. 24:40–41; Luke 17:34–35). In speaking of his second coming, Jesus says that there will be two men in a field (Matt.) or in a bed (Luke), and two women grinding at the mill. One of the men and one of the women will be taken, and the others left behind.

3. *Jesus' maternal concern for Jerusalem* (Matt. 23:37–39; Luke 13:34–35). Jesus looks upon Jerusalem and sees the people killing prophets and stoning other emissaries to them. As a result, the house of Jerusalem will be forsaken and desolate. Jesus laments, "How often would I have gathered your children together as a hen gathers her brood under her wings, and you would not!" Jesus has elsewhere pictured the heavenly Father in maternal terms; here he depicts himself under this imagery. He, too, exhibits the nurturing qualities found in a human mother or a hen.

4. *The pitiable fate of the daughters of Jerusalem* (Luke 23:27–31). On the way to the cross, a group of women

19. Ibid., pp. 150–51; Rebecca D. Pentz, "Can Jesus Save Women?" in *Encountering Jesus: A Debate on Christology*, ed. Stephen T. Davis (Atlanta: John Knox, 1988), p. 80.

followed, weeping and lamenting Jesus' fate. It was not uncommon for Jews to grieve and mourn an impending death, particularly of a relative or a famous person whose passing would mean a great loss.[20] Whether this group comprised disciples of Jesus or simply Jewish women who were spontaneously moved to sympathy by his plight, their public display could be dangerous to them in view of his being a convicted criminal. Their conduct forms an interesting contrast with that of the men disciples. Jesus' words to the women indicate that even in these last moments of his public ministry he was concerned about them and their future predicament as daughters of Israel. They should weep for themselves, for the days were coming when the barren would be considered blessed.

We must pause now to summarize what Jesus taught about women and their role:

1. Jesus spoke of the importance and sanctity of the family. While we must be careful to avoid reading in twentieth-century conceptions of the family, it is significant that he held the traditional roles of wife and mother in respect. In addition, his teaching about divorce stressed the permanence of marriage.
2. Jesus departed from the common conception of woman as the temptress, and placed responsibility in such matters as adultery upon the man. Unlike the religious teachings of his day, he held that women have the same rights in marriage as do men, and that the obligation to fidelity is as great upon the man as upon the woman. It is just as possible for a man to commit adultery against his wife as it is for a woman to commit adultery against her husband. Jesus appears to have taught a symmetry of responsibility.
3. Jesus used women as well as men to illustrate his teaching on spiritual matters. By so doing, he suggested that the qualities of women are no less suitable as analogies

20. Witherington, *Women*, p. 48.

of God and righteous behavior than are those of men, and he also provided women with imagery to which they could relate. At times, he appears to have gone out of his way to balance feminine and masculine examples.

Jesus' Treatment of Women

It will be instructive for us to observe the way in which Jesus related to various women. We will look first at some with whom he had a passing contact. Then we will focus on the women disciples, long-term followers such as Mary and Martha.

A first interesting case is that of the woman who anointed Jesus at the home of Simon (Luke 7:36–50). A righteous Jew, Simon had invited Jesus for dinner, perhaps out of a desire to learn more about him. While they ate, a sinful woman (probably a prostitute) came into the house. This in itself is not surprising, since the homes were of an open construction, and the Jews were instructed in their law to feed the poor. What the woman did, however, proved shocking to Simon. She proceeded to wash Jesus' feet with her tears, wipe them with her hair, kiss them, and anoint them. This aroused the ire of Simon, who said to himself, "If this man were a prophet, he would have known who and what sort of woman this is who is touching him, for she is a sinner" (v. 39). He saw the woman only in terms of her sinful acts, and thus only as a sex object. But the respect with which Jesus treated her shows that he saw her as just as much an object of divine concern and grace as was Simon; in fact, she was more loving and deserving of her sins' being forgiven (vv. 40–48). Neither her sinful life nor the fact that she was a woman presented any obstacle to Jesus.[21]

A second significant incident is the conversation between Jesus and the Samaritan woman (John 4:1–26). Here we have Jesus crossing a number of barriers, but for the moment we will focus upon the fact of her being a woman. The disciples marveled that he was talking to a woman in a public place (v. 27). And Jesus

---

21. While some scholars have seen the account of Jesus' handling of the woman taken in adultery (John 7:53–8:11) as a comparable instance, I do not believe it can legitimately be used. It is widely agreed that the passage is textually spurious, and attempts to argue that it nonetheless "rings true to what otherwise is known about Jesus" (Stagg and Stagg, *Woman*, p. 112) appear to me to be lacking in logical cogency.

was not making small talk. He was actually discussing theology with her, something which most Jewish men would have thought impossible. He took the initiative in the discussion, even though he knew the nature of her life, which was not such as to commend her. She had had five husbands (vv. 17–18). It was the custom in Judaism not to have more than three marriages in a lifetime. Legally, any number was permissible; morally, however, more than three was suspect.[22] In addition, living with a man to whom she was not married, she would have been ritually unclean, but Jesus seems unconcerned about such matters. (An interesting sidelight here is that Jesus' subsequent statement about sowing and reaping [vv. 34–38], though occasioned by the disciples' offer of food to him, occurs in a context where many Samaritans are coming to see and hear Jesus because of the woman's testimony. It is almost as if Jesus [and John] wishes to call attention to her role as a witness in his behalf.)

Another revealing narrative is the story of the poor widow and her two small coins (Mark 12:41–44; Luke 21:1–4). While there is no indication that Jesus actually confronted the woman and spoke with her, he observed her actions and drew certain conclusions about her. The scene was the temple treasury, where people could throw their gifts into the collection box. Many Pharisees threw in large gifts, doing so ostentatiously. Jesus, however, said that this poor widow had given more than them all, because they had put in out of their abundance, while she had given all that she had. Thus a woman was made an example for others to emulate. This whole episode is particularly striking in view of his immediately preceding statement about those who devour widows' households (Mark 12:40; Luke 20:47). Thus the moneys the rich threw into the treasury in such an ostentatious fashion may have derived at least in part from improper management of the resources of other widows. Ben Witherington says, "Jesus' special concern and admiration for women is perhaps nowhere more strikingly juxtaposed with His disgust over certain groups of privileged and supposedly pious men than here."[23]

---

22. Hermann L. Strack and Paul Billerbeck, *Kommentar zum Neuen Testament aus Talmud und Midrasch*, 6 vols. in 7 (Munich: C. H. Beck, 1974 reprint), vol. 2, p. 437.
23. Witherington, *Women*, p. 18.

Jesus also had contact with a number of women through his ministry of healing and other acts of compassion. One of the most striking cases was his healing of a crippled woman on the Sabbath (Luke 13:10–17). She had been possessed for eighteen years by a spirit of infirmity which left her doubled over. Apparently the illness did not make her unclean, for she was not ineligible to attend the Sabbath services. Jesus took several unusual steps. He interrupted his teaching and spoke to her in public. He healed her on the Sabbath, which brought a furious reaction from the synagogue official. Perhaps most surprising of all is his reference to her as a "daughter of Abraham." The expression *son of Abraham* was a standard phrase in Jewish literature to refer to a male member of the chosen people. Here, however, Jesus uses the expression of a woman, and does so in a context in which he contrasts her favorably with the males, and even the synagogue official, addressing them as "hypocrites"! Witherington's comment is instructive: "By using the title ['daughter of Abraham'], Jesus implies that she is as worthy of His concern and healing as any Jewish man and has as full a claim to her religious heritage as anyone."[24] Swidler's interpretation is similar: "For Jesus, women were also clearly full-fledged participants of the people and covenant of God."[25]

Jesus also healed a woman who had suffered an issue of blood for some twelve years (Matt. 9:20–22; Mark 5:24–34; Luke 8:43–48). This issue of blood made her ritually unclean (Lev. 15:19–30): she was unable to participate in any religious activity and consequently in some sense "displeasing to God." Anyone or anything she touched, or anyone who touched what she had touched, was similarly unclean. She managed, amid the crowd, to touch Jesus' cloak and was immediately healed. Jesus then singled her out and commended her for her faith, which he said had restored her to health. He showed that he was not afraid to be touched by an unclean person, thus by implication rejecting the blood taboo. And using her as an example, he also showed that women are capable of extraordinary acts of faith.[26]

Although none of the inner circle of twelve disciples was a

24. Ibid., p. 70.
25. Swidler, *Biblical Affirmations*, p. 182.
26. Witherington, *Women*, p. 73.

woman, there were several women who played prominent roles in Jesus' service. Except for his mother, Mary and Martha were undoubtedly the most important and prominent women in Jesus' life. They probably did not travel with him, but they provided hospitality for him in their home in Bethany, which was close to Jerusalem. One extremely instructive incident is found in Luke 10:38–42, sandwiched between the parable of the good Samaritan and the Lord's Prayer. Martha took the typically female role of hospitality and serving. Mary, however, "sat at the Lord's feet," a common way of referring to a disciple's learning from a rabbi. Martha complained to Jesus that Mary was leaving all the female work to her, and asked him to tell Mary to help. Jesus, however, commended what Mary was doing as choosing the better part. Here Jesus clearly broke from the culture and the stereotyped conceptions of women's roles. While women could attend the synagogue and even study if their husbands or masters were teachers, it was unheard of for a rabbi to come into a woman's house and teach her specifically.[27] Certainly Jesus was here indicating that an intellectual and spiritual life of study was fitting for women as well as for men.

In addition to Mary and Martha, we read in Luke 8:1–3 about a group of women who, with the other disciples, listened to Jesus and followed him about. The names of some of them are given: Mary Magdalene, Joanna, and Susanna. They were probably from Galilee, where the customs regarding women's conduct were not as forbidding as in Jerusalem. It is noteworthy that the gospel here cut across social classes, for Mary Magdalene, who had undoubtedly been avoided by many, and Joanna, the wife of Herod's steward, Chuza, were both members of this group. They had left home and family to travel with a rabbi, which was a most unusual breach of custom. Jesus apparently encouraged and approved of this—a factor to be kept in mind when he is charged with taking the traditional and conventional approach of having only male disciples.[28]

We ought also to notice the prominent role played by women disciples at the time of Jesus' death, burial, and resurrection. For

27. Ibid., p. 101.
28. Stagg and Stagg, *Woman*, pp. 123–25.

here we find women in a better light than his male disciples. Women who had followed Jesus and ministered to him were found at the cross (Matt. 27:55–56; Mark 15:40–41); they did not flee fearfully as had the male disciples (Matt. 26:56; Mark 14:50). We know that Jesus' mother was there, for he entrusted her to John. Among the other women present were her sister (Mary the wife of Clopas), Mary Magdalene, Mary the mother of James and Joseph, and Salome. The burial was also witnessed by at least two women, Mary Magdalene and Mary the mother of Joseph ("the other Mary," Matt. 27:61). Women, including at least Mary Magdalene, Mary the mother of James, and Salome, were the first to witness the empty tomb. They also were the first to bring this news to the disciples, who did not believe them (Matt. 28:1–8; Mark 16:1–8; Luke 24:1–11; John 20:1–10). They were the first ones to whom Jesus appeared, and thus first to proclaim the good news of his resurrection (Matt. 28:9–10; John 20:11–18). It appears that the women's faithfulness was the cause of their privilege. Because they had gone to the cross and later to the empty tomb, they were the first to be recipients and then proclaimers of the good news. They also believed when given the evidence, whereas the men disciples doubted. In connection with the most important events of Jesus' life and ministry, the faithfulness of women was impressive, and it was rewarded.

Both Jesus' treatment of women and the role they played in his life indicate that he was, by the standards of his time, something of a feminist.[29] Luke, who writes to a Gentile audience that would have been more inclined than the Jews to better the position of women, seems especially to select and amplify those incidents which reveal Jesus' positive attitude towards women.[30] It will be helpful to summarize briefly some of the innovative elements in Jesus' relationships:

1. Jesus did not reinforce the common conception that the place of women was in the home. On the contrary, they were encouraged to learn from him, just as did his male disciples.

29. Witherington, *Women*, pp. 123–24.
30. Ibid., pp. 46, 47, 52, 126–30.

2. Jesus broke with the traditions which prohibited public contact and conversation between a teacher and a woman. He even disregarded the blood taboo.
3. Jesus praised women for their faith and other spiritual virtues, even on occasion comparing them favorably with the official spiritual leaders of the Jews.
4. Jesus allowed women to accompany him and apparently to perform certain ministries for him. And they proved faithful. Not abandoning him in the hour of need, they consequently were privileged to be the first to see the empty tomb and the resurrected Christ, and to proclaim this good news to others.

It seems as if Jesus began to reverse some of the restrictive elements in Judaism. It is unlikely that we would find him, given his historical setting, to be a full practicing feminist, since the radical overturning of cultural mores that would have been involved, for example, in appointing women as some of the apostles, might have prevented his movement from ever obtaining a proper hearing. Nevertheless, there are enough serious breaks with the culture of the time to prove he had great sympathy with women.[31]

Jesus as Savior of Women

But do Jesus' teachings about and treatment of women render him sufficiently acceptable that women today can believe in and commit to him? That question is being addressed by a number of feminist theologians. One who has answered it in the affirmative is Rebecca Pentz. She seeks to respond to certain objections which some feminists have raised against Jesus.

The first objection is that even if we need not conclude that because Jesus, the supreme revelation of God, was male, God must be male, the characteristics of the God whom Jesus reveals are abhorrent to feminists. In particular, the idea of God as the transcendent Father communicates to feminists the idea of a tyrannical patriarch, the top dog in an oppressive hierarchy. Pentz applauds the efforts of feminists like Fiorenza, who have shown Jesus' opposition to hierarchies in which men exercise

31. Ibid., pp. 125–31.

dominance over women.[32] Pentz does not want an abrogation of one hierarchical structure, however, the one with Jesus and God on top.

Some argue that all hierarchies are essentially exploitative and dominating, so that the groups on top use their power to oppress those below. This, Pentz says, is a case of using "power over" as "power against."[33] It need not be so, however. She uses as an example the case of Bela Karolyi, the coach of Olympic gold-medalist gymnast Mary Lou Retton. He had almost complete power over her schedule and activities. This was not, however, power against, but power for, used to develop her potential to the fullest. So it is with God. There is no question that he has power over us. Because he is our Creator and has complete ability suited to his position, he has the right to exercise control. Yet he always uses his power over as power for, not power against. Although he has controlling power over us, he does not dominate us. He respects our freedom, allowing us to fail on our own and to succeed on our own as well.[34]

There is a lesson for women in God's use of his power. Sometimes women have shunned power, thinking it necessarily entails dominance. That need not be. The power used to ennoble, enlighten, and empower others is a kind of power that women should strive to attain.[35]

The second objection is that Jesus cannot be an example or model for women, for he had only male experiences. Pentz, however, notes that Jesus modeled different kinds of behavior when dealing with women alone and when dealing with men. He never, for example, washed a woman's feet and told her to do likewise.[36]

Valerie Saiving has proposed that there are particularly masculine as well as particularly feminine sins. Because of their biological makeup and roles, men are more inclined to sins of pride, will to power, and exploitation. Women are more self-giving and sacrificial, but these qualities have their own temptations, to "triviality, distractibility, and diffuseness." Contemporary theology, because it speaks from and to the male experience only, has rel-

32. Pentz, "Can Jesus Save Women?" pp. 78–80.
33. Ibid., p. 80.
34. Ibid., pp. 80–82.
35. Ibid., p. 82.
36. Ibid., p. 83.

egated women to their self-sacrifice rather than encouraging them to creativity and excellence.[37]

What of Jesus, however? Did he contribute to the uniquely feminine sins, and to the problems of women, by encouraging them to continue in their self-demeaning sin, being even more self-giving rather than finding an identity of their own and striving toward excellence? Pentz asserts that Jesus did not do this. In support of this contention, she appeals to three incidents in Jesus' ministry: his encounters with the Samaritan woman (John 4:7–30), with Martha (Luke 10:38–42), and with an unidentified woman in the crowd (Luke 11:27–28). In each of these cases, he did not encourage the typical feminine role. Rather, he called these women from their particularly feminine sins to excellence.[38]

Pentz goes on to declare that there is far more to Jesus' function than simply being a model for others, women included. She holds to the orthodox or traditional view that Christ's lifework "culminated in his death on the cross and his subsequent resurrection." These acts were intended to "save us from sin, restore us to God, and free us to be all God created us to be."[39] Here Pentz raises the question which forms the title of her essay: Can Jesus save women? In order to do so, she says, three conditions must be met: his act of salvation must be intended to cover women, it must be effective for them, and they must be able to accept his offer of salvation.

Pentz believes that all of these conditions are met. There can be no doubt that Jesus intended to save women. The way he treated women certainly argues for that. And if his salvation is effective for men, there is no reason why it should not also be so for women, for there is nothing especially intractable about the sins of triviality and diffuseness.[40] That leaves the third condition. Are women able to accept this salvation? Pentz gives two evidences that they are. First, while Jesus was on earth, women did respond to him. Second, if contemporary women understand what kind of Savior they are dealing with, they will not

---

37. Valerie Saiving, "The Human Situation: A Feminine View," in *Womanspirit Rising: A Feminist Reader in Religion*, ed. Carol P. Christ and Judith Plaskow (San Francisco: Harper and Row, 1979), p. 37.

38. Pentz, "Can Jesus Save Women?" pp. 84–96.

39. Ibid., p. 86.

40. Ibid., pp. 87–88.

feel alienated from him. He was not a self-aggrandizing, dominating person. In fact, Jesus' maleness is accidental to his meaning as Christ. Much in the act by which he saves us can be best described in human terms by the feminine metaphor of childbirth. He suffered in order to give us birth. Nor did his mothering of us end on the cross, for he continues to nurture us.[41]

What Pentz is arguing is that nothing in Jesus' maleness constitutes an inherent obstacle to women's accepting and committing themselves to him. It may be, of course, that some individuals will say, "We will accept only someone who is of our gender (or our race)." That, however, is insisting that God must meet our conditions. It is making God responsible to us, for we are prescribing the nature and grounds of the relationship. But then we have become gods ourselves. Then the issue is not merely Christology; it is a much larger issue of theology proper and even of worldview in general.

Jesus and Other Oppressed Groups

We have noted at some length Jesus' treatment of women. We made this our paradigm, for women are one group from which his incarnation automatically excluded him. It was not that he could not have been a woman, but that the act of becoming incarnate necessarily involved his being either male or female, thus excluding him from one half of the human race. But what of other social subgroups, the racially, socially, and economically oppressed? Can Jesus be their Savior also? We will look briefly at characteristics of Jesus which relate him in a positive way to three groups: the poor, the powerless or socially weak, and oppressed races.

The Poor

Jesus identified with the poor by entering their social class. He could have become incarnate in a family of virtually any social class without cutting off contact with the masses. He came, however, into one of the poorer families of Jewish society. That Joseph was a carpenter may, in view of the high wages earned by skilled construction workers today, seem to belie this,

41. Ibid., pp. 88–90.

but a carpenter in Israel had a rather modest income. There is another indication of the limited means of Jesus' family. As was the custom, the infant Jesus was taken to the temple to be consecrated, and a sacrifice was offered to make his mother ceremonially clean. The customary sacrifice was a lamb, but in cases of poverty two doves or two young pigeons, one for a burnt offering and the other for a sin offering, could be substituted (Lev. 12:8). It is notable that in the case of Jesus the substitute offering was presented (Luke 2:24).

Jesus' poverty continued throughout his ministry. On one occasion he and his disciples were liable for payment of a tax. Not having the money, he instructed Peter to catch a fish and to pay the tax with the coin he would find in its mouth (Matt. 17:24–27). On another occasion Jesus pointed out that he did not have a place of his own in which to lie down for the night (Matt. 8:20; Luke 9:58).

In addition to his personal circumstances, Jesus' preaching and teaching give indication of concern for the poor. He quoted and applied to himself Isaiah's words about preaching good news to the poor (Luke 4:18, 21). One of the signs offered to John the Baptist of Jesus' messiahship was that the poor had the gospel preached to them (Luke 7:22). He urged his hearers to invite not simply relatives, friends, and rich neighbors to their feasts, but also the poor, crippled, lame, and blind (Luke 14:12–14). The test of the rich young ruler's sincerity was his willingness to sell all his goods and give the proceeds to the poor (Matt. 19:21; Mark 10:21; Luke 18:22), and Zacchaeus's response to Jesus' teaching was an offer to give half of his possessions to the poor (Luke 19:8).

Hans Urs von Balthasar has argued that Jesus' teaching and preaching regarding the poor stand in the tradition of the Old Testament prophets in seeing the poor as oppressed, suffering injustice at the hands of the affluent. This emphasis continues in Jesus, although rather indirectly. He also introduces a new emphasis—the concept of voluntary poverty. He encourages selling what one has and giving away the proceeds for the sake of obedience to God and out of concern for the needs of others.[42]

42. Hans Urs von Balthasar, "The Poverty of Christ," *Communio: International Catholic Review* 13.3 (Fall 1986): 196–97.

Jesus himself in his coming to earth was the supreme example. In fact, "on the basis of a solidarity with the poorest . . . he considers as done to him what is done to them (Matt. 15:45) [sic; see 25:40, 45] and feels it accordingly (Acts 9:4)."[43]

One incident which may seem to run counter to what we have been saying is Jesus' anointing in the home of Simon the leper by a woman (Matt. 26:6–13; Mark 14:3–9; John 12:1–8). The disciples objected that the expensive perfume could have been sold at a high price and the money given to the poor. Jesus' response was that they would always have the poor with them, but they would not always have him with them. On the surface, this seems like a rather callous disregard of the needs of the poor. It must be seen and evaluated in its historical context, however. What Jesus was addressing was the timeliness of the woman's act. He would soon be taken from his disciples, and no such acts of devotion would any longer be possible. There would be other opportunities to help the poor, however.

The Powerless or Socially Weak

One of the clearest indications of Jesus' concern for the disadvantaged, weak, and defenseless was his care for widows. A number of instances are found in the Gospels. One is his denunciation of the scribes, whom he condemned for, among other things, their exploitation of widows: "Beware of the scribes . . . who devour widows' houses" was how he put it (Mark 12:38–40; Luke 20:46–47). There followed, by way of contrast, his commendation of the poor widow who cast all she had into the treasury, and who thus, according to Jesus, gave more than all of the others.

In the parable of the widow and the unjust judge (Luke 18:1–8) Jesus again used a widow as an example of the weakest and neediest. She found herself up against the male establishment. Through her persistence, she received what she sought.

One of Jesus' most striking and most moving actions was the raising of the son of the widow of Nain (Luke 7:11–17). The woman's predicament was an especially serious one. This was her only son, and so his death left her alone, without support,

43. Ibid., p. 197.

and with her family line cut off. When Jesus came upon the funeral procession, his heart went out to her and he said, "Do not weep!" (v. 13). He then violated rabbinic practice by stopping the funeral procession and touching the coffin. It was his mission to help the helpless.

Other Races

When we come to the matter of concern for people of other races and for minorities, we once again see Jesus breaking with contemporary customs. It is important that what he did and said be viewed in the context of the overall plan for his ministry. It was apparently the divine intention that the message first be taken to the people of Israel. They were not to have it exclusively, however, for it encompassed all races. The people of Israel were selected not merely to be recipients, but to be transmitters of God's message and grace. To insure that this would be accomplished, the initial effort was concentrated upon the Jews; then other races were gradually included. Thus we see Jesus, although reluctantly at first, responding favorably to the request of the Syrophoenician woman to include her in the blessings of his ministry (Mark 7:24–30).

We observed earlier (p. 583) Jesus' declaration that the queen of the South would someday condemn his wicked generation. That statement was remarkable because Jesus assigned not only to a woman, but to a Gentile woman besides, an honored role in the judgment.

It is in his attitude toward the Samaritans that Jesus showed most clearly his concern for other races, and particularly for the despised. The history of the ill will and conflict between Jews and Samaritans is well known. Three evidences indicate the concern which Jesus had for the Samaritans. The first is his conversation with the Samaritan woman. As we indicated earlier, several barriers had to be crossed here. That he pointedly offered salvation to her attests to the degree of his concern for and openness to people of other races. The second evidence is the parable of the good Samaritan. That Jesus chose a Samaritan as an example of the behavior he was commending was remarkable. So distasteful was this lesson to the lawyer to whom it was taught that he could not bring himself to identify the virtuous man of the story as a Samaritan, but could only say, "The one who showed mercy on him" (Luke 10:37). Finally, Jesus' commission to the disciples (Acts 1:8) pointedly included the Samaritans among those to whom they were to take the message. This made clear that these despised neighbors were also to receive the same grace as were the Jews.

We have responded to the objections of those who find Jesus sociologically unacceptable. Although he did not engage in revolutionary action, he did show his concern for the underprivileged and in special ways demonstrated his acceptance of them. He is indeed the Savior of all who are willing to trust him as their Lord.

24

The Incarnation
and the Problem of Evil

Theology, as we all know, is that discipline which seeks to study and give a reasoned explanation of God. As such, it deals not only with the divine person proper, but also with his relationships to the creation. Some of these relationships have posed special logical problems for the Christian faith; the problem of evil, or the question of the relationship of God's goodness and greatness to the obvious evil and suffering in the world, is perhaps the most difficult of all.

The Issue Under Consideration

The Nature of the Problem of Evil

We should not assume that the problem of evil is merely an intellectual challenge. It is a very existential problem, and anyone who has served as a pastor knows that far-reaching issues of spiritual care are involved here. When the problem of evil arises, it generally is not in a setting of abstract speculation, but of illness, death, or some other tragedy. Thus systematic theology is, ultimately, if we allow it, practical or pastoral theology.

In this chapter we shall attempt to relate two of the most difficult problems of Christian theology to one another: the problem of evil and the problem of orthodox incarnational Christology. By the latter we mean the doctrine that Jesus was both fully God and fully human. We will not limit our discussion to the fact of incarnation as such, but will seek to deal with several aspects of Christology as understood in light of the incarnation.

The problem of evil has been stated in many ways, most of which reduce to the contention that there is internal contradiction between three propositions. One of the best-known statements of the problem is that given by David Hume: "Is [God] willing to prevent evil, but not able? Then he is impotent. Is he able, but not willing? Then he is malevolent. Is he both able and willing? Whence then is evil?"[1] J. L. Mackie says, "In its simplest form the problem is this: God is omnipotent; God is wholly good; yet evil exists. There seems to be some contradiction between these three propositions, so that if any two of them were true the third would be false."[2] The problem of evil constitutes what a number of theologians have termed a trilemma.[3] Suggested solutions reject, reduce, or redefine one or more of the propositions.

Before attempting to make the problem simpler, I will first make it more complex. In my judgment, there is a fourth factor. For unless omniscience is part of omnipotence, one could respond by saying that while God is all-powerful and perfectly

---

1. David Hume, *Dialogues Concerning Natural Religion*, part X.8–9.
2. J. L. Mackie, "Evil and Omnipotence," in *The Philosophy of Religion*, ed. Basil Mitchell (London: Oxford University Press, 1971), p. 92.
3. E.g., Edgar Sheffield Brightman, *A Philosophy of Religion* (Englewood Cliffs, N.J.: Prentice-Hall, 1940), pp. 272–74.

good, he does not remove evil because he is not fully aware of its existence and extent. Thus the fourth proposition in what is now a "quadrilemma" is that God is fully aware of the existence of evil. And being aware of it, he must certainly know that it is undesirable (to say the least).

The Purpose of Grappling with the Issue

Testing the Truth of Christian Theism

In undertaking a study of the problem of evil, we are deliberately attempting to relate theology to empirical data. There are two benefits from such an endeavor. The first is that it is a way to test the truth of our doctrine. Both Christian believers, including theologians, and unbelievers have seen the powerful challenge which the problem of evil poses for theism. Basil Mitchell, for example, terms it "the most intractable of theological problems."[4] Some make even stronger assertions, affirming that the problem of evil refutes theism. Mackie claims that it shows not only "that religious beliefs lack rational support, but that they are positively irrational, that the several parts of the essential theological doctrine are inconsistent with one another, so that the theologian can maintain his position as a whole only by [an] extreme rejection of reason."[5]

Because the Christian system of doctrine constitutes a worldview, it must meet the criteria by which the truthfulness of worldviews is assessed. One of those criteria, as we spelled out in chapter 20, is adequacy to account for the manifold of experience. Among the most difficult segments of reality for any worldview to explain is the complex of factors which constitute the problem of evil. The ability of a worldview to deal with this issue is a major test of its credibility. We have no illusions that we will somehow resolve completely and finally the nettlesome problem of evil. The best theological minds in history, including Augustine and Thomas Aquinas, have grappled with this puzzle without totally unraveling it. It remains probably the most difficult of all challenges to the Christian faith and, for that matter, to any faith. The most we can hope for is some alleviation of the

4. Basil Mitchell, "Theology and Falsification," in *New Essays in Philosophical Theology*, ed. Antony Flew and Alasdair MacIntyre (New York: Macmillan, 1955), p. 103.
5. Mackie, "Evil and Omnipotence," p. 92.

problem, which in itself will be a worthy goal and a significant accomplishment.

Assuring the Meaningfulness of Christian Theism

Not only truth will be measured by our attempt to relate our theology to empirical data; meaningfulness also can be tested by such an endeavor. Logical positivism has taught us that the meaning of a proposition is at least in part to be found by showing with what it is inconsistent. If nothing counts against a proposition, then in a sense nothing counts for it either. We have long recognized the undue narrowness of the verifiability principle, which holds that a proposition is meaningless if it cannot in essence be verified or falsified by sense data; in fact, the verifiability principle is itself meaningless by that criterion.[6] Yet there is some merit to the contention that if a proposition is meaningful, we should be able to specify sense data that would count against it. Now in the traditional treatments of the problem of evil, it is often the case that nothing is allowed to count against some of the central tenets of theism (e.g., God's omnipotence and goodness), and thus they would seem to be meaningless. And while a statement can be meaningful and yet false, it has yet to be demonstrated that a meaningless statement (or one whose meaning cannot be explicated) can be true.

Consider John Macquarrie's story of a man who is narrowly missed by a bus, and who interprets his escape as a sign of divine love. Later, he is hit and injured by a bus, but sees in this episode another indication of God's love, for he was not killed. One day, however, he is hit and killed by a bus. His mourners see in this a sign of God's love, because God has taken him out of this unhappy and sinful world.[7] The question arises, Since nothing has been allowed to count against divine love, is there really any meaning to the concept? As we examine the problem of evil, we must make sure that our explications of divine omnipotence, knowledge, and goodness are not of such a nature that nothing is allowed to count against them, and Christian theism is thus exposed to the charge of meaninglessness.

---

6. Frederick Ferré, *Language, Logic, and God* (New York: Harper and Row, 1961), pp. 53–54.

7. John Macquarrie, *God-Talk: An Examination of the Language and Logic of Theology* (New York: Harper and Row, 1967), pp. 108–09.

There is another sense in which our endeavor will help assure the meaningfulness of theism. To some extent, the meaning of a proposition or a worldview (which is a system of propositions) is most evident if it answers questions that are being asked. Thus, if we can show that the incarnation was at least partly a response to the evil which occasions the problem of evil, we will have done much to increase our understanding of that doctrine.

Johnny Carson's Karnack jokes illustrate the cruciality of correlating our propositions to the questions being asked. Carson gives the answer to a question, opens an envelope, and reads the question. The meaning of the answer is then seen to be quite different from what one originally thought. The answer in one of my favorite Karnack jokes is, "Four score and seven years ago." The question is not, "How does Lincoln's Gettysburg Address begin?" but "What happens when a bases-loaded home run is hit, and when was the last one hit in a major-league all-star game?"

Another illustration is the ideologue who runs down the street, shouting, "I have the answer; I have the answer; who has a question?" Without a question, however, one may not really have an answer, or at least will not understand what it means.

What we are proposing here is something like Paul Tillich's method of correlation: theology gives answers to questions implied in the culture of the time. The content comes from the revelation; the form develops as one relates the message to the questions.[8] But there are perennial questions found in all cultures, times, and places. The problem of evil appears to be one of them. Although its urgency is greater in some situations and for some persons than others, it inevitably recurs. Thus it is appropriate to consider the central themes of providence, incarnation, and atonement as responses to the problem of evil, and the problem as an evocator of their meaning.

Approaching the Problem of Evil Through Incarnational Christology

There are two reasons to consider the doctrine of the person of Christ and, for that matter, the work of Christ as we wrestle with the problem of evil. First is the considerable biblical testi-

8. Paul Tillich, *Systematic Theology*, 3 vols. (Chicago: University of Chicago, 1951–1963), vol. 1, pp. 18–28.

mony that juxtaposes the two themes. One example is Romans 8:18–39. Having surveyed the presence of evil in the world and its widespread effects, Paul concludes by asking, "Who shall separate us from the love of Christ?" (v. 35). He then answers his own question: "For I am sure that neither death, nor life, nor angels, nor principalities, nor things present, nor things to come, nor powers, nor height, nor depth, nor anything else in all creation, will be able to separate us from the love of God in Christ Jesus our Lord" (vv. 38–39).

The second reason is experiential. It seems that committed Christians feel that the problem of evil poses an especially serious threat to their faith. This is not, I believe, solely because of the formal ideological conflict between the two conceptions. It is also because commitment to Christ and his teachings seems to sensitize the believer to the incongruity in a world riven by evil.

We may seem here to be attempting to explain the obscure by the more obscure, seeking to deal with a problem (evil) by bringing in a subject (incarnational Christology) which itself is problematic. What we are hoping to do, however, is to accomplish what I call a "plus three solution" to a problem. In social ethics the solution of a problem is frequently achieved only at the cost of aggravating or even creating another problem. When the benefit and the damage are approximately equal, we have a "zero solution," that is, a neutral situation. When the solution creates more good than evil, we have a "plus one solution." When it achieves good without any negative effects, we have a "plus two solution." But when the solution itself contributes to solving or alleviating another problem, then we have a "plus three solution," a very rare occurrence. For example, if the sludge from a municipal sewage-disposal plant could be transported from Chicago to downstate Illinois and spread over farmland to enrich the soil without any negative effect, then we would have a "plus three solution." We would dispose of waste while also increasing fertility. Most forms of recycling aim at some type of "plus three solution." This is what we are hopeful of here. If we can resolve the issues of Christology and in the process help alleviate the problem of evil, we have a nearly ideal type of theological explanation or, as we have termed it here, a "plus three solution."

Three possible solutions suggest themselves at this point:

S$_1$ God wishes to prevent evil, but is unable to do so.

S$_2$ God is able to prevent evil, but chooses not to.

S$_3$ God is able and willing to prevent evil, so the evil we see in our world must not be ultimately real, but only apparent.

It is possible that S$_1$ and S$_2$ will fare quite well when tested by the criteria dealing with the semantic and syntactic dimensions of meaning (see pp. 523–24). Thus they might describe life as we actually find it and fit well the broad sweep of our experience of reality. They might also show no inherent contradiction or lack of coherence, although some features of the biblical teaching would have to be revised. The pragmatic dimension, however, suffers under either of these solutions; and that is what originally occasioned the problem! For in a world in which there is no force capable of removing evil (S$_1$) or willing to do so (S$_2$), there is a question whether hope can be maintained. And hope, as Viktor Frankl has so well demonstrated, is essential for maintaining life.[9] The whole question of evil, then, is not a uniquely Christian or even a religious issue, but an existential problem.

We must here take special note of the way in which we will be approaching the problem of evil. Most attempts to resolve the problem are exercises in philosophical theology in which divine goodness and omnipotence and the nature of good and evil are discussed in abstract fashion. We, however, will be discussing divine goodness and divine power as those concepts are defined in Scripture rather than as they might be defined abstractly. (The reader may recall our distinction in chap. 22 between deity and humanity in abstraction and in the incarnation.)

Our response to the problem of evil seeks to take into account the specifics of Christian theology. Our argument is not simply a defense of theism or of a philosophy of life in general. It is the Christian world-and-life view that we are defending, and that provides our argument with the resources of the specifics of Christian theology. Diogenes Allen has put it thus: "This line of approach to the subject of suffering requires the use of specific

---

9. Viktor Frankl, *Man's Search for Meaning: An Introduction to Logotherapy* (New York: Washington Square, 1963).

Christian doctrines—Creation, Trinity, and Cross—which are often ignored in philosophic discussions of evil. Yet it is what is unique and central to Christianity which allows us to conceive of all suffering as the presence of God to us through the world (both natural and social), and enables us to find his love in and through the events of this life."[10]

We may need to change our thinking about some concepts. We may need, for instance, to alter our thinking about what is really evil and what is not. Here of course we must ultimately ask what the basis of such a judgment is, and that calls for some decisions about reality, human nature, and the good for humans. Beyond that, however, we must note that our reaction to the circumstances of life, and thus our judgment of what is evil, is a very individual matter, varying greatly from one person to another. We must ask ourselves about our own perception of what is good and what is evil. Members of the "me generation" may need to reexamine their complaints about the evil in the world. In a recent survey of Americans, 70 percent of those responding said that a microwave oven is indispensable to them, and 49 percent said that a telephone-answering machine is. Is the absence of one of these appliances really to be considered a case of evil? Allen says, "To approach nature with the expectation that we ought to be better looked after, makes it unlikely that we will learn from suffering."[11]

In a sense, what we will be attempting here is a variation of S_3. For we do not deny the reality of evil, claiming that it is illusory. Rather, we deny the ultimate reality of evil, and do so in the light of incarnational Christology. We will be contending that God has acted through his greatness and goodness to negate, cancel, or eliminate evil. We will, in the process, be carefully scrutinizing these aspects of God's nature to see whether we have correctly understood their biblical sense. This may lead to some redefinition of the traditional understanding of God's power or his love. We will be appealing to several key incarnational themes as we try to reach a solution.

10. Diogenes Allen, "Natural Evil and the Love of God," *Religious Studies* 16 (Dec. 1980): 455–56.

11. Ibid., p. 442.

Incarnational Themes
Related to the Problem of Evil

God's Personal Experience of Evil

When one views the severity of evil in the world and God's apparent failure to negate it, it seems as if God is either ignorant of its full impact or indifferent to the suffering of his creatures. This inference makes some sense. How can an infinite divine being really feel the full force of human suffering? He has no physical nature, so he is incapable of experiencing pain. He cannot die, being eternal and self-caused, so the agony of death that humans undergo is never his. To be sure, being all-knowing, he knows what death is and understands the physiology of suffering as none of us can. Similarly, he certainly understands the emotional and psychological basis of temptation, but he cannot be tempted (James 1:13). So his experience is not firsthand. It is like a physicist's understanding of a sunset. There may be complete intellectual comprehension of the physics involved, but apart from viewing a sunset in all of its beauty there is no real understanding.

There is a portion of Scripture which speaks directly to this concern, however. In Hebrews 4:15 the writer says of Jesus, "For we do not have a high priest who is unable to sympathize with our weaknesses, but we have one who has been tempted in every way, just as we are—yet was without sin" (NIV). The ancient doctrine of impassibility notwithstanding, it appears from this text that either we have to say that Jesus was only human, not divine, or we must interpret the incarnation as having affected the Triune God. There is a sense in which God is different for Jesus' having undergone temptation. In the incarnation God experienced firsthand the full nature of evil.

God's ability to sympathize through having actually experienced evil is seen in certain incidents from the life of Jesus, one of which is the death of Lazarus. Jesus had encountered death during his lifetime, and in a few cases had restored the dead to life. Here, however, was the death of one who had been close to Jesus. Jesus had accepted hospitality from Lazarus and his two sisters, Mary and Martha. He wept at the tomb (John 11:35), occasioning the Jews to say, "See how he loved him!" (v. 36). This death was different from the other deaths which Jesus had encountered. He had now experienced the death of someone close to him. Now the divine man knew firsthand what sorrow is like.

Other aspects of Jesus' experience are pertinent as well. God had, throughout the Old Testament, been rejected and abandoned by his people Israel. Now, however, Jesus experienced at first hand betrayal by one who had been part of his inner circle, who had sat at table with him, and who had been entrusted by him with the secrets of the kingdom of God. And Peter, who had been the spokesperson for the disciples on more than one occasion, and who had been entrusted with special leadership responsibilities, turned away from him, denying any prior knowledge of or relationship to him. This gave a firsthand knowledge of one of the most painful human experiences, the breaking of trust. Jesus also endured physical suffering, ridicule, and other abuse which God had not experienced firsthand prior to this time. Here yet another dimension was added to God's "knowledge" by the incarnation.

The objection that God is callous about human suffering assumes that he himself is not affected by suffering. But if, as we have been saying, God is no less a victim of the evil in the world than we are, his actions and attitude are as different from mere callousness as masochism is from sadism. Orthodox doctrine holds that God does indeed choose to permit evil to occur and continue, but that he does so with full knowledge of its consequences, for he himself is victimized by the force of evil.

Human parents often choose to endure certain kinds of suffering or inconvenience for the sake of their child. Sometimes these are situations in which the child also is caused discomfort. It is not uncommon for parents when administering a spanking to say, "This hurts me more than it hurts you." The parents may be genuinely pained by the child's suffering, just as they are when the child experiences hurt from some other source over which they have no control. In addition, parents may suffer because the child, instead of appreciating the value of the punishment, blames them for it. We seem to have a similar situation here. God's willingness to endure personally the adverse consequences of evil is a partial indication that in his judgment the evil must be achieving a salutary effect in the life of humans.

But does not this concept of God suffering, even in the crucifixion, conflict with the idea of divine perfection as long understood in Christian theology? A god who can suffer as humans do would seem to be less than the perfect God of Scripture. Thomas Aquinas, utilizing the thought of Aristotle, insisted that God, being completely immutable, is incapable of suffering. While love and joy belong to his nature, sadness and anger can be attributed to his absolute being only metaphorically.[12] Nor was this a distinctively Catholic doctrine. John Calvin declared that God is "not sorrowful or sad, but remains forever like Himself in his celestial and happy repose."[13] Calvin explained that biblical passages which seem to speak of God as suffering are merely anthropopathisms.[14]

But is such a conception of the divine perfection really biblical in origin, or does it derive from some other source such as Aristotelian philosophy? Here we must note a few biblical passages which seem to testify to a quite different conception of God. In Genesis 6:6 he is described as grieved by the sin of humanity. Psalm 103:13 says, "As a father pities his children, so the LORD pities those who fear him." Again and again God is pictured as grieving over Israel and its rebellion. It is difficult to dismiss these images as totally anthropomorphic. There must of course be an element of anthropomorphism, since God certainly does not suffer precisely as we do. As Paul Schilling has pointed out, God does not have a central nervous system, and therefore his endurance of pain cannot be equated with ours.[15] There must, however, be some univocal factor.

If we take seriously the idea of incarnation, the conception of divine suffering seems inescapable. Some theologians have sought to avoid this conclusion and to preserve the impassibility of God by maintaining that Jesus' suffering was a function only of his human nature. Gregory of Nyssa, for example, held that as God, the Son is impassible.[16] Augustine maintained that "passion," suggesting disturbance and changeableness, is incompatible with the divine nature.[17] This, however, seems not only to

12. Thomas Aquinas, *Summa theologica*, part I, question 9, article 1; part II, question 25, article1; *Summa contra Gentiles*, part II.25.

13. John Calvin, *Commentaries*, 22 vols. (Grand Rapids: Baker, 1979–1981 reprint), vol. 1, p. 249 (on Gen. 6:6).

14. Ibid.

15. S. Paul Schilling, *God and Human Anguish* (Nashville: Abingdon, 1977), p. 254.

16. Gregory of Nyssa *Adversus Eunomius* 6.1.

17. Augustine *City of God* 8.17.

impose upon Jesus a set of conceptions not based upon clear biblical witness, but to divide the unity of the two natures in the one person. It may in effect be a variety of incipient Nestorianism.

We need to note at this point that the pragmatic or experiential benefit of the idea that God suffers as we do is considerable. Nicolas Berdyaev said, "God can reconcile man to the sufferings of creation because he himself suffers, not because he reigns."[18] Simone Weil saw the cross as the supreme manifestation of God's love and therefore the only real hope for deliverance from the despair occasioned by the presence of evil in the world.[19]

There appear to be two dimensions to God's presence in our suffering. One is that we actually meet God in it. Suffering and affliction frequently have the effect of creating a sense that God is distant. This was one of the points which led the Death of God theologians to their very radical conclusions. Not only were they aware of the absence of an experience of God, but in the problem of evil they had the experience of the absence of God.[20] Even Jesus experienced the absence of God, for on the cross he cried out, "My God, my God, why have you abandoned me?" Yet in our suffering we are not limited to a feeling of being abandoned by God. Knowing that God was present in Christ and thus in his suffering makes us more aware of his presence with us.

The other dimension is the familiar role of suffering as soul making, emphasized in the Irenaean form of theodicy. When Paul said that "in everything God works [lit., 'with-works'] for good" (Rom. 8:28), he did not leave the good as an abstract concept. He went on to specify that the good consists in our being conformed to the image of God's Son (v. 29). Thus suffering often has the effect, if those experiencing it yield to its working, of producing humility, and consequently of making us like God. He is at work in our suffering and in the likeness to him which results.[21]

18. Nicolas Berdyaev, *Dream and Reality: An Essay in Autobiography* (New York: Macmillan, 1951), p. 179.

19. Simone Weil, *Gateway to God* (New York: Crossroad, 1982), pp. 77–91.

20. William Hamilton, "The Death of God Theologies Today," in Thomas J. J. Altizer and William Hamilton, *Radical Theology and the Death of God* (Indianapolis: Bobbs-Merrill, 1966), p. 28.

21. Allen, "Natural Evil," p. 447.

The Voluntariness of God's Suffering

It is important to emphasize that any suffering on God's part is completely voluntary. That God suffers the pain of evil is in no sense a threat to belief in his omnipotence. His choosing to limit himself to working in a certain way does not encroach upon his sovereign power, as long as the initial decision to take on the limitation was freely his.

God has at several points chosen to accept or create certain limitations for himself. He did this in the decision to create. Prior to that, his attributes were simply what some theologians have termed "absolute" or "intransitive" attributes. But at the time of creation his attributes or personal qualities became transitive in nature, for they now were expressed in relationship to the existing universe. In particular, his decision to create humans with wills of their own meant that his actions thereafter would have to be undertaken with some consciousness and consideration of how they would be affected.

Weil has tied the self-limitation of God in the act of creation to his corresponding acts of incarnation and atoning death. She points out that before creating, God was everything. By creating he has ceased to be everything. He has curtailed his absolute power. "Because he is creator, God is not all powerful. Creation is an abdication. But he is all-powerful in this sense that his abdication is voluntary. He knows its effects, and wills them. God has emptied himself. This means that both the Creation and Incarnation are included with the Passion."[22]

God was free to enter into certain covenants or not. His covenant with Abraham, and thus with the Hebrew people who descended from Abraham, was not something he was coerced or compelled to initiate. Once he did so, however, his moral character meant that he had certain limitations; that is, he was not completely free in what he could or could not do. He is incapable of denying his own word; thus, having pledged himself to act in a certain way, he cannot fail to fulfil it (Heb. 6:13–20). Further, although he need not have chosen to redeem humanity, and could perhaps have done so in a somewhat different way, once

22. Simone Weil, *First and Last Notebooks* (London: Routledge and Kegan Paul, 1972), p. 120.

he committed himself to the incarnation, he was obligated to experience all of its consequences.

This element of the voluntary runs through Jesus' own self-testimony. For example, he said of his life, "No one takes it from me, but I lay it down of my own accord. I have power to lay it down, and I have power to take it again; this charge I have received from my Father" (John 10:18). Struggling in the Garden of Gethsemane with his knowledge of the crucifixion which he was about to undergo, he prayed, "My Father, if it be possible, let this cup pass from me; nevertheless, not as I will, but as thou wilt" (Matt. 26:39).

God's Action in Christ's Death to Combat Evil

One complaint frequently raised in discussions of the problem of evil is, "Why does not God do something about the evil in the world?" To deal adequately with that question, we must look briefly at why there is evil in the world, although in itself this topic deserves major attention.

One of the Bible's most persistent answers to that question is that evil is ultimately traceable to and derives its power from human and angelic sin. Sin is understood as lack of conformity to the moral will of God; it can take the form of active or passive disobedience (rebellion or neglect). Many of the ills found within the creation derive from the fall (Gen. 3). In particular, Paul seems to view death as an effect of the fall (Rom. 5:12).

Individual sins, however, are not to be understood as the cause of specific evils. There have always been those who insist that evil circumstances are a punishment for the sin of the individual experiencing them. Job's friends, for instance, counseled him to confess his sin (e.g., Job 11:14); and Jesus' disciples asked whether the condition of the man born blind was to be explained by his sins or those of his parents (John 9:2). In both cases the hypothesis was rejected. Rather, we must recognize that there is a general situation of sin and evil in the world.

The question then becomes, "What has God done to counteract sin and its effects?" We spoke earlier of God's sympathy. But we do not really appreciate mere sympathy from someone who has the ability to remove the cause of our difficulty. This brings us squarely to consideration of the atonement. Jesus claimed that he had come to give his life as a ransom for many (Matt. 20:28). Paul, in the passage to which we have just alluded, paralleled the effect of Adam's sin with the effect of Christ's death (Rom. 5:15). Christ has negated sin's results.

The effect of Christ's death on evil will be seen in virtually any of the several theories of the atonement, although more powerfully in some than others. This is particularly true of the more objective theories, which hold that the effect of Christ's death was to cancel the consequences of sin. The subjective theories, on the other hand, see the major impact of Christ's death as being upon the human will: his act is viewed as either inspiring love and repentance or setting an example. The "classic" theory, which emphasizes Christ's triumph over evil,[23] and the penal-substitution theory, which sees Jesus as bearing the penalty of sin in the place of guilty humans,[24] are especially potent expressions of the effects of his death on evil.

We should note that the special ability of the atonement to resolve the problem that we are considering is based upon the incarnation. There has been rightful protest against any view of the atonement which holds that the penalty that one party was obligated to bear was transferred to some third party. Transferring to Jesus the penalty we deserved would be a particularly odious instance of injustice but for two considerations. The first is that the victim was not an unwilling victim. He indicated that he lay down his life of his own accord (John 10:17–18). The second is that the person administering the penalty was also the one bearing it. For according to the doctrines of the Trinity and the incarnation Jesus is God: he both participated in the decision to transfer the penalty for sin to himself and bore it.

It is important at this point to reiterate that this was an action voluntarily taken by God. It was not something into which God was forced. He need not have provided salvation from sin. Thus his power and greatness are not compromised. Rather, he voluntarily chose to provide atonement. The goodness of God is not only preserved, but emphasized.

---

23. Gustaf Aulen, *Christus Victor: An Historical Study of the Three Main Types of the Idea of the Atonement* (New York: Macmillan, 1931).
24. Anselm *Cur Deus homo?*

Actions of God Through Christ's Life to Combat Evil

Beyond the fact of Jesus' death, we have indications that in his life God was acting to negate some of the consequences or dimensions of sin in the world. Jesus' ministry involved healing the ill, restoring the dead, and casting out demons. That he saw himself as engaged in contest with the forces of evil is clear from his own comment in response to those who accused him of casting out demons by recourse to the strength of the prince of demons, Beelzebub (Matt. 12:22–37; Mark 3:22–30; Luke 11:14–23). His life was in large part dedicated to removing or rectifying the ills of the world in which he lived.

Jesus' teaching indicated that he was concerned as well about evils which transcended physical suffering and death. He spoke of the importance of loving one another and even one's enemy. He had come to heal the fractures found within the human race. The way of life which he advocated is characterized by unselfish love which is even willing to surrender one's own life for the sake of another person (John 15:13). He himself embodied this love and even exceeded the standard, for he did lay down his life, not only for his friends, but for those who hated him as well.

Historically, those who possess Plato's confidence in the power of rational thought have maintained that if only people know what is right and believe that they should do it, they will do it, and all will be right. Experientially, however, many of us find that what Paul expressed is true: "For I do not do the good I want, but the evil I do not want is what I do" (Rom. 7:19). Knowing what one ought to do is one thing, wanting to do what one knows one ought to do is another, and ability to do what one wills to do is yet another.

This is the problem with all methods of self-help. Good advice, such as "Don't worry!" and "Just do better!" is of little practical benefit. Many of us who have read Dale Carnegie's *How to Win Friends and Influence People* know what we should do in certain situations: smile at and compliment others. That does not avail, however, when what we want to do is physically or verbally smash the exasperating, obnoxious person before us. What is needed is not just good advice, but transformation into a different sort of person.

Jesus promised a supernatural alteration of human nature. To the disciples who asked whether anyone could enter the kingdom of God on his conditions, Jesus responded, "With men this is impossible, but with God all things are possible" (Matt. 19:26). Christians conceive of this supernatural transformation differently. For some, it is a matter of grace being conferred through the sacraments.[25] For others, it is a result of the exercise of faith alone.[26] For yet others, it occurs first on the macroscopic level and then on the microscopic, that is, through a social gospel which transforms society and consequently its individual members.[27] In all of these perspectives, except for the most naturalistic, divine activity is believed to bring about the transformation.

Of particular importance to understanding our transformation is the biblical theme that God acts in such a way as to bring good results out of evil conditions. This motif runs through many different parts of the Bible. Joseph, for example, saw God's bringing good out of the evil done to him (Gen. 45:5, 8; 50:20). He had an unusually clear understanding of how divine providence relates to evil human acts. The same theme is found in Paul's discussion of his "thorn in the flesh" (2 Cor. 12:7–10). Whatever it was, he does not blame God for its presence in his life, calling it a "messenger of Satan" (v. 7). It appears, however, that God used this thorn to good ends in Paul's life. It prevented him from becoming too elated (v. 7). It also became the means to the perfecting of divine power within his life, so that he actually rejoiced in and boasted of his weaknesses (vv. 9–10). He could say, "When I am weak, then I am strong" (v. 10).

This perspective is then applied to the matter of Jesus' death. Peter, in his Pentecost sermon, interpreted the death of Jesus as the act of sinful humans (Acts 2:23). He also, however, depicted it as being in accord with the plan and foreknowledge of God. For God raised Jesus up, thus "loos[ing] the pangs of death" (v. 24). The worst that evil could do to Jesus was to put him to death. We are not to blame God for this act of desperate evil, for he did not cause it, but merely permitted it. He then used it as the means to bring the greatest good to the world.

25. Joseph Pohle, *The Sacraments: A Dogmatic Treatise*, ed. Arthur Preuss, 4 vols. (St. Louis: B. Herder, 1942), vol. 1, p. 1.

26. An extreme case is Zane C. Hodges, *Absolutely Free!* (Grand Rapids: Zondervan, 1989), pp. 27–29.

27. Walter Rauschenbusch, *A Theology for the Social Gospel* (New York: Macmillan, 1917), pp. 95–130.

God's Suffering in Our Place

The witness of Scripture is that God has voluntarily suffered in our place. Rather than simply observing and empathizing with our suffering in a world of evil, God himself personally experienced it to restore us to those relationships from which sin had separated us.

Evil's most prominent form is human sin. The nature of sin, and the effect of sin, is to separate that which belongs together. In the biblical story of Adam and Eve, this is seen to be true on several different levels. There first was separation of Adam and Eve from God. Realizing their sin, they hid themselves from God (Gen. 3:8). Instead of loving and trusting God, they sought to avoid him. There also quickly came separation between humans. Adam sought to blame Eve for his own sin (v. 12). In the next chapter, friction leads Cain to murder his younger brother, Abel. There even is separation between humans and nature. Whereas formerly the creation was subject to humans and under their direction, now there are pain and toil within nature. It seems opposed to the man and the woman (3:16–19).

Reconciliation, the restoration of relationships that have been broken, always requires some cost, some pain. In quarrels there is an exchange of harsh statements. Each is followed by a similar or perhaps more bitter response. If the quarrel is to cease, someone must decline to respond or retaliate. This means forgoing the satisfaction of returning the pain to the other. And this decision means absorbing the pain into oneself.

This is what God has chosen to do. As the omnipotent ruler, he always has the privilege of the last word. He could have done anything he wished to finite humans, even destroy them. He chose, however, not to do this. Instead of having the satisfaction of returning evil for the evil which they have done, he has chosen to grant them forgiveness and salvation. And this means that God must in a sense suffer the consequences of human sin himself. He knows the pain that they would otherwise have known.

Jesus' Life and Death
the Supreme Instance of the Problem of Evil

In the life of Jesus, and particularly the crucifixion and the events surrounding it, we find the supreme case of the problem of evil. For here we find a person less deserving of the evil he experienced than anyone we can think of. Very few charges have ever been lodged against him. Very few persons whose lives can be ascertained with any degree of certainty even warrant comparison with him. In our day, only such persons as Mahatma Gandhi and Mother Teresa are even mentioned in the same sentence with him. The trial which led to his death was grossly unjust. The charges brought against him were unfair. No real effort was made to obtain impartial witnesses. He was put to death without having committed any capital crime, even by the measure of that day. Not only was he put to death, but the very manner of his execution was shameful and humiliating.

Sensitive persons deem the loss of human life under any circumstances unfortunate or regrettable at best. Even those who advocate capital punishment, while they think it to be right, usually do not think it to be good, unless they are consumed by hostility. They regard it as an unfortunate or unavoidable lesser of two evils. But most people, whether they believe in the practice of capital punishment or not, can at least see some justification for the evil (death) which comes upon the individual. More unfortunate is the accidental death of an innocent person. Here there seems to be no moral justification for what happens. We may be able to see some connection between certain nonmoral actions (e.g., failure to wear a seat belt or to yield the right of way) and the consequence, but that is a very different matter.

When we have the deliberate killing of a person without justification, our moral sensibilities are offended even more deeply. As abhorrent as killing in war may be, it is less so than murder. For in the latter case, the victim usually had no intention of harming the assailant. Similarly, we would be outraged if someone who was completely innocent of any crime liable to capital punishment and who had not been given a fair trial were to be executed. And if that person was innocent not only of any capital crime, but of any wrongdoing whatsoever, we would seem to have a supreme case of injustice and of the problem of evil.

In Christ, then, we have a paradigm case: the death of a person who is claimed to have done no wrong, who selflessly gave himself for others. As an extreme case, it will enable us to gain some additional understanding into how God will resolve the total problem of evil. A study of the outcome of Jesus' life and death should therefore be instructive to us.

In many ways, death is the epitome of evil. It has the power to bring to an end all unfulfilled hopes, dreams, aspirations. It has the power to sever us from those whom we love. This has been movingly expressed by Alfred, Lord Tennyson, in his poem "Break, Break, Break," inspired by his grief on the death of his friend Arthur Henry Hallam:

> Break, break, break,
> On thy cold gray stones, O Sea!
> And I would that my tongue could utter
> The thoughts that arise in me.
>
> O well for the fisherman's boy,
> That he shouts with his sister at play!
> O well for the sailor lad,
> That he sings in his boat on the bay!
>
> And the stately ships go on
> To their haven under the hill;
> But O for the touch of a vanish'd hand,
> And the sound of a voice that is still!
>
> Break, break, break,
> At the foot of thy crags, O Sea!
> But the tender grace of a day that is dead
> Will never come back to me.

Paul indicates that death is the last enemy (1 Cor. 15:26). If it takes place in a situation of suffering or shame, it is especially destructive. Death seems to be evil's ultimate weapon, the method used to destroy one's enemies in final fashion. Accordingly, those who opposed Jesus tried to rid themselves of him by having him put to death. What happened to death in the case of Jesus is therefore the answer of Christian faith to the most severe act of evil.

The resurrection of Jesus is the key to the biblical understanding of God's treatment of evil and its power. The basic Christian message about evil is that death is not the final word regarding Jesus, nor is it the final word regarding us. Paul acknowledges the power of death when he says that if Christ is not risen, there is little hope for believers: "If Christ has not been raised, your faith is futile and you are still in your sins. Then those also who have fallen asleep in Christ have perished. If for this life only we have hoped in Christ, we are of all men most to be pitied" (1 Cor. 15:17–19). The glorious message of Easter, however, is that Christ has been raised. And his resurrection points ahead to the resurrection of all believers. Paul makes resurrection the key to Christian hope and faith in the future (1 Cor. 15:20–23). This means that there need not be sorrow for those who have died (1 Thess. 4:16).

God's Eschatological Treatment of Evil

One other major theme that will help us understand how God deals with evil is the eschatological dimension. It is difficult to emphasize sufficiently the role which the otherworldly played in Jesus' teaching and its importance to the issue under discussion here. If our attempt to resolve the problem of evil uses only that which transpires within time and in this life here on earth, we are surely doomed to failure. In no way are most people's present experiences related equitably to the moral quality of their life. This is in part why the doctrine of reincarnation as found in Hinduism and some other Eastern religions has such a powerful appeal to many. It means that there is another chance, a second time around, in which the circumstances of a person's life are determined by and compensate for the way in which one lived in an earlier existence.

It must be said that in the final analysis there is no real solution to the problem of evil if there is no life beyond this one. In this life there do seem to be at times more pain and evil than good and pleasure. There often appears to be no justice. Thus the psalmist's complaint that the wicked seem to prosper (Ps. 73:1–14) rings true in many cases. Yet God's response is in terms of the end of these people, which seems to go beyond this life (vv. 17–28). In like manner, Christianity does not try to solve this problem by demonstrating that there is perfect justice here and now. Rather, it claims that this temporal existence is not all there is. In the life beyond, all will be set right, and the righteous will receive their rewards.

Jesus never claimed that there would be perfect equity within this life and world. Rather, he spoke of a coming world where there would be a judgment and a rectification of the evils and injustices of this life. It was for this reason that he urged his hearers not to lay up for themselves treasures on earth, but rather treasures in heaven (Matt. 6:19–21). He understood the life to come as being the more important, so that preparation for it is of paramount significance. He even declared that being maimed in this life is a far smaller evil than entering into hell with one's body perfectly intact (Mark 9:43–48).

Jesus' teaching made much of the idea of an afterlife. We have noticed his reference to accumulating treasures in heaven. The parable of the rich man and Lazarus seems among other things to be teaching that one's circumstances in the life beyond may be quite different from what they are in this life (Luke 16:19–31). A similarly strong intimation of the differences between the here and now and the transcendent kingdom is found in Jesus' contrast between the greatest and the least in the kingdom of God, which is a distinction between, on the one hand, those who in this life observed and taught the commandments and, on the other, those who broke them and taught others to do so (Matt. 5:19–20). Those who have been downtrodden and oppressed in this life will be given authority and participate in Christ's glory and rule. Jesus linked this coming situation to his own work, both present and future. He told his disciples that he was going to prepare a place for them (John 14:2). He also spoke of his return, which will usher in the new conditions. There will be judgment; justice will be done in the sense that a person's true character will be revealed. There will also be reward for faithfulness, punishment for unfaithfulness, and life everlasting (Matt. 25:31–46).

Paul speaks of this eschatological consummation in different but complementary fashion. For example, he points to the second coming as a basis for comforting those whose loved ones have died. They are not to sorrow, as do those who have no hope. For resurrection of the dead, which will entail the defeat of death and elimination of the sorrow which it causes, is tied to the second coming (1 Thess. 4:13–18). This sort of hope permeated Paul's thinking about the evils of this life. He could therefore write, "I consider that the sufferings of this present time are not worth comparing with the glory that is to be revealed to us" (Rom. 8:18). He then goes on to discuss the transformation which evidently will affect even the physical universe. Thus Paul speaks of a final great consummation in which even the creation, which somehow has been bound by the evil effects of human sin, will be liberated (vv. 19–23). In 2 Corinthians 4:17–18 he describes the present world as "this slight momentary affliction [which] is preparing for us an eternal weight of glory beyond all comparison." In light of this, he says, "we look not to the things that are seen but to the things that are unseen; for the things that are seen are transient, but the things that are unseen are eternal."

One objection that can be raised at this point, as well as at several other points, is that if God is truly omnipotent, he could have altered the situation so as to avoid the whole problem of evil. The answer usually given is that the particular goods which he sought to realize could be obtained only by using the particular means which he did. For example, if one of the virtues which humans need is patience, that cannot be accomplished in a moment. If obedience is needed, it may be necessary to allow for some failures in this area so that the consequences of disobedience will be realized. We find justification for this idea even in the life of Jesus himself, of whom it is said, "Although he was a son, he learned obedience from what he suffered and, once made perfect, he became the source of eternal salvation for all who obey him" (Heb. 5:8–9 NIV). It may well be that he learned obedience by observing the disobedience of others and its consequences.

But if God is truly omnipotent, could not this have been accomplished by some other means? Can he not only do everything, but do it through any means whatsoever? Here we need to look at the meaning of "omnipotence." As Mackie and others have set up the problem, "omnipotence" seems to be defined as the ability to do absolutely anything whatsoever.[28] But orthodox theology has usually insisted that God's "omnipotence" means the ability to do all things that are proper objects of his power. Perhaps we need another term, since "omnipotence" tends to carry the connotation of unqualified power. A term such as "omnicompetence" or "omnicapability" might be preferable. It would exclude the ability to do what is logically impossible or contrary to God's nature. Can God make a square circle? No. Can he conceive of a square circle? Yes, but he cannot believe in it. He can think of it only as nonexistent. He cannot state the term *square circle* without in effect adding, "It is not true." This

---

28. Mackie, "Evil and Omnipotence," p. 95.

is not to say that there are logical principles external to God to which he is bound, nor is it to say that he has volitionally created logic and could have chosen to create it differently. It is to say that logic is part of his very nature, and that he cannot choose to be different from what he is. So his inability to lie or to break his word is not a weakness (Heb. 6:18).

Now we do not know what characteristics desirable in human nature require the existence of evil and a future rather than an immediate rectification of the problem. Presumably, God could not have both made human beings as he intended them to be and also instituted immediate and total equity. But the inability to do this is not necessarily a weakness in the nature of God. It is so only on the basis of the assumptions which Mackie makes about omnipotence, assumptions which need not be made and do not seem to be required by the biblical teaching.

Another objection must be dealt with: the failure to eliminate evil, *and at the earliest possible time*, is a sign of lack of goodness on God's part. But how do we establish that goodness requires acting speedily? Presumably the answer is that failure to act as soon as possible heightens evil. The sooner justice is done, the less injustice there is. But that fails to take into account the values that may attach to delay. Omnipotence and total goodness would seem to require God to act at the time and in the way that would effect the greatest proportion of good.

What this seems to be saying is that God allows certain evils to occur in order to effect greater goods. This is a fairly common type of argument, but one to which both Mackie and Antony Flew object. As they state it, there are first-order evils, such as pain and misery. There are also first-order goods, such as pleasure and happiness. The usual argument of theism is that God permits first-order evil in order thereby to actualize second-order goods, such as benevolence and presumably sympathy, compassion, and mercy. Without first-order evil, second-order good would not be possible. The problem, however, is that this also makes possible second-order evils. It is possible to counter this by appeal to third-order goods, but these in turn lead to third-order evils. We are now caught in an infinite regress.[29]

---

29. Ibid., pp. 97–100; Antony Flew, "Divine Omnipotence and Human Freedom," in *New Essays in Philosophical Theology*, ed. Flew and MacIntyre, pp. 145–56.

But is this so on Christian grounds? To be sure, the argument seems to say that first-order evils are permitted so that there can be certain second-order goods. That is why God does not immediately rectify situations of evil and injustice. But we do not find ourselves caught in infinite regress, for the eschatological dimension of Christian biblical theism affirms that God will at some point eliminate the evils of every order.

We have come, at long last, to the provisional end of our investigation of evil and the incarnation. We do not claim to have resolved the problem of evil in any final fashion. We do contend, however, that some of the difficulties attaching to it come from assumptions made or stipulative definitions put forward by some nontheistic thinkers. We have chosen to deal with the problem not from the standpoint of abstract theism, but rather of biblical theism. We have argued that biblical theism does not make the same assumptions as do nontheists, and that, consequently, the incarnational Christology revealed in Scripture does alleviate the more severe dimensions of the problem of evil.

It will not be difficult to find problems and unresolved tensions within our explanation. We are not claiming to have resolved all of the conundrums connected with the problem of evil, but simply to have offered some resources for alleviating them. To those who may be disposed to criticize, we point out that it is not sufficient, when dealing with issues of this magnitude, to identify the difficulties in any given position. Here, as always, one must ask what the alternatives are. The experience of John Baillie may be instructive here. As a student, Baillie had written a paper in which he pointed out a number of difficulties with a particular theory. The professor wrote a telling comment on the paper: "Every theory has its difficulties, but you have not considered whether any other theory has less difficulties than the one you have criticized."[30]

It may well be that one solution to the problem, atheism, is quite satisfactory as an intellectual explanation. Mackie seems to think that the problem of evil is not a problem for atheism. Accepting the reality of evil, it rejects the concept of an omnipotent, benevolent God. There is, however, another dimension of

30. John Baillie, *Invitation to Pilgrimage* (New York: Scribner, 1942), p. 15.

experience that the atheistic explanation does not deal with: the pragmatic. For if there is no omnipotent, loving God, is there any real hope that evil will ever be removed? And how can there be meaningful life without hope? The problem of evil may not be a problem for atheism, but evil itself surely is.

Conclusion

We have come at last to the end of our long journey. We need to stop to note what we have attempted in this volume. We do not claim to have dealt with every issue of incarnational Christology or with every aspect of any individual issue. In some cases, the issues have been dealt with, but not in a direct or overt fashion.

One of the issues we have dealt with indirectly is the choice of basic methodology, "Christology from above" or "Christology from below." This is the question of whether one begins with the heavenly Second Person of the Trinity or with the earthly history of the human Jesus of Nazareth. In a sense, there are two different questions involved here, one ontological and the other epistemological. The ontological question is whether one assumes the deity of Christ and asks how the Second Person of the Trinity could become human (the problem of the incarnation), or asks how and in what sense a human, Jesus, could be divine.[1] Christology from above tends toward an emphasis upon the deity, Christology from below upon the humanity of Jesus.[2] At times, however, the issue is virtually epistemological: Does one begin with the kerygma of the early church or with the search

1. Wolfhart Pannenberg, *Jesus—God and Man* (Philadelphia: Westminster, 1968), pp. 33–39.
2. Gerald O'Collins, *What Are They Saying About Jesus?* (New York: Paulist, 1977), pp. 5–6.

625

for the earthly history of Jesus?[3] In Martin Kähler's terms, it is a question of the *historisch* Jesus or the *geschichtlich* Christ.[4]

Our starting point herein will be understood as a case of Christology from above. The question that has most concerned us is whether it is possible today to maintain the doctrine of the actual incarnation of God in an individual human being. Epistemologically, however, it should be noted that we have not simply assumed the deity, but have begun with a consideration of the possibility of reliable historical knowledge of Jesus. From that arose the contention that the biblical testimony, including Jesus' own self-witness, is that he was indeed divine. Thus, epistemologically, our approach has been from below.

Elsewhere I have suggested that the two approaches are neither completely exclusive nor exhaustive of the possibilities.[5] Indeed, Wolfhart Pannenberg, one of the chief contemporary exponents of Christology from below, grants some validity to the approach of Christology from above.[6] I would propose that the kerygma or the revelation of God supplies the interpretation of the phenomena of Jesus' life; that interpretation may then be tested by the use of the historical method. A pure Christology from below may never rise to understand the historical data, which, like Immanuel Kant's percepts, are blind. On the other hand, a pure Christology from above may be merely a fideistic belief, unsubstantiated and, like Kant's concepts, empty.

We have also not attempted to deal directly with all of the issues internal to biblical theology as such. In particular, biblical theologians may wish for an extended discussion of "trajectories" or of the titles for Jesus. Except for some mention of trajectories in chapter 11, there is little treatment of this subject, and the titles are discussed only to a small extent in chapter 18. In both cases, however, I would maintain that the issues involved have been treated in different form.

What have we accomplished, then? I would contend that we have established the following:

3. Pannenberg, *Jesus*, pp. 21–30.

4. Martin Kähler, *The So-Called Historical Jesus and the Historic Biblical Christ* (Philadelphia: Fortress, 1964).

5. Millard J. Erickson, *Christian Theology* (Grand Rapids: Baker, 1986), pp. 673–75.

6. Pannenberg, *Jesus*, p. 35.

1. We can determine, with a reasonable degree of certainty, enough about what Jesus said and did to form a picture of who and what he was.
2. Jesus believed himself to be, and was affirmed by the New Testament writers to be, the Son of God, fully divine in the same sense and to the same degree as God the Father.
3. The doctrine of Jesus Christ as fully God and fully human, and yet one person, while it is not totally comprehensible, is not a logically untenable or internally contradictory concept.
4. The bodily resurrection of Jesus is a historical occurrence. This event, which makes him unique among human beings, including the founders and leaders of other religions, justifies the claim that salvation is only through him.
5. Jesus showed his concern for all segments of society and is therefore able to be the Savior of all, no matter one's race, gender, or social class.
6. The teaching that in Jesus of Nazareth God was completely present in union with a fully human individual provides us with significant motifs for understanding and explaining the problem of evil in our world, and gives us basis for hope in the face of such evil.

If our presentation has been convincing, the reader should be led to belief in the incarnation: Jesus was truly God and man in one person. But more than intellectual belief in certain affirmations about his person is required. For, since Jesus is God, all of his words and claims must be taken seriously. He has the knowledge and the authority to prescribe what the truth is in religious matters, and he asserts that his work is the means of salvation, and that "no one comes to the Father, but by me" (John 14:6). It is not sufficient to believe that Jesus can provide salvation. Action to accept his work is what makes salvation possible for each of us. In the final analysis, it is our response to Jesus' call to new life that is the really important issue of Christology.

Scripture Index

5:26—31
5:26–27—30
5:27—31
5:30—31
5:32—31
5:37—31
5:41–44—30
5:42—30
6:15—31
6:27—30
6:35—27
6:37—31
6:38—74
6:48—27
6:57—31
6:61—30
6:62—29
6:63—27
7:18—30
7:29—30
7:41–42—416
7:46—30
7:52—419
8:1–11—208
8:12—28
8:15—27
8:16—31
8:24—28
8:28—28, 30
8:29—31
8:40—30
8:43—31
8:46—22
8:50–51—30
8:58—26, 29, 415
8:59—29
9:2—612
9:5—28
9:16—30
9:22—416, 419
9:35—30
10:1–5—444
10:7—28
10:10—28
10:11–13—444
10:14—530
10:14–18—28
10:15—30

10:17–18—613
10:18—31, 612
10:30—292
10:33—30
10:38—425
11:1–12:1—426
11:4—30
11:5—30
11:18—426
11:25–28, 460
11:33—30
11:34—31
11:35—30, 607
11:36—607
11:45–48—419
11:47—30
12:1–8—595
12:23—30
12:27—30
12:33–34—30
12:34—18
12:35–36—423
12:41—30
12:42—419, 420
13:21—30
13:31—30
13:32—31
14:2—620
14:6—28, 300, 460, 627
14:21—130
14:26—420
14:28—52
15:1—28
15:5—28
15:13—614
15:26—420
16:2—419, 420
16:12–13—420
17:1–2—30
17:2—31
17:3—52
17:5—29, 552
17:22—30
17:22–23—543
17:24—30, 31
17:24–26—31
18:11—31
18:28—427

18:34—31
19:7—231
19:13—427
19:14—427
19:25—392
19:26–27—30
19:28—30
19:37—447
20:1–10—589
20:11–18—589
20:17—457, 505
20:19—427
20:19–20—498
20:19–21—495
20:22—416
20:24–29—25, 570
20:27—505
20:28—461
20:30—416
20:31—25, 387
21:25—416

Acts

1—339
1:1—392
1:1–5—131
1:8—597
1:22—32
2:22—31, 32, 334
2:23—615
2:24—615
2:24–33—32
2:32–33—572
2:32–36—49
2:36—52, 100
3:1–10—204
3:6—31
3:15—32
3:20–21—100
3:26—32
4:2—32
4:10—31, 32
4:12—32, 300
4:33—32
5:30—32
5:30–31—572
6:1—464
7:55–56—470

Name and Subject Index

Millard J. Erickson, dean and professor of theology at Bethel Theological Seminary, is one of the most respected systematicians among evangelical theologians today. His concern for developing fresh full-orbed understandings of faith led to this generation's most complete systematic study of doctrine, *Christian Theology*. This same search for relevance is expressed in his books *The New Evangelical Theology, Relativism in Contemporary Christian Ethics, Contemporary Options in Eschatology,* and *Salvation*.